Multicultural Education

Issues and Perspectives

FIFTH EDITION UPDATE

NEW FEATURE ON HIGH STAKES: TESTING FOR TRACKING, PROMOTION, AND GRADUATION

Edited by

JAMES A. BANKS

University of Washington, Seattle

CHERRY A. McGEE BANKS

University of Washington, Bothell

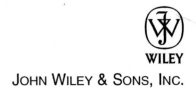

WILEY

JOHN WILEY & SONS, INC.

ACQUISITIONS EDITOR   Brad Hanson
EDITORIAL ASSISTANT   Lindsay Lovier
MARKETING MANAGER   Laura McKenna
SENIOR PRODUCTION EDITOR   Patricia McFadden
SENIOR DESIGNER   Dawn L. Stanley
PHOTO EDITOR   Lisa Gee
PRODUCTION MANAGEMENT SERVICES   Ingrao Associates
COVER PHOTO   Ernest Manewal/Superstock

This book is printed on acid-free paper. ∞

ISBN 0-471-71363-5

10 9 8 7 6 5 4 3

Preface

Since the Fourth Edition of this book was published, a number of national and world events have underscored the importance of teaching for social justice and multicultural literacy. The terrorist attacks of September 11, 2001, the war in Iraq, the intractable problems in the Middle East, and the ominous threat that terrorism poses throughout the world indicate that teaching students to become engaged citizens who can make reflective decisions in a troubled world should be major goals of the schools in a democratic and just society.

The cultural, racial, ethnic, and religious diversity within the United States provides an excellent context for students to acquire the multicultural understandings and skills needed to function effectively in their local communities, the nation, and the world. Political upheaval, world migration, and transnational economic linkages are bringing peoples throughout the world into increased contact, cultural interaction, and conflict within our national borders.

Racial, ethnic, language, class, and religious diversity is deepening within the United States as a consequence of worldwide population movements and the magnetic pull of the American Dream. Non-Hispanic Whites make up about 70 percent of the U.S. population. However, the U.S. Census projects that the non-Hispanic White percentage of the nation's population will decrease in the coming years and that racial, ethnic, cultural, and language diversity will deepen. If current demographic trends continue, non-Hispanic Whites are expected to make up 50 percent of the U.S. population by 2050.

Diversity in the United States is becoming increasingly reflected in the nation's schools, colleges, and universities. In 2003, 40 percent of the students enrolled in grades 1–12 in the public schools were students of color. It is projected that students of color will make up about 48 percent of the nation's school-age youth by 2020. The 2000 U.S. Census indicated that 18.4 percent of school-age youth spoke a language other than English at home. Consequently, large numbers of students in the nation's schools are English-language learners. It is projected that 20 to 25 percent of the students in U.S. public schools will be second-language learners by 2025.

Many of the nation's students are poor. In 2001, 32.9 million people in the United States were living in poverty, including one in five students. The gap between the rich and the poor is also widening. In 1976, the top 1 percent of Americans owned 20 percent of the nation's wealth. The top 1 percent owned 47 percent of U.S. wealth in 2001.

These demographic, social, and economic trends have important implications for teaching and learning in today's schools. As the nation's students become increasingly diverse, most of the nation's teachers remain White, middle-class, and female. In 2002, approximately 87 percent of the nation's teachers were White and 74 percent were female. Consequently, a wide gap exists between the racial, cultural, and language characteristics of U.S. students and teachers.

The increasing diversity within the nation's schools provides both opportunities and challenges. Diverse classrooms and schools make it possible to teach students from many different cultures and groups how to live together cooperatively and productively. However, racial prejudice and discrimination are challenges that arise when people from diverse groups come together. Teachers need to acquire the knowledge and skills needed to maximize the opportunities that diversity offers and to minimize its challenges. Teacher education programs should help teachers to attain the knowledge and behaviors needed to work effectively with students from diverse groups as well as to help students from mainstream groups develop cross-cultural knowledge, values, and competencies.

Multicultural Education: Issues and Perspectives, Fifth Edition, is designed to help current and future educators acquire the concepts, paradigms, and explanations needed to become effective practitioners in culturally, racially, and linguistically diverse classrooms and schools. This Fifth Edition has been revised to reflect current and emerging research, concepts, and debates about the education of students from both genders and from different cultural, racial, ethnic, and language groups. Exceptionality is a part of our concept of diversity because there are exceptional students in each group discussed in this book.

Chapters 4, 5, and 15 are new to this Fifth Edition. The chapters from the previous edition have been revised to reflect new research, theories, census data, statistics, interpretations, and developments. The Multicultural Resources in the Appendix have been substantially revised and updated. The Glossary has been revised to incorporate new census data and interpretations.

This book consists of six parts. The chapters in Part I discuss how race, gender, class and exceptionality interact to influence student behavior. This updated Fifth Edition contains a new **Feature** on "High Stakes: Testing for Tracking, Promotion and Graduation," which was written by the National Research Council's Committee on Appropriate Test Use. The National Research Council is a part of the National Academy of Sciences, which is a private, nonprofit institution specially created by a congressional charter in 1863 to advise the federal government. We are including this feature in this updated Fifth Edition because the testing of students has become a contentious and divisive issue in education since the passage of the No Child Left Behind Act of 2001. The feature on "High Stakes" gives sound guidelines for testing and assessment for all students, and provides thoughtful guidelines for using tests and assessments with special population groups, such as students with disabilities, low-income students, and students who are English language learners.

Social class and religion and their effects on education are discussed in Part II. Part III describes how educational opportunity differs for female and male students and how schools can foster gender equity. The issues, problems, and opportunities for educating students of color and students with language differences are discussed in Part IV. Chapter 11, on the colorblind perspective, highlights the importance of race even when it us unacknowledged by teachers. Part V focuses on exceptionality, describing the issues involved in creating equal educational opportunity for students who have disabilities and for those who are gifted. The final part, Part VI, discusses multicultural education as a process of school reform and ways to increase student academic achievement and to work more effectively with parents.

The Appendix consists of a list of books for further reading. The Glossary defines many of the key concepts and terms used throughout the book.

ACKNOWLEDGMENTS

We are grateful to the authors who revised their chapters for this Fifth Edition of *Multicultural Education* and to the authors who wrote new chapters.

We thank John J. Juelis, Caryn Park, and Amrita Zahir—research assistants in the Center for Multicultural Education at the University of Washington—for their work on the citations and references. We are grateful to Caryn Park for her careful work on updating the statistics in the parts of the book written by the editors. We extend special thanks to John J. Juelis for helping us prepare the **Feature** in this updated Fifth Edition for publication in this book.

Contents

Multicultural Education

A major goal of multicultural education is to help all students become effective citizens in a democratic society.

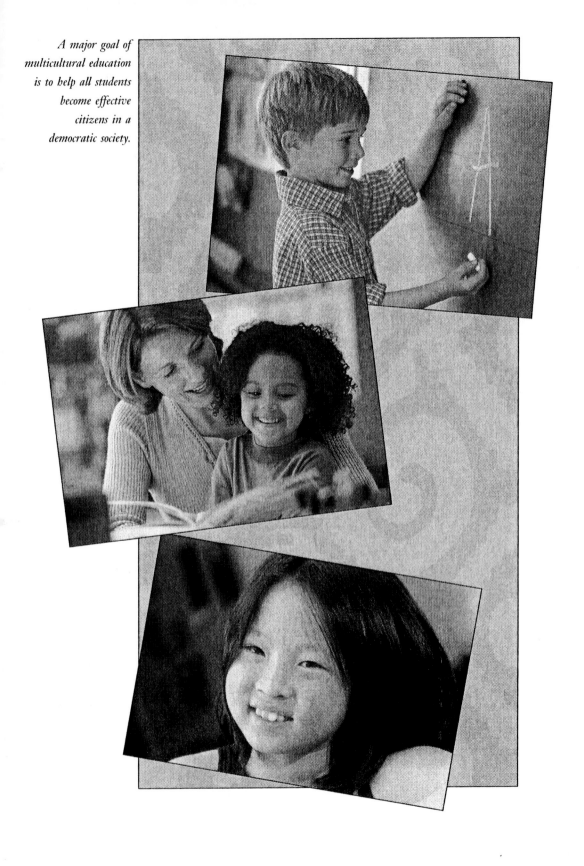

Issues and Concepts

The three chapters in Part I define the major concepts and issues in multicultural education, describe the diverse meanings of culture, and describe the ways in which such variables as race, class, gender, and exceptionality influence student behavior. Various aspects and definitions of culture are discussed. Culture is conceptualized as a dynamic and complex process of construction; its invisible and implicit characteristics are emphasized. The problems that result when culture is essentialized are described.

Multicultural education is an idea, an educational reform movement, and a process whose major goal is to change the structure of educational institutions so that male and female students, exceptional students, and students who are members of diverse racial, ethnic, language, and cultural groups will have an equal chance to achieve academically in school. It is necessary to conceptualize the school as a social system in order to implement multicultural education successfully. Each major variable in the school, such as its culture, its power relationships, the curriculum and materials, and the attitudes and beliefs of the staff, must be changed in ways that will allow the school to promote educational equality for students from diverse groups.

To transform the schools, educators must be knowledgeable about the influence of particular groups on student behavior. The chapters in this part of the book describe the nature of culture and groups in the United States as well as the ways in which they interact to influence student behavior.

CHAPTER 1

Multicultural Education: Characteristics and Goals

James A. Banks

THE NATURE OF MULTICULTURAL EDUCATION

Multicultural education is at least three things: an idea or concept, an educational reform movement, and a process. Multicultural education incorporates the idea that all students—regardless of their gender and social class and their ethnic, racial, or cultural characteristics—should have an equal opportunity to learn in school. Another important idea in multicultural education is that some students, because of these characteristics, have a better chance to learn in schools as they are currently structured than do students who belong to other groups or who have different cultural characteristics.

Some institutional characteristics of schools systematically deny some groups of students equal educational opportunities. For example, in the early grades, girls and boys achieve equally in mathematics and science. However, the achievement test scores of girls fall considerably behind those of boys as children progress through the grades (American Association of University Women Educational Foundation, 1998; Clewell, 2002; Francis, 2000). Girls are less likely than boys to participate in class discussions and to be encouraged by teachers to participate. Girls are more likely than boys to be silent in the classroom. However, not all school practices favor males. As Sadker and Sadker point out in Chapter 6, boys are more likely to be disciplined than are girls, even when their behavior does not differ from that of girls. They are also more likely than girls to be classified as learning disabled (Donovan & Cross, 2002). Males of color, especially African American males, experience a highly disproportionate rate of disciplinary actions and suspensions in school. Some writers have described the situation of African American males as a "crisis" and have called them "endangered" in U.S. society (Gibbs, 1988).

In the early grades, the academic achievement of students of color such as African Americans, Latinos, and American Indians is close to parity with the achievement of White mainstream students (Steele, 2003). However, the longer these students of color remain in school, the more their achievement lags behind that of White mainstream students. Social-class status is also strongly related to academic achievement. Persell, in Chapter 4, describes how educational opportunities are much greater for middle- and upper-income students than for low-income students. Knapp and Woolverton (2004), as well as Oakes, Joseph, and Muir (2004), describe the powerful ways in which social class influences students' opportunities to learn.

Exceptional students, whether they are physically or mentally disabled or gifted and talented, often find that they do not experience equal educational opportunities in the schools. The chapters in Part V describe the problems that such exceptional students experience in schools and suggest ways that teachers and other educators can increase their chances for educational success.

Multicultural education is also a reform movement that is trying to change the schools and other educational institutions so that students from all social-class, gender, racial, language, and cultural groups will have an equal opportunity to learn. Multicultural education involves changes in the total school or educational environment; it is not limited to curricular changes (Banks & Banks, 2004). The variables in the school environment that multicultural education tries to transform are discussed later in this chapter and illustrated in Figure 1.5. Multicultural education is also a process whose goals will never be fully realized.

Educational equality, like liberty and justice, is an ideal toward which human beings work but never fully attain. Racism, sexism, and discrimination against people with disabilities will exist to some extent no matter how hard we work to eliminate these problems. When prejudice and discrimination are reduced toward one group, they are usually directed toward another group or they take new forms. Whenever groups are identified and labeled, *categorization* occurs. When categorization occurs, members of in-groups favor in-group members and discriminate against out-groups (Stephan, 1999). This process can occur without groups having a history of conflict, animosity, or competition, and without their having physical differences or any other kind of important difference. Social psychologists call this process *social identity theory* or the *minimal group paradigm* (Rothbart & John, 1993; Smith & Mackie, 1995). Because the goals of multicultural education can never be fully attained, we should work continually to increase educational equality for all students. Multicultural education must be viewed as an ongoing process, not as something that we "do" and thereby solve the problems that are the targets of multicultural educational reform (Banks, 2001a).

HIGH-STAKES TESTING: A CHALLENGE TO TEACHING FOR SOCIAL JUSTICE

The No Child Left Behind Act is being widely interpreted and implemented as a testing and assessment initiative. The emphasis on testing, standards, and accountability that is mandated in most states compels many teachers to focus on narrow and basic skills in reading, writing, and math (Heubert & Hauser, 1999). In too many classrooms testing and test preparation are replacing teaching and learning. Research by Amrein and Berliner (2002) indicates that the emphasis on testing and accountability is having detrimental effects on student learning. Because of the ways in which accountability is being conceptualized and implemented, the professional role of teachers is being fractured and minimized.

The national focus on basic skills and testing is diverting attention from the broad liberal education that students need to live and function effectively in a multicultural nation and world. It is essential that all students acquire basic literacy and numeracy skills. However, students also need the knowledge, skills, and values that will enable them to live, interact, and make decisions with fellow citizens from different racial, ethnic, cultural, language, and religious groups.

The schools need to teach about social justice issues in addition to teaching basic skills. Teaching for social justice is very important because of the crises that the United States and the world face. An education that is narrowly defined as academic achievement and testing will not prepare students to become effective citizens who are committed to social justice. We should educate students to be reflective, moral, caring, and active citizens in a troubled world (Banks, 2004a). The world's greatest problems do not result from people being unable to read and write. They result from people in the world—from different cultures, races, religions, and nations—being unable to get along and to work together to solve the world's problems, such as global warming, the HIV/AIDS epidemic, poverty, racism, sexism, terrorism, international conflict, and war. Examples are the conflicts between the Western and Arab nations, North Korea and its neighbors, and the Israeli–Palestinian conflict.

MULTICULTURAL EDUCATION: AN INTERNATIONAL REFORM MOVEMENT

Since World War II, many immigrants and groups have settled in the United Kingdom and in nations on the European continent, including France, the Netherlands, Germany, Sweden, and Switzerland (Banks, 2004a; Figueroa, 2004). Some of these immigrants, such as the Asians and West Indians in England and the North Africans and Indochinese in France, have come from former colonies. Many Southern and Eastern European immigrants have settled in Western and Northern European nations in search of upward social mobility and other opportunities. Groups such as Italians, Greeks, and Turks have migrated to Northern and Western European nations in large numbers. Ethnic and immigrant populations have also increased significantly in Australia and Canada since World War II (Allan & Hill, 2004; Joshee, 2004).

Most of the immigrant and ethnic groups in Europe, Australia, and Canada face problems similar to those experienced by ethnic groups in the United States. Groups such as the Jamaicans in England, the Algerians in France, and the Aborigines in Australia experience achievement problems in the schools and prejudice and discrimination in both the schools and society at large. These groups also experience problems attaining full citizenship rights and recognition in their nation-states (Banks, 2004a).

The United Kingdom, various nations on the European continent, and Australia and Canada have implemented a variety of programs to increase the achievement of ethnic and immigrant students and to help students and teachers develop more positive attitudes toward racial, cultural, ethnic, and language diversity (Banks, 2004a; Figueroa, 2004).

THE HISTORICAL DEVELOPMENT OF MULTICULTURAL EDUCATION

Multicultural education grew out of the ferment of the civil rights movement of the 1960s. During this decade, African Americans embarked on a quest for their rights that was unprecedented in the United States. A major goal of the civil rights movement of the 1960s was to eliminate discrimination in public accommodations, housing, employment, and education. The consequences of the civil rights movement had a significant influence on educational institutions as ethnic groups—first African Americans and then other groups—demanded that the schools and other educational institutions reform their curricula so that they would reflect their experiences, histories, cultures, and perspectives. Ethnic groups also demanded that the schools hire more Black and Brown teachers and administrators so that their children would have more successful role models. Ethnic groups pushed for community control of schools in their neighborhoods and for the revision of textbooks to make them reflect the diversity of peoples in the United States.

The first responses of schools and educators to the ethnic movements of the 1960s were hurried. Courses and programs were developed without the thought and careful planning needed to make them educationally sound or to institutionalize them within the educational system. Holidays and other special days, ethnic celebrations, and courses that focused on one ethnic group were the dominant characteristics of school reforms related to ethnic and cultural diversity during the 1960s and early 1970s. Grant and Sleeter, in Chapter 3, call this approach "single-group studies." The ethnic studies courses developed and implemented during this period were usually electives and were taken primarily by students who were members of the group that was the subject of the course.

The visible success of the civil rights movement, plus growing rage and a liberal national atmosphere, stimulated other marginalized groups to take actions to eliminate discrimination against them and to demand that the educational system respond to their needs, aspirations, cultures, and histories. The women's rights movement emerged as one of the most significant social reform movements of the late twentieth century (Schmitz, Butler, Rosenfelt, & Guy-Sheftal, 2004). During the 1960s and 1970s, discrimination against women in employment, income, and education was widespread and often blatant. The women's rights movement articulated and publicized how discrimination and institutionalized sexism limited the opportunities of women and adversely affected the nation. The leaders of this movement, such as Betty Friedan and Gloria Steinem, demanded that political, social, economic, and educational institutions act to eliminate sex discrimination and to provide opportunities for women to actualize their talents and realize their ambitions (Steinem, 1995). Major goals of the women's rights movement included equal pay for equal work, the elimination of laws that discriminated against women and made them second-class citizens, the hiring of more women in leadership positions, and greater participation of men in household work and child rearing.

When *feminists* (people who work for the political, social, and economic equality of the sexes) looked at educational institutions, they noted problems similar to those identified by ethnic groups of color. Textbooks and curricula were dominated by men; women were largely invisible. Feminists pointed out that history textbooks were dominated by political and military history—areas in which men had been the main participants (Trecker, 1973). Social and family history and the history of labor and of ordinary people were largely ignored. Feminists pushed for the revision of textbooks to include more history about the important roles of women in the development of the nation and the world. They also demanded that more women be hired for administrative positions in the schools. Although most teachers in the elementary schools were women, most administrators were men.

Other marginalized groups, stimulated by the social ferment and the quest for human rights during the 1970s, articulated their grievances and demanded that institutions be reformed so they would face less discrimination and acquire more human rights. People with disabilities, senior citizens, and gay rights advocates were among the groups that organized politically during this period and made significant inroads in changing institutions and laws. Advocates for citizens with disabilities attained significant legal victories during the 1970s. The Education for All Handicapped Children Act of 1975 (P.L. 94–142), which required that students with disabilities be educated in the least restricted environment and institutionalized the word *mainstreaming* in education, was perhaps the most significant legal victory of the movement for the rights of students with disabilities in education (see Chapters 13 and 14).

HOW MULTICULTURAL EDUCATION DEVELOPED

Multicultural education emerged from the diverse courses, programs, and practices that educational institutions devised to respond to the demands, needs, and aspirations of the various groups. Consequently, as Grant and Sleeter point out in Chapter 3, multicultural education is not in actual practice one identifiable course or educational program. Rather, practicing educators use the term *multicultural education* to describe a wide variety of programs and practices related to educational equity, women, ethnic groups, language minorities, low-income groups, and people with disabilities. In one school district, multicultural education may mean a curriculum that incorporates the experiences of ethnic groups of color; in another, a program may include the experiences of both ethnic groups and women. In a third school district, this term may be used the way it is by me and by other authors, such as Nieto (2003) and Sleeter and Grant (2003); that is, to mean a total school reform effort designed to increase educational equity for a range of cultural, ethnic, and economic groups. This broader and more comprehensive notion of multicultural education is discussed in the last part of this chapter. It differs from the limited concept of multicultural education, in which it is viewed as curriculum reform.

THE NATURE OF CULTURE IN THE UNITED STATES

The United States, like other Western nation-states such as the United Kingdom, Australia, and Canada, is a multicultural society. The United States consists of a shared core culture as well as many subcultures. In this book, we call the larger shared core culture the *macroculture;* the smaller cultures, which are a part of the core culture, are called *microcultures.* It is important to distinguish the macroculture from the various microcultures because the values, norms, and characteristics of the mainstream (macroculture) are frequently mediated by, as well as interpreted and expressed differently within, various microcultures. These differences often lead to cultural misunderstandings, conflicts, and institutionalized discrimination.

Students who are members of certain cultural, religious, and ethnic groups are sometimes socialized to act and think in certain ways at home but differently at school (Ogbu, 2003). In her study of African American students and families in Trackton, Heath (1983) found that the pattern of language use in school was very different from the pattern used at home. At home, most of the children's interaction with adults consisted of imperatives, or commands. At school, questions were the dominant form of interactions between teachers and students. A challenge that multicultural education faces is how to help students from diverse groups mediate between their home and community cultures and the school culture. Students should acquire the knowledge, attitudes, and skills needed to function effectively in each cultural setting. They should also be competent to function within and across other microcultures in their society, within the national macroculture, and within the world community (Banks, 2004a).

The Meaning of Culture

Bullivant (1993) defines culture as a group's program for survival in and adaptation to its environment. The cultural program consists of knowledge, concepts, and values shared by group members through systems of communication. Culture also consists of the shared beliefs, symbols, and interpretations within a human group. Most social scientists today view culture as consisting primarily of the symbolic, ideational, and intangible aspects of human societies. The essence of a culture is not its artifacts, tools, or other tangible cultural elements but how the members of the group interpret, use, and perceive them. It is the values, symbols, interpretations, and perspectives that distinguish one people from another in modernized societies; it is not material objects and other tangible aspects of human societies (Kuper, 1999). People in a culture usually interpret the meanings of symbols, artifacts, and behaviors in the same or in similar ways.

Identifying and Describing the U.S. Core Culture

The United States, like other nation-states, has a shared set of values, ideations, and symbols that constitute the core or overarching culture. This culture is shared to some extent by all the diverse cultural and ethnic groups that make up the nation-state. It is difficult to identify and describe the overarching culture in the United States because it is such a diverse and complex nation. It is easier to identify the core culture within an isolated premodern society, such as the Maoris before the Europeans came to New Zealand, than within highly pluralistic, modernized societies such as the United States, Canada, and Australia (Lisitzky, 1956).

When trying to identify the distinguishing characteristics of U.S. culture, one should realize that the political institutions in the United States, which reflect some of the nation's core values, were heavily influenced by the British. U.S. political ideals and institutions were also influenced by Native American political institutions and practices, especially those related to making group decisions, such as in the League of the Iroquois (Weatherford, 1988).

Equality

A key component in the U.S. core culture is the idea, expressed in the Declaration of Independence in 1776, that "all men are created equal, that they are endowed by their Creator with certain unalienable rights, that among these are life, liberty, and the pursuit of happiness." When this idea was expressed by the nation's founding fathers in 1776, it was considered radical. A common belief in the eighteenth century was that human beings were not born with equal rights—that some people had few rights and others, such as kings, had divine rights given by God. When considering the idea that "all men are created equal" is a key component of U.S. culture, one should remember to distinguish between a nation's ideals and its actual practices, as well as between the meaning of the idea when it was expressed in 1776 and its meaning today. When the nation's founding fathers expressed this idea in 1776, their conception of men was limited to White males who owned property (Foner, 1998; Ladson-Billings, 2004). White men without property, White women, and all African Americans and Indians were not included in their notion of people who were equal or who had "certain unalienable rights."

Although the idea of equality expressed by the founding fathers in 1776 had a very limited meaning at that time, it has proven to be a powerful and important idea in the quest for human rights in the United States. Throughout the nation's history since 1776, marginalized and excluded groups such as women, African Americans, Native Americans, and other cultural and ethnic groups have used this idea to justify and defend the extension of human rights to them and to end institutional discrimination, such as sexism, racism, and discrimination against people with disabilities. As a result, human rights have gradually been extended to various groups throughout U.S. history. The extension of these rights has been neither constant nor linear. Rather, periods of extension of rights have often been followed by periods of retrenchment and conservatism. Schlesinger (1986) calls these patterns "cycles of American history." The United States is still a long way from realizing the ideals expressed in the Declaration of Independence in 1776. However, these ideals remain an important part of U.S. culture and are still used by marginalized groups to justify their struggles for human rights and equality.

Individualism and Individual Opportunity

Two other important ideas in the common overarching U.S. culture are individualism and individual social mobility (Stewart & Bennett, 1991). Individualism as an ideal is extreme in the U.S. core culture. Individual success is more important than commitment to family, community, and nation-state. An individual is expected to achieve success solely by his or her own efforts. Many people in the United States believe that a person can go from rags to riches within a generation and that every American-born boy can, but not necessarily will, become president.

Individuals are expected to achieve success by hard work and to pull themselves up by their bootstraps. This idea was epitomized by fictional characters such as Ragged Dick, one of the heroes created by the popular writer Horatio Alger. Ragged Dick attained success by valiantly overcoming poverty and adversity. A related belief is that if you do not succeed, it is because of your own shortcomings, such as being lazy or unambitious; failure is consequently your own fault. These beliefs are taught in the schools with success stories and myths about such U.S. heroes as George Washington, Thomas Jefferson, and Abraham Lincoln. The beliefs about individualism in U.S. culture are related to the Protestant work ethic. This is the belief that hard work by the individual is morally good and that laziness is sinful. This belief is a legacy of the British Puritan settlers in colonial New England. It has had a powerful and significant influence on U.S. culture.

The belief in individual opportunity has proven tenacious in U.S. society. It remains strong in American culture despite the fact that individuals' chances for upward social, economic, and educational mobility in the United States are highly related to the social-class, ethnic, gender, and other ascribed groups to which they belong (Knapp & Woolverton, 2004). The findings of social science research, as well as the chapters in this book, document the extent of social-class stratification in the United States and the ways in which people's opportunities in life are strongly influenced by the groups to which they belong (Rose, 1992; Willis, 1977). Yet the belief in individual opportunity remains strong in the United States.

Individualism and Groupism

Although the groups to which people belong have a major influence on their life chances in the United States, Americans—particularly those in the mainstream—are highly individualistic in their value orientations and behaviors. The nuclear family reinforces individualism in U.S. culture. One result of the strong individualism is that married children usually expect their older parents to live independently or in homes for senior citizens rather than with them.

The strong individualism in U.S. culture contrasts sharply with the groupism and group commitment found in Asian nations, such as China and Japan (Butterfield, 1982; Reischauer, 1981). Individualism is viewed rather negatively in these societies. One is expected to be committed first to the family and group and then to oneself. Some U.S. social scientists, such as Lasch (1978) and Bellah, Madsen, Sullivan, Swidler, and Tipton (1985), lament the extent of individualism in U.S. society. They believe it is harmful to the common national culture. Some observers believe that groupism is too strong in China and Japan and that individualism should be more valued in those nations. Perhaps modernized, pluralistic nation-states can best benefit from a balance between individualism and groupism, with neither characteristic dominating.

Expansionism and Manifest Destiny

Other overarching U.S. values that social scientists have identified include the desire to conquer or exploit the natural environment, materialism and consumption, and the belief in the nation's inherent superiority. These beliefs justified Manifest Destiny and U.S. expansion to the West and into other nations and the annexation of one-third of Mexico's territory in 1848. These observations, which reveal the less positive side of U.S. national values, have been developed by social scientists interested in understanding the complex nature of U.S. society (Appleby, Hunt, & Jacob, 1994).

In his discussion of the nature of values in U.S. society, Myrdal (1962) contends that a major ethical inconsistency exists in U.S. society. He calls this inconsistency "the American dilemma." He states that American creed values, such as equality and human dignity, exist in U.S. society as ideals. However, they exist alongside the institutionalized discriminatory treatment of African Americans and other ethnic and cultural groups in U.S. society. This variance creates a dilemma in the American mind because Americans try to reconcile their democratic ideals with their treatment of marginalized groups. Myrdal states that this dilemma has been an important factor that has enabled ethnic groups to fight discrimination effectively. In their efforts to resolve their dilemma when the inconsistencies between their ideals and actions are pointed out to them by human rights advocates, Americans, according to Myrdal, often support the elimination of practices that are inconsistent with their democratic ideals or the American creed. Some writers have refuted Myrdal's hypothesis and contend that most individuals in the United States do not experience such a dilemma (Ellison, 1995).

Microcultures in the United States

A nation as culturally diverse as the United States consists of a common overarching culture as well as a series of microcultures (see Figure 1.1). These microcultures share most of the

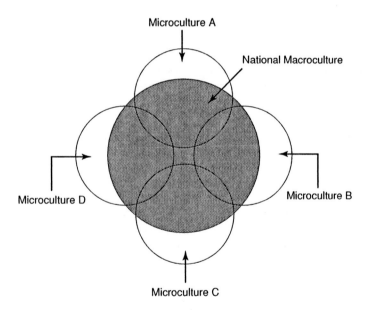

Figure 1.1   Microcultures and the National Macroculture

The shaded area represents the national macroculture. A, B, C, and D represent microcultures that consist of unique institutions, values, and cultural elements that are nonuniversalized and are shared primarily by members of specific cultural groups. A major goal of the school should be to help students acquire the knowledge, skills, and attitudes needed to function effectively within the national macroculture, their own microcultures, and within and across other microcultures.

Source: James A. Banks. *Cultural Diversity and Education: Foundations, Curriculum and Teaching*, 4th ed. (Boston: Allyn & Bacon), p. 73. Used with permission of the author.

core values of the nation-state, but these values are often mediated by the various microcultures and are interpreted differently within them. Microcultures sometimes have values that are somewhat alien to the national core culture. Also, some of the core national values and behaviors may seem somewhat alien in certain microcultures or may take different forms.

The strong belief in individuality and individualism that exists within the national macroculture is often much less endorsed by some ethnic communities and is somewhat alien within them. African Americans and Latinos who have not experienced high levels of cultural assimilation into the mainstream culture are much more group oriented than are mainstream Americans. Schools in the United States are highly individualistic in their learning and teaching styles, evaluation procedures, and norms. Many students, particularly African Americans, Latinos, and Native Americans, are group oriented (Irvine & York, 2001; Shade, Kelly, & Oberg, 1997). These students experience problems in the highly individualistic learning environment of the school. Teachers can enhance the learning opportunities of these students, who are also called field dependent or field sensitive, by using cooperative teaching strategies that have been developed and field-tested by researchers such as Slavin (2001) and Cohen and Lotan (2004).

Some theories and research indicate that female students may have preferred ways of knowing, thinking, and learning that differ to some extent from those most often preferred by males (Goldberger, Tarule, Clinchy, & Belenky, 1996; Halpern, 1986; Taylor, Gilligan, & Sullivan, 1995). Maher (1987) describes the dominant inquiry model used in social science as male constructed and dominated. She contends that it strives for objectivity: "Personal feelings, biases, and prejudices are considered inevitable limitations" (p. 186). Feminist pedagogy is based on different assumptions about the nature of knowledge and results in a different teaching method. According to Maher and Tetreault (1994), feminist pedagogy enhances the learning of females and deepens the insight of males. In Chapter 7, Tetreault describes feminist pedagogy techniques she uses to motivate students and to enhance their understandings.

After completing a major research study on women's ways of knowing, Belenky, Clinchy, Goldberger, and Tarule (1986) concluded that conceptions of knowledge and truth in the core culture and in educational institutions "have been shaped throughout history by the male-dominated majority culture. Drawing on their own perspectives and visions, men have constructed the prevailing theories, written history, and set values that have become the guiding principles for men and women alike" (p. 5).

These researchers also found an inconsistency between the kind of knowledge most appealing to women and the kind that was emphasized in most educational institutions. Most of the women interviewed in their study considered personalized knowledge and knowledge that resulted from first-hand observation most appealing. However, most educational institutions emphasize abstract, "out-of-context" knowledge (Belenky et al., 1986, p. 200). Ramírez and Castañeda (1974) found that Mexican American students who were socialized within traditional cultures also considered personalized and humanized knowledge more appealing than abstract knowledge. They also responded positively to knowledge that was presented in a humanized or story format.

Research by Gilligan (1982) provides some clues that help us better understand the findings by Belenky and her colleagues about the kind of knowledge women find most appealing. Gilligan describes caring, interconnection, and sensitivity to the needs of other people as dominant values among women and the female microculture in the United States.

By contrast, she found that the values of men were more characterized by separation and individualism.

A major goal of multicultural education is to change teaching and learning approaches so that students of both genders and from diverse cultural, ethnic, and language groups will have equal opportunities to learn in educational institutions. This goal suggests that major changes ought to be made in the ways that educational programs are conceptualized, organized, and taught. Educational approaches need to be transformed.

In her research on identifying and labeling students with mental retardation, Mercer (1973) found that a disproportionate number of African American and Mexican American students were labeled mentally retarded because the testing procedures used in intelligence tests "reflect the abilities and skills valued by the American core culture" (p. 32), which Mercer describes as predominantly White, Anglo-Saxon, and middle and upper class. She also points out that measures of general intelligence consist primarily of items related to verbal skills and knowledge. Most African American and Latino students are socialized within microcultures that differ in significant ways from the U.S. core culture. These students often have not had an equal opportunity to learn the knowledge and skills that are measured in mental ability tests. Consequently, a disproportionate percentage of African American and Latino students are labeled mentally retarded and are placed in classes for slow learners (Donovan & Cross, 2002). Mental retardation, as Mercer points out, is a socially determined status. When students are placed in classes for the mentally retarded, the self-fulfilling prophecy develops. Students begin to act and think as though they *are* mentally retarded (Banks, 2000).

Groups and Group Identification

Thus far, this chapter has discussed the various microcultures that make up U.S. society. Individuals learn the values, symbols, and other components of their culture from their social group. The group is the social system that carries a culture. People belong to and live in social groups (Bullivant, 1993). A group is a collectivity of persons who share an identity, a feeling of unity. A group is also a social system that has a social structure of interrelated roles (Theodorson & Theodorson, 1969). The group's program for survival, values, ideations, and shared symbols constitutes its culture (Kuper, 1999).

The study of groups is the major focus in sociology. Sociologists believe that the group has a strong influence on the behavior of individuals, that behavior is shaped by group norms, and that the group equips individuals with the behavior patterns they need in order to adapt to their physical, social, and metaphysical environments. Sociologists also assume that groups have independent characteristics; they are more than aggregates of individuals. Groups possess a continuity that transcends the lives of individuals.

Sociologists also assume that knowledge about groups to which an individual belongs provides important clues to and explanations for the individual's behavior. Goodman and Marx (1982) write, "Such factors as shared religion, nationality, age, sex, marital status, and education have proved to be important determinants of what people believe, feel, and do" (p. 7). Although membership in a gender, racial, ethnic, social-class, or religious group can provide us with important clues about individuals' behavior, it cannot enable us to predict behavior. Knowing one's group affiliation can enable us to state that a certain type of behavior

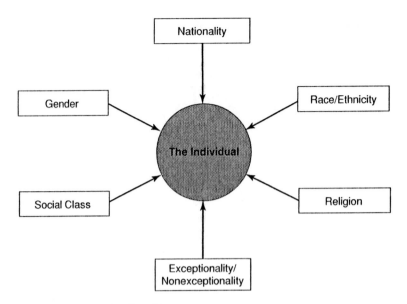

Figure 1.2 Multiple Group Memberships

An individual belongs to several different groups at the same time. This figure shows the major groups discussed in this book.

is probable. Membership in a particular group does not determine behavior but makes certain types of behavior more probable.

There are several important reasons that knowledge of group characteristics and modalities can enable us to predict the probability of an individual's behavior but not the precise behavior. This is, in part, because each individual belongs to several groups at the same time (see Figure 1.2). An individual may be White, Catholic, female, and middle class, all at the same time. She might have a strong identification with one of these groups and a very weak or almost nonexistent identification with another. A person can be a member of a particular group, such as the Catholic church, and have a weak identification with the group and a weak commitment to the tenets of the Catholic faith. Religious identification might be another individual's strongest group identification. Identification with and attachments to different groups may also conflict. A woman who has a strong Catholic identification but is also a feminist might find it difficult to reconcile her beliefs about equality for women with some positions of the Catholic church, such as its prohibiting women from being ordained as priests.

The more we know about a student's level of identification with a particular group and the extent to which socialization has taken place within that group, the more accurately we can predict, explain, and understand the student's behavior in the classroom. A knowledge of the importance of a group to a student at a particular time of life and within a particular social context will also help us understand the student's behavior. Ethnic identity may become more important to a person who becomes part of an ethnic minority when he or she previously belonged to the majority. Many Whites who have moved from the U.S. mainland to Hawaii have commented on how their sense of ethnic identity increased and they began to feel marginalized. Group identity may also increase when the group feels threatened, when a social movement arises to promote its rights, or when the group attempts to revitalize its culture.

The Teaching Implications of Group Identification

What are the implications of group membership and group identity for teaching? As you read the chapters in this book that describe the characteristics of the two gender groups and of social-class, racial, ethnic, religious, language, and exceptional groups, bear in mind that individuals within these groups manifest these behaviors to various degrees. Also remember that individual students are members of several of these groups at the same time. Above, the core U.S. culture is described as having highly individualistic values and beliefs. However, research by Gilligan (1982) indicates that the values of women, as compared with those of men, are more often characterized by caring, interconnection, and sensitivity to the needs of others. This observation indicates how core values within the macroculture are often mediated by microcultures within various gender, ethnic, and cultural groups.

As stated above, researchers have found that some students of color, such as African Americans and Mexican Americans, often have field-sensitive learning styles and therefore prefer more personalized learning approaches (Ramírez & Castañeda, 1974). Think about what this means. This research describes a group characteristic of these students, not the behavior of a particular African American or Mexican American student. It suggests that there is a higher probability that these students will have field-sensitive learning styles than will middle-class Anglo American students. However, students within all ethnic, racial, and social-class groups have different learning styles (Irvine & York, 2001). Those groups influence students' behavior, such as their learning style, interactively, because they are members of several groups at the same time. Knowledge of the characteristics of groups to which students belong, of the importance of each of these groups to them, and of the extent to which individuals have been socialized within each group will give the teacher important clues to students' behavior.

The Interaction of Race, Class, and Gender

When using our knowledge of groups to understand student behavior, we should also consider the ways in which such variables as class, race, and gender interact and intersect to influence student behavior. Middle-class and more highly assimilated Mexican American students tend to be more field-independent than do lower-class and less assimilated Mexican American students. African American students tend to be more field dependent (group oriented) than White students; females tend to be more field dependent than male students. Therefore, it can be hypothesized that African American females would be the most field dependent when compared to African American and White males and White females. This finding was made by Perney (1976).

Figure 1.3 illustrates how the major groups discussed in this book—gender, race or ethnicity, social class, religion, and exceptionality—influence student behavior, both singly and interactively. The figure also shows that other variables, such as geographic region and age, also influence an individual's behavior. The ways in which these variables influence selected student behaviors are described in Table 1.1.

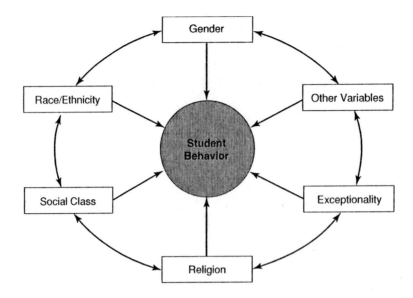

Figure 1.3 The Intersection of Variables

The major variables of gender, race or ethnicity, social class, religion, and exceptionality influence student behavior, both singly and interactively. Other variables, such as region and age, also influence student behavior.

Table 1.1   Singular and Combined Effects of Variables

Student Behavior	Gender Effects	Race/ Ethnicity Effects	Social- Class Effects	Religious Effects	Combined Effects
Learning Styles (Field Independent/Field Dependent)	X[a]	X			X
Internality/Externality			X		
Fear of Success	X	X			?
Self-Esteem	X	X			?
Individual vs. Group Orientation	X	X	X		?

[a]An X Indicates that the variable influences the student behavior that is described in the far-left column. An X in the far-right column means that research indicates that two or more variables combine to influence the described behavior. A question mark indicates that the research is unclear about the combined effects of the variables.

THE SOCIAL CONSTRUCTION OF CATEGORIES

The major variables and categories discussed in this book, such as gender, race, ethnicity, class, and exceptionality, are social categories (Berger & Luckman, 1967; Mannheim, 1936). The criteria for whether an individual belongs to one of these categories are determined by human beings and consequently are socially constructed. Religion is also a social category. Religious institutions, symbols, and artifacts are created by human beings to satisfy their metaphysical needs.

These categories are usually related to the physical characteristics of individuals. In some cases, as when they are individuals with severe or obvious physical disabilities, the relationship between the labels given to individuals and their physical characteristics is direct and would be made in almost any culture or social system. The relationship between categories that are used to classify individuals and their physical characteristics, however, is usually indirect and complex. Even though one's sex is determined primarily by physical characteristics (such as genitalia, chromosome patterns, etc.), gender is a social construction created and shaped by the society in which individuals and groups function.

Gender

Gender consists of the socially and psychologically appropriate behavior for males and females sanctioned by and expected within a society. Gender-role expectations vary across cultures and at different times in a society and within microcultures in the same society. Traditionally, normative behavior for males and females has varied among mainstream Americans, African Americans, Native Americans, and Hispanic Americans. Gender-role expectations also vary somewhat across social classes within the same society. In the White mainstream society in the 1940s and 1950s, upper-middle-class women often received negative sanctions when they worked outside the home, whereas women in working-class families were frequently expected to become wage earners.

Sexual Orientation

The discussion of gender roles provides an appropriate context for the examination of issues related to sexual orientation. The quest by gays and lesbians for human and civil rights has been an important development within the United States and throughout the Western world within the last several decades. Sexual orientation deserves examination when human rights and social justice are discussed because it is an important identity for individuals and groups and because many gay youths are victims of discrimination and hate crimes (*Harvard Educational Review*, 1996; Lipkin, 1999). Sexual orientation is often a difficult issue for classroom discussion for both teachers and students. However, if done sensitively, it can help empower gay and lesbian students and enable them to experience social equality in the college and university classroom. Recognition is one important manifestation of social equality (Gutmann, 2004).

Race

Race is a socially determined category that is related to physical characteristics in a complex way (Jacobson, 1998; Roediger, 2002). Two individuals with nearly identical physical characteristics, or phenotypes, can be classified as members of different races in two differ-ent societies (Nash, 1999; Root, 2004). In the United States, where racial categories are well defined and highly inflexible, an individual with any acknowledged or publicly known African ancestry is considered Black (Davis, 1991). One who looks completely Caucasian but who acknowledges some African ancestry is classified as Black. Such an individual would be con-sidered White in Puerto Rico. In Puerto Rico, hair texture, social status, and degree of emi-nence in the community are often as important as—if not more important than—physical characteristics in determining an individual's racial group or category. There is a saying in Puerto Rico that "money lightens," which means that upward social mobility considerably enhances an individual's opportunity to be classified as White. There is a strong relationship between race and social class in Puerto Rico and in most other Caribbean and Latin American nations.

Our discussion of race as a social category indicates that the criteria for determining the characteristics of a particular race vary across cultures, that an individual considered Black in one society may be considered White in another, and that racial categories reflect the social, economic, and political characteristics of a society.

Social Class

Social scientists find it difficult to agree on criteria for determining social class. The prob-lem is complicated by the fact that societies are constantly in the throes of change. During the 1950s, social scientists often attributed characteristics to the lower class that are found in the middle class today, such as single-parent and female-headed households, high divorce rates, and substance abuse. Today, these characteristics are no longer rare among the mid-dle class, even though their frequency is still higher among lower-class families. Variables such as income, education, occupation, lifestyle, and values are among the most frequently used indices to determine social-class status in the United States (Warner, 1949/1960). How-ever, there is considerable disagreement among social scientists about which variables are the most important in determining the social-class status of an individual or family.

Social-class criteria also vary somewhat among various ethnic and racial groups in the United States. Teachers, preachers, and other service professionals were upper class in many rural African American communities in the South in the 1950s and 1960s but were consid-ered middle class by mainstream White society. The systems of social stratification that exist in the mainstream society and in various microcultures are not necessarily identical.

Exceptionality

Exceptionality is also a social category. Whether a person is considered disabled or gifted is determined by criteria developed by society. As Shaver and Curtis (1981) point out, disabil-ities are not necessarily handicaps, and the two should be distinguished. They write, "A dis-ability or combination of disabilities becomes a handicap only when the condition limits or impedes the person's ability to function normally" (p. 1). A person with a particular disabil-ity, such as having one arm, might have a successful college career, experience no barriers to his achievements in college, and graduate with honors. However, he may find that when he tries to enter the job market, his opportunities are severely limited because potential employers view him as unable to perform well in some situations in which, in fact, he could perform effectively (Shaver & Curtis, 1981). This individual has a disability but was viewed as handicapped in one situation (the job market) but not in another (his university).

Mercer (1973) has extensively studied the social process by which individuals become labeled as persons with mental retardation. She points out that even though their physical characteristics may increase their chance of being labeled persons with mental retardation, the two are not perfectly correlated. Two people with the same biological characteristics may be considered persons with mental retardation in one social system but not in another one. An individual may be considered a person with mental retardation at school but not at home. She writes, "Mental retardation is not a characteristic of the individual, nor a meaning inherent in behavior, but a socially determined status, which [people] may occupy in some social systems and not in others" (p. 31). She states that people can change their role by changing their social group.

The highly disproportionate number of African Americans, Latinos, and particularly males classified as learning disabled by the school indicates the extent to which exceptionality is a social category (Donovan & Cross, 2002). Mercer (1973) found that the school labeled more people mentally retarded than did any other institution. Many African American and Latino students who are labeled mentally retarded function normally and are considered normal in their homes and communities. Boys are more often classified as mentally retarded than are girls. The school, as Mercer and other researchers have pointed out, uses criteria to determine the mental ability of students of color that conflict with their home and community cultures. Some students in all ethnic and cultural groups are mentally retarded and deserve special instruction, programs, and services, as the authors in Part V of this book suggest. However, the percentage of students of color in these programs is too high. The percentage of students in each ethnic group labeled mentally retarded should be about the same as the total percentage of that group in school.

Giftedness is also a social category (Sapon-Shevin, 1994). Important results of the socially constructed nature of giftedness are the considerable disagreement among experts about how the concept should be defined and the often inconsistent views about how to identify gifted students (Ford & Harris, 1999). The highly disproportionate percentage of middle- and upper-middle-class mainstream students categorized as gifted compared to lower-class students and students of color, such as African Americans, Latinos, and Native Americans, is also evidence of the social origin of the category.

Many students who are classified as gifted do have special talents and abilities and need special instruction. However, some students who are classified as gifted by school districts merely have parents with the knowledge, political skills, and power to force the school to classify their children as gifted, which will provide them with special instruction and educational enrichment (Sapon-Shevin, 1994).

Schools should try to satisfy the needs of students with special gifts and talents; however, they should also make sure that students from all social-class, cultural, language, and ethnic groups have an equal opportunity to participate in programs for academically and creatively talented students. If schools or districts do not have a population in their gifted programs that represents their various cultural, racial, language, and ethnic groups, steps should be taken to examine the criteria used to identify gifted students and to develop procedures to correct the disproportion. Both excellence and equality should be major goals of education in a pluralistic society.

THE DIMENSIONS OF MULTICULTURAL EDUCATION

When many teachers think of multicultural education, they think only or primarily of content related to ethnic, racial, and cultural groups. Conceptualizing multicultural education exclusively as content related to various ethnic and cultural groups is problematic for several reasons. Teachers who cannot easily see how their content is related to cultural issues will easily dismiss multicultural education with the argument that it is not relevant to their disciplines. This is done frequently by secondary math and science teachers.

The irrelevant-of-content argument can become a legitimized form of resistance to multicultural education when it is conceptualized primarily or exclusively as content. Math and science teachers often state, "Multicultural education is fine for social studies and literature teachers, but it has nothing to do with me. Math and science are the same, regardless of the culture or the kids." Multicultural education needs to be more broadly defined and understood so that teachers from a wide range of disciplines can respond to it in appropriate ways and resistance to it can be minimized.

Multicultural education is a broad concept with several different and important dimensions (Banks, 2004b). Practicing educators can use the dimensions as a guide to school reform when trying to implement multicultural education. The dimensions are (1) content integration, (2) the knowledge construction process, (3) prejudice reduction, (4) an equity pedagogy, and (5) an empowering school culture and social structure. Each dimension is defined and illustrated below.

Content Integration

Content integration deals with the extent to which teachers use examples and content from a variety of cultures and groups to illustrate key concepts, principles, generalizations, and theories in their subject area or discipline. The infusion of ethnic and cultural content into the subject area should be logical, not contrived.

More opportunities exist for the integration of ethnic and cultural content in some subject areas than in others. In the social studies, the language arts, and music, frequent and ample opportunities exist for teachers to use ethnic and cultural content to illustrate concepts, themes, and principles. There are also opportunities to integrate multicultural content into math and science. However, the opportunities are not as ample as they are in social studies, the language arts, and music.

The Knowledge Construction Process

The knowledge construction process relates to the extent to which teachers help students to understand, investigate, and determine how the implicit cultural assumptions, frames of reference, perspectives, and biases within a discipline influence the ways in which knowledge is constructed within it (Banks, 1996).

Students can analyze the knowledge construction process in science by studying how racism has been perpetuated in science by genetic theories of intelligence, Darwinism, and eugenics. In his important book *The Mismeasure of Man*, Gould (1996) describes how scientific racism developed and was influential in the nineteenth and twentieth centuries. Scientific racism has had and continues to have a significant influence on the interpretations of mental ability tests in the United States.

The publication of *The Bell Curve* (Herrnstein & Murray, 1994), its widespread and enthusiastic public reception, and the social context out of which it emerged provide an excellent case study for discussion and analysis by students who are studying knowledge construction (Kincheloe, Steinberg, & Gresson, 1996). Herrnstein and Murray contend that low-income groups and African Americans have fewer cognitive abilities than do other groups and that these differences are inherited. Students can examine the arguments made by the authors, their major assumptions, and how their conclusions relate to the social and political context.

Gould (1994) contends that Herrnstein and Murray's arguments reflect the social context of the times, "a historical moment of unprecedented ungenerosity, when a mood for slashing social programs can be powerfully abetted by an argument that beneficiaries cannot be helped, owing to inborn cognitive limits expressed as low I.Q. scores" (p. 139). Students should also study counterarguments to *The Bell Curve* made by respected scientists. Two good sources are *The Bell Curve Debate: History, Documents, Opinions*, edited by Jacoby and Glauberman (1995), and *Measured Lies: The Bell Curve Examined*, edited by Kincheloe, Steinberg, and Gresson (1996).

Students can examine the knowledge construction process in the social studies when they study such units and topics as the European discovery of America and the westward movement. The teacher can ask the students the latent meanings of concepts such as the European discovery of America and the New World. The students can discuss what these concepts imply or suggest about the Native American cultures that had existed in the Americas for about 40,000 years before the Europeans arrived. When studying the westward movement, the teacher can ask the students, "Whose point of view or perspective does this concept reflect, that of the European Americans or the Lakota Sioux?" "Who was moving west?" "How might a Lakota Sioux historian describe this period in U.S. history?" "What are other ways of thinking about and describing the westward movement?"

Prejudice Reduction

Prejudice reduction describes lessons and activities teachers use to help students develop positive attitudes toward different racial, ethnic, and cultural groups. Research indicates that children come to school with many negative attitudes toward and misconceptions about different racial and ethnic groups (Banks, 2001b; Stephan, 1999). Research also indicates that lessons, units, and teaching materials that include content about different racial and ethnic groups can help students to develop more positive intergroup attitudes if certain conditions exist in the teaching situation (Banks, 2001b). These conditions include positive images of the ethnic groups in the materials and the use of multiethnic materials in a consistent and sequential way.

Allport's (1954) *contact hypothesis* provides several useful guidelines for helping students to develop more positive interracial attitudes and actions in contact situations. He states that contact between groups will improve intergroup relations when the contact is characterized by these four conditions: (1) equal status, (2) cooperation rather than competition, (3) sanction by authorities such as teachers and administrators, and (4) interpersonal interactions in which students become acquainted as individuals.

An Equity Pedagogy

Teachers in each discipline can analyze their teaching procedures and styles to determine the extent to which they reflect multicultural issues and concerns. An equity pedagogy exists when teachers modify their teaching in ways that will facilitate the academic achievement of students from diverse racial, cultural, gender, and social-class groups (Banks & Banks, 1995). This includes using a variety of teaching styles and approaches that are consistent with the wide range of learning styles within various cultural and ethnic groups, being demanding but highly personalized when working with groups such as Native American and Alaskan students, and using cooperative learning techniques in math and science instruction in order to enhance the academic achievement of students of color (Cohen & Lotan, 2004; Slavin, 2001).

Several chapters in this book discuss ways in which teachers can modify their instruction in order to increase the academic achievement of students from different cultural groups and from both gender groups, including the chapters that constitute Parts III and IV.

An Empowering School Culture

Another important dimension of multicultural education is a school culture and organization that promotes gender, racial, and social-class equity. The culture and organization of the school must be examined by all members of the school staff. They all must also participate in restructuring it. Grouping and labeling practices, sports participation, disproportionality in achievement, disproportionality in enrollment in gifted and special education programs, and the interaction of the staff and the students across ethnic and racial lines are important variables that need to be examined in order to create a school culture that empowers students from diverse racial and ethnic groups and from both gender groups.

Figure 1.4 summarizes the dimensions of multicultural education described above. The next section identifies the major variables of the school that must be changed in order to institutionalize a school culture that empowers students from diverse cultural, racial, ethnic, and social-class groups.

THE SCHOOL AS A SOCIAL SYSTEM

To implement multicultural education successfully, we must think of the school as a social system in which all its major variables are closely interrelated. Thinking of the school as a social system suggests that we must formulate and initiate a change strategy that reforms the total school environment to implement multicultural education. The major school variables that must be reformed are presented in Figure 1.5.

Reforming any one of the variables in Figure 1.5, such as the formalized curriculum or curricular materials, is necessary but not sufficient. Multicultural and sensitive teaching materials are ineffective in the hands of teachers who have negative attitudes toward different racial, ethnic, and cultural groups. Such teachers are rarely likely to use multicultural materials or are likely to use them detrimentally. Thus, helping teachers and other members of the school staff to gain knowledge about diverse groups and democratic attitudes and values is essential when implementing multicultural programs.

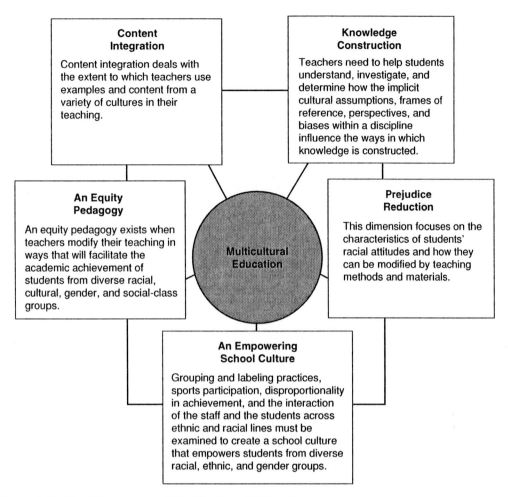

Figure 1.4 The Dimensions of Multicultural Education

To implement multicultural education in a school, we must reform its power relationships, the verbal interaction between teachers and students, the culture of the school, the curriculum, extracurricular activities, attitudes toward minority languages (Beykont, 2000), the testing program, and grouping practices. The institutional norms, social structures, cause–belief statements, values, and goals of the school must be transformed and reconstructed.

Major attention should be focused on the school's hidden curriculum and its implicit norms and values. A school has both a manifest and a hidden curriculum. The manifest curriculum consists of such factors as guides, textbooks, bulletin boards, and lesson plans. These aspects of the school environment are important and must be reformed to create a school culture that promotes positive attitudes toward diverse cultural groups and helps students

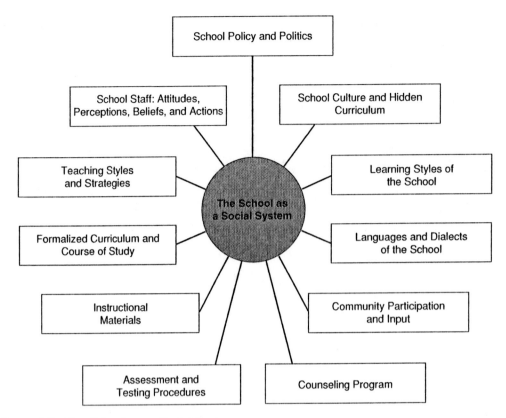

Figure 1.5 The School as a Social System

The total school environment is a system consisting of a number of major identifiable variables and factors, such as a school culture, school policy and politics, and the formalized curriculum and course of study. Any of these factors may be the focus of initial school reform, but changes must take place in each of them to create and sustain an effective multicultural school environment.

Source: Adapted with permission from James A. Banks (Ed.), *Education in the 80s: Multiethnic Education* (Washington, DC: National Education Association, 1981), Figure 2, p. 22.

from these groups experience academic success. However, the school's hidden or latent curriculum is often more important than is its manifest or overt curriculum. The latent curriculum has been defined as the one that no teacher explicitly teaches but that all students learn. It is that powerful part of the school culture that communicates to students the school's attitudes toward a range of issues and problems, including how the school views them as human beings and its attitudes toward males, females, exceptional students, and students from various religious, cultural, racial, and ethnic groups. Jackson (1992) calls the latent curriculum the "untaught lessons."

When formulating plans for multicultural education, educators should conceptualize the school as a microculture that has norms, values, statuses, and goals like other social systems.

The school has a dominant culture and a variety of microcultures. Almost all classrooms in the United States are multicultural because White students, as well as Black and Brown students, are socialized within diverse cultures. Teachers also come from many different groups. Many teachers were socialized in cultures other than the Anglo mainstream, although these may be forgotten and repressed. Teachers can get in touch with their own cultures and use the perspectives and insights they acquired as vehicles for helping them relate to and understand the cultures of their students.

The school should be a cultural environment in which acculturation takes place; teachers and students should assimilate some of the views, perspectives, and ethos of each other as they interact. Teachers and students will be enriched by this process, and the academic achievement of students from diverse groups will be enhanced because their perspectives will be legitimized in the school. Both teachers and students will be enriched by this process of cultural sharing and interaction.

SUMMARY

Multicultural education is an idea stating that all students, regardless of the groups to which they belong, such as those related to gender, ethnicity, race, culture, language, social class, religion, or exceptionality, should experience educational equality in the schools. Some students, because of their particular characteristics, have a better chance to succeed in school as it is currently structured than students from other groups. Multicultural education is also a reform movement designed to bring about a transformation of the school so that students from both genders and from diverse cultural, language, and ethnic groups will have an equal chance to experience school success. Multicultural education views the school as a social system that consists of highly interrelated parts and variables. Therefore, in order to transform the school to bring about educational equality, all the major components of the school must be substantially changed. A focus on any one variable in the school, such as the formalized curriculum, will not implement multicultural education.

Multicultural education is a continuing process because the idealized goals it tries to actualize—such as educational equality and the eradication of all forms of discrimination—can never be fully achieved in human society. Multicultural education, which was born during the social protest of the 1960s and 1970s, is an international movement that exists in nations throughout the world (Banks, 2004a). A major goal of multicultural education is to help students to develop the knowledge, attitudes, and skills needed to function within their own microcultures, the U.S. macroculture, other microcultures, and the global community.

Questions and Activities

1. What are the three components or elements of multicultural education?
2. How does Banks define multicultural education?
3. Find other definitions of multicultural education in several books listed under the category "Issues and Concepts" in the Appendix. How are the definitions of multicultural education in these books alike and different from the one presented in this chapter?

4. In what ways did the civil rights and women's rights movements of the 1960s and 1970s influence the development of multicultural education?

5. Ask several teachers and other practicing educators to give you their views and definitions of multicultural education. What generalizations can you make about their responses?

6. Visit a local school and, by observing several classes as well as by interviewing several teachers and the principal, describe what curricular and other practices related to multicultural education have been implemented in the school. Share your report with your classmates or workshop colleagues.

7. What is a macroculture? A microculture?

8. How is culture defined? What are the most important components of culture in a modernized society?

9. List and define several core or overarching values and characteristics that make up the macroculture in the United States. To what extent are these values and characteristics consistent with practices in U.S. society? To what extent are they ideals that are inconsistent with realities in U.S. society?

10. How is individualism viewed differently in the United States and in nations such as China and Japan? Why? What are the behavioral consequences of these varying notions of individualism?

11. What is the American dilemma defined by Myrdal? To what extent is this concept an accurate description of values in U.S. society? Explain.

12. How do the preferred ways of learning and knowing among women and students of color often influence their experiences in the schools as they are currently structured? In what ways can school reform help make the school environment more consistent with the learning and cognitive styles of women and students of color?

13. In what ways does the process of identifying and labeling students with mental retardation discriminate against groups such as African Americans and Latinos?

14. In what ways can the characteristics of a group help us understand an individual's behavior? In what ways are group characteristics limited in explaining an individual's behavior?

15. How do such variables as race, class, and gender interact to influence the behavior of students? Give examples to support your response.

16. What is meant by the "social construction of categories"? In what ways are concepts such as gender, race, social class, and exceptionality social categories?

17. List and define the five dimensions of multicultural education. How can these dimensions be used to facilitate school reform?

References

Allan, R., & Hill, B. (2004). Multicultural Education in Australia: Historical Development and Current Status. In J. A. Banks & C. A. M. Banks (Eds.), *Handbook of Research on Multicultural Education* (2nd. ed., pp. 979–995). San Francisco: Jossey-Bass.

Allport, G. W. (1954). *The Nature of Prejudice*. Reading, MA: Addison-Wesley.

American Association of University Women Educational Foundation. (1998). *Gender Gaps: Where Schools Still Fail Our Children*. Washington, DC: Author.

Amrein, A. L., & Berliner, D. C. (2002). High-Stakes Testing, Uncertainty, and Student Learning. *Education Policy Analysis Archives, 10*(8). Retrieved February 14, 2003, from http://eppa.asu.edu/eppa/v10n18/.

Appleby, J., Hunt, L., & Jacob, M. (1994). *Telling the Truth about History*. New York: Norton.

Banks, C. A. M., & Banks, J. A. (1995). Equity Pedagogy: An Essential Component of Multicultural Education. *Theory into Practice, 34*(3), 152–158.

Banks, J. A. (Ed.). (1996). *Multicultural Education, Transformative Knowledge, and Action*. New York: Teachers College Press.

Banks, J. A. (2000). The Social Construction of Difference and the Quest for Educational Equality. In R. Brandt (Ed.). *Education in a New Era* (pp. 21–45). Arlington, VA: Association for Supervision and Curriculum Development.

Banks, J. A. (2001a). *Cultural Diversity and Education: Foundations, Curriculum, and Teaching* (4th ed.). Boston: Allyn & Bacon.

Banks, J. A. (2001b). Multicultural Education: Its Effects on Students' Racial and Gender Role Attitudes. In J. A. Banks & C. A. M. Banks (Eds.), *Handbook of Research on Multicultural Education* (pp. 617–627). San Francisco: Jossey-Bass.

Banks, J. A. (Ed.). (2004a). *Diversity and Citizenship Education: Global Perspectives*. San Francisco: Jossey-Bass.

Banks, J. A. (2004b). Multicultural Education: Historical Development, Dimensions, and Practice. In J. A. Banks & C. A. M. Banks (Eds.), *Handbook of Research on Multicultural Education* (2nd ed., pp. 3–29). San Francisco: Jossey-Bass.

Banks, J. A., & Banks, C. A. M. (Eds.). (2004). *Handbook of Research on Multicultural Education* (2nd ed). San Francisco: Jossey-Bass.

Belenky, M. F., Clinchy, B. M., Goldberger, N.R., & Tarule, J. M. (1986). *Women's Ways of Knowing: The Development of Self, Voice, and Mind*. New York: Basic Books.

Bellah, R. N., Madsen, R., Sullivan, W. M., Swidler, A., & Tipton, S. M. (1985). *Habits of the Heart: Individualism and Commitment in American Life*. New York: Harper & Row.

Berger, P. L., & Luckman, T. (1967). *The Social Construction of Reality: A Treatise in the Sociology of Knowledge*. New York: Doubleday.

Beykont, Z. F. (Ed.). (2000). *Lifting Every Voice: Pedagogy and Politics of Bilingualism*. Cambridge, MA: Harvard Education Publishing Group.

Bullivant, B. (1993). Culture: Its Nature and Meaning for Educators. In J. A. Banks & C. A. M. Banks (Eds.), *Multicultural Education: Issues and Perspectives* (2nd ed., pp. 29–47). Boston: Allyn & Bacon.

Butterfield, F. (1982). *China: Alive in the Bitter Sea*. New York: Bantam.

Clewell, B. C. (2002). Breaking the Barriers: The Critical Middle School Years. In *The Jossey-Bass Reader on Gender in Education* (pp. 301–313). San Francisco: Jossey-Bass.

Cohen, E. G., & Lotan, R. (2004). Equity in Heterogeneous Classrooms. In J. A. Banks & C. A. M. Banks (Eds.), *Handbook of Research on Multicultural Education* (2nd ed., pp. 736–750). San Francisco: Jossey-Bass.

Davis, F. J. (1991). *Who Is Black? One Nation's Definition*. University Park: The Pennsylvania State University Press.

Donovan, M. S., & Cross, C. T. (Eds.). (2002). *Minority Students in Special and Gifted Education*. Washington, DC: National Academy Press.

Ellison, R. (1995). An American Dilemma: A Review. In J. F. Callahan (Ed.), *The Collected Essays of Ralph Ellison* (pp. 328–340). New York: The Modern Library.

Figueroa, P. (2004). Multicultural Education in the United Kingdom: Historical Development and Current Status. In J. A. Banks & C. A. M. Banks (Eds.), *Handbook of Research on Multicultural Education* (2nd ed., pp. 997–1026). San Francisco: Jossey-Bass.

Foner, E. (1998). *The Story of American Freedom*. New York: Norton.

Ford, D. Y., & Harris, J. J., III. (1999). *Multicultural Gifted Education*. New York: Teachers College Press.

Francis, B. (2000). *Boys, Girls and Achievement: Addressing the Classroom Issues*. London: Routledge/Falmer.

Gibbs, J. T. (Ed.). (1988). *Young, Black, and Male in America: An Endangered Species*. Dover, MA: Auburn House.

Gilligan, C. (1982). *In a Different Voice: Psychological Theory and Women's Development*. Cambridge, MA: Harvard University Press.

Goldberger, N., Tarule, J., Clinchy, B., & Belenky, M. (Eds.). (1996). *Knowledge, Difference, and Power*. New York: Basic Books.

Goodman, N., & Marx, G. T. (1982). *Society Today* (4th ed.). New York: Random House.

Gould, S. J. (1994). Curveball. *The New Yorker, 70*(38), 139–149.

Gould, S. J. (1996). *The Mismeasure of Man* (rev. & exp. ed.). New York : Norton.

Gutmann, A. (2004). Unity and Diversity in Democratic Multicultural Education: Creative and Destructive Tensions. In J. A. Banks (Ed.), *Diversity and Citizenship Education: Global Perspectives* (pp. 71–98). San Francisco: Jossey-Bass.

Halpern, D. F. (1986). *Sex Differences in Cognitive Abilities*. Hillsdale, NJ: Erlbaum.

Harvard Educational Review. (1996). Lesbian, Gay, Bisexual, and Transgender People and Education. Vol. 66 (2) [Special issue].

Heath, S. B. (1983). *Ways with Words: Language, Life, and Work in Communities and Classrooms*. New York: Oxford University Press.

Herrnstein, R. J., & Murray, C. (1994). *The Bell Curve: Intelligence and Class Structure in American Life*. New York: Free Press.

Heubert, J. P., & Hauser, R. M. (Eds.). (1999). *High Stakes Testing for Tracking, Promotion, and Graduation*. Washington, DC: National Academy Press.

Irvine, J. J., & York, E. D. (2001). Learning Styles and Culturally Diverse Students: A Literature Review. In J. A. Banks & C. A. M. Banks (Eds.), *Handbook of Research on Multicultural Education* (pp. 484–497). San Francisco: Jossey-Bass.

Jackson, P. W. (1992). *Untaught Lessons*. New York: Teachers College Press.

Jacobson, M. F. (1998). *Whiteness of a Different Color: European Immigrants and the Alchemy of Race*. Cambridge, MA: Harvard University Press.

Jacoby, R., & Glauberman, N. (Eds.). (1995). *The Bell Curve Debate: History, Documents, Opinions*. New York: Times Books/Random House.

Joshee, R. (2004). Citizenship and Multicultural Education in Canada: From Assimilation to Social Cohension. In J. A. Banks (Ed.), *Diversity and Citizenship Education: Global Perspectives* (pp. 127–156). San Francisco: Jossey-Bass.

Kincheloe, J. L., Steinberg, S. R., & Gresson, A. D., III (Eds.). (1996). *Measured Lies: The Bell Curve Examined.* New York: St. Martin's Press.

Knapp, M. S., & Woolverton, S. (2004). Social Class and Schooling. In J. A. Banks & C. A. M. Banks (Eds.), *Handbook of Research on Multicultural Education* (2nd ed., pp. 656–681). San Francisco: Jossey-Bass.

Kuper, A. (1999). *Culture: The Anthropologists' Account.* Cambridge, MA: Harvard University Press.

Ladson-Billings, G. (2004). Culture versus Citizenship: The Challenge of Racialized Citizenship in the United States. In J. A. Banks (Ed.), *Diversity and Citizenship Education: Global Perspectives* (pp. 99–126). San Francisco: Jossey-Bass.

Lasch, C. (1978). *The Culture of Narcissism.* New York: Norton.

Lipkin, A. (1999). *Understanding Homosexuality: Changing Schools.* Boulder, CO: Westview.

Lisitzky, G. (1956). *Four Ways of Being Human: An Introduction to Anthropology.* New York: Viking.

Maher, F. A. (1987). Inquiry Teaching and Feminist Pedagogy. *Social Education, 51*(3), 186–192.

Maher, F. A., & Tetreault, M. K. (1994). *The Feminist Classroom.* New York: Basic Books.

Mannheim, K. (1936). *Ideology and Utopia: An Introduction to the Sociology of Knowledge.* New York: Harcourt Brace.

Mercer, J. R. (1973). *Labeling the Mentally Retarded: Clinical and Social System Perspectives on Mental Retardation.* Berkeley: University of California Press.

Myrdal, G., with Sterner, R., & Rose, A. (1962). *An American Dilemma: The Negro Problem and Modern Democracy* (anniv. ed.). New York: Harper & Row.

Nash, G. B. (1999). *Forbidden Love: The Secret History of Mixed-Race America.* New York: Holt.

Nieto, S. (2003). *What Keeps Teachers Going.* New York: Teachers College Press.

Oakes, J., Joseph, R., & Muir, K. (2004). Access and Achievement in Mathematics and Science: Inequalities That Endure and Change. In J. A. Banks & C. A. M. Banks (Eds.), *Handbook of Research on Multicultural Education* (2nd ed., pp. 69–90). San Francisco: Jossey-Bass.

Obgu, J. U. (2003). *Black American Students in an Affluent Suburb: A Study of Academic Disengagement.* Mahwah, NJ: Earlbaum.

Perney, V. H. (1976). Effects of Race and Sex on Field Dependence–Independence in Children. *Perceptual and Motor Skills, 42,* 975–980.

Ramírez, M., & Castañeda, A. (1974). *Cultural Democracy, Bicognitive Development and Education.* New York: Academic Press.

Reischauer, E. O. (1981). *The Japanese.* Cambridge, MA: Harvard University Press.

Roediger, D. R. (2002). *Colored White: Transcending the Racial Past.* Berkeley: University of California Press.

Root, M. P. P. (2004). Multiracial Families and Children: Implications for Educational Research and Practice. In J. A. Banks & C. A. M. Banks (Eds.), *Handbook of Research on Multicultural Education* (2nd ed., pp. 110–124). San Francisco: Jossey-Bass.

Rose, S. J. (1992). *Social Stratification in the United States.* New York: The New Press.

Rothbart, M., & John, O. P. (1993). Intergroup Relations and Stereotype Change: A Social-Cognitive Analysis and Some Longitudinal Findings. In P. M. Sniderman, P. E. Telock, & E. G. Carmines (Eds.), *Prejudice, Politics, and the American Dilemma* (pp. 32–59). Stanford, CA: Stanford University Press.

Sapon-Shevin, M. (1994). *Playing Favorites: Gifted Education and the Disruption of Community.* Albany: State University of New York Press.

Schlesinger, A. M., Jr. (1986). *The Cycles of American History.* Boston: Houghton Mifflin.

Schmitz, B., Butler, J., Rosenfelt, D., & Guy-Sheftal, B. (2004). Women's Studies and Curriculum Transformation. In J. A. Banks & C. A. M. Banks (Eds.), *Handbook of Research on Multicultural Education* (2nd ed., pp. 882–905). San Francisco: Jossey-Bass.

Shade, B. J., Kelly, C., & Oberg, M. (1997). *Creating Culturally Responsive Classrooms.* Washington, DC: American Psychological Association.

Shaver, J. P., & Curtis, C. K. (1981). *Handicapism and Equal Opportunity: Teaching about the Disabled in Social Studies.* Reston, VA: Foundation for Exceptional Children.

Slavin, R. E. (2001). Cooperative Learning and Intergroup Relations. In J. A. Banks & C. A. M. Banks (Eds.), *Handbook of Research on Multicultural Education* (pp. 628–634). San Francisco: Jossey-Bass.

Sleeter, C. E., & Grant, C. A. (2003). *Making Choices for Multicultural Education: Five Approaches to Race, Class, and Gender* (4th ed.). New York: Wiley.

Smith, E. R., & Mackie, D. M. (1995). *Social Psychology.* New York: Worth.

Steele, C. (2003). Stereotype Threat and African-American Student Achievement. In T. Perry, C. Steele, & A. Hilliard III, *Young, Gifted and Black: Promoting High Achievement among African-American Students* (pp. 109–130). Boston: Beacon.

Steinem, G. (1995). *Outrageous Acts and Everyday Rebellions.* New York: Holt.

Stephan, W. G. (1999). *Reducing Prejudice and Stereotyping in Schools.* New York: Teachers College Press.

Stewart, E. C., & Bennett, M. J. (1991). *American Cultural Patterns: A Cross-Cultural Perspective.* Yarmouth, ME: Intercultural Press.

Taylor, J. M., Gilligan, C., & Sullivan, A. M. (1995). *Between Voice and Silence: Women and Girls, Race and Relationships.* Cambridge, MA: Harvard University Press.

Theodorson, G. A., & Theodorson, A. G. (1969). *A Modern Dictionary of Sociology.* New York: Barnes & Noble.

Trecker, J. L. (1973). Teaching the Role of Women in American History. In J. A. Banks (Ed.), *Teaching Ethnic Studies: Concepts and Strategies* (43rd Yearbook, pp. 279–297). Washington, DC: National Council for the Social Studies.

Warner, W. L., with Meeker, M., & Eells, K. (1960). *Social Class in America* (reissued ed.). New York: Harper Torchbooks. (Original work published 1949).

Weatherford, J. (1988). *Indian Givers: How the Indians of the Americas Transformed the World.* New York: Fawcett Columbine.

Willis, P. (1977). *Learning to Labor.* New York: Columbia University Press.

INTRODUCTION

High Stakes: Testing for Tracking, Promotion, and Graduation

In response to a congressional request, the National Research Council of the National Academy of Sciences established the Committee on Appropriate Test use to study the use, methods and implementation of large-scale testing as the primary form of assessment of student achievement in the US. Congressional interest in this subject stems from the widespread movement in the United States for standards-based school reform, and the increased reliance on achievement tests for various forms of accountability. Congress asked the National Academy of Sciences—through its National Research Council—for guidance in the appropriate and nondiscriminatory use of such tests. This study focuses on tests that, by virtue of their use for promotion, tracking, or graduation, have high stakes for individual students. The committee recognizes that accountability for students is related in important ways to accountability for educators, schools, and school districts. This report does not address accountability apart from the issue of students' participation in large-scale assessments. It is intended to apply to all schools and school systems in which tests are used.

The National Research Council's recommendations are based on a framework that emphasizes several basic principles of appropriate test use. Tests that are useful in curriculum planning or in school accountability are not appropriate for use in making high-stakes decisions about individual student's mastery unless the curriculum, the teaching, and the tests are aligned. A test score is not an exact measure of a student's knowledge or skill. Educational decisions that will have a major impact on a test taker should not solely or automatically be made on the basis of a single test score.

The Committee on Appropriate Test Use gives special attention to the problems that arise when special population groups—such as students with disabilities, low-income students, and students who are English language learners—take standardized tests. It decribes guidelines for making the use of tests with these groups fair and equitable.

Since the National Research Council's Committee on Appropriate Test Use issued its report in 1999, high-stakes tests have become a much more salient and contentious issue in the schools. In response to the leadership and urging by President George W. Bush, Congress passed the No Child Left Behind Act of 2001 (NCLB)(Public Law 107–110) (www.nochildleftbehind.gov). The NCLB Act requires states to implement statewide accountability in all schools. It also requires annual testing in reading and mathematics in grades 3 through 8. Assessments results and state progress must be shown by race, poverty, ethnicity, disability, and limited English proficient students. Significant negative sanctions are imposed on schools and states that cannot demonstrate progress toward stringent state goals (Guthrie, 2003).

The NCLB has caused acid debate and controversy among educators. Its supporters claim that it is a positive factor because it forces schools to focus attention on the academic achievement of low-income students, students with disabilities, language minority students, and students of color. Its critics argue that it holds schools accountable but does not provide the funds that schools need to implement meaningful reform required to increase the test scores of students from special population groups, such as students with disabilities and English language learners. Some of the most vocal and persistent critics of NCLB argue that it has limited the scope of a broad liberal and citizenship education because many teachers interpret it as requiring them to focus on low-level skills in reading and mathematics and on test preparation.

Tests and test preparation, argue the critics of NCLB, are driving the curriculum, rather than the needs of a diverse society that is part of a twenty first-century global age. Some emerging evidence indicates that the focus on tests and accountability is having negative consequences for some groups of students, such as low-income students and English language learners. Research by Amrein and Berlinger (2002) indicates that the emphasis on testing and accountability is having detrimental affects on student learning.

It is essential that all students master basic skills in reading, writing, and mathematics. Tests and assessments—when they have the characteristics described in the **Feature** that follows by the National Research Council Committee on Appropriate Test Use and are used in ways that the Committee recommends—can provide students, parents, and educators with helpful feedback that can be used to improve instruction and motivate students to learn. Tests and test preparation should facilitate and not divert attention from the broad liberal education that students need to live and function effectively in a multicultural nation and world (Banks, 2004).

References

Amrein, A. L., & Berliner, D. C. (2002). High-Stakes Testing, Uncertainty, and Student Learning. *Education Policy Analysis Archives, 10* (8). [On-line]. Retrieved February 14, 2003, from http://eppa.asu.edu/eppa/v10n18l.

Banks, J. A. (Ed.). (2004). *Diversity and Citizenship Education: Global Perspectives.* San Francisco: Jossey-Bass.

Guthrie, J. W. (Ed.). (2003). *Encyclopedia of Education* (6th ed.). New York: Macmillan Reference USA.

Recommended Books

Branson, J. D., Brown, A. L., & Cocking, R. R. (2000). *How People Learn: Brain, Mind, Experience, and School* (Expanded ed.). Washington, DC: National Academy Press.

Committee on Increasing High School Students' Engagement and Motivation to Learn (2004). *Engaging Schools: Fostering High School Students' Motivation to Learn.* Washington, DC: National Academy Press.

Elmore, R. L., & Rothman, R. (Eds.). (1999). *Testing, Teaching, and Learning: A Guide for States and School Districts.* Washington, DC: National Academy Press.

Heubert, J. P., & Hauser, R. M. (Eds.). (1999). *High Stakes: Testing for Tracking, Promotion and Graduation.* Washington, DC: National Academy Press.

Pellegrino, J. W., Chudowsky, N., & Glaser, R. (Eds.). (2001). *Knowing What Students Know: The Science and Design of Educational Assessment.* Washington, DC: National Academy Press.

Popham, W. J. (2005). *Classroom Assessment: What Teachers Need to Know* (4th ed.). Boston: Allyn and Bacon.

Taylor, C. S., & Nolen, S. B. (2005). *Classroom Assessment: Supporting Teaching and Learning in Real Classrooms.* Upper Saddle River, NJ: Merrill/Prentice Hall.

Wiggins, G., & McTighe, J. (1998). *Understanding by Design.* Alexandria, VA: Association for Supervision and Curriculum Development.

FEATURE

High Stakes: Testing for Tracking, Promotion, and Graduation

Jay P. Heubert and Robert M. Hauser, Editors

The Congress asked the National Academy of Sciences to "conduct a study and make written recommendations on appropriate methods, practices and safeguards to ensure that:

A. existing and new tests that are used to access student performance are not used in a discriminatory manner or inappropriately for student promotion, tracking or graduation; and

B. existing and new tests adequately access student reading and mathematics comprehension in the form most likely to yield accurate information regarding student achievement of reading and mathematics skills."

Congressional interest in this subject stems from the widespread movement in the United States for standards-based school reform, from the consideration of voluntary tests, and from the increased reliance on achievement tests for various forms of accountability; for schools systems, individual schools, administrators, teachers, and students. Moreover, there are sustained high levels of public support for high-stakes testing of individual students, even if it would lead to lower rates of promotion and high school graduation (Johnson and Immerwahr, 1994; Hochschild and Scott, 1998). Because large-scale testing is increasingly used for high-stakes purposes to make decisions that significantly affect the life chances of individual students, the Congress asked the National Academy of Sciences, through its National Research Council, for guidance in the appropriate and nondiscriminatory use of such tests.

This study focuses on tests that, by virtue of their use for promotion, tracking, or graduation, have high stakes for individual students. The committee recognizes that accountability for students is related in important ways to accountability for educators, schools, and school districts. This report does not address accountability at those other levels, apart from the issue of participation of all students in large-scale assessments. The report is intended to apply to all schools and school systems in which tests are used for student promotion, tracking, or graduation.

Source: Jay P. Heubert, & Robert M. Hauser (Eds.). (1999). *High Stakes: Testing for Tracking, Promotion, and Graduation.* Washington, DC: National Academy Press, pp. 273–307. Reprinted with the permission of The National Academy Press.

Test form (as mentioned in part B of the congressional mandate) could refer to a wide range of issues, including, for example, the balance of multiple-choice and constructed-response items, the use of student portfolios, the length and timing of the test, the availability of calculators or manipulatives, and the language of administration. However, in considering test form, the committee has chosen to focus on the needs of English-language learners and students with disabilities, in part because these students may be particularly vulnerable to the negative consequences of large-scale assessments. We consider, for these students, in what form and manner a test is most likely to measure accurately a student's achievement of reading and mathematics skills.

Two policy objectives are key for these special populations. One is to increase their participation in large-scale assessments, so that school systems can be held accountable for their educational progress. The other is to test each such student in a manner that accommodates for a disability or limited English proficiency to the extent that either is unrelated to the subject matter being tested, while still maintaining the validity and comparability of test results among all students. These objectives are in tension, and thus present serious technical and operational challenges to test developers and users.

ASSESSING THE USES OF TESTS

In its deliberations the committee has assumed that the use of tests in decisions about student promotion, tracking, or graduation is intended to serve educational policy goals, such as setting high standards for student learning, raising student achievement levels, ensuring equal educational opportunity, fostering parental involvement in student learning, and increasing public support for the schools.

Determining whether the use of tests for student promotion, tracking, or graduation produces better overall educational outcomes requires that the various intended benefits of high-stakes test use be weighed against unintended negative consequences for individual students and groups of students. The costs and benefits of testing should also be balanced against those of making high-stakes decisions about students in other ways, using criteria other than test scores; decisions about tracking, promotion, and graduation will be made with or without information from standardized tests. The committee recognizes that test use may have negative consequences for individual students even while serving important social or educational policy purposes. We believe that the development of a comprehensive testing policy should be sensitive to the balance among individual and collective benefits and costs.

The committee follows an earlier work by the National Research Council (1982) in adopting a three-part framework for determining whether a planned or actual test use is appropriate. The three principal criteria are (1) *measurement validity*—whether a test is valid for a particular purpose and the constructs measured have been correctly chosen; (2) *attribution of cause*—whether a student's performance on a test reflects knowledge and skill based on appropriate instruction or is attributable to poor instruction or to such factors as language barriers or construct-irrelevant disabilities; and (3) *effectiveness of treatment*—whether test scores lead to placements and other consequences that are educationally beneficial. This framework leads us to emphasize several basic principles of appropriate test use.

First, the important thing about a test is not its validity in general, but its validity when used for a specific purpose. Thus, tests that are useful in leading the curriculum or in school accountability are not appropriate for use in making high-stakes decisions about individual student mastery unless the curriculum, the teaching, and the tests are aligned.

Second, tests are not perfect. Test questions are a sample of possible questions that could be asked in a given area. Moreover, a test score is not an exact measure of a student's knowledge or skills. A student's score can be expected to vary across different versions of a test—within a margin of error determined by the reliability of the test—as a function of the particular sample of questions asked and/or transitory factors, such as the health of the student on the day of the test.

Third, an educational decision that will have a major impact on a test taker should not solely or automatically be made on the basis of a single test score. Other relevant information about the student's knowledge and skills should also be taken into account.

Finally, neither a test score nor any other kind of information can justify a bad decision. For example, research shows that tracking, as typically practiced, harms students placed in low-track classes. In the absence of better treatments, better tests will not lead to better educational outcomes. Throughout the report, the committee has considered how these principles apply to the appropriate use of tests in decisions about tracking, promotion, and graduation and to possible uses of the proposed voluntary national tests.

Blanket criticisms of testing and assessment are not justified. When tests are used in ways that meet relevant psychometric, legal, and educational standards, students' scores provide important information that, combined with information from other sources, can lead to decisions that promote student learning and equality of opportunity (Office of Technology Assessment, 1992). For example, tests can identify learning differences among students that the education system needs to address. Because decisions about tracking, promotion, and gradu-

ation will be made with or without testing, proposed alternatives to testing should be at least equally accurate, efficient, and fair.

It is also a mistake to accept observed test scores as either infallible or immutable. When test use is inappropriate, especially in the case of high-stakes decisions about individuals, it can undermine the quality of education and equality of opportunity. For example, it is wrong to suggest that the lower achievement test scores of racial and ethnic minorities and students from low-income families reflect inalterable realities of American society.[1] Such scores reflect persistent inequalities in American society and its schools, and the inappropriate use of test scores can legitimate and reinforce these inequalities. This lends a special urgency to the requirement that test use in connection with tracking, promotion, and graduation should be appropriate and fair. With respect to the use of tests in making high-stakes decisions about students, the committee concludes that statements about the benefits and harms of testing often go beyond what the evidence will support.

CROSS-CUTTING THEMES

In important ways, educational decisions about tracking, promotion, and graduation are different from one another. They differ most importantly in the role that mastery of past material and readiness for new material play as decision-making criteria and in the importance of beneficial educational placement relative to certification as consequences of the decision. Thus, we have considered the role of large-scale, high-stakes testing separately in relation to each type of decision. However, tracking, promotion, and graduation also share common features that pertain to appropriate test use

---

[1] For recent evidence of major changes in group differences in test scores, see Hauser (1998), Grissmer et al. (1998), Huang and Hauser (1998), and Ceci et al. (1998).

and to their educational and social consequences. These include the alignment between testing and the curriculum, the social and economic sorting that follows from the decisions, the range of educational options potentially linked to the decisions, the use of multiple sources of evidence, the use of tests among young children, and improper manipulation of test score outcomes for groups or individuals. Even though we also raise some of these issues in connection with specific decisions, each of them cuts across two or more types of decisions. We therefore discuss them jointly in this section before turning separately to the use of tests in tracking, promotion, and graduation decisions.

It is a mistake to begin educational reform by introducing tests with high stakes for individual students. If tests are to be used for high-stakes decisions about individual mastery, such use should follow implementation of changes in teaching and curriculum that ensure that students have been taught the knowledge and skills on which they will be tested. Some school systems are already doing this by planning a gap of several years between the introduction of new tests and the attachment of high stakes to individual student performance, during which schools may achieve the necessary alignment among tests, curriculum, and instruction. Others may see high-stakes student testing as a way of leading curricular reform, not recognizing the danger that a test may lack the "instructional validity" required by law (*Debra P. v. Turlington*, 1981)—that is, a close correspondence between test content and instructional content.

To the extent that all students are expected to meet "world-class" standards, there is a need to provide world-class curricula and instruction to all students. However, in most of the nation, much needs to be done before a world-class curriculum and world-class instruction will be in place (National Academy of Education, 1996). At present, curriculum does not usually place sufficient emphasis on student understanding

and application of concepts, as opposed to memorization and skill mastery. In addition, instruction in core subjects typically has been and remains highly stratified. What teachers teach and what students learn vary widely by track, with those in lower tracks receiving far less than a world-class curriculum. If world-class standards were suddenly adopted, student failure would be unacceptably high (Linn, 1998a).

Recommendation: Accountability for educational outcomes should be a shared responsibility of states, school districts, public officials, educators, parents, and students. High standards cannot be established and maintained merely by imposing them on students.

Recommendation: If parents, educators, public officials, and others who share responsibility for educational outcomes are to discharge their responsibility effectively, they should have access to information about the nature and interpretation of tests and test scores. Such information should be made available to the public and should be incorporated into teacher education and into educational programs for principals, administrators, public officials, and others.

Recommendation: A test may appropriately be used to lead curricular reform, but it should not also be used to make high-stakes decisions about individual students until test users can show that the test measures what they have been taught.

The consequences of high-stakes testing for individual students are often posed as a either-or propositions, but this need not be the case. For example, social promotion and simple retention in grade are really only two of many educational strategies available to educators when test scores and other information indicate that students are experiencing serious academic difficulty. Neither social promotion nor retention alone is an effective treatment, and schools can use a number of possible strategies to reduce the need for these either-or choices—for example, by coupling early identification of such students with effective remedial education. Similar observations hold for decisions about tracking and about high school graduation.

Recommendation: Test users should avoid simple either-or options when high-stakes tests and other indicators show that students are doing poorly in school, in favor of strategies combining early intervention and effective remediation of learning problems.

Large-scale assessments are used widely to make high-stakes decisions about students, but they are most often used in combination with other information, as recommended by the major professional and scientific organizations in testing (American Educational Research Association et al., 1985, 1998; Joint Committee on Testing Practices, 1988). For example, according to a recent survey, teacher-assigned grades, standardized tests, developmental factors, attendance, and teacher recommendations form the evidence on which most school districts say that they base promotion decisions (American Federation of Teachers, 1997). A test score, like any other source of information about a student, is not exact. It is an estimate of the student's understanding or mastery of the content that a test was intended to measure.

Recommendation: High-stakes decisions such as tracking, promotion, and graduation should not automatically be made on the basis of a single test score but should be buttressed by other relevant information about the student's knowledge and skills, such as grades, teacher recommendations, and extenuating circumstances.

Problems of test validity are greatest among young children, and there is a greater risk of error when such tests are employed to make significant educational decisions about children who are less than 8 years old or below grade 3—or about their schools. However, well-designed assessments may be useful in monitoring trends in the educational development of populations of students who have reached age 5 (Shepard et al., 1998).

Recommendation: In general, large-scale assessments should not be used to make high-stakes decisions about students who are less than 8 years old or enrolled below grade 3.

All students are entitled to sufficient test preparation, but it is not proper to expose them ahead of time to items that will actually be used on their test or to give them the answers to those questions. Test results may also be invalidated by teaching so narrowly to the objectives of a particular test that scores are raised without actually improving the broader set of academic skills that the test is intended to measure (Koretz et al., 1991). The committee also recognizes that the desirability of "teaching to the test" is affected by test design. For example, it is entirely appropriate to prepare students by covering all the objectives of a test that represents the full range of the intended curriculum. Thus, it is important that test users respect the distinction between genuine remedial education and teaching narrowly to the specific content of a test.

Recommendation: All students are entitled to sufficient test preparation so their performance will not be adversely affected by unfamiliarity with item format or by ignorance of appropriate test-taking strategies. Test users should balance efforts to prepare students for a particular test format against the possibility that excessively narrow preparation will invalidate test outcomes.

There is an inherent conflict of interest when teachers administer high-stakes tests to their own students or score their own students' exams. On one hand, teachers want valid information about how well their students are performing. On the other hand, there is often substantial external pressure on teachers (as well as principals and other school personnel) for their students to earn high scores. This external pressure may lead some teachers to provide inappropriate assistance to their students before and during the test administration or to mis-score exams. The prevalence of such inappropriate practices varies among and within states and schools. Consequently, when there is evidence of a problem, such as from observations or other data, formal steps should be taken to ensure the validity of the scores obtained. This could include having an external monitoring system with sanctions, or having someone external to the school administer the tests and ensure their security, or both. Only in this way can the scores obtained from high-stakes tests be trusted as providing reasonably accurate results regarding student performance.

Members of some minority groups, English-language learners, and low-socioeconomic (SES) students are overrepresented in lower-track classes and among those denied promotion or graduation on the basis of test scores. Moreover, these same groups of students are underrepresented in high-track classes, "exam" schools, and "gifted and talented" programs (Oakes et al., 1992). In some cases, such as courses for English-language learners, such disproportions are not problematic. We would not expect to find native English speakers in classes designed to teach English to English-language learners.

In other circumstances, such disproportions raise serious questions. For example, although the grade placement of 6-year-olds is similar among boys and girls and among racial and ethnic groups, grade retardation among children cumulates rapidly after age 6, and it occurs disproportionately among males and minority group members. Among children 6 to 8 years old in 1987, 17 percent of white females and 22 percent of black males were enrolled below the modal grade for their age. By ages 9 to 11, 22 percent of white females and 37 percent of black males were enrolled below the modal grade for their age. In 1996, when the same children were 15 to 17 years old, 29 percent of white females and 48 percent of black males were either enrolled below the modal grade level for their age or had dropped out of school (U.S. Bureau of the Census, *Current Population Reports,* Series P-20). These disproportions are especially disturbing in view of other evidence that grade retention and assignment to low tracks have little educational value.

The concentrations of minority students, English-language learners, and low-SES students among those retained in grade, denied high school diplomas, and placed in less demanding classes raise significant questions about the efficacy of schooling and the fairness of major educational decisions, including those made using information from high-stakes tests.

The committee sees a strong need for better evidence on the benefits and costs of high-stakes testing. This evidence should tell us whether the educational consequences of particular decisions are educationally beneficial for students, e.g., by increasing academic achievement or reducing school dropout. It is also important to develop statistical reporting systems of key indicators that will track both intended effects (e.g., higher test scores) and other effects (e.g., changes in dropout or special education referral rates). For example, some parents or educators may improperly seek to classify their students as disabled in order to take advantage of accommodation in high-stakes tests. Indicator systems could include measures such as retention rates, special education identification rates, rates of exclusion from assessment programs, number and type of accommodations, high school completion credentials, dropout rates, and indicators of access to high-quality curriculum and instruction.

> Recommendation: High-stakes testing programs should routinely include a well-designed evaluation component. Policymakers should monitor both the intended and unintended consequences of high-stakes assessments on all students and on significant subgroups of students, including minorities, English-language learners, and students with disabilities.

APPROPRIATE USES OF TESTS IN TRACKING, PROMOTION, AND GRADUATION

Tracking

The intended purpose of tracking is to place each student in an educational setting that is optimal given his or her knowledge, skills, and interests. Support for tracking stems from a widespread belief that students will perform optimally if they receive instruction in homogeneous classes and schools, in which the pace and nature of instructions are tailored to their achievement levels (Oakes et al., 1992; Gamoran and Weinstein, 1998). The research evidence on this point, however, is unclear (Mosteller et al., 1996).

"Tracking" takes many different forms, including: (1) grouping between classes within a grade level based on perceived achievement or skill level; (2) selection for exam schools or gifted and talented programs; (3) identification for remedial education programs, such as "intervention" schools; and (4) referral for possible placement in special education (Oakes et al., 1992; Mosteller et al., 1996). Tracking is common in American schools, but tracking policies and practices vary, not only from state to state and district to district, but also from school to school. Because tracking policies and procedures are both diverse and decentralized, it is

difficult to generalize about the use of tests in tracking.

Research suggests that (1) as a result of tracking, the difference in average achievement of students in different classes in the same school is far greater in the United States than in most other countries (Linn, 1998a); (2) instruction in low-track classes is far less demanding than in high-track classes (Welner and Oakes, 1996; McKnight et al., 1987); (3) students in low-track classes do not have the opportunity to acquire knowledge and skills strongly associated with future success; and (4) many students in low-track classes would acquire such knowledge and skills if placed in more demanding educational settings (Slavin et al., 1996; Levin, 1988; Title I of the Elementary and Secondary Education Act).

> Recommendation: As tracking is currently practiced, low-track classes are typically characterized by an exclusive focus on basic skills, low expectations, and the least-qualified teachers. Students assigned to low-track classes are worse off than they would be in other placements. This form of tracking should be eliminated. Neither test scores nor other information should be used to place students in such classes.

Some forms of tracking, such as proficiency-based placement in foreign language classes and other classes for which there is a demonstrated need for prerequisites, may be beneficial. We make no attempt here to enumerate all forms of beneficial tracking. The general criterion of what constitutes beneficial tracking is that a student's placement, in comparison with other available placements, yields the greatest chance that the student will acquire the knowledge and skills strongly associated with future success.

The role that tests play in tracking decisions is an important and subtle issue. Educators consistently report that, whereas test scores are routinely used in making tracking decisions, most within-grade tracking decisions are based not solely on test scores but also on students' prior achievement, teacher judgment, and other factors (White et al., 1996; Delany, 1991; Selvin et al., 1990). Research also suggests that "middle class parents intervene to obtain advantageous positions for their children" regardless of test scores or of teacher recommendations (Lucas, in press: 206). Nonetheless, even when test scores are just one factor among several that influence tracking decisions, they may carry undue weight by appearing to provide scientific justification and legitimacy for tracking decisions that such decisions would not otherwise have. Some scholars believe that reliance on test scores increases the disproportionate representation of poor and minority students in low-track classes. However, test use can also play a positive role, as when a relatively high test score serves to overcome a negative stereotype (Lucas, in press). Tests may play an important, even dominant, role in selecting children for exam schools and gifted and talented programs (Kornhaber, 1997), and they also play an important part in the special education evaluation process (Individuals with Disabilities Education Act, 1997).

Although standardized tests are often used in tracking decisions, there is considerable variation in what tests are used. Research suggests that some tests commonly employed for tracking are not valid for this purpose (Darling-Hammond, 1991; Glaser and Silver, 1994; Meisels, 1989; Shepard, 1991) but that other standardized tests are.

Although test use varies with regard to tracking, certain test uses are inconsistent with sound psychometric practice and with sound educational policy. These include: using tests not valid for tracking purposes; relying exclusively on test scores in making placement decisions; relying on a test in one subject for placement in other subjects—which in secondary schools may occur indirectly when placement in one class, combined with scheduling considerations, dictates track placements in other subjects (Oakes et al., 1992; Gamoran, 1988); relying on subject-matter tests in English, without appropriate accommodation, in placing English-language learners in certain classes; and failing to reevaluate students periodically to determine whether existing placements remain suitable. It is also inappropriate to use test scores or any other information as a basis for placing children in settings in which their access to higher-order knowledge and skills is denied or limited.

Recommendation: Since tracking decisions are basically placement decisions, tests and other information used for this purpose should meet professional test standards regarding placement.

Recommendation: Because a key assumption underlying placement decisions is that students will benefit more from certain educational experiences than from others, the standard for using a test or other information to make tracking decisions should be accuracy in predicting the likely educational effects of each of several alternative educational experiences.

Recommendation: If a cutscore is to be employed on a test used in making a tracking or placement decision, the quality of the standard-setting process should be documented and evaluated.

PROMOTION AND RETENTION

The intended purposes of formal promotion and retention policies are (1) to ensure that students acquire the knowledge and skills they need for successful work in higher grades and (2) to increase student and teacher motivation to succeed. Many states and school districts rely on large-scale assessments, some heavily, in making decisions about student promotion and retention at specified grade levels. In the great majority of states and school districts, promotion and retention decisions are based on a combination of grades, test scores, developmental factors, attendance, and teacher recommendations (American Federation of Teachers, 1997). However, the trend is for more states and school districts to base promotion mainly on test scores.

Much of the current public discussion of high-stakes testing is motivated by calls for an end to social promotion. For example, in the Clinton administration's proposals for educational reform, an end to social promotion is strongly tied to early identification and remediation of learning problems. The proposal also calls for "appropriate use of tests and other indicators of academic performance in determining whether students should be promoted" (Clinton, 1998:3). The key question is whether testing will be used appropriately in such decisions.

Grade retention policies typically have positive intentions but negative consequences. The intended positive consequences are that students will be more motivated to learn and will consequently acquire the knowledge and skills they need at each grade level. The negative consequences, as grade retention is currently practiced, are that retained students persist in low achievement levels and are likely to drop out of school. Low-performing students who have been retained in kindergarten or primary grades lose ground both academically and socially relative to similar students who have been promoted (Holmes, 1989; Shepard and Smith, 1989). In secondary school, grade retention leads to reduced achievement and much higher rates of school dropout (Luppescu et al., 1995; Grissom and Shepard, 1989; Anderson, 1994). At present, the negative consequences of grade retention policies typically outweigh the intended positive effects. Simple retention in grade is an ineffective intervention.

Social promotion and simple retention in grade are only two of the educational interventions available to educators when students are experiencing serious academic difficulty. Schools can use a number of possible strategies to reduce the need for these either-or choices, for example, by coupling early identification of such students with effective remedial education. In this model, schools would identify early those students whose academic performance is weak and would then provide effective remedial education aimed at helping them to acquire the knowledge and skills needed to progress from grade to grade. The effectiveness of such alternative approaches would depend on the quality of the instruction that students received. It is neither simple nor inexpensive to provide high-quality remedial instruction. In the current political environment, the committee is concerned about the possibility that such remediation may be neglected once higher promotion standards have been imposed.

The committee did not attempt to synthesize research on the effectiveness of interventions that combine the threat of in-grade retention with other treatments, such as tutoring, reduced class size, enrichment classes, and remedial instruction after school, on weekends, or during the summer. Some states and localities are carrying out such research internally.

Pressure for test-based promotion decisions has resulted from the common but mistaken perception that social promotion is the norm. In fact, large numbers of students are retained in grade, and grade retention has increased over most of the past 25 years. For example, the percentage of 6- to 8-year-olds enrolled below the modal grade for their age rose from 11 percent in 1971 to a peak of 22 percent in 1990, and it was 18 percent in 1996. The rise reflects a combination of early grade retention and later school entry. At ages 15 to 17, the percentage enrolled below the modal grade for their age rose from 23 percent in 1971 to 31 percent in 1996 (U.S. Bureau of the Census, *Current Population*

Reports, Series P-20). Thus, about 10 percent of students are held back in school between ages 6 to 8 and ages 15 to 17.

In some places, tests are being used inappropriately in making promotion and retention decisions. For example, achieving a certain test score has become a necessary condition of grade-to-grade promotion. This is inconsistent with current and draft revised psychometric standards, which recommend that such high-stakes decisions about individuals should not automatically be made on the basis of a single test score; other relevant information about the student's knowledge and skill should also be taken into account (American Educational Research Association et al., 1985: Standard 8.12; 1998). It is also inconsistent with the explicit recommendations of test publishers about using tests for retention decisions; for example, as noted by Hoover et al., (1994:12): "A test score from an achievement battery should not be used alone in making such a significant decision." Also, some tests used in making promotion decisions have not been validated for this purpose (Shepard, 1991); for example, tests are sometimes used for promotion decisions without having been aligned with the curriculum in either the current or the higher-level grade.

Recommendation: Scores from large-scale assessments should never be the only sources of information used to make a promotion or retention decision. No single source of information—whether test scores, course grades, or teacher judgments—should stand alone in making promotion decisions. Test scores should always be used in combination with other sources of information about student achievement.

Recommendation: Tests and other information used in promotion decisions should adhere, as appropriate, to psycho-metric standards for placement and to psychometric standards for certifying knowledge and skill.

Recommendation: Tests and other information used in promotion decisions may be interpreted either as evidence of mastery of material already taught or as evidence of student readiness for material at the next grade level. In the former case, test content should be representative of the curriculum at the current grade level. In the latter case, test scores should predict the likely educational effects of future placements—whether promotion, retention in grade, or some other intervention options.

Recommendation: If a cutscore is to be employed on a test used in making a promotion decision, the quality of the standard-setting process should be documented and evaluated—including the qualification of the judges employed, the method or methods employed, and the degree of consensus reached.

Recommendation: Students who fail should have the opportunity to retake any test used in making promotion decisions; this implies that tests used in making promotion decisions should have alternate forms.

Recommendation: Test users should avoid the simple either-or option to promote or retain in grade when high-stakes tests and other indicators show that students are doing poorly in school, in favor of strategies combining early identification and effective remediation of learning problems.

AWARDING OR WITHHOLDING HIGH SCHOOL DIPLOMAS

The intended purposes of graduation test requirements are (1) to imbue the high school diploma with some generally recognized meaning, (2) to increase student and teacher motivation, (3) to ensure that students acquire the knowledge and skills they need for successful work or study after high school, and (4) to provide accurate information to parents, educators, and policymakers about student achievement levels. Graduation exams initially focused on basic skills and minimum competencies, but recently there has been a trend toward graduation tests that assess higher-order skills (American Federation of Teachers, 1997).

In most states, individuals earn high school diplomas based on Carnegie units, which are defined by the number of hours the student has attended class. Because this simply ensures that students have passed certain courses, an imprecise and nonuniform measure of what students know at the end of high school, 18 states require that students also pass a competency exam in order to graduate, usually in addition to satisfactorily completing other requirements for graduation (Council of Chief State School Officers, 1998).

Very little is known about the specific consequences of passing or failing a high school graduation examination, as distinct from earning or not earning a high school diploma for other reasons. We do know that earning a high school diploma is associated with better health and with improved opportunities for employment, earnings, family formation and stability, and civic participation (Hauser, 1997; Jaeger, 1989).

The consequences of using high-stakes tests to grant or withhold high school diplomas may be positive or negative. For example, if high-stakes graduation tests motivate students to work harder in school, the result may be increased learning for those who pass the test and, perhaps, even for those who fail. Similarly, if high-stakes tests give teachers and other local educators guidance on what knowledge and skills are most important for students to learn, that may improve curriculum and instruction. In fact, minimum competency tests do appear to have affected instruction, by increasing the amount of class time spent on basic skills (Darling-Hammond and Wise, 1985; Madaus and Kellaghan, 1991; O'Day and Smith, 1993), but available evidence about the possible effects of graduation tests on learning and on high school dropout is inconclusive (e.g., Kreitzer et al., 1989; Reardon, 1996; Catterall, 1990; Cawthorne, 1990; Bishop, 1997).

If students have not have been exposed to subject matter included on the test—which is more likely to be the case when tests "lead" curricular change or when tests are for some other reason not aligned with curriculum—this may be inconsistent with relevant legal precedents. If failing to achieve a certain score on a standardized test automatically leads to withholding a diploma, this may be inconsistent with current and draft revised psychometric standards, which recommend that other relevant information also be taken into account in such a high-stakes decision.

The current standards-based reform movement, which calls for high standards for all students, presents states with possible dilemmas when graduation testing is concerned (Bond and King, 1995). First, states must be able to show that students are being taught what the high-standards tests measure. At present, however, advanced skills are often not well defined and ways of assessing them are not well established. Second, there is evidence that graduation tests geared to high performance levels, such as those currently used in the National Assessment of Educational Progress, would result, at least in the short run, in denying diplomas to a large proportion of students (Linn, 1998b).

The committee recognizes that the passing rate on a test is dependent on the choice of a cutoff or cutscore. Moreover, we recognize that setting a relatively high cutscore will probably lead to large differences in passing rates among groups differing by race or ethnicity, socioeconomic status, gender, level of English proficiency, and disability status, unless ways are found to improve educational opportunities for all. This could include using tests to provide early identification of students who are at risk of failing a graduation test and offering them instruction that would be effective in increasing their chances of passing.

An alternate approach to a single, test-based graduation examination would be to require students to pass each of a series of end-of-course exams. Another policy would allow students to offset a low score in one area with a high score in another. A third approach would be to offer "endorsed" diplomas to students who have passed a test without denying a diploma to those who have failed a graduation test but completed all other requirements. The committee did not attempt to synthesize research on the effectiveness of interventions that combine the threat of diploma denial with other treatments, such as remedial instruction after school, on weekends, and during the summer. We do not know how best to combine advance notice of high-stakes test requirements, remedial intervention, and opportunity to retake graduation tests. Research is also needed to explore the effects of different kinds of high school credentials on employment and other post-school outcomes.

Recommendation: High school graduation decisions are inherently certification decisions; the diploma should certify that the student has achieved acceptable levels of learning. Tests and other information used for this purpose should afford each student a fair opportunity to demonstrate the required levels of knowledge and skill in accordance with psychometric standards for certification tests.

Recommendation: Graduation tests should provide evidence of mastery of material taught. Thus, there is a need for evidence that the test content is representative of what students have been taught.

Recommendation: The quality of the process of setting a cutscore on a graduation test should be documented and evaluated—including the qualification of the judges employed, the method or methods employed, and the degree of consensus reached.

Recommendation: Students who are at risk of failing a graduation test should be advised of their situation well in advance and provided with appropriate instruction that would improve their chances of passing.

Recommendation: Research is needed on the effects of high-stakes graduation tests on teaching, learning, and high school completion. Research is also needed on alternatives to test-based denial of the high school diploma, such as endorsed diplomas, end-of-course tests, and combining graduation test scores with other indicators of knowledge and skill in making the graduation decision.

USING THE VOLUNTARY NATIONAL TESTS FOR TRACKING, PROMOTION, OR GRADUATION DECISIONS

The purpose of the proposed voluntary national tests (VNTs) is to inform students (and their parents and teachers) about the performance of the students in 4th grade reading and 8th grade mathematics relative to the standards of the National Assessment of Educational Progress (NAEP) and the Third International Mathematics and Science Study (TIMSS).

The VNT proposal does not suggest any direct use of the test scores to make decisions about the tracking, promotion, or graduation of individual students. Indeed, representatives of the U.S. Department of Education have stated that the VNT is not intended for use in making such decisions. Nonetheless, some civil rights organizations and other groups have expressed concern that test users would inappropriately use the scores for such purposes. Indeed, under the proposed plan, test users—including states, school districts, and schools—would be free to use the tests as they pleased, just as test users are now free to use commercial tests for purposes other than those recommended by test developers and publishers. Accordingly—and because this study was requested in the context of the discussion of the VNT—the committee has considered whether it would be appropriate to make tracking, promotion, or graduation decisions about individual students based on their VNT scores.

For tracking decisions, use of VNT scores would necessarily be limited to placement in 5th grade reading and 9th grade mathematics. Moreover, using the scores to make future class placements would be valid only to the extent that the VNT scores were predictive of success in future placements. VNT proficiency levels, which are expected to be the same as those of NAEP, do not correspond well with other common definitions of proficiency: those embodied in current state content and performance standards (Linn, 1998b), those found in such widely used tests as the SAT and advanced placement exams (Shepard et al., 1993), and those used in traditional tracking systems. Indeed, the large share of students who score below the basic level in NAEP has led to justifiable concerns

that reports of achievement on the VNT will provide little information about lower levels of academic performance.

For promotion decisions, there is no guarantee that the framework or content of the VNT assessments would be aligned with the curriculum that students have experienced or would experience in the next-higher grade. Moreover, to make reliable distinctions based on the NAEP proficiency levels, the tests should include many items near the levels of difficulty that separate proficiency levels. Even with a focus on the NAEP proficiency levels, some testing experts have been concerned about the accuracy of VNT results, and if the tests are not accurate enough for descriptive purposes, they will surely not be accurate enough to use in making high-stakes decisions about individual students.

The need for multiple versions of a promotion test conflicts with the plan to release all VNT test items and their correct answers. In high-stakes testing situations, demands for fairness, as well as our criteria of validity and reliability in measurement, require that students who fail a promotion test be permitted to retake comparable versions of the test. However, there is no plan to develop or release extra forms of the VNT assessments for use in "second-chance" administrations, and, if such extra forms were developed, this would add to problems of test security.

Similar concerns apply to the use of VNT scores in making high school graduation decisions. It is doubtful that there would be any potential use for the results of a 4th grade reading test in determining an individual's fitness to receive a high school diploma. Although some states have deemed achievement at the 8th grade level sufficient to meet their graduation standard in mathematics, the lack of alternative test forms to allow students opportunities to retake the test makes the VNT inappropriate for this purpose.

There are clear incompatibilities between features of the VNT that would facilitate its use as a tool for informing students, parents, and teachers about student achievement, on one hand, and possible uses of the scores in making decisions about tracking, promotion, or graduation of individual students, on the other hand.

Recommendation: The voluntary national tests should not be used for decisions about the tracking, promotion, or graduation of individual students.

Recommendation: If the voluntary national tests are implemented, the federal government should issue regulations or guidance to ensure that VNT scores are not used for decisions about the tracking, promotion, or graduation of individual students.

The committee takes no position on whether the VNT is practical or appropriate for its primary stated purposes.

FORMS OF TESTING: PARTICIPATION AND ACCOMMODATIONS

Students with Disabilities

Recent legislative initiatives at both the federal and state levels mandate that all students be included in large-scale assessment programs, including those with special language and learning needs (Goals 2000, 1994; Improving America's School Act, 1994). For students with disabilities, the mandate is particularly strong due to the recently amended Individuals with Disabilities Education Act of 1997 (IDEA), which requires states and districts to provide for such participation as a condition of eligibility. However, in many cases, the demands that full participation of these students place on assessment systems are greater than current assessment knowledge and technology can support.

Participation of students with disabilities in large-scale assessments is important to ensure that schools are held accountable for the educational performance of these students and to obtain a fully representative, accurate picture of overall student performance. When these assessments are used to make high-stakes decisions about individual students, the potential negative consequences are likely to fall most heavily on groups with special learning needs, such as students with disabilities.

More than 5 million students with disabilities participate in special education programs under the IDEA. They vary widely in the severity of disability, educational goals, and degree of involvement in the general education curriculum. Although federal legislation defines 13 categories of disability, 90 percent of all special education students have one of four disabilities: speech or language impairment, serious emotional disturbance, mental retardation and/or specific learning disabilities. This diversity has important implications for how students with disabilities participate in large-scale assessments: for example, some participate fully in ways that are indistinguishable from their general education peers, some require modifications or accommodations in the testing procedure, and others are exempted from participation entirely (National Research Council, 1997).

For a number of reasons, many students with disabilities have previously not been included in the large-scale assessment programs conducted by their states and districts (National Research Council, 1997). In order for some students with disabilities to participate, accommodations—such as braille versions, alternate settings, extended time, and calculators—will need to be provided during testing. The purpose of accommodations is to correct for the impact of a disability that is unrelated to the subject matter being tested; in essence, the disability interferes with the student's capacity to demonstrate what he or she truly knows about the subject (Willingham, 1988).

Validity will be improved when testing accommodations are designed to correct for distortions in scores caused by specific disabilities. However, accommodations should be independent of the construct being measured (Phillips, 1993, 1994; American Educational Research Association et al., 1985). Determining whether an accommodation is independent of the construct is difficult for some types of disability, especially cognitive disabilities. Moreover, there is little research on how to design accommodations, a problem that is exacerbated by the lack of a reliable taxonomy for describing disabilities. Some strategies, such as computer adaptive testing for students who need extra time, may accommodate a large share of students with special needs without threatening the validity of test results. However, more research and development—along with access to the technology—are needed to bring this and other strategies into widespread use.

Accommodations should therefore be offered for two purposes: (1) to increase the participation of students with disabilities in large-scale assessments and (2) to increase the validity of the test score information. These two objectives—obtaining valid information while still testing all students—create a sizable policy tension for the design of assessment systems, particularly when they involve high stakes.

> Recommendation: More research is needed to enable students with disabilities to participate in large-scale assessments in ways that provide valid information. This goal significantly challenges current knowledge and technology about measurement and test design and the infrastructure needed to achieve broad-based participation.

In addition, students with disabilities are rarely included in adequate numbers in the pilot samples when new assessments are being developed; oversampling may be necessary to permit key statistical analyses, such as determining the impact of accommodations on test scores, norm development, and analyses of differential item functioning (Olson and Goldstein, 1997).

> Recommendation: The needs of students with disabilities should be considered throughout the test development process.

As the stakes of testing become higher, there is a greater need to establish the validity of tests administered to students with disabilities. At present, policies on the kinds of testing accommodations offered and to whom they are offered vary widely from place to place (Thurlow et al., 1993). New federal regulations require that the individual education program (IEP) document the decisions made about each child's participation in assessments and the type and nature of the accommodations needed. The proportion of students that require accommodations will depend on the purpose, format, and content of the assessment.

Parents of students with disabilities play unique roles as advocates for their children's rights, important participants in the IEP process, and monitors of accountability and enforcement. If high stakes are to be attached to the assessment of students with disabilities, then parents and other members of the IEP team will need to be able to make informed choices about the nature and extent of a student's participation in the assessment and its possible implications for future education and postschool outcomes.

> Recommendation: Decisions about how students with disabilities will participate in large-scale assessments should be guided by criteria that are as systematic and objective as possible. They should also be applied on a case-by-case basis as part of the child's individual education program and consistent with the instructional accommodations that the child receives.

Recommendation: If a student with disabilities is subject to an assessment used for promotion or graduation decisions, the IEP team should ensure that the curriculum and instruction received by the student through the individual education program is aligned with test content and that the student has had adequate opportunity to learn the material covered by the test.[2]

Although the basic principle should be to include all students with disabilities in the large-scale assessments, and to provide accommodations to enable them to do so, some number of students is likely to need to participate in a different or substantially modified assessment; the size of this group will depend on the nature of the assessment and the content being assessed. Obtaining meaningful information about the educational achievement and progress of these students is difficult. However, when the stakes are high, such as in deciding whether a student receives a diploma, it is critical for students who cannot take the test to have alternate ways of demonstrating proficiency. For students whose curriculum differs substantially from the general curriculum, there may also be a need to develop meaningful alternative credentials that can validly convey the nature of the student's accomplishments.

Recommendation: Students who cannot participate in a large-scale assessment should have alternate ways of demonstrating proficiency.

Recommendation: Because a test score may not be a valid representation of the skills and achievement of students with disabilities, high-stakes decisions about these students should consider other sources of evidence such as grades, teacher recommendations, and other examples of student work.

English-Language Learners

Federal and state mandates increasingly require the inclusion of English-language learners in large-scale assessments of achievement (Goals 2000 [P.L. 103-227], Title 1 (Helping Disadvantaged Children Meet High Standards] and Title VII [Bilingual Education] of the Improving America's Schools Act of 1994 [P.L. 103-382]). In particular, high-stakes tests are used with English-language learners for decisions related to tracking, promotion, and graduation, as well as for system-wide accountability. The demands that full participation of English-language learners make on assessment systems are greater than current knowledge and technology can support. In addition, there are fewer procedural safeguards for English-language learners under federal law than for students with disabilities.

When English-language learners are not proficient in the language of the assessment, their scores will not accurately reflect their knowledge. Thus, requiring those who are not proficient in English to take an English-language version of a test without accommodations will produce invalid information about their true achievement (American Educational Research Association et al., 1985; National Research Council and Institute of Medicine, 1997). This can lead to poor decisions about individuals and about English-language learners as a group, as well as about school systems in which they are heavily represented.

---

[2]To the extent that tracking decisions are based on readiness rather than mastery, there might not be any need to assume that the student has been exposed to particular curricular content. Thus, this recommendation does not pertain to tracking decisions.

Understanding the performance of English-language learners on achievement assessments requires satisfactory assessments of English-language proficiency, in order to determine whether poor performance is attributable to lack of knowledge of the test content or weak skills in English. Lack of a clear or consistent definition of language proficiency, and of indicators or measures of it, contributes to the difficulty of making these decisions more systematically (Olson and Goldstein, 1997).

Research evidence to date does not allow us to be certain about the meaning of test scores for students who are not yet proficient in English and who have received accommodations or modifications in test procedures. For any examination system employing accommodations or modifications, test developers or test users should conduct research to determine whether the constructs measured are the same for all children (Hambleton and Kanjee, 1994; Olson and Goldstein, 1997).

Accommodations and alternative tests should be provided (1) to increase the participation of English-language learners in large-scale assessments and (2) to increase the validity of test results. These two objectives—obtaining valid information while still testing all English-language learners—create a sizable policy tension for the design of assessment systems, particularly when they involve high stakes.

Recommendation: Systematic research that investigates the impact of specific accommodations on the test performance of both English-language learners and other students is needed. Accommodations should be investigated to see whether they reduce construct-irrelevant sources of variance for English-language learners without disadvantaging other students who do not receive accommodations. The relationship of test accommodations to instructional accommodations should also be studied.

Recommendation: Development and implementation of alternative measures, such as primary-language assessments, should be accompanied by information regarding the validity, reliability, and comparability of scores on primary-language and English assessments.

A sufficient number of English-language learners should be included when items are developed and pilot-tested and in the norming of assessments (Hambleton and Kanjee, 1994). Experts in the assessment of English-language learners might work with test developers to maintain the content difficulty of items while making the language of the instructions as well as actual test items more comprehensible. These modifications would have to be accomplished without making the assessment invalid for other students.

Recommendation: The learning and language needs of English-language learners should be considered during test development.

Various strategies can be used to obtain valid information about the achievement of English-language learners in large-scale assessments. These include native-language assessments and modifications that decrease the English-language load. Such strategies, however, are often employed inconsistently from place to place and from student to student. Monitoring of educational outcomes for English-language learners as a group is needed to determine the intended and unintended consequences of their participation in large-scale assessments.

Recommendation: Policy decisions about how individual English-language learners will participate in large-scale assessments—such as the language and accommodations to be used—should balance the demands of political accountability with professional standards of good testing practice. These standards require evidence that such accommodations or alternate forms of assessment lead to valid inferences regarding performance.

Recommendation: States, school districts, and schools should report and interpret disaggregated assessment scores of English-language learners when psychometrically sound for the purpose of analyzing their educational outcomes.

In addition, the role of the test score in decision making needs careful consideration when its meaning is uncertain. For example, invalid low scores on the test may lead to inappropriate placement in treatments that have not been demonstrated to be effective. Multiple sources of information should be used to supplement test score data obtained from large-scale assessment of students who are not language proficient, particularly when decisions will be made about individual students on the basis of the test (American Educational Research Association et al., 1985).

Recommendation: Placement decisions based on tests should incorporate information about educational accomplishments, particularly literacy skills, in the primary language. Certification tests (e.g., for high school graduation) should be designed to reflect state or local deliberations and decisions about the role of English-language proficiency in the construct to be assessed. This allows for subject-matter assessment in English only, in the primary language, or using a test that accommodates English-language learners by providing English-language assistance, primary language support, or both.

Recommendation: As for all learners, interpretation of the test scores of English-language learners for promotion or graduation should be accompanied by information about opportunities to master the material tested. For English-language learners, this includes information about educational history, exposure to instruction in the primary language and in English, language resources in the home, and exposure to the mainstream curriculum.

POTENTIAL STRATEGIES FOR PROMOTING APPROPRIATE TEST USE

The two existing mechanisms for promoting and enforcing appropriate test use—professional standards and legal enforcement—are important but inadequate.

The Joint Standards, and the Code of Fair Testing Practices in Education, ethical codes of the testing profession, are written in broad terms and are not always easy to interpret in particular situations. In addition, enforcement of the Joint Standards and the Code depends chiefly on professional judgment and goodwill. Moreover, professional self-regulation does not cover the behavior of individuals outside the testing profession. Many users of educational test results—policymakers, school administrators, and teachers—are unaware of the Joint Standards and are untrained in appropriate test use (Office of Technology Assessment, 1992).

Litigation, the other existing mechanism, also has limitations. Most of the pertinent statutes and regulations protect only certain groups of students, and most court decisions are not binding everywhere. Court decisions in different jurisdictions sometimes contradict one another (*Larry P. v. Riles*, 1984; *Parents in Action on Special Education v. Hannon*, 1980). Some courts insist that educators observe the principles of test use in the Joint Standards (Office of Technology Assessment, 1992:73–74) and others do not

(*United States v. South Carolina,* 1977). And court challenges are often expensive, divisive, and time-consuming. In sum, federal law is a patchwork of rules rather than a coherent set of norms governing proper test use, and enforcement is similarly uneven.

The committee has explored four possible alternative mechanisms that have been applied to problems similar to that of improper test use and about which empirical literature exists. It offers these as alternatives, some less coercive and others more so, that could supplement professional standards and litigation as means of promoting and enforcing appropriate test use.

• **Deliberative forums:** In these forums, citizens would meet with policymakers to discuss and make important decisions about testing. In this model, all participants have equal standing and are more likely to accept decisions, even those with which they disagree, because they feel that they have had an opportunity to influence the outcome. All parties with a stake in assessments would be represented. Such discussions could help define what constitutes "educational quality" and "achievement to high standards," the role that tests should play in shaping and measuring progress toward those goals, and the level of measurement error that is acceptable where test scores are used in making high-stakes decisions about students.

Broad public interest in testing makes this a good time to consider the establishment of such forums. We note, however, the importance of considering potential limitations of this strategy, including: a scarcity of successful examples, the reluctance of those with authority to part with it, and the large amounts of time and patience it would require.

• **An independent oversight body:** George Madaus and colleagues have proposed creating an independent organization to monitor and audit high-stakes testing programs (Madaus, 1992; Madaus et al., 1997). It would not have regulatory powers but would provide information to the public about tests and their use, highlighting best practices in testing. It could supplement a labeling strategy (see below) by educating policy-makers, practitioners, and the public about test practice. It could deter inappropriate test use by creating adverse publicity (Ernest House, personal communication 1998).

The shortcomings of this proposal include the monitoring body's lack of formal authority to require test publishers or school administrators to submit testing programs for review. Similarly, test users would be under no obligation to accept the body's judgments. It will be important for policymakers interested in the work of such a body to prevent unintended negative consequences.

• **Labeling:** Test producers could be required to report to test users about the appropriate uses and limitations of their tests. A second target of a labeling strategy would be test consumers: parents, students, the public, and the media. Relevant information could include the purpose of the test, intended uses of individuals' scores, consequences for individual students, steps taken to validate the test for its intended use, evidence that the test measures what students have been taught, other information used with test scores to make decisions about individual students, and options for questioning decisions based on test scores.

Limitations of this strategy include limited data on its effectiveness, the obstacles many parents face when they seek to challenge policies and actions with which they disagree, and the ineffectiveness of test labeling when the real problem is poor instruction rather than improper test use.

• **Federal regulation:** Federal statutes could be amended to include standards of appropriate test use. Title I regulations could be revised to ensure that large-scale assessments comply with established professional standards. State Title I plans could address the extent to which state and local assessment systems meet these professional norms. Title VI of the Civil Rights Act of 1964 and Title IX of the Education Amendment of 1972 prohibit federal fund recipients from discriminating on the basis of race, national origin, or sex; both have been cited in disputes about tests that carry high stakes for students. Under existing regulations, when a test has disproportionate adverse impact, the recipient of federal funds must demonstrate that the test and its use are an "educational necessity." Federal regulations do not, however, define this term. Thus, federal regulations could define educational necessity in terms of compliance with professional testing standards.

The advantages of this strategy would include its applying to all 50 states and virtually all school districts. Federal regulations could also be a powerful tool for educating policymakers and the public about appropriate test use. And relying on them would make use of existing administrative and judicial mechanisms to promote adherence to testing standards that are rarely enforced.

The risks of the regulatory approach are that the sanctions available for failure to comply—cutting off federal aid—make it unwieldy. Moreover, there is political resistance to federal regulation, creating the risk of a backlash that would make it more difficult for the U.S. Department of Education to guide local practice in testing and other areas. This strategy would also be subject to many of the usual disadvantages of administrative and judicial enforcement.

The committee is not recommending adoption of any particular strategy or combination of strategies, nor does it suggest that these four approaches are the only possibilities. We do think, however, that ensuring proper test use will require multiple strategies. Given the inadequacy of current methods, practices, and safeguards, further research is needed on these and other policy options to illuminate their possible effects on test use. In particular, we would suggest empirical research on the effects of these strategies, individually and in combination, on testing products and practice, and an examination of the associated potential benefits and risks.

REFERENCES

American Educational Research Association, American Psychological Association, & National Council on Measurement in Education. (1985). *Draft Standards for Educational and Psychological Testing*. Washington, DC: American Psychological Association.

American Educational Research Association, American Psychological Association, & National Council on Measurement in Education. (1998). *Standards for Educational and Psychological Testing*. Washington, DC: American Psychological Association.

American Federation of Teachers. (1997). *Passing on Failure: District Promotion Policies and Practices*. Washington, DC: American Federation of Teachers.

Anderson, D. K. (1994). *Paths through Secondary Education: Race/Ethnic and Gender Differences*. Unpublished doctoral dissertation. Ithaca, NY: Cornell University.

Bishop, J. H. (1997). *Do Curriculum-Based External Exit Exams Systems Enhance Student Achievement?* Ithaca, NY: Cornell University, Consortium for Policy Research in Education, Center for Advanced Human Resource Studies.

Bond, L.A., & King, D. (1995). *State High School Graduation Testing: Status and Recommendations*. Portland, OR: North Central Regional Educational Laboratory.

Catterall, J. S. (1990). *A Reform Cooled-Out: Competency Tests Required for High School Graduation* (CSE technical report 320). University California at Los Angeles, Center for Research on Evaluation, Standards, and Student Assessment.

Cawthorne, J. E. (1990). *"Tough" Graduation Standards for "Good" Kids.* Boston College, Center for the Study of Testing, Evaluation and Educational Policy.

Ceci, S. J., Rosenblum, T.B., & Kumph, M. (1998). The Shrinking Gap between High- and Low-Scoring Groups: Current Trends and Possible Causes. In U. Neisser (Ed.), *The rising curve* (pp. 287–302). Washington, DC: American Psychological Association Books.

Clinton, W. J. (1998). *Memorandum to the Secretary of Education: Press Release.* Washington, DC: The White House.

Council of Chief State School Officers (1998). *Survey of State Student Assessment Programs.* Washington, DC: Council of Chief of State School Officers.

Darling-Hammond, L. (1991). The Implications of Testing Policy for Quality and Equality. *Phi Delta Kappan, 73(3),* 220–225.

Darling-Hammond, L., & Wise, A. (1985). Beyond Standardization: State Standards and School Improvement. *Elementary School Journal 85(3),* 315–336.

Debra P. v. Turlington, 474 F. Supp. 244 (m.D. Fla 1979); aff'd in aprt and rev'd in part, 644 F. 2d 397 (5th Cir. 1981); rem'd 564 F. Supp. 177 (M.D. Fla. 1983), aff'd 730 F.2d 1405 (11th Cir. 1984).

Delany, B. (1991). Allocation, Choice, and Stratification within High Schools: How the Sorting Machine Copes. *American Journal of Education 99(2),* 181–207.

Gamoran, A. (1988). *A Multi-Level Analysis of the Effects of Tracking.* Paper presented at the annual meeting of the American Sociological Association. Atlanta, GA.

Gamoran, A., & Weinstein, M. (1998). Differentiation and Opportunity in Restructured Schools. *American Journal of Education, 106,* 385–415.

Glaser, R., & Silver, E. (1994). *Assessment, Testing, and Instruction: Retrospect and Prospect.* Los Angeles, CA: National Center for Research on Evaluation, Standards, and Student Testing.

Goals 2000, Educate America Act, 20 U.S.C. Sections 5801 et seq.

Grissmer, D., Williamson, S., Kirby, S. N., & Berends, M. (1998). Exploring the Rapid Rise in Black Achievement Scores in the United States (1970–1990). In U. Neisser (Ed.), *The Rising Curve* (pp. 251–285). Washington, DC: American Psychological Association Books.

Grisom, J. B., & Shepard, L. A. (1989). Repeating and Dropping Out of School. In L. A. Shepard & M. L. Smith (Eds.), *Flunking Grades* (pp. 34–63). London: Falmer.

Hambleton, R. K., & Kanjee, A. (1994). Enhancing the Validity of Cross-Cultural Studies: Improvements in Instrument Translation Methods. In T. Husen, & T. N. Postlewaite (Eds.), *International Encyclopedia of Education* (2nd ed., Vol. 11, pp. 6328–6334). Oxford, UK: Pergammon Press.

Hauseer, R. M. (1997). Indicators of High School Completion and Dropout. In R. M. Hauser, B. V. Brown, & W. R. Prosser (Eds.), *Indicators of Children's Well-Being.* New York: Russell Sage Foundation.

Hauser, R. M. (1998). Trends in Black-White Test Score Differentials: Uses and Misuses of NAEP/SAT Data. In U. Neisser (Ed.), *The Rising Curve* (pp. 219–249). Washington DC: American Psychological Association Books.

Hochschild, J., & Scott, B. (1998). Trends: Governance and Reform of Public Education in the United States. *Public Opinion Quarterly 62(1),* 79–120.

Holmes, C. T. (1989). Grade Level Retention Effects: A Meta-Analysis of Research Studies. In L. A. Shepard, & M. L. Smith (Eds.), *Research and Policies on Retention* (pp. 16–33). London: Falmer Press.

Hoover, H. D., Hieronymus, A. N., & Frisbie, D. A. (1994). *Interpretive Guide for School Admistrators: Iowa Test of Basic Skills,* Levels 5–14. Itasca, Il: Riverside.

Huang, M.H., & Hauser, R.M. (1998). Trends in Black-White Test Score Differentials: The Wordsum Vocabulary Test. In U. Neisser (Ed.), *The Rising Curve* (pp. 303–332). Washington, DC: American Psychological Association Books.

Improving America's Schools Act, 1994. Retrieved August 16, 2004, from http://www.evenstart.org/hrb.htm

Jaeger, R. M. (1989). Certification of Student Competence. In R. L. Linn (Ed.), *Educational Measurement* (pp. 485–514). New York: Macmillan.

Johnson, J., & Immerwahr, J. (1994). *First Things First: What Americans Expect from the Public Schools.* New York: Public Agenda.

Joint Committee on Testing Practices (1988). *Code of Fair Testing Practices.* Washington, DC: National Council on Measurement.

Koretz, D. M., Linn, R. L., Dunbar, S. B., & Shepard, L. A. (1991). *The Effects of High-Stakes Testing on Achievement: Preliminary Findings about Generalization across Tests.* Paper presented at the annual meeting of the American Educational Research Association and National Council on Measurement in Education, Chicago, IL.

Kornhaber, M. (1997). *Seeking Strengths: Equitable Identification for Gifted Education and the Theory of Multiple Intelligences.* Unpublished doctoral dissertation. Harvard University.

Kreitzer, A. E., Madaus, F., & Haney, W. (1989). Competency Testing and Dropouts. In L. Weis, E. Farrar, & H. G. Petrie (Eds.), *Dropouts from School: Issues, Dilemmas, and Solutions* (pp. 129–152). Albany: State University of New York Press.

Larry P. v. Riles, 495 F. Supp. 926 (N.D. Cal. 1979); aff'd 793 F. 2d 969 (9th Cir 1984).

Levin, H. (1988). *Accelerated Schools for At-Risk Students.* New Brunswick, NJ: Center for Policy Research in Education.

Linn, R. (1998a). *Assessments and Accountability.* Paper presented at the annual meeting of the American Educational Research Association. San Diego.

Linn, R. (1998b). Validating Inferences from National Assessment of Educational Progress Achievement-Level Setting. *Applied Measurement in Education, 11(1),* 23–47.

Lucas, S. R. (1999). *Tracking Inequality: Stratification and Mobility in American High Schools.* New York: Teachers College Press.

Luppescu, S., Bryk, A. S., Deabaster, P., Easton, J.Q., & Thum, Y.M., (1995). *School Reform Retention Policy, and Student Achievement Gains.* Chicago, IL: Consortium on Chicago School Research.

Madaus, G. F., Haney, W., Newton, K. B., & Kreitzer, A. E. (1993). *A Proposal for a Monitoring Body of Tests Used in Public Policy.* Boston: Center for the Study of Testing, Evaluation, and Public Policy.

Madaus, G. F., Haney, W., Newton, K. B., & Kreitzer, A. E. (1997). *A Proposal to Reconstitute the National Commission on Testing and Public Policy as an Independent, Monitoring Agency for Educational Testing.* Boston: Center for the Study of Testing, Evaluation, and Public Policy.

Madaus, G. F., & Kellaghan, T. (1991). *Examination Systems in the European Community: Implications for a National Examination System in the U.S.* Paper presented for the Science, Education, and Transportation Program, Office of Technology Assessment, U.S. Congress, Washington, DC.

McKnight, C. C., Crosswhite, F. J., Dossey, J. A., Kifer, E., Swafford, S. O., Travers, K., & Cooney, T. J. (1987). *The Underachieving Curriculum: Assessing U.S. School Mathemathics from an International Perspective*. Champaign, IL: Stipes.

Meisels, S. J. (1989). *Testing, Tracking, and Retaining Young Children: An Analysis of Research and Social Policy*. Commissioned paper for the National Center for Education Statistics.

Mosteller, F., Light, R., & Sachs, J. (1996). Sustained Inquiry in Education: Lessons from Skill Grouping and Class Size. *Harvard Educational Review, 66(4)*, 797–843.

National Academy of Education (R. Linn, & G. Bohrnstedt, Eds.). (1996). *Quality and Utility: The 1994 Trial State Assessment in Reading*. Stanford, CA: National Academy of Education, Panel on the Evaluation of the NAEP Trial State Assessment.

National Research Council—Committee on Child Development Research and Public Policy (K. A. Heller, W. H. Holtzman, S. Messick, Eds.). (1982). *Placing Children in Special Education: A Strategy for Equity*. Washington, DC: National Academy Press.

National Research Council—Committee on Goals 2000 and the Inclusion of Students with Disabilities (L. M. McDonnell, M. L. Mclaughlin, P. Morrison, Eds.). (1997). *Education One and All: Students with Disabilities and Standards Based Reform*. Washington, DC: National Academy Press.

O'Day, J. A., & Smith, M. S. (1993). Systemic Reform and Educational Opportunity. In S. H. Fuhrman (Ed.), *Designing Coherent Educational Policy* (pp. 250–312). San Francisco: Jossey-Bass.

Oakes, J. A., Gamoran, A., & Page, R. (1992). Curriculum Differentiation: Opportunities, Outcomes, and Meanings. In P. Jackson (Ed.), *Handbook of Research on Curriculum* (pp. 570–608). New York: Macmillan.

Office of Technology Assessment. (1992). *Testing in American Schools: Asking the Right Questions*. Washington, DC: U.S. Government Printing Office OTA-SET-519.

Olson, J. F., & Goldstein, A. A. (1997). *The Inclusion of Students with Disabilities and Limited English Proficient Students in Large-Scale Assessments: A Summary of Recent Progress*. Washington, DC: U.S. Department of Education, Office of Educational Research and Improvement, NCES 97-482.

Parents in Action on Special Education (PASE) v. Hannon, 506 F. Supp. 831 (N. D. Ill. 1980).

Phillips, S. E. (1993). Testing Accommodations for Disabled Students. *Educational Law Reporter, 80*, 9–32.

Phillips, S. E. (1994). High-Stakes Testing Accommodations: Validity versus Disabled Rights. *Applied Measurement in Education, 7(2)*, 93–120.

Reardon, S. F. (1996). *Eighth Grade Minimum Competency Testing and Early High School Dropout Patterns*. Paper presented at the annual meeting of the American Educational Research Association, New York.

Selvin, M. J., Oakes, J., Hare, S., Ramsey, K., & Schoeff, D. (1990). *Who Gets What and Why: Curriculum Decision Making at 3 Comprehensive High Schools*. Santa Monica, CA: Rand.

Shepard, L. A. (1991). Negative Policies for Dealing with Diversity: When Does Assessment and Diagnosis Turn into Sorting and Segregation? In E. Hiebert (Ed.), *Literacy for a Diverse Society* (pp. 278–298). New York: Teachers College Press.

Shepard, L. et al. (1993). Evaluating Test Validity. *Review of Research in Education, 19*, 405–450.

Shepard, L. A., Kagan, S., & Wurtz, E. (Eds.). (1998). *Principles and Recommendations for Early Childhood Assessments*. Washington, DC: National Educational Goals Panel.

Shepard, L. A., & Smith, M. L. (1989). Academic and Emotional Effects of Kindergarten Retention in One School District. In L. A. Shepard, & M. L. Smith (Eds.), *Flunking Grades: Research and Policies on Retention* (pp. 79–107). London: Falmer.

Slavin, R. E., Madden, N. A., Dolan, L. J., & Wasik, B. A. (1996). *Every Child, Every School: Success for All*. Thousand Oaks, CA: Corwin Press.

Thurlow, M. L., Ysseldyke, J. E., & Silverstein, B. (1993). *Testing Accommodations for Students with Disabilities: A Review of Literature (Synthesis Report 4)*. Minneapolis, MN: National Center on Educational Outcomes.

Title 1, Elementary and Secondary Education Act, 20 U.S.C. Sections 6301 et seq. United States v. South Carolina.

Welner, K. G., & Oakes, J. (1996). (Li)ability Grouping: The New Susceptibility of School Tracking Systems to Legal Challenges. *Harvard Educational Review, 66(3)*, 451–470.

White, P. Gamoran, A., Smithson, J., & Porter, A. (1996). Upgrading the High School Math Curriculum: Math Course-Taking Patterns in Seven High Schools in California and New York. *Educational Evaluation and Policy Analysis, 18(4)*, 285–307.

Willingham, W. W. (1988). Introduction. In W. W. Willingham, M. Ragosta, R. E. Bennett, H. Braun, D.A. Rock, & D. E. Powers (Eds.), *Testing Handicapped People* (pp. 1–16). Boston: Allyn & Bacon.

Questions and Activities

1. Examine a standardized test used by a school district or a state. Determine the strengths and weaknesses of a large-scale assessment for students in a particular school in your community. Whose interests are best served by the test? Whose interests are not served by it? What are the goals of the test? What other forms of assessment could be used to provide a more comprehensive view of student achievement?

2. How does the National Research Council's Committee on Appropriate Test Use define *validity?* Using the Committee's definition, examine the validity of a standardized test. How could the test better serve students, teachers, and school districts to meet state and federal standards?

3. The Committee on Appropriate Test Use recommends that students receive balanced preparation for standardized test experiences without "excessively narrow preparation." Given the already crowded school curriculum, how can teachers best prepare students for standardized tests without "teaching to the test?"

4. The Committee on Appropriate Use discusses key policy objectives for including special populations in large-scale assessments. How does the Committee define special populations? What are the policy objectives identified by the Committee? How can these objectives be actualized in district practices?

5. How do tracking, promotion and graduation differ? How and to what extent should these issues be influenced by test scores or methods of assessment?

6. How can schools and districts avoid using large-scale testing as the only indicator of students' mastery of knowledge?

7. Identify and discuss the strategies described by the Committee on Appropriate Test Use for promoting appropriate test use at the school district and state levels.

8. What specific guidelines does the Committee on Appropriate Use give for using tests with special population groups such as students with disabilities and English language learners? What problems might teachers encounter in trying to implement these guidelines? How might these problems best be solved?

CHAPTER 2

Culture in Society and in Educational Practices

Frederick Erickson

A group of first graders and their teacher are in the midst of a reading lesson in a classroom in Berkeley, California. The children read aloud in chorus from their reading book:

1 T: All right, class, read that and remember your endings.

2 CC: What did Little Duck see? (final t of "what" deleted)

3 T: What. (emphasizing final t)

4 CC: What (final t deleted as in turn 2)

5 T: I still don't hear this sad little "t."

6 CC: What did—what did—what—(final t's deleted)

7 T: What.

8 T&CC: What did Little Duck see? (Final t spoken)

9 T: OK, very good

(Piestrup, 1973, pp. 96–97)

What is cultural in this picture? How are those aspects of culture, and other aspects as well, related to issues of multicultural education? This chapter tries to answer these questions by considering various ways in which culture has been thought of and how those varying definitions of culture have relevance for education in general and for multicultural education in particular. The chapter first surveys a number of issues broadly in an overview. Later in the chapter, as the issues are revisited more closely, pertinent citations are included.

CULTURE: AN OVERVIEW

In a sense, everything in education relates to culture—to its acquisition, its transmission, and its invention. Culture is in us and all around us, just as is the air we breathe. It is personal, familial, communal, institutional, societal, and global in its scope and distribution.

31

Yet culture as a notion is often difficult to grasp. As we learn and use culture in daily life, it becomes habitual. Our habits become for the most part invisible to us. Thus, culture shifts in and outside our reflective awareness. We do not think much about the structure and characteristics of culture as we use it, just as we do not think reflectively about any familiar tool in the midst of its use. If we hammer things a lot, we do not think about the precise weight or chemical composition of the steel of the hammer, especially as we are actually hammering; and when we speak to someone we know well, we are unlikely to think reflectively about the sound system, grammar, vocabulary, and rhetorical conventions of our language, especially as we are doing things in the midst of our speaking.

Just as hammers and languages are tools by which we get things done, so is culture; indeed, culture can be thought of as the primary human toolkit. Culture is a product of human creativity in action; once we have it, culture enables us to extend our activity still further. In the sense that culture is entirely the product of human activity, an artifact, it is not like the air we breathe. By analogy to computers, which are information tools, culture can be considered as the software—the coding systems for doing meaning and executing sequences of work—by which our human physiological and cognitive hardware is able to operate so that we can make sense and take action with others in daily life. Culture structures the "default" conditions of the everyday practices of being human.

Another way to think of culture is as a sedimentation of the historical experience of persons and social groupings of various kinds, such as nuclear family and kin, gender, ethnicity, race, and social class, all with differing access to power in society. We have become increasingly aware that the invention and sharing of culture (in other words, its production and reproduction) happen through processes that are profoundly political in nature, having to do with access to and distribution of social power. In these processes of cultural production and reproduction, the intimate politics of immediate social relations face to face are combined with a more public politics in the social forces and processes of economy and society writ large. How does the sedimentation of historical experience as culture take place? What are the micro- and macropolitical circumstances in which culture is learned and invented? How does culture get distributed, similarly and differently, within and across human groups and within and between human generations?

These are questions not only for social scientists or for social philosophers to address; they also are questions that raise issues that are essential for educators to consider. Culture, as it is more and less visible and invisible to its users, is profoundly involved in the processes and contents of education. Culture shapes and is shaped by the learning and teaching that happen during the practical conduct of daily life within all the educational settings we encounter as learning environments throughout the human life span—in families, in school classrooms, in community settings, and in the workplace. There is some evidence that we begin to learn culture in the womb, and we continue to learn new culture until we die. Yet people learn differing sets and subsets of culture, and they can unlearn culture—shedding it as well as adopting it. At the individual and the group level, some aspects of culture undergo change and other aspects stay the same within a single human life and across generations.

Educators address these issues every time they teach and every time they design curricula. They may be addressed by educators explicitly and with conscious awareness, or they may be addressed implicitly and without conscious awareness. But at every moment in the conduct of educational practice, cultural issues and choices are at stake. This chapter makes some of those issues and choices more explicit.

Two final orienting assumptions are implicit in the previous discussion. First, everybody is cultural, and although there is no evidence base on which to decide that any particular cultural ways are intrinsically more valuable than others—more inherently superior or inferior—it is a plain political fact that not all cultural practices are equal in power and prestige in the United States or in any other country. Every person and social group possesses and uses culture as a tool for the conduct of human activity. This means that culture is not the possession or characteristic of an exotic other, but of all of us, the dominant and the dominated alike. In other words, and to put it more bluntly, within U.S. society White people are just as cultural as are people of color (indeed the terms *White* and *people of color* represent cultural categories that are socially constructed). Moreover, White Anglo-Saxon Protestants (WASPs) are just as cultural as are Jews or Catholics; men are just as cultural as women; adults are just as cultural as teenagers; Northerners are just as cultural as Southerners; English speakers are just as cultural as the speakers of other languages; and native-born Americans are just as cultural as immigrants or citizens who reside in other countries. This is to say, Americans of African or European or Asian descent are just as cultural as people who live in Africa, Europe, or Asia. To reiterate, everybody in the world is cultural, even though not all cultures are equal in power or prestige.

The second orienting assumption is that everybody is multicultural. Every person and every human group possesses both culture and cultural diversity. For example, Americans of Mexican descent are not culturally identical to Puerto Ricans who live on the mainland, but not all Mexican Americans or Puerto Ricans (or White Episcopalians, for that matter) are culturally identical even if they live in the same neighborhood and attend the same school or church. Members of the same family also are culturally diverse. In fact, we often encounter cultural difference as individual difference, as well as encountering culture in its more institutionalized manifestations, such as school literacy, the legal system, or the broadcast media. An important way we meet culture is in the particular people with whom we interact daily.

It is not possible for individuals to grow up in a complex modern society without acquiring differing subsets of culture—differing software packages that are tools that can be used in differing kinds of human activity, tools that in part enable and frame the activities in which they are used. Through the nuclear family, through early and later schooling, through peer networks, and through life at work, we encounter, learn, and to some extent help create differing microcultures and subcultures. Just as everyone learns differing variants and styles of the various languages we speak, so that everybody is multilingual (even those of us who only speak English), so, too, is everybody multicultural. No matter how culturally isolated a person's life may appear, in large-scale modern societies (and even in small-scale traditional societies) each member carries a considerable amount of that society's cultural diversity inside. This insight is very clearly stated in an article by Goodenough (1976)—"Multiculturalism as the Normal Human Experience."

If it is true that every person and human group is both cultural and multicultural, then a multicultural perspective on the aims and conduct of education is of primary importance. That assumption guides this chapter. First, it considers a variety of definitions of culture. Then it discusses how culture is organized and distributed in society, and this raises issues that have special relevance for education. The discussion comments on teaching and learning in multicultural classrooms in the light of the conceptions of culture previously discussed. The chapter concludes with further discussion of the diversity of culture not only within society but also within the person and the implications of that diversity for multicultural education.

ALTERNATIVE DEFINITIONS AND CONCEPTIONS OF CULTURE

Attempts at formal definitions of culture have not been fruitful; even the experts have not been able to agree on what culture *really* is. Yet some ways of thinking about culture seem increasingly to be inadequate and misleading and others are more useful. Presented here is a range of definitions, emphasizing the differing conceptions of culture that underly the various definitions. I begin with two initial definitions, the first of which was in use by the eighteenth century and the second of which became current in the nineteenth century. Then I consider five more contemporary conceptions of culture.

I. Culture as Cultivation

All conceptions of culture imply a distinction between the cultural and the natural. Cultivation transforms the natural in a social sense just as agriculture transforms nature in a biological and chemical sense. Cultivating the soil makes for fewer weeds than in nature (indeed, the distinction between what is considered weed and what is considered plant is a cultural one). Cultivation requires effort and method—it evokes images of straight furrows, of working, and of planning for the future harvest.

The agricultural metaphor for culture bears a family resemblance to an artistic one. In the fine arts, cultivation also involves disciplining the natural—the fingers learn to find keys on the piano; the painter's eye and hand and the ballerina's feet are schooled by artistic convention. Thus, in ordinary use, culture has come to mean high culture—what we find in the museum, the symphony hall, the theater, the library. In those institutions we find cultural products whose value is defined by elite tastes, which are defined and framed reflexively by those cultural products.

In contrast to prestigious high culture, there is also low culture—popular culture—which is another sense in which the term *culture* is used. Some artifacts of U.S. popular culture, such as blue jeans and popular music, have been adopted throughout the world. In the realm of popular culture, fashions change across time and across various social groups and social sectors, just as they do in the realm of high culture. We have diverse artifacts and practices of popular culture with differential appeal, such as classic rock'n'roll, rap, country, and Cajun music. We have Western cowboy boots, motorcycle boots, hiking boots, upland game hunting boots, and Nike basketball sneakers, each with a different resonance among subgroups within U.S. society and each potentially able to serve as badges of personal and group identity.

In the social sciences, the term *culture* refers to phenomena that are less mystifying than those of so-called high culture and less sensational than those of popular culture. In the social scientific sense, culture is seen as something everyone has and makes use of routinely, regardless of social position. It refers to the patterns for sense-making that are part of the organization of the conduct of everyday life.

This egalitarian notion of culture arose among Western Europeans in the Enlightenment (Vico, 1744/1968), and it developed further in the early Romantic period, foreshadowed by Rousseau and continued by the brothers Grimm and by von Humboldt. The Grimms collected folktales from German peasants whose language and folk knowledge had been made fun of by aristocrats in earlier times. This shift toward greater respect for the lifeways of ordinary people happened between the mid-eighteenth and the early nineteenth centuries.

2. Culture as Tradition

By the early nineteenth century, culture was beginning to be seen as tradition—that which is handed down across generations. Within anthropology during the nineteenth century, culture was seen as a sum total of social inheritance. In 1871, the anthropologist Sir Edward Burnett Tylor (1871/1970) presented this broad definition: "Culture or Civilization . . . is that complex whole which includes knowledge, belief, art, morals, law, custom, and any other capabilities and habits acquired by man as a member of society" (p. 1).

As genetic theory was developing, culture came to be seen as a kind of gene pool existing at the level of social symbolism and meaning rather than biology. By 1917, a U.S. anthropologist called culture the "superorganic," meaning that it had an ideational rather than material existence (Kroeber, 1917). Following Tylor and others, Kroeber assumed that culture was a whole system consisting of interrelated parts, not literally a living organism but metaphorically similar to one.

Yet the notion of culture remained fuzzy among social scientists. Near the end of his career, Kroeber collaborated with Kluckhohn in a review of the uses of the term *culture*. Their review of anthropology and sociology publications turned up hundreds of citations and differing shadings of meaning for the word (Kroeber & Kluckhohn, 1952). Since then, no scholar has tried to put forward a single, authoritative meaning of the term.

3. Culture as Information Bits

Let us turn now to contemporary definitions of culture. Currently, one conception of culture considers it analogous to information bits in a computer as well as to genetic information in a breeding population. According to this view, culture can be thought of as consisting of many small chunks of knowledge that are stored as a large pool of information within a bounded social group (see Goodenough, 1981). No single member of the group has learned all knowledge that is possessed by the group as a whole. The amounts and kinds of information known are seen as varying widely across individuals and subgroups within the total population.

This variation can be understood by analogy to language. What we call a *language* has a sound system (pronunciation), a syntax (grammar), and a lexicon (vocabulary). Those who understand the literal meaning of a sound system, a syntax, and a lexicon are termed members of the same *language community*. Subsets of the language are called dialects—they are spoken by members of subgroups within the overall language community. Dialects may vary in some aspects of pronunciation of vowels or consonants, or in some aspects of grammar, or in vocabulary, but any dialect is still intelligible overall to speakers of other dialects within the language. Each person within a language community speaks a unique form of that language, called an *idiolect* (i.e., no one individual actually speaks "English"; all individuals pronounce the language sounds in slightly differing ways and use grammar and vocabulary in individually distinct ways, in a kind of personal dialect). By this analogy, an overall general culture = language, while dialect = subculture, and idiolect = microculture, which can be thought of as a personal or immediately local variation on a subculture or general culture.

4. Culture as Symbol System

Another conception considers culture as a more limited set of large chunks of knowledge—conceptual structures that frame or constitute what is taken as "reality" by members of a social group (Geertz, 1973). These central organizing constructs—core symbols—are seen as being shared widely throughout the group. The routine ways of acting and making sense that are used by members of the group tend to repeat the major framing patterns again and again, just as within a musical composition many variations can be written on a few underlying thematic elements. This conception of culture emphasizes relatively tight organization of patterns, coherence in the overall meaning system, and identical (or at least closely shared) understandings of symbols and shared sentiments regarding those symbols among the members of the social group.

5. Culture as Motive and Emotion

Another current approach considers both the cognitive and the emotional/motivational force of culture (Lutz, 1990). We learn customs, but why do we become emotionally attached to them? How do we come to desire and work for ends and to use means for reaching those ends that are culturally enjoined? We do not act on culturally defined goals simply because we are forced to do so, although in situations of unequal power subordinates may fake it—they may feign more allegiance to cultural norms, such as politeness or diligence, than they in fact are feeling. Still, culturally defined love objects are genuinely yearned for, culturally defined careers do become the objects of genuine aspiration and striving, and customs that are culturally defined as repulsive, such as eating sea slugs, evoke strong emotional reactions of disgust in some social groups, even though those same food practices are seen as normal or even highly desirable in other social groups.

Contemporary neuroscience shows that engaging in routine activities activates not only the neural networks that involve prior cognitive learning (i.e., neural connections to the cerebral cortex) but also the neural connections to our emotional states at the time of initial learning (i.e., neural connections to the limbic system). Thus, our repetition of certain customary activities evokes and reinforces emotional feelings as well as thoughts and skills (D'Andrade & Strauss, 1992). Through continued participation in daily life we thus require cultural models for its conduct that involve feeling in our knowing. In an important sense that went unrecognized in earlier cognitive psychology, all of our cognitions are "hot cognitions," and learning is a profoundly emotional activity as well as a cognitive one.

6. Culture as Distributed along Lines of Power in Society

A sixth conception treats the distribution of power and culture in modern societies as intertwined (Bourdieu, 1977; Bourdieu & Passeron, 1977; Williams, 1983). The fourth and fifth conceptions of culture could be applied to small-scale traditional societies as well as to large-scale modern ones. The sixth conception attempts to account for the production, distribution, and reproduction of culture as this distinctly happens in large-scale modern societies or in modernizing ones. It considers the basic social unit as the nation-state.

Some work within this stream of approaches emphasizes the diversity of cultural knowledge within a state (Barth, 1969, 1989). Cultural difference is seen as tracing lines of status, power, and political interest within and across the subgroups and institutions found in the nation-state as a total social unit. This variation in cultural difference within a whole modern society can be seen as analogous to the ways in which differences in air pressure or temperature are displayed on a weather map. There is variation in temperature in the earth's atmosphere, and it is nonrandomly distributed. There is variation in culture within a human society, and it, too, is nonrandomly distributed, closely related to the differential allocation of power and prestige within the society, across lines of social class, race, ethnicity, gender, language, and religious affiliation. For many who take this view of culture, the connections between social-class difference and cultural difference have been seen as primary.

One school of thought within this sixth mode sees culture not as being a cognitive template for the routine conduct of everyday life but as residing in the conduct of everyday life itself (Bourdieu, 1977; Ortner, 1984). This conduct is seen as practice, as routine activity that is habitual and goal directed (Connell, 1982). Practices are daily and customary, but they also tend toward a projected outcome, although the aims in such "projects" may not be entirely conscious ones. Thus, the person engaged in the practical conduct of everyday life can be seen as not simply following cultural "rules" (as in the second and third conceptions of culture listed previously) or as responding to cultural symbols always in the same ways (as is implied in the fourth conception of culture), but as being strategic—an active agent who uses culture as tools adaptively, employing novel means when necessary to achieve desired ends.

The second, third, fourth, and fifth conceptions of culture can be criticized as presuming that human actors are the passive recipients of shaping by their social circumstances and that once having acquired culture through learning they are on "automatic pilot," capable only of following general cultural rules or scripts and incapable of acting adaptively in unique local circumstances. These views consider the cultural actor as a robot or as a "social dope" (Garfinkel & Sacks, 1970); they leave no room for human agency. Practice theory, on the other hand, takes realistic account of how habitual and conservative our daily conduct is, but it leaves room for the assumption that individuals can make sense adaptively within their practices, rather than simply following cultural rules.

The schools of thought that see culture as inherently related to issues of social structure and power also tend to see culture as arising through social conflict, with the possibility of differing interest groups becoming progressively more culturally different across time even though the groups may be in continual contact.

Overall, the sixth conception of culture emphasizes three related points: (1) the systematic variation of culture in relation to the allocation of power in society; (2) social conflict as a fundamental process through which cultural variation is organized, through which traditional culture is being simultaneously forced on people and contested, and through which new culture is continually being invented; and (3) human agency in the use of cultural tools, both tools inherited through tradition and tools invented through their use in practice within changing circumstances (Giddens, 1984).

7. Culture as Residing in Local Communities of Practice

A seventh conception sees culture as the practices of specific sets of persons interacting within local communities of practice. In this view, not only is culture what persons do but it is what particular persons do in mutual influence upon one another as they associate regularly together. A particular family household group is one kind of local community of practice whose members possess distinct funds of knowledge (Moll, 1998; Moll & Greenberg 1990). A particular school classroom is another local community of practice, a religious congregation is another, and a particular work setting is another—not the classroom or workplace considered abstractly as general social forms, but local gatherings of particular people considered as specific communities of practice. Individuals play roles of apprenticeship within such communities of practice, and those roles change over time as newcomers become more proficient in and centrally participatory in the sets of practices that are customary in a particular community of practice. Learning, from this perspective, can be defined as change over time in individuals' forms of participation within a local community of practice (see Lave & Wenger, 1990; Rogoff, 2003; Wenger, 1999).

The sources of the practices are in part nonlocal and in part local; that is, some practices may derive from the social-class, racial, ethnic, linguistic, and gender backgrounds of persons and groups in society at large (as in the sixth conception of culture), but the particular versions of these practices are locally distinct. They are partly the result of unique local invention. Thus, the class-based practices of one family are not identical to those of another family—there are subtle yet important differences between them. Moreover, across the life cycle individuals participate in multiple communities of practice, acquiring multiple microcultural repertoires as their own personal culture, and these repertoires differ from one individual to the next among persons within the "same" social category (e.g., class, race, gender). This seventh conception of culture, in other words, accounts for the acquisition of personal culture (the implications of distinctive diversity of culture within the individual will be explored later in this chapter). One's personal culture is acquired by showing up regularly in certain settings of practice rather than in others. Where one shows up, in which local communities of practice and how often, provides each individual with opportunities for cultural learning that are so distinct, so site specific and person specific, that they are literally unique.

This conception of culture also accounts for "bottom-up" cultural change, in the distinct local versions of practices that arise through invention and sharing within local communities of practice. Local communities of practice are thus seen as sites of cultural innovation. As a new member joins the group or as a current member begins to act differently within the group, this influences what other members do interactionally; the social ecology of the group changes as a result of the learning and/or the subtle cultural innovations that are continually taking place and are being manifested in the improvised actions of individual members. Some of this innovation may then be adopted by other local communities of practice in processes of social and cultural change within which the practices that originated locally come to influence the general society (Rogoff, 2003). Currently we don't understand well how the cultural innovation that initially takes place in local communities of practice comes to be adopted more widely within society. But bottom-up cultural change does happen, and cultural innovation is always occurring within local communities of cultural practice; that is, tactical innovation is inherent in the everyday conduct of work—of local practice (for a general argument along these lines, see Erickson, 2004).

From this perspective, the emphasis is not on culture as a general integrated system but on the content of cultural knowledge and practice within the specific life situations of the persons and groups by whom such knowledge is held and such practices are undertaken. This position assumes that new culture—whether conceived as small information bits or as larger structures of concept and activity—is being transformed continually within the contradictions experienced by particular persons in their daily lives. These new cultural forms are either accepted, learned, and remembered, or rejected, ignored, and forgotten, depending on where one sits in the social order and depending on the particular circumstances in the situation in which the new culture is invented.

Summary Discussion

Now, more than 40 years since Kroeber and Kluckhohn's review of social scientists' use of the term *culture*, formal definitions, while overlapping, still do not agree exactly (Kuper, 1999). Yet culture is generally seen as a product of human activity that is used as a tool. It is seen as being learned and transmitted from our elders and also as being invented (or incrementally transformed) through recurrent improvisation within current situations of practice. How much and in what ways culture is shared within and between identifiable human groups are issues on which there is much debate currently. Power and politics seem to be involved in the processes by which culture is learned, shared, and changed. Culture, in other words, takes shape in the weight of human history. Some aspects of culture are explicit, and others are implicit, learned, and shared outside conscious awareness. Our moods and desires as well as our thoughts are culturally constructed.

Culture can be thought of as a construction—it constructs us and we construct it. That is, all thoughts, feelings, and human activity are not simply natural but are the result of historical and personal experiences that become sedimented as culture in habit. Culture varies, somehow, from one person or group to another. Since our subjective world—what we see, know, and want—is culturally constructed, and since culture varies, persons really do not inhabit the same subjective worlds even though they may seem to do so. Even though some of us show up at what seems to be the same event, how we experience it is never quite the same across the various individuals who have joined together in interaction. Thus, no single or determinative human world is a fixed point of reference. Individually and collectively, we make cultural worlds and they are multiple. This point has profound implications for educators, as is discussed in the following sections.

As human beings not only do we live in webs of meaning, caring, and desire that we ourselves create and that create us, but those webs also hang in social gravity (Geertz, 1973). Within the webs all our activity is vested in the weight of history; that is, in a social world of inequality all movement is up or down. Earlier conceptions of culture described it and human actions guided or framed by it as existing in a universe without gravity. Movement was thus unconstrained; it had no effort, no force. There was no domination or subordination, no resistance or compliance in such a cultural world. In more recent conceptions of culture, we are coming to see that, living as we do in a gravity-ridden social and cultural universe, we always have weight. We are culturally constructed and constructing beings, and in that construction we are never standing still.

CULTURAL ISSUES IN EDUCATION, IN SOCIETY, AND IN PERSONS

The previous discussion provides a framework for the four main issues that have special relevance for educators: (1) the notion of culture as invisible as well as visible, (2) the politics of cultural difference in school and society, (3) the inherent diversity of cultures and subcultures within human social groups, and (4) the diversity of cultures within the individual—a perspective on the self as multiculturally constructed.

Invisible Culture

The distinction between visible and invisible culture has also been called explicit/implicit or overt/covert (Hall, 1959, 1976; Philips, 1983). Much of culture is not only held outside conscious awareness but is also learned and taught outside awareness; hence, neither the cultural insiders nor the newcomers are aware that certain aspects of their culture exist. In multicultural education and in discussions of cultural diversity more generally, the focus has been on visible, explicit aspects of culture, such as language, dress, food habits, religion, and aesthetic conventions. While important, these visible aspects of culture, which are taught deliberately and learned (at least to some extent) consciously, are only the tip of the iceberg of culture.

Implicit and invisible aspects of culture are also important. How long in clock time one can be late before being impolite, how one conceives or experiences emotional or physical pain, how one displays such pain behaviorally, what topics should be avoided at the beginning of a conversation, how one shows interest or attention through listening behavior, how loud is too loud or not loud enough in speaking, how one shows that one would like the speaker to move on to the next point—these are all aspects of culture that we learn and use without realizing it. When we meet other people whose invisible cultural assumptions and patterns of action differ from those we have learned and expect implicitly, we usually do not recognize what they are doing as cultural in origin. Rather, we see them as rude or uncooperative. We may apply clinical labels to the other people—passive-aggressive or suffering from low self-esteem.

Differences in invisible culture can be troublesome in circumstances of intergroup conflict. The difficulty lies in our inability to recognize others' differences in ways of acting as cultural rather than personal. We tend to naturalize other people's behavior and blame them—attributing intentions, judging competence—without realizing that we are experiencing culture rather than nature.

Modern society exacerbates the difficulties that can result from differences in invisible culture. Formal organizations and institutions, such as hospitals, workplaces, the legal system, and schools, become collection sites for invisible cultural difference. If the differences were more visible, we might see less misattribution, in the absence of intergroup conflict. For example, if we were to meet a woman in a hospital emergency room who was wearing exotic dress, speaking a language other than English, and carrying food that looked and smelled strange, we would not assume that we understood her thoughts and feelings or that she necessarily understood ours. Yet when such a person is dressed similarly to us, speaks English, and does not differ from us in other obvious ways, we may fail to recognize the invisible cultural orientations that differ between us, and a cycle of mutual misattribution can start.

Anthropologists with linguistic and cognitive orientations have identified aspects of invisible culture (Gumperz, 1982; Hymes, 1974). They make a helpful distinction between language community and speech community or network. People in the same language community share knowledge of the sound system, grammar, and vocabulary of a language. But within the same language community there are diverse speech communities or networks—sets of persons who share assumptions about the purposes of speaking, modes of politeness, topics of interest, ways of responding to others. Those cultural assumptions concerning ways of speaking differ considerably, even though at a general level all are uttering the same language. That is, language community differences are visible, but speech community differences are often invisible.

Yet cultural difference, visible and invisible, does not always lead to trouble between people. These differences become more troublesome in some circumstances than in others. That leads to a consideration of the circumstances of intercultural contact.

The Politics of Cultural Difference: Boundaries and Borders

The introductory discussion states that cultural difference demarcates lines of political difference and often of domination. By analogy to a weather map, boundaries of cultural difference can be seen as isobars of power, rank, and prestige in society. One can trace boundaries of networks of members who share cultural knowledge of various sorts, such as language, social ideology and values, religious beliefs, technical knowledge, preferences in aesthetic tastes—in recreation and sport, in personal dress and popular music tastes, and in cultivated tastes in the fine arts, cuisine, and literature. Because these preferences have differing prestige value, they have been called cultural capital (Bourdieu, 1977; Bourdieu & Passeron, 1977). Such preferences also become symbols, or badges of group identity—markers of ethnicity, religion, gender, or social class.

The presence of cultural difference in society does not necessarily lead to conflict, however, nor need it lead to difficulty in education. The presence of conflict depends on whether cultural difference is being treated as a *boundary* or as a *border* (Barth, 1969; Giroux, 1991; McDermott & Gospodinoff, 1981). *A cultural boundary refers to the presence of some kind of cultural difference.* As noted earlier, cultural boundaries are characteristic of all human societies, traditional as well as modern. *A border is a social construct that is political in origin.* Power is exercised across a border, as in the political border between two nations.

When a cultural boundary is treated as a cultural border, differences in rights and obligations are powerfully attached to the presence or absence of certain kinds of cultural knowledge. Consider, for example, the political/cultural border between the United States and Mexico. On either side of the border are people who speak English and people who speak Spanish; that is, the boundaries of language community cross over the lines demarcating national citizenship. Yet on either side of the border, fluency in Spanish—which is an aspect of cultural knowledge—is differentially rewarded or punished. On the Mexican side of the border, fluency in Spanish is an advantage legally, educationally, and in the conduct of much daily life, while on the U.S. side, the same cultural knowledge is disadvantaged; indeed in parts of south Texas, speaking Spanish is still stigmatized.

When one arrives at a cultural border, one's cultural knowledge may be held up for scrutiny—stopped and frisked. An ancient example comes from the biblical Book of Judges.

In approximately 800 B.C., the Hebrews were not yet fully unified politically under a monarch and they had not yet completely occupied the territory of Canaan. They were a loose federation of kinship groups or clans that periodically came together in an unstable, tense alliance against common enemies. A dispute broke out between soldiers of two of the clans, the men of Ephraim and the men of Gilead. After defeat in a battle with the Ammonites, the common enemy, the men of Ephraim were trying to escape across fords in the Jordan River. The fords were guarded on the Hebrew-occupied side of the river by Gileadites. The men of Gilead checked the clan identity of the retreating soldiers by testing their cultural knowledge: "When any of the fugitives of Ephraim said, 'Let me go over,' the men of Gilead said to him, 'Are you an Ephraimite?' When he said, 'No,' they said to him, 'Then say Shibboleth.' He said 'Sibboleth,' for he could not pronounce it correctly. Then they seized him and slew him at the fords of the Jordan" (Judges 12:5b–6a, RSV). The two clans of Hebrews differed in their pronunciation of the initial sibilant in the word *Shibboleth*. The Gileadites used the /sh/ phoneme for that consonant, while the Ephraimites used the /s/ phoneme. The Gileadite soldiers were aware of this cultural difference and made use of it to construct a sociolinguistic test at a geographic and political border, which, because of the test imposed, became a cultural border as well.

In modern societies the same thing can happen when one enters the emergency room of a hospital and speaks to an admitting clerk or when one speaks to the maitre d' at a restaurant. It also can happen in school classrooms. Yet cultural boundaries (the objective presence of cultural difference) need not necessarily be treated as cultural borders. This is a matter of socially constructed framing.

The framing of cultural difference as boundary or as border can change over time. Sometimes that change is very rapid, as in the following example (Fanon, 1963). In Algeria shortly before France gave up colonial rule, the pronunciation of the announcers on the state radio was made a cultural border issue by the independence movement. Complaints were voiced that Radio Algiers was not employing native Algerians. This practice was seen as another symbol of colonial oppression by France. Radio Algiers sent out a statement that its announcers were in fact Algerians. The independence movement then asked why the radio announcers spoke cosmopolitan French rather than the Algerian dialect. The complaints about the announcers became increasingly strident in the independence-oriented press, right up to Independence Day. After that day the announcers on Radio Algiers continued to speak cosmopolitan French but public complaint ended instantly. The reason for the complaint was gone, and so a small feature of cultural difference, which had been framed for a time as a cultural border, was reframed as a cultural boundary.

These two examples suggest that cultural difference, rather than being considered a cause of conflict in society (and in education), is more appropriately seen as a resource for conflict. If people have a reason to look for trouble, cultural difference—especially one that becomes a badge of social identity—can be used to start a fight. But the causes of the fight go beyond the cultural difference itself.

Cultural Differentiation as a Political Process

What happens over time when certain aspects of cultural difference get treated as border issues? Examples from language suggest that the differences become more extreme on either side. This suggests that political conflict, explicit and implicit, is a major engine of culture change. Such conflict generates cultural resistance. Labov (1963) found that on Martha's Vineyard, a small island off the coast of Massachusetts, certain sound features in the islanders' dialect became increasingly divergent from the more standard English spoken by summer tourists as the number of tourists staying on the island in the summer increased over time, although the islanders were not aware that this was happening. First-hand contacts with a standard model of American English had been increasing for the islanders, but across a generation their speech was becoming more different from that of the mainlanders.

A similar process of divergence was reported as taking place across the time span of half-hour interviews in experimental situations (Giles & Powesland, 1975). Speakers of differing British regional dialects were paired for two-person discussions. In some discussions, mild discomfort and conflict were experimentally introduced, while in other discussions conflict was not introduced. In the discussions with conflict and discomfort, by the end of a half-hour each person was speaking a broader form of his or her regional dialect than before the discussion began. In other words, if a Yorkshireman were talking to a person from Dorsetshire, he would become more distinctly Yorkshire in his pronunciation and the Dorset man would become more Dorsetshire in his pronunciation as the conversation between the two progressed. Conversely, when conflict was not introduced and the two parties spoke comfortably, pronunciation features that differed between their two dialects became less distinct—they were converging in speech style rather than diverging.

This example suggests that cultural divergence is a result rather than a cause of social conflict. Bateson, Jackson, Hally, and Weakland (1972) called the tendency of subsystems to evolve in increasingly differentiated ways complementary *schismogenesis*, which seems to be the process by which cultural resistance over time results in culture change. It should be emphasized, however, that such change can occur entirely outside the conscious awareness of those involved in it as well as in situations of more explicit, conscious awareness in which people are deliberate regarding the change they are struggling to produce.

The classic view of culture in social science was as a total system with integrated parts, the operation of which tended toward maintaining a steady state. As we have seen, culture now seems to be more labile than that—variable in the moment. This raises the question of how we conceive of culture change—as loss, as gain, as a mixture of both, or less evaluatively as change. We must also consider how culture is shared within human groups. We usually think of ethnic and racial groups (and perhaps of gender categories as well) as necessarily identifying cultural boundaries. Such groups, we may assume, are defined by shared culture among their members. Barth (1969) contends, however, that culture sharing is not the crucial defining attribute of ethnic group membership. Rather, the ethnic or racial group is more appropriately considered as an economic and political interest group. Features of culture may be considered as identity badges, indicating group membership. But culture sharing is not essential for this, according to Barth. There may be much cultural diversity within the same named social category. He used as an example the Pathans (also called Pashtun), who live as a numerical minority on one side of the border between Pakistan and Afghanistan and as a majority on the other side. Some Pathans are herders—more so on the Afghan side of the border. Other Pathans are farmers—more so on the Pakistani side. Yet both herders and farmers will identify as Pathan and are so regarded by other ethnic groups on either side of the border. Their ethnic identification is at least as strong as is their identification with the nation-state within whose border they reside; that became apparent during the war in Afghanistan in 2002.

Culture Change as Culture Loss—or Not

When we think of ethnic/racial groups and cultural groups as having the same boundaries—the traditional view—we sometimes think of culture change as culture loss. Members of an ethnic group can blame themselves for losing a language, a religion, a household practice. Native Americans, for example, have mourned the passing of old culture and have gone beyond mourning to self-blame, considering themselves less Indian than their forebears. Yet if a Koyukon Athabaskan now uses a snowmobile rather than a dog team and sled, does that mean he or she is any less Koyukon than before? Not necessarily, if we follow Barth's analysis. What is essential for the maintenance of ethnic groups and ethnic identities are not the specifics of culture traits practiced by the members; rather, being ethnic counts economically and politically in the larger society. Even the specific ways in which it counts to be ethnic can change; yet if there continue to be economic and political consequences of being identified as ethnic, especially if that is to the advantage of the members, then the ethnic group continues.

The classic view makes culture the defining attribute of ethnic identity. It becomes easy, then, to see culture change as culture loss. This can be thought of as the leaky bucket perspective on culture change—as if culture were held in a human group as water is contained in a bucket. Change then becomes the holes in the bucket. As one carries such a bucket over time and space, the water gradually drains out. Alternatively, we can conceive of the bucket of culture as always full. Air may replace the water, but the bucket is never empty. The contemporary Koyukon society, with its snowmobile practices, can be considered just as full culturally as the Koyukon society in the days of sled and dog team. What is in the bucket is different now, but the bucket is still not empty. During the summer people in an Odawa community in northern Ontario wear T-shirts as they fish from aluminum boats powered by outboard motors. They no longer wear buckskin and use birchbark canoes. Yet they continue to fish, and they do so with differing fishing rights from those of White Canadians. Moreover, they still consider themselves Odawa, as distinct from White Canadians in neighboring villages who also fish from aluminum boats while wearing T-shirts.

Culture and Collective Identity Formation

To call something cultural has in itself political implications. Because so many aspects of culture are transparent to its users in their use, ordinarily we do not think about or notice them. Yet in complex and diverse modern societies, as ethnic, racial, religious, and gender identifications become self-aware among identification group members, they begin to notice their customary practices and to identify them as cultural. As with ethnic identification, cultural identification is always relational and comparative—with reference to an other. In the early nineteenth century, for example, German *Kultur* began to be invoked by German intellectuals in contrast and opposition to the French and Italians, whose tastes in literature and music, architecture, and clothing had previously set the standard of what was desirable in upper-class polite society. Without the presence of French and Italian models to compete with, Germans may not have become so aware of their own Germanness. This awareness progressed beyond rediscovery to invention, with German intellectuals such as Wagner helping to create a Germanic heritage with the support of the ruling interests in German society. With this rise in in-group awareness and solidarity came a heightened awareness of boundaries with non-Teutonic others. To the extent that this perception of out-groups was invidious, the boundaries became borders.

We see a similar phenomenon today with the rise of religious nationalism and of ethnic and racial nationalism. With in-group identification there is always the possibility for treating boundaries as borders. Especially when heightening of cultural awareness and identification is used as a political strategy for changing power relations in society, or for legitimating territorial or colonial expansion, in-group solidarity and identification can become demonic. As Said (1978) notes in commenting on the colonial relationship between Europe and a perceived Orient that was a cultural creation of Europeans themselves, when more powerful nations or interest groups identify some Other as exotic and different, there can be a tendency for the more powerful to project their own flaws, contradictions, and hostilities on the constructed Other. Such projections are reciprocated by those who have been "Othered" in a process of mutual border framing. Through this process of projective "Othering," negative cultural stereotypes result, making the fostering of intercultural and multicultural awareness a tricky business indeed.

Ethnic identification need not necessarily lead to Othering in the negative sense, however—the comparisons with those who differ from "Us" need not be invidious. Cultural differences can be framed as boundaries rather than as borders even though such framing takes effort to maintain. It should be noted, however, that an increase in the deliberateness and intensity of cultural awareness necessarily involves a comparative awareness. The construction of in-group identity is a relational process through which a definition of Other as well as of Self, of Them as well as of Us—and in the case of subordinated groups a specific identification of aspects of oppression—becomes more focal in conscious awareness.

TEACHING AND LEARNING MULTICULTURALLY

Emphasizing Invisible as Well as Visible Culture

Schools can support or hinder the development of healthy identity and of intergroup awareness. The discussion now turns to teaching and learning in classrooms (see Wills, Lintz & Mehan, 2004). This chapter emphasizes the importance of culture and criticizes our tendencies to essentialize it. When we essentialize culture, assuming that all persons in a given social category are culturally similar and focusing on the unitary cultures of various Others without reflecting on our own cultures and their diversity, we open a Pandora's box of opportunity for negative attribution. Sometimes social scientific notions of culture, especially of culture as unified system and of group membership as culturally defined, have provided a justification for intergroup stereotypes. When these stereotypes come with social scientific warrant, we call them neostereotypes.

Teaching about the cultural practices of other people without stereotyping or misinterpreting them and teaching about one's own cultural practices without invidiously characterizing the practices of other people should be the aims of multicultural education. In situations of intergroup conflict these aims can be ideals that are difficult to attain. Educators should face such difficulty realistically.

One problem in multicultural curriculum and pedagogy is the overemphasis on visible (explicit) culture at the expense of the invisible and implicit. Focusing mainly on explicit culture can be misleading. Even when we do this respectfully of the lifeways of others, focus on visible culture easily slides into too comfortable a stance for considering other people—a stance of cultural romance or cultural tourism.

Particular traits of visible culture, often treated in isolation, have become the basis for much of what we teach about cultural diversity in schools. Some educators speak critically of "piñata curriculum," "snowshoe curriculum," and "holidays and heroes" in characterizing this approach. By treating cultural practices as sets of static facts, we trivialize them in superficiality and we make it seem as if culture were necessarily unchanging. What if Mexican Americans were to have a party and not break a piñata? Would they be any less Mexican? They are only if we adopt an essentialist view of culture, with its accompanying leaky bucket image of culture change.

A way to teach about explicit culture without overgeneralizing about the lifeways of other people is to emphasize the variability of culture within social groups and the continual presence of cultural change as well as cultural continuity across time. Unfortunately, published multicultural materials that have an essentialist emphasis may not lend themselves well to this method. Yet in every classroom there is a resource for the study of within-group cultural diversity as well as between-group diversity. That resource is the everyday experience and cultural practices of the students and teachers themselves. (This is most easily done in a self-contained classroom, and so this discussion may seem most relevant for elementary school teaching, but many of the issues and approaches mentioned can be undertaken by high school and college teachers as well.)

Critical Autobiography as Curriculum and as Action Research

Critically reflective autobiographies by students and oral histories of their families—a form of community action research—can become important parts of a multicultural curriculum. Even in a classroom with a student population highly segregated by race or by social class, reflective investigation of their own lives and of family and local community histories by students will reveal diversity as well as similarity (hooks, 1993; Skilton Sylvester, 1994; Torres-Guzmán, 1992; Wiggington, 1986; Witherell & Noddings, 1991). Not all the Italian Americans in a classroom have had the same family experience of immigration. Not all the African American students whose forebears moved from the rural South to a large city have had the same experience of urbanization. As a result of differing life experiences, there are differences in cultural funds of knowledge between families who on the surface appear to be demographically similar—differences in family microcultures (see Moll, 1990, 1998).

Just as students can engage in critical autobiography, so their teachers need to identify the particular cultures of their individual students through observation of and dialogue with those students. An index for the individual student's distinctive cultural repertoire is that student's distinctive *daily round*—where the student shows up and what is happening there, in the specific sequences and ranges of engagement of the student in local communities of practice inside and outside school. By learning which particular communities of practice a student has had access to, and the kinds of participation in those communities that a student has engaged in, a teacher can come to understand the personal culture of each student—to see each student as "cultural" without stereotyping the student simplistically as "Anglo" or "African American," as "lower class" or "upper middle class," as "boy" or "girl." In order to develop this kind of non-stereotypical understanding of actual students, a teacher must spend time outside school in the school community(ies) from which the teacher's students come as well as pay attention to the communities of practice that are found during the school day in places beyond that teacher's own classroom. There is no substitute for this first-hand knowledge of the everyday interactional circumstances of the particular children one teaches—without it one adopts stereotypic, categorical "cultural" labels for students that are too general to be able to take accurate account of the actual lives, the personal cultures, that those specific children are developing.

A close look at particular families and at the daily rounds of individuals can reveal similarity as well as distinctiveness—as in variations on a common theme of life experience such as that of the experience of racism by African Americans or of language prejudice by those who grow up speaking Spanish in the United States. But not all the experiences, even of racism within a given racial group, are identical. Thus, diversity and similarity always accompany one another in the real stories of people in human groups. Those stories have involved struggles to change, to resist. Contemporary community issues, as students address them through local community study, also provide opportunities for students to take action to improve the circumstances of their lives and, in the process, come to see themselves and their families not simply as passive recipients of social and cultural influences, but as active agents who are making sense and making their lives.

Direct connections between the daily lives of students outside the classroom and the content of instruction in history, social studies, and literature can make the stated curriculum come alive. These connections also afford the teacher an opportunity to learn the cultural backgrounds and cultural diversity that he or she confronts with each set of students. As stated earlier, formal organizations in modern societies become collection sites for cultural diversity. This is true for every school classroom. Each new set of students represents a unique sampling from the universe of local cultural diversity present in the school area. Simply knowing that one has three Haitian students and four Cambodian students—or seventeen girls and eleven boys—in a certain classroom, for example, does not tell that teacher anything (necessarily) about the specific cultural backgrounds of those students and their families and their assumptions about ethnicity, race, or gender, given the cultural diversity that is possible within any social category. The teacher's tasks are to know not only about Haitians or Cambodians in general, or about girls and boys in general, but also about these students in particular. By making particular student culture and family history a deliberate object of study by all the students in the classroom, the teacher can learn much about what he or she needs to know in order to teach the particular students in ways that are sensitive and powerfully engaging, intellectually and emotionally.

As our standards for what students need to learn change from the lower-order mastery of facts and simple skills to higher-order reasoning and the construction of knowledge that is personally distinctive and meaningful (in other words, as we move from an essentialist understanding of curriculum, teaching, and learning to a more constructivist one), our conceptions of culture in multicultural education also need to become more constructivist and less essentialist. Teaching about culture as socially constructed and continually changing is thus consistent with contemporary definitions of good pedagogy as well as consistent with recent developments in culture theory and social theory.

Reframing Borders as Boundaries in the Classroom

This approach frames the cultural diversity to be found in the classroom in terms of cultural boundaries rather than cultural borders. Even when cultural difference and group identity are highly politicized in the wider society, by approaching the culture of students forthrightly in the classroom they can be depoliticized to a remarkable extent (or perhaps we might think of it as being repoliticized in a positive rather than negative frame).

A problem comes with teaching second-culture skills and knowledge as morality rather than as pragmatic skills for survival and success. Delpit (1995) observes that for students of color in the United States, the school's "second culture" often appears alien and dominating. Culturally mainstream ways of speaking and writing represent a "language and culture of power" that minority students need to master for success in the wider society. But this culture of power can be taught unsuccessfully in two ways. In the first, the teacher attempts to teach the second-culture skills in a moralizing way—the right way to act and to be. This approach is likely to stimulate student resistance and thus is a teaching strategy that risks student refusal to learn. (Consider the word *ain't*. Teachers for generations have been teaching working-class students not to say *ain't* as a moral lesson. Yet inside and outside the classroom the students still say *ain't*.)

Another unsuccessful way to teach a second-culture skill is implicitly, according to Delpit. She observes that among well-meaning middle-class White teachers, some aspects of the language of power are part of the teacher's own invisible culture. Taking it for granted themselves, they do not teach it explicitly to working-class African American students.

Delpit (1995) recommends an alternative approach—to teach second-culture skills explicitly and carefully but without moralizing. The school's language and culture of power can be presented as a situational dialect to be used pragmatically for special situations, such as job interviews, formal writing, and college admissions interviews. When combined with reflective self-study of the student's own language use in the family, among peers, and in the neighborhood—study by which the student explores his or her own repertoire of differing speech styles used in differing situations—explicit teaching and learning of the language of power can be framed as a matter not of cultural borders but of cultural boundaries. This approach takes a critical and strategic view of multiculturalism for survival reasons.

Multicultural Pedagogy as Emancipatory

Other multicultural educators recommend a critical approach to cultures of domination and to the phenomenon of domination. Ladson-Billings (1994) describes African American and White teachers who are effective with African American students. They taught in a variety of styles, but one common approach was to deal directly and explicitly with issues of injustice and oppression and the privileging of mainstream knowledge and perspectives as they came up in the curriculum and in the reported daily experiences of their students. Trueba (1994), Nieto (1999), McCarthy (1993), Perry and Fraser (1993), Sleeter and Grant (1993), Apple (1996), and Giroux (1991) all recommend a similar approach, sometimes called critical pedagogy, counter-hegemonic pedagogy, or emancipatory pedagogy.

Cultural hegemony refers to the established view of things—a commonsense view of what is and why things happen that serves the interests of those people already privileged in a society. When the school presents a comfortable established view of the nature of U.S.

society and of the goodness and inherent rightness of school knowledge and school literacy, that is hegemonic. Students whose lives are not affirmed by the establishment seem intuitively not to accept hegemonic content and methods of instruction. They often resist, consciously or unconsciously, covertly as well as overtly.

Multicultural education has an opportunity and a challenge to be counter-hegemonic. When such issues as racism, class privilege, and sexism are left silent in the classroom, the implicit message for students of color appears to be that the teacher and the school do not acknowledge that experiences of oppression exist. If only the standard language, the standard American history, and the voices and lives of White men appear in the curriculum, then the further implicit message (by what is left in and what is left out of the knowledge presented as legitimate by the school) seems to be that the real United States and real school are only about the cultural mainstream and its establishment ideology. This approach especially marginalizes the students of color who come to school already marginalized by life experience and by the historical experience of oppression in their ethnic or racial communities. Such a hegemonic approach also marginalizes female students (Sadker & Sadker, 1994). Marginalization is alienating, and one response to alienation is resistance—the very thing that makes teaching and learning more difficult for students and their teachers.

Ironically, for teachers to name and acknowledge tough social issues, rather than turning students against school and the teacher, makes it more possible for students who have experienced oppression to affiliate with the teacher and with school learning. By taking the moralizing that characterizes culturally hegemonic teaching out of the picture, reframing second-culture acquisition as strategically instrumental rather than inherently right, a teacher facilitates second-culture learning by students from nonmainstream backgrounds. Through such teaching, cultural borders are reframed as boundaries, and the politics of the dominant culture and cultures are, to some extent at least, depoliticized in the classroom. The cycles of resistance and schismogenesis that are stimulated by hegemonic curriculum and teaching do not get set off.

The role of resistance to cultures of domination in student disaffiliation from school learning is a fundamental issue in public education in the United States, Canada, and Australia, as well as Britain and the rest of Europe (Apple, 1996; Giroux, 1983; Willis, 1977). Ogbu (1987) has argued that for students of "caste-like" minority background in the United States (from groups with historic experiences of stigma and limitation of economic opportunity, such as African Americans, Mexican Americans, Puerto Ricans, and Native Americans), resistance to school is almost inevitable because of the effects of group history. Fordham (1996) has shown that African American high school students in Washington, D.C., defined achieving in school as "acting White." Other scholars (Erickson, 1987; Foley, 1991; Trueba, 1994) have acknowledged Ogbu's insight while observing that student resistance can result not only from a group history of oppression but also from oppressive and alienating circumstances surrounding teaching and learning within the school itself. Another difficulty with Ogbu's position is that it leaves no room for the possibility of school change.

A major theme here is that when business is done as usual in school, student resistance results from that, as well as from influences from the wider society on students. In the short run, we cannot change the wider society. But we can make school learning environments less alienating. Multicultural education, especially critical or antiracist multicultural education, is a way to change the business-as-usual of schools. When that happens, as Ladson-Billings (1994) and others have shown, minority students of backgrounds categorized as "caste-like" rise to the occasion. When treated with dignity and taught skillfully, such students affiliate with the school and achieve. As noted earlier, Moll and Greenberg (1990; see also Moll, 1998) show that minority students' families maintain *funds of knowledge* in their cultural practices that can be made use of in curriculum as teachers learn what those practices are and the kinds of knowledge and skill they entail. Gutierrez, in a series of compelling studies of classroom teaching (Gutierrez, Baquedano-López, Alvarez, & Chiu 1999; Gutierrez, Baquedano-López, & Tejeda 1999; Gutierrez, Rymes, & Larson 1995), shows that learning is enhanced (as is student morale—the will to learn) when teachers in classroom discourse make use of language and speech styles from students' homes and from popular culture. This bridging pedagogy between official school knowledge and unofficial knowledge creates an intermediate "third space"—a hybrid discourse that allows students to use the voices they bring to the classroom as they begin to affiliate with school voices and discourses and to appropriate them as their own. In such classrooms the price of school success is not that one give up one's own self and voice to adopt a new and alien one. Rather, the student adds new voices and discourses to those already possessed, and the teacher through his or her own language use respects both the voices that are familiar to the student and those that are new.

A group history of oppression no doubt makes students and parents wary of school and its claims that the standard ways of teaching are good for you. That is, trust of a school's good intentions, especially by students and parents of color, is not automatic. But relationships of mutual trust and respect can be established between teachers and students in the classroom. Sensitive multicultural pedagogy is one foundation for such trust.

Conventional Teaching as Cultural Border Wars

Conversely, for teachers to treat the dominant culture in the curriculum as a matter of cultural borders rather than of boundaries can make the classroom an unsafe place for students. It makes the classroom learning environment untrustable and can invite student resistance. A vivid example of such culture conflict is seen in the first-grade reading lesson cited at the beginning of this chapter and repeated here:

1 T: All right, class, read that and remember your endings.

2 CC: What did Little Duck see? (final t of "what" deleted)

3 T: What. (emphasizing final t)

4 CC: What (final t deleted as in turn 2)

5 T: I still don't hear this sad little "t."

6 CC: What did—what did—what—(final t's deleted)

7 T: What.

8 T&CC: What did Little Duck see? (final t spoken)

9 T: OK, very good

(Piestrup, 1973, pp. 96–97)

The example comes from first-grade classrooms in Berkeley, California, attended by both predominantly working-class African American children and predominantly middle-class White children. In some classrooms the teachers were African American, and in others they were White.

Piestrup (1973) found the phenomenon of language-style divergence that increases over time in situations of conflict, also reported by Labov (1963) and Giles and Powesland (1975). At the beginning of the school year many of the African American children spoke Black dialect (sometimes termed Black nonstandard vernacular). In the classrooms in which the teachers—whether African American or White—negatively sanctioned the children's use of Black dialect, by the end of the year the children spoke a broader form of the dialect in the classroom than they had done at the beginning of the year. The converse was also true in Piestrup's findings. Regardless of whether the teacher was African American or White, if the teacher did not publicly rebuke children for speaking Black dialect, by the end of the year those children's classroom speech more closely approached standard English.

The transcribed example shows one scene of rebuke for a language style that Piestrup found in a number of the classrooms. Here, the teacher was correcting African American children's nonstandard pronunciation. An alternative focus of instruction could have been comprehension—understanding what was in the story. The teacher chose to focus on final consonant deletion (the final /t/ in the word *what*). In so doing, the teacher was making that cultural feature of language style a cultural border issue—just as the Ephraimites treated the pronunciation of the final sound in the word *Shibboleth* so long ago. But the children's not articulating the final /t/ in *what* could have been treated as a cultural boundary issue.

Framed in that way, the speech-style difference (which probably did not interfere with the teacher's ability to hear the child's speech as intelligible in terms of literal, referential meaning) need not have gotten in the way of the discussion. Rather, the teacher, the child, and the other children in the group could have gone on to consider what Little Duck saw. There is now considerable evidence that pronouncing words in a nonstandard way does not interfere with children's ability either to decode written standard English (that is, to read letter combinations as identifiable words) or to understand the sense of a written passage at the level of a sentence or paragraph.

Why did the teacher insist on the final /t/? One explanation could be class bias or some other source of ethnocentrism, since final consonant deletion is not correct in terms of the dominant cultural style of official school literacy. Another, related explanation is possible. Deletion of a final /t/ also violates a key cultural assumption in one of the professional sub-cultures of educators—the assumption from behaviorist learning theory that mastery of subskills (such as pronouncing the final consonant) must necessarily precede mastery of more complex skills (such as comprehension at the word or sentence level). This ladder-of-skills cultural belief of educators is increasingly being challenged by advocates of whole-language approaches to literacy as well as by sociolinguists and cognitive psychologists who study the processes of learning to read.

Both sets of beliefs can be seen as hegemonic, reinforcing one another's commonsense validity. The general cultural value of correctness of standard English seems to be confirmed by the professional cultural belief in a ladder-of-skills approach to pedagogy. Of course, the teacher should correct mistakes, the reasoning goes; that's the teacher's job. Thus, we see how what may have begun as an ethnic and social-class marker in speech style (standard

English) gets used as a sociolinguistic test at a cultural border in what seems to be a professionally responsible pedagogy. The justification of that pedagogy results in ways of teaching that are culturally biased and needlessly alienating for students who come to school speaking a dialect other than the culturally dominant one.

Between teachers and students, the discomfort of such interchanges as shown in the example, repeated day after day across the school year, according to Piestrup, led to dialect divergence on the part of the students. Considering that these were first graders, not adolescents, we can see the dialect divergence as a nondeliberate form of resistance on the part of the students, outside their conscious awareness. These regressive social relationships between teachers and students, which become more negative, can happen for many reasons, not only because of cultural difference. When cultural difference is treated as a border issue in the classroom, it becomes a rich resource for ongoing conflictual relationships between teachers and students (McDermott & Gospodinoff, 1981).

In the previous example, the cultural assumptions behind the standard pedagogy are so much a part of professional common sense that we might consider them an aspect of invisible culture. The teacher might say, "I wasn't doing anything cultural; I was just teaching the children to read correctly." The children's lack of cooperation might not be seen as cultural resistance. Rather, the cultural issue might be clinicalized. The uncooperative children might be seen as passive-aggressive or as suffering from low self-esteem. If they shifted in their seats a lot, they might be considered hyperactive.

Aspects of invisible culture are often used as diagnostic indicators with clinical significance, especially in the early grades. For example, if a child comes from a home in which adults do not routinely ask him or her teacherlike known-information questions (questions to which the adults already know the answer), such questions by a teacher can initially seem confusing or intimidating (Heath, 1983). "What color is this?" the kindergarten teacher says on the first day of school, holding up a red piece of construction paper in front of an African American child whose mother is on welfare. "Aonh-oh' (I don't know)," the child replies, thinking there must be some trick, because anybody can see that the paper is red. "Lacking in reading readiness," the teacher thinks, writes this in the child's permanent record, and assigns the child to the bottom reading group.

Once again we find ourselves with the Ephraimites on the banks of the Jordan River, witnessing the consequences of a cultural border test. Yet because we do not recognize knowing about teacherlike questions as a distinct cultural skill, we may not see the teacher's informal readiness test as cultural or as culturally biased. Such framing of cultural difference as a border can be done inadvertently by teachers who are themselves members of the student's ethnic group and speech community as well as by teachers who are of majority background. Recall that Piestrup (1973) found the African American students' speech style diverging from the standard style in classrooms where such speech style was rebuked, regardless of whether the teacher was White or African American. What mattered was not the race of the teacher but whether the teacher's pedagogy was culturally responsive or unresponsive.

The cultural responsiveness or relevance of a classroom learning environment can differ in contradictory ways between the visible and the invisible aspects of culture. For example, in the same multiracial kindergarten or first-grade classroom in which a teacher uses informal tests of reading readiness that treat invisible cultural knowledge and skill as a cultural border (such as recognition of teacher questions and how to answer them), the teacher may have put a picture of Frederick Douglass on the wall, read a book about his life, presented information of West Africa in a positive light, and taught basic vocabulary in Yoruba or Swahili. Yet hanging a picture of Douglass, the African American abolitionist, on the wall next to a picture of George Washington, the White slave holder, or introducing students to an African language does not make that classroom fully multicultural if invisible aspects of the communicative cultural practices of African American students are still being treated in invidious ways.

Such contradictions between formal and informal culture must be confusing and alienating for students, even though that alienation may be experienced by them outside conscious awareness. This is why attention to issues of invisible informal culture as well as those of visible formal culture seems so important for the success of attempts at multicultural education. And in all this work we must critically investigate our notions of failure and success itself, for "school failure" and "school success" are themselves cultural constructions, generally within society and locally within each classroom (see Varenne & McDermott, 1998).

CONCLUSION: ON DIVERSITY OF TONGUES AND THEIR EDUCATIONAL POTENTIAL

The Russian literary critic Bakhtin (1981) provides us with a final way to consider culture in its continuity and in its diversity, as transmitted across generations and as invented in the present moment. He studied the novel as it emerged in the sixteenth and eighteenth centuries in Spain and France and in England, respectively, and as it developed in England, France, and Russia in the nineteenth century. Bakhtin noted that the classic novelists depicted a variety of ways of speaking across their various characters who differed in social class, gender, and region. That diversity he called *heteroglossia*, from the Greek meaning "differing tongues." He believed that a fine novel encapsulated key aspects of the total diversity in speech styles found in the society at the historical moment in which that novel was written. To produce such a text convincingly, the author must have incorporated the diversity of tongues present in the society.

Bakhtin (1981) also observed a personal heteroglossia within the characters of the novel akin to that in its author. For example, in Cervantes's *Don Quixote* Bakhtin noticed that usually the good Don, of bourgeois background, spoke in an imitation of the literary romance. Thus, his speech style sounded like the Spanish of the nobility. Sancho Panza, the peasant, usually spoke in the speech style of the lower classes. Yet once in a while, when engaged with the Don, or when reflecting to himself on what he had been experiencing, Sancho's speech drifted slightly toward the more prestigious style of Spanish. This tendency, apparent from the beginning of the modern novel, was more pronounced in nineteenth-century French and Russian novels. Russian serfs, for example, were depicted as speaking in a variety of speech styles, what Bakhtin called "social languages"—some more elevated and agentive, some more subordinated and passive. Worldview, personal status, and agency seemed to shift, as did the characters' language style.

Bakhtin's insights suggest ways of understanding how cultural diversity is organized and distributed within a society and within persons. There is heteroglossia within a society. Members of distinct social categories and social networks speak more often than not in differing ways (reminiscent of the "speech community" notion discussed earlier). Men do tend to speak differently from women, African Americans from Whites, working-class people from upper-middle-class people, gay from straight, fundamentalist Christians from Unitarians, physicians from lawyers (and physicians from nurses). These ways of speaking are relatively continuously distributed within the various social groupings; they become badges of identity of such group-ings; and for the most major social categories such as class, gender, race and ethnicity, and reli-gion; these social languages tend to persist across generations. In other words, social divisions and cultural and linguistic diversity appear to be consistently reproduced in society across time.

Moreover, the differing ways of speaking carry with them differing points of view that are the result of the differing life experiences of the speakers and, as the feminist slogan puts it, "the personal is political." Thus, the historical experience of a group and its particular political interests in assuming that things are really one way rather than some other—its ide-ology—come with the social language of the group, as uttered by a particular member of that group. Ways of speaking, then, are discourses—whole sets of assumptions about the world and roles for being in the world that are entailed in certain ways of creating oral and written texts (Foucault, 1979; Gee, 1990). Much more is involved than language style alone. To the extent that various group interests and their discourses are involved with the distri-bution of power in society, there can be conflict and contradiction between ways of speaking and thinking as well as between social groupings. A discourse is in a sense a social institution or a subculture.

Yet the consistency of cultural reproduction is not unitary or absolute. There is also het-eroglossia within persons. Each person's life experiences differ somewhat from those of other people, and every person lives in a variety of social situations each day. Differing social sit-uations provide differing ecologies of relationship with other people. They evoke differing aspects of the individual's overall repertoire of ways of speaking. One speaks differently to one's mother than to one's siblings, to one's teacher than to one's mother. Sometimes in com-plex relationships, such as that between an employee and supervisor who are also friends or between spouses who are simultaneously lovers, parents, and administrators of household resources, a variety of interrelated voices are evoked from moment to moment in what appears to be the same social situation. The utterances of persons in dialogue lean on one another in mutual influence, Bakhtin claimed. Thus, the phenomenon of ways of speaking (and of discourses) is inherently labile as well as stable. Culture at the group level varies in part because individuals differ among one another and within themselves as they find them-selves in differing social circumstances. In other words, there is an inherent hybridity in cul-tural practices (see Arteaga, 1994; Gutierrez, Baquedano-López, & Tejeda, 1999; Valle & Torres, 1995)—a blending of sources and voices in which new combinations and recombi-nations of old elements with new ones are continually being made.

As diverse persons show up in the scenes of daily life, they bring their heteroglossia with them. There can be affiliation as well as conflict across those cultural differences. And dis-courses can be contested; they can be interrupted or interrogated. When that happens, the assumptions of the discourse become visible and available for criticism. If a person or a group were to change discourses in a conflict, that would be to take a different stance in the world. One may feel as if that is not permitted or as if that is one's right.

Since the discourses vary within persons as well as between groups, whatever conflict or affiliation there may be between the discourses in society is experienced within the personality.

This means that the diversity of tongues and of voices within the person has profound emotional content and profound significance for personal identity and wholeness.

Schools are collection sites for a diversity of voices and identities. Schools ask of students that they try on new discourses, new ways of speaking and thinking, new ways of being a self, and to appropriate them as their own. At their best, schools ask this of teachers as well, in order that they may come into closer awareness of and engagement with the voices of their students and also develop intellectually within their careers, appropriating within themselves more of the various discourses and literacies of their society. That is personally risky business, for both students and teachers. When discourses, or cultures, are in conflict in society, then conflict can be experienced within the self over which discourses are being tried on.

As we have seen, students and teachers come to school already having appropriated multiple voices and cultures. One task of education can be reflection on the voices one already has. Multicultural education, especially that which considers invisible as well as visible culture, can assist in that process of personal and group reflection. Teachers and students, by looking within themselves, can come to see that everybody is cultural and multicultural, including themselves. By listening to the discourses around them and also within them and by testing how those discourses feel—more like self, more like other, owned or alienated— students and their teachers can valorize many discourses, treating them as inherently of equivalent worth, even though not all the discourses and cultures are treated as equal in power and prestige in the world outside the classroom. If school is a secure place to try on new cultures and voices, if cultural diversity is treated as boundaries rather than as borders, then students and their teachers can establish safe "third spaces" in which to explore growing relationships with new cultures and old ones. This third-space pedagogy (Gutierrez, Baquedano-López, Alvarez, & Chiu, 1999) makes legitimate within the walls of the classroom the cultural hybridity that students and teachers bring to it.

Ultimately, for persons in complex multicultural societies, growth into maturity involves coming to terms with the diversity of voices and cultures within. This is especially the case when the cultures and voices have been in conflict in the wider society and when the person is a member of a dominated group. Then, coming to terms with one's own diversity means making some kind of just peace with the voices within. For example, in every man there are the voices of women, and in every woman there are the voices of men. Are these voices alien and in conflict within the person, or have they been appropriated within the self? Can a woman come to terms with the male voices within without acquiescing to male hegemony and adopting an alienated self? In every White person in the United States, because of our historical experience, there are not only White voices but also Black ones. What do those voices sound more like—Amos and Andy or Frederick Douglass? Aunt Jemima or Alice Walker? How have those voices been appropriated within the person, and what role has the school played in facilitating that process? In every African American in the United States, there are not only Black voices but also White ones. How can the African American come to terms with the White voices within, forgiving and making peace with them, coming to own them while at the same time affirming and owning the Black voices, holding a continuing sense of the injustice of continuing racism? Doing all of that is necessary to mature into full adulthood as a African American (Cross, 1991; Helms, 1990).

To come to terms with the diversity of voices within is an educative task for society, for the individual, and for the school. It is what growing up means in a multicultural society and in a multicultural world. When the voices of the school curriculum and of its teaching and learning are fully multicultural, then the appropriation of multiple voices—in dignity and without coercion, keeping a critical stance without despair—becomes possible for all students. This is a noble aim for multicultural education. How difficult it is to achieve, yet how necessary. This becomes more apparent to educators as we become able to think more deeply about culture, its nuances, and its diversity in school and in society.

AFTERWORD

> What we are talking about is creating a new tradition, telling "new stories" that are fundamentally different by virtue of the role that the lives of the historically oppressed have assumed in their construction. This is a matter of redefining American culture, not once and for all, but in the negotiated meanings that are always emerging out of a curricular process. It is in the day-to-day interactions of teachers and students, dealing with a transformed curriculum and attempting to create a transformed, democratic classroom, that the new common culture will be created and continually re-created. (Perry & Fraser, 1993, pp.19–20)

Questions and Activities

1. The author describes seven conceptions of culture: (1) culture as cultivation, (2) culture as tradition, (3) culture as information bits, (4) culture as symbol system, (5) culture as motive and emotion, (6) culture as distributed along lines of power in society, and (7) culture as residing in local communities of practice. Form groups in your class or workshop to explore the diverse meanings of culture. Ask one student or workshop participant in each group to become an expert on one conception of culture given by the author. Discuss how the different conceptions of culture are both alike and different. Explain each definition by giving examples.

2. What does the author mean by "implicit and invisible aspects of culture"? In what ways are these aspects of culture important? Give some examples of invisible aspects of culture. What are some nonexamples of the concept?

3. In what ways might differences in invisible culture cause conflict? Give specific examples.

4. According to the author, what problems result when teachers focus on visible (explicit) culture at the expense of invisible (implicit) culture? What kinds of educational practices result when teachers focus on visible and tangible aspects of culture?

5. How does the author distinguish between a cultural boundary and a cultural border? Why is this distinction important? Is a cultural boundary always a cultural border? Explain.

6. According to the author, does cultural change necessarily mean cultural loss? Explain why or why not.

7. The author states that we sometime "essentialize" culture. What does he mean? What problems result, in his view, when culture is essentialized?

8. The author states that "our conceptions of culture in multicultural education need to become more constructivist and less essentialist." Explain what he means by this statement and its implications for educational practice.

9. The author states that "multicultural education has an opportunity and a challenge to be counter-hegemonic." Explain the meaning of this statement and give examples of how this might be done by classroom teachers.

References

Apple, M. W. (1996). *Cultural Politics and Education.* Buckingham, UK: Open University Press.

Arteaga, A. (1994). *An Other Tongue: Nation and Ethnicity in the Linguistic Borderlands.* Durham, NC: Duke University Press.

Bakhtin, M. M. (1981). *The Dialogic Imagination* (M. Holquist, Ed; C. Emerson & M. Holquist, Trans.). Austin: University of Texas Press.

Barth, F. (1969). *Ethnic Groups and Boundaries: The Social Organization of Culture Difference.* Boston: Little, Brown.

Barth, F. (1989). The Analysis of Culture in Complex Societies. *Ethnos, 54,* 120–142.

Bateson, G., Jackson, D., Haley, J., & Weakland, J. (1972). Toward a Theory of Schizophrenia. In G. Bateson, *Steps toward an Ecology of Mind* (pp. 201–227). New York: Ballantine.

Bourdieu, P. (1977). *Outline of a Theory of Practice* (Cambridge Studies in Social Anthropology No. 16). New York: Cambridge University Press.

Bourdieu, P., & Passeron, J. C. (1977). *Reproduction: In Education, Society and Culture.* Beverly Hills, CA: Sage.

Connell, R. (1982). *Making the Difference: Schools, Families, and Social Division.* Sydney, Australia: Allen & Unwin.

Cross, W. E. (1991). *Shades of Black: Diversity in African American Identity.* Philadelphia: Temple University Press.

D'Andrade, R. G., & Strauss, C. (Eds.). (1992). *Human Motives and Cultural Models.* New York: Cambridge University Press.

Delpit, L. (1995). *Other People's Children: Cultural Conflict in the Classroom.* New York: New Press.

Erickson, F. (1987). Transformation and School Success: The Politics and Culture of Educational Achievement. *Anthropology and Education Quarterly, 18*(4), 335–356. (Reprinted in E. Jacob & C. Jordan (Eds.), *Minority Education: Anthropological Perspectives.* Norwood, NJ: Ablex, 1992.)

Erickson, F. (2004). *Talk and Social Theory: Ecologies of speaking and listening in everyday life.* Cambridge, England: Polity Press.

Fanon, F. (1963). *The Wretched of the Earth* (C. Farrington, Trans.). New York: Grove.

Foley, D. E. (1991). Reconsidering Anthropological Explanations of Ethnic School Failure. *Anthropology and Education Quarterly, 22*(1), 60–86.

Fordham, S. (1996). *Blacked Out: Dilemmas of Race, Identity, and Success at Capital High*. Chicago: University of Chicago Press.

Foucault, M. (1979). *Discipline and Punish: The Birth of the Prison*. New York: Random House/Vintage.

Garfinkel, H., & Sacks, H. (1970). The Formal Properties of Practical Actions. In J. C. McKinney & E. A. Tiryakian (Eds.), *Theoretical Sociology* (pp. 331–336). New York: Appleton-Century-Crofts.

Gee, J. (1990). *Social Linguistics and Literacies: Ideology in Discourses*. Philadelphia: Falmer.

Geertz, C. (1973). *The Interpretation of Cultures*. New York: Basic Books.

Giddens, A. (1984). *The Constitution of Society: Outline of the Theory of Structuration*. Berkeley: University of California Press.

Giles, H., & Powesland, P. F. (1975). *Speech Style and Social Evaluation*. London: Academic Press.

Giroux, H. A. (1983). Theories of Reproduction and Resistance: A Critical Analysis. *Harvard Educational Review*, 53, 257–293.

Giroux, H. (1991). *Border Crossings: Cultural Workers and the Politics of Education*. New York: Routledge.

Goodenough, W. (1976). Multiculturalism as the Normal Human Experience. *Anthropology and Education Quarterly*, 7(4), 4–7.

Goodenough, W. (1981). *Culture, Language and Society*. Menlo Park, CA: Benjamin/Cummins.

Gumperz, J. J. (1982). *Discourse Strategies*. New York: Cambridge University Press.

Gutierrez, K., Baquedano-López, P., Alvarez, H., & Chiu, M. (1999). Building a Culture of Collaboration through Hybrid Language Practices. *Theory into Practice*, 38(2), 87–93.

Gutierrez, K., Baquedano-López, P., & Tejeda, C. (1999). Rethinking Diversity: Hybridity and Hybrid Language Practices in the Third Space. *Mind, Culture, and Activity*, 6(4) 286–303.

Gutierrez, K., Rymes, B., Larson, J. (1995). Script, Counterscript, and Underlife in the Classroom: James Brown versus *Brown* vs. *Board of Education*. *Harvard Educational Review*, 65(3), 445–471.

Hall, E. T. (1959). *The Silent Language*. New York: Doubleday.

Hall, E. T. (1976). *Beyond Culture*. New York: Doubleday.

Heath, S. B. (1983). *Ways with Words: Language, Life, and Work in Communities and Classrooms*. New York: Cambridge University Press.

Helms, J. (1990). *Black and White Racial Identity*. New York: Greenwood.

Hooks, B. (1993). Transformative Pedagogy and Multiculturalism. In T. Perry & J. W. Fraser (Eds.), *Freedom's Plow: Teaching in the Multicultural Classroom* (pp. 91–98). New York: Routledge.

Hymes, D. H. (1974). *Foundations in Sociolinguistics: An Ethnographic Approach*. Philadelphia: University of Pennsylvania Press.

Kroeber, A. L. (1917). The Superorganic. *American Anthropologist*, 19, 163–213.

Kroeber, A. L., & Kluckhohn, C. (1952). *Culture: A Critical Review of Concepts and Definitions*, Vol. 47(1). Cambridge, MA: Peabody Museum of American Archaeology and Ethnology, Harvard University.

Kuper, A. (1999). *Culture: The Anthropologists' Account*. Cambridge, MA: Harvard University Press.

Labov, W. (1963). The Social Motivation of a Sound Change. *Word*, 19, 273–309.

Ladson-Billings, G. (1994). *The Dreamkeepers: Successful Teachers of African-American Children*. San Francisco: Jossey-Bass Publishers.

Lave, J., & Wenger, E. (1990). *Situated Learning: Legitimate Peripheral Participation*. Cambridge: Cambridge University Press.

Lutz, C. A. (1990). *Language and the Politics of Emotion.* New York: Cambridge University Press.

McCarthy, C. (1993). After the Canon: Knowledge and Ideological Representation in the Multicultural Discourse on Curriculum Reform. In C. McCarthy & W. Crichlow (Eds.), *Race, Identity, and Representation in Education* (pp. 289–305). New York: Routledge.

McDermott, R. P., & Gospodinoff, K. (1981). Social Contexts for Ethnic Borders and School Failure. In A. Wolfgang (Ed.), *Nonverbal Behavior: Applications and Cultural Implications* (pp. 175–195). New York: Academic Press.

Moll, L. C. (Ed.). (1990). *Vygotsky and Education: Instructional Implications and Applications of Sociohistorical Psychology.* New York: Cambridge University Press.

Moll, L. (1998, February). *Funds of Knowledge for Teaching: A New Approach to Culture in Education.* Keynote address delivered to the Illinois State Board of Education, 21st Annual Statewide Conference for Teachers of Linguistically and Culturally Diverse Students, Springfield, IL.

Moll, L., & Greenberg, J. (1990). Creating Zones of Possibilities: Combining Social Contexts for Instruction. In L. C. Moll (Ed.), *Vygotsky and Education* (pp. 319–348). New York: Cambridge University Press.

Nieto, S. (Ed.). (1999). *The Light in Their Eyes: Creating Multicultural Learning Communities.* New York: Teachers College Press.

Ogbu, J. U. (1987). Variability in Minority School Performance: A Problem in Search of an Explanation. *Anthropology and Education Quarterly, 18*(4), 312–334.

Ortner, S. B. (1984). Theory in Anthropology since the Sixties. *Comparative Studies in Society and History, 26*(1), 126–166.

Perry, T., & Fraser, J. W. (Eds.). (1993). *Freedom's Plow: Teaching in the Multicultural Classroom.* New York: Routledge.

Philips, S. U. (1983). *The Invisible Culture: Communication in School and Community on the Warm Springs Indian Reservation.* New York: Longman.

Piestrup, A. M. (1973). *Black Dialect Interferences and Accommodations of Reading Instruction in First Grade.* Washington, DC: National Institute of Mental Health. (ERIC Document Reproduction Service No. ED 119113).

Rogoff, B. (2003). *The Cultural Nature of Human Development.* Oxford: Oxford University Press.

Sadker, M., & Sadker, D. (1994). *Failing at Fairness: How America's Schools Cheat Girls.* New York: Scribner's.

Said, E. W. (1978). *Orientalism.* New York: Pantheon.

Skilton Sylvester, P. (1994). Elementary School Curricula and Urban Transformation. *Harvard Educational Review, 64,* 309–331.

Sleeter, C. E., & Grant, C. A. (1993). *Making Choices for Multicultural Education.* New York: Merrill/Macmillan.

Torres-Guzmán, M. (1992). Stories of Hope in the Midst of Despair: Culturally Responsive Education for Latino Students in an Alternative High School in New York City. In M. Saravia-Shore & S. F. Arvizu (Eds.), *Cross-Cultural Literacy: Ethnographies of Communication in Multiethnic Classrooms* (pp. 477–490). New York: Garland.

Trueba, H. T. (1994). Reflections on Alternative Visions of Schooling. *Anthropology and Education Quarterly, 25*(3), 376–393.

Tylor, E. B. (1970). *Primitive Culture: Researches into the Development of Mythology, Philosophy, Religion, Language, Art, and Custom.* London: Murray. (Original work published 1871).

Valle, V., & Torres, R. (1995). The Idea of Mestizaje and the "Race" Problematic: Racialized Media Discourse in a Post-Fordist Landscape. In A. Darder (Ed.), *Culture and Difference: Critical Perspectives on the Bicultural Experience in the United States* (pp. 139–153). Westport, CT: Bergin & Garvey.

Varenne, H., & McDermott, R. (1998). *Successful Failure: The School America Builds.* Boulder, CO: Westview.

Vico, G. (1968). *The New Science of Giambattista Vico* (rev. ed.) (T. G. Bergin & M. H. Frisch, Trans.). Ithaca, NY: Cornell University Press. (3rd ed. published 1744).

Wenger, E. (1999). *Communities of Practice.* New York: Cambridge University Press.

Wiggington, S. (1986). *Sometimes a Shining Moment: The Foxfire Experience.* Garden City, NY: Anchor.

Williams, R. (1983). *Culture and Society.* New York: Columbia University Press.

Willis, P. E. (1977). *Learning to Labor: How Working-Class Kids Get Working-Class Jobs.* New York: Columbia University Press.

Wills, J. S., & Lintz, A. & Mehan, H. (2004). Ethnographic Studies of Multicultural Education in Classrooms and Schools. In J. A. Banks & C. A. M. Banks (Eds.), *Handbook of Research on Multicultural Education,* (2nd ed., pp. 163–183). New York: Macmillan.

Witherell, C., & Noddings, N. (1991). *Stories Lives Tell: Narrative and Dialogue in Education.* New York: Teachers College Press.

CHAPTER 3

Race, Class, Gender, and Disability in the Classroom

Carl A. Grant and
Christine E. Sleeter

Schools have always been a focal point of debate. What should be taught? How should students be organized for instruction? How should teachers be prepared? What constitute acceptable standards, and who should set them? As we enter the twenty-first century, several developments and tensions in society have fueled renewed debate about schooling.

First, the September 11 attacks and then the war with Iraq have led to a strong wave of patriotism and reluctance on the part of many people to criticize any aspect of U.S. culture or policy. As a reform movement, multicultural education has critiqued racism, sexism, and other forms of social stratification within the United States as well as globally. In the wake of September 11 and the war with Iraq, the slogan "United We Stand" is displayed ubiquitously on cars, walls, fences, building interiors, and so forth, and those who question are often silenced. For example, in an effort to recognize the racial diversity of World Trade Center rescue workers, many people argued that the WTC monument should be multiracial rather than all White; but this was countered with angry charges of "political correctness" gone awry. The American Council of Trustees and Alumni published a report charging university faculty with being the "weak link" in the U.S. response to terrorism because of questions many have raised about U.S. policies (Gonzalez, 2001). Figures such as Congresswoman Barbara Lee of California and the actor Danny Glover were strongly criticized for questioning a loss of civil liberties and the U.S. war on terrorism. How does one condemn terrorism against civilians and at the same time question U.S. policies both at home and abroad, particularly when questioning is branded as assisting terrorists? This dilemma is leading many people to silence.

Second, the United States has experienced tremendous growth in ethnic and racial diversity, especially through immigration, and public debate about what that diversity should mean has become prolific. By 2000, the population was 75 percent White, 12 percent African American, 4 percent Asian and Pacific Islander, 1 percent Native American, 2 percent more than one race, and 6 percent some other race. About 12 percent of the population classify themselves as Hispanic (U.S. Bureau of the Census, 2000). Whites were no longer the majority in many cities. In California and Hawaii, no racial or ethnic group was a majority in the public schools. About half of the nation's immigrants during the 1990s were from Central and South America and the Caribbean, the largest number coming from Mexico ("Foreign-Born Population," 1998). Of the U.S. population, 86 percent spoke only English at home, while 14 percent spoke a language other than English.

In the wake of September 11, public sentiment about diversity has rapidly become more negative, particularly toward people of Arab descent. According to a Gallup poll, 58 percent of Americans thought Arab Americans should undergo more intense security checks than the rest of the population; 49 percent favored making Arab Americans have special ID cards. In another survey, 31 percent of respondents favored putting Arab Americans in detention camps (Sen, 2002). Many Japanese American communities have actively come to the support of Arab Americans, remembering the treatment Japanese Americans experienced 60 years ago.

Third, the work of schools is being increasingly driven by a rapidly growing standards and testing movement. This movement began with the report *A Nation at Risk: The Imperative for Educational Reform*, written by the National Commission on Excellence in Education (1983). It warned that U.S. preeminence on the world stage was being eroded by the mediocre performance of its educational institutions. A call to raise student achievement levels led to the 1989 Educational Summit in Charlottesville, Virginia, where President George Bush and the nation's governors unveiled Goals 2000, declaring that every child in the United States would meet rigorous standards of academic achievement by the year 2000. After a brief attempt to develop national standards in the early 1990s, the task of standard writing quickly devolved to the states. At the state level, task forces across the nation wrote or elaborated on state standards for student and teacher performance, and systems of testing were put into place, spurred on by passage of the No Child Left Behind Act at the federal level. As a vice principal recently remarked to one of us, "Everything in our school is being driven by tests." Many advocates of multicultural education quickly found attention to diversity and equity being replaced by attention to standards and student test scores. At the same time, universities had become actively engaged in promoting diversity. The amount of multicultural research and curriculum mushroomed (Banks & Banks, 2004), advancing perspectives that differed in some cases sharply from those of most political and economic leaders.

Fourth, the gradually rising levels of educational attainment have not been accompanied by a rising quality of life. As transnational corporations exported jobs to Third World nations in order to cut wages, many middle-class and working-class people in the United States experienced an erosion of their lifestyles, and the poverty level rose, especially among women and children. Compared to the postwar economic boom, the 1980s and 1990s were decades in which people in the United States had to learn to settle for less. Fewer jobs were available, prices rose, real income of a large proportion of the population fell, and White middle-class families experienced some of the hard times poor families had always lived with (Newman, 1993; Rivlin, 1992; Shor, 1986).

Between 1983 and 1995, the average household net worth of the 1 percent of the wealthiest families grew by 17 percent, while the average net worth of the bottom 95 percent fell; that of the poorest 40 percent of U.S. households dropped by 79 percent (Collins, Leondar-Wright, & Sklar, 1999). Between 1970 and 1987, the White–African American education gap closed from 2.3 years to 3 months (U.S. Census Bureau, 1989) and has since remained at 3 to 4 months (U.S. Department of Education, 1998). At the same time, however, poverty and unemployment hit communities of color harder than White communities (U.S. Census Bureau, 2000). Communities of color experienced assaults on legal protections, such as passage of Propositions 187 (aimed at reducing immigration), 209 (aimed at ending affirmative action), and 227 (aimed at ending bilingual education) in California. Prisons became a growth industry. More jails were built than hospitals or schools (Zukin, 1995).

Many leaders of color view the explosion of prison populations as a new form of slavery, a warehousing of unemployed young men of color. Indeed, between 1977 and 1985, "when the prison population almost tripled, 70 percent of new inmates were African American, Latino, or other nonwhite minorities," a fact that had been downplayed by classifying Latinos as White (Chanse, 2002, p. 3). Even Asian Americans, held up as the model group who had made it, were not nearly as uniformly successful as the media suggested. It is revealing that some of the most outspoken critics of the "model minority" stereotype have been Japanese Americans, the group often touted as most successful (Jiobu, 1988; Omatsu, 1994; Suzuki, 1989; Takaki, 1989).

People in the United States with disabilities have also experienced both gains and losses. Although special education had expanded services to students with disabilities in schools, it, too, was disproportionately hit by economic losses and threatened by the raising of standards in schools. A triumph was passage of the Americans with Disabilities Act, designed to protect people with disabilities from discrimination. At the same time, most disabled adults are either unemployed or employed part time, often earning below the poverty level. For example, in 1998, only one-third of disabled high school graduates were employed (McNeil, 2000).

Furthermore, domestic social problems such as drug use and teen pregnancy seemed to be concentrated in a growing underclass dependent on welfare. Middle-class people in the United States, increasingly concerned about their ability to maintain their own standard of living, have become less tolerant of those who are poor. As schooling has become increasingly a prerequisite for employment, its payoff has seemed less certain, and competition for the good jobs has seemed keener.

All of this may seem removed from you and your classroom. But students whose parents have been experiencing the tensions discussed here are in your classroom, and local community and business leaders as well as spokepersons for oppressed groups are recommending what they believe schools should do to address these issues. And you have probably come across reports of tensions surrounding these issues in the media. For example, as the states of California and New York have wrestled with what a multicultural curriculum should look like, and as universities have begun requiring multicultural coursework, critics have charged minority groups with attempting to tear the United States apart (Schlesinger, 1992). Yet multicultural education theorists argue that most curricula are no more than cosmetically multicultural (Sleeter & Grant, 1991) and that weak treatments of historical injustices mask very real concerns.

A major thread running through the debates about schooling is the relative importance of preparing students for jobs versus preparing them as citizens. Schools have always done both, but recently much of the talk about what schools should do has emphasized job preparation and test scores; little has been said about citizenship. What kind of a nation do we want for ourselves and our children, given the challenges and problems we have been facing? How should limited resources be distributed, given our diversity and virtually everyone's desire for a good life? How should we address the fact that there are not enough good jobs to go around? And who gets to decide the most effective ways of educating children from diverse backgrounds?

Students we teach usually give one of three reasons for wanting to become teachers: (1) they love kids, (2) they want to help students, (3) they want to make school more exciting than when they were students. If one of these is the reason you chose to enter the teaching profession, then we hope you will see the demographic and social trends described above as being challenging and will realize that your love and help are needed not just for some students but for all students.

This chapter discusses the importance of race, class, gender, language, and disability in classroom life and provides alternative approaches to dealing with these issues in the classroom.

RACE, CLASS, GENDER, LANGUAGE, DISABILITY, AND CLASSROOM LIFE

Ask yourself what you know about race, class, gender, language, and disability as they apply to classroom life. Could you write one or two good paragraphs about what these words mean? How similar or different would your meanings be from those of your classmates? How much do these dynamics of social organization influence the way you think about teaching? If you and your classmates organize into small discussion groups (try it) and listen closely to each other, you will probably notice some distinct differences in the ways you see the importance of these dynamics. The point of such an exercise is not to show that you have different ideas and interpretations, but to challenge you to think clearly about what your ideas and interpretations mean for working with your students: How will you teach with excellence and equity?

Race, social class, and gender are used to construct categories of people in society. On your college application form, you were probably asked to indicate your race, ethnicity, gender, disability, and parents' place of employment. Most institutions want to know such information. It provides the institution with the ability to analyze and report data related to any or all of your ascribed characteristics. Social scientists studying school practices often report results according to race, class, home language, or gender. As a teacher, it is essential for you to understand how the dynamics of race, class, language, gender, and disability can influence your knowledge and understanding of your students. It is also important for you to consider these dynamics collectively, not separately. Each of your students is a member of multiple status groups, and these simultaneous memberships, in interaction with dynamics in the broader society, influence the students' perceptions and actions.

For example, a child in the classroom may be not just Asian American but also male, middle class, native–English-speaking, and not disabled. Thus, he is a member of a historically marginalized group—but also of a gender group and a social class that have historically oppressed others. Therefore, his view of reality and his actions based on that view will differ from those of a middle-class Asian American girl whose first language is Korean or a lower-class Asian American boy whose first language is Hmong and who has spina bifida. A teacher's failure to consider the integration of race, social class, and gender can lead to an oversimplified or inaccurate understanding of what occurs in schools and, therefore, to an inappropriate or simplistic prescription for educational equity and excellence. You may have noticed, for example, teachers assuming (often mistakenly) that Mexican American students identify strongly with each other and that they view issues in much the same way, or that African American male students have the same goals and views as African American female students.

We often begin working with teacher education students by having them take a self-inventory of the sociocultural groups they have been exposed to in their own schooling, religious, or work situations. The more honest you are in thinking about your familiarity with the backgrounds of different children, the more readily you can begin to learn about people to whom you have had little exposure. It will be a much greater limitation on your ability to teach well if you assume you know more about different students than you actually know than if you recognize whose lives are unfamiliar to you, so that you can learn.

APPROACHES TO MULTICULTURAL EDUCATION

Educators often work with students of color, students from low-income backgrounds, and White female students according to one of five approaches to multicultural education. As we briefly explain these approaches, ask yourself which approach you are most comfortable using in your teaching. Before we begin this discussion, you should understand two important points. First, space does not allow for a complete discussion of each approach; for a thorough discussion, please refer to *Making Choices for Multicultural Education: Five Approaches to Race, Class, and Gender* (Sleeter & Grant, 2003). Second, if you discover that you are a true eclectic or that none of the approaches satisfy your teaching style, that is fine, as long as you are not straddling the fence. Indecision, dissatisfaction, and frustration in teaching style and technique may confuse your students. Also, to be the dynamic teacher you want to be, you need a teaching philosophy that is well thought out and makes learning exciting for your students. Good teaching requires that you have a comprehensive understanding of what you are doing in the classroom, why, and how you are doing it.

Teaching the Exceptional and the Culturally Different

If you believe that a teacher's chief responsibility is to prepare all students to fit into and achieve within the existing school and society, this approach may appeal to you. It may be especially appealing if students of color, special education students, White female students, language-minority students, or low-income students are behind in the main subject areas of the traditional curriculum. The goals of this approach are to equip students with the cognitive skills, concepts, information, language, and values traditionally required by U.S. society, and eventually to enable them to hold a job and function within society's institutions and culture. Teachers using this approach often begin by determining the achievement levels of students, comparing their achievement to grade-level norms, and then working diligently to help those who are behind to catch up.

A good deal of research documents learning strengths of students of different sociocultural groups, suggesting that if a teacher learns to identify and build on their strengths, students will learn much more effectively than if a teacher assumes the child cannot learn very well. For example, based on a study of high-performing Hispanic schools, Reyes,

Scribner, and Scribner (1999) found that these schools share four characteristics. (1) The schools proactively involved families and communities. (2) The schools were organized around collaborative governance and leadership that was clearly focused on student success. (3) Culturally responsive pedagogy was widely used. Teachers viewed children as capable of high levels of achievement and viewed their cultural background as a valuable resource on which to build. (4) The schools used advocacy-oriented assessment, which was used to support high achievement by giving information that could improve instruction and guide intervention on a day-to-day basis. Language sensitivity was part of this process. Teachers who understand how to build on the culture and language of students will read the classroom behavior of such children more accurately and adjust their instructional processes accordingly without lowering their expectations for learning.

As another example, gender differences in math achievement may be due partly to instructional styles that favor males. Fennema and Peterson (1987) suggest that girls learn math better when taught through cooperative rather than competitive procedures. More recently, Pearson (1992) discovered that, at the college level, the majority of the female students studied preferred a more collaborative and intimate learning environment. Based on a review of research on bilingual education, Snow (1994) concludes that developing a strong foundation in children's primary language provides a sturdy base for literacy development and cognitive growth. Programs that treat languages other than English as a problem to remediate rather than as a resource to develop cut off language-minority children from language skills with which they enter school.

Starting where the students are and using instructional techniques and content familiar to them are important. For example, one teacher who used this approach helped two African American students who had moved from a large urban area to a much smaller college town to catch up on their writing skills by having them write letters to the friends they had left behind in the city. A second teacher grouped the girls in her ninth-grade class who were having problems in algebra, allowing them to work together, support one another, and not be intimidated by the boys in the class who had received the kind of socialization that produces good math students. A third teacher provided two students with learning disabilities with materials written at their reading level that covered concepts comparable to those the rest of the class was reading about. A fourth teacher placed two Latino students with limited English-speaking abilities into a transitional bilingual program. A teacher may believe that only one or two students in the classroom need this approach or that all of them do, especially if the school is located in an inner-city community or barrio.

In sum, the heart of this approach is building bridges for students to help them acquire the cognitive skills and knowledge expected of the so-called average White middle-class student. This approach accepts that there is a body of knowledge all students should learn but proposes that teachers should teach that knowledge in whatever way works so students understand and learn it.

Human Relations Approach

If you believe that a major purpose of the school is to help students learn to live together harmoniously in a world that is becoming smaller and smaller, and if you believe that greater social equality will result if students learn to respect one another regardless of race, class, gender, or disability, then this approach may be of special interest to you. Its goal is to promote a feeling of unity, tolerance, and acceptance among people: "I am okay and you are okay."

The human relations approach engenders positive feelings among all students, promotes group identity and pride for students of color, reduces stereotypes, and works to eliminate prejudice and biases. For example, a teacher of a fourth-grade multiracial, mainstreamed classroom spends considerable time during the first two weeks of each semester, and some time thereafter, doing activities to promote good human relations in the class. Early in the semester he uses a sociogram to learn student friendship patterns and to make certain that every child has a buddy. He also uses this activity to discover how negative or positive the boy–girl relationships are. He uses sentence-completion activities to discover how students are feeling about themselves and their family members. Based on these data, he integrates into his curriculum concepts of social acceptance and humanness for all people, the reduction and elimination of stereotypes, and information to help students feel good about themselves and their people. Also, he regularly brings to his classroom speakers who represent the diversity in society to show all students that they, too, can be successful.

The curriculum for the human relations approach addresses individual differences and similarities. It includes contributions of the groups of which the students are members and provides accurate information about various ethnic, racial, disability, gender, or social-class groups about whom the students hold stereotypes. Instructional procedures include a good deal of cooperative learning, role playing, and vicarious or real experiences to help the students develop appreciation of others. Advocates of this approach suggest that it should be comprehensive, integrated into several subject areas, and schoolwide. For example, a school attempting to promote gender equality is working at cross-purposes if lessons in language arts teach students to recognize sex stereotypes, while in the science class girls are not expected to perform as well as boys and thus are not pushed to do so. These contradictory attitudes simply reaffirm sex stereotypes.

While the teaching-the-exceptional-and-the-culturally-different approach emphasizes helping students acquire cognitive skills and knowledge in the traditional curriculum, the human relations approach focuses on attitudes and feelings students have about themselves and each other.

Single-Group Studies Approach

We use the phrase *single-group studies* to refer to the study of a particular group of people, for example, Asian American studies or Native American studies. The single-group studies approach seeks to raise the social status of the target group by helping young people examine how the group has been oppressed historically and what its capabilities and achievements have been. Unlike the two previous approaches, this one (as do the next two) views school knowledge as political rather than neutral and presents alternatives to the existing Eurocentric, male-dominant curriculum. It focuses on one specific group at a time so the history, perspectives, and worldview of that group can be developed coherently, rather than piecemeal. It also examines the current social status of the group and actions taken historically as well as contemporarily to further the interests of the group. Its advocates hope that students will develop more respect for the group and also the knowledge and commitment to work to improve the group's status in society.

Single-group studies are oriented toward political action and liberation. For example, in his discussion of the development of Asian American studies, Omatsu (1994) explains that

> the redefinition [of the Asian American experience] began with an analysis of power and domination in American society. It provided a way for understanding the historical forces surrounding us. And most importantly, it presented a strategy and challenge for changing our future. (p. 33)

Women's studies, according to Westkott (1983), is intended "to change the sexist world." Women's studies corrects history that has been written almost solely by White men about White men. It teaches students about the oppression women face and provides female students with accurate knowledge, purpose, and understanding of themselves. For students of color, ethnic studies provides the intellectual offensive for the social and political struggle for liberation and cultural integrity (Cortada, 1974). The student works to develop what Freire (1973) calls a "critical consciousness." Similarly, gay, lesbian, and transsexual studies helps students develop a consciousness about the history and current status of struggles around sexual orientation; and disability studies focuses on reframing disability from a deficit orientation to a difference orientation.

Since the late 1960s and early 1970s, scholars have generated an enormous amount of research about various oppressed groups and have begun to map out new conceptual frameworks within various disciplines. For example, Afrocentric scholars redefined the starting point of African American history from slavery to ancient Africa, in the process rewriting story lines for African American history. Beginning history with a group other than European males enables one to view historical events very differently. A group's story may begin in Asia and move east, or begin in South or Central America and move north, or begin in Europe and move west, or begin right here on the North American continent thousands of years ago. Further, the story is different if one views the group as having started from a position of strength (for example, African civilizations [Gates, 1999]), then having been subjugated, and now attempting to rebuild that strength, rather than starting from a position of weakness (such as slavery) and now attempting to rise.

A single-group studies curriculum includes units or courses about the history and culture of a group (for example, African American history, Chicano literature, disability studies). It teaches how the group has been victimized and has struggled to gain respect as well as about current social issues facing the group. It is essential that such curricula be based on scholarship by people who have studied the group in depth, rather than on your own ideas about what you think might be important.

Beginning in the late 1980s, Afrocentric curricula and schools received considerable publicity and discussion. As reported in *Education Week,*

> School districts in Atlanta, Indianapolis, Milwaukee, Pittsburgh, Washington, and other cities are in various stages of adopting Afrocentric programs inspired, in part, by a curriculum pioneered in the predominantly white Portland, Ore. school system. (Viadero, 1990, p. 11)

Afrocentric schools represent a serious attempt to implement the single-group studies approach because of the failure of schools to successfully educate African American children. Afrocentric public schools received considerable publicity during the 1990s. However, Ratteray (1990) points out that more than 400 independent African American schools exist, a few being more than 100 years old. The main rationale for such schools is that "current practice, even in desegregated settings, effectively excludes African American males from the mainstream culture" (Leake & Leake, 1992, p. 25). African American females, to a lesser degree are also excluded Pollard and Ajirotutu (1999) reported a five-year study of one Afrocentric middle school in Milwaukee. The greatest problem they found was high staff turnover, making consistent implementation of school reform difficult. Over the five years, student attendance improved, and suspensions and truancy dropped. Academic achievement gains were mixed. Their major recommendation was that such schools need a stable staff, with a consistent program of staff development, led by an administrative team with a clear vision.

Developments such as this have sparked much controversy. While many African American educators maintain that they are an antidote to the "colonial Western approach to history and academic work" and that they develop strong self-concepts in African American students, opponents maintain that such curricula are too politicized and stretch the truth (Leo, 1990). From our perspective, all curricula and school programs are political and try to teach someone's version of the truth; at least Afrocentric curricula are more direct about this than are traditional Eurocentric, male-dominant curricula.

Although single-group studies focus mainly on the curriculum, they also give some attention to instructional processes that benefit the target group. Women's studies programs, for example, have developed what is known as "feminist pedagogy" (see Chapter 7). This is a teaching approach that attempts to empower students. The main idea is that in the traditional classroom, women are socialized to accept other people's ideas. By reading text materials that were written mainly by men and provide a male interpretation of the world, women learn not to interpret the world for themselves. In the feminist classroom, women learn to trust and develop their own insights. The feminist teacher may assign material to read and may encourage students to generate discussion and reflections about the material. The discussion and personal reflection are important parts of the process, during which "control shifts from me, the teacher, the arbiter of knowing, to the interactions of students and myself with the subject matter" (Tetreault, 1989, p. 137).

In summary, the single-group studies approach is aimed toward social change. It challenges the knowledge normally taught in schools, arguing that knowledge reinforces control by wealthy White men over everyone else. It offers an in-depth study of oppressed groups for the purpose of empowering group members, developing in them a sense of pride and group consciousness, and helping members of dominant groups understand where others are coming from.

Multicultural Education Approach

Multicultural education has become the most popular term used by educators to describe education for pluralism. We apply this term to a particular approach that most multicultural education theorists prefer. As you will notice, this approach synthesizes many ideas from the previous three approaches.

The societal goals of this approach are to reduce prejudice and discrimination against oppressed groups, to work toward equal opportunity and social justice for all groups, and to effect an equitable distribution of power among members of the different cultural groups. The multicultural education approach attempts to reform the total schooling process for all children, regardless of whether the school is an all-White suburban school or a multiracial urban school. Schools that are reformed around principles of pluralism and equality would then contribute to broader social reform.

Various practices and processes in the school are reconstructed so that the school models equality and pluralism. For example, the curriculum is organized around concepts basic to each discipline, but content elaborating on those concepts is drawn from the experiences and perspectives of several different U.S. groups. If you are teaching literature, you select literature written by members of different groups. This not only teaches students that groups other than Whites have produced literature; it also enriches the concept of literature because it enables students to experience different literature forms that are common to all writing. For example, the universal struggle for self-discovery and cultural connection within a White-dominant society can be examined by reading about a Puerto Rican girl in *Felita* (Mohr, 1990), a Chinese girl in *Dragonwings* (Yep, 1975), an African American boy in *Scorpions* (Myers, 1990), a European American girl in *The Great Gilly Hopkins* (Paterson, 1987), and Iranian youth in *Teenage Refugees from Iran Speak Out* (Strazzabosco, 1995).

It is also important that the contributions and perspectives you select depict each group as the group would depict itself and show the group as active and dynamic. This requires that you learn about various groups and become aware of what is important and meaningful to them. For example, teachers wishing to teach about famous Native Americans should ask members of different Native American tribes whom they would like to see celebrated, instead of holding up to their students Pocahantas, Kateri Tekakwitha, or Sacajawea. These Native Americans are often thought among their people to have served White interests more than Native American interests. Additionally, African Americans are becoming increasingly concerned because the African American athlete or entertainer is often held up as the hero and heroine for the group, instead of African Americans who have done well in other areas of life, such as science or literature.

In this approach, instruction starts by assuming that students are capable of learning complex material and performing at a high level of skill. Each student has a personal, unique learning style that teachers discover and build on when teaching. The teacher draws on and uses the conceptual schemes (ways of thinking, knowledge about the world) that students bring to school. Cooperative learning is fostered, and both boys and girls are treated equally in a nonsexist manner. A staff as diverse as possible is hired and assigned responsibilities nonstereotypically. More than one language is taught; all students become at least bilingual. The multicultural education approach, more than the previous three, advocates total school reform to make the school reflect diversity. It also advocates giving equal attention to a variety of cultural groups regardless of whether specific groups are represented in the school's student population.

Education That Is Multicultural and Social Reconstructionist

Reflect back on the various forms of social inequality mentioned at the opening of this chapter. Education that is multicultural and social reconstructionist deals more directly than the other approaches have with oppression and social structural inequality based on race, social class, gender, and disability. Its purpose is to prepare future citizens to reconstruct society so that it better serves the interests of all groups of people, especially those who are of color, poor, female, and/or with disabilities. The phrase *education that is multicultural*, Grant (1978) explains, means that the entire education program is redesigned to reflect the concerns of diverse (racial, class, gender, and disability) groups. Its orientation and focus are on the whole education process. Social reconstructionism seeks to reconstruct society toward greater equity in race, class, gender, and disability. This approach also questions ethics and power relations embedded in the new global economy. It draws on the penetrating vision of George Bernard Shaw, who exclaimed, "You see things, and you say, 'Why?' But I dream things that never were, and I say, 'Why not?'"

As noted above, this approach extends the multicultural education approach, in that the curriculum and instruction of these two approaches are very similar. However, there are four practices unique to education that is multicultural and social reconstructionist.

First, democracy is actively practiced in the schools. Having students read the U.S. Constitution and hear lectures on the three branches of government is a passive way to learn about democracy. For students to understand democracy, they must live it. They must practice politics, debate, social action, and the use of power. In the classroom this means that students will be given the opportunity to direct a good deal of their learning and to learn how to be responsible for that direction. This does not mean that teachers abdicate the running of their classroom to the students, but rather that they guide and direct students so they learn how to learn and develop skills for wise decision making. Shor (1980) describes this as helping students become subjects rather than objects in the classroom, and Freire (1985) says it will produce individuals "who organize themselves reflectively for action rather than men [and women] who are organized for passivity" (p. 82).

Second, students learn how to analyze institutional inequality within their own life circumstances. Freire (1973) distinguished between three kinds of consciousness: critical consciousness, magical consciousness, and naive consciousness:

> Critical consciousness represents things and facts as they exist
> empirically, in their causal and circumstantial correlations, naive
> consciousness considers itself superior to facts, in control of
> facts, and thus free to understand them as it pleases. Magic
> consciousness, in contrast, simply apprehends facts and attributes
> them to a superior power by which it is controlled and to which it
> must therefore submit. (p. 44)

To put it another way, a person with critical consciousness wants to know how the world actually works and is willing to analyze the world carefully for himself or herself. A person with naive or magic consciousness does not do that. If one sees the world through magic, one assumes that one cannot understand or affect the world; things just happen. If one sees the world naively, one assumes cause–effect relationships that one wants to assume or that one has been told exist, without investigating them or thinking critically for oneself.

In a stratified society, Freire (1973) argued, most ordinary people see the world naively or magically, as the elite would wish them to see it. Either they believe that they have no power to change the way the world works for them or they believe that their problems have no relationship to their position in the power hierarchy. For example, students are taught that education is the doorway to success and that if they obey the teacher and do their work, they will succeed. However, studies indicate that many students of color who comply with school rules and teachers' requests still do not receive the career guidance and schoolwork necessary for becoming successful (Grant & Sleeter, 1986). Furthermore, education pays off better for White males than for all others. For example, in 1997 the average full-time working White male with four years of high school earned $29,298, whereas the average Black and Latino full-time working male with the same amount of education earned $22,440 and $22,253, respectively. For full-time working women, these figures were $17,166 (White women), $15,789 (Black women), and $15,949 (Latino women) (U.S. Bureau of the Census, 1989). This approach teaches students to question what they hear about how society works from other sources and to analyze the experiences of people like themselves in order to understand more fully what the problems actually are so they can prepare themselves to change unfair social processes.

Third, students learn to use social action skills. Bennett (1990) describes social action skills as "the knowledge, attitudes and skills that are necessary for active citizen participation" (p. 307). In this approach, the school is seen as a laboratory or training ground for preparing students to be more socially active. Banks (1994) says that oppressed ethnic groups

> must also develop a sense of political efficacy, and be given practice
> in social action strategies which teaches them how to get power
> without violence and further exclusion. . . . A curriculum designed
> to help liberate marginalized ethnic groups should emphasize
> opportunities for social action, in which students have experience
> obtaining and exercising power. (p. 216)

For example, some stories that elementary school children read could deal with issues involving discrimination and oppression and could suggest ways to deal with such problems. Students of all ages can be taught to identify sexist advertising of products sold in their community and how to take action to encourage advertisers to stop these types of practices. Advocates of this approach do not expect children to reconstruct the world, but they do expect the schools to teach students how to do their part in helping the nation achieve excellence and equity in all areas of life.

Fourth, bridges are built across various oppressed groups (e.g., people who are poor, people of color, and White women) so they can work together to advance their common interests. This is important because it can energize and strengthen struggles against oppression. However, getting groups to work together is difficult because members often believe that they would have to place some of their goals second to those of other groups. Further, racial groups find themselves divided along gender and class lines to the extent that middle-class males of all colors fail to take seriously the concerns of women and of lower-class members of their own groups. Childs (1994) describes "transcommunal" organizations, such as the African American/Korean alliance in Los Angeles, which bring different groups together to identify and work on common concerns. Albrecht and Brewer's (1990) *Bridges of Power: Women's Multicultural Alliances* addresses concerns and issues women face in attempting to coalesce across racial and social-class lines.

You now have an idea of the approaches used to teach multicultural education. Which one best suits your teaching philosophy and style? An equally important question is, Which approach will best help to bring excellence and equity to education? This chapter next provides an example of how one teacher brings both excellence and equity to her classroom.

MS. JULIE WILSON AND HER APPROACH TO TEACHING

The following example describes a few days in the teaching life of Ms. Julie Wilson, a first-year teacher in a medium-large city. Which approach to multicultural education do you think Ms. Wilson is using? With which of her teaching actions do you agree or disagree? What would you do if assigned to her class?

May 23

Julie Wilson was happy but also sad that she had just completed her last exam at State U. As she walked back to her apartment, she wondered where she would be at this time next year. She had applied for 10 teaching positions and had been interviewed three times. As Julie entered her apartment building, she stopped to check the mail. A large, fat, white envelope addressed to her was stuffed into the small mailbox. She hurriedly tore it open and quickly read the first sentence. "We are pleased to offer you a teaching position." Julie leaped up the stairs three at a time. She burst into the apartment, waving the letter at her two roommates. "I've got a job! I got the job at Hoover Elementary. My first teaching job, a fifth-grade class!"

Hoover Elementary had been a part of a desegregation plan that brought together students from several different neighborhoods in the city. Hoover was situated in an urban-renewal area to which city officials were giving a lot of time and attention and on which they were spending a considerable amount of money. The city officials wanted to bring the Whites back into the city from suburbs and to encourage the middle-class people of color to remain in the city. They also wanted to improve the life chances for the poor. Julie had been hired because the principal was looking for teachers who had some record of success in working with diverse students. Julie had a 3.5 grade point average and had worked with a diverse student population in her practicum and student-teaching experience. She had strong letters of recommendation from her cooperating teacher and university supervisor. Julie also had spent her last two summers working as a counselor in a camp that enrolled a wide diversity of students.

August 25

Julie was very pleased with the way her classroom looked. She had spent the last three days getting it ready for the first day of school. Plants, posters, goldfish, and an old rocking chair added to the warmth of an attractive classroom. There was also a big sign across the room saying "Welcome Fifth Graders." Tomorrow was the big day.

August 26

Twenty-eight students entered Julie's classroom: fifteen girls and thirteen boys. There were ten White students, two Hmong students, six Latino students, nine African American students, and one Bosnian student. Three of the students were learning disabled, and one was in a wheelchair. Eleven of the students were from middle-class homes, nine were from working-class homes, and the remaining eight were from very poor homes. Julie greeted each student with a big smile and a friendly hello as they entered the room. She asked their names and told them hers. She then asked them to take the seat with their name on the desk.

After the school bell rang, Julie introduced herself to the whole class. She told them that she had spent most of her summer in England and that while she was there she had often thought about this day—her first day as a teacher. She talked briefly about some of the places she had visited in England as she pointed to them on a map. She concluded her introduction by telling them a few things about her family. Her mother and father owned a dairy farm in Wisconsin, and she had one older brother, Wayne, and two younger sisters, Mary and Patricia. Julie asked if there were any students new to the school. Lester, an African American male, raised his hand, along with a female Hmong student, Mai-ka; a Bosnian female student, Dijana; and two Latino students, Maria and Jesus. Julie asked Mai-ka if she would like to tell the class her complete name, how she had spent her summer, and one favorite thing she liked to do. Then she asked the same of the other four. After all five had finished introducing themselves, Julie invited the other students to do the same. Julie then asked Lourdes, a returning student, to tell Mai-ka, Maria, Dijana, Jesus, and Lester about Hoover Elementary. As she listened to the students, she realized that Dijana and Jesus were both newcomers to the United States and neither spoke English fluently. To assist them, she asked two other students to buddy with them for the day. She realized that she would need to figure out a good buddy system, and she would also need help making her teaching accessible to these students while they learned English.

Once the opening greetings were completed, Julie began a discussion about the importance of the fifth grade and how special this grade was. She explained that this was a grade and class where a lot of learning would take place, along with a lot of fun. As Julie spoke, the students were listening intently. Julie radiated warmth and authority. Some of the students glanced at each other unsmilingly as she spoke of the hard work; however, when she mentioned "a lot of fun," the entire class perked up and looked at each other with big grins on their faces.

Julie had begun working on her educational philosophy in the Introduction to Education course at State U. Although she was continually modifying the way she thought about teaching, her basic philosophical beliefs had remained much the same. One of her major beliefs was that the students should actively participate in planning and shaping their own educational experiences. This, she believed, was as important for fifth graders as twelfth graders.

Julie asked the class if they were ready to take care of their classroom governance—deciding on rules, helpers, a discipline code, and time for classroom meetings. The class responded enthusiastically. The first thing the students wanted to do was to decide on the class rules. Several began to volunteer rules:

> "No stealing."
>
> "No rock throwing on the playground."
>
> "No sharpening pencils after the bell rings."
>
> "No fighting."

As the students offered suggestions, Julie wrote them on the chalkboard. After giving about sixteen suggestions, the class concluded. Julie commented, "All the rules seem very important"; she then asked the class what they should do with the rules. One student, Richard, suggested that they be written on poster board and placed in the upper corner of the room for all to see. Other class members said, "Yes, this is what we did last year in fourth grade." William, however, said, "Yes, we did do this, but we rarely followed the rules after the first day we made them." Julie assured the class this would not be the case this year and that they would have a weekly classroom meeting, run by an elected official of the class. She then asked if they thought it would be helpful if they wrote their rules using positive statements, instead of "no" or negative statements. The class said yes and began to change statements such as "no stealing" to "always ask before borrowing" and "no rock throwing" to "rock throwing can severely hurt a friend." Once the rules were completed, the class elected its officers.

After the classroom governance was taken care of, Julie asked the students if they would like her to read them a story. An enthusiastic yes followed her question. Julie glanced at the clock as she picked up *To Break the Silence* (Barrett, 1986) from the desk. The book is a varied collection of short stories, especially for young readers, written by authors of different racial backgrounds. It was 11:35. She could hardly believe the morning had gone by so quickly. She read for twenty minutes. All the students seemed to be enjoying the story, except Lester and Ben, two African American male students. Lester and Ben were drawing pictures, communicating nonverbally between themselves, and ignoring the rest of the class members. Julie decided that because they were quiet and not creating a disturbance, she would leave them alone.

After lunch, Julie had the class do two activities designed to help her learn about each student both socially and academically. She had the students do a self-concept activity, in which they did sentence completions that asked them to express how they felt about themselves. Then she had them play math and reading games to assess informally their math and reading skills. These activities took the entire afternoon, and Julie was as pleased as the students when the school day came to an end.

When Julie arrived at her apartment, she felt exhausted. She had a quick dinner and shower and then crawled into bed. She set the alarm for 7:00 P.M. and quickly fell asleep.

By 10:30 that night she had examined the students' self-concept activity and compared the information she had collected from the informal math and reading assessment with the official information from the students' cumulative record cards. She thought about each student's achievement record, social background, race, gender, and exceptionality. She said aloud, "I need to make plans soon to meet every parent. I need to find out about the students' lives at home, the parents' expectations, and if I can get some of them to volunteer."

Julie turned off her desk lamp at 11:45 to retire for the evening. She read a few pages from Anne Fadiman's (1997) *The Spirit Catches You and You Fall Down*, which tells the story of a Hmong child and the culture clash she experienced with American doctors. Then she turned out the light. Tonight she was going to sleep with less tension and nervousness than she had the night before. She felt good about the way things had gone today and was looking forward to tomorrow. As Julie slept, she dreamed of her class. Their faces and most of their names and backgrounds floated through her mind.

Eight of the ten White students were from Briar Creek, a middle-class single-unit housing community; these students were performing at grade level or above in all scholastic areas, and each of them was at least a year ahead in some core-area subject. Charles, who had used a wheelchair since being in an automobile accident three years ago, was three years ahead in both reading and math. However, Elaine and Bob had chosen a mixture of positive and negative adjectives when doing the self-concept activity, and this concerned Julie. She would keep her eye on them to try to determine the cause of their problems.

Estelle and Todd, the other two White students, were between six months and a year behind in most academic areas. Estelle had been diagnosed as learning disabled (LD), but the information in her personal cumulative folder seemed ambiguous about the cause of her problem. Julie wondered whether Estelle was classified as LD based on uncertain reasons. She recalled an article that discussed the learning-disability label as being a social construction rather than a medical condition.

Both of the Hmong students were at grade level or very close in their subjects. However, both of them, Mai-ka and Chee, were having some difficulty speaking English. Chee's family owned a restaurant in the neighborhood. The rumor mill reported that they were doing very well financially, so well that they had recently opened a restaurant in the downtown area of the city. Five of the six Latino students were Mexican American, born in the United States. Maria, José, and Lourdes were bilingual; Richard and Carmen were monolingual, with English being their primary language; and Jesus spoke mainly Spanish. Maria, José, and Lourdes were from working-class homes, and Richard, Jesus, and Carmen were from very poor homes. Lourdes, Carmen, and Richard's achievement scores were at least two years ahead of their grade level. José was working at grade level, and Maria and Jesus were one to two years behind. Jesus had immigrated to the U.S. only a year ago.

Five of the African American students—Lester, Ben, Gloria, Sharon, and Susan—were all performing two years behind grade level in all core-area subjects. All five lived in the Wendell Phillips low-rent projects. Two African American students—Shelly and Ernestine—lived in Briar Creek and were performing above grade level in all academic areas. Dolores and Gerard lived in Chatham, a working-class, predominantly African American neighborhood. Dolores was performing above grade level in all subjects; Gerard was behind in math. Gerard had also chosen several negative words when doing the self-concept activity.

Finally, Dijana, who had immigrated recently from Bosnia, did not know enough English to participate very well in any of the day's activities. Julie was glad that Shelley seemed to be taking an interest in helping her. Julie realized that she would need to think regularly about how to make sure Dijana was following along and would need to make sure both Dijana and Jesus were being tested for the English as a Second Language program.

All students in Julie's class were obedient and came from families that encouraged getting a good education.

May 25, 7:30 A.M.

Julie liked arriving early at school. The engineer, Mike, usually has a pot of coffee perking when she arrived. This was her time to get everything ready for the day. She had been teaching for almost one school year and was proud and pleased with how everything was going. The school principal, Mr. Griffin, had been in her class three times for formal visits and had told others, "Julie is an excellent teacher." He usually offered her one or two minor suggestions, such as "Don't call the roll every day; learn to take your attendance silently" and "The museum has an excellent exhibit on food and the human body your class may enjoy."

Julie had also been surprised by several things. She was surprised at how quickly most of the teachers left school at the end of the day. Out of a staff of twenty classroom teachers, only about five or six came early or stayed late. Even more surprising to her was how she and the other teachers who either came early or stayed late were chided about this behavior. She was surprised at the large number of worksheets and ditto sheets used and at how closely many teachers followed the outline in the books regardless of the needs of students. Also, she noticed, there was a common belief among the staff that her instructional style would not work.

Julie had made several changes in the curriculum. She had adopted a tradebook approach to reading and integrated that with her language arts. She made available to the students a wide assortment of books that featured different races, exceptionalities, and socioeconomic classes. In some stories, both males and females were featured doing traditional as well as nontraditional activities. Stories were set in urban and rural settings, and some featured children with disabilities. It had taken Julie several months to acquire such a diverse collection of books for her students, and she had even spent some of her own money for the books, but the excitement the students had shown about the materials made the expense worthwhile. She made sure she was teaching the kinds of reading and language arts skills her students would be tested on but refused to sacrifice the richness of a literature-based curriculum for "test prep." Thankfully, her principal was supportive of her.

She also had several computers in her class. A computer lab was down the hall, but Julie wanted her students to use the computer on a regular basis. When she discovered that Richard's father owned a computer store, she convinced him to lend the class two iMacs, and she convinced Mr. Griffin to purchase six more at cost. Several of the students from Briar Creek had computers at home. Charles and Elaine, Julie discovered, were wizards at the computer. Julie encouraged them to help the other students (and herself—sicne she had taken only one computer course at State U). The two students enjoyed this assignment and often had a small group of students remain after school to receive their help. Julie was pleased at how well Charles and Elaine handled this responsibility. Lester and Ben were Charles's favorite students; they liked the computer, but Julie believed they liked Charles and his electric wheelchair even more. Julie had heard them say on several occasions that Charles was "cool." Lester's and Ben's work was showing a steady improvement, and Charles enjoyed having two good friends. This friendship, Julie believed, had excellent mutual benefits for all concerned, including herself.

Julie's mathematics pedagogy was built on two principles. First, she built on the thinking and life experiences of the students. Second, she sought to provide students with insights into the role of mathematics in the various contexts of society. These two principles of mathematics pedagogy guided her daily teaching. Julie often took her class to the supermarket, to the bank, and to engineering firms. She made certain that she selected firms that employed men and women of color and White women in positions of leadership. She often requested that a representative from these groups spend a few minutes with the students, explaining their roles and duties. On one occasion, Julie's students questioned a federal government official about the purpose and intent of the U.S. Census. One biracial student asked, "How are racial categories constructed?"

Julie took the students on field trips to supermarkets in different areas of town so the students could compare the prices and quality of products (e.g., fruit, meat, and vegetables) between the suburban area and the inner-city area. On two occasions this led to a letter-writing campaign to the owner of the food chain to explain their findings. The students also wondered why the cost of gas was cheaper in the suburban areas than in the inner-city area. This became a math, social studies, and language arts lesson. Letters were written and interviews conducted to ascertain the cost of delivering the gas to the inner city as compared to the suburban area of the city, and to ascertain the rental fee for service station property in the inner city in comparison to the suburban areas. Math skills were used to determine whether there needed to be a difference in gas prices between the areas after rental fees and delivery charges were taken into consideration.

Julie used advertisements and editorials from newspapers and magazines to help students see the real-life use of such concepts as sexism, justice, and equity. Julie supplemented her social studies curriculum on a regular basis. She found the text biased in several areas. She would integrate into the assigned curriculum information from the history and culture of different racial and ethnic groups. For example, when teaching about the settling of the local community years ago, she invited a Native American female historian and a White historian to give views on how the settling took place and on problems and issues associated with it. She invited an African American historian and a Latino historian to discuss what was presently happening in the area. She had her students identify toys that had been made in Third World countries, and she explored with them the child labor and low-wage work that many transnational corporations had put in place in order to maximize corporate profits.

Students were usually encouraged to undertake different projects in an effort to provide a comprehensive perspective on the social studies unit under study. Choices were up to the student, but Julie maintained high expectations and insisted that excellence in every phase of the work was always necessary for each student. She made certain that during the semester each student was a project leader. She also made certain that boys and girls worked together. For example, Julie knew that Ben, Lester, and Charles usually stayed close together and did not have a girl as a member of their project team. She also knew that Carmen was assertive and had useful knowledge about the project on which they were working. She put Carmen on the project team.

By the end of the year, her students were scoring well on the district-mandated achievement tests; on average, they compared with other fifth-grade students. Julie was especially pleased to see how well her new immigrant students, Jesus and Dijana, had learned to work with the curriculum and the rest of the class. Where they had been quiet and timid at the beginning of the semester, they were now talkative and inquisitive.

Julie did have two problems with her class that she could not figure out. Shelly and Ernestine did not get along well with any of the other African American students, especially Ben and Lester. George and Hank, two White boys from Briar Creek, had considerable difficulty getting along with José and went out of their way to be mean to Lourdes and Maria. Julie was puzzled by George's and Hank's behavior; she did not think it was racially motivated because both of the boys got along pretty well with Shelly. She labored over this problem and discussed it with the school counselor. She wondered whether she had a problem related to a combination of race, class, and gender in George's and Hank's relationship with

José, Lourdes, and Maria. She also concluded that she might have a social-class problem among the African American students.

Julie decided to discuss her concerns with the students individually. After some discussion, she discovered that Shelly's and Ernestine's problem with Ben and Lester was related to social class and color. Both Shelly and Ernestine had very fair skin color. They had grown up in a predominantly White middle-class community and had spent very little time around other African American students. Ben and Lester were dark-skinned male students who lived in a very poor neighborhood. Julie felt that if her assumptions were true, she would need help with this problem. She was successful in getting an African American child psychiatrist to talk to her class. She did this in relationship to an art unit that examined "color, attitude, and feelings." His discussion enabled Julie to continue her discussion with Shelly and Ernestine and get them to examine their prejudice.

George and Hank admitted to Julie, after several discussions, that they did not care too much for any girls. But Hispanic girls who wore funny clothes and ate non-American foods were a big bore. It took Julie several months of talking with George and Hank, using different reading materials and having them all work on a group project under her direction, to get George and Hank to reduce some of their prejudices. At the end of the semester, Julie still believed this problem had not been completely resolved. Thus, she shared it with the sixth-grade teacher.

At the end of the school year, Julie felt very good about her first year. She knew she had grown as a teacher. She believed her professors at State U, her cooperating teacher, and her university supervisor would give her very high marks. They had encouraged her to become a reflective teacher—committed, responsible, and wholehearted in her teaching effort. Julie believed she was well on her way to becoming a reflective teacher, and she looked forward to her second year with enthusiasm.

She also realized that her sensitivity to things she did not know had grown, and she planned to engage in some learning over the summer. As she had become aware of resentments that students from low-income families felt toward students from upper-income families, she began to wonder what the city was doing to address poverty. She heard that the NAACP (National Association for the Advancement of Colored People), some Latino community leaders, and heads of homeless shelters were trying to work with the city council, and she wanted to find out more about how these groups viewed poverty in the city. She decided to join the NAACP so she could become more familiar with its activities. She also wanted to spend time with some Latino families, because before her teaching experience she had never talked directly with Latino adults; her principal suggested she should meet Luis Reyes, who directed a local community center and could help her do this. In addition, Julie felt somewhat overwhelmed by the amount of background information she had never learned about different groups in the United States and decided to start reading; because she enjoyed novels, she would start with some by Toni Morrison, Louise Erdrich, James Baldwin, and Maxine Hong Kingston. She would also read the novel by Sylvia Plath, *The Bell Jar*.

From what you know of Julie, what is her approach to multicultural education? Would you be comfortable doing as Julie did? Discuss Julie's teaching with your classmates. How would you change it?

CONCLUSION

In Julie's classroom, as in yours, race, class, gender, and disability are ascribed characteristics students bring to school that cannot be ignored. To teach with excellence, Julie had to affirm her students' diversity. Why do we say this?

For one thing, Julie needed to pay attention to her students' identities in order to help them achieve. She needed to acknowledge the importance of African American males to American life to hold the interest of Lester and Ben; she needed to acknowledge Mai-ka's, Chee's, Jesus's, and Dijana's prior learning to help them learn English and school material; she needed to become familiar with her students' learning styles so her teaching would be most effective.

For another thing, Julie needed to pay attention to her students' personal and social needs to help them perceive school as a positive experience. Some of her students disliked other students because of prejudices and stereotypes. Some of her students did not know how to relate to people in wheelchairs or to people who looked or talked differently. Some of her students felt negative about their own abilities. These attitudes interfere not only with achievement but also with one's quality of life, both today as students and later as adults in a pluralistic society.

Julie realized over the year the extent to which schools are connected with their social context. She remembered having to take a course called School and Society and had not understood why it was required. She remembered reading about societal pressures on schools; during the year, she had come to see how societal pressures translated into funding, programs, and local debates that directly affected resources and guidelines in her classroom. Further, she realized the extent to which students are connected with their own cultural context. The African American students, for example, emphasized their African American identity and did not want to be regarded as White; teachers who tried to be colorblind regarded this as a problem, but teachers who found the community's diversity to be interesting saw it as a strength. On the other hand, immigrant students tried hard to fit in; Julie would not have understood why without considering why their families had immigrated and the pressures the children experienced.

Julie also knew that the future of the United States depends on its diverse children. Her students will all be U.S. adults one day, regardless of the quality of their education. But what kind of adults will they become? Julie wanted them all to be skilled in a variety of areas, to be clear and critical thinkers, and to have a sense of social justice and caring for others. Julie had some personal selfish motives for this: She knew her own well-being in old age would depend directly on the ability of today's children to care for older people when they become adults. She also knew her students of today would be shaping the society in which her own children would one day grow up. She wanted to make sure they were as well prepared as possible to be productive citizens who had a vision of a better society. She drew from all of the approaches, at one time or another, to address specific problems and needs she saw in the classroom. But the approach she emphasized, and the one that guided her planning, was education that is multicultural and social reconstructionist.

How will you approach excellence and equity in your own classroom? We can guarantee that all your students will have their identities shaped partly by their race, social class, and gender; all of them will notice and respond in one way or another to people who differ from themselves; and all of them will grow up in a society that is still in many ways racist, sexist, and classist. You are the only one who can guarantee what you will do about that.

Questions and Activities

1. Why is it important for teachers to strive to attain both excellence and equity for their students? What can you do to try to achieve both goals in your teaching?

2. What does each of these terms mean to you in relationship to classroom life: *race, language, class, gender,* and *disability?* How are your notions of these concepts similar to and different from those of your classmates?

3. Give an example of how such variables as race, language, class, and gender interact to influence the behavior of a particular student.

4. Name the five approaches to multicultural education identified by Grant and Sleeter. What are the assumptions and instructional goals of each approach?

5. In what significant ways does the "education that is multicultural and social reconstructionist" approach differ from the other four approaches? What problems might a teacher experience when trying to implement this approach in the classroom? How might these problems be reduced or solved?

6. Visit a school in your community and interview several teachers and the principal about activities and programs the school has implemented in multicultural education. Using the typology of multicultural education described by the authors, determine what approach or combination of approaches to multicultural education are being used within the school. Share your findings with your classmates or fellow workshop participants.

7. Which approach to multicultural education is Julie using? Which aspects of her teaching do you especially like? Which aspects would you change?

8. Which approach to multicultural education described by the authors would you be the most comfortable using? Why?

References

Albrecht, L., & Brewer, R. (1990). *Bridges of Power: Women's Multicultural Alliances.* Philadelphia: New Society Publishers.

Banks, J. A. (1994). *Multiethnic Education: Theory and Practice* (3rd ed.). Boston: Allyn & Bacon.

Banks, J. A., & Banks, C. A. M. (2004). *Handbook of Research on Multicultural Education.* San Francisco: Jossey-Bass.

Barrett, P. A. (Ed.). (1986). *To Break the Silence.* New York: Dell.

Bennett, C. E. (1990). *Comprehensive Multicultural Education* (2nd ed.). Boston: Allyn & Bacon.

Chanse, S. (2002). Racefile. *Colorlines, 5*(1), 3.

Childs, J. B. (1994). The Value of Transcommunal Identity Politics. *Z Magazine, 7*(7/8), 48–51.

Collins, C., Leondar-Wright, B., & Sklar, H. (1999). *Shifting Fortunes: The Perils of the Growing American Wealth Gap.* Boston: United for a Fair Economy.

Cortada, R. E. (1974). *Black Studies: An Urban and Comparative Curriculum.* Greenwich, CT: Xerox Publishing Group.

Fadiman, A. (1997). *The Spirit Catches You and You Fall Down.* New York: Noonday.

Fennema, E., & Peterson, P. L. (1987). Effective Teaching for Girls and Boys: The Same or Different? In D. C. Berliner and B. V. Rosenshine (Eds.), *Talks to Teachers* (pp. 111–125). New York: Random House.

Foreign-Born Population Tops 25 Million. (1998, April 9). *Monterey County Herald,* p. A7.

Freire, P. (1973). *Education for Critical Consciousness.* New York: Seaburg.

Freire, P. (1985). *The Politics of Education: Culture, Power, and Liberation* (D. Macedo, Trans.). Boston: Bergin & Garvey.

Gates, H. L., Jr. (1999). *Wonders of the African World.* New York: Knopf.

Gonzalez, R. J. (2001, December 13). Lynne Cheney–Joe Lieberman Group Puts Out a Blacklist. *San Jose Mercury News.* Retrieved May 29, 2003, from http://www.commondreams.org/views01/1213-05.htm.

Grant, C. A. (1978). Education That Is Multicultural—Isn't That What We Mean? *Journal of Teacher Education, 29,* 45–49.

Grant, C. A., & Sleeter, C. E. (1986). *After the School Bell Rings.* Philadelphia: Falmer.

Jiobu, R. (1988). *Ethnicity and Assimilation.* Albany: State University of New York Press.

Leake, D. O., & Leake, B. L. (1992). Islands of Hope: Milwaukee's African American Immersion Schools. *The Journal of Negro Education, 61*(1), 24–29.

Leo, J. (1990, November 12). A Fringe History of the World. *U.S. News and World Report,* pp. 25–26.

McNeil, J. M. (2000). Employment, Earnings, and Disability. Paper presented at Annual Conference of the Western Economic Association International. Vancouver: British Columbia.

Mohr, N. (1990). *Felita.* New York: Bantam.

Myers, W. D. (1990). *Scorpions.* New York: Harper Trophy.

National Commission on Excellence in Education. (1983). *A Nation at Risk: The Imperative for Educational Reform.* Washington, DC: U.S. Department of Education.

Newman, K. S. (1993). *Declining Fortunes: The Withering of the American Dream.* New York: Basic Books.

Omatsu, G. (1994). The "Four Prisons" and the Movements of Liberation: Asian American Activism from the 1960s to the 1990s. In K. Aguilar-San Juan (Ed.), *The State of Asian America* (pp. 19–70). Boston: South End Press.

Paterson, K. (1987). *The Great Gilly Hopkins.* New York: Harper Trophy.

Pearson, C. S. (1992). Women as Learners: Diversity and Educational Quality. *Journal of Developmental Education, 16*(2), 2–4, 6, 8, 10, 38–39.

Reyes, P., Scribner, J. D., & Scribner, A. P. (Eds.). (1999). *Lessons from High-Performing Hispanic Schools.* New York: Teachers College Press.

Rivlin, A. M. (1992). *Reviving the American Dream: The Economy, the States, and the Federal Government.* Washington, DC: Brookings Institution Press.

Schlesinger, A. M. (1992). *The Disuniting of America.* New York: Norton.

Sen, R. (2002). Durban and the war. *Colorlines*, 5(1): 7–9.

Shor, I. (1980). *Critical Teaching and Everyday Life*. Boston: South End Press.

Shor, I. (1986). *Culture Wars*. Boston: Routledge & Kegan Paul.

Sleeter, C. E., & Grant, C. A. (1991). Textbooks and Race, Class, Gender, and Disability. In M. W. Apple & L. K. Christian-Smith (Eds.), *Politics of the Textbook* (pp. 78–110). New York: Routledge, Chapman & Hall.

Sleeter, C. E., & Grant, C. A. (2002). *Making Choices for Multicultural Education: Five Approaches to Race, Class, and Gender* (4th ed.). New York: Wiley.

Snow, M. A. (1994). Primary Language Instruction: A Bridge to Literacy. In C. F. Leyba (Ed.), *Schooling and Language Minority Students: A Theoretical Framework* (2nd ed., pp. 133–164). Los Angeles: Evaluation, Dissemination and Assessment Center at California State University, Los Angeles.

Strazzabosco, G. (1995). *Teenage Refugees from Iran Speak Out*. New York: Rosen.

Suzuki, B. (1989, November/December). Asian Americans as the "Model Minority." *Change*, pp. 13–19.

Takaki, R. (1989). *The Fourth Iron Cage: Race and Political Economy in the 1990's*. Paper presented at the Green Bay Colloquium on Ethnicity and Public Policy, Green Bay, WI.

Tetreault, M. K. T. (1989). Integrating Content about Women and Gender into the Curriculum. In J. A. Banks & C. A. M. Banks (Eds.), *Multicultural Education: Issues and Perspectives* (pp. 124–144). Boston: Allyn & Bacon.

U.S. Census Bureau (1989). *Statistical Abstract of the United States, 1989*. Washington, DC: U.S. Government Printing Office.

U.S. Census Bureau (2000). Statistical Abstract of the United States, 2000. Washington, D.C.: U.S. Government Printing Office.

U.S. Department of Education, National Center for Education Statistics (1998). NAEP 1996 Trends in Academic Progress (NCES 97–985). Retrieved August 16, 2002 from http://nces.ed.gov/quicktables/Detail.asp?Key=345.

Viadero, D. (1990, November 28). Battle over Multicultural Education Rises in Intensity. *Education Week*, *10*, 11.

Westkott, M. (1983). Women's Studies as a Strategy for Change: Between Criticism and Vision. In G. Bowles and R. D. Klein (Eds.), *Theories of Women's Studies* (pp. 210–218). London: Routledge & Kegan Paul.

Yep, L. (1975). *Dragonwings*. New York: Harper & Row.

Zukin, S. (1995). Whose Culture? Whose City? In R. T. LeGates & F. Stout (Eds.), *The City Reader* (2nd ed., pp. 131–142). London: Routledge Taylor & Francis Group.

Students from diverse groups experience equal status when teachers successfully implement multicultural education in their classrooms.

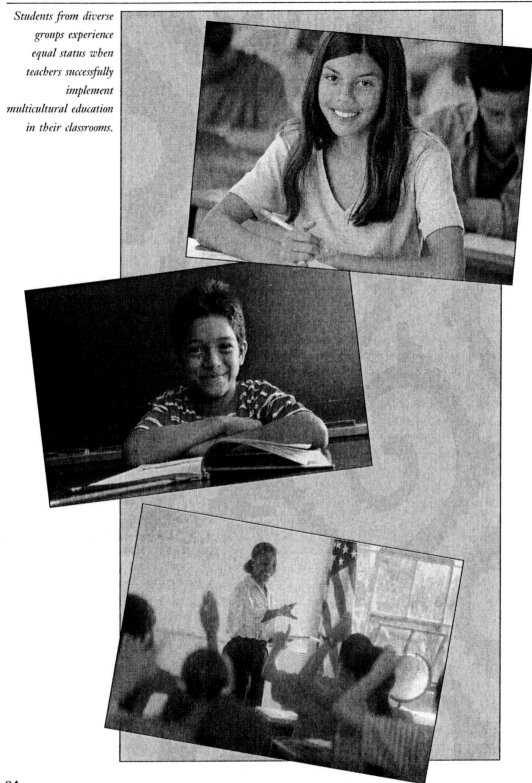

Social Class
and Religion

The two chapters in Part II discuss the effects of two powerful variables on student behavior, beliefs, and achievement: social class and religion. Social class is a powerful variable in U.S. society despite entrenched beliefs about individual opportunity in the United States. As Persell points out in Chapter 4, students who attend affluent middle- and upper-class schools have more resources, better teachers, and better educational opportunities than do students who attend low-income, inner-city schools. Students from the lower, middle, and upper classes usually attend different kinds of schools and have teachers who have different beliefs and expectations about their academic achievement. The structure of educational institutions also favors middle- and upper-class students. Structures such as tracking, IQ tests, and programs for gifted and mentally retarded students are highly biased in favor of middle- and upper-class students.

Students who are socialized within religious families and communities often have beliefs and behaviors that conflict with those of the school. Religious fundamentalists often challenge the scientific theories taught by schools about the origin of human beings. They also attack textbooks and fictional books assigned by teachers that they believe violate or contradict their doctrines. Conflicts about the right to pray in the school sometimes divide communities. The school should help students mediate between their home culture and the school culture. Lippy, in Chapter 5, describes the religious diversity within the United States and some of its educational implications.

CHAPTER 4

Social Class and Educational Equality

Caroline Hodges Persell

Picture three babies born at the same time, but to parents of different social-class backgrounds. The first baby is born into a wealthy, well-educated business or professional family. The second is born into a middle-class family in which both parents attended college and have middle-level managerial or social service jobs. The third is born into a poor family in which neither parent finished high school or has a steady job. Will these children receive the same education? Although the United States is based on the promise of equal opportunity for all people, the educational experiences of these three children are likely to be quite different.

Education in the United States is not a single, uniform system that is available to every child in the same way. Children of different social classes are likely to attend different types of schools, to receive different types of instruction, to study different curricula, and to leave school at different rates and times. As a result, when children end their schooling, they differ more than when they entered, and these differences may be used by society to legitimate adult inequalities. If we understand better how schools can help construct inequalities, we may be in a better position to try to change them.

The nature and meaning of social class are issues often debated by social scientists. U.S. researchers often measure social class by asking survey questions about a person's or a family's educational level, occupation, rank in an organization, and earnings. A few have tried to include measures of wealth such as home ownership or other assets. Several features of social class in the United States are worth special mention. Social-class inequality is greater in the United States than in any other industrial or postindustrial society in the world. Germany, Japan, Italy, France, Switzerland, England, Sweden, the Netherlands, you name it—all have considerably less social-class inequality than the United States. The countries with the least amount of class-based educational inequality are Sweden and the Netherlands, and they are also the countries where a family's social-class background is less related to their children's school achievement (Blossfeld & Shavit, 1993). Furthermore, income inequality has widened in the United States during the last twenty years, increasing inequality among children as well (Lichter & Eggebeen, 1993; Mayer, 2001).

The growing economic inequality in the United States affects how much education people receive. In states with bigger gaps between high- and low-income families (i.e., more income inequality), young people who grow up in high-income families obtain more education and children in low-income families obtain less education, compared to states with smaller gaps between high- and low-income families, where family income is not so strongly related to the amount of education children obtain (Mayer, 2001). The explanation for these differences seems to be more state spending for schooling and higher economic returns to schooling in states with greater income inequality (Mayer, 2001). At the same time, the United States has a historical belief in opportunity for all, regardless of their social origins.

This paradox of great and growing inequality and the belief in opportunity for all creates a special problem for the United States, namely, the "management of ambition" (Brint & Karabel, 1989, p. 7). Many more people aspire to high-paying careers than can actually enter them. One result has been the growth of educational credentialism, which means that more and more education is required for all jobs, especially professional and managerial occupations (Collins, 1979). This means that education is playing an ever-increasing role in the process of sorting people into their highly unequal adult positions. This sorting does not happen randomly, however.

Social class has been consistently related to educational success through time (Coleman et al., 1966; Gamoran, 2001; Goldstein, 1967; Grissmer, Kirby, Berends, & Williamson, 1994; Hanson, 1994; Mare, 1981; Mayeske & Wisler, 1972; Persell, 1977). Although there are a number of exceptions, students from higher social-class backgrounds tend to get better grades and to stay in school longer than do students from lower-class backgrounds. The question is, why does this happen? Does the educational system contribute to the widening of educational results over time? If so, what might change it—and how? I argue that three features of American education affect educational inequalities:

1. The structure of schooling in the United States
2. The beliefs held by many members of U.S. society and hence by many educators
3. Teachers, curricula, and teaching practices in U.S. schools

The *structure of schooling* refers to such features as differences among urban, rural, and suburban schools as well as differences between public and private schools. *Educational beliefs* include beliefs about IQ (intelligence quotient) and testing. *Teachers, curricula, and teaching practices* include teacher training and recruitment, tracking of students into certain curricula, teachers' expectations about what different children can learn, and differences in the quantity and quality of what is taught.

This chapter reviews research showing differences in educational structures, beliefs, and practices; examines how these differences are related to the social-class backgrounds of students; considers the consequences they have for student achievement; and analyzes how they affect individuals' adult lives. Lest this be too depressing an account, at the end of the chapter I suggest some ways in which teachers, other educators, and parents might work to improve education.

EDUCATIONAL STRUCTURES

The three babies described above are not likely to attend the same school, even if they live in the same area. Most students in the United States attend schools that are relatively alike with respect to the social-class backgrounds of the other students. One reason this happens is that people in the United States tend to live in areas that are fairly similar with respect to class and race. If they attend their neighborhood school, they are with students from similar backgrounds. If children grow up in a fairly diverse area such as a large city, mixed suburb, or rural area, they are less likely to attend the same schools. The states with the most private schools, for example, are the states with the largest concentrations of urban areas (Coleman, Hoffer, & Kilgore, 1982). If, by chance, students of different backgrounds do attend the same school, they are very likely to experience different programs of study because of tracking and ability grouping.

In older suburbs or cities, children of higher-class families are more likely to attend homogeneous neighborhood schools, selective public schools, or private schools, and to be in higher tracks; lower-class children are also likely to attend school together. Middle-class families try to send their children to special public schools, parochial schools, or private schools if they can afford them.

Private day and boarding schools are also relatively similar with respect to social class, despite the fact that some scholarships are awarded. Researchers who studied elite boarding schools, for example, found that 46 percent of the families had incomes of more than $100,000 per year in the early 1980s (Cookson & Persell, 1985). This is undoubtedly true of many more than half the families today.

Let's look more closely at elite private schools and exclusive suburban schools, which are overwhelmingly attended by upper- and upper-middle-class students; at parochial schools, attended by middle-class and working-class students; and at large urban public schools, heavily attended by lower-class pupils. Although these descriptions gloss over many distinctions within each major type of school, they do convey some of the range of differences that exist under the overly broad umbrella we call U.S. education.

Schools of the Upper and Upper-Middle Classes

At most upper- and upper-middle-class high schools, the grounds are spacious and well kept; the computer, laboratory, language, and athletic facilities are extensive; the teachers are well educated and responsive to students and parents; classes are small; nearly every student studies a college preparatory curriculum; and considerable homework is assigned.

At private schools, these tendencies are often intensified. The schools are quite small, with few having more than 1,200 students. Teachers do not have tenure or belong to unions, so they can be fired by the headmaster or headmistress if they are considered unresponsive to students or parents. Classes are small, often having no more than fifteen students and sometimes fewer. Numerous advanced placement courses offer the possibility of college credit. Students remark that it is "not cool to be dumb around here" (Cookson & Persell, 1985, p. 95). Most students watch very little television during the school week and do a great deal of homework (Cookson & Persell, 1985). They have many opportunities for extracurricular activities, such as debate and drama clubs, publications and music, and the chance to learn sports that colleges value, such as crew, ice hockey, squash, and lacrosse. Research suggests that participating in one or more extracurricular activities increases students' desire to attend school. Students have both academic and personal advisers who monitor their progress, help them solve problems, and try to help them have a successful school experience.

Affluent suburban communities have a robust tax base to support annual costs, which in the 2000s often exceed $15,000 per pupil. School board members are elected by members of the community who are likely to know them. Private schools are run by self-perpetuating boards of trustees, many of whom are graduates of the school. The school head is chosen by the board of trustees and may be replaced by them if they are not satisfied.

Private Parochial Schools

Many differences exist among parochial schools, but in general these schools are also relatively small. More of the high school students in them study an academic program and do more homework than do their public school peers. They are also subjected to somewhat stricter discipline (Coleman et al., 1982). The classes, however, are often larger than elite private, suburban, or urban school classes, with sometimes as many as forty or fifty pupils per class. Some non-Catholic middle- and working-class parents, especially those in urban areas, send their children to parochial schools (Coleman et al., 1982).

The costs at parochial schools are relatively low, especially compared to private schools, because these schools are subsidized by religious groups. These schools have relatively low teacher salaries and usually have no teachers' unions. Currently there are more lay teachers and fewer nuns, priests, and brothers as teachers. The schools are governed by the religious authority that runs them.

Urban Schools

Urban schools are usually quite large, and they are part of an even larger school system that is invariably highly bureaucratic. They usually offer varied courses of study, including academic, vocational, and general curricular tracks. The school systems of large cities and older, larger suburbs tend to lack both political and economic resources. These systems are generally highly centralized, with school board members generally elected on a citywide basis. School board members are often concerned members of the community who may send their own children to private schools, and they may have little knowledge about or power over the daily operations of the public system. The authority of professional educators is often buttressed by bureaucratic procedures and by unionization of teachers and administrators (Persell, 2000). Some observers (Rogers, 1968; Rogers & Chung, 1983) have described the system as one of organizational paralysis rather than governance.

Economically, the large city school systems are also relatively powerless. Because schools are supported by local property taxes, and because there is a great deal of housing segregation by social class as well as race in the United States, students who live in low-income areas are very likely to attend schools with lower per-pupil expenditures. Some schools with very high per-pupil spending even raise additional private funds to supplement the generous tax monies used to support the school. Thus, they are able to provide additional educational enrichments to the students attending such schools.

Unequal educational expenditures have serious consequences for the condition of school buildings, libraries and laboratories, computer equipment, the richness of curricular offerings, the ability to hire experienced and certified teachers, class size, and the variety of extracurricular offerings. Such disparities in educational opportunities affect how much children learn, how long they stay in school, their graduation rates, and the rates at which they successfully pursue further education after high school. While the question of whether money makes a difference in educational achievement has long been debated (Coleman et al., 1966; Hanushek, 1989, 1996), more recent research has refined the question so as to see money as a threshold condition that is necessary but not always sufficient for achievement. How the money is spent certainly matters (Elliott, 1998; Gamoran, Secada, & Marret, 2000; Wenglinsky, 1997). Expenditures need to be connected to opportunities to learn effectively (Gamoran et al., 2000), to having good teachers (Darling-Hammond, 2001), to inquiry-based teaching methods (Elliott, 1998), and to good equipment, especially in the case of science (Elliott, 1998).

Because of the importance of funding equity, twenty states have faced court challenges, resulting in court decisions requiring them to provide all students with equal access to quality schools (Dively & Hickrod, 1992; "A Truce in New Jersey's School War," 2002). Perhaps the most extensive and bitterly contested of these suits is *Abbott v. Burke* in New Jersey, brought in 1981. This case produced eight court rulings, ordering equal funding in urban and suburban schools, a high-quality preschool program for poor districts, and standards-based reforms to close the achievement gap between rich and poor students. In January 2002, after years of delay, newly elected New Jersey Governor James McGreevey announced that he would abide by the court's rulings. This court case has been described by some as perhaps "the most significant education case since the Supreme Court's desegregation ruling nearly 50 years ago" ("A Truce in New Jersey's School War," 2002). It affects 30 underprivileged districts in the state and may have implications for other states facing such court challenges.

In general, then, a child's social-class background is related to the school attended, the size of the school, the political and economic resources available to the school, the curricula offered, and the ensuing educational opportunities (Persell, Cookson, & Catsambis, 1992).

EDUCATIONAL BELIEFS

Since the last century, ideas about testing students have permeated education. For decades the concept of measuring intelligence, or IQ testing, played a major role in education. The concept of IQ has been used to explain why some children learn more slowly than others, why African American children do less well in school than White children, and why lower-class children do less well than middle- and upper-middle-class children. The latest example of this argument is presented by Richard Herrnstein and Charles Murray (1994) in their highly controversial book. IQ tests are often used to justify variations in education, achievement, and rewards. The justification usually is that because some people are more intelligent than others, they are entitled to more opportunities and rewards, including curricular track placement and exposure to special educational programs and resources.

Critics of IQ tests have raised a number of good points about the accuracy of the tests. For example, IQ tests do not measure such important features of intelligence as creative or divergent thinking, logic, and critical reasoning. The idea of multiple intelligences is well developed by Howard Gardner (1983) in *Frames of Mind*. Stephen Jay Gould's (1981) *The Mismeasure of Man* may still be the single best critical analysis of IQ tests.

In the last several decades, increasing emphasis has been placed on the use of large-scale achievement tests. This so-called high-stakes testing has been used as the basis for deciding the educational "track" to which students are assigned, whether a student moves to the next grade in school, and whether a student graduates from high school. Such tests may also be used to hold educators, schools, and school districts accountable. The focus here is on how the use of tests affects individuals and whether it is discriminatory or unfair for students of certain social-class backgrounds.

The purposes of using such tests include setting high standards for student learning and raising student achievement. However, when some students do poorly on a test, schools and teachers can respond in several different ways. They can work harder with the students obtaining low scores, providing them with more personal attention, tutoring, and additional learning experiences in an effort to improve their achievement test scores. Such responses usually require additional resources, which many schools, especially ones that are already underfunded, may not have. Another possible response is that schools try to get rid of students with lower scores, by encouraging them to drop out or transfer, or through other means. This is clearly an unintended consequence of high-stakes testing and one that impacts most severely on the most educationally needy and vulnerable students. One set of researchers has observed that the educational achievement gaps between poor and rich students are larger in states with more extensive student testing programs and that student accountability decreases opportunities for learning for all students (Schiller & Muller, 2002). More research is needed on how schools respond to accountability (Schiller & Muller, 2002).

Similarly, Amrein and Berliner (2002) found that "while students show consistent improvement on the state exams, the opposite is true of their performance on other, independent measures of academic achievement" (cited in Winter, 2002, p. A1) and that "once states tie the standardized tests to graduation, fewer students tend to get diplomas" (Winter, 2002, p. A15). On the other hand, Winter points out that some researchers such as Carnoy and Loeb as well as Raymond and Hanushek "make the case that do-or-die exams . . . have brought about at least a modicum of academic progress, especially for minority students who may get scant attention otherwise" (Winter, 2003, p. B9).

It is important to note that all of these results are simply correlations and that there is not enough evidence to say that the tests *cause* either of these types of results. Many teachers, while not opposed to high standards, say that the existence of mandatory testing leads to "teaching in ways that contradicted their own ideas of sound educational practice" (Winter, 2003, p. B9).

In 1997, the U.S. Congress asked the National Academy of Sciences to conduct a study and make written recommendations on appropriate methods that would ensure that tests are "not used in a discriminatory manner or inappropriately for student promotion, tracking or graduation" (Heubert & Hauser, 1999, p. 7). Among the committee's recommendations are the following:

- Because a test score is not exact, "high-stakes educational decisions should not be made solely or automatically on the basis of a single test score but should also take other relevant information into account" such as grades, developmental factors, attendance, and teacher recommendations. (p. 6)

- "Tests should be used for high-stakes decisions about individual mastery only after implementing changes in teaching and curriculum that ensure that students have been taught the knowledge and skills on which they will be tested." (p. 6) In other words, students should not be tested until they have been taught the content.

- Everyone involved in education, including parents, educators, and public officials, should understand "the nature and interpretation of test scores." (p. 5)

- Students who receive low test scores should be offered a range of alternatives, such as effective remedial education, not just an either–or consequence of social promotion or grade repetition.[1]

- Appropriate test use carries over to appropriate student preparation. Students should not see test items in advance, nor should teaching be narrowly geared to just what is on the test, without "improving the broader set of academic skills that the test is intended to measure." (p. 7)

- Students with disabilities and English-language learners require special consideration to ensure validity and fairness.

- Finally, there is a need for research on whether using particular tests is "educationally beneficial for students—for example, by increasing academic achievement or reducing dropout rates." (p. 8)

TEACHERS, CURRICULUM, AND TEACHING PRACTICES

The relatively recent growth of high-stakes testing may deflect attention from essential features of schools that affect learning. Educational equity requires that we examine not only the educational funding but also what that funding is used for and how it affects education. Three features of schools highlight how students' educational experiences vary depending on their social class—specifically, the teachers they get, curricular tracking, and teachers' expectations.

Teachers

Schools with more low-income students are more likely to have teachers who are not certified at all or who are teaching out of their area of certification (Ingersoll, 1999). Large shortages

---

[1]Retaining students in grade leads to declines in both their achievement and social-emotional measures compared to students of equal achievement levels who are promoted (Holmes & Matthews, 1984; Shephard & Smith, 1986, both cited in Darling-Hammond, 2001, p. 475). They are also more likely to drop out (Darling-Hammond, 2001).

of certified teachers in such major urban areas as New York City in recent years have led to several changes. The schools chancellor developed an alternative, abbreviated path to temporary certification, aimed at career-changers and recent college graduates with no teaching experience. The alternative path to provisional certification involves a month of intensive education courses. At the end of this time, these teachers are placed in the 100 lowest-performing schools from the prior year. About 30 percent of the new certified teachers in the fall of 2002 in New York City had this alternative certification. In addition, New York and other cities received recruits from Teach for America, a non-profit organization that recruits college graduates, provides a summer of intensive training, and places them in troubled schools.

Like New York, many school districts around the country, including Los Angeles, Atlanta, and Washington, D.C., have alternative certification programs in an effort to address the shortage of qualified teachers. However, there is considerable debate over the abbreviated training that alternative-route certification involves. Arthur Levine, President of Teachers College at Columbia University, points out that the definition of a certified teacher has been changed, but the net result "is that we will still have large numbers of students this fall whose teachers are unprepared to teach them" (cited in Goodnough, 2002, p. 83). On the other hand, Rod Paige, the U.S. secretary of education, has "dismissed the pedagogical course work offered by schools of education—like Teachers College—as cumbersome and often ineffective" (Goodnough, 2002, p. B3). Research by Gomez and Grobe (1990, cited in Darling-Hammond, 2001, p. 472) finds that alternative-route teacher candidates had more uneven performance ratings compared to trained beginners, particularly in the area of classroom management and in their knowledge of instructional techniques. Their students, in turn, scored significantly lower in language arts, compared to students of fully prepared beginning teachers, when students' initial achievement levels were held constant (Gomez & Grobe, 1990, cited in Darling-Hammond, 2001, p. 472).

As Darling-Hammond (2001) notes, "policy makers have nearly always answered the problem of teacher shortages by lowering standards, so that people who have had little or no preparation for teaching can be hired" (p. 471). It is notable that this issue does not surface in more affluent suburban public schools, because they have very low percentages of teachers who are not certified or are teaching outside their areas of certification (Ingersoll, 1999). One reason that such areas can attract and retain certified teachers better than inner-city schools is that they pay higher salaries on the average.

In 2002, New York City improved its ability to attract more certified teacher applicants as well as those with alternative certification because it raised the starting salaries of entry-level teachers from $31,910 to $39,000. It also raised the maximum yearly salary that certified teachers hired from other districts could initially earn from $43,370 to nearly $61,000. In 1986, Connecticut also solved its teacher shortage by dramatically raising and equalizing beginning teacher salaries (Darling-Hammond, 2001).

The question will be whether New York or other urban school systems can retain the new teachers they have hired. Teacher turnover rates are much higher in low-income and urban school districts than in more affluent areas (Darling-Hammond, 1990, 1992; Grissmer & Kirby, 1987; Wise, Darling-Hammond, & Berry, 1987). Thus, teacher mentoring, professional development, and support remain important issues to address if educational equality is to be achieved. The effective professional development of teachers has been found to enhance student learning (Gamoran et al., 2000).

Teachers, however, work within educational structures that contribute to unequal learning opportunities. This is especially true of the educational practice of tracking.

Tracking

The first recorded instance of tracking was the Harris plan in St. Louis, begun in 1867. Since then, tracking has followed a curious pattern in the United States of alternate popularity and disuse. In the 1920s and 1930s, when many immigrants came to the United States, tracking increased greatly. Thereafter, it fell into decline until the late 1950s, when it was revived, apparently in response to the USSR's launching of *Sputnik* and the United States's competitive concern with identifying and educating the gifted (Conant, 1961; Oakes, 1985). That period was also marked by large migrations of rural southern African Americans to northern cities and by an influx of Puerto Rican and Mexican American migrants into the United States. Darling-Hammond (2001) points out that "tracking is much more extensive in U.S. schools than in most other countries" (p. 474). This observation prompts us to ask why this is the case. There are two differences between the United States and European countries that might account for the difference. The United States has more racial and economic inequality than European countries, and educational achievement and attainment are more important for a person's (more unequal) occupation, earnings, and other life chances in the United States than in European countries.

Tracking today is widespread, particularly in large, diverse school systems and in schools serving primarily lower-class students. It is less prevalent, and less rigid when it occurs, in upper-middle-class suburban and private schools and in parochial schools (Jones, Vanfossen, & Spade, 1985). Schools with more low-income students have smaller academic tracks and larger remedial and vocational programs, while schools serving affluent students may have only academic tracks and no vocational or remedial programs (Oakes, 1992). Differences in the courses students take, especially in such areas as mathematics, science, and foreign language, go a long way toward explaining differences in achievement test scores (Darling-Hammond, 2001).

What exactly is tracking? To address this question, we need to examine the distinction between ability grouping and curriculum differentiation. Proponents of ability grouping stress flexible subject-area assignment. By this they mean that students are assigned to learning groups on the basis of their background and achievement in a subject area at any given moment and that skills and knowledge are evaluated at relatively frequent intervals. Students showing gains can be shifted readily into another group. They might also be in different ability groups in different subjects, according to their own rate of growth in each subject. This practice suggests a common curriculum shared by all students, with only the mix of student abilities being varied. It also assumes that, within that curriculum, all groups are taught the same material.

In fact, it seems that group placement becomes self-perpetuating, that students are often grouped at the same level in all subjects, and that even a shared curriculum may be taught differently to different groups. This is especially likely to happen in large, bureaucratic, urban public schools. Quite often, different ability groups are assigned to different courses of study, resulting in simultaneous grouping by curriculum and ability. Rosenbaum (1976) notes that although ability grouping and curriculum grouping may appear different to educators, in fact they share several social similarities: (1) students are placed with those defined as similar to themselves and are segregated from those deemed different, and (2) group placement is done on the basis of criteria such as ability or postgraduate plans that are unequally esteemed. Thus, group membership immediately ranks students in a status hierarchy, formally stating that some students are better than others (Rosenbaum, 1976). Following Rosenbaum's usage, the general term *tracking* is applied here to both types of grouping.

On what basis are students assigned to tracks? Three major criteria have been noted in the literature: (1) standardized test scores; (2) teacher grades, recommendations, or opinions about pupils; and (3) pupil race and socioeconomic class. Test scores are usually based on large group-administered aptitude tests, a method considered least valid by test-givers. Teacher opinions about students may be influenced by test scores, pupil social class, or ethnicity, as discussed below. Social class and ethnicity have been found in some research studies to be directly related to track assignments as well, even when ability and teacher recommendations were similar (Brookover, Leu, & Kariger, 1965). This is partly because of prior educational placements and experiences, partly because of counselors' advice (influenced by their view of students' futures), and partly because parents are more likely to intervene effectively in tracking decisions for students of higher social classes (Darling-Hammond, 2001).

Thus, the social-class background of students is related to the prevalence of tracking in the schools, to the nature of the available tracks, and to the ways track assignments are made. Furthermore, while there is some relationship between tested ability and track placement, it is highly imperfect (Dreeben & Barr, 1988; Pallas, Entwisle, Alexander, & Stluka, 1994).

Once students are assigned to different tracks, what happens to them? Researchers suggest that tracking has effects through at least three mechanisms. These are instructional, social, and institutional in nature, and all three may operate together. The major *instructional processes* that have been observed to vary according to track placement include the unequal allocation of educational resources, the instruction offered, student–teacher interactions, and student–student interactions. Dreeben and Barr (1988) found variations in the content, pacing, and quantity of instruction in different tracks. Higher-ranked reading groups were taught more (and learned more) words than lower-ranked reading groups, according to Gamoran (1984, 1986).

Hallinan (1987) studied within-class ability grouping in thirty-four elementary school classes. She found that ability grouping affects the learning of students in higher and lower groups because it influences their opportunities for learning, the instructional climate, and the student aptitudes clustered in the different groups. High-ability groups spend more time on-task during class; that is, more class time is devoted to actual teaching activities. Also, teachers use more interesting teaching methods and materials. Finally, teachers hold higher expectations and the other students support learning more in the higher-ability groups. As a result, the aptitude of students in the higher groups tends to develop more than does the aptitude of students in the lower group (Hallinan).

In secondary schools, college-track students consistently receive better teachers, class materials, laboratory facilities, field trips, and visitors than their lower-track counterparts (Findley & Bryan, 1975; Goodlad, 1984; Oakes, 1985; Rosenbaum, 1976; Schafer, Olexa, & Polk, 1973). Oakes observed that teachers of high-track students set aside more time for student learning and devoted more class time to learning activities. Fewer students in these classes engaged in "off-task" activities (Oakes, 1985, p. 111). Oakes (1985) also found that "students are being exposed to knowledge and taught behaviors that differ not only educationally but also in socially important ways. Students at the top are exposed to the knowledge that is highly valued in our culture, knowledge that identifies its possessors as 'educated'" (pp. 91–92). Similarly, those students are taught critical thinking, creativity, and independence. Students at the bottom are denied access to these educationally and socially important experiences (Oakes, 1985).

Freiberg (1970) found that higher-track students received more empathy, praise, and use of their ideas, as well as less direction and criticism, than did lower-track students. Oakes (1985) observed that teachers spent more time in low-track classes on discipline and that students in those classes perceived their teachers as more punitive than did students in high-track classes.

Socially, tracks may create settings that shape students' self-esteem and expectations about academic performance. For example, Rosenbaum (1976) reported that more than one-third of lower-track (noncollege) students mentioned "blatant insults directed at them by teachers and administrators. 'Teachers are always telling us how dumb we are'" (p. 179). One articulate general-track student in that study reported that he sought academic help from a teacher but was told that he was not smart enough to learn the material. Several students reported that a lower-track student who asks a guidance counselor for a change of classes is not only prevented from changing but is also insulted for being so presumptuous as to make the request (Rosenbaum, 1976). Rosenbaum was told by one teacher, "You're wasting your time asking these kids for their opinions. There's not an idea in any of their heads." As the researcher notes, "This comment was not expressed in the privacy of the teacher's room; it was said at a normal volume in a quiet classroom full of students!" (p. 180).

Students have been observed to pick up on the negative evaluations associated with lower-track placement. They may make fun of lower-track students, call them unflattering names, or stop associating with them (Rosenbaum, 1976). Hence, a major result of tracking is differential respect from peers and teachers, with implications for both instruction and esteem.

Institutionally, tracking creates groups of students who are understood by teachers and parents as having certain qualities and capacities, above and beyond the actual skills they possess. The symbolic value of track placement thus creates expectations in teachers and parents, independent of student performance. These expectations affect placement in subsequent levels of the educational system (Gamoran, 1984). Ability groups limit teachers' perceptions of what grades are appropriate for students in different tracks (Reuman, 1989). Both parents and teachers rated children in higher reading groups as more competent and likely to do better in the future than children in low reading groups, even when children's initial performance levels and parents' prior beliefs about their children's abilities were held constant (Pallas et al., 1994, p. 41). Further consequences of tracking include segregation of students by social class and ethnicity (Esposito, 1973; *Hobson v. Hansen*, 1967; New York Education Department, 1969; Oakes, 1985), unequal learning by students in different tracks (Findley & Bryan, 1970; Oakes, 1985; Rosenbaum, 1976; Shafer et al., 1973), and unequal chances to attend college (Alexander, Cook, & McDill, 1978; Alexander & Eckland, 1975; Jaffe & Adams, 1970; Jones, Spade, & Vanfossen, 1987; Rosenbaum, 1976, 1980). The percentage of students in an academic curriculum may be the single most significant structural difference between different types of schools. Noncollege preparatory programs may foreclose future opportunities for young persons by failing to provide them with the courses or training necessary for admission to institutions of higher education or for pursuit of particular college majors (Hallinan, 1987; Oakes, Joseph, & Muir, 2004).

Darling-Hammond (2001) suggests that tracking persists because few teachers "are prepared to manage heterogeneous classrooms effectively" (p. 474). In the 1980s, tracking came under considerable attack, and a movement toward "detracking" gained support (Braddock & McParland, 1990; Oakes, 1985, 1992; Wheelock, 1992). But even when teachers have a strong ideology of detracking and have succeeded in ending tracking in some communities, they have encountered serious resistance and opposition from parents. In their three-year longitudinal case studies of ten racially and socioeconomically mixed secondary schools that were participating in detracking reform, Oakes, Wells, Jones, and Datnow (1997) found that detracking is a "highly normative and political endeavor that confronts deeply held cultural beliefs, ideologies, and fiercely protected arrangements of material and political advantage in local communities" (p. 507). For example, being in an honors course confers advantages in the competition for college admissions. Detracking was able to occur when politically savvy teachers were able to involve powerful parents in meaningful ways in the process of implementing it (Oakes et al., 1997).

Teachers' Expectations

Educational structures such as schools that are socioeconomically homogeneous, the growing use of standardized achievement tests, and practices such as tracking go a long way toward shaping the expectations teachers hold about students. Teacher training and textbooks have tended to attribute educational failures to deficiencies in the children. Often, such deficiencies are assumed to reside in the social characteristics of the pupils, such as their social-class background, ethnicity, language, or behavior, rather than in social structure. In a review of relevant research, Persell (1977) found that student social class was related to teacher expectations when other factors such as race were not more salient, when expectations were engendered by real children, or when teachers had a chance to draw inferences about a student's social class rather than simply being told his or her background. Sometimes social class was related to teacher expectations even when the children's current IQ and achievement were comparable. That is, teachers held lower expectations for lower-class children than for middle-class children even when those children had similar IQ scores and achievement.

Teachers' expectations may also be influenced by the behavior and physical appearance of the children (Ritts, Patterson, & Tubbs, 1992). Social class may influence teacher expectations directly or indirectly through test scores, appearance, language style, speed of task performance, and behavior. All of these traits are themselves culturally defined and are related to class position. Moreover, teacher expectations are influenced more by negative information about pupil characteristics than by positive data. It is important to know this because much of the information teachers gain about low-income children seems to be negative.

Another factor that may influence teacher expectations and pupil performance is the operation of the cultural capital possessed by families of higher social classes. As used here, the term *cultural capital* refers to the cultural resources and assets that families bring to their interactions with school personnel. By virtue of their own educational credentials and knowledge of educational institutions, parents, especially mothers, are able to help their children get the right teachers and courses and do extra work at home if necessary (Baker & Stevenson, 1986; Grissmer et al., 1994; Lareau, 1989; Useem, 1990).

If teacher expectations are often influenced by the social class of students, do those expectations have significant consequences for students? Research on this question has produced seemingly contradictory results. The controversy began with the publication of *Pygmalion in the Classroom* (Rosenthal & Jacobson, 1968). That book suggested that the expectations of classroom teachers might powerfully influence the achievement of students. Hundreds of studies on the possibility of "expectancy effects" have been conducted since then (see Cooper & Good, 1983). One thing is clear: Only expectations that teachers truly believe are likely to affect their behaviors.

When teachers hold higher expectations for pupils, how does this affect their behavior? Their expectations seem to affect the frequency of interaction they have with their pupils and the kinds of behaviors they show toward different children. Teachers spend more time interacting with pupils for whom they have higher expectations (Persell, 1977). For example, Brophy and Good (1970) found that students for whom teachers held high expectations were praised more frequently when correct and were criticized less frequently when wrong or unresponsive than were pupils for whom teachers had low expectations.

Rosenthal (1974) believes that teachers convey their expectations in at least four related ways. He bases this judgment on his review of 285 studies of interpersonal influence, including at least 80 in classrooms or other settings. First, he sees a general climate factor, consisting of the overall warmth a teacher shows to children, with more shown to high-expectancy students. Second, he sees students for whom high expectations are held as receiving more praise for doing something right than do students for whom low expectations are held. Third, Rosenthal notes that high-expectancy students are taught more than are low-expectancy students. This is consistent with research by others and summarized by Persell (1977). Fourth, Rosenthal indicates that expectancy may be affected by a response-opportunity factor. That is, students for whom the teacher has higher expectations are called on more often and are given more chances to reply, as well as more frequent and more difficult questions.

A fifth way teachers convey their expectations, which Rosenthal does not mention but which has been observed by others, is the different type of curricula teachers may present to children for whom they have different expectations. One study found that teachers report that they present completely different types of economics to students of differently perceived abilities (Keddie, 1971). Another study reported that teachers use more reading texts and more difficult ones with the top reading group (Alpert, 1975). Clearly, there is evidence that at least some teachers behave differently toward students for whom they hold different expectations. The critical question remains: Do these expectations and behaviors actually affect students? Do the students think differently about themselves or learn more as a result of the expectations teachers hold? Therein lies the heart of the "Pygmalion effect" controversy.

Students report being aware of the different expectations teachers have for them, and they notice differences in the way teachers treat them. For example, students studied by Ferguson (2001) reported that when they asked the teacher a question, they received only a brief one-sentence reply, but when other students (for whom the teacher had higher expectations) asked the same question, the teacher spoke at length in response.

When teachers hold definite expectations and when those expectations are reflected in their behavior toward children, these expectations are related to student cognitive changes, even when pupil IQ and achievement are controlled. Moreover, negative expectations, which can be observed only in natural settings because it is unethical to induce negative expectations experimentally, appear to have even more powerful consequences than do positive expectations. Moreover, socially vulnerable children (i.e., younger, lower-class, and minority children) seem to be more susceptible to lower teacher expectations (Rosenthal & Jacobson, 1968).

CONSEQUENCES OF SOCIAL CLASS AND EDUCATIONAL INEQUALITY

This profile of social-class differences in education in the United States is oversimplified, but considerable evidence suggests that the general patterns described here do exist. Social-class backgrounds affect where students go to school and what happens to them once they are there. As a result, lower-class students tend to encounter less prepared teachers, are less likely to be exposed to valued curricula, are taught less of whatever curricula they do study, and are expected to do less work in the classroom and outside of it. Hence, they learn less and are less well prepared for the next level of education.

Although students have many reasons for dropping out of school or for failing to continue, their experiences in school may contribute to their desire to continue or to quit. Coleman et al. (1982) found that 24 percent of public high school students dropped out, compared to 12 percent of Catholic and 13 percent of other private school students. Social class is a more important cause of lost talent among U.S. youth in the late high school and post–high school years than gender or race, according to Hanson (1994).

Similarly, college attendance depends on a number of factors, including access to the necessary financial resources. Nevertheless, it is striking how differently students at different schools fare. Graduation from a private rather than a public high school is related to attending a four-year (rather than a two-year) college (Falsey & Heyns, 1984), attending a highly selective college (Persell et al., 1992), and earning higher income in adult life (Lewis & Wanner, 1979). Even within the same school, track placement is related to college attendance (Alexander et al., 1978; Alexander & McDill, 1976; Jaffe & Adams, 1970; Rosenbaum, 1976, 1980). College attendance, in turn, is related to the adult positions and earnings one attains (Kamens, 1974; Tinto, 1980; Useem, 1984; Useem & Karabel, 1986). In 1999, women with bachelor's degrees earned slightly more than $30,000 on average compared to women with high school degrees, who earned about $16,000, while men with bachelor's degrees earned $46,000 compared to men with high school degrees, who earned about $30,000 on average (U.S. Department of Commerce, 1999). Thus, educational inequalities help create and legitimate economic and social inequalities.

However, most educators do not want to enhance and legitimate social inequalities. Therefore, it seems reasonable to ask, What can they do to try to change these patterns?

RECOMMENDATIONS FOR ACTION

Teachers, educators, and concerned citizens might consider the following actions:

1. Working politically and legally to increase the educational resources available to all children, not just those in wealthy school districts, and not just the gifted and talented. Those concerned might do this by joining a political party that works to advance the interests of the less advantaged members of society, by attending political meetings, by holding candidates accountable for their positions on education, and by supporting class-action lawsuits for educational equity. We can join other people interested in scrutinizing candidates' records of support for education and contribute time, money, or both to the campaigns of candidates seeking to defeat incumbents who have not supported quality education for all children.

2. Working to reduce economic inequalities in society. This can be done by supporting income tax reforms at the national level that benefit hardworking low- and middle-income families, by opposing tax cuts for the rich, by supporting job programs at reasonable wages and health care programs for those who can work, and by providing aid for poor parents who are unable to work.

3. Working to build economically and racially integrated communities. This can be done by choosing to live in such a community, by supporting federal subsidies for low-income housing in mixed-income areas, and by opposing efforts to restrict access to certain communities by members of particular ethnic or income groups. Such restrictions might take the form of zoning that prohibits the construction of high-rise housing for low-income groups or limits housing lots to a large size, such as two acres, or of red-lining by banks that refuse to provide mortgages in certain neighborhoods.

4. Working to support prenatal care for all pregnant women. In 1989, about one-quarter of them received no prenatal care. Helping all pregnant women could reduce or eliminate perhaps one-third of all learning disorders (Hodgkinson, 1989).

5. Working to support Head Start programs for all eligible children. In 1988, only 16 percent of low-income children eligible for the preschool program for four-year-olds were enrolled in it, yet Head Start has a proven track record. Every dollar invested in quality preschool education yields $4.75 because of lower costs later on for special education, public assistance, and the incarceration of people who commit crimes (Children's Defense Fund, 1988; Weikart & Schweinhart, 1984).

6. Using tests for diagnosing rather than dismissing students. For example, instead of taking a low test score as evidence that a child cannot learn, we can examine what parts of a particular test were difficult for that child. If necessary, we can obtain further, individual testing to identify and analyze what skills the child needs to develop and devise strategies for teaching those specific skills. We can try alternative teaching strategies with each child until we find one that works. If a child has difficulty learning to read phonetically, for example, we might try teaching that child a different way, perhaps visually. We can help children with

various kinds of learning disabilities learn ways to compensate for their difficulties. For example, planning their work in advance, organizing it so that they have enough time to complete the necessary steps, and allowing time for someone else to check their spelling are all compensatory strategies that can be adopted to good effect by children trying to overcome various learning disabilities.

7. Working on finding the abilities students do have, rather than on deciding that they don't have any. For example, for students who have strong artistic, musical, athletic, or auditory talents, but are weaker in the verbal or mathematical areas, we can help them find ways into the academic subjects through their strengths.

8. Supporting efforts at detracking.

9. Learning about and using collaborative teaching techniques, such as those developed by Elizabeth Cohen and her colleagues at Stanford University, that work effectively in heterogeneous classes (Cohen, 1994, 2000; Cohen & Lotan 1997; Sharan, 1980).

10. Committing to the use of a variety of pedagogical techniques, curricular assignments, and projects that address the learning needs of individual children.

11. Expecting and demanding a lot from students in the way of effort, thought, and work. We can help students take pride in themselves and their work by teaching them what first-rate work should look like. The written materials students get from teachers and schools and the appearance of the classrooms and hallways should all convey a sense of care, quality, and value. We can carefully check the work students do, suggest constructive ways they might improve it, and expect them to do better the next time.

12. Teaching students content and subject matter. We can show students that we value them and their learning by devoting class time to pedagogically useful tasks, by refusing to waste class time on frivolous activities, and by trying to stick to an annual schedule of curricular coverage.

13. Helping students see how education is relevant and useful for their lives, perhaps by bringing back graduates who have used school as a springboard to better themselves and their worlds. Schools might keep a roster of successful graduates and post pictures and stories about them for current students to see. We can bring in examples that link learning with life accomplishments so students can begin to see connections between school and life. For example, we might invite people who run their own business to talk about how they use math or bring in people who work in social service organizations to show how they use writing in their daily work.

SUMMARY

This chapter explores how educational structures, beliefs, and practices contribute to unequal educational outcomes. To achieve greater educational equality, educators must understand what social-class differences presently exist in those structures, beliefs, and practices. If these differences are understood, then the educational experiences of students of all social classes might be made more similar.

The higher one's social-class background, the more likely one is to attend a smaller school with more resources, including better teachers, smaller classes, and an academic curriculum. Achieving greater educational equality means making such school experiences available to all students, regardless of their social-class backgrounds.

Widespread confidence in educational testing and the growing use of high-stakes testing runs the risk of blaming students for their failure and diverting attention from how the social organization of schools may help to create failures. Instead, we should be examining how teachers, curricula, and teaching practices of schools attended by children of different social classes influence their learning.

The educational process of tracking refers to the segregation of students into different learning or curriculum groups that are unequally ranked in a prestige hierarchy. Whether based on ability grouping or curricular grouping, such tracking tends to reduce learning opportunities for students in the lower groups, while increasing such opportunities for students in higher groups. As a result, this educational practice contributes to educational inequalities. The detracking movement represents an important effort toward achieving greater educational equality, but it has encountered some resistance from certain parents.

Teachers may unconsciously form different learning expectations about students of different social-class backgrounds. When teachers hold higher expectations for students, they tend to spend more time interacting with those students, praise them more, teach them more, call on them more often, and offer them a more socially valued curriculum. When teachers hold higher expectations, and when those expectations are evident in their behavior, they increase student learning. Thus, achieving greater educational equality means that teachers' expectations for lower-class students need to be raised.

Because the educational structures, beliefs, and practices examined here are related to unequal educational attainment, and because educational success is related to lifetime occupations and earnings, it is important that educational inequalities be reduced. This chapter recommends a number of steps that concerned educators and citizens can take to promote educational and social equality.

Questions and Activities

1. According to Persell, in what ways do schools contribute to inequality? What evidence does the author give to support her position?

2. Give examples of how each of the following factors contributes to educational inequality: (a) educational structures, (b) funding inequities, (c) testing practices, and (d) teachers and curriculum.

3. What are the major characteristics of each of the following types of schools: (a) elite private schools and exclusive suburban schools, (b) parochial schools, and (c) large urban public school systems?

4. Why do students from different social-class backgrounds often attend different schools or get assigned to different tracks when they attend the same schools? How does the social-class background of students influence the kind of education they often receive?

5. Visit and observe in (a) a local elite private school, (b) a school in an upper-middle-class suburb, and (c) an inner-city school. How are these schools alike? How are they different? Based on your visits and observations, what tentative generalizations can you make about education, social class, and inequality? To what extent are your generalizations similar to and different from those of Persell?

6. What cautions should teachers, principals, policy makers, and parents keep in mind when interpreting standardized achievement tests?

7. What is the self-fulfilling prophecy? How does it affect teacher expectations?

8. What is tracking? Why do you think tracking is more widespread in large, diverse school systems and in schools serving primarily lower-class students than in upper-middle-class suburban, private, and parochial schools?

9. How do the school experiences of students in lower and higher tracks differ? How does tracking contribute to educational inequality? What is detracking?

10. Why does tracking persist?

11. How do factors related to social class influence teacher expectations of students?

12. How do teacher expectations influence how teachers and pupils interact, what students are taught, and what students achieve?

References

Alexander, K. L., Cook, M., & McDill, E. L. (1978). Curriculum Tracking and Educational Stratification: Some Further Evidence. *American Sociological Review, 43*(1), 47–66.

Alexander, K. L., & Eckland, B. K. (1975). Contextual Effects in the High School Attainment Process. *American Sociological Review, 40*(3), 402–416.

Alexander, K. L., & McDill, E. L. (1976). Selection and Allocation within Schools: Some Causes and Consequences of Curriculum Placement. *American Sociological Review, 41*(6), 963–980.

Alpert, J. L. (1975). Do Teachers Adapt Methods and Materials to Ability Groups in Reading? *California Journal of Education Research, 26*(3), 120–123.

Amrein, A. L., & Y Berliner, D. C. (2002). High-Stakes Testing, Uncertainty, and Student Learning. *Education Policy Analysis Archives, 10*(18). Retrieved February 14, 2003, from http://epaa.asu.edu/epaa/v10n18/.

Baker, D. P., & Stevenson, D. L. (1986). Mothers' Strategies for Children's School Achievement: Managing the Transition to High School. *Sociology of Education, 59*(3), 156–166.

Blossfeld, H. P., & Shavit, Y. (1993). Persisting Barriers: Changes in Educational Opportunities in Thirteen Countries. In Y. Shavit & H. P. Blossfeld (Eds.), *Persistent Inequality: Changing Educational Attainment in Thirteen Countries* (pp. 1–23). Boulder, CO: Westview.

Braddock, J. H., II, & McPartland, J. M. (1990). Alternatives to Tracking. *Educational Leadership, 47*(7), 76–79.

Brint, S., & Karabel, J. (1989). *The Diverted Dream: Community Colleges and the Promise of Educational Opportunity in American, 1900–1985.* New York: Oxford University Press.

Brookover, W. B., Leu, D. J., & Kariger, R. H. (1965). *Tracking.* Unpublished manuscript (mimeo), Western Michigan University, Kalamazoo, MI.

Brophy, J. E., & Good, T. L. (1970). Teachers' Communication of Differential Expectations for Children's Classroom Performance: Some Behavioral Data. *Journal of Educational Psychology, 61*(5), 365–374.

Children's Defense Fund. (1988). *A Call for Action.* Washington, DC: Author.

Cohen, E. G. (1994). Restructuring the Classroom: Conditions for Productive Small Groups. *Review of Educational Research, 64*(1), 1–35.

Cohen, E. G. (2000). Equitable Classrooms in a Changing Society. In M. T. Hallinan (Ed.), *Handbook of the Sociology of Education* (pp. 265–283). New York: Kluwer Academic/Plenum.

Cohen, E. G., & Lotan, R. A. (Eds.). (1997). *Working for Equity in Heterogeneous Classrooms: Sociological Theory in Practice.* New York: Teachers College Press.

Coleman, J. S., Campbell, E. Q., Hobson, C. J., McPartland, J., Alexander, M., Mood, A. M., Weinfeld, F. D., & York, R. L. (1966). *Equality of Educational Opportunity.* Washington, DC: U.S. Government Printing Office.

Coleman, J. S., Hoffer, T., & Kilgore, S. (1982). *High School Achievement.* New York: Basic Books.

Collins, R. (1979). *The Credential Society.* New York: Academic Press.

Conant, J. B. (1961). *Slums and Suburbs.* New York: McGraw Hill.

Cookson, P. W., Jr., & Persell, C. H. (1985). *Preparing for Power: America's Elite Boarding Schools.* New York: Basic Books.

Cooper, H. M., & Good, T. L. (1983). *Pygmalion Grows Up.* New York: Longman.

Darling-Hammond, L. (1990). Teacher Quality and Equality. In J. Goodlad & P. Keating (Eds.), *Access to Knowledge: An Agenda for Our Nation's Schools* (pp. 237–258). New York: College Entrance Examination Board.

Darling-Hammond, L. (1992). Teaching and Knowledge: Policy Issues Posed by Alternate Certification for Teachers. *Peabody Journal of Education, 67*(2), 123–154.

Darling-Hammond, L. (2001). Inequality and Access to Knowledge. In J. A. Banks & C. A. M. Banks (Eds.), *Handbook of Research on Multicultural Education* (pp. 465–483). San Francisco: Jossey-Bass.

Dively, J. A., & Hickrod, G. A. (1992). Update of Selected States' School Equity Funding Litigation and the "Boxscore." *Journal of Education Finance, 17*(2), 352–363.

Dreeben, R., & Barr, R. (1988). Classroom Composition and the Design of Instruction. *Sociology of Education, 61*(3), 129–142.

Elliott, M. (1998). School Finance and Opportunities to Learn: Does Money Well Spent Enhance Students' Achievement? *Sociology of Education, 71*(3), 223–245.

Esposito, D. (1973). Homogeneous and Heterogeneous Ability Grouping: Principal Findings and Implications for Evaluating and Designing More Effective Educational Environments. *Review of Educational Research, 43*(2), 163–179.

Falsey, B., & Heyns, B. (1984). The College Channel: Private and Public Schools Reconsidered. *Sociology of Education, 57*(2), 111–122.

Ferguson, R. F. (2001, December 13). Talk presented at New York University. "Closing the Achievement Gap: What Schools Can Do."

Findley, W. G., & Bryan, M. M. (1970). *Ability Grouping: 1970–1 The Impact of Ability Grouping on School Achievement, Affective Development, Ethnic Separation and Socioeconomic Separation.* Athens: University of Georgia Center for Educational Improvement. (ERIC Document Reproduction Service No. ED 048382).

Findley, W. G., & Bryan, M. M. (1975). *The Pros and Cons of Ability Grouping.* Bloomington: Phi Delta Kappa.

Freiberg, J. (1970). *The Effects of Ability Grouping on Interactions in the Classroom.* (ERIC Document Reproduction Service No. ED 053194).

Gamoran, A. (1984). *Teaching, Grouping, and Learning: A Study of the Consequences of Educational Stratification.* Unpublished doctoral dissertation, Department of Sociology, University of Chicago.

Gamoran, A. (1986). Instructional and Institutional Effects of Ability Grouping. *Sociology of Education, 59*(4), 185–198.

Gamoran, A. (2001). American Schooling and Educational Inequality: A Forecast for the 21st Century. *Sociology of Education, 34*, 135–153.

Gamoran, A., Secada, W. G., & Marrett, C. B. (2000). The Organizational Context of Teaching and Learning. In M. T. Hallinan (Ed.), *Handbook of the Sociology of Education* (pp. 37–63). New York: Kluwer Academic/Plenum.

Gardner, H. (1983). *Frames of Mind.* New York: Basic Books.

Goldstein, B. (1967). *Low Income Youth in Urban Areas: A Critical Review of the Literature.* New York: Holt, Rinehart & Winston.

Goodlad, J. I. (1984). *A Place Called School.* New York: McGraw-Hill.

Goodnough, A. (2002, August 23). Shortage Ends as City Lures New Teachers. *New York Times,* pp. A1, B3.

Gould, S. J. (1981). *The Mismeasure of Man.* New York: Norton.

Grissmer, D. W., & Kirby, S. N. (1987). *Teacher Attrition: The Uphill Climb to Staff the Nation's Schools.* Santa Monica, CA: RAND.

Grissmer, D. W., Kirby, S. N., Berends, M., & Williamson, S. (1994). *Student Achievement and the Changing American Family.* Santa Monica, CA: RAND.

Hallinan, M. T. (1987). Ability Grouping and Student Learning. In M. T. Hallinan (Ed.), *The Social Organization of Schools: New Conceptualizations of the Learning Process* (pp. 41–69). New York: Plenum.

Hanson, S. L. (1994). Lost Talent: Unrealized Educational Aspirations and Expectations among U.S. Youths. *Sociology of Education, 3*(3), 159–183.

Hanushek, E. A. (1989). The Impact of Differential Expenditures on School Performance. *Educational Researcher, 18*(4), 45–51.

Hanushek, E. A. (1996). School Resources and Student Performance. In G. Burtless (Ed.), *Does Money Matter?* (pp. 43–73). Washington, DC: Brookings Institution Press.

Herrnstein, R. J., & Murray, C. (1994). *The Bell Curve.* New York: Free Press.

Heubert, J. P., & Hauser, R. M. (Eds.). (1999). *High Stakes: Testing for Tracking, Promotion, and Graduation.* Washington, DC: National Academy Press.

Hobson v. Hansen. (1967, June 21). *Congressional Record* 6721–16766.

Hodgkinson, H. L. (1989). *The Same Client: The Demographics of Education and Service Delivery Systems.* Washington, DC: Institute for Educational Leadership.

Ingersoll, R. M. (1999, August). *Teachers Teaching Out of Area of Certification.* Paper presented at the American Sociological Association annual meeting, Chicago.

Jaffe, A., & Adams, W. (1970). *Academic and Socio-Economic Factors Related to Entrance and Retention at Two- and Four-Year Colleges in the Late 1960's.* New York: Bureau of Applied Social Research, Columbia University.

Jones, J. D., Spade, J. N., & Vanfossen, B. E. (1987). Curriculum Tracking and Status Maintenance. *Sociology of Education, 60*(2), 104–122.

Jones, J. D., Vanfossen, B. E., & Spade, J. Z. (1985, August). *Curriculum Placement: Individual and School Effects Using the High School and Beyond Data.* Paper presented at the American Sociological Association Annual Meeting, Washington, DC.

Kamens, D. (1974). Colleges and Elite Formation: The Case of Prestigious American Colleges. *Sociology of Education, 47*(3), 354–378.

Keddie, N. (1971). Classroom Knowledge. In M. F. D. Young, (Ed.), *Knowledge and Control* (pp. 133–160). London: Collier-Macmillan.

Lareau, A. (1989). *Home Advantage.* Philadelphia: Falmer.

Lewis, L. S., & Wanner, R. A. (1979). Private Schooling and the Status Attainment Process. *Sociology of Education, 52*(2), 99–112.

Lichter, D. T., & Eggebeen, D. J. (1993). Rich Kids, Poor Kids: Changing Income Inequality among American Children. *Social Forces, 71*(3), 761–780.

Mare, R. (1981). Change and Stability in Educational Stratification. *American Sociological Review, 46*(1), 72–87.

Mayer, S. E. (2001). How Did the Increase in Economic Inequality between 1970 and 1990 Affect Children's Educational Attainment? *American Journal of Sociology, 107*(1), 1–32.

Mayeske, G. W., & Wisler, C. E. (1972). *A Study of Our Nation's Schools.* Washington, DC: U.S. Government Printing Office.

New York Education Department. (1969). *Racial and Social Isolation in the Schools.* Albany: New York State Education Department.

Oakes, J. (1985). *Keeping Track: How Schools Structure Inequality.* New Haven, CT: Yale University Press.

Oakes, J. (1992). Can Tracking Research Inform Practice? Technical, Normative, and Political Considerations. *Educational Researcher, 21*, 12–21.

Oakes, J., Joseph, R., & Muir, K. (2004). Access and Achievement in Mathematics and Science: Inequalities That Endure and Change. In J. A. Banks & C. A. M. Banks (Eds.), *Handbook of Research on Multicultural Education* (2nd ed., pp. 69–90). San Francisco: Jossey-Bass.

Oakes, J., Wells, A. S., Jones, M., & Datnow, A. (1997). Detracking: The Social Construction of Ability, Cultural Politics, and Resistance to Reform. *Teachers College Record, 98*(3), 482–510.

Pallas, A. M., Entwisle, D. R., Alexander, K. L., & Stluka, M. F. (1994). Ability-Group Effects: Instructional, Social, or Institutional? *Sociology of Education, 67*(1), 27–46.

Persell, C. H. (1977). *Education and Inequality: The Roots and Results of Stratification in America's Schools.* New York: Free Press.

Persell, C. H. (2000). Values, Control, and Outcomes in Public and Private Schools. In M. T. Hallinan (Ed.), *Handbook of Sociology of Education* (pp. 387–407). New York: Kluwer Academic/Plenum.

Persell, C. H., Cookson, P. W., Jr., & Catsambis, S. (1992). Family Background, High School Type, and College Attendance: A Conjoint System of Cultural Capital Transmission. *Journal of Research on Adolescence, 2*(1), 1–23.

Reuman, D. A. (1989). How Social Comparison Mediates the Relation between Ability-Grouping Practices and Students' Achievement Expectancies in Mathematics. *Journal of Educational Psychology, 81*(1), 78–89.

Ritts, V., Patterson, M. L., & Tubbs, M. E. (1992). Expectations, Impressions, and Judgments of Physically Attractive Students: A Review. *Review of Educational Research, 62*(4), 413–426.

Rogers, D. (1968). *110 Livingston Street: Politics and Bureaucracy in the New York City School System.* New York: Random House.

Rogers, D., & Chung, N. H. (1983). *110 Livingston Street Revisited: Decentralization in Action.* New York: New York University Press.

Rosenbaum, J. E. (1976). *Making Inequality.* New York: Wiley-Interscience.

Rosenbaum, J. E. (1980). Track Misperceptions and Frustrated College Plans: An Analysis of the Effects of Tracks and Track Perceptions in the National Longitudinal Survey. *Sociology of Education, 53*(2), 74–88.

Rosenthal, R. (1974). The Pygmalion Effect: What You Expect Is What You Get. *Psychology Today Library Cassette, #12.* New York: Ziff-Davis.

Rosenthal, R., & Jacobson, L. (1968). *Pygmalion in the Classroom.* New York: Holt, Rinehart & Winston.

Schafer, W. E., Olexa, C., & Polk, K. (1973). Programmed for Social Class: Tracking in American High Schools. In N. K. Denzin (Ed.), *Children and Their Caretakers* (pp. 220–226). New Brunswick, NJ: Transaction Books.

Schiller, K., & Muller, C. (2002, August). *Raising the Bar: State Policies and Students' Mathematics and Science Course-Taking.* Paper presented at the American Sociological Association annual meeting, Chicago.

Sharan, S. (1980). Cooperative Learning in Small Groups: Recent Methods and Effects on Achievement, Attitudes, and Ethnic Relations. *Review of Educational Research, 50,* 241–271.

Tinto, V. (1980). College Origin and Patterns of Status Attainment. *Sociology of Work and Occupations, 7*(4), 457–486.

"A Truce in New Jersey's School War." (2002, February 9). *New York Times,* p. A18.

U.S. Department of Commerce, Bureau of the Census (1999). *Money Income in the United States: 1999.* (Current Population Reports, Series P-60). Washington, DC; U.S. Government Printing Office. Retrieved from: http://nccs.ed.gov/pubs2002/digest2001/ch5.asp August 31, 2003.

Useem, E. L. (1990, April). *Social Class and Ability Group Placement in Mathematics in the Transition to Seventh Grade: The Role of Parental Involvement.* Paper presented at the annual meeting of the American Educational Research Association, Boston.

Useem, M. (1984). *The Inner Circle: Large Corporations and the Rise of Business Political Activity in the U.S. and U.K.* New York: Oxford University Press.

Useem, M., & Karabel, J. (1986). Educational Pathways to Top Corporate Management. *American Sociological Review, 51*(2), 184–200.

Weikart, D., & Schweinhart, L. J. (1984). *Changed Lives: The Effects of the Perry Preschool Program on Youths through Age 19.* Ypsilanti, MI: High Scope.

Wenglinsky, H. (1997). How Money Matters: The Effect of School District Spending on Academic Achievement. *Sociology of Education, 70,* 221–237.

Wheelock, A. (1992). *Crossing the Tracks: How "Untracking" Can Save America's Schools.* New York: New Press.

Winter, G. (2002, December 28). Rigorous School Tests Grow, but Big Study Doubts Value. *New York Times,* pp. A1, A15.

Winter, G. (2003, April 23). New Ammunition for Backers of Do-or-Die Exams. *New York Times,* p. B9.

Wise, A. E., Darling-Hammond, L., & Berry, B. (1987). *Effective Teacher Selection: From Recruitment to Retention.* Santa Monica, CA: RAND.

CHAPTER 5

Christian Nation or Pluralistic Culture: Religion in American Life

Charles H. Lippy

Two threads in the tapestry representing American religious culture seem paradoxical, if not contradictory:

1. The United States is a Christian nation, founded on religious principles deriving from the Bible still embedded in the laws under which we live. While other religious communities are tolerated, Christianity in its many forms has been and remains the dominant religious influence in our common life.

2. Religious freedom prevails in the United States because of the principle of "separation of church and state." Hence Americans are free to believe whatever they want and to worship however they want. Consequently, many religious alternatives flourish side by side, with none dominating.

Both perceptions have long histories; both are vital to understanding the religious dynamics of American culture in the early twenty-first century.

EUROPEANS PLANT CHRISTIANITY IN NORTH AMERICA

When the thirteen colonies that became the United States broke away from Great Britain in 1776, European settlement in those areas stretched back less than 175 years. Most of those who came from England brought with them a religious consciousness shaped by Protestant Christianity (Lippy, Choquette, & Poole, 1992). In southern areas like Virginia, although there were some variations of belief, colonial arrangements included legal establishment of the Church of England. Establishment meant that Church of England parishes and the few clergy serving them were supported by public tax money and that all who lived there would in theory be expected to be part of a parish.

To the north, first to Plymouth and then to other areas of Massachusetts, came settlers who had deep ties to the Church of England. However, they were unhappy with what they saw as compromises the Church of England had made with Roman Catholic ways in trying to craft a religious establishment with broad appeal. These dissenters came to New England to set up churches that reflected their own understanding of religious truth. Generally, we label all of them Puritans, for all sought a more pure form of Protestant Christianity than they found in the Church of England. But there were important differences. The Pilgrims who came to Plymouth in 1620 believed that the Church of England was hopelessly engulfed in religious falsehood; therefore, the only way to assure their own salvation was to separate from the church by moving away and setting up their own religious institutions. The Puritans who settled much of the rest of New England still identified with the Church of England, but they thought that their abandoning a structure that relied on the authority of bishops and their simpler worship rendered them a more pure form of that church.

Regardless, both thought that relocating to North America would give them religious freedom, unwittingly giving birth to the idea that the United States was founded on the principle of religious freedom. In actuality, neither Plymouth Pilgrims nor other Puritans believed that those who disagreed with them should have any religious freedom; indeed, alternative points of view were seen as dangerous. For example, Massachusetts authorities banished Roger Williams in the 1630s because he was too much a religious seeker. Later acclaimed a bulwark of religious freedom whose perspective influenced Baptist developments, Williams then was regarded as a dangerous heretic. But all he needed to do was move a few miles away to what is now Rhode Island. There Massachusetts authorities had no control over him, and he was free to set up a church reflecting his own views.

Before the end of the seventeenth century, however, political changes in Britain mandated in the colonies a broader toleration of variant forms of Protestantism, so long as they did not disrupt public order and peace. Roman Catholics, however, were still not formally recognized, although they had carved a presence for themselves when Maryland was established. They later flourished, especially in Pennsylvania, where the Quaker-dominated government supported what the founder William Penn called a "holy experiment" of allowing persons of whatever religious persuasion to settle so long as they supported the commonweal.

EARLY SIGNS OF DIVERSITY

Even so, patterns of immigration generated a far greater diversity in many parts of the English colonies than was recognized by public policy. From the arrival of the first slave ships in Virginia in 1619, an African tribal substratum made most southern Christian life diverse, since many congregations in time became biracial. White Christians were at first reluctant to share their religion with the slaves, fearing that conversion would automatically bring freedom from the bonds of slavery. When more sustained efforts were made to preach Christianity to African Americans from the middle of the eighteenth century on, the result was a vibrant fusion of African ways with evangelical Protestantism. The chant, song, and dance central to much tribal religiosity fused with the enthusiastic and often emotional style of evangelicalism to give African American Christianity a distinctive expression that grew and developed alongside the churches with European roots. Those whose forced migration from Africa brought them first to the Caribbean added other twists that endured in practices popularly associated with voodoo once they planted those rituals on American soil. Both

European Americans and African Americans were drawn to slaves with a gift for preaching. However, few Whites recognized how often the power of the slave preacher echoed that of the tribal conjurer, a blending that endured in the person of many African American clergy even after the abolition of slavery and the emergence of separate African American denominations. In addition, some of the first slaves were Muslims, although the conditions of slavery made it impossible for Muslim practice to last very long among the African population.

Ethnicity also contributed to other manifestations of diversity. The Dutch who had originally settled in New York (New Netherlands) brought with them their Calvinistic Reformed faith; even after the English took control, they remained a strong presence. To what became New Jersey, clusters of Scandinavian immigrants brought their Lutheran religion with them. Various communities of German immigrants who came to Pennsylvania carried a variety of religious labels, most still within the orbit of Protestant Christianity. And almost from the inception of the colonies came Jewish immigrants, who remained on the margins of colonial religious life but established synagogues and communities in places such as Charleston, South Carolina; Savannah, Georgia; New York; and Newport, Rhode Island. Often unrecognized, because they were not understood even by well-intentioned Christian colonists as religious, were the practices of the Native American tribes on whose lands the Europeans settled. They, too, are part of the larger picture of diversity.

By the middle of the eighteenth century, Scots-Irish immigrants had planted their own form of Presbyterianism, especially in the middle colonies and then farther south as they settled along the eastern slopes of the Appalachian mountain chain. By mid-century, too, those inclined to Methodism, then a "new religion" in England, had made their way to North America. Even so, when the new United States conducted its first national census in 1790, statistics showed that only around 10 percent of the population were formal members of a religious group. But that figure is misleading, for it underestimates the influence of the churches in colonial and early national life and fails to take into account the conviction prevailing then that joining a church—actually becoming a member—was a serious, important step not to be taken lightly. Many who regularly attended worship and who tried to live by the moral codes of the churches never took that step.

English control did not extend to all areas of North America that eventually became part of the United States. The presence of Spanish settlements in areas from Florida through Texas and the Southwest to California adds another layer to the tale of diversity. The last of the Spanish missions, the one in San Francisco, was founded in 1776, the same year that the English colonies proclaimed their independence from Britain. In addition, a Catholicism reflecting the French experience flourished in areas along the Gulf of Mexico from Mobile to New Orleans and along the southern Mississippi River. When these areas became part of the United States, they intensified the story of diversity because of the long history of both Spanish and French Catholicism that had supported adjoining colonial empires.

COMMON THEMES

Presbyterians and Methodists, Lutherans and Dutch Reformed, Congregationalist Puritans and Baptists—all were part of the larger Protestant heritage that had marked European Christianity since the Reformation of the sixteenth century. And while there were differences, there were also common features that became more evident in the first half-century or so when the United States was struggling with what it meant to be a republic, a representative democracy. Perhaps the most important feature was some sense that vital religion was based on personal experience, although there was considerable difference as to whether one had such experience of one's own volition or whether an experience of conversion, a sense of salvation, was something determined only by God. Congregationalists, Presbyterians, and Dutch Reformed, all looking back to the sixteenth-century reformer John Calvin, were more inclined to attribute all to the work of God, while Methodists were convinced that human beings had to accept God's gift of salvation of their own free will. Among Baptists, some emphasized free will and some believed that God alone determined who would be saved. Anglicans—those who were part of the Church of England—and Lutherans also showed some diversity, although many simply regarded the work of God in salvation as a mystery revealed to those who faithfully attended worship and accepted the doctrines of the church.

In the middle of the eighteenth century, the centrality of personal religious experience got a big boost when waves of revivals swept through the colonies, revivals that historians call the Great Awakening, although some debate whether historians invented both the phenomenon and the label. For about a decade or so after 1740, folks seemed to exhibit a renewed interest in religion. Many talked about being converted, some because they were convinced that God had given them signs that they were chosen for salvation and others because they believed they had willingly accepted God's gracious offer of salvation. The revival enriched the biracial character of Christianity in the southern colonies, for evangelical preachers, as already noted, were among the first who actively sought converts among enslaved African Americans.

Although church members remained a minority in the whole population, Protestant denominations emphasizing personal decision and free will in matters of religion were those whose influence grew immensely in the first half of the nineteenth century. Even those who stressed election by God in salvation began to move away from that idea. Free will and choice seemed consistent with the idea of democracy taking root in American political life, for in this approach, all persons were equal, whether as sinners or as those who chose salvation. Just as wealth and rank were not supposed to matter in the public order in a democracy, so, too, they had no clout in the evangelical denominations, like the Methodists and Baptists, that offered salvation to all. These groups—along with Presbyterians, who were gradually jettisoning the idea that God predestined some to salvation—were more aggressive in going to where ordinary folk were in order to present their message.

As the American population grew and began to move westward, evangelicals were among the major proponents of the camp meeting, which brought together those who lived isolated lives on the frontier for times of preaching and fellowship. Then, as factory towns developed along the rivers and canals in the North (the Erie Canal in New York is a prime example), enterprising urban evangelists adapted the techniques of the frontier camp meeting and made revivalism a major device for spreading the influence of Protestant Christianity. Revivalists and itinerant evangelists earned their reputations because their preaching moved the minds and emotions of their audiences, not because of formal education in the rigors of theology once favored by New England Puritans. Denominations that still expected their clergy to have more formal training saw their influence dwindling; few had the time or the money to prepare for ministry in this way. Table 5.1 shows the relative growth of Christian groups from 1650 to 1996.

Table 5.1   Number of Places of Worship

	1650	1750	1850	1950	1996
Baptist	2	132	9,375	77,000	98,228
Congregationalist	62	465	1,706	5,679	6,748
Episcopal	31	289	1,459	7,784	7,517
Presbyterian	4	233	4,824	13,200	14,214
Methodist	0	0	13,328	54,000	51,311
Roman Catholic	6	30	1,221	15,533	22,728
Jewish	0	5	30	2,000	3,975
Holiness/Pentecostal	0	0	0	21,705	52,868
Lutheran	4	138	1,217	16,403	19,077

Adapted from Gaustad and Barlow (2001), p. 390.

THE SPREAD OF EVANGELICAL PROTESTANTISM

These currents helped make a broad evangelical Protestantism the dominant style of Christianity in the United States by the time of the Civil War. Even the arrival of thousands of Roman Catholics from Ireland in the 1830s and 1840s did not diminish that influence, for Protestant folk were also the ones who ran the developing businesses and industries and usually the ones elected or appointed to political office. This Protestant Christian character became deeply etched into American culture more subtly as public education began to develop in the 1830s. The well-known *McGuffey Readers* (Westerhoff, 1978; Williams, 1980) were standard fare in primary education for generations of students. A quick look at the content of those readers reveals that they simply assumed that pupils shared a broad evangelical Protestant background, making the emerging public schools almost arms of the Protestant denominations in their fusion of Protestant beliefs, moral values, and sound learning. Hence, even though there were other groups present—Irish Catholics, German Catholics, Jews, and more—this broad evangelical Protestantism influenced every sector of common life, reinforcing the image of the United States as a Christian nation.

The decades between the close of the Civil War and the outbreak of World War I, when immigration from Europe reached its peak, brought challenges to that hegemony. Most of the millions who arrived on American shores in those decades came not from Protestant or even Catholic areas of Northern and Western Europe, but from Southern, Central, and Eastern Europe. The majority were not Protestants, but Roman Catholics, Eastern Orthodox Christians, and Jews. Many Catholic parishes established parochial or parish schools, in part because Protestant assumptions pervaded the public school curriculum and instruction. But some of those in positions of social, economic, and political power recoiled not only at the religious orientation of these immigrants but also at their cultural and ethnic folkways. Calls to Americanize the immigrants, however, were also most often quite clearly calls to Protestantize them, to force them into the dominant religious style and therefore perpetuate the image of the United States as a (Protestant) Christian nation.

The congregationalist Josiah Strong, who worked for the interdenominational Evangelical Alliance, in his *Our Country* (1886/1964) of the mid-1880s, identified the religions of the immigrants, along with their concentration in the nation's cities and the rapid industrialization that their presence in the work force propelled, as major threats to American identity. But they were threats only if one assumed that an American identity was wedded to evangelical Protestant Christianity.

Adding another layer to the *de facto* diversity was the steady growth of African American Protestant denominations, most associated with the Methodist and Baptist traditions. By no means mirror images of their White counterparts, these groups played a critical role in allowing an indigenous leadership to develop, centered in the churches, that realized much of its potential in the civil rights movement of the twentieth century. In much of the South, where legal discrimination replaced slavery, churches were frequently the only property actually owned by African Americans, and the preachers who served them often the only ones who had received a higher education. The churches became more than religious centers; in the rural South especially they became broad social institutions, serving as centers for community life and offering an array of social welfare programs that remained essential as long as legal racism penetrated the larger society.

Nonetheless, Protestants from the mainline denominations continued to exert an influence in the business and political affairs of the nation that was increasingly out of proportion to their numbers in the whole population. Hence, after World War I, when Congress enacted the first laws restricting immigration overall, there had already been earlier legislation affecting primarily Chinese and Japanese immigration to California and other areas of the West. The new quotas assured that the bulk of those allowed to enter the United States each year would give at least tacit assent to Protestant Christian belief and thus preserve the image of the U.S. as a Christian nation. Table 5.2 presents data on religious affiliation from 1830 to 1990.

RELIGIOUS FREEDOM AND THE SEPARATION OF CHURCH AND STATE

Countervailing forces always assured that a vital undercurrent challenged the reality of the image of the United States as a Christian nation and sustained the conviction that religious diversity and pluralism flourished in the culture. In this view, the United States has never been a Christian nation per se, but one where religious freedom prevailed and no one religious group or tradition, like Christianity, dominated. Those who trumpet this religious freedom point to the First Amendment to the Constitution, which says simply that "Congress shall make no law respecting an establishment of religion, or prohibiting the free exercise thereof." Ever since the adoption of the Bill of Rights, courts and pundits have debated precisely what those words mean.

Table 5.2   Percentage of Those Claiming Religious Affiliation

	1830	1890	1990
Baptist	25.0%	18.0%	20.0%
Congregationalist	12.3	2.5	1.5
Episcopal	5.0	2.6	1.8
Presbyterian	17.0	6.2	2.7
Methodist	23.4	22.3	11.8
Roman Catholic	4.2	30.2	38.9
Jewish	*	*	4.4
Holiness/Pentecostal	*	*	4.4
Lutheran	3.4	6.0	6.0

*Less than 1 percent.

Adapted from Gaustad and Barlow (2001), p. 389.

In the context of the early Republic, one reason for refraining from having a nationally established religion was pragmatic. If most citizens of the new United States identified with one of the numerous Christian bodies, primarily Protestant ones, no one denomination or sect could count a majority as adherents, much less as members. Already Baptists, Methodists, Presbyterians, Quakers, Lutherans of many ethnic varieties, Episcopalians, and a host of others had learned to live in relative peace and harmony. This diversity, which some later would celebrate as a kind of pluralism, meant that it would be unfair—undemocratic—to single out one group to receive governmental support. Another assumption undergirded this nod to diversity—namely, a conviction that regardless of label, all such groups inculcated the same values and morals that made their followers good citizens. Differences of theological doctrine paled in importance to this ethical bent.

At the same time, many of the leading political thinkers of the age embraced ideas of rationality and freedom of thought associated with the philosophical currents of the Enlightenment. The Age of the Revolution was also the Age of Reason. Thomas Jefferson, Benjamin Franklin, George Washington, and a host of others all subscribed to Enlightenment ideas. Contrary to later lore, they were not twenty-first-century fundamentalists disguised as eighteenth-century political leaders; nor were they what a later age would call secular humanists. Most accepted the idea that an overarching Providence worked through human affairs, a Providence that the more orthodox called God. All believed that religious doctrines, even if they did not subscribe to them individually, were useful because doctrines helped mold people into moral citizens and therefore supported peace and social order. All were suspicious of what could not be demonstrated on the basis of logic. Yet logic and reason also decreed that one had a right to think as one wished, to follow the truth given by one's own mind, without interference from others.

The rationalist emphasis on what the eighteenth-century Boston pastor Jonathan Mayhew (1749) called the "right of private judgment" and the more evangelical Protestant emphasis on a dynamic personal experience of conversion or election were actually two sides of the same coin. Both, albeit in different ways, made the individual—not churches, ministers, priests, or even Scripture—the final authority in matters of personal belief and practice. Just as no one could have an experience of conversion for another person, so only the individual could determine what the mind saw as right and true. Most who looked to reason as a guide were confident—some would say naively optimistic—that what was true would look pretty much the same to everyone. But there was no guarantee. Hence a democratic social order had no choice but to allow for latitude of belief among its citizens. If different minds arrived at different truths, so be it, so long as such difference did not disrupt civil order.

From the point of view of reason, the danger in having government endorse a particular belief system, no matter how worthy it was, or in giving official status to any one religious group or tradition, no matter how pervasive its influence, was the potential tyranny such a belief or group could exert over others. If a religious community could call on the coercive power of the state to force conformity to its beliefs and practices, it lost its legitimacy. It no longer had to persuade people of its truth on rational grounds or to move people to experience for themselves the reality of the salvation it offered.

Even before ratification of the Bill of Rights, the state of Virginia had adopted a statute providing for near-total religious freedom. Inspired by Thomas Jefferson, the Virginia statute became something of a model for other states, since the Constitution restricted only the Congress from establishing a religion. When the Bill of Rights was adopted, a few New England states still had constitutions that provided for the payment of salaries of teachers of religion and morals from public funds. The last state to drop such a provision was Massachusetts in 1833.

The phrase with which later generations are familiar, *separation of church and state*, is not strictly speaking part of the constitutional or legal heritage of the nation. Rather, it comes from a letter written in 1802 by Thomas Jefferson, while president, to a group of Connecticut Baptists in which he referred to a "wall of separation between church and state." Jefferson concurred with the Baptists who had written to him, noting that he, too, believed that "religion is a matter which lies solely between man and his God, that he owes account to none other for his faith or his worship" and "that the legislative powers of government reach actions only, and not opinions" (cited in Wilson, 1965, pp. 75–76). To be sure, Jefferson acknowledged the reality of God; what he wanted to avoid was government involvement in determining what individuals should believe and how they should put that belief into practice.

The legal provisions for religious freedom did not mean, however, that all sorts of fanatics made their way to the United States, although numerous individuals tried to drum up a following for their own particular points of view. In historical context, one result paralleled other Enlightenment-era shifts in Europe—namely, assuring that there were no political disabilities attached to Jewish identity. For centuries, Jews had been forced into ghettoes, prohibited from practicing certain occupations in the larger communities, denied access to political life, and restricted in their educational opportunities in much of Europe. The idea of separation of church and state, a phrase that uses a Christian term (*church*) as a symbol for all religion, would make that impossible in the United States, although it did not eradicate either the overt or the covert anti-Semitism that ran through American culture.

This legal arrangement did mean that the United States became a nation where extraordinary religious experimentation and diversity prevailed just beneath the surface, even if a broadly evangelical Protestantism centered around a few denominations dominated public life. In the 1830s in upstate New York, for example, Joseph Smith reported having a vision that led to the founding of the Latter-Day Saints, better known as the Mormons. Although the Mormons were not well received for a generation or so because their teachings seemed to undermine orthodox Protestant doctrine, they were able to move from one location to another. They garnered more followers as they went until they finally wound up around the Great Salt Lake, ironically just before the Utah area was transferred from Mexican to U.S. control. The Saints represent what some historians regard as the first genuinely "new" religion to emerge in the American context.

Around the same time, John Humphrey Noyes relocated from Vermont to Oneida in upstate New York, where he preached his own version of the gospel and drew scores to his communitarian enterprise with its practice of complex marriage. In the 1830s as well, the Shakers, although planted on North American soil by their founder Ann Lee and a handful of adherents just before the American Revolution, also reached their peak. About 6,000 men and women were leading the simple, celibate life in hopes of salvation in nearly two dozen different communities, several of them in upstate New York and New England. Countless other groups followed the lead of an inspired teacher, each carving a niche for itself because government would not interfere in matters of personal belief and practice. Many experimented with communal living. As in a marketplace, each group competed to gain a following, with those best able to convince men and women of their truth reaping the largest number of adherents.

Immigration in the first decades of the nineteenth century also assured that the U.S. would be home to a significant Jewish population. Although there had been several small Jewish communities in the English colonies, with synagogues early flourishing in places such as Newport, Rhode Island, and Charleston, South Carolina, the immigration of Jews from German cultures in Europe laid the foundation for diversity within the Hebrew tradition itself. Eager to seize the opportunities for fuller participation in public life that followed the Enlightenment and ended centuries of forced exclusion from society, many Jews were drawn to Reform Judaism. The Reform movement sought to abandon nonessential features of Jewish practice that were thought to be inextricably wedded to ancient Near Eastern culture and times and to take on a more modern appearance.

Later generations of Jewish immigrants would wonder whether Reform was not too radical, willing to yield too much. Those who resisted most strongly became known as Orthodox Jews, while in time the largest body became known as Conservative Jews. Conservative Jews were willing to make some modifications to traditional practice to accommodate life in a modern, religiously pluralistic culture but thought that Reform had jettisoned too much. Although various forms of Christianity continued to dominate American religious life, by the middle of the nineteenth century it was clear that a vibrant Jewish culture would remain a dynamic alternative.

The first half of the nineteenth century also saw other religious teachers who preached their own understanding of the truth at frontier camp meetings or who worked the lecture circuit, a form of popular entertainment, in the larger cities. Along the frontier, for example, several sought to restore what they believed to be the actual practice of first-century

New Testament Christianity. That meant shedding denominational structure and, in some cases, even religious professionals like clergy. Out of that swirl of interest came groups that later coalesced into the Disciples of Christ and the Churches of Christ.

In cities like New York, individuals such as William Miller drew crowds to their presentations on biblical prophecy. Miller, renowned for predicting the imminent return of Christ to usher in the millennial age, even fixed a date when the Second Advent would transpire, more than once revising his calculations when the Second Advent did not occur on schedule. Although most of his followers scattered because of the "great disappointment" that ensued, his teaching formed part of the background for the Seventh-Day Adventists and the doctrines advocated by their early leader, Ellen G. Harmon White.

By the end of the nineteenth century, many other groups had emerged, some reflecting the religious styles of the continuing streams of immigrants and others arising from ideas offered by dynamic speakers and writers. Among the better-known immigrant communities are the Amish and their religious cousins, the Mennonites, who sought to live their version of a simple life without involvement in a larger society that they saw as hopelessly corrupted by modernity. Their major immigration to the United States and Canada came in the decades after the Civil War. That epoch was also a time of increasing interest in science and the application of scientific techniques to religious expression. Mary Baker Eddy, for example, called her approach to using mental power in faith to effect healing Christian Science, and her influence grew rapidly as she published summaries of her views and as practitioners of her way fanned out across the country, promoting her ideas.

These few examples demonstrate some of the diversity and pluralism beginning to color American religious life, a diversity and pluralism made possible in part because of the legal arrangements embedded in the First Amendment. Other factors aided this religious experimentation. The seemingly vast amount of land available in the expanding nation literally meant that there was room for various religious teachers and groups to go about their business without really interrupting or interfering with the lives of those around them. Consequently, the American experience helped demolish a myth that had helped buttress Western civilization from the days of the Roman Empire onward, namely, that some sort of religious uniformity—or at least tacit conformity to one religious tradition—was a necessary precondition for political stability and social harmony.

DIVERSITY, RELIGIOUS FREEDOM, AND THE COURTS

At the same time, some religious groups seemed to many Americans, primarily those identified with Protestant denominations, to push the limits of freedom too far. After all, they were minority groups on the margins of the larger religious culture. If their beliefs and practices were too far out of step with the majority, should they not be restrained or curtailed before they undermined the dominant religious style? In one sense, the basic issues were how much diversity free exercise allowed before it became dangerous and how much control government should wield to protect a presumed majority before it became tyrannical.

One example emerged when the Latter-Day Saints founder Joseph Smith advocated the practice of plural marriage. A revelation he believed to be from God convinced him that the ancient Hebrew practice, recorded in the Bible, of men having more than one wife was appropriate for his own followers. However, most Americans were aghast at the idea of polygamy, and most states forbade polygamous practice when the Utah Territory was seeking admission to the Union. The situation was convoluted, and historians are not of a single mind as to exactly how subsequent Mormon teaching came to prohibit the practice. But until there were restrictions on polygamy, which the Saints once believed part of their free exercise of religion, Utah would not be admitted as a state. In the process, the U.S. Supreme Court heard two cases dealing with plural marriage, *Reynolds v. United States* in 1878 and *Davis v. Beason* in 1890 (Miller & Flowers, 1987). Even after the official position changed and Utah was admitted as a state with a constitution prohibiting plural marriage, some individuals who identified themselves as Mormons continued the practice. At the dawn of the twenty-first century, occasional cases still came to the attention of the media and the courts, although most are ignored since practitioners tend to live in remote rural areas where local folks often overlook what does not upset public order.

Laws protecting Sabbath observance go back to the colonial period. Among the earliest was a provision in Virginia, part of "Dale's Laws" issued in 1610, that not only required attendance at Christian worship but also prohibited "any gaming" in public or private on Sunday. As the Jewish population of the United States grew, those identified with Orthodox Judaism, with its emphasis on strict observance of the Sabbath from sundown Friday until sundown Saturday, found laws favoring Sunday as the Sabbath discriminatory. However, because the numbers of Jews were small and the Jewish population fairly scattered, there were few challenges to the status quo.

Sunday laws also affected Seventh-Day Adventists, who, as their name indicates, hold to the Hebrew practice of keeping the Sabbath, the seventh day or Saturday, as sacred. Most Christian groups, whether Protestant, Catholic, or Orthodox, that represented the majority of Americans believed that the Christian practice or keeping Sunday, the first day, as a sacred and holy day superseded seventh-day sabbath observance. Well into the twentieth century, many states and local communities legally restricted what kinds of work could be done on Sunday, whether and what goods and products could be sold, and access to certain recreational activities. Popularly known as "blue laws," such regulations aroused little concern when the overwhelming majority of citizens in a town or area accepted the Christian practice for themselves. They tended to keep the day sacred even without such legal restraint. But what about those for whom the seventh day was holy?

Most legal challenges involving Seventh-Day Adventists and Orthodox Jews remained in local and state courts. Some early challenges to Sunday blue laws that reached the U.S. Supreme Court did not directly involve religious groups, although the issues at stake did. For example, the arrest of discount store employees for selling on Sunday products restricted by law propelled *McGowan v. Maryland* (1961), and in *Two Guys from Harrison-Allentown, Inc. v. McGinley* (1961), there was a similar situation, but with sufficient factual differences to require a separate decision. In both, the Court upheld Sunday blue laws on the grounds of "argument from history" and insisted that even if blue laws originally supported specifically Christian observance, they had come to promote the general welfare by mandating a day of rest once in seven. But bringing such cases to the Supreme Court unwittingly set in motion moves to repeal most blue laws on a state and local level.

In times of war, court cases at every level have centered on those who refused to engage in military combat and sometimes in any activity that supported such combat. Although hundreds have been imprisoned, generally the courts concluded that persons who were members of religious groups, such as the Quakers, the Mennonites, the Church of the Brethren, and other historic "peace churches," could refuse to serve, although most were required to perform alternative service. In the age of protest against the U.S. military presence in Vietnam, the protection of conscientious objection was extended to individuals who opposed all war on grounds of personal belief, regardless of whether they were formal members of any religious group.

Over the years, court cases involving groups that reject certain medical procedures (e.g., blood transfusions), like the Jehovah's Witnesses and the Church of Christ, Scientist, have also raised questions about free exercise. Generally, the courts have upheld the right of persons of legal age to refuse medical treatment on religious grounds, but the situation has been much more complex when it comes to parents who refuse to authorize medical procedures for their minor children on religious grounds. Here the issue has been whether the overriding responsibility of government to promote the welfare of minors could require treatments that the faith communities in which they were being raised opposed on religious grounds.

Where and how to draw the line between the duty of government to promote the welfare of the people and the right of free exercise also informed many of the cases, mostly on a state level, that concerned the ritual handling of serpents and ingesting of poisonous liquids such as strychnine. Serpent handlers claimed a biblical basis for the practice in the Gospel of Mark, Chapter 16, and insisted that they were doing what Scripture required. But did the possibility of death from snake bite make serpent handling a practice that so undermined the general welfare that government was obligated to prohibit the practice? Since serpent-handling groups are concentrated in the mountains of central Appalachia, most of the laws making serpent handling illegal were passed by states where the practice was not uncommon. But few of the laws were regularly enforced, and most of them had been rescinded by the end of the twentieth century.

The most familiar cases wrestled with whether practices sanctioned by law resulted in a *de facto* establishment of religion, particularly in areas affecting education in public schools. Some of the earliest concerned children who were Jehovah's Witnesses. On religious grounds, Witnesses refuse to salute the flag, insisting that reciting the Pledge of Allegiance places a blasphemous loyalty to the state before their allegiance to God. Most cases brought by Witnesses came decades before the recent controversy over whether the phrase *under God* that was inserted into the Pledge of Allegiance by Congress in 1954 represented unconstitutional support for religion. Until the rights of the Witnesses received legal protection, episodes in several communities resulted in children who were Witnesses being expelled from school and their parents being prosecuted. At first, though, the Supreme Court was reluctant to see refusal to recite the Pledge of Allegiance as an exercise of religious freedom. In *Minersville School District v. Gobitis* (1940), the Court decreed that the social cohesion resulting from requiring students to recite the pledge superseded free exercise. But in *West Virginia State Board of Education v. Barnette*, which came just three years later, the court reversed its earlier opinion, setting a precedent that has prevailed since.

As noted above, when public education began to become the norm in the United States in the nineteenth century, a majority of students came from families with ties to mainline Protestant denominations, and curriculum materials often reflected the beliefs and practices of those groups. Christian holidays, such as Christmas and Holy Week before Easter, were times when classes were suspended; Jewish holy days did not as a rule receive such preferential treatment, although Jewish children were not penalized for absences on religious holidays. In some school districts school facilities were used, primarily by Protestant groups, for religious instruction, occasionally held during the regular class day. In 1948, in *McCollum v. Board of Education*, the Supreme Court ruled against using school facilities and class time for instruction in a particular faith tradition, even when participation was voluntary.

Some accommodation was reached in 1952 in *Zorach v. Clauson*, when the Court sanctioned dismissing children early from regular classes to attend voluntary off-site religious instruction. For a couple of decades after *Zorach v. Clauson*, there were a host of cooperative endeavors by Protestant churches as well as programs set up for Roman Catholic children not enrolled in parochial schools to be dismissed from school an hour early one day a week. By the last third of the twentieth century, when it became difficult for groups to recruit volunteers to staff such programs and other extracurricular options expanded, most were dismantled.

The greatest controversy, however, has revolved around Bible reading and prayer in the public schools and whether such activities represent a tacit establishment or favoring of a particular religious tradition. In local communities there have been other cases, most notably those that challenged prayers at athletic events, such as those included in pregame ceremonies at football games or commencement exercises. The most famous cases to reach the Supreme Court came in the early 1960s. In 1962, the decision in *Engel v. Vitale* struck down a practice mandated by the New York State Board of Regents that required public school students to recite a presumably generic, nonsectarian prayer at the start of each school day. Before the furor over that judgment had abated, the Court announced its verdict the next year in *Abington v. Schempp*. It declared unconstitutional the reading of any portion of the Bible for devotional purposes and any recitation of the Lord's Prayer, even if those for whom the prayer was not an act of worship were not required to participate.

Four decades later, school districts and state legislatures still wrangle with ways to get around these decisions. Subsequent cases, mostly in lower courts, have whittled away at the absolute prohibitions by allowing in some cases for student-initiated prayers at certain events and for use of facilities for voluntary student religious groups outside normal class hours on the same basis that they are available for other extracurricular programs. But all the controversy has frequently overlooked the Supreme Court's insistence that prohibiting devotional practices associated with particular religions did not ban the academic study of religion in public schools, something rather different from instruction in the teachings of a particular faith tradition as ultimate truth. Nor did it mean that sacred texts such as the Bible could not be studied from literary and historical perspectives. That study was seen as different from using the scriptures of any religious tradition to promote personal belief and commitment. In reality, however, most public school systems have been reluctant to offer the academic study of religion lest it be misconstrued, curriculum materials developed for such courses are limited, and few teachers are given the formal background to teach religion as an academic subject.

In the early twenty-first century, debates continued over what separation of church and state involved and how to assure the free exercise of religion. Some echoed earlier themes, such as a case involving whether Santeria was a religion and therefore its ritual of sacrificing chickens a protected religious practice. Others touched on dimensions of how religion and education might legally be linked, such as whether states or communities could provide vouchers that citizens could use to defray the cost of parochial or church-sponsored education. Yet others focused on whether creationism was a science and should be included in biology textbooks if theories of evolution were also presented.

In retrospect, it seems that early cases concerned how to protect the rights of religious minorities, but some had come to believe that later cases imposed minority rule on the majority. Regardless, the array of legal cases concerning religion suggested that a deep and abiding diversity marked American life, even if in an earlier epoch a broadly based evangelical Protestantism had exercised dominant influence.

PLURALISM BECOMES THE NORM

The controversial court cases of the 1960s concerning prayer and Bible reading came at a time when the evangelical consensus that buttressed the image of the United States as a Christian nation was already unraveling. As early as 1955, Will Herberg, one-time labor union organizer and Jewish theologian who taught sociology of religion at Methodism's Drew Theological Seminary, in his *Protestant, Catholic, Jew* (1960) argued that the vast majority of Americans regarded the many forms of Protestantism, Roman Catholicism, and Judaism as equally valid in molding adherents into responsible citizens. What mattered was that one had a religious label as a badge of social worth, not what that label was. For Herberg, the downside was the emergence of a culture of religion, what he called the "religion of the American Way of Life," that emphasized materialism and conspicuous consumption in place of the commitment and discipleship permeating biblical faith. That unconscious push to a common ground minimizing denominational particularities and even distinctions among faith traditions echoes in the oft-quoted statement attributed to President Eisenhower: The government of the United States "makes no sense unless it is founded on a deeply felt religious faith—and I don't care what it is" (cited in Herberg, 1960, p. 95).

Service in the military during World War II introduced thousands of Americans to persons of other religious persuasions; the shared experience of battle minimized faith differences. As veterans reentered civilian life at the close of World War II, employment opportunities frequently entailed relocation. The long-standing model of Americans going through childhood, coming to maturity, and ultimately dying in communities where they had been born or at least near to their places of birth quickly disappeared. Relocation for many meant finding a new church with which to affiliate, often chosen for reasons other than its denominational label. If the denomination of one's birth had no congregation nearby, it was a simple matter to affiliate with another one.

The suburban sprawl accompanying the rise in mobility also contributed to this gradual erosion of denominational loyalty. Mainline Protestant denominations raced to build new churches in rapidly growing suburban communities, often cooperating with each other so as not to "overchurch" a particular area. Church bureaucrats knew that families were likely to identify with a church, regardless of denomination, with programs oriented toward young families. Denominational switching became the norm. Denominations could no longer take for granted that those raised within the fold would retain a lifelong identification with a particular tradition. Individuals lost a sense of deep linkage to a particular heritage, relating only to the specific local congregation where they worshiped or held membership. Those not steeped in a certain tradition could hardly be expected to rear their own children with a firm bond to that heritage.

The rush to the nation's colleges and universities in the immediate postwar years, spurred by the famous G.I. Bill, in a different way undermined enduring denominational loyalty. The collegiate environment, like military experience, introduced many to a variety of ways of being religious. It was not, as some feared, that the colleges intentionally sought to destroy religious faith. Rather, those with sustained exposure to persons from other faiths or even from other Protestant denominations lost much of their apprehension of alternative religions. As a result, they began to see the various faith communities as functionally equivalent, with none having an exclusive claim to ultimate truth. Some Protestants did demur, believing this sort of exposure dangerous since it led to compromise with falsehood and contamination of authentic faith.

Mobility, military service, and collegiate experience were all catalysts for the sharp increase in interreligious marriage as the nation moved into the Cold War era. Marriage across Protestant denominational lines had long been common. Now there came a dramatic increase in marriages between Protestants and Roman Catholics and between Christians and Jews; the boundaries separating these larger faith traditions had previously proved far more unyielding than those between Protestant denominations. Then, too, hundreds of Protestant Americans who served in the Pacific during the war brought home spouses from various Asian or Pacific cultures, who, like other immigrants, sought to retain their religions of origin. As individual families carved out a religious identity of their own, ties to religious communities brought together in a single household varied. Some compromised by identifying with yet another religious group; sometimes husbands and wives went their separate ways in terms of religious affiliation, with children exposed to both, sometimes just to one, often to none. Many quietly dropped out of organized religion.

However families resolved the multiple religious heritages within the household, new dimensions of pluralism were taking on increasing importance in the daily lives of millions. The burgeoning ecumenical movement, primarily among Protestants, also contributed. Cooperative endeavors through various councils of churches, mergers of denominations even within the same religious family such as the reunion of northern and southern Presbyterians in the 1980s, and talks of church union spearheaded by the Consultation on Church Union formed in the early 1960s all created the impression that all Protestant bodies were pretty much alike, that denominations per se made no difference and had no distinctive ways of determining what Christian faith was all about. If labels made no difference, then a passionate loyalty to a particular denomination made no difference. In promoting unity among Protestants, the ecumenical movement unwittingly eroded denominational loyalty.

In addition, social forces unleashed by the civil rights movement and then the antiwar efforts associated with U.S. military involvement in Vietnam challenged all forms of authority within American life, including the authority of religious groups and their leaders. The baby-boom generation, reaching adulthood during that turbulent epoch, tended more than earlier generations to shun commitment to all social institutions, including religious ones. Reared during a time when denominational loyalty was no longer paramount, they lacked a sense of identification with organized religion. Although earlier generations had drifted away from religious communities in late adolescence and early young adulthood, they had generally returned when they began to raise their own families, if only to provide some moral or religious anchor for their children. Boomers did not return in the same proportion. Many, however, identified themselves as spiritual, even if they shunned the designation of being religious.

Robert Wuthnow (1998) has argued that in the second half of the twentieth century, Americans exchanged the idea of a religious "home" or center, usually fixed around a religious tradition or group, for a religious "quest," something far more individualistic and idiosyncratic. An article in a popular journal captured the mood in its subtitle: "Design Your Own God" (Creedon, 1998). Women from the boomer generation, for example, have probed resources that take them well beyond the standard denominations to forge a spirituality that speaks to the female experience. Some draw on pagan and pre-Christian forms of religious expression, sparking panic in some Christian circles that feminist spirituality threatens the integrity of the churches. All of the following signal a dynamism of spirituality that exists alongside and frequently outside organized religious institutions:

1. Those who gather in forest groves to celebrate rituals marking passages unique to women from childbirth to menopause

2. Those who rarely attend worship but claim to be very spiritual because they occasionally read the Bible along with practicing Zen meditation techniques

3. Those who fashion altars in their homes that may have a cross juxtaposed with New Age crystals

4. Those who sport WWJD (What Would Jesus Do?) bracelets the way a previous generation took the cross and made it a piece of jewelry

5. Those who walk the universal mandala, the labyrinth, in silence because organized religion has become too noisy

At the same time, those Christian groups that have been growing have also tended to be those that have resisted this privatization of spirituality. At the peak of the civil rights and antiwar movements, careful analysts recognized that among Protestants, those denominations and especially those independent congregations that were more orthodox in their religious teaching, more inclined to variations of fundamentalist and Pentecostal expression, were growing (Kelley, 1977). For generations, it had been easy to consign such forms of Christianity to the periphery. Scholars had mistakenly assumed that fundamentalism and Pentecostalism drew only from the economically disadvantaged and politically powerless.

Fundamentalists, Pentecostals, and other evangelicals had developed networks of association that forged enduring bonds and provided resources to build solid foundations for vital institutions during their time on the margins (Carpenter, 1997). They gathered strength from the abiding conviction that truth could not be questioned, thereby protecting the basis for belief and practice from the cultural attacks on authority that marked the larger culture in the last half of the twentieth century. If mainline Protestants and Catholics were torn apart by debates over civil rights, Vietnam, and feminism, these expressions of Christianity offered a refuge, a sense of direction, and a secure way of looking at the world, one not battered by social controversy but buttressed by a certainty that they still had a corner on the Truth. Their presence also complicates efforts to discern any common religious base to American culture.

Some talk about a "Judeo-Christian tradition," an artificial construct at best, as reflecting the dominant religious mood. In the opening years of the twenty-first century, particularly in the wake of the terrorist attacks of September 2001, many of those who called for the posting of the Ten Commandments in courthouses, schools, and other public buildings reflected a hope that this amorphous amalgamation of traditions with roots in the biblical text could still provide a base for social cohesion. But their efforts were undercut by another facet of the religious pluralism that had become characteristic of American society—namely, the dramatic increase in the number of Americans who identified with religious traditions such as Islam, Buddhism, and Hinduism.

THE NEW FACES OF PLURALISM

Changes in immigration laws in 1965 have resulted in a dramatic increase in immigrants from both Latin America and Asia, and with them has come a burgeoning interest in the religions indigenous to those areas and fresh awareness of the links between ethnicity and religious style. In the last decade of the twentieth century, the greatest proportional growth in immigration from Latin America, the Near East, and Asia came in the Sun Belt. Twenty-five counties in Georgia, more than in any other state, reported an increase of at least 50 percent in immigration between 1990 and 1998. For example, in Georgia's Whitfield County, the heart of the state's carpet industry, Hispanic Americans now constitute almost 50 percent of the population, and more than 50 percent of students in the lower grades of the public schools are Hispanic (Mahoney, 2002).

In most urban areas across the nation, Roman Catholic parishes have added services in Spanish, recognizing that Hispanic Catholicism brings a rich blend of traditions to Catholic life, many reflecting the cultures of Central and South America. Cuban immigrants in the Miami area, for example, have erected a shrine to Our Lady of Charity that signals both a particular religious sensibility and a Cuban nationalism (Tweed, 1997). In a sense, these immigrants are simply doing what Italian and Irish Catholics and others did more than a century before—namely, bringing with them the festivals, patron saints, and fusion of religious and ethnic ways that give them a sense of identity and cultural cohesion.

Some Protestant denominations have launched special ministries to Spanish-speaking Americans, while many Pentecostal congregations, like their Roman Catholic counterparts, now provide services and programs designed to reflect the spirituality and concerns of Hispanic followers. Theologically, Hispanic Americans—both Protestant and Catholic—tend to be more traditional and conservative in their thinking, even as their practice reveals considerable syncretism in its expression. Even within the Christian tradition, it has become impossible to look at Anglo-American styles as normative.

Immigration from Asia swelled the ranks of Hindus, Buddhists, and Muslims in the United States. American interest in Asian religious cultures has a long history. In the nineteenth century, Transcendentalist writers such as Ralph Waldo Emerson were drawn to Asian religious philosophy, while thousands devoured reports of seemingly exotic religious practices in Asia through letters from missionaries published in scores of popular religious magazines. But, except for a relatively small number of immigrants from China and Japan on the West Coast, few Americans had first-hand experience with these religions; even fewer were inclined to practice them.

A more direct exposure came with the World's Parliament of Religions, held in Chicago in 1893 in conjunction with the Columbian Exposition that marked the four-hundredth anniversary of Columbus's first voyage to America. Representatives from a number of religions, including Hindus and Buddhists, were invited to Chicago; some, like the Hindu philosopher Vivekananda, remained in the United States for an extended period, speaking in the nation's larger cities and attracting some interest, primarily among intellectuals, in the philosophy behind these religious approaches. With American involvement in military endeavors in Asia in World War II, the Korean War, and the Vietnam War, thousands had more direct exposure to Asian ways of being religious. Some brought spouses back to the United States who sought to continue the religious ways in which they had been nurtured.

The 1960s also witnessed a spate of Asian religious figures who sought to gain American converts, particularly from among those who were disenchanted with traditional American religious life and who saw the dominant religious institutions as mired in racism and torn apart over government policy in Vietnam. The International Society of Krishna Consciousness, more popularly known as Hare Krishna, became a familiar presence in cities and college towns; thousands were drawn to practices like Transcendental Meditation, promoted by the Maharishi Mahesh Yogi and made fashionable by celebrities like the Beatles. A generation later, the Dalai Lama would become a symbol of American interest in Tibetan Buddhism, aided by the devotion of well-known figures like Richard Gere.

While some forms of Buddhism, such as that promoted by the Dalai Lama, and some popular forms of Hinduism, like Krishna Consciousness, have attracted primarily American devotees, the majority of American Buddhists, Hindus, and Muslims come from families who are doing what Americans have done for centuries—practicing the religion that the first generation of immigrants brought with them, albeit adapting it to the American context. What is changing the face of pluralism in the first decade of the twenty-first century is the steadily growing presence of immigrants for whom these traditions represent the heritages they bring with them when they come to the United States. Table 5.3 illustrates their relative growth.

Estimates suggest that the United States was home to only 30,000 Buddhists in 1900, but to two million a century later; to a mere 1,000 Hindus in 1900, but 950,000 at century's

Table 5.3   Estimates of Adherents of Asian Religions

	1900	1970	2000
Buddhists	30,000	200,000	2,000,000
Hindus	1,000	100,000	950,000
Muslims*	10,000	800,000	3,950,000

*Not including the Nation of Islam.
Figures based on data from the U.S. Bureau of the Census

end; to just 10,000 Muslims in 1900, but perhaps—and the estimates vary widely here—between two and one-half to four million a century later, not counting those affiliated with the Nation of Islam (U.S. Census Bureau, 2000). The Hindu tradition has never been inclined to proselytize; in other cultural contexts, Buddhists and Muslims have been more active in seeking converts. However, in the U.S. context, there is relatively little association among the various immigrant Buddhist communities and the centers that cater primarily to American converts to the various stands of Buddhism. American Muslims report that they are reticent to proselytize because popular perception links Muslims to international terrorism. Those Americans who have converted to Islam are more likely to be persons of African descent; they join a small but growing number of African immigrants who are also Muslim.

The growth of these groups signals the pluralism that marks American religious life and the impossibility of regarding a single tradition as normative or perhaps even culturally dominant in the twenty-first century.

SUMMARY AND EDUCATIONAL IMPLICATIONS

From the colonial period to the twenty-first century, the American landscape became ever more religiously diverse. If the first European invaders brought with them a range of Protestant sensibilities, their efforts to plant a Christian culture in America always faced challenges. These challenges came from the Native Americans whose tribal religions once flourished in the same places where Europeans settled as well as from enslaved Africans who managed to sustain an African religious consciousness despite the horrors of slavery. They also came from a variety of other groups who promoted alternative ways of being religious. Diversity was part of the American religious experience from the outset.

That diversity received acknowledgment when the Bill of Rights added an amendment to the U.S. Constitution guaranteeing the free exercise of religion. But the questions of what free exercise means and how to balance the religious sensibilities of the majority with those of many minorities have challenged the courts ever since. In the twentieth century, many of those challenges concerned the role of religion in public education.

Immigration has been a major force enhancing religious diversity over the centuries. Immigration helped cement a Roman Catholic and Jewish presence in American life in the nineteenth century. By the dawn of the twenty-first century, immigration was swelling the ranks of Buddhists, Hindus, Muslims, and a variety of others who called the United States home.

If public education in its early years in the middle third of the nineteenth century could assume that the bulk of students shared a broadly based evangelical Protestant background, by the end of that century those assumptions were no longer viable, although they had by no means vanished. By the end of the twentieth century, however, it was clear that religious pluralism rendered it impossible for education or any other dimension of the public sector to presume that a majority shared common beliefs and values—or even a common religious sensibility. What has proved more difficult is to determine how to study the religious mosaic that is the United States without either presuming allegiance to a particular faith tradition or granting any one faith community a privileged position.

RESOURCES

Jon Butler and Harry S. Stout (1998) have edited a seventeen-volume series of texts on religion in American life suitable for classroom use at the secondary level. Published by Oxford University Press, some are chronological in focus (colonial America, the nineteenth century, the twentieth century), some treat particular groups (Catholics, Jews, Mormons, Protestants, Muslims, Buddhists, Hindus, Sikhs), and others deal with specific topics (African American religion, church and state, immigration, women, Native American religion, alternative religions). The concluding volume is a biographical supplement and index. All are by leading scholars.

Numerous materials appropriate for classroom use are identified in the several sections of the website for the Religion and Public Education Resource Center based at the California State University at Chico: www.csuchico.edu/rs/rperc.

Also specializing in teaching resources about American religious culture is the Wabash Center: www.wabashcenter.wabash.edu.

The Pluralism Project at Harvard University has focused primarily on the new diversity represented by the growth of Buddhism, Hinduism, and Islam in the last half-century. Its website includes not only state-by-state maps but also a directory of religious centers, news summaries, profiles of groups, and teaching resources: http://www.pluralism.org.

There are also helpful websites on particular groups or topics that illustrate the diversity within American religious life. On African American religious history, for example, see: http://northstar.vassar.edu.

The Cushwa Center at Notre Dame University offers many resources on facets of U.S. Roman Catholic life and history: www.nd.edu/~cushwa.

Similarly, the American Jewish Historical Society identifies much that is useful to tracking the American Jewish experience: www.ajhs.org.

Questions and Activities

1. The principle of separation of church and state is a keystone of religious freedom in the United States. Investigate how closely church and state are tied together in the United States today. For example, can churches receive federal funding? If so, under what conditions? Can parochial and other religious schools receive support from public school districts? If so, what kind of support can they receive and what conditions do they need to meet in order to qualify for support?

2. Large numbers of African Americans and European Americans are members of Protestant churches and share religious traditions. However, services in African American and European American churches can be very different. Visit a Methodist church service and an African Methodist Episcopal (AME) church service. Compare the services at the two churches by identifying factors such as the length of service, the music, and the enthusiasm of the minister. Discuss your findings with your classmates. An informative reference for this activity is *The Black Church in the African American Experience* (Lincoln & Mamiya, 1990).

3. The media have become a powerful force for disseminating religious messages that are tied to political positions. Form a group of approximately five students and identify five different religious television programs to watch over a one-month period. Record key themes that are embedded in the programs. Analyze the themes and ideas to determine whether they include political messages. Discuss the extent to which the paradox that Lippy discusses at the beginning of the chapter is being exacerbated by the media.

4. Most racial and ethnic groups in the United States are members of the major faith communities. However, most faith communities in the United States are segregated. Investigate churches, mosques, and temples in your community to find out the extent to which faith communities are segregated. Interview heads of religious communities. Ask them why they think faith communities tend to be predominately made up of one racial or ethnic group. Also ask them whether they have made efforts to desegregate their faith communities.

5. Revivals continue to play an important role in evangelical Protestant churches. Go to the Internet and investigate the types of revivals that are being held today, where they are being held, their goals, and their intended audience. To what extent do modern revivals reflect Lippy's discussion about the new faces of pluralism?

6. Religion in the United States is frequently associated with the roles that men have played in formulating religious ideas and institutions. However, women have made significant contributions to religious life in the United States. Read the biographies of women religious leaders such as Mary Baker Eddy and Ellen G. Harmon White. Also read *Righteous Discontent: The Women's Movement in the Black Church, 1880–1920* (Higginbotham, 1993). Discuss how gender has influenced the lives of women in the church.

7. How does social class intersect with religion? Are religious congregations primarily composed of people from the same social-class background? How do different religious organizations respond to low-income people? How do low-income people in your community feel about religious organizations? Study these questions by dividing the class into groups.

References

Butler, J., & Stout, H. S. (Eds.). (1998). *Religion in America: A Reader*. New York: Oxford University Press.

Carpenter, J. A. (1997). *Revive Us Again: The Reawakening of American Fundamentalism*. New York: Oxford University Press.

Creedon, J. (1998, July–August). God with a Million Faces: Design Your Own God. *Utne Reader*, pp. 42–48.

Gaustad, E. S., & Barlow, P. L. (2001). *New Historical Atlas of Religion in America*. San Francisco: Harper.

Herberg, W. (1960). *Protestant, Catholic, Jew: An Essay in American Religious Sociology* (rev. ed.) Garden City, NY: Doubleday.

Higginbotham, E. B. (1993). *Righteous Discontent: The Women's Movement in the Black Church, 1880–1920*. Cambridge, MA: Harvard University Press.

Kelley, D. M. (1977). *Why Conservative Churches Are Growing* (2nd ed.). New York: Harper.

Lincoln, C. E., & Mamiya, L. M. (1990). *The Black Church in the African American Experience*. Durham, NC: Duke University Press.

Lippy, C. H., Choquette, R., & Poole, S. (1992). *Christianity Comes to the Americans, 1492–1776*. New York: Paragon House.

Mahony, P. (2002, July 26). Study Says Hispanic Buying Power Rising. *Chattanooga Times Free Press*. Retrieved May 16, 2003 from www.timesfreepress.com/2002/july/26jul/disposableincomehispanic.html.

Mayhew, J. (1749). *Seven Sermons*. Boston: Rogers & Fowle.

Miller, R. T., & Flowers, R. B. (Eds.). (1987). *Toward Benevolent Neutrality: Church, State, and the Supreme Court* (3rd ed.). Waco, TX: Baylor University Press.

Strong, J. (1964). *Our Country* (J. Herbst, Ed.). Cambridge, MA: Harvard University Press. (Original work published 1886).

Tweed, T. A. (1997). *Our Lady of the Exile: Diasporic Religion at a Cuban Catholic Shrine in Miami*. New York: Oxford University Press.

U.S. Bureau of the Census. (2000). *Statistical Abstract of the United States*. Retrieved May 1, 2003, from www.census.gov/statab/www/.

Westerhoff, J. H. (1978). *McGuffey and His Readers: Piety, Morality, and Education in Nineteenth Century America*. Nashville, TN: Abingdon.

Williams, P. W. (1980). *Popular Religion in America: Symbolic Change and the Modernization Process in Historical Perspective*. Englewood Cliffs, NJ: Prentice-Hall.

Wilson, J. F. (Ed.). (1965). *Church and State in American History*. Boston: Heath.

Wuthnow, R. (1998). *After Heaven: Spirituality in America Since the 1950s*. Berkeley: University of California Press.

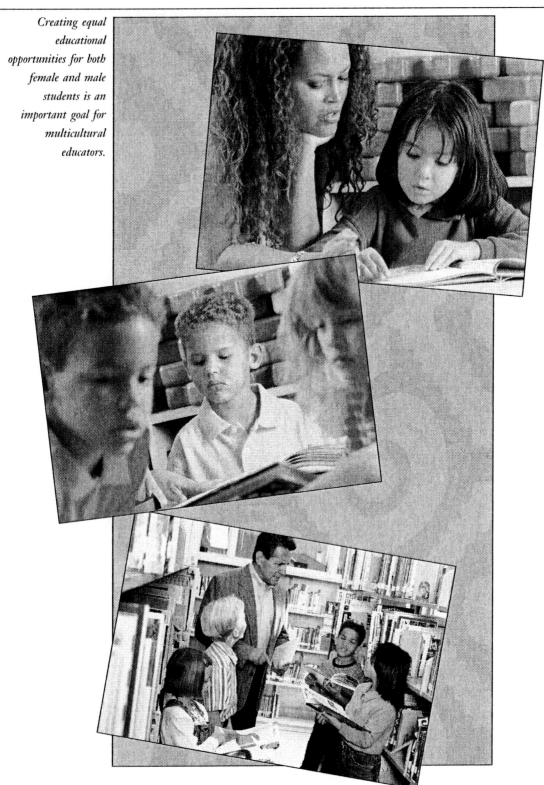

Creating equal educational opportunities for both female and male students is an important goal for multicultural educators.

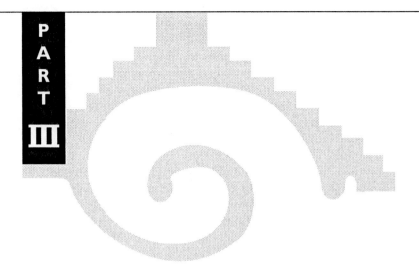

Gender

Social, economic, and political conditions for women have improved substantially since the women's rights movement emerged as part of the civil rights movement of the 1960s and 1970s. However, gender discrimination and inequality still exist in schools and in society at large. In 1998, the median earnings for women who were full-time workers were 73 percent of those for men, up from 70.2 percent in 1988. The status of women in the United States within the last two decades has changed substantially. More women are now working outside the home than ever before, and more women are heads of households. In 1997, 83.6 percent of women worked outside the home, making up 46.2 percent of the total work force. In 1998, 21.7 percent of households in the United States were headed by women. A growing percentage of women and their dependents constitute the nation's poor. Some writers use the term *the feminization of poverty* to describe this development. In 1996, 61 percent of poor families in the United States were headed by women.

The three chapters in Part III of this book describe the status of women in the United States, the ways in which schools perpetuate gender discrimination, and strategies that educators can use to create equal educational opportunities for both female and male students. As Sadker and Sadker point out in Chapter 6, both males and females are harmed by sex stereotypes and gender discrimination. Tetreault, in Chapter 7, describes how school knowledge is dominated by male perspectives and how teachers can infuse their curricula with perspectives from both genders and thereby expand their students' thinking and insights. In Chapter 8, Butler discusses how women of color have often been ignored by the women's movement, which is predominately a White, middle-class phenomenon. She describes perspectives and content that will enable teachers to integrate their curricula with the experiences and cultures of women of color.

CHAPTER 6

Gender Bias: From Colonial America to Today's Classrooms

David Sadker and
Myra Sadker[1]

The anthropologist Margaret Mead once suggested that if fish were anthropologists, the last thing they would discover would be the water. We are all like those fish, swimming in a sea of sexism, but few of us "see" the water, the gender bias that engulfs us. So common (and vexing) is our bias myopia that the term *gender blindness* has been coined to capture this cultural shortsightedness (Bailey, Scantlebury, & Letts, 1997). Gender blindness influences virtually every aspect of our lives, including how we teach and learn.

In *Failing at Fairness* (Sadker & Sadker, 1994a), Myra and I referred to the gender blindness we uncovered in schools as "a syntax of sexism so elusive that most teachers and students were completely unaware of its influence" (p. 2). It is still elusive, and many teachers still miss it. Teacher education and staff development programs do little to prepare teachers to "see" the subtle, unintentional, and damaging gender bias that shortchanges children. Many educators hold the costly misperception that gender bias is a "female" issue, one with little relevance for males. The violence and shootings in schools across the nation offer powerful reminders of the cost associated with the male sex-role stereotype. Unfortunately, many of today's boys and girls, unaware of the struggle that was waged to gain even rudimentary educational rights for females, disdain the term *feminist* and lack the perspective and tools necessary to confront the continuing challenges posed by sexism in school.

This chapter provides a context for understanding gender bias. It includes (1) a brief historical overview of women's struggle for educational opportunity; (2) an update of the

---

[1]In 1995, Myra Sadker died while undergoing treatment for breast cancer. This was one of many writings that she originally co-authored. For more about her life and work and her organization, Myra Sadker Advocates, visit her website: www.sadker.org.

progress made and the gains yet to be made in promoting gender equity in schools; (3) an analysis of gender bias in curriculum; (4) recent research findings concerning gender bias in instruction; (5) a preview of some of the emerging trends and challenges concerning gender issues; and (6) a dozen suggestions for creating gender-equitable classrooms.

THE HIDDEN CIVIL RIGHTS STRUGGLE

The education of America's girls was so limited that less than one-third of the women in colonial America could even sign their names. For centuries, women fought to open the schoolhouse door. Although a woman gave the first plot of ground for a free school in New England, female children were not allowed to attend the school. In fact, women were commonly viewed as being mentally and morally inferior to men, relegated to learning only domestic skills. Not until the 1970s and 1980s did they win the right to be admitted to previously all-male Ivy League colleges and universities, and not until the 1990s did they breach the walls of the Citadel and the Virginia Military Institute. It is rare indeed that such a monumental civil rights struggle—so long, so recent, and impacting so many—has remained so invisible. Let us take a brief look at this hidden civil rights struggle, one unknown to most people in the United States.

During the colonial period, dame schools educated very young boys and girls (with few exceptions, *White* boys and girls) in the homes of women who had the time and desire to teach. Girls lucky enough to attend such schools would learn domestic skills along with reading (so that they could one day read the Bible to their children). For the boys, such schools also taught them how to write and prepared them for further, more formal education. Girls graduated to the kitchen and the sewing area, focusing on their futures as wives and mothers.

With a new democracy came new ideas and the promise of greater educational opportunities for females. Elementary schools gradually opened their doors to females, and for the families financially able, secondary schools became possible in the form of *female seminaries*. Seminaries provided a protected and supervised climate melding religious and academic lessons. In New York, Emma Hart Willard battled to establish the Troy Female Seminary, and in Massachusetts, Mary Lyon created Mount Holyoke, a seminary that eventually became a noted women's college. Seminaries often emphasized self-denial and strict discipline, considered important elements in molding devout wives and Christian mothers. By the 1850s, with help from Quakers such as Harriet Beecher Stowe, Myrtilla Miner established the Miner Normal School for Colored Girls in the nation's capital, providing new educational opportunities for African American women. While these seminaries sometimes offered a superior education, they were also trapped in a paradox they could never fully resolve: They were educating girls for a world not ready to accept educated women. Seminaries sometimes went to extraordinary lengths to reconcile this conflict. Emma Willard's Troy Female Seminary was devoted to "professionalizing motherhood" (and who could not support motherhood?). But en route to reshaping motherhood, seminaries reshaped teaching.

For the teaching profession, seminaries became the source of new ideas and new recruits. Seminary leaders such as Emma Hart Willard and Catherine Beecher wrote textbooks on how to teach and how to teach more humanely than was the practice at the time. They denounced corporal punishment and promoted more cooperative educational practices.

Since school was seen as an extension of the home and another arena for raising children, seminary graduates were allowed to become teachers—at least until they decided to marry. More than 80 percent of the graduates of Troy Female Seminary and Mount Holyoke became teachers. Female teachers were particularly attractive to school districts—not only because of their teaching effectiveness but also because they were typically paid one-third to one-half the salary of male teachers.

By the end of the Civil War, a number of colleges and universities, especially tax-supported ones, were desperate for dollars. Institutions of higher learning experienced a serious student shortage due to Civil War casualties, and women became the source of much-needed tuition dollars. But female wallets did not buy on-campus equality. Women often faced separate courses and hostility from male students and professors. At state universities, such as the University of Michigan, male students would stamp their feet in protest when a woman entered a classroom, a gesture some professors appreciated.

While an economic necessity for many colleges, educating women was not a popular idea, and some people even considered it dangerous. In *Sex in Education*, Dr. Edward Clarke (1873), a member of Harvard's medical faculty, argued that women attending high school and college were at medical risk. According to Dr. Clarke, the blood destined for the development and health of their ovaries would be redirected to their brains by the stress of study. Too much education would leave women with "monstrous brains and puny bodies . . . flowing thought and constipated bowels" (pp. 120–128). Clarke recommended that females be provided with a less demanding education, easier courses, no competition, and "rest" periods so that their reproductive organs could develop. The female brain was too small, and the female body too vulnerable, for such mental challenges. He maintained that allowing girls to attend places such as Harvard would pose a serious health threat to the women themselves, with sterility and hysteria potential outcomes. The famous psychologist G. Stanley Hall (1905) agreed with the Harvard doctor's prescription. It would take another century before Harvard and other prestigious men's colleges would finally admit women.

Dr. Clarke's ideas constructed some powerful fears in women. M. Carey Thomas, future president of Bryn Mawr and one of the first women to earn a Ph.D. in the United States, wrote of the fears created by writers like Clarke. "I remember often praying about it, and begging God that if it were true that because I was a girl, I could not successfully master Greek and go to college, and understand things, to kill me for it" (cited in Sadker & Sadker, 2000, p. 438). In 1895, the faculty of the University of Virginia concluded that "women were often physically unsexed by the strains of study" (cited in Sadker & Sadker, 2000, p. 438). Parents, fearing for the health of their daughters, would often place them in less demanding programs reserved for females or would keep them out of advanced education entirely. Even today, the echoes of Clarke's warnings resonate—some people still see well-educated women as less attractive, or view advanced education as "too stressful" for females, or believe that education is more important for males than for females.

There were clear racist overtones in Clarke's writing. The women attending college were overwhelmingly White, and education delayed marriage and decreased childbearing. As a result, while women of color were reproducing at "alarming" rates, wealthy White women were choosing college rather than motherhood. The dangers to the White establishment were clear.

By the twentieth century, women were winning greater access to educational programs at all levels, although well into the 1970s gender-segregated programs were the rule. Although females attended the same schools as males, they often received a less valuable education. "Commercial courses" prepared girls to become secretaries, while "vocational programs" channeled them into cosmetology and other low-paying occupations. After World War II it was not unusual for a university to require a married woman to submit a letter from her husband granting her permission to enroll in courses before she would be admitted. With the passage of Title IX of the Education Amendments of 1972, females saw significant progress toward gaining access to educational programs, but not equality.

Title IX of the 1972 Education Amendments Act become law as the women's movement gained momentum. The opening section of Title IX states:

> No person in the United States shall, on the basis of sex, be
> excluded from participation in, be denied the benefits of, or be
> subjected to discrimination under any education program or
> activity receiving federal financial assistance.

While most people have heard of Title IX in relation to sports, it reaches far beyond the athletic field. Every public school and most of the nation's colleges and universities are covered under Title IX, which prohibits discrimination in school admissions, in counseling and guidance, in competitive athletics, in student rules and regulations, and in access to programs and courses, including vocational education and physical education. Title IX also applies to sex discrimination in employment practices, including interviewing and recruitment, hiring and promotion, compensation, job assignments, and fringe benefits. Although enforcement remains sporadic, even this weakened entitlement of educational rights was targeted for elimination by the conservative political movement of the 1990s.

In *Backlash*, Susan Faludi (1991) documents the negative impact on women resulting from the conservative political gains of the 1980s and 1990s. Most of the federal educational programs designed to assist girls and women have been eliminated, and Title IX itself is often under attack. In high school and college, a "glass wall" still keeps women from entering the most lucrative careers and keeps men from entering traditionally "female" jobs. In certain vocational areas, such as engineering, physics, chemistry, and computer science, few women can be found. In nursing, teaching, library science, and social work, few men can be found. Even in high-status careers where tremendous progress has been made, like medicine and law, a second generation of bias persists. In both professions, women find themselves channeled into the least prestigious, least profitable specialties. Being aware of these historical threads, the channeling of females into certain specialties, and the devaluation of their worth as students or employees can help us to tease out the subtle (and not-so-subtle) biases that persist today.

By the mid-1990s, a militant cadre of political conservatives alleged that the feminist movement had gone too far and claimed that the real victims of sexism were males. After all, they point out, boys receive lower report card grades, are assigned in greater numbers to special education classes, are disciplined more, and are more likely to drop out of school. While many of their criticisms of educational research were politically motivated, they did remind us of the problems faced by males. While today's gender bias is typically less problematic than in the past, the bias is still virulent. Let's take a look at some of the salient statistics.

REPORT CARD: THE COST OF SEXISM IN SCHOOLS

Below is a report card you will not find in any elementary or secondary school, yet these statistics document the loss that both girls and boys suffer because of sex bias in society and in education. Decades after the passage of Title IX, gender inequities continue to permeate schools and shortchange our children (American Association of University Women, 1998a; American Psychological Association, 1999; Levante, 1996; Mid-Atlantic Equity Center, 1999; National Coalition for Women and Girls in Education, 2002; Sadker & Sadker, 1994a; Women's Educational Equity Act, 1999).

Academic

Girls

- In the early grades, girls score ahead of boys in verbal skills; their academic performance is equal to that of boys in math and almost equal to boys in science. However, as they progress through school, many of their high-stakes achievement test scores (such as the SATs) decline. Girls are the only group in our society to begin school with a testing advantage, yet they leave school with a testing disadvantage.

- Males outperform females on both the verbal and mathematics sections of the Scholastic Assessment Test (SAT). Gender differences on the American College Testing Program Examination (ACT) are less pronounced, with females ahead in verbal scores and males in mathematics.

- Female enrollment in mathematics and science courses has increased dramatically in recent years. However, boys still take more advanced courses, all three core science courses—biology, chemistry, and physics—and score higher on competitive tests, such as the Advanced Placement tests.

- Computer science and technology, exciting growth fields, reflect continuing gender (and racial) disparities. Boys not only enroll in more of these courses, but they also enroll in the more advanced courses. Girls are more likely to be found in word-processing and clerical support courses. Girls are also less likely to use computers outside school, and girls from all ethnic groups rate themselves considerably lower than boys on technological ability. Current software products are more likely to reinforce these gender stereotypes than to reduce them.

- In spite of the performance decline on many standardized achievement tests, girls frequently receive better grades in school. This may be one of the rewards they receive for more quiet and docile classroom behavior. However, their silence may be at the cost of achievement, independence, and self-reliance.

- Females experience fewer academic contacts in class. They are less likely to be called on by name, are asked fewer complex and abstract questions, receive less praise or constructive feedback, and are given less direction on how to do things for themselves. In short, girls are more likely to be invisible members of classrooms.

- Girls who are gifted, especially in math and science, are less likely to participate in special or accelerated programs to develop their talent, and this is particularly true for African American and Hispanic girls. Girls who suffer from learning disabilities are also less likely to be identified or enrolled in special education programs than are learning-disabled boys.

- Girls who repeat grades are more likely to drop out of school than are boys. The overall dropout rate (percentage of girls 16 to 24 years of age who are not in school and have not completed high school) is approximately 11 percent. That dropout rate is approximately twice as high for African American girls, three times higher for Latinas, and almost five times as high for American Indian females.

- By 1996, about 24 percent of the U.S. population aged 25 or older had at least four years of college. That group included 24 percent of White females and 29 percent of White males; 14 percent of African American women and 12.5 percent of African American men; and 10 percent of Latinas and 11 percent of Latinos. (Data are not available for American Indians.) Only 16 percent of all women with disabilities are likely to have any college education, compared with 28 percent of men with disabilities.

- Although more women than men (approximately 56 percent to 44 percent) are college students, overall women still lag behind men in earning Ph.D.s and professional degrees.

Boys

- Boys are more likely to be scolded and reprimanded in school, even when their misbehavior is equivalent to that of females. Males are more likely to be referred to school authorities for disciplinary action than are girls.

- Boys are far more likely to be identified as exhibiting learning disabilities, reading problems, and mental retardation. As a result, they are more likely to be enrolled in classes for the learning disabled and emotionally disturbed.

- Males receive lower report card grades from elementary school through college. In their elementary and high school years, they are more likely to be grade repeaters.

- Boys are disciplined more harshly, more publicly, and more frequently than are girls. They constitute 71 percent of school suspensions.

- The mismatch between male norms and school norms contributes to the male dropout rate. As a result, boys are more likely to drop out of school than are girls.

- Males enroll in fewer English, sociology, psychology, foreign-language, and fine arts courses than do females.

- African American males are about half as likely as African American females to take Advanced Placement exams.
- Males lag behind females in a variety of extracurricular areas, including school government, literary activities, and the performing arts.
- The National Assessment of Educational Progress indicates that males perform significantly below females in writing achievement.
- Men are the minority (44 percent) of students enrolled in both undergraduate and graduate institutions, and they lag behind women in degree attainment at the associate (39 percent), bachelor's (44 percent), and master's (44 percent) levels. Although White males and females attend college in fairly equal proportions, African American and Hispanic males are particularly underrepresented at all levels of education.

Psychological and Physical

Girls

- One in five girls reports sexual or physical abuse, although these incidents are frequently not communicated to the authorities.
- Girls are sexually harassed more often than are boys and report more serious and more damaging consequences.
- About half of adolescent girls report having dieted, most in order to "look better."
- About one million U.S. teenage girls get pregnant each year, a higher relative percentage than in most Western nations. Between 1991 and 1996, the teen birthrate for African Americans decreased by 17 percent and by 9 percent for non-Hispanic Whites. The Hispanic birthrate has not declined.
- Teenage pregnancy is related to a constellation of factors, including poverty, low self-esteem, academic failure, and the perception of few life options. Forty-three percent of girls gave marriage or pregnancy as a reason for dropping out of school.
- One in four girls does not receive necessary health care.
- Both girls and boys believe that girls will have a more difficult time achieving their aspirations than will boys, and adolescent girls report higher levels of stress and depression and a lower level of confidence. Females exhibit lower self-esteem than do males during secondary and higher education.
- Despite extraordinary strides made by females in high school athletics, females exercise far less than do males and female sports programs receive only half the amount of money as male programs.

Boys

- Boys are taught stereotyped behaviors earlier and more harshly than are girls; there is a greater probability that such stereotyped behavior will stay with them for life.

- Society socializes boys into an active, independent, and aggressive role. But such behavior is incongruent with school norms and rituals that stress quiet behavior and docility. This results in a pattern of role conflict for boys, particularly during the elementary years.

- Hyperactivity is estimated to be nine times more prevalent in boys than in girls. Boys are more likely to be identified as having emotional problems, and statistics indicate a higher suicide rate among males.

- Conforming to the male sex-role stereotype takes a psychological toll. Boys who score high on sex-appropriate behavior tests also score highest on anxiety tests.

- Boys are underdiagnosed for depression and are more likely to be involved in alcohol or drug abuse.

- Males are less likely than females to be close friends with one another. When asked, most men identify women as their closest friends.

- In terms of school violence, three times as many boys as girls carry weapons, and twice as many have been threatened, injured with weapons, or hurt in physical fights. In general, African American and Latino boys are more likely than others to be involved with crime and violence on school property.

- Male gang members outnumber females fifteen to one.

- In some areas of the country, it is more likely for a Black male between the ages of 15 and 25 to be the victim of homicide than it was for a U.S. soldier to be killed on a tour of duty in Vietnam.

- One in eight teenage dating relationships involves abuse. Until recently, programs focusing on adolescent sexuality and teen pregnancy were directed almost exclusively at females. Males were ignored, and this permissive "boys will be boys" attitude translated into sexual irresponsibility.

- Males are more likely to succumb to serious disease and be victims of accidents or violence. The average life expectancy of men is approximately eight years shorter than that of women.

Career and Family Relationships

Women

- On average, a female college graduate of any racial, ethnic, socioeconomic, or ability group still earns less than a White male with a college degree.

- Women overall earned seventy-four cents for every dollar earned by men; Latinas earned fifty-four cents, African American women earned sixty-three cents, White women earned seventy-two cents, and Asian American women earned eighty cents.

- More women than ever before are in the work force, but gender stereotypes still limit female options. Women constitute only 16.9 percent of electricians and electronic technicians, 11.1 percent of engineers, 2 percent of construction workers, 4 percent of mechanics, 2.5 percent of firefighters, and 4.1 percent of sheet metal workers.

- Within the few broad occupational categories in which women continue to be concentrated, further segregation also exists by race. For example, the occupations with the highest concentrations of African American women are nursing aides, cashiers, and secretaries; for Native American women, it is welfare aides, child-care workers, and teacher's aides; and for White women, it is administrative support workers, dental hygienists and assistants, and occupational therapists. In contrast, the three occupations with the highest concentrations of White men are executive and managerial workers, airplane pilots, and sales engineers.
- College programs are highly segregated, with women earning between 75 percent and 90 percent of the degrees in education, nursing, home economics, library science, psychology, and social work. Women receive only about 16 percent of undergraduate and 11 percent of doctorate degrees in engineering, less than 2 percent of doctorate degrees in math and physical sciences, and 28 percent of undergraduate and 15 percent of doctorate degrees in computer and information sciences.
- Between 1970 and 1996, the percentage of women earning first professional degrees increased dramatically. For example, in dentistry women increased from less than 10 percent to 36 percent; in medicine women increased from less than 10 percent to 41 percent; and in law women increased from less than 10 percent to 44 percent.
- Women are 73 percent of the elementary and secondary school teachers but only 35 percent of the principals.

Men

- Even well-meaning teachers and counselors often advise boys to enter sex-stereotyped careers and limit their potential in occupations such as kindergarten teacher, nurse, or clerical worker.
- Many boys build career expectations that are higher than their abilities. This can result in later compromise, disappointment, and frustration.
- Gender segregation continues to limit the academic and career majors of all students. Male college students account for only 12 percent of elementary education majors, 11 percent of special education majors, 12 percent of library science majors, and 14 percent of those majoring in social work.
- Current parenting patterns reinforce male stereotyping. Many families accept the notion that adolescent boys are naturally aggressive, withdrawn, and emotionally unexpressive, and they support these characteristics as normal development.
- As a result of the limited range of masculinity role models, boys tend to define themselves in opposition to others, either as nonfemale, nonhomosexual, or anti-authority (e.g., schools, parents). Adolescent boys, in particular, see female qualities as unacceptable for males, contributing to an antigay and antifemale disposition.
- Both at school and at home, males are taught to hide or suppress their emotions; as husbands and fathers, they may find it difficult or impossible to show positive feelings toward their wives and children.

- Men and women vary in their beliefs about a father's role. Men emphasize the need for the father to earn a good income and to provide solutions to family problems. Women, on the other hand, stress the need for fathers to assist in caring for children and in responding to the emotional needs of the family. These differing perceptions of fatherhood increase family strain and anxiety.

- Few schools provide programs that encourage boys to understand and prepare for the parenting role. As a result, through absence and apathy, many men become not so much parents as "transparents."

- The male propensity for violence is too often manifested in family life by fathers and husbands who perpetrate physical abuse on spouses and children.

Research Summary

The report card reflects the volatile state of gender equity in and beyond school; while some gender barriers are crumbling, others seem impervious to change. During the past two decades, the gender gap has decreased in mathematics, biology, and chemistry, and in professional careers such as law and medicine. In fact, these rapid changes underscore the profound power of schools and society to radically alter age-old cultural norms (Hyde, Fenneman, & Lamon, 1990; Hyde & Lynn, 1988). Yet other areas have been resistant to change: computer science, technology, physics, and engineering, for example, remain male domains, while elementary and preschool teachers are overwhelmingly female. To complicate matters further, an array of gender-related psychological and physical dynamics impact both males and females, in very different but often harmful ways. Gender equity has reached a new stage; just as the blatant bias and discrimination of the past has become less frequent, subtle and pervasive bias continues to plague schools and to shortchange both girls and boys.

For the typical classroom teacher, gender equity emerges as a continuing challenge on at least two levels. First, gender is often the invisible issue in the curriculum, with the contributions and experiences of women absent. At other times, when the information is present, it is frightfully distorted. Second, female students typically receive less active instruction. Teachers focus more of their time and talent on male students. As a result, in the pages of books and in the voices of the classroom, females struggle to be heard (Hahn, 1996; Loewen, 1995). To help teachers tease out the subtle biases that persist in classrooms, we focus on two central areas of classroom life—student–teacher interaction and the curriculum.

GENDER BIAS IN TODAY'S CLASSROOMS: THE CURRICULUM

Today's curriculum, both "low-tech" books and "high-tech" computers, often set the pace and the tone of classroom instruction. Studies (Woodward & Elliot, 1990) suggest that students spend as much as 80 to 95 percent of classroom time using textbooks and that teachers make a majority of their instructional decisions based on the textbook. In recent years, the Internet and enhanced media options, such as cable and satellite television broadcasting, have offered students a greater array of curricular resources than ever before. Today, both print and electronic resources typically determine what is taught and not taught in U.S. classrooms.

In the 1970s and 1980s, textbook companies and professional associations, such as the American Psychological Association, issued guidelines for nonracist and nonsexist books, suggesting how to include and fairly portray different groups in the curriculum. As a result, textbooks became more balanced in their description of underrepresented groups; but problems of biased instructional material persist. In science textbooks, two-thirds to three-quarters of drawings are male, and not one of the five texts examined contained an image of a female scientist (Bazler & Simons, 1990). Seventy percent of music-related figures found in school textbooks were male (Koza, 1992). A 1989 language arts textbook had twice as many males as females represented and far more stories featuring male characters (Sadker & Sadker, 1994b; Women's Educational Equity Act, 1999). In Addison-Wesley's 1991 *World History: Traditions and New Directions,* five times more men than women are pictured; the text index cites 41 women and 596 men, and only one page of text (in a 819-page book) discusses women. Prentice-Hall's 1992 *History of the United States,* by Daniel Boorstin and Brooks Mather Kelley, offers four times more illustrations of males than females, and less than 3 percent of the text relates the lives, experiences, and contributions of women (Sadker & Sadker, 1994b, pp. 130–131.) Unfortunately, bias is alive and flourishing in today's curriculum.

How can teachers detect such bias? Perhaps the first step is to be able to understand the different manifestations of bias. Following is a description of seven forms of bias that can be used to assess instructional materials. These forms of bias can be based not only on gender, race, or ethnicity, but they can also help identify prejudice against the elderly, people with disabilities, non-English speakers, gays and lesbians, and limited-English speakers. In short, any group can be inaccurately portrayed through one or more of these seven forms of bias.

Invisibility

Women have made significant contributions to the growth and development of the United States, contributions mostly ignored in history textbooks. This form of bias (invisibility, or omission) characterizes not only history books but also texts in reading, language arts, mathematics, science, spelling, and vocational education.

A 1970 study of history texts found that students had to read more than 500 pages before they found 1 page of information about women (Trecker, 1977). New history texts, published in the 1990s, continue to devote only 2 or 3 percent of book space to the experiences or contributions of women (Women's Educational Equity Act, 1999). When girls and women are systematically excluded from curricular material, students are deprived of information about half the nation's people. The result is that both boys and girls lower their opinions about the importance of females in creating the United States. For example, when asked to name twenty famous women from American history, most students cannot do it. Typically, they list fewer than five (Sadker & Sadker, 1994b). A similar case can be made for the invisibility of males in parenting and other roles nontraditional to their gender.

Linguistic Bias

The use of masculine terms and pronouns was one of the earliest forms of gender bias to be detected, and authors and publishers quickly set about to correct the language. As a result, newer texts are less likely to use terms such as *caveman, forefather,* or *policeman.* Yet some linguistic bias persists, especially in the use of selected adjectives. The conservative nineteenth-century diplomat Klemens von Metternich is described in one recent and popular high school history book as a man whose "charm" worked well with "elegant ladies"—words and facts of dubious historical import, but not without prurient interest (Beck, Black, Krieger, Naylor, & Shabaka, 1999). The German use of *fatherland* to describe Germany and the Russian use of *motherland* to describe Russia are examples of gendered nouns that offer insights into different national consciousness; such gender and linguistic insights are frequently left unexplained in texts.

In addition to these subtle forms of linguistic bias that persist in newer textbooks, more overt linguistic bias continues to emerge in classroom life. Many economically strapped districts are forced to use texts that are ten, twenty, or even thirty years old, books replete with gender bias. And teachers themselves may unintentionally perpetrate linguistic bias through the materials they create for instruction and in their spoken language. Too often teachers resort to the familiar sexist words of their own past, using pronouns such as *he* or nouns such as *mankind* to refer to all people or using unnecessary modifiers, such as *female doctor*, which serve to promote sexist assumptions. Linguistic bias is certainly less common in today's classrooms, but it is far from extinct.

Stereotyping

Stereotyping persists when one gender is portrayed exhibiting one set of values, behaviors, and roles and the other gender is in possession of a different set of values, behaviors, and roles. From traditional phonics reading texts to current computer software, boys have routinely been shown as ingenious, creative, brave, athletic, achieving, and curious, and men are seen as the movers and shakers of history, the scientists of achievement, and the political leaders. Not all the male action figures in the curriculum have been positive, since males are also portrayed as the evildoers in history or as the violent and unruly ones at home.

Girls are more often portrayed as dependent, passive, fearful, docile, and even as victims, with a limited role in or impact on the world. In a study of seventy-seven basal readers published between 1980 and 1982, books that are still in use in some classrooms today, Britton and Lumpkin (1983) found a total of 5,501 careers depicted; 64 percent were attributed to Anglo males, 14 percent to Anglo females, 17 percent to males of color, and 5 percent to females of color.

The most common careers shown for Anglo males were soldier, farmer, doctor, and police officer. The most frequently shown role models for males of color were worker, farmer, warrior, Indian chief, and hunter. The most common careers for White women were mother, teacher, author, and princess. For females of color, mother and teacher also headed the list, followed by slave, worker, porter, and artist (Britton & Lumpkin, 1983). Unfortunately, even with instructional materials published more recently, gender stereotypes persist. A 1990s study of elementary mathematics software revealed that when gender-identifiable characters were present (about 40 percent of the time), only 12 percent of the characters were female. Reinforcing stereotypes, female characters were portrayed passively as mothers and princesses while male characters were shown as active and as "heavy equipment operators, factory workers, shopkeepers, mountain climbers, hang gliders, garage mechanics, and as a genie providing directions" (Hodes, 1995–1996).

Imbalance

Textbooks perpetuate bias by presenting only one interpretation of an issue, situation, or group of people, avoiding subtleties and complexities. Sometimes the reason for imbalance is to simplify a difficult issue or to squeeze a complex topic into limited book space. At other times, only one point of view is present to avoid potential controversy and to ensure that school board members, educational administrators, and teachers or parents are not offended.

The suffrage movement is one example of imbalance in history texts. The fight to enfranchise half the population and the efforts made by women like Elizabeth Cady Stanton are described as a time when women were "given" the vote (Sewall, 1992). Few texts report the bravery and sacrifices of the suffrage leaders that eventually "won" the right to vote.

Unreality

Textbooks the world over share this common form of bias called unreality. In this technique, controversial topics such as discrimination and prejudice are glossed over in favor of a more fanciful, favorable, and traditional view of national history or current issues. Like imbalance, this unrealistic portrayal is done to avoid offending adults who are the decision-makers in purchasing textbooks. For example, almost 50 percent of all marriages in the United States end in divorce, and one-third of all children will live with a single parent during part of their lives (U.S. Department of Education, 1996). Some texts provide sensitive and accurate portrayals of these new demographic realities; others find them difficult to confront. For example, one text reports: "In some cultures, the basic unit is the nuclear family, or a mother, father, and their children. This pattern is common in industrial nations such as the United States, Great Britain, and Germany" (Jacobs, LeVasseur, & Randolph, 1998). When difficult issues are papered over, students are denied the information they will need to confront and resolve real social challenges (Noddings, 1992).

Fragmentation

Did you ever read a textbook that separates the discussion of women into a disconnected chapter or perhaps a separate section or insert? This is called fragmentation (or isolation) and communicates to readers that while women are an interesting diversion, their contributions do not constitute the mainstream of history or literature or the sciences. Fragmentation also occurs when group members are depicted as interacting only among themselves and as having little or no influence on society as a whole. For example, textbook discussions of feminism often talk about how women are affected by this contemporary movement, but there is little analysis of the impact of the women's movement on men, politics, or the business community.

Cosmetic Bias

Cosmetics can provide an illusion of an up-to-date, well-balanced textbook; yet beneath the superficial appearance, bias persists. Cosmetic bias emerges in a science textbook that features a glossy pullout of female scientists but includes precious little narrative of the scientific contributions of women. Another example is a music book with an eye-catching, multiethnic cover that projects a world of diverse songs and symphonies, yet behind the cover, traditional White male composers dominate the book. This illusion of equity is really a marketing strategy directed at potential adopters who flip the pages and might be lured into purchasing books that appear current, diverse, and balanced.

RECENT PROGRESS

The last thirty years have witnessed uneven progress in creating fairer textbooks. In the 1970s, professional associations and publishers created and distributed guidelines for creating nonsexist books (NCTE Committee, 1973). These guidelines recommended that the achievements of women be included in their textbooks; that women and girls be given the same respect as men and boys; that abilities, traits, interests, and activities should not be assigned on the basis of male or female stereotypes; and that sexist language be avoided. Today, most textbook publishers edit books for sexist language and work to include more equitable presentations of females and people of color. For example, a study of story problems in mathematics textbooks from the mid-1930s to the late 1980s found a greater proportion of story problems about women in textbooks used in the 1980s than in the 1970s or before (Nibbelink, Stockdale, & Mangru, 1986). A study of the Newbery Medal Award books in the 1970s and 1980s found that the portrayal of women and girls was less stereotypic and that the number of girls and women as the main character had increased substantially (Kinman & Henderson, 1985). A study of the illustrations in seven elementary science textbook series found that female children were represented with greater frequency than were male children, a change from previous findings (Powell & Garcia, 1985). Unfortunately, progress can be slow, and the contributions of women in most history texts are still minimized (Crocco, 1997; Davis, Ponder, Burlbaw, Garza-Lubeck, & Moss, 1986; Sadker & Sadker, 1994a). In short, today's instructional materials are less biased, but they are not yet bias-free. Teachers still must exercise care in selecting and using curriculum materials.

Educators who choose gender-fair materials can encourage positive growth in students. Bias-free materials in literature expand students' knowledge of changing sex roles and encourage greater flexibility in attitudes regarding appropriate behavior for females and males. In science and math, gender-fair materials provide females with encouragement to enter careers in traditionally male areas. Such a curriculum can teach boys to consider their future family roles and the importance of involved and caring fathers. But gender-fair curricular materials by themselves are not sufficient to create a nonsexist educational environment. Attention must also be paid to the process of instruction.

GENDER BIAS IN TODAY'S CLASSROOMS: INSTRUCTION

The following scene, an updated general music class in action, reflects the subtle ways in which gender bias can permeate the instructional process (Carter, 1987).

As the bell rings, students take their seats. The girls are clustered in the front and on the right-hand side of the room, while the boys are predominantly on the other side of the room and in the back. This seating arrangement doesn't bother the students; they choose their own seats. It doesn't seem to bother their teacher, Mrs. Howe, who feels that students should have the right to sit where they choose (unless of course, there is racial segregation; Mrs. Howe has little patience for that). Everyone seems comfortable with the boys and girls creating their own seating areas.

Mrs. Howe starts the lesson by playing part of Mozart's Symphony Concertante on the CD player. After about five minutes, she turns to the class with questions.

MRS. HOWE: Who can tell me the name of this composer?

(A few hands are raised when John shouts out "Ricky Martin." After the laughter dies down, Mrs. Howe calls on Mitch.)

MITCH: Haydn.

MRS. HOWE: Why do you think so?

MITCH: Because yesterday you played Haydn.

MRS. HOWE: Close. Enrique, what do you think?

ENRIQUE: I don't know.

MRS. HOWE: Come on, Enrique. During the last two weeks we have been listening to various classical period composers. Out of those we've listened to, who wrote this piece? (Silence)

MRS. HOWE: John, can you help Enrique out?

JOHN: Beethoven.

MRS. HOWE: No, it's not Beethoven. Beethoven was more a Romantic period composer. Think!

(Mrs. Howe finally calls on Pam, who has had her hand half-raised during this discussion.)

PAM: I'm not sure, but is it Mozart?

MRS. HOWE: Uh-huh. Anyone else agree with Pam?

MITCH (calls out): It's Mozart. It's similar to the Mozart concerto you played yesterday.

MRS. HOWE: Very good. Can you tell us if this is another concerto he wrote?

MITCH: Yes, it's a violin concerto.

MRS. HOWE: That's almost right. It's a special concerto written for two instruments. To help you figure out the other instrument, let's listen to more of the piece.

(Mrs. Howe plays more of the piece and calls on Mitch.)

MITCH: Another violin.

MRS. HOWE: Peter?

PETER: A cello.

MRS. HOWE: You're all close. It's another string instrument, but it's not another violin or a cello.

RUTH (calls out): What about a viola?

MRS. HOWE: Ruth, you know I don't allow shouting out. Raise your hand next time. Peter?

PETER: A viola.

MRS. HOWE: Very good. This is a special kind of concerto Mozart wrote for both the violin and viola called Symphony Concertante. One reason why I want you to listen to it is to notice the difference between the violin and the viola. Let's listen to the melody as played first by the violin then the viola. Listen for the similarities and differences between the two.

This scenario demonstrates several important interaction patterns; in this gender-segregated classroom, Mrs. Howe called on the boys more often than on the girls and asked them more higher-order and lower-order questions. She gave male students more specific feedback, including praise, constructive criticism, and remediation. Research (Sadker & Sadker, 1985) shows that from grade school to graduate school, most classrooms demonstrate similar instructional patterns.

One large study (Sadker & Sadker, 1984) conducted in the fourth, sixth, and eighth grades in more than 100 classrooms in four states and the District of Columbia found that teachers gave boys more academic attention than they gave girls. They asked them more questions and gave them more precise and clear feedback concerning the quality of their responses. In contrast, girls were more likely to be ignored or given vague evaluation of the academic quality of their work (D'Ambrosio & Hammer, 1996; Sadker & Sadker, 1994a). Other research shows that these same patterns are prevalent at the secondary and postsecondary levels (Sadker, Sadker, & Klein, 1991).

One reason boys get more teacher attention is that they demand it (Altermatt, Jovanovic, & Perry, 1998). More likely to shout out questions and answers, they dominate the classroom airwaves. However, when boys call out, teachers often accept their comments. In contrast, when girls call out, teachers usually reprimand them by saying things like, "In this class, we raise our hands before talking."

Another factor allowing boys to dominate interaction is the widespread gender segregation that characterizes classrooms. Occasionally teachers divide their classrooms along gender-segregated lines in groups, work and play areas, and seating. More frequently, students gender-segregate themselves. Drawn to the sections of the classroom where the more assertive boys are clustered, the teacher is positioned to keep interacting with male students.

The conclusion of most interaction studies is that teachers give more attention (positive, negative, and neutral) to male students. However, some researchers emphasize that low-achieving males get most of the negative attention, while high-achieving boys get more positive and constructive academic contacts (Babad, 1998). But no matter whether they are high or low achievers, female students are more likely to be invisible and ignored (Brophy & Good, 1974; Francis, 2000; Jones & Gerig, 1994; Sadker & Sadker, 1994b; Sadker & Sadker, 1994c).

The gender difference in classroom communications is more than a mere counting game of who gets the teacher's attention and who does not. Teacher attention is a vote of high expectations and commitment to a student. Decades of research show that students who are engaged are more likely to achieve and to express positive attitudes toward schools and learning (Flanders, 1970; Good & Brophy, 1994).

Most teachers are unaware of these biases, and when they are made aware, they want to adopt fairer strategies. Unfortunately, there are few resources available to help them become more equitable. Federal programs designed to eliminate classroom bias have been removed from the federal budget, and teacher education programs do little to correct this problem. In a content analysis of twenty-three teacher education textbooks, Zittleman and Sadker (2002) found that introductory teacher education textbooks devote only about 7 percent of their content space to issues related to gender, and much of this coverage describes the achievement of a few notable women educators. Yet even this minimal treatment is problematic, since the stories of female pioneers are given far less coverage than those of males. Methods textbooks, those focusing on the skills and resources for teachers, devote only 1 percent of content space to gender concerns. Future teachers looking for information about the special problems boys encounter in reading, or girls encounter in science, will likely not even read that such problems exist. And if they should find the rare text that discusses such problems, it is unlikely that they will be given any ideas, strategies, or resources to untangle these puzzles. While most of today's teacher education textbooks voice support for gender-equity goals, they include precious few practical steps on how to achieve them. This is unfortunate because studies show that with resources, awareness, and training, educators can eliminate gender bias in their teaching (Campbell & Sanders, 1997; Sadker, Sadker, & Shakeshaft, 1992; Zittleman & Sadker, 2002).

TRENDS AND CHALLENGES

At both the beginning and the end of the twentieth century, gender and education were in the national spotlight (Sadker, 1999). In the early 1900s, people worried about the negative physical consequences of educating girls, and many girls were kept out of school "for their own good" (Sadker & Sadker, 1994a). By the 1990s, some educators were again concerned with gender problems in school, but they found an old solution to try to resolve the problem: separation. Many public schools began experimenting with single-sex education as a way to make schools work better for both girls and boys. At the same time, school violence made its way into the headlines, as shootings erupted on school grounds. Most instances of physical attacks, bullying, sexual harassment, antigay acts, and shootings were being perpetrated by males, often White males, and some writers began exploring the connection between school violence and the male stereotype. For many Americans, however, the gender connection to violence remained invisible, while boys' academic problems were very visible. Although the problems boys were having in school were not new, some found a convenient new target for these difficulties: feminists. Critics argued that women had created "feminine" school climates that hurt boys, and a "gender war" was declared. These gender issues were emerging in schools that were being transformed by the information age, as bytes and bits were added to the school curriculum. But even this brave new world of computers reminded us of an earlier time with the persistence of the gender gap, as males far outpaced females in technological training, careers, and salaries. Let's take a brief look at some of these current themes.

The Backlash

By the mid-1990s, gender equity and feminism were fair game for ultraconservative commentators who not only attacked the movement but also suggested that girls had few if any problems in school. They argued that if gender bias exists at all, it was the boys who were the real victims. When Wellesley College and the American Association of University Women (AAUW) assembled a literature review of gender-related research studies documenting how gender bias harmed girls in school, the publication was quickly attacked as biased, an example not of research but of organizations promoting a political position (Sommers, 1995). Although only a few of the more than 1,000 studies cited in that report were actually criticized, and most of those criticisms were flimsy at best, public and political support for gender-equity programs was weakened. Gender-equity research was now characterized as biased and political, and discounted as "advocacy research." Those reading these criticisms were often unaware that the backlash critics themselves were not independent researchers but funded by ultraconservative foundations. While decrying "advocacy research," these critics were in fact modeling it. As an example, the author of this chapter was telephoned by one such backlash writer and asked to photocopy and mail hundreds of pages of a fifteen-year-old research report. When I suggested that the caller go to a library and read the report, the backlash critic chose instead to write a number of articles claiming that because the report was not mailed, it never existed (Kleinfeld, 1999). That erroneous story of the "mysterious missing report" was repeated by others (Sommers, 2000) and soon found its way into publications ranging from the *Weekly Standard* to the *Atlantic Monthly*. To the public, unaware of such tactics, this seemed to confirm the lack of evidence about gender bias in school. Although many of these critical backlash stories were replete with errors and omissions, and themselves lacked peer-reviewed final reports, few media outlets ever pursued that line of inquiry (Sadker, 1996).

Despite these inaccuracies, the charge that schools are being run by feminists at the expense of boys resonated with many, particularly those who were never comfortable with the social changes brought about by the women's movement. While evidence shows that boys as well as girls face problems and challenges in school (this chapter has already documented some of the problems faced by boys), the crux of the backlash argument was that feminist educators were promoting an anti-male agenda and that the resources spent on female achievement in school were coming at the expense of boys (Sommers, 2000).

A more careful account of school history would reflect a very different picture. It was in fact female teachers who crusaded to improve school life for all children, particularly boys. As females became teachers, they were shocked and dismayed at the inhumane practices they found in many schools. Female teachers fought not against boys but against the corporal punishment and autocratic teaching styles that were used to "control" male behavior. In fact, the problems that backlash critics lay on the doorstep of female teachers were actually far worse before females entered teaching. Many of the recommendations advocated by the backlash critics are themselves of dubious merit. For example, they argue that to better meet the needs of boys, schools should introduce stronger discipline, sponsor more school competitions, and teach boys how to read by using more "war" poetry in school (Sommers, 2000). It is evident that the gender debate has grown beyond female gender roles into how society views males as well.

Single-Sex Schools and Classes

From the 1960s through the early part of the 1990s, there was a precipitous decline in U.S. single-sex secondary and postsecondary schools. The number of women's colleges dwindled from almost 300 to fewer than 100, and single-gender high school statistics reflected a similar decline. The widespread belief that single-sex education was an anachronism led many such schools to become coeducational institutions or to close their doors.

By the early 1990s, single-sex education was "in" again, and there was a resurgence of interest in girls' schools and women's colleges (Stabiner, 2002). Why the turnaround? Many writers and researchers, as well as conservative and liberal political leaders, have reconsidered the single-sex school option and found it attractive, although for different reasons. Conservatives argue that sex-separate education is more effective than coeducation because it eliminates hormone-driven social distractions, creating a more focused academic performance. On the other hand, many liberals believe that gender bias is so much a part of coeducation that only single-sex schools can offer girls a fair educational chance. As a result, individuals from across the political spectrum have turned to single-gender classes and schools as an answer to the gender challenges. In fact, by the late 1990s California had funded several local single-gender school experiments. However, because of the lack of resources, lack of a clear purpose, and multiple pressures, most of these schools closed their doors within a few years (Herr & Arms, 2002). Although the California experiment failed, the momentum toward single-sex education grew (Woody, 2002).

What does research say about single-sex education? The findings, unfortunately, are far from uniform. Some studies suggest that for females, at least, single-sex education may indeed offer advantages, including increased academic achievement, self-esteem, and career salience, as well as a decrease in sex-role stereotyping (Cairns, 1990; Hollinger, 1993; Tyack & Hansot, 1990). One study found that students in girls' schools in the United States expressed greater interest in both mathematics and English, took more mathematics courses, did more homework, and had more positive attitudes toward academic achievement than girls attending coeducational institutions (Lee & Bryk, 1986). Girls in single-sex schools showed more interest in the feminist movement and were less sex-role stereotyped than were their peers in coeducational schools (Lee & Marks, 1990; Riordan, 1990, 2002; Sadker & Sadker, 1994b). Yet other studies showed far less dramatic results for girls, and several educators argued that the effectiveness of single-sex schools might have little or nothing to do with the gender nature of these schools. Rather, they held that these schools were successful because they modeled effective school practices, including small class size, skilled teachers, academically oriented learning communities, and committed and involved parents (Datnow & Hubbard, 2002).

Others urged caution, arguing that the lack of a clear purpose for making the transition to single-sex education, the absence of meaningful teacher training related to this new approach, and the threat of intensifying gender stereotypes should be considered before coeducation is abandoned (Campbell & Sanders, 2002; Sadker, 2002). While the efficacy of girls' schools evades an easy consensus, questions about segregating boys raises even greater doubts. While a few studies indicated that some boys, particularly boys of lower socioeconomic status, benefit from single-sex schools and classes (Riordan, 2002), other studies show little or no benefits for boys at all (AAUW, 1998b). The lack of conclusive evidence on the effectiveness of single-sex schools did not slow their implementation. The second Bush administration initiated a review of Title IX to make certain that the law's restrictions against single-sex education would not interfere with creating such schools, but several scholars believed that single-sex public schools would be legal even under the old Title IX regulations (Salomone, 2002).

Title IX

Widely known for its application to sports, Title IX of the 1972 Educational Amendments also prohibits sex discrimination in counseling, discipline, testing, admissions, medical facilities, the treatment of students, financial aid, and a host of educational activities. By now, some people might have hoped that Title IX would have eliminated sex bias, since it became the law of the land more than three decades ago. In reality, despite some sparkling advances (women's soccer and increased college enrollments, to name two striking examples), Title IX may be weakened in the years ahead. As this chapter goes to press, several Title IX regulations are under attack. President George W. Bush established two commissions to consider eliminating Title IX prohibitions on single-sex schooling and lowering the level of funding for female athletes (Suggs, 2002). In 2001, the Supreme Court barred individuals from bringing lawsuits against Title VI—civil rights legislation that is similar to Title IX—and in January 2002, the National Wrestling Coaches Association joined other groups in a federal lawsuit challenging Title IX's athletic regulations. There is a growing likelihood that Title IX will be weakened in the years ahead. But even if no changes were made, the reality is that Title IX has never been well enforced and even current requirements are often ignored (National Coalition for Women and Girls in Education, 2002). Too often, sexist school practices persist because parents and students are unaware of their rights under the law, school administrators are unresponsive or uninformed, or the Office of Civil Rights is less than vigorous in enforcing the law. With little funding provided to promote awareness or enforcement of Title IX, gender bias continues to be a daily part of the school life for both students and teachers.

Violence and the Male Stereotype

Research studies indicate that while most males do not perpetrate violence, most gendered violence is perpetrated by males (Foulis & McCabe, 1997; Schwartz, 1997). A more violent and physical disposition seems to begin for males at an early age. In the first three years of school, research indicates that young boys initiate most of the teasing and bullying incidents, that teachers and adults frequently ignore such incidents, and that both boys and girls are the targets of bullying and sexual harassment. For boys, harassment takes the form of challenging their heterosexuality. Typically, males respond with a physical reaction to such taunts, feeding the cycle of violence. Male taunts regarding sexuality underscore the deep homophobia in male youth (AAUW, 1993). For girls, the response to harassment or bullying is more likely to be verbal and ineffective (Froschl, Sprung, & Mullin-Ridler, 1998). For gay, lesbian, and bisexual students, taunts and physical attacks, usually from males, have become commonplace. In one survey, nine out of ten such youth reported verbal or physical attacks, and in 15 percent of the cases, the attacks were so severe that medical services were required (Safe Schools Coalition of Washington, 1995).

Males adhering to traditional sex-role stereotypes and perceptions are more likely to harass or commit violence, more likely to see such acts as normal, and less likely to take responsibility for their actions (LeJeune & Folette, 1994; Perry, Schmidtke, & Kulik, 1998). Males have perpetrated the majority of gun violence and shootings in U.S. schools. Educators and psychologists are investigating male socialization patterns, seeking not only reasons for this violence connection but also strategies to prevent such incidents. In a very real sense, the male voice, more likely to be read in the curriculum and heard in the classroom, is now being heard on a national stage.

By the late 1990s, volumes about boys were cascading into bookstores. These tomes varied dramatically in quality and approach. Some books called for greater parental understanding of the pressures boys faced and emphasized the need for more love and communication between adults and boys. Some authors indicted the cultural pressures on males for creating an unspoken "boy code," a set of rules and societal expectations that pushed boys into limited, unrealistic, and damaging roles (Pollack, 1998). Other books focused on boy "risk factors," condemning the contemporary tide of boy-initiated violence and decrying the "culture of cruelty" in male peer groups (Garbarino, 1999; Gilligan, 1997; Kindlon & Thompson, 1999; Miedzian, 1992). Several books focused on thoughtful, practical strategies and advice for parents and educators concerned with raising caring males of integrity (Kivel, 1999; Salisbury & Jackson, 1995; Silverstein & Rashbaum, 1995). Unfortunately, a few books chose to lash out at females, in a sense perpetuating male aggression by targeting women for causing the problems boys face. These books argued that inappropriate mothering, female teachers, and the drive for female rights interfered with natural male biology. Other authors maintained a testosterone-based explanation of gender differences, explaining that males and females were "wired" differently from birth and that traditional male aggression and behavior must be recognized and can best be channeled only by other males (Gurian, 1997). As the sweeping targets and disparate reasoning found in these new books suggest, the rebirth of interest in the male role offers both promises and pitfalls.

Technology

The swift advent of computers, the Internet, and high-tech innovations has dramatically affected the nation's economy, culture, and schools. Many of today's students are preparing for, and some are already profiting from, these information age changes. However, the painful statistics reveal that the new technology is a mostly male phenomenon. On the Advanced Placement exams required for college credit, high school girls account for fewer than 20 percent of introductory test takers and just over 10 percent of the advanced computer test takers (National Coalition for Women and Girls in Education, 2002). Only in computer courses that focus on data entry do females dominate, and these are the very courses that lead to lower-paying clerical careers (AAUW, 1998a). Girls are also less likely to use computers outside of school, and girls from all ethnic groups rate themselves considerably lower than boys on computer ability. Certainly this situation is not helped by current software products, which are more likely to reinforce gender stereotypes and bias than to reduce them. Without appropriate teacher training, more equitable software, and programs designed to build technological self-confidence and self-competence among girls, women workers in the twenty-first century are likely to see this technology gap grow into a costly income gap (AAUW, 1998a).

A DOZEN STRATEGIES FOR CREATING GENDER-FAIR CLASSROOMS

Some of these recent trends are discouraging, but they are not the final word. Teachers can make an enormous difference in the lives of their students. The following suggestions consist of ways to make your own classroom a nonsexist one (AAUW, 1998a; Sadker, Sadker, & Klein, 1986, 1991).

1. If the textbooks and software that you are given are biased, you may wish to confront this bias rather than ignore it. Discuss the issue directly with your students. It is entirely appropriate to acknowledge that instructional materials are not always perfect. By engaging your students in a conversation about curricular omission and stereotyping, you can introduce them to important social issues and help them to develop critical literacy skills as well.

2. Supplementary materials can offset the influence of limited textbooks. School, university, and local libraries, as well as the Internet, can offer information on the lives and contributions of women and other underrepresented groups.

3. Have your students help you assemble bulletin boards, websites, and other instructional displays. Teach them about the forms of bias and make sure that the displays, projects, and products are bias-free.

4. Analyze your seating chart to determine whether there are pockets of race or gender segregation in your classroom. Make certain that you do not teach from one area of the room, investing your time and attention on one group of students while ignoring others. When your students work in groups, construct the groups to reflect diversity. Monitor student groups for equitable participation and decision making.

5. Role modeling is central to learning. Students are taught less by what adults say and more by what adults do. This is particularly true in the classroom, where teachers' words are measured against their actions. A male teacher who cooks or weaves, or a female teacher active on the athletic fields or skillful with machines, teaches students believable and powerful lessons about the range of gender behaviors.

   Educators can extend these lessons by inviting multicultural guest speakers to the classroom, speakers who can address interests and competencies that break stereotypic boundaries. For younger children, inviting male nurses and female physicians to the classroom widens the career horizons of both genders. Even for older children, an engineer or a graphic artist who describes the exact tasks involved in their jobs (specifics that often elude even adults!) can enlighten both girls and boys to the amazing possibilities of the workplace.

6. Technology's promise can be short-circuited by curricular and instructional biases. Teachers should schedule computer time equally for all students. A schedule is better than the democratic-sounding phrase *free time*, which can result in the very undemocratic domination of the keyboard by a few of the more aggressive students. Schedules create more equitable access. In addition to creating rules for computer access, software needs to be analyzed. Newer technologies are no guarantee that old and destructive biases will not reappear. Teachers and students need to make certain that new technology does not reinforce racial, ethnic, gender, or any other form of destructive bias.

7. Peer tutoring and cooperative learning can encourage positive gender and racial relationships. Moreover, these techniques increase achievement not only for the students being helped but for those doing the helping. Both peer tutoring and cooperative learning are much more powerful when students receive training in how to work constructively with others. Where such training is not given, boys tend to dominate cooperative learning groups.

8. Positive reinforcement can be effective for increasing the amount of time boys and girls work and play in coeducational arrangements. In some studies (Holden, 1993; Petersen, Johnson, & Johnson, 1991; Schmuck & Schmuck, 1992) teachers made a consistent effort to praise girls and boys who were working and playing cooperatively together. When teachers praised in this way, the amount of time girls and boys spent working and playing cooperatively increased.

9. Most teachers find it difficult to track their own questioning patterns while they are teaching. Try to have someone do this for you. Make arrangements to have a professional whose feedback you value (a supervisor, your principal, another teacher) come into your classroom and observe. Your observer can tally how many questions you ask boys and how many you ask girls as well as how many questions you ask students of different racial and ethnic groups. Then you can consider the race and sex of the active students and silent students in your class. Determine whether one group is receiving more than its fair share of your time and attention.

10. Because teachers may find it difficult to have professional observers come into their classrooms on a regular basis, many have found it helpful to have students track interaction patterns, counting who gets questions and who is likely to be left out. Before you do this, you may want to explain to the class how important it is for all students to become involved in classroom discussion. Sharing your commitment to equity with your students is itself an important and genuine technique for promoting fairness in and beyond the classroom.

11. Do not tolerate harmful words, bullying, or harassment in your classroom. Do not say "Boys will be boys" to excuse sexist comments or behaviors. Nor are racist or antigay comments to be ignored, laughed at, or tolerated. As a teacher, you are the model and the norm setter: If you do not tolerate hurtful prejudice, your students will learn to honor and respect each other.

12. Because research on gender equity in education is occurring at a rapid pace, it is important to continue your reading and professional development in this area. Be alert for articles and other publications on the topic, and be careful that your own rights are not denied because of sex discrimination. Also, be discerning as you read related topics. Remember that research publications are less susceptible to political agendas than are the popular press or politically funded organizations.

Questions and Activities

1. The authors of this chapter list seven forms of gender bias that you can use when evaluating instructional materials: (1) invisibility, (2) stereotyping, (3) linguistic bias, (4) imbalance, (5) unreality, (6) fragmentation, and (7) cosmetic bias. In your own words, define each form of bias. Examine a sample K–12 textbook in your teaching area and determine whether it contains any of these forms of gender bias. Are there forms of bias reflected against any other groups? Share your findings with your classmates or workshop participants.

2. Give three examples of how teachers can supplement textbooks to eliminate the seven forms of gender bias identified in item 1 above. Now go online and search for equity websites that provide supplementary resources.

3. Why have centuries of female efforts to gain educational access gone almost unnoticed and unrecognized? How has that experience differed from civil rights efforts undertaken by African Americans, Latinos, and other groups? How has it been similar?

4. In what ways do Mrs. Howe's interactions with the boys and girls during the music lesson indicate gender bias? How might you help Mrs. Howe change her behavior and make it more gender-fair?

5. Observe lessons being taught in several classrooms that include boys and girls and students from different racial and ethnic groups. Create a seating chart and count the interactions between the teacher and each student. Did the ways in which the teachers interacted with males and female students differ? If so, in what ways? Did the teachers interact with students from various ethnic groups differently? If so, in what ways? Did you notice any ways in which gender and ethnicity combined to influence the ways the teachers interacted with particular students? If so, explain.

6. How can you use technology to supplement classroom materials and promote gender equity? Can you find some useful equity websites for your students that augment information missing from textbooks?

7. Girls start out in school ahead of boys in speaking, reading, and counting. Boys surpass girls in math performance by junior high school. Why do you think this happens? Recent research indicates that the disparities in the academic achievement of boys and girls are declining. Why do you think this achievement gap is shrinking?

8. In what ways, according to the authors, are single-sex schools beneficial for females? Why do you think all-girl schools are making a comeback? Why is the research on the effectiveness of boys' schools less persuasive? Do you think this trend toward single-sex schooling should be halted or supported? Why or why not?

9. After reading this chapter, do you think there are some ways in which you can change your behavior to make it more gender-fair? If yes, in what ways? If no, why not?

10. How are the rights of gay and lesbian students related to gender-equity issues? How does homophobia endanger the rights of all students? What can teachers do to create safe and effective classroom climates for all students?

11. Identify six classroom strategies that can encourage girls to develop both technological confidence and competence.

12. Check out the requirements of Title IX. Prepare a brief list to remind yourself of some of the ways in which the law is designed to ensure gender equity. (The Internet is a good source for this information. Try www.nw/c.org.)

13. Consider how gender bias impacts males by creating questions based on the report card findings in this chapter. Interview boys of various ages and collect their insights about male and female roles. How aware are your interviewees about the dangers of the male stereotype? How do they describe their roles as adult men?

References

Altermatt, E. R., Jovanovic, J., & Perry, M. (1998). Bias or Responsivity? Sex and Achievement-Level Effects on Teachers' Classroom Questioning Practices. *Journal of Educational Psychology, 90*(3), 516–527.

American Association of University Women Educational Foundation (AAUW). (1993). *Hostile Hallways: The AAUW Survey of Sexual Harassment in America's Schools.* Washington, DC: Author.

American Association of University Women Educational Foundation (AAUW). (1998a). *Gender Gaps: Where Schools Still Fail Our Children.* Washington, DC: Author.

American Association of University Women Educational Foundation (AAUW). (1998b). *Separated by Sex: A Critical Look at Single-Sex Education for Girls.* Washington, DC: Author.

American Psychological Association, APA Public Policy Office. (1999). Is Youth Violence Just Another Fact of Life? In *Raising Children to Resist Violence: What You Can Do.* Washington, DC: Author.

Babad, E. (1998). Preferential Affect: The Crux of the Teacher Expectancy Issue. In J. Brophy (Ed.), *Advances in Research on Teaching: Expectations in the Classroom* (pp. 183–214). Greenwich, CT: JAI Press.

Bailey, B. L., Scantlebury, K., & Letts, W. J. (1997). It's Not My Style: Using Disclaimers to Ignore Issues in Science. *Journal of Teacher Education, 48*(1), 29–35.

Bazler, J., & Simons, D. (1990). Are Women Out of the Picture? *Science Teacher, 57*(9), 24–26. [See also Potter, E., & Rosser, S. (1992). Factors in Life Science Textbooks That May Deter Girls Interest in Science. *Journal of Research in Science Teaching, 57*(9), 669–686.]

Beck, R., Black, L., Krieger, L., Naylor, P., & Shabaka, D. (1999). *World History: Patterns of Interaction*. Evanston, IL: McDougal Littell.

Britton, G., & Lumpkin, M. (1983). Females and Minorities in Basal Readers. *Interracial Books for Children Bulletin, 14*(6), 4–7.

Brophy, J., & Good, T. (1974). *Teacher-Student Relationships: Causes and Consequences*. New York: Holt, Rinehart & Winston.

Cairns, E. (1990). The Relationship between Adolescent Perceived Self-Competence and Attendance at Single-Sex Secondary School. *British Journal of Educational Psychology, 60*(3), 207–211.

Campbell, P. B., & Sanders, J. (1997). Uninformed, but Interested: Findings of a National Survey on Gender Equity in Preservice Teacher Education. *Journal of Teacher Education, 48*(1), 69–75.

Campbell, P. B., & Sanders, J. (2002). Challenging the System: Assumptions and Data behind the Push for Single-Sex Schools. In A. Datnow & L. Hubbard (Eds.), *Gender in Policy and Practice: Perspectives on Single-Sex and Coeducational Schooling* (pp. 31–46). New York: Routledge/Falmer.

Carter, R. (1987). Unpublished class paper. American University, Washington, DC. Used with permission.

Clarke, E. H. (1873). *Sex in Education: Or, a Fair Chance for Girls*. Boston: Houghton Mifflin.

Crocco, M. S. (1997). Making Time for Women's History: When Your Survey Course Is Already Filled to Overflowing. *Social Education, 6*(1), 32–37.

D'Ambrosio, M., & Hammer, P. S. (1996, April). *Gender Equity in the Catholic Elementary Schools*. Paper presented at the annual convention and exposition of the National Catholic Education Association, Philadelphia.

Datnow, A., & Hubbard, L. (Eds.). (2002). *Gender in Policy and Practice: Perspectives on Single-Sex and Coeducational Schooling*. New York: Routledge/Falmer.

Davis, O. L., Jr., Ponder, G., Burlbaw, L., Garza-Lubeck, M., & Moss, A. (1986). *Looking at History: A Review of Major U.S. History Textbooks*. Washington, DC: People for the American Way.

Faludi, S. (1991). *Backlash: The Undeclared War against American Women*. New York: Crown.

Flanders, N. (1970). *Analyzing Teaching Behaviors*. Reading, MA: Addison-Wesley.

Foulis, D., & McCabe, M. P. (1997). Sexual Harassment: Factors Affecting Attitudes and Perceptions. *Sex Roles: A Journal of Research, 37*(9–10), 773–798.

Francis, B. (2000). *Boys, Girls, and Achievement: Addressing the Classroom Issues*. London: Routledge/Falmer.

Froschl, M., Sprung, B., & Mullin-Ridler, N. (1998). *Quit It! A Teacher's Guide on Teasing and Bullying for Use with Students in Grades K–3*. New York: Equity Concepts; Wellesley, MA: Wellesley College Center for Research on Women; Washington, DC: NEA.

Garbarino, J. (1999). *Lost Boys: Why Our Sons Turn Violent and How We Can Save Them*. New York: Free Press.

Gilligan, J. (1997). *Violence: Reflections on a National Epidemic*. New York: Vintage.

Good, T. L., & Brophy, J. E. (1994). *Looking in Classrooms*. New York: HarperCollins College Publishers.

Gurian, M. (1997). *The Wonder of Boys*. New York: Tarcher/Putnam.

Hahn, C. L. (1996). Gender and Political Learning. *Theory and Research in Education, 24*(1), 8–35.

Hall, G. S. (1905). *Adolescence: Its Psychology and Relations to Physiology, Anthropology, Sociology, Sex, Crime, Religion, and Education.* New York: D. Appleton.

Herr, K., & Arms, E. (2002). The Intersection of Educational Reforms: Single-Gender Academies in a Public Middle School. In A. Datnow & L. Hubbard (Eds.), *Gender in Policy and Practice: Perspectives on Single-Sex and Coeducational Schooling* (pp. 31–46). New York: Routledge/Falmer.

Hodes, C. L. (1995–1996). Gender Representations in Mathematics Software. *Journal of Educational Technology Systems, 24,* 67–73.

Holden, C. (1993). Giving Girls a Chance: Patterns of Talk in Co-Operative Group Work. *Gender & Education, 5,* 179–89.

Hollinger, D. (Ed.). (1993). *Single-Sex Schooling: Perspectives from Practice and Research.* Washington, DC: Office of Educational Research and Improvement, U.S. Department of Education.

Hyde, J., Fenneman, E., & Lamon, S. (1990). Gender Differences in Mathematical Performance: A Meta-Analysis. *Psychological Bulletin, 107,* 139–155.

Hyde, J., & Lynn, M. (1988). Gender Differences in Verbal Activity: A Meta-Analysis. *Psychological Bulletin, 104,* 53–69.

Jacobs, H., LeVasseur, M., & Randolph, B. (1998). *Western Hemisphere Geography, History, Culture* (Prentice-Hall World Explorer Program). Upper Saddle River, NJ: Prentice-Hall.

Jones, G. M., & Gerig, T. M. (1994). Silent Sixth-Grade Students: Characteristics, Achievement, and Teacher Expectations. *The Elementary School Journal, 95*(2), 169–182.

Kindlon, D., & Thompson, M. (1999). *Raising Cain.* New York: Ballantine.

Kinman, J., & Henderson, D. (1985). An Analysis of Sexism in Newberry Medal Award Books from 1977 to 1984. *The Reading Teacher, 38,* 885–889.

Kivel, P. (1999). *Boys Will Be Men: Raising Our Sons for Courage, Caring, and Community.* Gabriola Island, B.C., Canada: New Society Publishers.

Kleinfeld, J. (1999). Student Performance: Males versus Females. *The Public Interest, 134,* 3–20.

Koza, J. E. (1992). The Boys in the Band: Sexism and the Construction of Gender in Middle School Textbook Illustrations. *Educational Foundations, 6*(3), 85–105.

Lee, V., & Bryk, A. (1986). Effects of Single-Sex Secondary Schools on Student Achievement and Attitudes. *Journal of Educational Psychology, 78*(5), 381–395.

Lee, V., & Marks, H. (1990). Sustained Effects of the Single-Sex Secondary School Movement on Attitudes, Behaviors, and Values in College. *Journal of Educational Psychology, 82*(3), 578–592.

LeJeune, C., & Folette, V. (1994). Taking Responsibility: Sex Differences in Reporting Dating Violence. *Journal of Interpersonal Violence, 9*(1), 133–140.

Levante, R. (1996). New Psychology of Men. *Professional Psychology Research and Practice, 27,* 259–265.

Loewen, J. (1995). *Lies My Teacher Told Me.* New York: New Press.

Mid-Atlantic Equity Center. (1999). *Adolescent Boys: Statistics and Trends (A Fact Sheet).* Chevy Chase, MD: Author.

Miedzian, M. (1992). *Boys Will Be Boys: Breaking the Link between Masculinity and Violence.* New York: Doubleday.

National Coalition for Women and Girls in Education. (2002, June). *Title IX at 30: Report Card on Gender Equity.* Washington, DC: Author.

NCTE Committee on the Role and Image of Women in the Council and in the Profession. (1973). Guidelines for Publishers. *Elementary English, 50*(7), 1019.

Nibbelink, W., Stockdale, S., & Mangru, M. (1986). Sex Role Assignments in Elementary School Mathematics Textbooks. *The Arithmetic Teacher, 34*(2), 19–21.

Noddings, N. (1992). Social Studies and Feminism. *Theory and Research in Social Education, 20*(3), 230–241.

Perry, E. L., Schmidtke, J. M., & Kulik, C. T. (1998). Propensity to Sexually Harass: An Exploration of Gender Differences. *Sex Roles: A Journal of Research, 38*(5–6), 443–460.

Petersen, R., Johnson, D., & Johnson, R. (1991). Effects of Cooperative Learning on Perceived Status of Male and Female Pupils. *Journal of Social Psychology, 131*, 717–735.

Pollack, W. (1998). *Real Boys: Rescuing Our Sons from the Myths of Boyhood*. New York: Random House.

Powell, R., & Garcia, J. (1985). The Portrayal of Minorities and Women in Selected Elementary Science Series. *Journal of Research in Science Teaching, 22*(6), 519–533.

Riordan, C. (1990). *Girls and Boys in School: Together or Separate?* New York: Teachers College Press.

Riordan, C. (2002). What Do We Know about the Effects of Single-Sex Schools in the Private Sector? Implications for Public Schools. In A. Datnow & L. Hubbard (Eds.), *Doing Gender in Policy and Practice: Perspectives on Single-Sex and Coeducational Schooling* (pp. 10–30). New York: Routledge/Falmer.

Sadker, D. (1996, September 4). Where the Girls Are? *Education Week*, Commentary, pp. 49–50.

Sadker, D. (1999). Gender Equity: Still Knocking at the Classroom Door. *Educational Leadership, 56*(7), 22–26.

Sadker, D. (2002). At Issue: Should Federal Regulations Make It Easier for School Districts to Establish Single-Sex Schools or Classes? *Congressional Quarterly Researcher, 12*(25), 585.

Sadker, M., & Sadker, D. (1984). *Year 3: Final Report: Promoting Effectiveness in Classroom Instruction.* Washington, DC: National Institute of Education. ED257819.

Sadker, M., & Sadker, D. (1985, March). Sexism in the Classroom of the 80s. *Psychology Today*, pp. 54–57.

Sadker, M., & Sadker, D. (1994a; updated for this chapter). *Failing at Fairness: How America's Schools Cheat Girls.* New York: Scribners. (The Report Card copyright of David & Myra Sadker. All rights reserved; no part may be reproduced or transmitted without permission from the authors.)

Sadker, M., & Sadker, D. (1994b). *Failing at Fairness: How America's Schools Cheat Girls.* New York: Scribners.

Sadker, M., & Sadker, D. (1994c). Sex Equity: Assumptions and Strategies. In *International Encyclopedia of Education* (pp. 5441–5445). Oxford, UK: Pergamon.

Sadker, M., & Sadker, D. (2000). *Teachers, Schools, and Society* (5th ed.). Boston: McGraw-Hill.

Sadker, M., Sadker, D., & Klein, S. (1986). Abolishing Misperceptions about Sex Equity in Education. *Theory into Practice, 25*, 220–226.

Sadker, M., Sadker, D., & Klein, S. (1991). The Issue of Gender in Elementary and Secondary Education. In G. Grant (Ed.), *Review of Research in Education* (Vol. 17, pp. 269–334). Washington, DC: American Educational Research Association.

Sadker, M., Sadker, D., & Shakeshaft, C. (1992). Sexuality and Sexism in School: How Should Educators Be Prepared? In S. S. Klein (Ed.), *Sex Equity and Sexuality in Education* (pp. 363–375). Albany: State University of New York Press.

Safe Schools Coalition of Washington. (1995). *1995 Seattle Teen Health Risk Survey.* Seattle, WA: Author. (Reprinted from the *Third Annual Report of the Safe Schools Anti-Violence Project.*)

Salisbury, J., & Jackson, D. (1995). *Challenging Macho Values: Practical Ways of Working with Adolescent Boys.* London: Falmer.

Salomone, R. (2002). The Legality of Single-Sex Education in the United States: Sometimes "Equal" Means "Different." In A. Datnow & L. Hubbard (Eds.), *Doing Gender in Policy and Practice: Perspectives on Single-Sex and Coeducational Schooling* (pp. 47–72). New York: Routledge/Falmer.

Schmuck, R., & Schmuck, P. (1992). *Group Processes in the Classroom* (6th ed.). Dubuque, IA: Brown.

Schwartz, M. D. (1997). *Sexual Assault on the College Campus: The Role of Male Peer Support.* Thousand Oaks, CA: Sage.

Sewall, G. (1992). Do Textbooks Shortchange Girls? *Social Studies Review: A Bulletin of the American Textbook Council, 11,* 3–9.

Silverstein, O., & Rashbaum, B. (1995). *The Courage to Raise Good Men.* New York: Penguin.

Sommers, C. H. (1995). *Who Stole Feminism? How Women Have Betrayed Women.* New York: Simon & Schuster.

Sommers, C. H. (2000). *The War against Boys: How Misguided Feminism Is Harming Our Young Men.* New York: Simon & Schuster.

Stabiner, K. (2002). *All Girls: Single-Sex Education and Why It Matters.* New York: Riverhead.

Suggs, W. (2002, September 6). Federal Commission Considers Reinterpreting Title IX. *The Chronicle of Higher Education, 49*(2), A54.

Trecker, J. L. (1977). Women in U.S. History High-School Textbooks. In J. Pottker & A. Fishel (Eds.), *Sex Bias in the Schools: The Research Evidence* (pp. 146–161). Cranbury, CT: Associated University Presses.

Tyack, D., & Hansot, E. (1990). *Learning Together: A History of Coeducation in American Schools.* New Haven, CT: Yale University Press.

U.S. Bureau of the Census. (1997). *Current Population Reports.* Washington, DC: U.S. Government Printing Office.

U.S. Department of Education. (1996). *Youth Indicators.* Washington, DC: Author.

Women's Educational Equity Act. (1999). *1999 Fact Sheet on Women's and Girls' Educational Equity.* Newton, MA: Educational Development Corporation.

Woodward, A., & Elliot, D. L. (1990). Textbook Use and Teacher Professionalism. In D. L. Elliot & A. Woodward (Eds.), *Textbooks and Schooling in the United States,* 89th Yearbook of the National Society for the Study of Education (pp. 178–193). Chicago: University of Chicago Press.

Woody, E. (2002). Constructions of Masculinity in California's Single Gender Academies. In A. Datnow & L. Hubbard (Eds.), *Doing Gender in Policy and Practice: Perspectives on Single-Sex and Coeducational Schooling* (pp. 280–303). New York: Routledge/Falmer.

Zittleman, K., & Sadker, D. (2002). Gender Bias in Teacher Education Texts: New (and Old) Lessons. *Journal of Teacher Education, 53*(2), 168–179.

CHAPTER 7

Classrooms for Diversity: Rethinking Curriculum and Pedagogy

Mary Kay Thompson Tetreault

> It's time to start learning about things they told you you didn't
> need to know . . . learning about me, instead of learning about
> them, starting to learn about her instead of learning about him. It's
> a connection that makes education education. (A student of
> European and African American ancestry)

This student's reflection on her education signals a twin transformation that is pushing us to rethink our traditional ways of teaching. The first is that students in our classrooms are increasingly more diverse and the second is that traditional course content has been enriched by the new scholarship on women, cultural studies, and multiculturalism. It is in the classroom that these transformations intersect, and it rests on the teacher to make education "education" for this student and for the majority who feel their education was not made for them—women of all backgrounds, people of color, and men who lack privilege because of their social class—by bringing the two together. The current challenges to classroom teachers are not only to incorporate multiple perspectives into the curriculum but also to engage in pedagogical practices that bring in the voices of students as a source for learning rather than managing or controlling them.

FEMINIST PHASE THEORY

One of the most effective ways I have found to set a frame for envisioning a gender-balanced, multicultural curriculum, while at the same time capturing the reforms that have occurred over the past thirty years, is feminist phase theory. Conceptually rooted in the scholarship on women, feminist phase theory is a classification system of the evolution in thought about the incorporation of women's traditions, history, and experiences into selected disciplines. The model I have developed identifies five common phases of thinking about women:

male-defined curriculum, contribution curriculum, bifocal curriculum, women's curriculum, and *gender-balanced curriculum.* A gender-balanced perspective, one that is rooted in feminist scholarship, takes into account the experiences, perspectives, and voices of women as well as men. It examines the similarities and differences between women and men and also considers how gender interacts with such factors as ethnicity, race, culture, and class.

The language of this system or schema, particularly the word *phase*, and the description of one phase and then another suggest a sequential hierarchy in which one phase supplants another. Before reviewing the schema, please refrain from thinking of these phases in a linear fashion; envision them as a series of intersecting circles, or patches on a quilt, or threads in a tapestry, which interact and undergo changes in response to one another. It is more accurate to view the phases as different emphases that coexist in feminist research. The important thing is that teachers, scholars, and curriculum developers ask and answer certain questions at each phase.

The following section identifies key concepts and questions articulated initially at each phase, using examples from history, literature, and science; it then discusses how the phases interact and undergo changes in response to one another. The final part of this chapter shows teachers grappling with the intersection of changes in the disciplines and changes in the student population and presents four themes of analysis: mastery, voice, authority, and positionality. The chapter concludes with specific objectives, practices, and teaching suggestions for incorporating content about women into the K–12 curriculum in social studies, language arts, and science.

Male-Defined Curriculum

Male-defined curricula rest on the assumption that the male experience is universal, that it is representative of humanity, and that it constitutes a basis for generalizing about all human beings. The knowledge that is researched and taught, the substance of learning, is knowledge articulated by and about men. There is little or no consciousness in it that the existence of women as a group is an anomaly calling for a broader definition of knowledge. The female experience is subsumed under the male experience. For example, feminist scientists have cited methodological problems in some research about sex differences that draws conclusions about females based on experiments done only on males or that uses limited (usually White, middle-class) experimental populations from which scientists draw conclusions about all males and females.

The incorporation of women into the curriculum has not only taught us about women's lives but has also led to questions about our lopsided rendition of men's lives, wherein we pay attention primarily to men in the public world and conceal their lives in the private world. Historians, for example, are posing a series of interesting questions about men's history: What do we need to unlearn about men's history? What are the taken-for-granted truths about men's history that we need to rethink? How do we get at the significant masculine truths? Is man's primary sense of self defined in relation to the public sphere only? How does it relate to boyhood, adolescence, family life, recreation, and love? What do the answers to these questions imply about the teaching of history?

Feminist scholarship, like African American, Native American, Latino, and Asian American scholarship, reveals the systematic and contestable exclusions in the male-defined

Table 7.1 Male-Defined Curriculum

Characteristics of Phase	Questions Commonly Asked about Women in History*	Questions Commonly Asked about Women in Literature*	Questions Commonly Asked about Women in Science*
The absence of women is not noted. There is no consciousness that the male experience is a "particular knowledge" selected from a wider universe of possible knowledge and experience. It is valued, emphasized, and viewed as the knowledge most worth having.	Who is the author of a particular history? What is her or his race, ethnicity, religion, ideological orientation, social class, place of origin, and historical period? How does incorporating women's experiences lead to new understandings of the most fundamental ordering of social relations, institutions, and power arrangements? How can we define the content and methodology of history so it will be a history of us all?	How is traditional humanism, with an integrated self at its center and an authentic view of life, in effect part of patriarchal ideology? How can the objectivist illusion be dismantled? How can the idea of a literary canon of "great literature" be challenged? How are writing and reading political acts? How do race, class, and gender relate to the conflict, sufferings, and passions that attend these realities? How can we study language as specific *discourse*, that is, specific linguistic strategies in specific situations, rather than as universal language?	How do scientific studies reveal cultural values? What cultural, historical, and gender values are projected onto the physical and natural world? How might gender be a bias that influences choice of questions, hypotheses, subjects, experimented design, or theory formation in science? What is the underlying philosophy of an andocentric science that values objectivity, rationality, and dominance? How can the distance between the subject and the scientific observer be shortened so that the scientist has some feeling for or empathy with the organism? How can gender play a crucial role in transforming science?

*New questions generated by feminist scholars.

curriculum. When we examine it through the lens of this scholarship, we are forced to reconsider our understanding of the most fundamental conceptualization of knowledge and social relations within our society. We understand in a new way that knowledge is a social construction, written by individual human beings who live and think at a particular time and within a particular social framework. All works in literature, science, and history, for example, have an author, male or female, White or ethnic or racial minority, elite or middle class or occasionally poor, with motivations and beliefs. The scientist's questions and activities, for instance, are shaped, often unconsciously, by the great social issues of the day (see Table 7.1). Different perspectives on the same subject will change the patterns discerned.

Contribution Curriculum

Early efforts to reclaim women's rightful place in the curriculum were a search for missing women within a male framework. Although there was the recognition that women were missing, men continued to serve as the norm, the representative, the universal human being. Outstanding women emerged who fit this male norm of excellence or greatness or conformed to implicit assumptions about appropriate roles for women outside the home. In literature, female authors were added who performed well within the masculine tradition, internalizing its standards of art and its views on social roles. Great women of science who made it in the male scientific world, most frequently Marie Curie, for example, were added.

Examples of contribution history can be seen in U.S. history textbooks. They now include the contributions of notable American women who were outstanding in the public sphere as rulers or as contributors to wars or reform movements to a remarkable degree. Queen Liliuokalani, Hawaii's first reigning queen and a nationalist, is included in the story of the kingdom's annexation. Molly Pitcher and Deborah Sampson are depicted as contributors to the Revolutionary War, as is Clara Barton to the Civil War effort. Some authors have also included women who conform to the assumption that it is acceptable for women to engage in activities outside the home if they are an extension of women's nurturing role within the family. Examples of this are Dorothea Dix, Jane Addams, Eleanor Roosevelt, and Mary McLeod Bethune (Tetreault, 1986).

The lesson to be learned from understanding these limitations of early contribution history is not to disregard the study of notable women but to include those who worked to reshape the world according to a feminist reordering of values. This includes efforts to increase women's self-determination through a feminist transformation of the home, to increase education, political rights, and women's rights to control their bodies, and also to improve their economic status. A history with women at the center moves beyond paying attention to caring for the unfortunate in the public sphere to how exceptional women influenced the lives of women in general (see Table 7.2). Just as Mary McLeod Bethune's role in the New Deal is worth teaching to our students, so is her aggressive work to project a positive image of Black women to the nation through her work in Black women's clubs and the launching of the *Afro-American Woman's Journal*.

Bifocal Curriculum

In bifocal curricula, feminist scholars have made an important shift from a perspective that views men as the norm to one that opens up the possibility of seeing the world through women's eyes. This dual vision, or bifocal perspective, generated global questions about women and about the differences between women and men. Historians investigated the separation between the public and the private sphere and asked, for example, how the division between them explains women's lives. Some elaborated on the construct by identifying arenas of female power in the domestic sphere. Literary critics aimed to provide a new understanding of a distinctively female literary tradition and a theory of women's literary creativity. They sought to provide models for understanding the dynamics of female literary response to male literary assertion and coercion. Scientists grapple with definitions of woman's and man's nature by asking how the public and private, biology and culture, and personal and impersonal inform each other and affect men and women, science, and nature.

Scholars have pointed out some of the problems with bifocal knowledge. Thinking about women and men is dualistic and dichotomized. Women and men are thought of as having different spheres, different notions of what is of value in life, different ways of imagining the

Table 7.2 Contribution Curriculum

Characteristics of Phase	Questions Commonly Asked about Women in History	Questions Commonly Asked about Women in Literature	Questions Commonly Asked about Women in Science
The absence of women is noted. There is a search for missing women according to a male norm of greatness, excellence, or humanness. Women are considered exceptional, deviant, or other. Women are added into history, but the content and notions of historical significance are not challenged.	Who are the notable women missing from history and what did they and ordinary women contribute in areas or movements traditionally dominated by men, for example, during major wars or during reform movements, like abolitionism or the labor movement? What did notable and ordinary women contribute in areas that are an extension of women's traditional roles, for example, caring for the poor and the sick? How have major economic and political changes like industrialization or extension of the franchise affected women in the public sphere? How did notable and ordinary women respond to their oppression, particularly through women's rights organizations? *Who were outstanding women who advocated a feminist transformation of the home, who contributed to women's greater self-determination through increased education, the right to control their bodies, an increase in their political rights, and the improvement of their economic status? *What did women contribute through the settlement house and labor movements?	Who are the missing female authors whose subject matter and use of language and form meet the male norm of "masterpiece"? What primary biological facts and interpretations are missing about major female authors?	Who are the notable women scientists who have made contributions to mainstream science? How is women's different (and inferior) nature related to hormones, brain lateralization, and sociobiology? Where are the missing females in scientific experiments? What is the current status of women within the scientific profession? *How does adding minority women into the history of science reveal patterns of exclusion and recast definitions of what it means to practice science and to be a scientist? *How is the exclusion of women from science related to the way science is done and thought? *What is the usual pattern of women working in science? How is it the same as or different from the pattern of notable women? *How do our definitions of science need to be broadened to evaluate women's contributions to science? Do institutions of science need to be reshaped to accommodate women? If so, how?

*New questions generated by feminist scholars.

human condition, and different associations with nature and culture. But both views are valued. In short, women are thought of as a group that is complementary but equal to men; there are some truths for men and there are some truths for women. General analyses of men's and women's experiences often come dangerously close to reiterating the sexual stereotypes scholars are trying to overcome. Because many people believe that the public sphere is more valuable than the private sphere, there is a tendency to slip back into thinking of women as inferior and subordinate.

The generalized view of women and men that predominates in the bifocal curriculum often does not allow for distinctions within groups as large and as complex as women and men. Important factors like historical period, geographic location, structural barriers, race, paternity, sexual orientation, and social class, to name a few, clearly make a difference.

Other common emphases in the bifocal curriculum are the oppression of women and the exploration of that oppression. Exposés of woman-hating in history and literature are common. The emphasis is on the misogyny (the hatred of women) of the human experience, particularly the means men have used to advance their authority and to assert or imply female inferiority. The paradoxes of women's existence are sometimes overlooked with this emphasis on oppression. For example, although women have been excluded from positions of power, a few of them as wives and daughters in powerful families were often closer to actual power than were men. If some women were dissatisfied with their status and role, most women adjusted and resisted efforts to improve women's lot. Too much emphasis on women's oppression perpetuates a patriarchal framework presenting women as primarily passive, reacting only to the pressures of a sexist society. In the main, it emphasizes men thinking and women being thought about.

Women's scholarship from the 1970s through the 1990s (Collins, 1998; Goldberger, Tarule, Clinchy, & Belenky, 1996; Schmitz, Butler, Rosenfelt, & Guy-Sheftall, 1995) has helped us see that understanding women's oppression is more complex than we initially thought. We do not yet have adequate concepts to explain gender systems founded on a division of labor and sexual asymmetry. To understand gender systems, it is necessary to take a structural and experiential perspective that asks from a woman's point of view where we are agents and where we are not, where our relations with men are egalitarian and where they are not. This questioning may lead to explanations of why women's experiences and interpretations of their world can differ significantly from men's.

Further, the concepts with which we approach our analysis need to be questioned. Anthropologists have pointed out that our way of seeing the world—for instance, the idea of complementary spheres for women (the private sphere) and men (the public sphere)—is a product of our experience in a Western, modern, industrial, capitalistic state with a specific history. We distort our understanding of other social systems by imposing our worldview on them. Feminist critics are calling for rethinking not only of categories like the domestic versus the public sphere, and production and reproduction, but also even of categories like gender itself.

Feminist scholars have helped us see the urgency of probing and analyzing the interactive nature of the oppressions of race, ethnicity, class, and gender (Collins, 1998). We are reminded that we can no longer take a liberal reformist approach that does not probe the needs of the system that are being satisfied by oppression. We have to take seriously the model of feminist scholarship that analyzes women's status within the social, cultural, historical, political, and economic contexts. Only then will issues of gender be understood in relation to the economic needs of both male dominance and capitalism that undergird such oppressions.

One of the most important things we have learned about a bifocal perspective is the danger of generalizing too much, of longing for women's history instead of writing histories about women. We must guard against establishing a feminist version of great literature and then resisting any modifications or additions to it. We have also learned that the traditional disciplines are limited in their ability to shed light on gender complexities, and it becomes apparent that there is a need for an interdisciplinary perspective (see Table 7.3).

Women's Curriculum

The most important idea to emerge in women's scholarship is that women's activities, not men's, are the measure of significance. What was formerly devalued, the content of women's everyday lives, assumes new value as scholars investigate female rituals, housework, childbearing, child rearing, female sexuality, female friendship, and studies of the life cycle. For instance, scientists investigate how research on areas of interest primarily to women—menstruation, childbirth, and menopause—challenge existing scientific theories. Historians document women's efforts to break out of their traditional sphere of the home in a way that uses women's activities, not men's, as the measure of historical significance. These activities include women's education, women's paid work, and volunteer work outside the home, particularly in women's clubs and associations. Of equal importance is the development of a collective feminist consciousness, that is, of women's consciousness of their own distinct role in society. Analyses begun in the bifocal phase continue to explore what sex and gender have meant for the majority of women.

As scholars look more closely at the complex patterns of women's lives, they see the need for a pluralistic conceptualization of women. Although thinking of women as a monolithic group provides valuable information about patterns of continuity and change in those areas most central to women's lives, generalizing about a group as vast and diverse as women leads to inaccuracies. The subtle interactions among gender and other variables are investigated. Historians ask how the particulars of race, ethnicity, social class, marital status, and sexual orientation challenge the homogeneity of women's experiences. Third World feminists critique hegemonic "Western" feminisms and formulate autonomous, geographically, historically, and culturally grounded feminist concerns and strategies (Mohanty, Russo, & Torres, 1991).

Questions about sex and gender are set within historical, ideological, and cultural contexts, including the culture's definition of the facts of biological development and what they mean for individuals. Researchers ask, for example, Why are these attitudes toward sexuality prevalent at this time in history? What are the ways in which sexual words, categories, and ideology mirror the organization of society as a whole? What are the socioeconomic factors contributing to them? How do current conceptions of the body reflect social experiences and professional needs?

Life histories and autobiographies shed light on societies' perceptions of women and women's perceptions of themselves. Women's individual experiences are revealed through these stories and contribute to the fashioning of the human experience from the perspective of women.

Table 7.3 Bifocal Curriculum

Characteristics of Phase	Questions Commonly Asked about Women in History	Questions Commonly Asked about Women in Literature	Questions Commonly Asked about Women in Science
Human experience is conceptualized primarily in dualist categories: male and female, private and public, agency and communion. Emphasis is on a complementary but equal conceptualization of men's and women's spheres and personal qualities. There is a focus on women's oppression and on misogyny. Women's efforts to overcome the oppression are presented. Efforts to include women lead to the insight that the traditional content, structure, and methodology of the disciplines are more appropriate to the male experience.	How does the division between the public and the private sphere explain women's lives? Who oppressed women, and how were they oppressed? *What are forms of power and value in women's world? *How have women been excluded from and deprived of power and value in men's sphere? *How do gender systems create divisions between the sexes such that experience and interpretations of their world can differ significantly from men's? *How can we rethink categories like public and private, productive and reproductive, sex and gender?	Who are the missing minor female authors whose books are unobtainable, whose lives have never been written, and whose works have been studied casually, if at all? How is literature a record of the collective consciousness of patriarchy? What myths and stereotypes about women are present in male literature? How can we critique the meritocratic pretensions of traditional literary history? How can we pair opposite-sex texts in literature as a way of understanding the differences between women's and men's experiences? How is literature one of the expressive modes of a female subculture that developed with the distinction of separate spheres for women and men? *How can feminist literary critics resist establishing their own great canon of literature and any additions to it?	How have the sciences defined (and misdefined) the nature of women? Why are there so few women scientists? What social and psychological forces have kept women in the lower ranks or out of science entirely? How do women fit into the study of history of science and health care? How do scientific findings, originally carried out on males of a species, change when carried out on the females of the same species? How do the theories and interpretations of sociobiology require constant testing and change to fit the theory for males and females with regard to competition, sexual selection, and infanticide? How does the science/gender system—the network of associations and disjunctions between public and private, personal and impersonal, and masculine and feminine—inform each other and affect men and women, science and nature? *What are the structural barriers to women in science?

*New questions generated by feminist scholars.

Scholars find it necessary to draw on other disciplines for a clearer vision of the social structure and culture of societies as individuals encounter them in their daily life. Likewise, there are calls for new unifying frameworks and different ways to think of periods in history and literature to identify concepts that accommodate women's history and traditions. There is also a more complex conceptualization of historical time. The emphases in much history are on events, a unit of time too brief to afford a sense of structural change, changes in the way people think about their own reality, and the possibilities for other realities. L'Ecole des Annales in France (a group of historians who pioneered the use of such public records as birth, marriage, and death certificates in historical analysis) has distinguished between events and what they call the *longue durée* (Letters to the Editor, 1982). By the *longue durée* they mean the slow, glacial changes, requiring hundreds of years to complete, that represent significant shifts in the way people think.

Examples of areas of women's history that lend themselves to this concept are the structural change from a male-dominated to an egalitarian perspective and the transformation of women's traditional role in the family to their present roles as wives, mothers, and paid workers outside the home. Also important is the demographic change in the average number of children per woman of childbearing age from seven to fewer than two children between 1800 and 1990 (see Table 7.4).

Gender-Balanced Curriculum

This phase continues many of the inquiries begun in the women's curriculum phase, but it articulates questions about how women and men relate to and complement one another. Conscious of the limitations of seeing women in isolation and aware of the relational character of gender, researchers search for the nodal points at which women's and men's experiences intersect. Historians and literary critics ask if the private, as well as the public, aspects of life are presented as a continuum in women's and men's experience.

The pluralistic and multifocal conception of women that emerged in the women's curriculum phase is extended to human beings. A central idea in this phase is *positionality* (Alcoff, 1988; Haraway, 1997; Harding, 1991). Positionality means that important aspects of our identity (for example, our gender, our race, our class, our age, and so on) are markers of relational positions rather than essential qualities. Their effects and implications change according to context. Recently, feminist thinkers have seen knowledge as valid when it comes from an acknowledgment of the knower's specific position in any context, one always defined by gender, race, class, and other variables.

Scientists ask explicit questions about the invention and reinvention of nature. For example, they ask questions about the meanings of the behavior and social lives of monkeys and apes and male–female relations in animals and inquire about how such variables as age, species, and individual variation challenge current theories. They also explore contemporary technoscience—its stories and dreams, its facts and delusions, its institutions and politics, and its scientific advances (Haraway, 1991, 1997).

Accompanying this particularistic perspective is attention to the larger context, for example, the interplay among situation, meaning, economic systems, family organization, and political systems. Thus, historians ask how gender inequities are linked to economics, family organization, marriage, ritual, and politics. Research scientists probe how differences

Table 7.4 Women's Curriculum

Characteristics of Phase	Questions Commonly Asked about Women in History	Questions Commonly Asked about Women in Literature	Questions Commonly Asked about Women in Science
Scholarly inquiry pursues new questions, new categories, and new notions of significance that illuminate women's traditions, history, culture, values, visions, and perspectives.	What were the majority of women doing at a particular time in history? What was the significance of these activities?	What does women's sphere—for example, domesticity and family, education, marriage, sexuality, and love—reveal about our culture?	How do the cultural dualisms associated with masculinity and femininity permeate scientific thought and discourse?
A pluralistic conception of women emerges that acknowledges diversity and recognizes that variables besides gender shape women's lives—for example, race, ethnicity, and social class.	How can female friendship between kin, mothers, daughters, and friends be analyzed as one aspect of women's overall relations with others?	How can we contrast the fictional image of women in literature with the complexity and variety of the roles of individual women in real life as workers, housewives, revolutionaries, mothers, lovers, and so on?	How do women's actual experiences, as compared to the physician's analysis or scientific theory, challenge the traditional paradigms of science and of the health care systems?
Women's experience is allowed to speak for itself. Feminist history is rooted in the personal and the specific; it builds from that to the general.	What kind of productive work, paid and unpaid, did women do and under what conditions?	How do the particulars of race, ethnicity, social class, marital status, and sexual orientation, as revealed in literature, challenge the thematic homogeneity of women's experiences?	How does research on areas of primary interest to women, for instance, menopause, childbirth and menstruation/estrus, challenge existing scientific theories?
The public and the private are seen as a continuum in women's experiences.	What were the reproductive activities of women? How did they reproduce the American family?		
Women's experience is analyzed within the social, cultural, historical, political, and economic contexts.	How did the variables of race, ethnicity, social class, marital status, and sexual preference affect women's experience?	How does literature portray what binds women together and what separates them because of race, ethnicity, social class, marital status, and sexual orientation?	How do variables other than sex and gender, such as age, species, and individual variation, challenge current theories?
Efforts are made to reconceptualize knowledge to encompass the female experience. The conceptualization of knowledge is not characterized by disciplinary thinking but becomes multidisciplinary.	What new categories need to be added to the study of history, for instance, housework, childbearing, and child rearing? How have women of different races and classes interacted throughout history? What are appropriate ways of organizing or periodizing women's history? For example, how will examining women's experiences at each stage of the life span help us to understand women's experiences on their own terms?	How does the social and historical context of a work of literature shed light on it?	How do the experience of female primates and the variation among species of primates—for example, competition among females, female agency in sexuality, and infanticide—test the traditional paradigms?

between the male and female body have been used to justify a social agenda that privileges men economically, socially, and politically. In this phase, a revolutionary relationship comes to exist between things traditionally treated as serious, primarily the activities of men in the public sphere, and those things formerly perceived as trivial, namely the activities of women in the private sphere.

This new relationship leads to a recentering of knowledge in the disciplines, a shift from a male-centered perspective to one that includes both females and males. This reconceptualization of knowledge works toward a more holistic view of the human experience. As in the previous stage, the conceptualization of knowledge is characterized by multidisciplinary thinking.

Feminist scholars have cautioned against moving too quickly from women's curricula to gender-balanced curricula. As the historian Gerda Lerner observed in the 1980s, our decade-and-a-half-old investigation of women's history is only a speck on the horizon compared to the centuries-old tradition of male-defined history. By turning too quickly to studies of gender, we risk short-circuiting important directions in women's studies and again having women's history and experiences subsumed under those of men. It remains politically important for feminists to defend women as women in order to counteract the male domination that continues to exist. The French philosopher Julia Kristeva (cited in Moi, 1985) and, more recently, Judith Butler (1990, 1993) push us to new considerations when they urge women (and men) to recognize the falsifying nature of masculinity and femininity, to explore how the fact of being born male or female determines one's position in relation to power, and to envision more fluid gender identities that have the potential to liberate both women and men to a fuller personhood (see Table 7.5). Of particular interest to teachers is the work of Barry Thorne (1993), who draws upon her daily observations in the classroom and on the playground to show how children construct gender and experience gender in the school.

CHANGING TRADITIONAL WAYS OF TEACHING

Feminist scholarship has helped us understand that all knowledge, and therefore all classroom knowledge, is a social construction. This insight affirms the evolving nature of knowledge and the role of teachers and students in its ongoing construction. For me, the term *pedagogy* applies not just to teaching techniques but also to the whole classroom production of knowledge; it encompasses the full range of relationships among course materials, teachers, and students. Such broadened conceptualizations of pedagogy challenge the commonly held assumptions of the professor as a disinterested expert, the content as inherently "objective," and the method of delivery as irrelevant to the message (hooks, 1994). To educate students for a complex, multicultural, multiracial world, we need to include the perspectives and voices of those who have not been traditionally included—women of all backgrounds, people of color, and females and males who perceive their education as not made for them.

Feminist teachers are demonstrating how they transform courses through their attention to cultural, ethnic, and gender diversity and give concrete form to the complexity of the struggles over knowledge, access, and power (hooks, 1994; Maher & Tetreault, 1994, 2001; Weiler, 1988). In *The Feminist Classroom*, Frances Maher and I (Maher & Tetreault, 2001)

Table 7.5 Gender-Balanced Curriculum

Characteristics of Phase	Questions Commonly Asked about Women in History	Questions Commonly Asked about Women in Literature	Questions Commonly Asked about Women in Science
A multifocal, gender-balanced perspective is sought that weaves together women's and men's experiences into multilayered composites of human experience. At this stage, scholars are conscious of positionality. Positionality represents the insight that all women and men are located in historical contexts, contexts defined in terms of race, class, culture, and age, as well as gender, and that they gain their knowledge and their power from the specifics of their situations. Scholars begin to define what binds together and what separates the various segments of humanity. Scholars have a deepened understanding of how the private as well as public form a continuum in individual experience. They search for the nodal points at which comparative treatment of men's and women's experience is possible. Efforts are made to reconceptualize knowledge to reflect this multilayered composite of women's and men's experience. The conceptualization of knowledge is not characterized by disciplinary thinking but becomes multidisciplinary.	What is the knower's specific position in this historical context? How is gender asymmetry linked to economic systems, family organizations, marriage, ritual, and political systems? How can we compare women and men in all aspects of their lives to reveal gender as a crucial historical determinant? Are the private, as well as the public, aspects of history presented as a continuum in women's and men's experiences? How is gender a social construction? What does the particular construction of gender in a society tell us about the society that so constructed gender? What is the intricate relation between the construction of gender and the structure of power? How can we expand our conceptualization of historical time to a pluralistic one that conceives of three levels of history: structures, trends, and events? How can we unify approaches and types of knowledge of all social sciences and history as a means of investigating specific problems in relational history?	How does the author's specific position, as defined by gender, race, and class, affect this literary work? How can we validate the full range of human expression by selecting literature according to its insight into any aspect of human experience rather than according to how it measures up to a predetermined canon? Is the private as well as the public sphere presented as a continuum in women's and men's experiences? How can we pair opposite-sex texts in literature as a way of understanding how female and male characters experience "maleness" and "femaleness" as a continuum of "humanness"? How do the variables of race, ethnicity, social class, marital status, and sexual orientation affect the experience of female and male literary characters? How can we rethink the concept of periodicity to accentuate the continuity of life and to contain the multitude of previously ignored literary works, for example, instead of Puritanism, the contexts for and consequences of sexuality? How can we deconstruct the opposition between masculinity and femininity?	What explicit questions need to be raised about the invention and reinvention of nature? What is the meaning of male–female relations in animals? How do variables such as age, species, and individual variation challenge current theories? What are the limits to generalizing beyond the data collected on limited samples to other genders, species, and conditions not sampled in the experimental protocol? How have sex differences been used to assign men and women to particular roles in the social hierarchy? How have differences between the male and female body been used to justify a social agenda that privileges men economically, socially, and politically?

show how all students may benefit from, and how some are even inspired by, college courses transformed by their professor's attention to cultural, ethnic, and gender diversity. We have found that the themes we used to analyze teaching and learning in seventeen classrooms on six campuses across the country apply to elementary and secondary classrooms as well. The four themes—*mastery, authority, voice,* and *positionality*—all relate to issues present in today's classroom. Although all four deal with reconstituted relationships between new students and new disciplinary frameworks, the themes of mastery and authority focus on knowledge and its sources; voice and positionality on the students themselves.

Mastery has traditionally meant the goal of an individual student's rational comprehension of the material on the teacher's and expert's terms. Women (and other marginalized groups) must often give up their voices when they seek mastery on the terms of the dominant culture. We found classrooms undergoing a shift away from unidimensional sources of expertise to a multiplicity of new information and insights. Students were no longer mastering a specific body of material, nor were they emphasizing subjective experiences that risk excluding students from a wealth of knowledge. Rather, they were struggling through or integrating often widely various interpretations of texts, scientific research, and social problems. These teachers redefined mastery as interpretation, as increasingly sophisticated handling of the topics at hand, informed by but not limited to the students' links to the material from their own experience. For example, a Japanese American student reread an Emily Dickinson poem about silences and invisibilities to comment on her gender and ethnic marginality:

> I couldn't help thinking of the idea of a mute culture within a dominant culture. A "nobody" knowing she's different from the dominant culture keeps silent. . . . But to be somebody! How dreary! How public! So when you become a somebody and buy into the dominant culture, you have to live in their roles.
>
> A silly example: It's like watching a Walt Disney movie as a child where Hayley Mills and these other girls dance and primp before a party singing "Femininity," how being a woman is all about looking pretty and smiling pretty and acting stupid to attract men. As a child I ate it up, at least it seemed benign. But once your eye gets put out and you realize how this vision has warped you, it would split your heart to try and believe that again, it would strike you dead.

Students were stretched by such broadenings of interpretative frameworks and indeed became authorities for one another. A White male student in the same class said:

> I could read Dickinson a thousand times and probably never try to relate to that because it just would never make an impression on me, but having the girls in that class interested in that particular topic, "How does that relate to me as a woman?" then I sit back and I think that's a really good question. Although I'm male I can learn how women react to women's text as opposed to maybe the way I react to it or the teacher reacts to it.

The teachers in our study consciously used their *authority* to give students responsibility for their own learning (Finke, 1993). Students and professors became authorities for one another to the extent that they were explicit about themselves as social and political actors with respect to a text or an issue (Tetreault, 1991). The teachers also struggled with reconceptualizing the grounds for their own authority, both over the subject matter and with students, because their traditional positions as the sole representatives of expertise were called into question by these multiple new sources of knowledge. These professors shared a sense of their authority as being grounded in their own experiences and in their intellectual engagement with feminist scholarship and other relevant fields.

As important as the rethinking of the disciplines is the power of expression that these new forms of knowledge, coming from the students' questions as well as from new topics, give to women and to other previously silenced groups. We explored the effects on students through our theme of voice. *Voice* is frequently defined as the awakening of the students' own responses. However, we came to think of these classrooms as arenas where teachers and students fashion their voices rather than "find" them, as they produce relevant experiences to shape a narrative of an emerging self.

Our fourth theme is *positionality*, which is defined in the section on gender-balanced curriculum. Positionality helps us to see the multiple ways in which the complex dynamics of difference and inequality, which come from outside society, also operate powerfully inside the classroom itself. Much of our emphasis in the past three decades has been on the consequences of sexism and racism on females and on students of color. We have learned much about how universalizing the position of maleness leads to intellectual domination.

Some educators and theorists are arguing that we need to become conscious in similar ways about the effects of universalizing the position of Whiteness (Frankenberg, 1993, 1997; McIntosh, 1990; Morrison, 1993; Tatum, 1992). For example, how does the norm of Whiteness or maleness shape the construction of knowledge in classrooms? How do those assumptions contribute to the intellectual domination of groups? Why is it that when we think of the development of racial identity in our students, we think primarily of students of color rather than of White students? What happens in classrooms where Whiteness is marked, revealed as a position? In our culture, the presumptions of Whiteness or maleness act to constrict voice by universalizing the dominant positions, by letting them float free of "position."

Frances Maher and I revisited data presented in *The Feminist Classroom* to examine how assumptions of Whiteness shape the construction of knowledge as it is produced and resisted in the classroom (Maher & Tetreault, 1997). We saw how the dominant voices continue to call the tune—that is, to maintain the conceptual and ideological frameworks through which suppressed voices are distorted or not fully heard. We saw more clearly the ways in which a thorough pedagogy of positionality must entail an excavation of Whiteness in its many dimensions and complexities. Understanding all the ways in which positionality shapes learning is a long, interactive process.

The lessons that follow attempt to model teaching that is constructed to reveal the particular and the common denominators of human experience. These sample lessons are organized by the subject areas of language arts, science, and social studies, but they can be adapted to other subject areas as well.

Language Arts

Analyzing Children's Literature
Suggested Activities

Ask students to locate five of their favorite children's books, to read or reread them, and to keep a written record of their reactions to the books. Either on the chalkboard or on a sheet of newsprint, keep a record of the students' (and your) book choices. Divide the class into small groups according to the same or similar favorite books and have students share their written reactions to the books. Ask the groups to keep a record of the most noteworthy ideas that emerge from their small-group discussions. When you bring the small groups together, ask each group to present its noteworthy ideas. Ideas that emerge may be as follows:

> How differently they read the book now than at the time of their first reading
>
> The differences and similarities in so-called girls' books and boys' books
>
> The importance of multicultural or international perspectives
>
> What the stories reveal about the culture in which the stories are set

A follow-up activity could be to interview grandparents, parents, teachers, and other adults about characters and stories they remember from childhood. Questions to ask include, How do they recall feeling about those stories? Have images of female and male behavior or expectations in children's stories changed? Is race or ethnicity treated similarly or differently?

Pairing Female and Male Autobiographies
Suggested Activities

Pairings of autobiographies and fiction by male and female authors can contribute greatly to students' multifocal, relational understanding of the human experience. Two pairings I have found to be particularly illuminating are *Black Boy*, by Richard Wright (1945/2000), and *Woman Warrior*, by Maxine Hong Kingston (1976). Other interesting pairings are Maya Angelou's *I Know Why the Caged Bird Sings* (1969) and Mark Twain's *The Adventures of Huckleberry Finn* (Twain, 1912/1985); *The Autobiography of Frederick Douglass* (Douglass, 1994) and *Incidents in the Life of a Slave Girl* (Jacobs, 1861/1988); *The Adventures of Tom Sawyer* (Twain, 1910/1996) and *Little Women* (Alcott, 1880/1995).

One professor we observed at Lewis and Clark College, Dorothy Berkson, uses teaching logs to demystify the process of interpretation by linking the students' emotional connections to texts with their intellectual analysis. She asks her students to select a passage that puzzles or engages them or triggers a strong emotional reaction. Believing that some of the best criticism starts with such reactions, she asks the students next to paraphrase the passage they have chosen, to understand what it means, or, in a sense, to master it. They are then asked to look at it again, to become conscious of what cannot be captured by paraphrase as well as any concerns or questions that escaped them before. They finally place the passage in the context of the entire text, using the following questions: Where does it happen? Are there other passages that relate to it? That contradict it? That confirm it? That raise more questions about it? Concluding with a summary of where this procedure has taken them, they turn in these logs at the end of each class. Returned to the students with Berkson's comments, the logs then become the basis for the students' formal paper. This process forces students to reengage with the text over and over again, to engage in continuous reinterpretation of the text rather than to think they have arrived at some final mastery.

Science

Fear of Science: Fact or Fantasy?
Suggested Activities

Fear of science and math and the stereotyping of scientists contribute to the limited participation of some students, most often female, in math and science classes. Their inadequate participation limits their choice of most undergraduate majors that depend on a minimum of three years of high school mathematics. In *Aptitude Revisited: Rethinking Math and Science Education for America's Next Century*, David E. Drew (1996) argues that the people least encouraged to study mathematics and science in our society are those who have the least power—especially students from poverty, minority students, and young women. Policy makers, teachers, and even parents often steer certain students away from math and science for completely erroneous reasons. The result, Drew contends, is not simply an inadequately trained work force: This educational discrepancy is widening the gap between the haves and the have-nots in our society. He challenges the conventional view that science and math are too boring or too hard for many students to argue that virtually all students are capable of mastering these subjects.

The following exercise was designed by the Math and Science Education for Women Project at the Lawrence Hall of Science (Fraser, 1982).[1] The purpose of the exercise is to decrease female and male students' fear of science by enabling them to function as researchers who define the problem and generate solutions to it.

Ask students to complete the following sentence by writing for about fifteen minutes:

> When I think about science, I . . .

When they are finished, divide students into groups of five or six to discuss their responses to the cue. Ask each group to state the most important things it has learned. Discuss fear of science with the class and whether there is a difference in how girls and boys feel about science. What could be some reasons for these differences or similarities? When the findings from this exercise are clear, suggest to students that they broaden their research to include other students and teachers in the school. Have each group brainstorm questions that might appear on a science attitude questionnaire. Put the questions on the chalkboard. Analyze the questions and decide on the ten best questions.

Decide with the class what group of students and teachers you will research and how you will do it, for example, other science classes, all ninth-grade science classes, or the entire school during second period. Obtain permission to conduct the survey from the administration

---

[1]Adapted from *Fact or Fantasy* (adapted from *Spaces: Solving Problems of Access to Careers in Engineering and Science*). Sherry Fraser, Project Director. Lawrence Hall of Science, Regents of University of California. Used with permission.

and other teachers or classes involved in your research project. Have the class do the survey or questionnaire as a pilot activity. Analyze the questions for sex differences and make minor revisions before giving the survey and questionnaire to your research group. Distribute the survey or conduct interviews. Have the students decide how to analyze the information. Let each group decide how it will display findings and information. Current statistics of male and female scientists in biology, chemistry, physics, and other sciences can be found in the NSF Science and Engineering Indicators on the World Wide Web at www.nsf.gov/sbe/srs/seind98/start.htm.

Another valuable resource is *Re-Engineering Female Friendly Science*, by Sue Rosser (1997).

Have each group give (1) a report to the class on what it found, using graph displays to convey the information, and (2) recommendations for decreasing science anxiety in the school. Place the entire student research project in the school library, main office, or gymnasium, where the rest of the school population can see the results. Have a student summarize and write an article for the school paper.

Doing Science

Suggested Activities

Evelyn Fox Keller's (1983) biography of Barbara McClintoch, *A Feeling for the Organism*, allows students to explore the conditions under which dissent in science arises, the function it serves, and the plurality of values and goals it reflects. Questions her story prompts are: What role do interests, individual and collective, play in the evolution of scientific knowledge? Do all scientists seek the same kinds of explanations? Are the kinds of questions they ask the same? Do differences in methodology between different subdisciplines ever permit the same kinds of answers? Do female and male scientists approach their research differently? This book is difficult reading for high school or college students, but it is manageable if they read carefully and thoroughly. The best way I have found to help them manage is to ask them to read a chapter or section and to come to class with their questions about the reading and to propose some answers.

Social Studies

My Family's Work History
Suggested Activities

Women and men of different social classes, ethnic groups, and geographic locations have done various kinds of work inside and outside their homes in agricultural, industrial, and postindustrial economies. Before introducing students to the history of work, I pique their interest by asking them to complete a Family Work Chart (see Table 7.6). When their charts are complete, the students and I build a work chronology from 1890 to the present. Our work chronology contains information gleaned from the textbook and library sources about important inventions, laws, demographics, and labor history.

I then reproduce the work chronology on a chart so they can compare their family's history with key historical events. By seeing their families' histories alongside major events in our collective work history, students can see how their family was related to society. A sample of items from our chart looks like this (Chapman, 1979):

Table 7.6 Family Work Chart

| | | Work Experience | | |
| | | | AFTER MARRIAGE | |
	YEAR OF BIRTH	BEFORE MARRIAGE	WHILE CHILDREN WERE YOUNG	WHEN CHILDREN WERE GROWN
Your maternal side				
Mother				
Grandmother				
Grandfather				
Great-grandmother				
Great-grandfather				
Great-great-grandmother				
Great-great-grandfather				
Your paternal side				
Father				
Grandmother				
Grandfather				
Great-grandmother				
Great-grandfather				
Great-great-grandmother				
Great-great-grandfather				

This activity was developed by Carol Frenier. Reprinted with permission from the Education Development Center from Adeline Naiman, Project Director, *Sally Garcia and Family Resource Guide*, Unit 3 of *The Role of Women in American Society* (Newton, Mass.: Education Development Center, Inc., 1978), p. 62.

Historical Events	*Your Family History*
1890 Women are 17 percent of the paid labor force	
1915 Telephone connects New York and San Francisco	
1924 Restriction of immigration	

Students conclude this unit by writing about a major theme in their family's work history. They might focus on how the lives of the women in the family differed from the lives of the men. They might focus on how their family's race or ethnicity shaped their work history.

Integrating the Public and Private Spheres
Suggested Activities

Human life is lived in both the public and the private spheres in wartime as well as in peacetime. By asking students consciously to examine individuals' lives as citizens, workers, family members, friends, members of social groups, and individuals, they learn more about the interaction of these roles in both spheres. War is an extraordinary time when the nation's underlying assumptions about these roles are often put to the test. By having students examine the interaction of these roles in wartime, they can see some of our underlying assumptions about the roles and how they are manipulated for the purposes of war. Through researching the histories of their families, and by reading primary source accounts, viewing films, and reading their textbook, they will see the complexity and variety of human experiences in the United States during World War II.

Students research their family's history during World War II by gathering family documents and artifacts and by interviewing at least one relative who was an adult during World War II. Students draw up questions beforehand to find out how the individual's social roles were affected by the war. During the two weeks they are researching their family's history, two class periods are spent on this project. During the first period, students give oral reports to a small group of fellow students in read-around groups.

Appropriate readings and films on World War II are widely available. Studs Terkel's (1984) *The Good War* is particularly useful because of the variety of people the author interviewed. For instance, students can read about the internment of Japanese Americans and can role-play an account read. Their textbook may provide good background information. A moving account written by an author who was interned is *Desert Exile: The Uprooting of a Japanese-American Family*, by Yoshiko Uchida (1982). My students answer two questions in this unit: World War II has been described as a "good war." From the materials you have examined, was it a good war for individuals' lives as citizens, workers, family members, friends, and members of social groups? How were their experiences similar to or different from those of your relatives?

SUMMARY

This chapter has illustrated how women's studies is challenging male domination over curricular content. The evolution of that challenge is illuminated by understanding the different emphases that coexist in male-defined, contribution, bifocal, women's, and gender-balanced curricula. We now have a conceptual framework for a curriculum that interweaves issues of gender with ethnicity, culture, and class. This framework acknowledges and celebrates a multifocal, relational view of the human experience.

The idea of the phases of feminist scholarship as a series of intersecting circles, or patches on a quilt, or threads on a tapestry, suggests parallel ways to think about a class of students.

Each student brings to your classroom a particular positionality that shapes his or her way of knowing. Your challenge as a teacher is to interweave the individual truths with course content into complex understandings that legitimize students' voices.

This relational knowledge, with the authority of the school behind it, has the potential to help students analyze their own social, cultural, historical, political, and economic contexts. The goal of relational knowledge is to build a world in which the oppressions of race, gender, and class, on which capitalism and patriarchy depend, are challenged by critical citizens in a democratic society.

Questions and Activities

1. What is a gender-balanced, multicultural curriculum?

2. What is feminist phase theory?

3. Define and give an example of each of the following phases of the feminist phase theory developed and described by the author: (a) male-defined curriculum, (b) contribution curriculum, (c) bifocal curriculum, (d) women's curriculum, (e) gender-balanced curriculum.

4. What problems do the contribution and bifocal phases have? How do the women's curriculum and gender-balanced curriculum phases help solve these problems?

5. The author states that "knowledge is a social construction." What does this mean? In what ways is the new scholarship on women and ethnic groups alike? In what ways does the new scholarship on women and ethnic groups challenge the dominant knowledge established in society and presented in textbooks? Give examples.

6. Examine the treatment of women in a sample of social studies, language arts, mathematics, or science textbooks (or a combination of two types of textbooks). Which phase or phases of the feminist phase theory presented by the author best describe the treatment of women in the textbooks you examined?

7. What is the *longue durée?* Why is it important in the study of social history, particularly women's history?

8. Research your family history, paying particular attention to the roles, careers, and influence of women in your family's saga. Also describe your ethnic heritage and the influence of ethnicity on your family's past and present. Share your family history with a group of your classmates or workshop participants.

References

Alcoff, L. (1988). Cultural Feminism versus Post-Structuralism: The Identity Crisis in Feminist Theory. *Signs, 13,* 405–436.

Alcott, L. M. (1880/1995). *Little Women.* New York: Scholastic.

Angelou, M. (1969). *I Know Why the Caged Bird Sings.* New York: Bantam.

Butler, J. (1990.). *Gender Trouble: Feminism and the Subversion of Identity.* New York: Routledge.

Butler, J. (1993). *Bodies That Matter: On the Discursive Limits of "Sex."* New York: Routledge.

Chapman, A. (Ed.). (1979). *Approaches to Women's History.* Washington, DC: American Historical Association.

Collins, P. H. (1998). *Fighting Words: Black Women and the Search for Justice.* Minneapolis: University of Minnesota Press.

Douglass, F. (1855/1994). *The Autobiography of Frederick Douglass.* New York: Penguin.

Drew, D. E. (1996). *Aptitude Revisited: Rethinking Math and Science Education for America's Next Century.* Baltimore: John Hopkins University Press.

Finke, L. (1993). Knowledge as Bait: Feminism, Voice, and the Pedagogical Unconscious. *College English,* 55(1), 7–27.

Frankenberg, R. (1993). *White Women, Race Matters: The Social Construction of Whiteness.* Minneapolis: University of Minnesota Press.

Frankenberg, R. (Ed.). (1997). *Displacing Whiteness: Essays in Social and Cultural Criticism.* Durham, NC: Duke University Press.

Fraser, S. (1982). *Spaces: Solving Problems of Access to Careers in Engineering and Science.* Berkeley: University of California, Lawrence Hall of Science.

Goldberger, N., Tarule, J., Clinchy, B., & Belenky, M. (Eds.). (1996). *Knowledge, Difference, and Power.* New York: Basic Books.

Haraway, D. J. (1991). *Simians, Cyborgs, and Women.* New York: Routledge.

Haraway, D. J. (1997). *Modest-Witness@-Second-Millennium.* New York: Routledge.

Harding, S. (1991). *Whose Science? Whose Knowledge? Thinking from Women's Lives.* Ithaca, NY: Cornell University Press.

hooks, b. (1994). *Teaching to Transgress: Education as the Practice of Freedom.* New York: Routledge.

Jacobs, H. (1861/1988). *Incidents in the Life of a Slave Girl.* New York: Oxford University Press.

Kingston, M. H. (1976). *Woman Warrior.* New York: Knopf.

Letters to the Editor. (1982). *Social Education,* 46(6), 378–380.

Maher, F., & Tetreault, M. K. (1994). *The Feminist Classroom.* New York: Basic Books.

Maher, F., & Tetreault, M. K. (1997). Learning in the Dark: How Assumptions of Whiteness Shape Classroom Knowledge. *Harvard Educational Review,* 67(2), 321–349.

Maher, F., & Tetreault, M. K. (2001). *The Feminist Classroom* (2nd ed.). New York: Rowman & Littlefield.

McIntosh, P. (1990). White Privilege and Male Privilege. In M. L. Andersen & P. J. Collins (Eds.), *Race, Class and Gender* (pp. 70–81). Boston: Wadsworth.

Mohanty, C., Russo, A., & Torres, L. (1991). *Third World Women and the Politics of Feminism.* Bloomington: Indiana University Press.

Moi, T. (1985). *Sexual/Textual Politics.* New York: Methuen.

Morrison, T. (1993). *Playing in the Dark: Whiteness and the Literary Imagination.* New York: Vintage.

Rosser, S. V. (1997). *Re-Engineering Female Friendly Science.* New York: Teachers College Press.

Schmitz, B., Butler, J. E., Rosenfelt, D., & Guy-Sheftall, B. (1995). Women's Studies and Curriculum Transformation. In J. A. Banks & C. A. M. Banks (Eds.), *Handbook of Research on Multicultural Education* (pp. 708–728). New York: Macmillan.

Tatum, B. (1997). *"Why Are All the Black Kids Sitting Together in the Cafeteria?" and Other Conversations about Race.* New York: Basic Books.

Terkel, S. (1984). *The Good War: An Oral History of World War II.* New York: Pantheon.

Tetreault, C. (1991). *Metacommunication in a Women's Studies Classroom.* Unpublished senior honors thesis, Vassar College, Poughkeepsie, NY.

Tetreault, M. K. T. (1986). Integrating Women's History: The Case of United States History Textbooks. *The History Teacher, 19*(2), 211–262.

Thorne, B. (1993). *Gender Play: Girls and Boys in School.* New Brunswick, NJ: Rutgers University Press.

Twain, M. (1910/1996). *The Adventures of Tom Sawyer.* New York: Oxford University Press.

Twain, M. (1912/1985). *The Adventures of Huckleberry Finn.* New York: Collier.

Uchida, Y. (1982). *Desert Exile: The Uprooting of a Japanese-American Family.* Seattle: University of Washington Press.

Weiler, K. (1988). *Women Teaching for Change: Gender, Class, and Power.* South Hadley, MA: Bergin & Garvey.

Wright, R. (1945/1983). *Black Boy.* New York: Harper & Brothers.

CHAPTER 8

Transforming the Curriculum: Teaching about Women of Color

Johnnella E. Butler

Many efforts to include women and issues of gender into what is called the mainstream curriculum focus on White, middle-class women from the United States and on women from other nations and cultures. Generally, we have taken the White, middle-class woman's experience as the norm when examining and talking about women's lives. When we want to know about women's lives that differ from that norm, we generally have explored the global experience (Gross, 1987), despite the tremendous number of texts both by and about women of color in the United States across disciplines (Collins, 1998).

Curiously, when we deal with cultures of other nations, we seem to grasp that before we can have a proper understanding of the women in these cultures, we must adopt a multicultural perspective. It seems less apparent to us that to understand the lives of women in the United States, a cross-ethnic, multiethnic perspective that takes into account the effects of the structures and representations of racism, classism, ethnocentrism, sexism, and heterosexism on the goals and life experiences of women is necessary. Such a perspective is based on the recognition of the interconnections of various aspects of human identity and the consequent interconnectedness among structures hostile to those identities. This chapter provides an approach for studying women of color in the United States that is rooted in the exploration of connections that reveal the dynamics of similarity or sameness and dissimilarity or difference.

To talk about, study, and analyze racism is often a very frustrating endeavor. On one end of the spectrum, many scholars argue that racism is a thing of the past and that we need to move on to class analyses and return with more vigor to gender analyses or to analyses of other forms of difference through which power is negotiated. Other people who share this perspective also question the wisdom of examining the United States as a multicultural society, determining that such an examination invites a division. On the other end, many people argue that while race is indeed a social construction, both *institutional racism* (racism that is integral to our various structures of human social, political, cultural, and economic organization) and *individual racism* (racism that is manifested in individual behavior and supported by racist beliefs) shape the existence and actions of all people in the United States. While references to these various positions are too numerous and various to list here, Michael Omi and Howard Winant (1994) in *Racial Formation in the United States* provide an excellent grounding for understanding the origins and the evolution of these positions.

Examples are provided throughout the chapter to keep the theory from seeming abstract and unrelated to people involved in the teaching process—the student and the teacher. Although the chapter does not include suggested activities for kindergarten and grades 1 through 12, it does provide information and a conceptual framework, the appropriate starting points for such activities. The appendix of this book includes bibliographic resources for content about the lives of women of color. These resources also provide a starting point. Much work has yet to be done to make this information available to most teachers.

IDENTITY, KNOWLEDGE, AND EXPERIENCE

Paula Moya (2000), in *Realist Theory and the Predicament of the Postmodern*, expresses succinctly the predicament we find ourselves in today regarding identity:

> "Identity" remains one of the most urgent—as well as hotly disputed—topics in literary and cultural studies. For nearly two decades, it has been a central focus of debate for psychoanalytic, poststructuralist, and cultural materialist criticism in areas ranging from postcolonial and ethnic studies to feminism and queer theory. Oddly enough, much of what has been written about identity during this period seeks to delegitimate, and in some cases eliminate, the concept itself by revealing its ontological, epistemological, and political limitations. Activists and academics alike have . . . conclud[ed] that (social or cultural) identity, as a basis for political action, is theoretically incoherent and politically pernicious. (pp. 1–2)
>
> The first problem with essentialist conceptions of identity, according to critics, is the tendency to posit one aspect of identity (say, gender) as the sole cause or determinant constituting the social meanings of an individual's experience. The difficulty, critics of identity point out, is that identities are constituted differently in different historical contexts. . . . They remind us that insofar as every woman differs from every other woman in more or less significant ways, it is impossible to determine the (racial, class, cultural, etc.) identity of the "authentic woman" and thus to unify different women under the signifier "woman." (p. 3)

Simon Woolley, a British activist and head of Operation Black Vote, commented during a 2003 luncheon discussion about identity at the London U.S. Embassy that such an approach to identity obscured its salience and made it "impossible to move from A to B" in bringing people together in coalition. The very term *women of color* derives from and points to the possibility of coalition, of cultural and aesthetic expression, social and political action based on shared experience and shared values. It is important to clarify, then, the approach to identity in this chapter, for simply invoking the term *women of color* may to some appear, at first glance, reductionist or essentialist, that is, characterizing women and women of color as one-dimensional or monologic.

Identities are not fixed essences. One is not a woman or a man, or a Latina or a Baptist, in a unified, homogeneous way that does not change over time. Rather, identities matter enormously, reflecting and revealing knowledge about the world. As Hames-García demonstrates (2000), identity is multiple, that is:

> Memberships in various social groups combine with and mutually constitute one another. Membership in one group (e.g., "femaleness") thus means something different in the context of some simultaneous group memberships (e.g., "blackness") than in others (e.g., "motherhood"). The totality of these relations in their mutual constitution comprises the self. One important consequence of this fact is that one cannot understand a self as the sum of so many discrete parts, that is femaleness + blackness + motherhood. The whole self is constituted by the mutual interaction and relation of its parts to one another. Politically salient aspects of the self, such as race, ethnicity, sexuality, gender and class, link and imbricate themselves in fundamental ways. (p. 103)

This chapter is intended to show how teaching about women of color can transform our understanding of how identity functions in experience and in producing knowledge. Women of color reflect most directly the multiplicity Hames-García describes and therefore, in their individual and collective complex experiences, can shed light on concepts key to a curriculum that not only recognizes sociocultural diversity but also engages, produces knowledge about, and learns from that diversity in ways that certainly move us from A to B.

WHY WOMEN OF COLOR?

The term *women of color* came into use gradually during the 1970s. It immediately brings to mind differences of race and culture. It also makes clear that African American women are not the only women of color in a nation where the Black racial experience historically and legally operates both to define and to obscure racial dynamics between Whites and other racialized ethnic groups (see, for example, Brodkin, 1998). Moreover, in a democratically structured society with a great power imbalance signified by race and class privilege, labels representative of reality for people outside the realm of power are difficult to determine. The form of that power is both cultural and political and consequently further complicates labeling. Selecting the phrase *women of color* by many women of U.S. ethnic groups of color is part of their struggle to be recognized with dignity for their humanity, racial heritage, and cultural heritage as they work within the women's movement of the United States. The effort of women of color to name themselves is similar to attempts by African Americans and other ethnic groups to define with dignity their race and ethnicity and to counter the many stereotypical names bestowed on them. Because we tend to use the word *women* to be all-inclusive and general, we usually obscure both the differences and the similarities among women.

With the decline of the civil rights movement of the 1960s, the women's movement in the second half of the twentieth century got under way. Not long after, African American women began to articulate the differences they experienced as African American women, not only because of the racism within the women's movement or the sexism within the African American community, but also because of their vastly differing historical reality. One major question posed by Toni Cade Bambara's (1970) pioneering anthology, *The Black Woman*, remains applicable: How relevant are the truths, the experiences, the findings of White women to Black women? Are women after all, simply women? Bambara answers the question then as it might still be answered today:

> I don't know that our priorities are the same, that our
> concerns and methods are the same, or even similar enough so
> that we can afford to depend on this new field of experts (White,
> female). It is rather obvious that we do not. It is obvious that we
> are turning to each other. (p. 9)

This anthology served as a turning point in the experience of the African American woman.

Previously, White males, for the most part, had interpreted her realities, her activities, and her contributions. *The Negro Family: The Case for National Action* (1965), whose primary author was Daniel Patrick Moynihan, was the most notable example of this scholarship. It was widely publicized and well received by most U.S. readers. Blaming African American social and economic problems on the Black family, Moynihan argued that Black families, dominated by women, are generally pathological and pathogenic. His scholarship directly opposed the scholarship of Billingsley and others, which demonstrates the organizational differences between Black and White family units, the existence of a vital African American culture on which to base solutions to the problems, and the effects of racism, sexism, classism, and ethnocentrism in shaping the Black reality and government policy and societal attitudes toward that reality (Billingsley, 1968; Ladner, 1973; McAdoo, 1981; Moynihan, 1965). Bambara's (1970) anthology responded directly to such attacks and resulting policy, calling for Black women's direct involvement in both defining the problems and fashioning the solutions.

Although we are beyond the point of the complete invisibility and complete distortion of women of color in the academic branch of the women's movement (women's studies), African American women must still demand to be heard, must insist on being dealt with from the perspective of the experiences of women of color, just as they did in 1970, as the blurb on the paperback edition of *The Black Woman* (Bambara, 1970) implies: "Black Women Speak Out. A Brilliant and Challenging Assembly of Voices That Demand to Be Heard." By the latter part of the 1970s, the logic of a dialogue among women of color became a matter of course. We find, as in Bambara's *The Black Woman*, Black women speaking to one another in publications such as *Conditions, Five: The Black Women's Issue* (1979), and women of color speaking in the pioneering *This Bridge Called My Back: Writings by Radical Women of Color* (Moraga & Anzaldúa, 1981). The academic community began to recognize U.S. women of color who identify with the Third World, both for ancestral heritage and for related conditions of colonization; in 1980, for example, we saw the publication of Dexter Fisher's (1980) anthology *The Third Woman: Minority Women Writers of the United States,* another milestone giving greater access to the voices of U.S. women of color. Unfortunately, this dialogue has waned considerably due to the postmodern critiques of identity, discussed above, and to the political fragility of coalition that is constantly undermined by racism. Late twentieth- and early twenty-first-century interest in mixed-race identity, the work of Gloria Anzaldúa and her colleagues in *Borderlands/La Frontera* (Anzaldúa, 1987) and *The Bridge We Call Home: Radical Visions of Transformation* (Anzaldúa & Keating, 2003) and the anthology *The Woman That I Am: The Literature and Culture of Contemporary Women of Color* (Madison, 1994) are keeping the dialogue alive.

The most familiar ethnic groups of color are the Asian Americans, African Americans, Hispanic Americans, and Native Americans. Yet within each group there are cultural, class, and racial distinctions. These ethnic groups can be further delineated: Asian Americans consist of Chinese Americans, Japanese Americans, Filipino Americans, Korean Americans, and the more recent immigrants from Southeast Asia. African Americans consist of the U.S. African American and the West Indian or African Caribbean immigrants. The number of African immigrants is most likely too small and diverse to consider as a group; however, their presence should be acknowledged. Hispanic Americans, or Latino Americans as some people prefer, are largely Puerto Rican, Chicano, and Cuban. The Native American is made up of many nations, such as Sioux, Apache, Navajo, and Creek.

The phrase *women of color* helps women of all these groups acknowledge both their individual ethnicity and their racial solidarity as members of groups that are racial minorities in the United States, as well as a majority as people of color in the world. The concept also acknowledges similarity in historical experiences and position in relation to the White American. In addition, the use of the phrase and the concept *women of color* implies the existence of the race and ethnicity of White women, for whom the word *women* most often is used to indicate an assumed norm for all women or to exclude other women.

WHAT WE LEARN FROM STUDYING WOMEN OF COLOR

When we study women of color, we raise our awareness and understanding of the experiences of all women either implicitly or directly. Quite significantly, because of the imbalanced power relationship between White women and women of color, information about one group tends to make more apparent the experiences of the other group. It is well known, for example, that ideals of beauty in the United States are based on the blond, blue-eyed model. Dialogue about the reactions to that model in the experience of women of color, both within their ethnic groups and as they relate to White women, ultimately reveals that White women often judge themselves by that model of beauty. White women also serve simultaneously as reminders or representatives of that ideal to women of color and, most frequently, to themselves as failures to meet the ideal.

Another way of stating this is that a way of understanding an oppressor is to study the oppressed. Thus, we come to another level of awareness and understanding when we study women of color. We see clearly that White women function both as women who share certain similar experiences with women of color and as oppressors of women of color. This is one of the most difficult realities to cope with and still maintain productive, generative dialogue among women while teaching and conducting scholarship. White women who justifiably see themselves as oppressed by White men find it difficult to separate themselves from the effects of and power shared with White men. White women share with White men an ethnicity, an ancestral heritage, racial dominance, and certain powers and privileges by virtue of class, race, and ethnicity, by race and ethnicity if not class, and always by virtue of White skin privilege (Brodkin, 1998; Frye, 1983; Lipsitz, 1998; McIntosh, 1987; Roediger, 1991, 1994).

The growing scholarship on women of color gives us much to teach about women's lives, their joys and celebrations, and their oppressions. I cannot begin to relate the content you must deal with in order to know women's lives. However, the books in the appendix can provide a beginning guide for you to become familiar with the history and culture of women of color. When we study women of color, we raise our awareness and understanding of the experiences of all women either explicity or implicitly. Once we realize that all women are not White, and once we understand the implications of this realization, we see immediately the importance of race, ethnicity, and class when considering gender. Interestingly, much scholarship that intends to illustrate and analyze class dynamics is blind to racial and ethnic dynamics. In similar fashion, much scholarship that illustrates and analyzes racial dynamics and class dynamics fails to see ethnic dynamics. Other scholarship gives short shrift to, or even ignores, class. We have begun to grapple with the connectedness of the four big isms— racism, sexism, classism, and ethnocentrism.

Much scholarship in women's studies, however, fails to work within the context of race, class, ethnicity, and gender and their related isms, which modulate each other to a greater or lesser extent. Elizabeth V. Spelman (1982) illustrates how the racist equating of Blackness with lustfulness in Western culture modulates sexism toward African American women. One resulting stereotype is that the African American woman has a bestial sexuality and, as such, deserves or expects to be raped. This racism is also modulated by an ethnocentrism that further devalues the African American woman, thereby justifying the sexism.

Classism may also modulate this sexism if the perpetrator is of a higher class status than are most African American women. However, if this cannot be claimed, then racism, ethnocentrism, or both may elevate the status of other people over the African American woman institutionally or socially. Nonetheless, each is operative to some degree. Lower-class Whites or Whites of the same economic class as African Americans can invoke skin privilege to differentiate within the class common denominator. The categories of race, class, ethnicity, and gender are connected and interrelated; likewise, their related isms and their correctives.

Attention to race makes us aware of the differing perspectives that women have about race and skin color—perceptions of what is beautiful, ugly, attractive, or repulsive, and what is ordinary or exotic, pure or evil, based on racist stereotypes, on the role that color plays in women's lives, and on the norms by which women judge themselves physically. Attention to race also brings us to a realization that White women, too, are members of a race with stereotypes about looks and behavior. Attention to race in women's lives, with the particular understanding that race has a function for White women as well, reveals the oppression of racism, from the point of view of both one who is oppressed and of one who oppresses or participates in oppression by virtue of privilege.

Attention to class reveals, among other things, that because of different historical experiences, class means different things to different groups. Not necessarily measured by financial status, neighborhood, and level of education, class status is frequently measured by various ways in which one approximates variations on the Anglo American norm of middle to upper class. Simultaneously, our society insists on formally measuring class status by economic means. The market/consumer representation of people in the United States drives goals and concepts of self-worth and continues today in variations on the themes of representations that gained currency during the 1980s, such as those in the television show *Dynasty* and the yuppie (young urban professionals) and buppie (Black urban professionals) popular culture images. Yet for the woman of color, as for the man of color, the dynamic of social class becoming a measure for success is particularly insidious, threatening to destroy the affirmation of ethnic strengths that may be closely related to a generative self-identity. For example, Chinese Americans who have reached a high education level may move from Chinatown in a conflicting effort to succeed and participate in U.S. society. Adherence to the Anglo-American norm dictates certain dress, foods, and lifestyle, as well as a sense of superiority of the Anglo values. Ties to family and friends may be questioned, and the very traditions and understandings that provided the source of strength for coping in the White world may be devalued and discarded rather than transformed and adapted to the U.S. context.

Ethnicity, as a category of analysis, reveals the cultural traditions, perspectives, values, and choices that shape women's lives and their position in society, ranging from hairstyles and jewelry adornment to modes of worship and ways of perceiving a divine force, from values to the perception of women's roles and men's roles. Ethnicity, our cultural and historical heritage, shapes our perception of race and racism, sex and sexism, class and classism.

The element of power or lack of power has a great deal to do with the benefits or deficits of race and ethnicity. Similar to the example regarding classism, the ethnic traditions, kinships, and values that are sustaining in the context of an ethnic group that is a minority—and thus powerless—may become deficits when interacting with the majority or dominant society. On the other hand, when one becomes secure in one's ethnic identity, deficits of powerlessness and the moves to various levels of success (access to limited power) can be negotiated through variations on those strengths. Kinship networks, for example, are of primary importance to people of color for cultural reasons and for survival. Women's friendships often have particular significance, specifically friendships of younger women with older women. The structure of the larger U.S. society does not make allowances for such friendships. Most of us do not live in extended families or in neighborhoods near relatives. Women of color frequently insist that they maintain such relationships over great distances. Time spent with family, especially extended family, must have priority at various times during the year, not just for tradition's sake but for maintaining a sense of rootedness, for a dose of shared wisdom, a balanced perspective of who you are, and often simply for that affirmation that Mama or Grandpa loves you. Ethnic identity provides a basis on which women of color celebrate who they are and where they come from in the awareness that they are not simply victims of ethnocentrism and other isms.

Ethnicity is important in women's lives. Most important, ethnicity reveals that besides the usually acknowledged European American ethnic groups, White Anglo-Saxon Protestants are an ethnic group. Even though it is an ethnicity that boasts a defining dominance that makes it unnecessary to name itself, it is an ethnicity. That it is an ethnicity to which many Whites have subscribed, rather than one to which they belong by lineage, is frequently cause for confusion. However, it is no less an ethnicity for this reason.

The presence of Anglo American ethnicity within the ethnicity of ethnic groups of color is often cause for confusion. Nonetheless, U.S. ethnic groups of color manifest ethnicities that constantly balance, integrate, and synthesize the Western European Anglo American with what has become, with syncretism over the years, Chinese American, Japanese American, African American, Chicano, Native American, and Puerto Rican American. In a similar fashion, the English who came here syncretized with the values that emanated from being on this continent and became English Americans. They maintained a position of power so that other Europeans who syncretized to their English or colonial American culture eventually resulted in their being called Americans. Ethnic consciousness, beginning in the 1970s and inspired by the Black Power movement, resulted in open celebration of various European heritages among the assimilated White Americans.

Religion is closely related to ethnicity. Its values are sometimes indistinguishable from ethnic values, and it defines women's experiences in similar ways. Ethnicity as a category of analysis reveals sources of identity and sources of sustenance and celebration as well as the cultural dynamics that shape women's experience. It makes apparent the necessity of viewing women pluralistically.

Once we view women pluralistically, gender roles begin to assume differing degrees of importance. By virtue of the modulation of the other categories, women may see gender, sexual identity, sexism, and homophobia to be of lesser or greater importance. Gender roles for women of color are more apparently designated, determined, or modulated by ethnicity, race, and sexism. Therefore, racism may assume primary importance as an oppressive force with which to reckon. The African American woman harassed in the workplace because she wears her hair in intricate braids and wears clothes associated with her African heritage receives harsh treatment because of racism, not sexism. Racism also caused African American women to be denied the right to vote after White women gained suffrage rights. Gender, sexual identity, and race become related targets for discrimination as a result of ethnic and/or religious values; an individual's conceptualization of gender roles may be in conflict with that of her racial/ethnic group. Thus, while key aspects of women's identities are connected and interrelated, they can be so in conflict as well as in harmony.

WOMEN OF COLOR: THE AGENT OF TRANSFORMATION

In dealing with the commonalities and differences among women (a necessity in teaching about women of color), I am reminded that the title of Paula Giddings's (1984) work on African American women is taken from Anna J. Cooper's observation: "When and where I enter, then and there the whole . . . race enters with me" (p. 82). Repeated in many forms by women of color, from the nineteenth-century struggle for the vote to present-day women's organizing, this truth ultimately contains the goal of transformation of the curriculum: a curriculum that reflects all of us, egalitarian, communal, nonhierarchical, and pluralistic. Women of color are inextricably related to men of color by virtue of ethnicity and traditions as well as by common conditions of oppression. Therefore, at minimum, their struggle against sexism and racism is waged simultaneously. The experiences and destinies of women and men of color are linked. This reality poses a special problem in the relationship between White women and women of color. Moreover, in emphasizing the commonalities of privilege between White men and women, the oppressive relationship between men of color and White men, women of color and White men, and men of color and White women—all implied in Anna J. Cooper's observation—the teaching about women of color provides the naturally pluralistic, multidimensional catalyst for transformation. As such, women of color are agents of transformation.

This section defines transformation and provides the theoretical framework for the pedagogy and methodology of transformation. The final section discusses aspects of the process of teaching about women of color, which, though closely related to the theoretical framework, manifest themselves in very concrete ways.

A review of feminist pedagogy over the past twenty years or so reveals a call for teaching from multifocal, multidimensional, multicultural, pluralistic, interdisciplinary perspectives. This call, largely consistent with the pedagogy and methodology implied thus far in this chapter, can be accomplished only through *transformation*. Although many theorists and teachers now see this point, the terminology has still to be corrected to illustrate the process. In fact, we often use the words *mainstreaming, balancing, integration,* and *transformation* interchangeably. Mainstreaming, balancing, and integration imply adding women to an established, accepted, and unchangeable body of knowledge. The experience of White, middle-class women has provided a norm in a way that White Anglo American male ethnicity provides a norm. All other women's experience is added to and measured by those racial, class, ethnic, and gender roles and experiences.

Transformation, which emphasizes the multiplicity of identity, allows us to see the many aspects of women's lives. Understanding the significance of naming the action of treating women's lives through a pluralistic process—transformation—leads naturally to a convergence between women's studies and ethnic studies. This convergence is necessary to give us the information that illuminates the function and content of race, class, and ethnicity in women's lives and in relation to gender. In similar fashion, treating the lives of people of color through a pluralistic process leads to the same convergence, illuminating the functions and content of race, class, and gender in relation to lives of ethnic Americans and in relation to ethnicity.

We still need to understand exactly what is meant by this pluralistic, multidimensional, interdisciplinary scholarship and pedagogy; much of the scholarship on, about, and even frequently by women of color renders them systematically invisible, erasing their experience or part of it. White, middle-class, male, and Anglo American are the imposed norms corresponding to race, class, gender, and ethnicity. In contrasting and comparing experiences of pioneers, White males and females when dealing with Native Americans, for example, often speak of "the male," "the female," and "the Indian." Somehow, those of a different ethnicity and race are assumed to be male. Therefore, both the female and the male Indian experiences are observed and distorted. They must be viewed both separately and together to get a more complete view, just as to have a more complete view of the pioneer experience, the White male and White female experiences must be studied both separately and together. Thus, even in our attempts to correct misinformation resulting from measurement by one norm, we can reinforce measurement by other norms if we do not see the interaction of the categories, the interaction of the isms, as explained in the previous section. This pluralistic process and eye are demanded in order to understand both the particulars and the generalities of people's lives.

Why is it so easy to impose these norms effectively to erase the experience of others? I do not think erasing these experiences is always intentional. I do, however, think that it results from the dominance of the Western cultural norms of individuality, singularity, rationality, masculinity, and Whiteness at the expense of the communal, the plural, the intuitive, the feminine, and people of color. A brief look at Elizabeth Spelman's (1982) seminal work, "Theories of Race and Gender: The Erasure of Black Women," explains the important aspects of how this erasure comes about. Then a consideration of the philosophical makeup of transformation tells us both how our thinking makes it happen and how we can think to prevent it from happening.

Spelman gives examples of erasure of the Black woman, similar to the examples provided in this chapter. She analyzes concepts that assume primacy of sexism over racism. Furthermore, she rejects the additive approach to analyzing sexism, an approach that assumes a sameness of women modeled on the White, middle-class, Anglo-oriented woman. Spelman shows that it is premature to argue that sexism and racism are either mutually exclusive, totally dependent on one another, or in a causal relationship with one another. She discusses how women differ by race, class, and culture or ethnicity. Most important, she demonstrates that Black does not simply indicate victim. Black signifies African diasporic cultural identity—in the United States, African American identity. She suggests, then, that we present women's studies in a way that makes it a given that women are diverse, that their diversity is apparent in their experiences with oppression and in their participation in U.S. culture. To teach about women in this manner, our process must not be additive, that is, integrating, mainstreaming, or balancing the curriculum. Rather, *transformation* is the process that leads to this goal.

Essentially, transformation is the process of revealing unity among human beings and the world, as well as revealing important differences. Transformation implies acknowledging and benefiting from the interaction among sameness and diversity, groups and individuals. The maxim on which transformation rests may be stated as an essential affirmation of the West African proverb, "I am because we are. We are because I am." The communality, the human unity implicit in the proverb, operates in African traditional (philosophical) thought in regard to human beings and to other categories of life—categories of knowledge and ways of thinking and being (Davidson, 1969; Mbiti, 1975). Traditional African thought is in opposition to the European, Western pivotal axiom, on which integration, balancing, and mainstreaming rest (as expressed through the White, middle-class, Anglo norm in the United States)—"I think; therefore, I am," as expressed by Descartes.

Traditional African thought is in tune with a pluralistic, multidimensional process; the European Western axiom with a monolithic, one-dimensional process. Stated succinctly as "I am we," the West African proverb provides the rationale for the interaction and modulation of the categories of race, class, gender, and ethnicity; for the interaction and modulation of their respective isms; for the interaction and modulation of the objective and subjective, the rational and the intuitive, the feminine and the masculine—all those things that we, as Westerners, see as either opposite or as standing rigidly alone. This view is the breakdown of what is called feminist pedagogy, or multifocal teaching, when the ends are the comprehension of and involvement with cultural, class, racial, and gender diversity toward not tolerance but rather an egalitarian world based on communal relationships within humanity. It also indicates the multiplicity and complexity of identity that evolves from dialogue among individuals and community, cultural, social, political, and economic institutions, as in the Hames-García reference above. Elsa Barkley Brown (1989) gives us an insightful and useful discussion of teaching African American women's history in a way consistent with transformation as described here. This way of teaching creates "a polyrhythmic, 'nonsymmetrical,' nonlinear structure in which individual and community are not competing entities" (p. 926).

To realize this transformation, we must redefine categories and displace criteria that have served as norms in order to bring about the life context (norms and values) as follows:

1. Nonhierarchical terms and contexts for human institutions, rituals, and action

2. A respect for the interaction and existence of both diversity and sameness (a removal of measurement by norms perpetuating otherness, silence, and erasure)

3. A balancing of and interaction between the individual and the group

4. A concept of humanity emanating from interdependence of human beings on one another and on the world environment, both natural and human-created

5. A concept of humanity emanating from a sense of self that is not totally abstract and totally individually defined (I think; therefore, I am), but that is both abstract and concrete, individually and communally defined (I am we; I am because we are; we are because I am).

Such a context applies to pedagogy and scholarship in the dissemination and ordering of knowledge in all disciplines and fields. Within this context (the context in which the world does operate and against which the Western individualistic, singular concept of humanity militates), it becomes possible for us to understand the popular music form rap as an Americanized, Westernized version of African praise singing, functioning, obviously, for decidedly different cultural and social reasons. It becomes possible to understand the syncretization of cultures that produced Haitian voudon, Cuban santería, and Brazilian candomblé from Catholicism and the religion of the Yoruba. It becomes possible to understand what is happening when a Japanese American student is finding it difficult to reconcile traditional Buddhist values with her American life. It becomes possible to understand that Maxine Hong Kingston's (1976) *Woman Warrior* is essentially about the struggle to syncretize Chinese ways within the United States, whose dominant culture devalues and coerces against syncretization, seeking to impose White, middle-class conformity.

Thinking in this manner is foreign to the mainstream of thought in the United States, although it is alive and well in Native American traditional philosophy, in Taoist philosophy, in African traditional philosophy, and in African American folklore. It is so foreign, in fact, that I realized that in order to bring about this context, we must commit certain so-called sins. The philosopher Elizabeth Minnich suggested that these sins might be more aptly characterized as heresies, because they are strongly at variance with established modes of thought and values (see, e.g., Minnich, 1990).

The following heresies challenge and ultimately displace the ways in which the Western mind orders the world (for related discussions, see Freire, 1969, 1973; Hord & Lee, 1995; Yancy, 1998; Young, 1990). These heresies emanate from the experiences of people of color, the nature of their oppression, and the way the world operates. Adopting them is a necessity for teaching about women of color. Using the heresies to teach women's studies, to teach about the lives of all women, becomes natural when we study women of color, and it leads to the transformation of the curriculum to a pluralistic, egalitarian, multidimensional curriculum.

- **Heresy #1** The goal of interaction among human beings, action, and ideas must be seen not only as synthesis but also as the identification of opposites and differences. These opposites and differences may or may not be resolved; they may function together by virtue of the similarities identified and the tensions they generate as they move ultimately toward resolution.

- **Heresy #2** We *can* address a multiplicity of concerns, approaches, and subjects without a neutral or dominant center. Reality reflects opposites as well as overlaps in what are perceived as opposites. There exist no pure, distinct opposites. Human experience has multiple, interconnected centerings.

- **Heresy #3** It is not reductive to look at gender, race, class, and culture as mutually interactive and related parts of a multiply consituted, complex whole. The more different voices we have, the closer we are to the whole.

- **Heresy #4** Transformation demands an understanding of ethnicity that takes into account the differing cultural continua (in the United States, Western European, Anglo American, African, Asian, Native American) and their similarities.

- **Heresy #5** Transformation demands a relinquishing of the primary definitiveness of gender, race, class or culture, and ethnicity as they interact with theory, methodology, pedagogy, institutionalization, and action, both in synthesis and in a dynamic that functions as opposite and same simultaneously. A variation on this heresy is that although all isms are not the same, they are connected and operate as such; likewise, their correctives.

- **Heresy #6** The Anglo-American, and ultimately the Western, norm must be seen as only one of many norms, and also as one that enjoys privilege and power that has colonized, and may continue to colonize, other norms.

- **Heresy #7** Feelings are direct lines to better thinking. The intuitive as well as the rational is part of the process of engaging experience and moving from the familiar to the unfamiliar in acquiring knowledge.

- **Heresy #8** Knowledge is identity and identity is knowledge. All knowledge is explicitly and implicitly related to who we are, both as individuals and as groups. (For an extended discussion of this point, see Mohanty, 2000)

Engaging transformation through these eight heresies means addressing the connections among human beings, among human beings and the environment, and among experiences, categories of identity. It means using the intuitive and the cognitive, displacing dominating norms, exploring the comparative and relational aspects of various norms as well as the conflictual aspects, and acknowledging the power of knowledge to define self, others, and experience. Transformation, then, provides the basis of a pedagogy that stems from teaching about the experience of women of color in a way that engages both how women of color are constructed as subject and an implicit understanding of how the student is constructed as subject.

Such an approach may prove helpful in teaching other content to today's postmodern youth, whom Henry Giroux (1994) describes as "border youth," that is, youth for whom "plurality and contingency—whether mediated through the media or through the dislocations spurned by the economic system, the rise of new social movements or the crisis of representation—have resulted in a world with few secure psychological, economic, or intellectual markers. . . . [They] increasingly inhabit shifting cultural and social spheres marked by a plurality of languages and cultures" (p. 355). As stated at the beginning of this chapter, the content, context of, and pedagogy for teaching about women of color in the United States is part of the needed dialogue between modernism and postmodernism. The fragmentation and dislocation of women of color in relation to what and how we teach frequently reflect and refract the objectification of the student when we teach as if we are filling empty repositories, fulfilling Freire's (1969) banking concept.

As the agent of transformation, women of color as subject content in the humanities and social sciences provide an excellent point for engaging our modern/postmodern conflict. It also provides a philosophical perspective, transformation, for a generative pedagogy that fosters students as subjects, generates knowledge and understanding through building on the interconnections among student, teacher, and content, and engages the conflictive from the strength of the multiply-centered, relational context.

TEACHING ABOUT WOMEN OF COLOR

The first six heresies cited above essentially address content and methodology for gathering and interpreting content. They inform decisions such as the following:

1. Not teaching Linda Brent's *Incidents in the Life of a Slave Girl* (1861/1973) as the single example of the slave experience of African American women in the nineteenth century, but rather presenting it as a representative example of the slave experience of African American women that occurs within a contradictory, paradoxical world that had free Black women such as Charlotte Forten Grimke and African American abolitionist women such as Sojourner Truth. The picture of Black women that emerges then becomes one that illuminates their complexity of experiences and their differing interactions with White people rather than an aberrant or unidimensional experience.

2. Not simply teaching about pioneer women in the West, but teaching about Native American women, perhaps through their stories, which they have passed on to their children and their children's children, using the word to advance those concepts crucial to cultural survival. The picture of settling the West becomes more balanced, suggesting clearly to students the different perspectives and power relationships. The Native American becomes a subject—one who acts and interacts—rather than an object of Whites, portrayed as the only subjects.

3. Not choosing a single biography each for children to read of a White woman, an Asian American woman, and an African American woman, but rather finding ways through biography, poetry, and storytelling to introduce children to different women's experiences—different according to race, class, ethnicity, and gender roles and sexual identity—as well as ways to discuss women's lives comparatively.

The last two heresies directly address process. After accurate content, process is the most important part of teaching. Students who learn in an environment that is sensitive to their feelings and that supports and encourages the pursuit of knowledge will consistently meet new knowledge and new situations with the necessary openness and understanding for human development and progress. If this sounds moralistic, we must remember that the stated and implied goal of critical pedagogy and feminist pedagogy, as well as of efforts to transform the curriculum with content about women and ethnicity, is to provide an education that more accurately reflects the history and composition of the world, that demonstrates the relationship of what we learn to how we live, and that implicitly and explicitly reveals the relationship between knowledge and social action. Process is most important, then, in helping students develop ways throughout their education to reach the closest approximation of truth toward the end of a better, more democratic human condition.

The key to understanding the teaching process in any classroom in which teaching about women of color from the perspective of transformation is a goal is recognizing that the content alters all students' perceptions of themselves. First, they begin to realize that we can never say *women* to mean all women, that we must particularize the word as appropriate to context and understanding (for example, White, middle-class women; Chinese American, lower-class women; Mexican American, middle-class women). Second, students begin to understand that using White, middle-class women as the norm will seem distortingly reductive. White women's ethnic, regional, class, and gender commonalities and differences soon become apparent, and the role in oppression of the imposed Anglo-American ethnic conformity stands out. Third, students begin to see that experience shapes identity and that identity shapes experience (Hames-García 2000; Mohanty, 2000).

Student reactions may range from surprise, to excitement about learning more, to hostility and anger. In *Gendered Subjects*, Margo Culley (1985) details much of what happens. Her opening paragraph summarizes her main thesis:

> Teaching about gender and race can create classrooms that are charged arenas. Students enter these classrooms imbued with the values of the dominant culture: they believe that success in conventional terms is largely a matter of will and that those who do not have it all have experienced a failure of will. Closer and closer ties between corporate America and higher education, as well as the "upscaling" of the student body, make it even harder to hear the voices from the margin within the academy. Bringing those voices to the center of the classroom means disorganizing ideology and disorienting individuals. Sometimes, as suddenly as the fragments in a kaleidoscope rearrange to totally change the picture, our work alters the ground of being for our students (and perhaps even for ourselves). When this happens, classrooms can become explosive, but potentially transformative arenas of dialogue. (p. 209)

Even though Culley's observation is almost 20 years old, reports from graduate students and faculty in various workshops I conduct nationwide suggest that it still holds.

"Altering the ground of being" happens to some extent on all levels. The White girl kindergarten pupil's sense of the world is frequently challenged when she discovers that heroines do not necessarily look like her. Awareness of the ways in which the world around children is ordered occurs earlier than most of us may imagine. My niece, barely four years old, told my father in a definitive tone as we entered a church farther from her home than the church to which she belongs, "Gramps, this is the Black church." We had not referred to the church as such, yet clearly that Catholic congregation was predominantly Black and the girl's home congregation predominantly White. Her younger sister, at age three, told her mother that the kids in the day school she attended were "not like me." She then pointed to the brown back of her hand. Young children notice difference. We direct what they do with and think of that difference.

Teaching young children about women of color gives male and female children of all backgrounds a sense of the diversity of people, of the various roles in which women function in U.S. culture, of the various joys and sorrows, triumphs and struggles they encounter. Seeds of awareness of the power relationships between male and female, among racial, ethnic, and class groups are sown and nurtured.

Teaching about women of color early in students' academic experience allows the voices of the margin to be heard and to become a part of the matrix of reality. Teaching about women of color reveals race, ethnicity, gender, and class as essential components of human identity and also questions ideology and ways of being. It encourages an openness to understanding, to difference and similarity, and to the foreign and the commonplace necessary to the mind-set of curiosity about and fascination for knowledge that we all want to inspire in our students no matter what the subject. Moreover, it highlights connections among human beings and human experiences and reveals relationships among actions.

Culley (1985) also observes that "anger is the energy mediating the transformation from damage to wholeness," the damage being the values and perspectives of the dominant culture that have shaped opinions based on a seriously flawed and skewed American history and interpretation of the present (p. 212). Certain reactions occur and are part of the process of teaching about women of color. Because they can occur at all levels to a greater or lesser extent, it is useful to look for variations on their themes.

It is important to recognize that these reactions occur within the context of student and teacher expectations. Students are concerned about grading; teachers, about evaluations by superiors and students. Frequently, fear of, disdain for, or hesitancy about feminist perspectives by some students may create a tense, hostile atmosphere. Similarly, fear of, disdain for, or hesitancy about studying people different from you (particularly by the White student) or people similar to you (particularly by the student of color or of a culture related to people of color) may also create a tense, hostile atmosphere. Student expectations of teachers, expectations modulated by the ethnicity, race, class, and gender of the teacher, may encourage students to presume that a teacher will take a certain position. The teacher's need to inspire students to perform with excellence may become a teacher's priority at the expense of presenting material that may at first confuse the students or challenge their opinions. It is important to treat these reactions as though they are as much a part of the process of teaching as are the form of presentation, the exams, and the content, for, indeed, they are. Moreover, they can affect the success of the teaching of the material about women of color.

Specifically, these reactions are part of the overall process of moving from the familiar to the unfamiliar. As Heresy #7 guides us, "Feelings are direct lines to better thinking." Affective reactions to content, such as anger, guilt, and feelings of displacement, when recognized for what they are, lead to the desired cognitive reaction—the conceptualization of the facts so that knowledge becomes useful as the closest approximation to the truth. As Japanese American female students first read accounts by Issei (first-generation) women about their picture-bride experiences, the students' reactions might at first be mixed. Raising the issue of Japanese immigration to the United States during the late nineteenth century may not only challenge the exotic stereotype of the Japanese woman, but it may also engender anger toward Japanese males because of students' incomplete access to history. White students may respond with guilt or indifference because of the policy of a government whose composition is essentially White and Anglo-oriented and with which they identify. Japanese American male students may become defensive, desirous of hearing Japanese American men's stories about picture-bride marriages. African American male and female students may draw analogies between the Japanese American experience and the African American experience. Such analogies may be welcomed or resented by other students. Of course, students from varied backgrounds may respond to learning about Issei women with a reinforced or instilled pride in Japanese ancestry or with a newfound interest in immigration history.

Teacher presentation of Issei women's experience as picture brides should include, of course, lectures, readings, films, and videos about the experience of male Issei immigrants to the United States during the first quarter of the twentieth century—the cheap labor they provided, the impossibility of return to Japan due to low wages, the male–female ratio of Japanese Americans at the turn of the century, and the tradition of arranged marriage in Japan. Presentations should also anticipate, however, student reaction based on their generally ill-informed or limited knowledge about the subject. Discussion and analysis of the students' initial perspectives on Issei women, of how those perspectives have changed given the historical, cultural, and sociological information, allow for learning about and reading Issei women's accounts to become an occasion, then, for expressing feelings of guilt, shame, anger, pride, interest, and curiosity, and for getting at the reasons for those feelings.

Understanding those feelings and working with them to move the student from a familiar that may be composed of damaging misinformation and even bigotry to a balanced understanding sometimes becomes a major portion of the content, especially when anger or guilt is directed toward a specific group—other students, the teacher, or perhaps even the self. Then it becomes necessary for the teacher to use what I call pressure-release sessions. The need for such sessions may manifest itself in many ways. For example,

> the fear of being regarded by peers or by the professor as racist, sexist or "politically incorrect" can polarize a classroom. If the [teacher] participates unconsciously in this fear and emotional self-protection, the classroom experience will degenerate to hopeless polarization, and even overt hostility. He or she must constantly stand outside the classroom experience and anticipate such dynamics. . . . "Pressure release" discussions work best when the teacher directly acknowledges and calls attention to the tension in

the classroom. The teacher may initiate the discussion or allow it
to come about in whatever way he or she feels most comfortable.
(Butler, 1985, p. 236)

The hostility, fear, and hesitancy "can be converted to fertile ground for profound academic
experiences . . . 'profound' because the students' knowledge is challenged, expanded, or reinforced" by a subject matter that is simultaneously affective and cognitive, resonant with the
humanness of life in both form and content (Butler, 1985, p. 236). Students learn from these
pressure-release sessions, as they must learn in life to achieve balance and harmony in whatever pursuits, that paradoxes and contradictions are sometimes resolved and sometimes stand
separately yet function together (recall Heresy #1).

Teaching about women of color can often spark resistance to the teacher or cause students to question subject veracity. For example, students usually are taught that the latter
part of the nineteenth century and the turn of the twentieth century was a time of expansion for the United States—the Progressive Era. Learning of the experiences of Native
American and Mexican women who were subjected to particular horrors as the United States
pushed westward, or reading about restrictions on Chinese immigrant women who were not
allowed to enter the United States with the Chinese men who provided what was tantamount
to slave labor for the building of the railroads, students begin to realize that this time was
anything but progressive or expansive.

Teaching about Ida Wells-Barnett, the African American woman who waged the anti-
lynching campaigns at the end of the nineteenth century and well into the twentieth century,
also belies the progress of that time. Ida Wells-Barnett brings to the fore the horror of lynch-
ings of African American men, women, and children; the inhuman practice of castration that
was part of the lynching of Black males; the stereotyped ideas of African American men and
women, ideas that were, as Giddings (1984) reminds us, "older than the Republic itself—for
they were rooted in the European minds that shaped America" (p. 31). Furthermore, Wells-
Barnett's life work reveals the racism of White women in the suffragist movement of the
early twentieth century, a reflection of the racism in that movement's nineteenth-century
manifestation.

The ever-present interaction of racism and sexism, the stereotyping of African American
men and women as bestial, the unfounded labeling of African American men as rapists in
search of White women, and the horrid participation in all of this by White men and women
in all stations of life make for difficult history for any teacher to teach and for any student
to study. The threat to the perfect founding fathers and Miss Liberty versions are apparent.
Such content is often resisted by African American and White students alike, perhaps for
different reasons, including rage, anger, or shame that such atrocities were endured by people like them; indifference in the face of reality because "nothing like that will happen again;"
and anger, guilt, or shame that people of their race were responsible for such hideous
atrocities. Furthermore, all students may resent the upsetting of their neatly packaged understandings of U.S. history and of their world.

The teacher must know the content and be willing to facilitate the pressure-release sessions that undoubtedly will be needed. Pressure-release sessions should help students sort
out facts from feelings and, most of all, must clarify the relevance of the material to understanding the world in which we live and to preventing such atrocities from recurring. Also,

in teaching about the Issei women and about the life of Ida Wells-Barnett, teachers must never let the class lose sight of the vision these women had, how they dealt with joy and sorrow, the triumphs and struggles of their lives, the contributions to both their own people and to U.S. life at large. It is most important, also, to remind students of the contributions of many Whites such as John Brown, the militant, hanged abolitionist; or Viola Liuzzo, the murdered Italian American civil rights worker; or the persistent civil rights lawyer Morris Dees. The possibility of coalition among people from different, and even conflicting experiences, should always be modeled as we examine the often brutal failures of humanity.

In addition to variations on anger, guilt, and challenges to credibility in learning about women of color, students become more aware of the positive aspects of race and ethnicity and frequently begin to take pride in their identities. As Heresy #8 states, "Knowledge is identity and identity is knowledge. All knowledge is explicitly and implicitly related to who we are, both as individuals and as groups." The teacher, however, must watch for overzealous pride as well as for unadmitted uneasiness with one's ethnic or racial identity. White students, in particular, may react in a generally unexpected manner. Some may predictably claim their Irish ancestry; others may be confused as to their ethnicity, for they may come from German and Scottish ancestry, which early on assumed Anglo American identity. Students of Anglo-American ancestry, however, may hesitate to embrace that terminology, for it might suggest to them, in the context of the experiences of women and men of color, an abuse of power and "all things horrible in this country," as one upset student once complained to me. Here, teachers must be adept not only at conveying facts but also at explaining the effects of culture, race, gender, and ethnicity in recording and interpreting historical facts. Teachers also must be able to convey to students both the beautiful and the ugly in all of us. Thus, the African American teacher may find himself or herself explaining the cultural value of Anglo-American or Yankee humor, of Yankee precision in gardening, of Yankee thriftiness, of the conflicting values of the founding fathers, and how we all share, in some way, that heritage. At whatever age this occurs, students must be helped to understand the dichotomous, hierarchical past of that identity and to move toward expressing their awareness in a pluralistic context.

Now that we have explored the why of the phrase *women of color*, identified the essence of what we learn when we study women of color, discussed the theory of transformation and its heresies, and identified and discussed the most frequent reactions of students to the subject matter, in conclusion we focus on the teacher.

CONCLUSION

Teaching about women of color should result in conveying information about a group of people largely invisible in our curricula in a way that encourages students to seek further knowledge and ultimately to begin to correct and reorder the flawed perception of the world based on racism, sexism, classism, and ethnocentrism. To do so is no mean feat. Redefining one's world involves not only the inclusion of previously ignored content but also the revision, deletion, and correction of accepted content in light of missing and ignored content. As such, it might require a redesignation of historical periods, a renaming of literary periods, and a complete reworking of sociological methodology to reflect the ethnic and cultural standards at work. Fundamentally, it demands a rethinking about and a reclaiming of identity and its multiple, complex, and vital role in theorizing about the world and in the development of knowledge.

This chapter, then, is essentially an introduction to the journey that teachers must embark on to begin providing for students a curriculum that reflects the reality of the past, prepares students to deal with and understand the present, and creates the basis for a more humane, productive, caring future. The implications of teaching about women of color are far-reaching, involving many people in many different capacities. New texts need to be written for college-level students. Teacher education must be restructured to include not only the transformed content but also the pedagogy that reflects how our nation and the world are multicultural, multiethnic, multiracial, multifocal, and multidimensional. College texts, children's books, and other materials need to be devised to help teach this curriculum. School administrators, school boards, parents, and teachers need to participate in and contribute to this transformation in all ways that influence what our children learn.

For teachers and those studying to be teachers, the immediate implications of a transformed curriculum can seem overwhelming, for transformation is a process that will take longer than our lifetimes. Presently, we are in the formative stages of understanding what must be done to correct the damage in order to lead to wholeness. I suggest that we begin small. That is, decide to include women of color in your classes this year. Begin adding some aspect of that topic to every unit. Pay close attention to how that addition relates to what you already teach. Does it expand the topic? Does it present material you already cover within that expansion? Can you delete some accepted, repetitive material and still meet your objectives? Does the new material conflict with the old? How? Is that conflict a valuable learning resource for your students? Answering such questions will move you quickly from simply adding to revisioning and transforming. Continue to do this each year. Gradually, other central topics will emerge about men of color, White men, White women, class, race, ethnicity, and gender. By beginning with studying women of color, the curriculum then will have evolved to be truly pluralistic.

This chapter pays the most attention to the student. The teacher, who embarks on this long journey, must be determined to succeed. Why? Because all the conflicting emotions, the sometimes painful movement from the familiar to the unfamiliar, are experienced by the teacher as well. We have been shaped by the same damaging, ill-informed view of the world as our students have. Often, as we try to resolve their conflicts, we are simultaneously working through our own. Above all, we must demand honesty of ourselves before we can succeed.

Another important task of the teacher is changing how, in our attempts to change the construction of the student as object, a receptacle of information, we have constructed the student as a distant, theoretical, abstract subject. John Shilb (1992) cogently describes what it means to change how we construct the student as subject:

> Changing how the student is constructed as subject entails a number of related teaching practices. It means considering how social differences can affect the interests, backgrounds, learning styles, and degrees of confidence that students bring to the classroom. It means examining how authority operates there as well as in the larger society, analyzing how traditional power relations might be rethought or merely reinforced when teachers

and students meet. It means taking students' accounts of their own experiences as at least potentially legitimate avenues to knowledge. It means recognizing that learning can involve intuition and emotion, not just cold, hard logic. Overall, it means taking as a central classroom aim the empowerment of students as conscious, active subjects in the learning process, thereby enhancing their capacity to develop a more democratic world. (p. 65)

The difficulty of the process of transformation is one factor contributing to the maintenance of the status quo.

Often, we look for the easiest way out. It is easier to work with students who are not puzzled, concerned, or bothered by what they are studying. We, as teachers, must be willing to admit that we do not know everything but that we do know how to go about learning in a way that reaches the closest approximation of the truth. Our reach must always exceed our grasp, and, in doing so, we will encourage the excellence, the passion, the curiosity, the respect, and the love needed to create superb scholarship and encourage thinking, open-minded, caring, knowledgeable students.

Questions and Activities

1. When Butler uses the phrase *women of color,* to what specific ethnic groups is she referring? Why did this phrase emerge, and what purpose does it serve?

2. How can a study of women of color help broaden our understanding of White women? Of women in general?

3. In what ways, according to Butler, is ethnicity an important variable in women's lives? Give specific examples from this chapter to support your response.

4. How does racism, combined with sexism, influence the ways in which people view and respond to women of color?

5. What does the author mean by *transformation* and a *transformed curriculum?* How does a transformed curriculum differ from a mainstream or balanced curriculum?

6. How can content about women of color serve as a vehicle for transforming the school curriculum?

7. The author lists eight heresies, or assumptions, about reality that differ fundamentally from dominant modes of thought and values. Why does she believe these heresies are essential when teaching about women of color?

8. The author states that teaching about women of color may spark resistance to the teacher, the subject, or both. What examples of content does she describe that may evoke student resistance? Why, according to Butler, might students resist this content? What tips does she give teachers for handling student resistance?

9. Develop a teaching unit in which you incorporate content about women of color, using the transformation approach described in this chapter. Useful references on women of color are found in the Appendix ("Gender" section).

References

Anzaldúa, G. E. (1987). *Borderlands/La Frontera*. San Francisco: Spinsters, Aunt Lute.

Anzaldúa, G. E., & Keating, A. (Eds.). (2002). *The Bridge We Call Home: Radical Visions of Transformation*. New York: Routledge.

Bambara, T. C. (Ed.). (1970). *The Black Woman: An Anthology*. New York: New American Library.

Billinglsey, A. (1968). *Black Families in White America*. Englewood Cliffs, NJ: Prentice-Hall.

Brent, L. (1861/1973). *Incidents in the Life of a Slave Girl* (L. M. Child, Ed.). New York: Harcourt.

Brodkin, K. (1998). *How Jews Became White Folks and What That Says about Race in America*. New Brunswick, NJ: Rutgers University Press.

Brown, E. B. (1989). African American Women's Quilting: A Framework for Conceptualizing and Teaching African American Women's History. *Signs: Journal of Women in Culture and Society, 14*(4), 921–929.

Butler, J. E. (1985). Toward a Pedagogy of Everywoman's Studies. In M. Culley & C. Portuges (Eds.), *Gendered Subjects: The Dynamics of Feminist Teaching* (pp. 230–239). Boston: Routledge & Kegan Paul.

Collins, P. H. (1998). *Fighting Words: Black Women and the Search for Justice*. Minneapolis: University of Minnesota Press.

Conditions, Five. (1979). The Black Woman's Issue, *2*(3).

Culley, M. (1985). Anger and Authority in the Introductory Women's Studies Classroom. In M. Culley & C. Portuges (Eds.), *Gendered Subjects: The Dynamics of Feminist Teaching* (pp. 209–217). Boston: Routledge & Kegan Paul.

Davidson, B. (1969). *The African Genius*. Boston: Little, Brown.

Fisher, D. (Ed.). (1980). *The Third Woman: Minority Women Writers of the United States*. Boston: Houghton Mifflin.

Freire, P. (1969). *Pedagogy of the Oppressed*. New York: Seabury.

Freire, P. (1973). *Education for Critical Consciousness*. New York: Seabury.

Frye, M. (1983). On Being White: Toward a Feminist Understanding of Race and Race Supremacy. In M. Frye (Ed.), *The Politics of Reality: Essays in Feminist Theory* (pp. 110–127). Trumansburg, NY: Crossing Press.

Giddings, P. (1984). *When and Where I Enter: The Impact of Black Women on Race and Sex in America*. New York: Morrow.

Giroux, H. (1994). Slacking Off: Border Youth and Postmodern Education. *Journal of Advanced Composition, 14*(2), 347–366.

Gross, S. H. (1987). Women's History for Global Learning. *Social Education, 51*(3), 194–198.

Hames-García, M. (2000). "Who Are Our Own People?" Challenges for a Theory of Identity. In P. Moya & M. Hames-García (Eds.), *Reclaiming Identity: Realist Theory and the Predicament of Postmodernism* (pp. 102–129). Berkeley: University of California Press.

Hord, F. L., & Lee, J. (1995). *I Am Because We Are: Readings in Black Philosophy*. Amherst: University of Massachusetts Press.

Kingston, M. H. (1976). *The Woman Warrior: Memories of a Girlhood among Ghosts*. New York: Random House.

Ladner, J. (Ed.). (1973). *The Death of White Sociology.* New York: Vintage.

Lipsitz, G. (1998). *The Possessive Investment in Whiteness: How White People Profit from Identity Politics.* Philadelphia: Temple University Press.

Madison, D. S. (1994). *The Woman That I Am: The Literature and Culture of Contemporary Women of Color.* New York: St. Martins Griffin.

Mbiti, J. (1975). *Introduction to African Religion.* London: Heinemann.

McAdoo, H. (Ed.). (1981). *Black Families.* Beverly Hills, CA: Sage.

McIntosh, P. (1987, June). *Understanding Correspondence between White Privilege and Male Privilege through Women's Studies Work.* Paper presented at the annual meeting of the National Women's Studies Association, Atlanta, GA.

Minnich, E. (1990). *Transforming Knowledge.* Philadelphia: Temple University Press.

Mohanty, S. P. (2000). The Epistemic Status of Cultural Identity: On *Beloved* and the Postcolonial Condition. In P. Moya and M. Hames-García (Eds.), *Reclaiming Identity: Realist Theory and the Predicament of Postmodernism* (pp. 29–66). Berkeley: University of California Press.

Moraga, C., & Anzaldúa, G. E. (Eds.). (1981). *This Bridge Called My Back: Writings by Radical Women of Color.* Watertown, MA: Persephone Press.

Moya, P. (2000). Introduction: Reclaiming Identity. In P. Moya & M. Hames-García (Eds.), Reclaiming Identity: *Realist Theory and the Predicament of Postmodernism* (pp. 1–26). Berkeley: University of California Press.

Moynihan, D. P. et. al., (1965). *The Negro Family, the Case for National Action.* Washington, D.C: U.S. Government Printing Office.

Omi, M., & Winant, H. (1994). *Racial Formation in the United States, from the 1960s to the 1990s* (2nd ed.). New York: Routledge.

Roediger, D. R. (1991). *The Wages of Whiteness: Race and the Making of the American Working-Class.* London: Verso.

Roediger, D. R. (1994). *Towards the Abolition of Whiteness: Essays on Race, Politics, and Working-Class History.* London: Verso.

Shilb, J. (1992). Poststructuralism, Politics, and the Subject of Pedagogy. In M. Kecht (Ed.), *Pedagogy Is Politics: Literary Theory and Critical Teaching* (pp. 62–85). Urbana: University of Illinois Press.

Spelman, E. V. (1982). Theories of Gender and Race: The Erasure of Black Women. *Quest: A Feminist Quarterly,* 5(4), 36–62.

Yancy, G. (Ed.). (1998). *African American Philosophers: 17 Conversations.* New York: Routledge.

Young, R. (1990). *White Mythologies: Writing History and the West.* New York: Routledge.

Because of the growing diversity in our nation's schools teachers need to develop the knowledge, attitudes, and skills needed to work effectively with students from diverse racial, ethnic, social-class, and language groups.

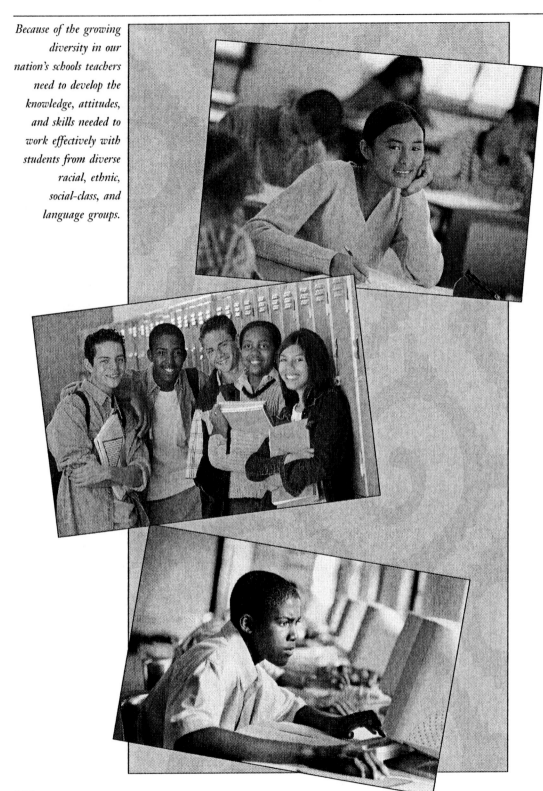

Race, Ethnicity, and Language

The drastic increase in the percentage of students of color and of language-minority students in the nation's schools is one of the most significant developments in education in the last several decades. The growth in the percentage of students of color and of language-minority students in the nation's schools results from several factors, including the new wave of immigration that began after 1968 and the aging of the White population. The nation's classrooms are experiencing the largest influx of immigrant students since the beginning of the 20th century. The United States receives nearly 1 million immigrants annually, most of whom come from nations in Asia and Latin America. However, the Immigration and Naturalization Service reported that in 2001, 16.5 percent of all legal immigrants came from Europe, many of them from nations in the Russian Federation. Between 1990 and 1996, nearly 1 million immigrants entered the United States each year. Another 3.3 million arrived between January of 2000 and March of 2002.

Demographers predict that if current trends continue, about 46 percent of the nation's school-age youths will be of color by the year 2020. In 2002, 40 percent of students in grades 1 to 12 in public schools were members of a minority group, an increase of 16 percentage points since 1976. They were a majority of the students in the state of California as well as in many major cities, such as Seattle, San Francisco, Chicago, and Washington, D.C. Another important characteristic of today's students is the large percentage who are poor and who live in female-headed households. Today, about one out of every five students lives in a poor family.

While the nation's students are becoming increasingly diverse, most of the nation's teachers remain White (87 percent), female (74 percent), and middle-class. The percentage of teachers of color remains low. In 2002, teachers of color made up only 13 percent of the nation's teachers. The growing racial, cultural, and income gap between teachers and students underscores the need for all teachers to develop the knowledge, attitudes, and skills needed to work effectively with students from diverse racial, ethnic, social-class, and language groups. The four chapters in this part of the book present concepts, knowledge, and strategies that all teachers will find helpful in working with students from diverse groups.

CHAPTER 9

Educational Equality
for Students of Color

Geneva Gay

Educational equality in the United States is popularly understood to mean the *physical access* of African Americans, Latinos, Asian Americans, and Native Americans to the same schools and instructional programs as middle-class European American students. The prevailing assumption is that when these groups become students in majority schools, equal educational opportunity is achieved. Until recently, little attention was given to the quality of the curriculum content and instructional processes as key factors in formulas for educational equity.

For people who accept a strictly *de jure*, or legal, conception of desegregation, the issue of educational inequality is largely resolved. After all, they argue, federal and state laws now exist prohibiting educational discrimination on the basis of race, color, creed, gender, nationality, and social class. For these people, the persisting discrepancies between the academic achievement, quality of school life, and other indicators of school success of students of color and European Americans are not a result of differences in educational opportunities at all. Rather, these problems are matters of personal abilities, aspirations, and responsibilities. Students of color and poverty do not do as well in school as their middle-class European American counterparts because of individual deficiencies, not because of discrepancies in opportunities perpetuated by schools that serve systematically to their detriment.

Legal mandates guaranteeing the accessibility of schooling to all students do not ensure quality unless the opportunities themselves are of equal status (Astin, 1985). And under no circumstances can identical educational opportunities for very diverse groups and individuals (whether that diversity stems from class, gender, race, ethnicity, nationality, or personal traits) constitute equality. Their diversity demands variability in treatment so that students in each group can have the best chances to perform at maximum capabilities. Thus, equality of educational opportunities should be understood to mean *equity, parity,* and *comparability* of instructional treatment based on diagnosed needs of diverse individuals and groups. How can this be accomplished? Should the *processes of schooling* be given much more attention in efforts to achieve educational equality for students of color? Or, as Grant and Sleeter (1985) might ask, what should happen "after the school bell rings" for students of color if

211

they are to receive educational equality? Answers to these questions are contingent on a clear understanding of the various inequalities that now exist. These issues and inequities and some possible solutions to them are discussed in the subsequent sections of this chapter.

EDUCATIONAL ATTAINMENT FOR STUDENTS OF COLOR

Most elementary and secondary schools in the United States continue to be racially segregated (Orfield, Eaton, & the Harvard Project on School Desegregation, 1996). These demographic divisions have some profound implications for providing ethnically diverse students with equal access to high-quality educational opportunities and outcomes.

Enrollment Distributions and Persistence Rates

In 1996 (most recent available data) students of color constituted the majority population in 70 of the nation's 130 largest school districts (with 36,000 students or more), and this distribution is increasing yearly (U.S. Department of Education, 1999a). The percentages of their representation range from 50.7 in Toledo, Ohio, to 96.9 in Brownsville, Texas. In 37 of these districts, students of color are 75 percent or higher, with 6 districts having 95 percent or more (San Antonio, Texas; Detroit, Michigan; New Orleans, Louisiana; Washington, D.C.; Santa Ana, California; Brownsville, Texas). In addition to the largest school districts with majority students of color, another 9 have 45.0 to 49.9 percent. In the 449 school districts with 15,000 or more (which comprise a total of almost 18.5 million) students of color are 54.7 percent. The percentage distributions among African Americans, Latinos, Asian Americans/Pacific Islanders, and Native American/Alaskans are 26.9 percent, 21.4 percent, 5.7 percent, and 0.7 percent, respectively (U.S. Department of Education, 1999a).

Furthermore, ethnically diverse students are not necessarily attending school with each other. Districts with the highest representations of students of color are either predominately African American or Latino. In 41 of the largest school districts with majority students of color, African American predominate. When the other districts are added in which students of color are not the majority, the number in which African Americans are the largest group increases to 75. Latinos are predominant in 25 of the 70 large school districts with majority students of color, and 8 of the other 130 largest in the United States. Asian Americans have the highest representation in only 6 large districts with majority students of color. These districts are Sacramento, California; Seattle, Washington; St. Paul, Minnesota; Elk Grove, California; the state of Hawaii; and San Francisco. African American, Latino, and Asian American students are almost equally represented in only 4 of the 130 largest school districts (e.g., Fairfax, Virginia; Montgomery County, Maryland; San Juan, California; and Cherry Creek, Colorado), but their composite totals do not constitute a majority in any of them. Native Americans/Alaskans are the largest group of color only in Anchorage, Alaska (with 11.3 percent of the enrollment). Their other relatively sizable representations are in Tulsa (8.2 percent), Minneapolis (6.3 percent), and Oklahoma City (5.3 percent) (U.S. Department of Education, 1999a). Students of color also are geographically distributed unequally throughout the United States: African Americans are clustered in the Southeast and the Great Lakes areas; Latinos in the Southwest; Asian Americans along the Pacific Coast; and Native Americans in the Great Plains, Pacific Northwest, and Alaska.

Yet the ethnicity of teachers, administrators, and policy makers in these districts is the reverse. European Americans far outnumber educators of color in all school leadership and instructional positions. In fact, the numbers of schoolteachers and administrators of color declined steadily for about fifteen years. The percentage of African American teachers declined from 12.0 in 1970 to an all-time low of 6.9 percent in 1987. By 1996 this percentage had increased slightly, to 7.3. Latino Americans make up 4.9 percent of all elementary and secondary teachers in the United States. The percentage of Native American/Alaskan and Asian American/Pacific Islander teachers is 0.9 and 1.1 percent, respectively (U.S. Department of Education, 1999a). Traditionally, urban schools (which most students of color attend) have had less money, fewer resources and poorer facilities, larger numbers of inexperienced teachers, greater management problems, and higher turnover rates among teachers, administrators, and students (see Chapter 4 for a more detailed discussion). All of these factors can have negative effects on the educational opportunities and outcomes of students of color.

The high school completion rates in 1997 for 25 to 29 year-old European Americans was 92.9 percent, compared to 86.9 percent for African Americans and 61.8 percent for Latino Americans (U.S. Department of Education, 1999b). (No data were reported for the high school graduation rates of Native American/Alaskans or Asian Americans/Pacific Islanders.) These data indicate that dropout rates are declining for all ethnic groups except European Americans. Between 1990 and 1997, dropout rates for 18- and 19-year-old African Americans declined from 16.6 to 14.9 percent, while those of European Americans remained approximately the same (11.1 percent and 11.2 percent, respectively). While the dropout rates of Latino 18- to 19-years-olds declined from 34.2 percent in 1990 to 25.2 percent in 1997, they are still more than twice those of European Americans and one and one-third times those of African Americans. For all ethnic groups, males dropped out of school at higher rates than did females in 1997. This is a change for African Americans from 1990, when 17.6 percent of 18- to 19-year-old females dropped out of school, compared to 15.5 percent of males. The pattern has reversed for Latinos since 1995, when the female dropout rate (35 percent) exceeded that for males (27 percent) by 8 percentage points (U.S. Department of Education, 1999a).

Another school attendance factor that contributes to the educational inequality of students of color is *school delay*. Defined by Nielsen (1986) as "the discrepancy between the educational level reached by students and the normal level corresponding to their age" (p. 79), school-delay rates are substantially greater for African Americans, Latinos, and Native Americans than for European and Asian Americans. These three groups repeat grades more often and generally take longer to complete school. Since 1980 the percentage of students of color below modal grade (the grade in which most children of a certain age are enrolled) has increased substantially. African American males have the highest below-modal grade averages. By age thirteen almost one-half of African American males and one-third of Latinos have repeated a grade at least once (Miller-Lachmann & Taylor, 1995).

School delays have serious ramifications for the educational equality of students of color. They may initiate a cumulative process that ultimately results in the youth leaving school completely. Delayed students are more likely to be declared academically inadequate and assigned to special category, low academic, or vocational-track curricula. As these students fall behind their age group, they become stigmatized as slow learners and become socially isolated in schools. Teachers tend to have low expectations of achievement for delayed students. Together, these situations increase failure rates and the chances that the affected students will become school dropouts.

SAT Test Scores

Even for students of color who remain in school, their academic achievement levels are significantly lower than those of European Americans. These differences exist on all measures for every age group at all levels of schooling, in every region of the country, and at every socioeconomic level (College Board, 1999, 2002; Gougis, 1986). Some Asian Americans (notably students of Japanese, Korean, and Chinese origins) are exceptions to these patterns.

One powerful and frequently referenced indication of achievement among high school students is performance on college entrance tests, especially the Scholastic Achievement Test (SAT) and the American College Test (ACT). Trends in SAT scores offer both encouraging and discouraging news about the achievement of students of color. The good news is that the combined average verbal and math scores on the SAT for all test-takers increased from 999 in 1991 to 1020 in 2001. Also, SAT takers are becoming more ethnically, racially, and economically diverse. According to the College Board, which administers the SAT, students of color constituted more than one-third of the test-takers in 2002; this was an increase of 25 percent from 1989. The specific ethnic distribution included 11 percent African Americans, 10 percent Asian Americans, 1 percent Native Americans, 4 percent Mexican Americans, 1 percent Puerto Ricans, and 4 percent other Latinos. For those students for whom English was not their first language, 39 percent were Asian Americans and 25 percent each were Mexican Americans and Puerto Ricans (College Board, 2002).

The bad news is that long-established ethnic group patterns of performance on the SAT persist largely unchanged despite some improvements in the scores of groups of color. As the data in Table 9.1 show, the greatest gains for the decade between 1991 and 2002 occurred for Asian Americans/Pacific Islanders (a verbal–math combined increase of 37 points), Puerto Ricans (32 points), European Americans (30 points), Native Americans/Alaskans (24 points), and African

Table 9.1   SAT Scores by Selected Ethnic Groups for 1991 and 2002

Ethnic Groups	Verbal Scores			Math Scores		
	1991	2002	DIF.	1991	2002	DIF.
African Americans	427	430	+3	419	427	+8
Asian Americans/Pacific Islanders	485	501	+16	548	569	+21
European Americans	518	527	+9	513	533	+21
Mexican Americans	454	446	−8	459	457	−2
Native Americans/Alaskans	470	479	+9	468	483	+15
Puerto Ricans	436	456	+20	439	451	+12
Other Latinos	458	458	0	462	464	+2

Sources: College Board, 2002; U.S. Department of Education, 2002c.

Americans (11 points). The smallest gains were made by other Latinos (2 points). Mexican Americans were the only group that experienced a decline in SAT scores over this decade (a combined total of −10 points). The distribution of these increases favored math performance over verbal for all ethnic groups except Puerto Ricans, whose verbal increase on the SAT was 20 points over the decade, compared to a 12-point increase in math. The performance of Mexican Americans followed the pattern of the other ethnic groups. Although both sets of their SAT scores declined, this was less so on math (−2 points) than verbal performance (−8 points). The largest math–verbal increase differential occurred for European Americans, whose increase in math scores was 12 points higher than for verbal scores. For Asian Americans/Pacific Islanders, African Americans, Native Americans, and other Latinos the math advantage over the decade was smaller, at 5, 5, 6, and 2 points, respectively (College Board, 2002).

Even for Latinos, African Americans, and Native Americans who do well on the SAT and other college admission tests, the grades they achieve at predominately White colleges and universities are significantly lower than those for European and Asian Americans. This phenomenon holds true even for students who attend selective, highly prestigious institutions such as Harvard, Yale, and Stanford (College Board, 1999).

The gaps among groups of color on the SAT continue to be significant. The performance of African Americans is the lowest of all groups. In 2002 there was a combined verbal–math gap of 50 points between them and Puerto Ricans and 46 points between them and Mexican Americans, the groups whose performance is closest to theirs. Differences in the combined scores of African Americans and Asian and European Americans were 213 and 203 points, respectively. The single largest performance gap on the SAT in 2002 among groups of color occurred in math for African Americans and Asian Americans (a total of 142 points). Despite having the highest combined verbal–math scores in 2002 (1070), Asian Americans had the biggest gap between verbal (501) and math (569) scores, a total of 65 points. These performance trends suggest that the achievement gaps between groups of color and European Americans, as well as among themselves, as measured by SAT scores, is not narrowing significantly. Major disparities continue to exist even as the overall scores of all groups, except Mexican Americans, have increased over the last decade (College Board, 2002; U.S. Department of Education, 1999a, 1999b).

The achievement patterns by ethnic groups evident in the SAT scores are virtually identical to those on the ACT. This test measures reasoning abilities in English, math, reading, and science, and most of the students taking it are college-bound. The highest score that anyone can receive is 36. The 2002 results of this measure of achievement by ethnic groups and subject areas are presented in Table 9.2. Again, African Americans consistently score lower than all other ethnic groups, and the gap is significant (a composite average of 16.8). They performed the highest in science (17.1) and the lowest in English (16.2). European and Asian American scored the highest, and their performances are comparable. For example, while European Americans had an average score of 21.2 in English, 21.3 in math, 21.1 in reading, and 21.6 in science, the scores of Asian Americans in the same subjects were 20.5, 22.9, 21.2 and 21.3, respectively. The performances of Native Americans, Puerto Ricans, and Mexican Americans also were comparable, but Puerto Ricans scored slightly higher than the other two groups in all areas except science. In that subject the 2002 ACT scores were 19.0 for Native Americans, 18.5 for Mexican Americans, and 18.9 for Puerto Ricans ("ACT National and State Scores," 2002).

Table 9.2   2002 Average ACT Scores by Ethnic Groups and Subjects

Ethnic Group	Subjects				
	English	Math	Reading	Science	Composite
African Americans	16.2	16.7	16.8	17.1	16.8
Asian Americans	20.5	22.9	21.2	21.3	21.6
European Americans	21.2	21.3	21.1	21.6	21.7
Mexican Americans	17.1	18.4	18.3	18.5	18.2
Native Americans	17.6	18.4	19.1	19.0	18.6
Puerto Ricans	17.9	18.9	19.1	18.9	18.2

Source: "ACT National and State Scores," 2002.

Another indicator of the achievement gaps among ethnic groups is the grade point averages (GPA) of high school SAT takers. These parallel other performance measures. According to information presented by the College Board in 2001 Asian American and European American SAT takers had the highest GPAs (3.41 and 3.35, respectively), and African Americans (2.94) and Puerto Ricans (3.06) had the lowest. The GPAs of the other ethnic groups of color, from highest to lowest, were 3.21 for Mexican Americans, 3.14 for Native Americans, and 3.13 for other Latinos (College Board, 2002).

NAEP Report Cards

Performance on proficiency tests given by the National Assessment of Educational Progress (NAEP) is another high-stakes, high-status measure of student achievement. The scores on these tests suggest major discrepancies in the educational quality of different ethnic groups. NAEP presents achievement data for nine-, thirteen-, and seventeen-year-olds (or grades 4, 8, and 12) on a regular basis in eight skill areas. In these "Report Cards," reading and mathematics proficiency is assessed every two years, science and writing every four years, and geography and U.S. history every six years. In 1997, for the first time, students were tested in music, theater, and the visual arts, but only thirteen-year-olds were involved. Civics was tested in 1998 for all three age groups. Foreign languages will be added to the assessment schedule for grade 12 in 2004, and economics in 2006 (U.S. Department of Education, n.d.).

Student achievement is usually reported by gender and for the ethnic group clusters of European Americans, African Americans, Latino Americans, Native Americans/Alaskan Natives, and Asian Americans/Pacific Islanders. The performance of Native Americans and Asian Americans has been specified only in the most recent assessment cycles. Their exclusion from earlier reports was due to the small sample sizes. According to the National Center for Education Statistics, because these groups constitute only 1 percent of U.S. school enrollments, they are not represented in sufficient numbers in national education studies to permit reliable and valid generalizations about their characteristics (U.S. Department of Education, 1995).

Achievement gaps between students of color and European Americans tend to narrow somewhat across all subjects as grade levels increase, but which group accounts for this progress varies. However, the differences continue to be significant and usually greater for African Americans than other groups. These patterns are graphically illustrated by the scores different ethnic groups attained in ten subject areas: math, science, writing, reading, geography, U.S. history, civics, music, visual arts, and theater. The latest results were attained on NAEP tests administered between 1997 and 2001, which are summarized in Table 9.3. The varying dates by subjects are indicative of where they fall within the testing cycles.

Table 9.3   Latest Available NAEP Achievement by Subject, Grade, and Ethnic Groups

Subject and Ethnic Group	Grade 4	Grade 8	Grade 12
GEOGRAPHY, 2001			
European American	222	273	291
African American	181	234	260
Latino Americans	184	240	270
Asian Americans/Pacific Islanders	212	266	286
Native Americans	199	261	288
U.S. HISTORY, 2001			
European American	220	271	292
African American	188	243	269
Latino Americans	186	243	274
Asian Americans/Pacific Islanders	213	267	295
Native Americans	197	249	277
MATHEMATICS, 2000			
European American	236	286	308
African Americans	205	247	274
Latino Americans	212	253	283
Asian American/Pacific Islanders		289	319
Native Americans	216	255	293
SCIENCE, 2000			
European American	160	162	154
African American	124	122	123
Latino Americans	129	128	128
Asian Americans/Pacific Islanders		156	154
Native Americans	140	134	139

(continued)

Table 9.3 Continued

Subject and Ethnic Group	Grade 4	Grade 8	Grade 12
READING, 1998/2000*			
European American	226	272	298
African American	193	243	270
Latino Americans	197	244	275
Asian Americans/Pacific Islanders	232	271	289
Native Americans	196	248	276
WRITING, 1998			
European American	157	158	156
African Americans	131	131	134
Latino Americans	134	131	135
Asian Americans/Pacific Islanders	164	159	152
Native Americans	138	132	129
CIVICS, 1998			
European American	159	159	158
African American	132	133	131
Latino Americans	126	127	130
Asian Americans/Pacific Islanders	153	153	151
Native Americans	137	134	129
MUSIC, 1997**			
European American		158	
African American		130	
Latino Americans		127	
Asian Americans/Pacific Islanders		152	
Native Americans		—	
VISUAL ARTS, 1997**			
European American		159	
African Americans		124	
Latino Americans		128	
Asian Americans/Pacific Islanders		153	
Native Americans		—	

Table 9.3 Continued

THEATER, 1997**	
European American	159
African American	120
Latino Americans	139
Asian Americans/Pacific Islanders	—
Native Americans	—

*Only fourth graders were assessed in 2000.

**1997 scores reported mean proficiency; the mean score established for each age group tested was 150. Only eighth graders were assessed in music, arts and theater.

Sources: U.S. Department of Education, n.d., 1999c, 2002c.

Fourth-, eighth-, and twelfth-grade African Americans scored 41, 39, and 31 points, respectively, lower than did European Americans on the geography test of 2001. The gaps for Latinos were 38, 33, and 21 points. Asian Americans came closest to matching the performance of European Americans in grade 4 (10 points less) and grade 8 (7 points less). In grade 12 this position was held by Native Americans, whose geography scores were only 3 points less than European Americans. For most groups of color the achievement gap narrows as grade level increases when their scores are compared to European Americans and to each other. For example, there was a 38-point difference between the geography scores of fourth-grade Latinos and European Americans. It declined to 33 points in grade 8 and 21 in grade 12. A Latino–Asian American comparison shows differential scores (favoring Asian Americans) of 28, 26, and 16 in grades 4, 8, and 12, respectively. This pattern reversed in the comparison of African Americans and Latinos. On the fourth-grade geography tests Latinos scored 3 points higher than African Americans. This gap increased to 6 points in grade 8 and to 10 points in grade 12. Although Native Americans scored 13 points less than Asian Americans in grade 4, and 5 points less in grade 8, their performance was 3 points higher in grade 12.

In the 2001 U.S. history assessments, some established achievement patterns prevailed but others did not. European Americans and Asian Americans again performed the highest of all groups, and Native Americans performed better than African Americans and Latinos at all three grade levels. The performance of African Americans was higher than Latinos in grade 4 and equal in grade 8, but lower in grade 12. European Americans scored better than African Americans by 32 points in grade 4, 29 in grade 8, and 23 in grade 12. Differences with Latinos were 34, 29, and 18 points, respectively. The history scores of Asian Americans were only 7 points lower than European Americans in grade 4, and 4 points less in grade 8. They scored higher than European American in grade 12 by 3 points. The performance of Native Americans was 23 points less than European Americans in grade 4 and 12 in grade 8, but only 3 points lower in grade 12. They scored higher than African Americans by 11, 6, and 8 points in grades 4, 8, and 12, respectively. In comparison to Latinos, the positive point differences for Native Americans, beginning with grade 4, were 11, 6, and 3 (see Table 9.3).

Generally, the size of the achievement gaps among ethnic groups in U.S. history is somewhat smaller than in geography. For example, while the performance of Latinos in geography was 3 to 10 points higher than African Americans across the three grades tested, it was only 0 to 5 points different in history. This pattern is reversed in the comparison of Native Americans and Asian Americans. On the geography tests the differences in their performance were 13 points in grade 4 and 5 points in grade 8, favoring Asian Americans. In grade 12 Native Americans had the higher score by 2 points. However, on the history tests Asian Americans scored better than Native Americans in all three grades and with a wider point spread—16 in grade 4 and 18 each in grades 8 and 12.

Overall, African Americans and Latinos perform better in history than in geography across the grades, but Natives Americans do better in geography than history The performance of European Americans is comparable in both subjects and all grades. The achievement of Asian Americans in geography and history is also comparable but only in grades 4 and 8. In grade 12 it is higher in history than geography. In both subjects, the performance of twelfth-grade African Americans was lower than eighth-grade European Americans. This also was the case for twelfth-grade Latinos in geography.

Mathematics test scores between 1996 and 2000 fluctuated by ethnic groups and grades. The most consistent pattern occurred among Europeans Americans, who showed a decline in all three grades. The performance of African Americans and Latinos increased in grades 4 and 8 but declined in grade 12. The fourth-grade scores of Native Americans were the same in 1996 and 2000, declined in grade 8, and increased in grade 12. Some errors in the data collected led to no math scores being reported for fourth-grade Asian Americans in 2000 and eighth graders in 1996. Twelfth graders showed no losses or gains between 1996 and 2000. Students in all ethnic groups at all three ages tested better in areas of mathematical knowledge (recalling and recognizing facts) and skills (performing computations and manipulations) than in applications (reasoning and problem solving) (U.S. Department of Education, n.d.).

Other patterns of performance among ethnic groups that are evident in other subjects prevailed in mathematics as well. The sequential order of achievement in 2000 among groups of color, from highest to lowest, was Asian Americans, Native Americans, Latino Americans, and African Americans. Asian Americans performed better than European Americans by 3 points in grade 8 and 11 points in grade 12. No comparisons are possible for grade 4. The scores of African Americans were lower than European Americans by 31, 39, and 34 point for grades 4, 8, and 12, respectively. The gaps followed a similar pattern for Latino Americans but were less extreme, with point spreads of 24, 33, and 25 for the same grades. The math achievement of Native Americans followed suit and maintained the position established in other subject areas. Their fourth-grade scores were 20 points less than European Americans. This gap increased to 31 points at grade 8 but dropped to 15 points at grade 12. The actual average math scores of these ethnic groups by grades for the 2000 testing cycle are presented in Table 9.3.

The overall science proficiency among ethnic groups declined slightly between 1996 and 2000. Some small gains (1 to 4 points) were made in grade 8 by European Americans and African Americans and in grades 8 and 12 by Asian Americans (4 and 5 points, respectively). A decline occurred for all other groups of color in grade 12, where there was an overall 3-point decline in the average scores of students. In grade 4, the scores of Native Americans and

Latino Americans also declined, while those of European Americans and African Americans remained the same. The largest decline in science scores was for Native Americans in grade 8, which dropped by 14 points from 1996 to 2000. The second-largest decreases in science performance occurred in grade 12, with 7 points for Native Americans and 5 points for European Americans (U.S. Department of Education, n.d., 2002b). The actual average science scores for 2000 by ethnic groups and grades are summarized in Table 9.3. NAEP reports them according to a baseline score of 250 for each grade tested. However, that score represents different skills for different grades.

Despite some apparent disruptions in performance trends, which may suggest that the science achievement gap is narrowing for some groups of color because European Americans are making less progress, other disparities persist. There was only one instance in which the performance of a group of color equaled that of European Americans. This was the scores of twelfth-grade Asian Americans (see Table 9.3). The largest achievement gaps occurred for African Americans. Their scores at grades 4, 8, and 12 were lower than European Americans by 36, 40, and 31 points, respectively. Latino Americans performed slightly better but still significantly lower than European Americans—by 31 points for nine-year-olds, 34 for thirteen-year-olds, and 26 for seventeen-year-olds. For some unexplained reasons the gaps in the 2000 NAEP science assessment scores of African Americans and Latinos were greater in grade 8 than in grades 4 and 12. The same pattern also was apparent for Native Americans. They performed lower than European Americans by 20 points in grade 4, 28 points in grade 8, and 15 points in grade 12 (see Table 9.3).

These patterns of performance are further confirmed by distributions by percentile scores and competency levels. Performance in all percentile rankings (10th, 25th, 50th, 75th, 90th) between 1996 and 2000 remained the same in grade 4, declined in the three lower percentiles for grade 8 but increased slightly for the top two percentiles, and declined in all percentiles in grade 12 (U.S. Department of Education, 2002b). Furthermore, the ethnic patterns of performance in science prevail when analyzed by percent of students by groups at various levels of proficiency. In grade 12 almost two-thirds (62 percent) of European Americans and 59 percent of Asian Americans performed at or above the basic achievement level. This level denotes partial mastery of scientific knowledge and skills necessary to function at grade level. This level of achievement was significantly lower for Native Americans (44 percent), Latino Americans (30 percent), and African Americans (22 percent). As the levels of knowledge increase, the percentage of students reaching them decreases for all ethnic groups, such that no groups in any of the three grades tested reached advanced performance in science in 2000. Even at the level of proficiency, which indicates competency in subject-matter knowledge, application to real-world situations, and analytical skills, the percentages in all ethnic groups dropped radically. In 2000 the highest percent of twelfth graders achieving proficiency on the NAEP test was Asian Americans (26 percent). They were followed next by European Americans at 23 percent. Less than 10 percent of each of the other three ethnic groups reached the proficiency level of achievement in science—9 percent of Native Americans, 7 percent of Latino Americans, and 3 percent of African Americans (U.S. Department of Education, 2002b).

The reading achievement scores presented in Table 9.3 include scores from the 2000 test for grade 4 but 1998 results for grades 8 and 12, since the last two were not tested in 2000. For the most part, the same patterns of performance by ethnic groups are evident in reading as in other subjects. African Americans continued to perform lower than all other ethnic groups in all three grades tested; the achievement gap between students of color and European Americans declined somewhat as the grades increased, except for Asian Americans; and the fourth-grade reading scores declined between 1998 and 2000, except for Latinos (+1 point) and Asian Americans (+7 points) (U.S. Department of Education, 2002a). While Asian Americans in grade 4 scored higher in reading than European Americans by 6 points, this advantage was lost at grade 8 since their scores were 1 point less, and again in grade 12 when the gap increased to 9 points. Native Americans performed better than African Americans by 3 points in grade 4 in 2000 but 1 point less than Latino Americans. In 1998 their differences in reading achievement increased to 4 points over Latinos and 5 points over African Americans. In grade 12 the Native American differential over Latino Americans dropped back to 1 point but increased to 6 points over African Americans.

Differences in the reading achievement of African Americans, Native Americans, and Latinos when compared to European Americans are profound at the three grade levels tested, even though they decrease slightly as the grades increase. At grade 4 the differences were 33 points for African Americans, 30 points for Native Americans, and 29 points for Latino Americans. This is one of the few instances in which Latinos scored higher than Native Americans across all the subjects and grades tested for which scores are available for all groups of color (see Table 9.3). In grades 8 and 12 the sequence of performance among these groups returned to the more typical pattern. The differences in their scores compared to European Americans, from largest to smallest, and beginning with African Americans, were 29, 28, and 24 points in grade 8, and 28, 23, and 22 points in grade 12.

As is the case with science, most students in all ethnic groups are not reaching the highest levels of achievement in reading (U.S. Department of Education, 1999b, 2002a). For example, more fourth-grade Asian Americans (46 percent) than European Americans (40 percent) performed at or above the proficiency achievement level in 2000. This means that they were able to extend ideas presented in the text by making inferences, drawing conclusions, and making connections to their own lived experiences. The numbers of students achieving at proficiency level was radically lower for the other three ethnic groups—17 percent for Native Americans, 16 percent for Latino Americans, and only 12 percent for African Americans (U.S. Department of Education, 2002a).

NAEP used a scale similar to that used in science and civics to report the 1998 writing test results in that a baseline score of 150 was established for each of the three grades. For the most part, ethnic group patterns look very much like those in reading, science, and mathematics, but the gaps are not quite as wide (see Table 9.3). Asian Americans are making more progress in narrowing the achievement gap with European Americans than other groups. Their scores were higher in grades 4 and 8 by 7 and 1 points, respectively. However, their twelfth-grade writing scores were 4 points lower than European Americans. The gaps among Native Americans, African Americans, and Latinos were also narrower than in some of the other subjects tested. For example, in grade 8 they were separated by only 1 point, in favor of Native Americans; Latinos and African Americans had identical scores. In grade 12 Native Americans performed lower than the other two groups—6 points lower than Latinos and 5 points lower than African Americans. This is a deviation from other established patterns. The achievement gap between Native Americans and African Americans was the widest in grade 4, at 7 points. At the same grade Native Americans performed better than Latinos by only 4 points. When the writing achievements of students of color (except Asian Americans) are compared with European Americans, the results are much more dismal. The scores for African Americans in grades 4, 8, and 12 were 26, 27, and 22 points lower, respectively; the scores for Latino Americans were 23, 27, and 21 points lower; and the scores for Native Americans were 29, 26, and 27 points lower. The actual test scores used to calculate these differences are presented in Table 9.3.

The civics report card of 1998 indicates both continuity and variance in established patterns of achievement among ethnic groups. Because of changes in how test results were presented, the actual scores of students across age levels cannot be compared. For all three ages tested, European Americans and Asian Americans continued the pattern established in other areas of achievement by performing better than other ethnic groups. African Americans deviated from their achievement patterns in other areas by not performing the lowest of all groups. They scored better than Latinos in grades 4, 8, and 12, and better than Native Americans in grade 12. Latinos had the lowest performance of all ethnic groups in grades 4 and 8 but not in grade 12, where their civics scores were higher than those of Native Americans by 1 point. While the achievement levels of European Americans and Asian Americans were close (6 to 7 points difference across the three grades tested, favoring European Americans), they are substantially lower for other ethnic groups. Differences between the scores of African Americans and European Americans for grades 4, 8, and 12 were 27, 26, and 27 points, respectively; for Latinos the differences were 33, 32, and 28 points; and for Native Americans the differences were 22, 25, and 29 points (U.S. Department of Education, n.d.). The test scores on which the comparisons are based are presented in Table 9.3.

NAEP presented a report card in 1997 for the first time on performance in music, theater, and the visual arts. But only eighth graders were tested, and a 0-to-300 point scale was used. The pattern of performance by ethnic groups established in other years and subjects was largely replicated once again. The order of achievement, from highest to lowest, was European Americans, Asian Americans, Latinos, and African Americans. Two exceptions were noted—African Americans performed higher than did Latinos in music, and data were presented for Asian Americans in music and visual arts but not theater. Differences in the scores of the various ethnic groups were as low as 6 points (between European Americans and Asian Americans in music) and as high as 39 points (between African Americans and European Americans in theater). Other differences in the performance of European Americans and African Americans were 28 points in music and 35 points in visual arts. The performances of Latinos and African Americans were close, separated by only 3 points in music and 4 points in visual arts. Differences in their performance in theater (19 points) were much more substantial (see Table 9.3). All of these differences favored Latinos (U.S. Department of Education, n.d., 1999a, 1999b).

MIXED SIGNALS IN ACHIEVEMENT PATTERNS

The fact that students of color in all three age groups tested made small but steady gains in science and mathematics achievement is encouraging. But it is disheartening and troublesome that this pattern is not true for reading and writing. In general, Latinos seem to be making more academic progress than are African Americans even though their dropout rates are higher. Consequently, the gaps between their achievement levels and those of European American students are decreasing somewhat, while those of African Americans remain about the same. Although recent improvements by students of color on standardized tests show that they are making some gains on low-level cognitive skills, such as decoding, computation, factual recognition, and recall, they are not developing high-level skills, such as making inferences, critical thinking, analyzing and synthesizing information, logical reasoning, and creative expression.

Another good-news/bad-news dilemma associated with the achievement profiles is that the data are largely not disaggregated. The test scores presented earlier in this discussion are composite profiles for large groups and large clusters of skills. As such, they do not identify what aspects of the various subjects and skills were easy or difficult for students taking the tests. Nor do they give any detailed information on how individuals within ethnic groups were distributed across the range of skills included in the various tests. For instance, it is impossible to discern from the scores whether comprehension, vocabulary, making inferences, or some other component skill of reading was most challenging for Mexican Americans, Puerto Ricans, or Cuban Americans. How individuals' membership in ethnic groups is assigned and where they are placed for analysis also may distort some of the achievement patterns. Data on the educational achievement of African Americans are never distributed by subcategories, such as the various Afro-Caribbean groups (e.g., Jamaican, Trinidadans, Guyanese). Nor is the performance of Asian Americans specified by component ethnic groups (such as Japanese, Chinese, Koreans, or Vietnamese) or Native Americans by particular tribal identity (e.g., Navajo, Cherokee, Yakama). Furthermore, no distinctions are made between the performances of immigrant and U.S.-born members of different ethnic groups, such as Nigerian, Ethiopian, and Kenyan among African Americans, and Japanese and Mexican immigrants as opposed to Japanese Americans and Mexican Americans.

All these demographic details affect performance patterns and have serious implications for reforming instruction to improve educational equality for ethnically diverse students. For example, Asian Americans are often considered the model minority and are perceived to be high achievers in all aspects of schooling and on all measures of achievement. This positive stereotype overlooks the immense diversity by national origin of Asian American ethnic groups; the serious language and social adjustment problems that some Southeast Asian new immigrants encounter; the great disparities in Asian American verbal and math achievement; the self-concept dilemmas of even many higher-achieving Asian Americans; the special educational needs of individual students; and the high dropout rates among some Asian groups, such as Hmongs, Cambodians, and Vietnamese (Gibbs & Nahme-Huang, 1989; Igoa, 1995; Miller-Lachmann & Taylor, 1995; Pang, 2001; Pang & Cheng, 1998; Pang, Mizokawa, Morishima & Olstad, 1985; Yu, Doi, & Chang, 1986). Osajima (1991) cautions that

> beneath the awards and accomplishments lie struggles, conflicts,
> and uncertainties that manifest racism's hidden and subtle
> impacts. . . . The quiet demeanor of Asian students, which has
> heretofore only garnered praise, may in fact be problematic, for
> this survival mechanism could also leave them isolated with their
> doubts about identity and belonging. (pp. 130–131)

Understanding Mixed-Achievement Signals

How can the mixed results that are apparent in the achievement profiles of students of color be explained? One possible explanation is that teachers and instructional programs are still not acknowledging and responding to these students' unique cultural orientations, values, and learning styles. The failure to do so is negatively affecting their achievement outcomes. As Boateng (1990) explains, the "deculturalization" of students of color in schools interferes with their ability to focus on and master academic tasks.

Achievement patterns may be a direct result of the curriculum differentiations that exist for students of color and for European American students in elementary and secondary schools. These students are not necessarily enrolled in similar kinds of courses, nor are they receiving equal-status instruction. It is not surprising, then, that there is so much variance in their academic achievement. Another possibility is that all students are not receiving the best-quality education possible. Rarely do students from any ethnic group receive scores on NAEP tests that symbolize advanced levels of proficiency such as the ability to do critical thinking and complex problem solving in math, science, geography, and history.

Other possible explanations of these variations in achievement may be found in students' attendance patterns and dropout rates. Many of the most problematic students of color may drop out of school before age seventeen. Those who remain should be more like their European counterparts and, therefore, have similar achievement levels. This possibility may be counteracted by disproportionately low percentages of high school students of color enrolled in academic courses of study. The combination of these possibilities gives credence to the contention that the longer African American, Latino, and Native American youths stay in school, the further they fall behind academically. Ralph, Keller, and Crouse (1994) explained this phenomenon further by pointing out that even after eight additional years of schooling, seventeen-year-olds who were at the 10th percentile in math and the 25th percentile in reading and science at age nine still have not attained achievement scores equal to those of the 95th percentile of their cohort at age seventeen.

Another explanation is that students of color know much more than standardized achievement test scores indicate. Despite their frequent use, these tests may not be valid measures to use in determining the academic abilities of culturally and ethnically different students. The lack of sensitivity of these techniques, in both their content and administration procedures, to the cultural nuances of students of color may have a negative effect on their total scores. In other words, the lack of culturally relevant content, test-taking skills, and other preferred performance styles may mediate against some ethnic groups doing well on the SAT and NAEP tests of academic proficiency. Measures of achievement that are culturally sensitive, employ diverse techniques, and access multidimensional sites of performance, such as curriculum content and classroom instructional interactions, may produce very different results.

The unequal curriculum and instruction systems that exist in U.S. schools undoubtedly account for many of the disparities in achievement among students of color and European Americans. This inequity has been firmly established by research. For example, in its *Mexican-American Education Study*, conducted between 1971 and 1974, the U.S. Civil Rights Commission (1971–1974) attributed quality and equality of educational experiences to the opportunities different students receive to participate in classroom interactions with teachers.

It found that Mexican Americans were not receiving as many opportunities as were European Americans to participate in classroom interactions, as evidenced by fewer and lower-level questions asked of them, the time allowed to give responses, and the praise and encouragement teachers gave for students' efforts. Gay (1974) found similar results for African American students interacting with both African American and European American teachers. Teachers, regardless of their own ethnic identity, tended to give preferential treatment and more quality opportunities to participate in the substance of instruction to European American students.

Other disparities in curriculum options and instructional interactions available to racially and ethnically different groups have been reported by Goodlad (1984), Oakes (1985), Persell (1977), and Harry (1992). The studies by these researchers indicate that students of color are disproportionally enrolled in special education and vocational programs. Furthermore, the placement of students of color in vocational courses occurs earlier, and the programs differ substantially in kind and content from those for European Americans. Students of color are often assigned to courses that train specifically for low-status occupations (e.g., cosmetology, mill and cabinet shop, building maintenance, television repair, retail sales, clerical jobs). By comparison, European American students enroll more often in courses that offer managerial training, business and finance skills, and general industrial arts skills. To receive their training, youths of color must leave the school campus more often than do European Americans, thus isolating them from many of the social activities and "cultural capital" of the school (Oakes, 1985) that could help to socialize them into the test-taking modes and ethos.

The enrollment of students of color in high-stakes, high-status academic programs is also unequally distributed. They are highly underrepresented in college preparatory, gifted-and-talented, and gateway programs or courses leading to higher educational success, such as calculus, chemistry, and advanced placements. Although college-bound African American and Latino seniors are as likely as European Americans to have taken three or more years of mathematics, they are less likely to have taken algebra, geometry, trigonometry, and calculus and more likely to have taken general and business math (U.S. Department of Education, 1994). Students in low-income and predominately children-of-color schools have less access to computers, have fewer qualified teachers trained in the use of computers, and tend to use computers more for drill and practice in basic skills rather than for conceptual knowledge or programming instruction (College Entrance Examination Board, 1985; U.S. Department of Education, 1999b; Winkler, Stravelson, Stasz, Robyn, & Fiebel, 1984). In 1997 approximately 61 percent of European American high school students used computers at home, compared to 22 percent of African Americans and Latinos. These figures represent more than a 100 percent increase from 1993 for students of color and a 75 percent increase for European Americans. Elementary students use computers at home less often, but the increase over time is similarly significant (U.S. Department of Education, 1999b).

The system of tracking routinely used to organize students for instruction is a very effective way to deny educational equality to students of color. These inequities include over-representation of Latinos, African Americans, Native Americans, and poor students from all ethnic groups in low-track, low-status instructional programs. These programs tend to offer low-quality instruction and emphasize compliance-type behaviors and attitudes, classroom management, discipline, and procedural matters. High-track students are advantaged by participating in subjects and curricula perceived to be high status; by having better teachers, equipment, materials, and more provocative learning experiences; by being taught leadership and high-order intellectual skills such as critical thinking and problem solving; by receiving high expectations of achievement from teachers; and by having more instructional time allocated to academic tasks (Goodlad, 1984; Grant & Sleeter, 1985; Morgan, 1977; Oakes, 1985; Oakes & Guiton, 1995; Persell, 1977; Verdugo, 1986). These disparities are discussed in greater detail in Chapter 4.

Because African Americans, Latinos, and Native Americans are overrepresented in low-track curriculum programs, they are consistently and systematically denied equal access to the substance of quality education. *In effect, tracking is a process for the legitimization of the social inequalities that exist in the larger society.* It serves the instrumental functions of social selection, creating castes among students and closing off paths for personal advancement for students in the lower levels (Morgan, 1977). Through this practice, students learn to accept the unequal patterns of social and political participation in society and all its institutions as the natural order of things.

In the final analysis, access to high-status knowledge and high quality of instructional interactions between students and teachers defines educational equality. These processes are what ultimately determine which students are educated for intellectual rigor, personal self-determination, and social empowerment, and which ones are trained for a life of institutional compliance, economic dependence, and for the social underclass (College Entrance Examination Board, 1985). The current educational status of students of color in the United States suggests that too many of them are being educated for the underclass.

WHY EDUCATIONAL INEQUALITY EXISTS FOR STUDENTS OF COLOR

The various resources used in the educational process have a direct effect on the level and quality of student achievement. When different groups of students are exposed to qualitatively different resources, their achievements also differ. In the debate on educational equality, a crucial question is whether the resources used in teaching students of color are comparable to those used with European Americans on measures of accuracy, technical quality, relevance, and appropriateness. These resources include facilities, personnel, financing, instructional materials and programs, and environmental settings.

The relative value of instructional resources cannot be determined independently of environmental context, intended users, and expected outcomes. Even when students of color and European Americans receive similar educational resources, the effects are not identical. Sometimes resources that benefit and facilitate the academic achievement of European Americans block or retard the educational development of students of color. How is this possible? One way is how school systems treat curricular and instructional options that are highly populated by students of color relative to performance expectations and resource allocations. They receive fewer laboratory facilities, fewer out-of-classroom learning experiences, less qualified teachers, and less commitment, concern, and effort from teachers (Oakes, 1985; Oakes & Guiton, 1995).

Despite being overrepresented in low-track, nonacademic, and special education programs, most students of color are enrolled in a wide spectrum of *regular* curriculum options, including general education, academic, and college preparatory courses. If educational resources are allocated by programs and if these programs receive a fair share of them, then how is it that students of color are denied comparable access? Several ways are possible. First, the sameness of educational resources for diverse individuals and groups does not constitute comparability of quality or opportunity. To believe that they do is to assume that students of African, Latino, Native, Asian, and European origin are identical in personal, social, cultural, historical, and family traits.

Second, most graduates of typical teacher education programs know little about the cultural traits, behaviors, values, and attitudes that different children of color bring to the classroom and how they affect students' responses to instructional situations. Most teachers do not know how to understand and use the school behaviors of these students, which differ from their own normative expectations, as aids to teaching. Therefore, they often misinterpret these students as deviant and treat them punitively. Because most teachers' cultural backgrounds and value orientations are highly compatible with middle-class and European American culture, they can use these cultural connections and shared frames of reference to facilitate the learning of White students. The absence of these cultural connections in routine classroom instruction for students of color places them at a learning disadvantage.

Third, like teacher education, most curriculum designs and instructional materials are Eurocentric. When attempting to learn academic tasks, European American students may not have the additional burden of working across irrelevant instructional materials and methods. More of their efforts and energies can be directed toward mastering the substance of teaching. Students of color are often placed in double academic jeopardy. They must divide their energies and efforts between coping with instructional materials and methods that are not culturally relevant to them and mastering the academic knowledge and tasks being taught. Because this division of efforts dissipates their concentration on learning tasks, they do not receive the same kinds of educational opportunities to learn the substance of teaching as do European Americans.

Fourth, the school environments in which students live and learn are not comparable for racially majority and minority students. When students and teachers arrive at school, they do not leave their cultural backgrounds at home. This is not a problem for most European Americans, since school culture and rules of behavior are reflections and extensions of their home cultures. These students do not experience much social-code incompatibility or need for cultural style shifting to adjust to the behavioral rules and expectations of schools. The converse is true for most students of color. Many of the social codes for succeeding in school are unfamiliar to them or are diametrically opposed to the codes they have learned in their home cultures. When learning situations do not reflect the cultures of the students, gaps exist "between the contexts of learning and the contexts of performing" (John-Steiner & Leacock, 1979, p. 87). These gaps are greatest for students from ethnic cultures and communities that are not part of the mainstream culture, and such gaps can mediate against effective teaching and learning. Therefore, the causes of many of the disparities that are apparent in the educational attainment of different ethnic groups are situated in cultural, procedural, and contextual incompatibilities (Gay, 2000).

Most educators do not think to teach students of color the skills on how to survive and succeed in school—for example, how to study across ethnic learning styles, how to adjust talking styles to accommodate school expectations, how to interact appropriately with school administrators and classroom teachers, and how to identify and adapt to the procedural rules for functioning in different instructional classrooms. Instead, educators tend to operate on the assumption that school codes of behavior are universal and commonly understood and are acquired from simply living in the broader culture that surrounds schools. What most of these educators forget is that many students of color live only marginally in mainstream culture. Furthermore, their parents may not be able to pass on to them a legacy of how to "do" schooling successfully because they did not experience it themselves.

These differences in socialization mean that students of color may have to learn how to survive in school while simultaneously learning what is taught. If they fail to master the social codes, they may never get a chance to try the academic tasks. As Holliday (1985) suggests, mastery of the social protocols and managerial procedures of schooling is frequently a prerequisite to receiving opportunities to participate in substantive instructional interactions and for academic learning to occur. Also, the in-class success of students of color is often determined more by mastery of social-skills (such as compliance to institutional expectations and having pleasant or accommodating personality traits) than by academic performance. In assessing the performance of students of color, some teachers give less credit to academic factors than to nonacademic ones such as "being nice, cooperative, and not troublemakers," "feeling sorry for students," and "work being neat, if not of very high substantive quality." In comparison, the performance of European American students is assessed more on academic criteria ("he studies hard," "she is a good thinker," "they are very attentive in class," "she asks provocative questions" "his writing is clear and cogent").

Closely related to the issue of comparable-quality material and pedagogical resources is the role of teacher attitudes, expectations, and competencies in perpetuating educational inequality for students of color. The essence of this issue is: How can teachers who have grown up in ethnically isolated communities and in a racist society teach students whom they do not know, may not value, and may even fear? This question is crucial in equations of educational equality, especially when most teachers are racially White, culturally Eurocentric, middle class, and female, and when their professional preparation is grounded almost exclusively in Eurocentric cultural orientations. Therefore, they enter the profession assuming that all students can be taught as if they were European Americans. Teachers of color who receive the same kind of professional socialization frequently begin their careers with the same kind of expectations, attitudes, and values. Research shows that

> teachers form expectations about children based directly upon race
> and social class . . . pupil test scores, appearance, language style,
> speed of task performance, and behavior characteristics which are
> themselves culturally defined. Moreover, teacher expectations are
> more influenced by *negative* information about pupil characteristics
> than positive data. (Persell, 1977, p. 112)

Teachers transmit these attitudes and expectations in what they say and do in the classroom. Students respond in ways that become self-fulfilling prophecies. Many children of color come to believe that they are destined to fail, and they act accordingly. Most European and Asian American students internalize the high expectations teachers have of them, believe they are destined to succeed and do succeed.

The behaviors of educators reflect their performance expectations of different students. For example, teachers who do not have high academic expectations for students of color tend to ask them low-level memory, recall, and convergent questions; do not praise or encourage them as often as they praise European Americans; use lower standards for judging the quality of their work; and do not call on them as frequently (Good & Brophy, 1994; Oakes, 1985; Oakes & Guiton, 1995). Guidance counselors who do not believe students of color can master high-level math and science skills do not schedule them into these classes. School administrators who expect greater discipline problems from students of color tend to treat their rule infractions with harsher punishment. In general, low expectations of educators cause them to feed African Americans, Latinos, Native Americans, and some Southeast Asians (notably Vietnamese and Cambodians) academic pabulum.

These educators then wonder why these students do not do well on standardized measures of school achievement. Students of color for whom educators have low expectations are suspected of dishonesty and cheating when they defy these expectations by performing well. When low expectations produce low performance, teachers make comments such as "What else can you expect?" European American students who do not live up to high expectations are described as underachievers, and low-performing students who exceed expectations are called overachievers. These attitudes cause wide disparities in how educators interact with European Americans and students of color in the day-to-day operations of schools and thereby perpetuate educational inequalities.

A similar argument holds for the content and substance of student evaluations. All achievement tests are designed to determine what students know. Presumably these tests reflect what is taught in schools. This is a reasonable expectation, and there would be no issue of ethnic inequality if schools taught equally relevant curricula equally well to all students. But they do not. Although progress has been made in the last three decades in making school curricula more inclusive of ethnic and cultural diversity, most of the knowledge taught, and consequently the achievement tests, continues to be Eurocentric.

Even skill mastery is transmitted through Eurocentric contexts. For instance, achievement tests may embed skills in scenarios about situations that are not relevant to the cultural backgrounds and life experiences of students of color. These students then have to decipher the contexts in order to extrapolate the skill content. One example is asking immigrant students from the Caribbean who have never experienced snow to engage in problem solving from a composition on the challenges and dilemmas of a blizzard. They may know the skill, but unfamiliarity with the contextual scenario (problems associated with snow) interferes with them effectively demonstrating their ability to do problem solving. Most European American students do not have these kinds of contextual-interference problems. They are familiar with both the context and the performance format because these formats are extracted from cultural orientations the students share with schools. If they know the skill, they therefore are advantaged in demonstrating their mastery. This is not to say that students of color should not take achievement tests, that their school performance should not be evaluated, or that high levels of achievement should not be expected of them.

ACHIEVING EDUCATIONAL EQUALITY

The College Entrance Examination Board (1985) concluded its report *Equality and Excellence* with the observation that "excellence for Black students will not become a reality until they receive enriched curricular opportunities in elementary and secondary schools, sufficient financial assistance to pursue higher education opportunities, and instruction from well-qualified teachers" (p. 4). A more recent report, *Reaching the Top* (College Board, 1999), declares that "the rapid changes that are occurring in the racial and ethnic composition of the nation bring a new sense of urgency" to improving the educational opportunities and outcomes of students of color (p.1). This need has become

> a moral and pragmatic imperative [because] when a great many individuals—and entire groups of people—do not have a genuine chance to develop their academic talents fully, our society is much poorer for their lack of educational opportunities. . . . This is fundamentally unjust and potentially an enormous source of social divisiveness. (College Board 1999, pp. 2, 5)

Gay (1994) suggests that *comparability in culturally relevant learning experiences for ethnically diverse students* is essential to achieving educational equality and high-level achievement for them.

Redefining Access

To accomplish these goals, reform efforts should begin with a redefinition of educational equality for students of color as *access to a variety of instructional processes that are informed by and responsive to their cultural orientations and learning styles.* In operational terms, this means affirming that problems in learning are located not so much in the inabilities of students as in culturally unequal, insensitive, and hegemonic practices used in the schools they attend. It also means that schools should be more responsive to human variability; spend less time manipulating students of color to make them comply to institutional structures; and implement programs and processes that empower students through access to high-quality, high-status, and high-power knowledge, skills, and experiences (Fantini, 1979). Translating these conceptions of educational equality into practice requires reform in teacher preparation, curriculum design, classroom instruction, grouping of students for instruction, school climates, and how students' needs are diagnosed and their achievement assessed. All of these issues cannot be discussed in great detail here. Because of the crucial role teachers play in determining the quality of learning opportunities students receive in classrooms, more attention is given to their professional preparation.

Changing Tracking and Testing

All forms of tracking should be eliminated entirely. Even under the best of circumstances, tracking denies equal educational opportunities to students of color and to other students who populate the lower levels. It closes rather than opens pathways to social and academic advancement, and it commits some students early to a permanent educational and social underclass. Tracking should be replaced with flexible and frequently changed cooperative and heterogeneous groupings of students for specific instructional tasks or skill development purposes. For example, students grouped together to learn geographical directions should remain together only until that skill is mastered. Then other kinds of arrangements should be constructed to deal with new learning skills, tasks, and experiences.

Norm-referenced standardized tests for evaluating student achievement should be used infrequently, cautiously, and only in conjunction with other performance measures. More emphasis should be placed on evaluating students against their own records, with *range of improvement between different points of reference being the focus of attention,* as opposed to performance at isolated points in time. This requires that schools and classrooms use multiple techniques and procedures, including academic, social, psychological, and emotional measures, as well as verbal, visual, observational, participatory, and kinetic means, to assess students' knowledge and skills. This variety is necessary to prevent any one technique that is highly advantageous to one ethnic group from being used to the exclusion of others. Both the *content and process* of performance appraisal should be revised to incorporate more fully the cultural contributions, experiences, orientations, and styles of the full range of ethnic groups in the United States.

These approaches should always be *culturally contextualized and designed to serve diagnostic and developmental learning and teaching functions.* That is, they should be used to determine how and why students are proceeding with specific learning tasks, and the formats these approaches take should reflect the cultural orientations and nuances of the students being assessed. They should be administered frequently, and instructional programming should be changed according to the results obtained. Thus, students of color should be put in self-referenced and self-paced programs to complete their schooling. Narrative reports, developmental profiles, student–teacher–parent conferences, and anecdotal records should replace or complement letter and symbol grades for reporting student progress.

Curriculum Reform

School curricula, too, must be reformed if students of color are to be assured equal educational opportunities and outcomes. However, greater content quantity as the measure of educational quality is not the answer. More of the same irrelevant school subjects will not improve the educational equality and achievement quality of students of color. If Latinos, Native Americans, and African Americans are already failing science, simply taking more of it without multiculturalizing any of its content or techniques means that these students will have even greater opportunities to fail. If low-track students are already taking substantially different kinds of mathematics courses than are high-track students, then the gap in the substantive content they are learning widens as the high-track students take even more advanced courses and the low-track students take even more remedial math courses.

What schools consider to be essential knowledge and skills for all students to learn and how these skills are understood and taught need to be revised to incorporate cultural pluralism. These revisions should reflect the *comprehensive demographic, social, cultural, and linguistic realities of U.S. society and the world,* not just the technological, economic, and political sides of life. This means, first, that school curricula should demonstrate and emulate the *interdisciplinary nature of human life, knowledge, values, skills, and experiences.* Second, they should teach and model the *interdependence of the world*—a world in which Whites are a small numerical minority and one in which the control of natural resources, social aspirations, and power negotiations is gradually shifting from Western to non-Western, non-White nations. Third, a concerted effort should be made to achieve a *greater balance between technological developments and humanistic concerns,* where skills in ethics, morality, and aesthetics are as important as cognition. These kinds of curricular reforms increase the likelihood that students of color will identify with and relate better to schooling and improve their performance.

Multicultural Teacher Education

Because teachers play such a central role in the kinds of educational opportunities students of color receive in classrooms, their reeducation and training are fundamental to providing educational equality. This training should have four primary emphases. The first is *self-knowledge.* Teachers, counselors, and administrators need to become conscious of their own cultural values and beliefs, of how these affect their attitudes and expectations toward students from different ethnic groups, and of how they are habitually exhibited in school behaviors. They also need to understand the effects of their values and beliefs on students, relative to the students' self-concepts, academic abilities, educational opportunities, and achievement outcomes.

Spindler and Spindler (1993) offer a model for how teacher self-knowledge can be facilitated. Called "cultural therapy," it is "a process of bringing one's own culture, in its manifold forms—assumptions, goals, values, beliefs, and communicative modes—to a level of awareness that permits one to perceive it as a potential bias in social interaction and in the acquisition or transmission of skills and knowledge" (p. 28). Cultural therapy has elements of *self-reflection, self-monitoring,* and *self-transcendence.* This cultural consciousness is imperative "so that potential conflicts, misunderstandings, and blind spots in the perception and interpretation of behavior can be anticipated" (p. 28) and unequal power relationships in school and the larger society can be explicated. Cultural therapy can help teachers to identify, understand, and analyze reasons they may find the values and behaviors of ethnically different students objectionable, shocking, and irritating (Spindler & Spindler, 1993). Its ultimate goals are to empower teachers and to implement the principle that social reforms begin with individuals.

Merely telling teachers about how their cultural assumptions can lead to low expectations and negative consequences for students of color will not suffice. Nor will reading the impressive body of research that documents these effects. Instead, teachers need to *see and understand* how they behave toward culturally diverse students in their classrooms. This can be accomplished by projecting mirror images of or replaying their classroom behaviors back to them and training them to be participant-observers of their own classroom dynamics and to use different techniques systematically to analyze their instructional behaviors. Inexpensive technology, such as camcorders, makes it possible to accomplish such training with ease and expediency. Audio- and videotapes of teaching behaviors are invaluable for showing teachers what they actually do in classrooms. They are much better than are outside observers, because recorders and cameras do not interpret or misrepresent what actually occurs. Training in ethnographic techniques, interactional analysis, questioning strategies, frame analysis, self-reflection, feedback mechanisms, and participatory action research can help teachers to look systematically at these recorded behaviors and to monitor their change efforts.

In addition to *learning how to culturally decode their attitudes and behaviors* from an insider's viewpoint, teachers need to learn how to analyze these attitudes and behaviors from the perspectives of "others," especially those of their students of color. These skills are not acquired automatically; they must be deliberately taught. Without training, most educators cannot see the cultural biases and prejudices of their routine school behaviors. Suggestions to the effect that they are not treating students of color and European Americans equally tend to be associated with deliberate and blatant acts of discrimination. Teachers do not understand how thoroughly and subtly cultural nuances permeate all of their behaviors and can generate negative effects in instructional actions toward students who do not share their cultural frames of reference.

These cultural influences need to be counteracted by developing skills in *critical consciousness and culturally relevant pedagogy* for use with ethnically diverse students. Several contributing authors to the *Handbook of Research on Multicultural Education* (Banks & Banks, 2004), to *Culture, Style, and the Educative Process* (Shade, 1989), and to *Teaching Diverse Populations* (Hollins, King, & Hayman, 1994) explain what this means specifically for Native, African, Latino, and Asian American students. Their explanations include teaching about the cultural heritages and contributions of ethnic groups of concern; developing social and interpersonal relationships between students and teachers that convey a sense of personal kindredness, interdependence, connectedness, and caring; using cultural frames of reference to make the content of teaching personally meaningful to ethnically diverse students; showing concern for the affective and moral as well as the cognitive development of students; and cultivating social and cultural consciousness, solidarity, and responsibility. Thus, culturally appropriate or responsive pedagogy "empowers students intellectually, socially, emotionally, and politically by using cultural referents to impart knowledge, skills, and attitudes" (Ladson-Billings, 1992, p. 382).

A second emphasis in teacher reeducation for educational equality is *understanding differences in cultural values and behavioral codes* between themselves as middle-class European Americans and students of color and how instructional processes can be restructured to better accommodate them. Teachers cannot begin to treat African, Latino, Native, Asian, and European American students equitably until they accept that they all have comparable human worth and that differences do not automatically mean inferiorities. This acceptance begins with acquiring knowledge about the cultural backgrounds, life experiences, interactional patterns, and learning styles of different ethnic groups to replace racial myths and stereotypes. Once teachers understand the structures and motivations behind these cultural behaviors, they can begin to design more culturally compatible instructional options and thereby improve the quality of the learning experiences for students of color. This is the logic behind Pai's (1990) and Gay's (1994) contentions that knowledge of cultural diversity is an essential foundation for equality and excellence in both the processes and outcomes of education. These ideas are further elaborated in research reported by Foster (1989, 1991), Allen and Boykin (1992), Au (1993), Lee (1993), and Losey (1997). The findings consistently indicate that *cultural connectedness* in the educational process improves the academic achievement of students of color.

The third focus of teacher reeducation should be the development of *pedagogical skills* appropriate for use with students of color. The point of departure for this training should be understanding the specific traits of different teaching styles and ethnic learning styles. This knowledge should be combined with learning how to diversify teaching strategies culturally; to create more culturally diverse supportive environments for learning and demonstrating achievement; to reduce stress, tension, and conflict in ethnically pluralistic classrooms; to select materials that have high-quality interest appeal for different ethnic groups; and to develop and use learning activities that are meaningful, involving, enabling, and empowering for students of color. In other words, teachers need to learn how to ethnically integrate the structural arrangements and curricular materials for teaching, to culturally diversify their instructional and assessment strategies, and to make democratic the environments constructed for learning. These general skills can be made operational by helping teachers learn how to use specific instructional techniques with students of color, such as questioning, feedback and reinforcement, cooperative learning, inductive teaching, social-context learning, and auditory and visual learning.

The approaches used in teacher training to develop these skills should be four-dimensional—including *diagnosis, development and implementation, analytical debriefing and reflection,* and *refinement*—with teachers-in-training actively involved in each aspect. The training process should begin with a careful assessment of the value of and problems associated with using various instructional strategies with students of color. Examples of actual teaching behaviors should be used for this purpose. The training should then proceed to having teachers develop alternative curriculum designs and instructional strategies that incorporate cultural diversity and try them out in real or simulated teaching situations and under careful supervision. After these development efforts have been piloted or field-tested, they should be examined thoroughly through the filters of some established cultural diversity design and implementation criteria in order to determine their strengths and weaknesses. Central to this analysis should be discerning features of the new teaching strategies that facilitate or continue to inhibit the improvement of educational opportunities and achievement for students of color. Finally, the insights gained from these experiences and analyses should be used to further refine the multicultural curriculum designs and instructional strategies.

A fourth emphasis in the retraining of teachers, counselors, and school administrators for educational equality is *public relations skill development.* Major reform is needed in how educators are prepared to communicate and interact with parents of color and to mobilize their community resources to help in the educational process. Currently, there is a strong tendency for educators to blame the school failure of students on the lack of involvement of their parents in school affairs. This buck-passing is counterproductive to improving the education of students. It is a form of blaming and indicting the victims and of educators abdicating their own responsibility for teaching youths of color.

Certainly, parents of color should be more actively involved in their children's education, but it is understandable why they are reluctant or unable to do so. The schools that are failing their children are the same ones that failed many of them when they were students. Educators usually approach parents about their children only when the children get into trouble with the school system. This punitive, adversarial posture is not conducive to cooperation among educators and parents of color. Furthermore, teachers and administrators do not fully understand or appreciate the fact that many parents do not have the time, the personal resources, or the technical skills to assist in the education of their children in ways the teachers typically expect. How can parents effectively supervise their children's homework or come to the schools on demand when they are unfamiliar with the latest pedagogical strategies used in schools and when they are working at hourly wages or low-salaried jobs that do not permit them to take time off without significant cost? How can non- or limited-English-speaking mothers and fathers even understand their children's language arts assignment, let alone supervise and help them complete it? Professional development programs should help pre- and in-service educators understand these real-life social and cultural factors, the effects they have on parents' reactions to invitations and challenges to being educational partners, and how to develop novel, culturally sensitive strategies to overcome these obstacles.

This retraining process should include *culturally appropriate public relations skill development* for use with different ethnic communities. It should be a part of all levels of professional preparation, undergraduate and graduate, pre-service and in-service. It should start with acquiring an accurate knowledge base about the cultural dynamics of different ethnic communities, who the power brokers are in these communities, and how interactions and relationships are negotiated. It should also include specific strategies and skills about how to establish credibility and trust with different ethnic communities and parents. Specifically, this might include such skills as identifying and accessing the informal community networks of influence; understanding different ethnic groups' social protocols; establishing consultancy relations with parents and community organizations; establishing equal-status relationships with parents of color and other community members; being cultural brokers or mediators across the cultural systems of homes and schools; diffusing the threat and intimidation often associated with schools for parents of color; translating educational jargon into language styles that are meaningful for parents from different ethnic, social, and linguistic backgrounds; and identifying neutral sites or zones where parents and educators can meet, consult, confer, and collaborate.

All of these are elements of *cultural diplomacy* that classroom teachers, guidance counselors, and school administrators need to master in order to develop more constructive and cooperative relations with parents and communities of color. These elements, like the components of cultural therapy, literacy in ethnic and cultural diversity, and culturally responsive pedagogy, are fundamental to improving the quality of educational opportunities and outcomes for students of color.

CONCLUSION

Educational achievement among many students of color continues to be disturbingly low, even after more than five decades of deliberate legal reforms and funding policies designed to improve it. Some improvements are apparent, but they are not significant enough to alter long-established patterns. Consistently across time, place, and indicators of achievement, African Americans have the lowest academic proficiency levels of all ethnic groups, followed in sequence by Latinos and Native Americans. These trends are unequivocal in the math, science, reading, writing, history, and geography report cards issued at two-, four-, and six-year intervals by the National Assessment of Educational Progress (NAEP). African Americans perform somewhat better in civics, with scores higher than those of Latinos. The fact that school attendance and graduation rates are increasing for all students of color makes their low academic achievement even more troubling. If staying in school has positive consequences for mediating educational, social, and economic disadvantaged conditions, as theory claims, then as graduation rates increase and dropout rates decline students of color should perform academically much better than they are.

The failure of most students of color to achieve significant educational improvements from year to year gives credence to the position taken by Miller-Lachmann and Taylor (1995) that while funds and laws are necessary variables in providing educational equality, they are not sufficient. Something significantly different in *instructional quality* must be done to provide better educational opportunities and outcomes for students of color. Culturally responsive pedagogy and multicultural education offer ideologies and strategies that can facilitate these changes.

When the cultures of students and teachers are not congruent, someone loses out. Invariably, who loses out are the students and also the effectiveness of their learning, especially if they are members of racially visible groups, such as African, Native, Latino, and Asian Americans. Not understanding, accepting, or using their culture as instructional tools means that these students do not have access to high-quality instructional opportunities and interactions comparable to those of their European American counterparts. It is not surprising, then, that disparities in achievement outcomes exist. These situations will be reversed only when educators accept the fact that culture is a crucial, if not the ultimate, mediating factor in the quality of educational opportunities students of color receive and the levels of academic performance they achieve. As John Goodlad (1984) suggests, the central problem of both educational equality and excellence for today and tomorrow is "no longer access to school. It is access to knowledge for all" (p. 140). This access is not maximally possible for students of color unless their cultural orientations are used as filters for teaching and learning. Therefore, *culturally responsive pedagogy* must be used to better educate students from diverse ethnic and cultural backgrounds.

Questions and Activities

1. How do popular conceptions of educational equality differ from the view of this concept presented by Gay, the author of this chapter? What unfortunate assumptions, according to Gay, underlie these popular nations of educational equality?

2. What general patterns about the educational status of students of color are evident across different measures of achievement? What accounts for these trends?

3. In what ways did the educational status of students of color decline during the 1990s? What are some reasons for this decline?

4. How does the reference to Asian Americans as the model minority oversimplify their educational status? Give specific examples from this chapter to support your response.

5. How do school and curriculum practices such as tracking, vocational courses, and special education classes deny students of color equal educational opportunities?

6. The author argues that students of color are often placed in double jeopardy in school, in part because of differences between their cultures and the culture of the school. Explain what the author means by this concept. How can teachers help reduce the problems students of color experience in the schools?

7. How does testing, according to the author, promote educational inequality for low-income students and for students of color? How can assessment programs be changed so they will contribute to educational equality for all students?

8. According to the author, how can curriculum reforms related to ethnic diversity contribute to educational equality?

9. Gay contends that educational equality for students of color cannot be achieved short of "massive schoolwide reform." What factors in the school environment and in teacher education does she think require reform? What specific recommendations does she make for attaining these reforms?

10. Explain why Gay believes that multicultural education has the potential for improving educational equality and achievement for students of color.

11. Construct a descriptive profile of the concept of educational equality as developed by the author of this chapter.

12. Observe for several days in a school that has a large percentage of students of color. Look for evidence of the existence of the inequities discussed in this chapter. In what ways do your observations substantiate Gay's conclusions about the problems that students of color experience in schools? What programs, policies, and practices are being implemented in the school you observed to improve the educational status of students of color, and to what extent are they effective?

References

ACT National and State Scores. (2002). Average ACT Scores by Academic Preparation for Different Ethnic Groups. Retrieved May 22, 2003, from http://www.act.org/news/data/02/data.html.

Allen, B. A., & Boykin, A. W. (1992). African-American Children and the Educative Process: Alleviating Cultural Discontinuity through Prescriptive Pedagogy. *School Psychology Review, 21*(4), 586–598.

Astin, A. A. (1985). *Achieving Educational Excellence: A Critical Assessment of Priorities and Practices in Higher Education.* San Francisco: Jossey-Bass.

Au, K. H. (1993). *Literacy Instruction in Multicultural Settings.* New York: Harcourt Brace.

Banks, J. A., & Banks, C. A. M. (Eds.). (2004). *Handbook of Research on Multicultural Education* (2nd. ed.). San Francisco: Jossey-Bass.

Boateng, F. (1990). Combatting Deculturalization of the African-American Child in the Public School System: A Multicultural Approach. In K. Lomotey (Ed.), *Going to School: The African American Experience* (pp. 73–84). Albany: State University of New York Press.

College Board. (1999). *Reaching the Top: A Report of the National Task Force on Minority High Achievement.* New York: Author.

College Board. (2002). 2002 College-Bound Seniors: A Profile of SAT Program Test Takers. Retrieved May 22, 2003, from http://www.collegeboard.com.

College Entrance Examination Board. (1985). *Equality and Excellence: The Educational Status of Black Americans.* New York: Author.

Fantini, M. D. (1979). From School System to Educational System: Policy Considerations. In D. A. Wilkerson (Ed.), *Educating All of Our Children: An Imperative for Democracy* (pp. 134–153). Westport, CT: Mediax.

Foster, M. (1989). It's Cooking Now: A Performance Analysis of the Speech Events of a Black Teacher in an Urban Community College. *Language in Society, 18*(1), 1–29.

Foster, M. (Ed.). (1991). *Readings on Equal Education: Qualitative Investigations into Schools and Schooling* (Vol. 11). New York: AMS Press.

Gay, G. (1974). *Differential Dyadic Interactions of Black and White Teachers with Black and White Pupils in Recently Desegregated Social Studies Classrooms: A Function of Teacher and Pupil Ethnicity.* Washington, DC: Office of Education, National Institute of Education.

Gay, G. (1994). *At the Essence of Learning: Multicultural Education.* West Lafayette, IN: Kappa Delta Pi.

Gay, G. (2000). *Culturally Responsive Teaching: Theory, Research, and Practice.* New York: Teachers College Press.

Gibbs, J. T., & Nahme-Huang, L. (Eds.). (1989). *Children of Color: Psychological Interventions with Minority Youth.* San Francisco: Jossey-Bass.

Good, T. L., & Brophy, J. E. (1994). *Looking in Classrooms* (6th ed.). New York: Harper Collins.

Goodlad, J. I. (1984). *A Place Called School: Prospects for the Future.* New York: McGraw-Hill.

Gougis, R. A. (1986). The Effects of Prejudice and Stress on the Academic Performance of Black Americans. In U. Neisser (Ed.), *The Achievement of Minority Children: New Perspectives* (pp. 145–158). Hillsdale, NJ: Erlbaum.

Grant, C. A., & Sleeter, C. E. (1985). Equality, Equity, and Excellence: A Critique. In P. G. Altbach, G. P. Kelly, & L. Weis (Eds.), *Excellence in Education: Perspectives on Policy and Practice* (pp. 139–159). Buffalo, NY: Prometheus.

Harry, B. (1992). *Cultural Diversity, Families, and the Special Education System: Communication and Empowerment.* New York: Teachers College Press.

Holliday, B. G. (1985). Towards a Model of Teacher–Child Transactional Processes Affecting Black Children's Academic Achievement. In M. B. Spencer, G. K. Brookins, & W. R. Allen (Eds.), *Beginnings: The Social and Affective Development of Black Children* (pp. 117–130). Hillsdale, NJ: Erlbaum.

Hollins, E. R., King, J. E., & Hayman, W. C. (Eds.). (1994). *Teaching Diverse Populations: Formulating a Knowledge Base.* Albany: State University of New York Press.

Igoa, C. (1995). *The Inner World of the Immigrant Child.* New York: St. Martin's.

John-Steiner, V. P., & Leacock, E. (1979). Transforming the Structure of Failure. In D. A. Wilkerson (Ed.), *Educating All of Our Children: An Imperative for Democracy* (pp. 79–91). Westport, CT: Mediax.

Ladson-Billings, G. (1992). Liberatory Consequences of Literacy: A Case of Culturally Relevant Instruction for African American Students. *The Journal of Negro Education, 61*(3), 378–391.

Ladson-Billings, G. (1994). *The Dreamkeepers: Successful Teachers of African-American Children.* San Francisco: Jossey-Bass.

Lee, C. (1993). *Signifying as a Scaffold to Literary Interpretation: The Pedagogical Implications of a Form of African American Discourse.* Urbana, IL: National Council of Teachers of English.

Losey, K. M. (1997). *Listen to the Silences: Mexican American Interaction in the Composition Classroom and Community.* Norwood, NJ: Ablex.

Miller-Lachmann, L., & Taylor, L. S. (1995). *Schools for All: Educating Children in a Diverse Society.* New York: Delmar.

Morgan, E. P. (1977). *Inequality in Classroom Learning: Schooling and Democratic Citizenship.* New York: Praeger.

Nielsen, F. (1986). Hispanics in High School and Beyond. In M. A. Olivas (Ed.), *Latino College Students* (pp. 71–103). New York: Teachers College Press.

Oakes, J. (1985). *Keeping Track: How Schools Structure Inequality.* New Haven, CT: Yale University Press.

Oakes, J., & Guiton, G. (1995). Matchmaking: The Dynamics of High School Tracking Decisions. *American Educational Research Journal, 32*(1), 3–33.

Orfield, G., Eaton, S. E., & the Harvard Project on School Desegregation. (1996). *Dismantling Desegregation: The Quiet Reversal of Brown v. Board of Education.* New York: New Press.

Osajima, K. (1991). Breaking the Silence: Race and the Educational Experiences of Asian-American College Students. In M. Foster (Ed.), *Readings on Equal Education: Qualitative Investigations into Schools and Schooling* (Vol. 11, pp. 115–134). New York: AMS Press.

Pai, Y. (1990). *Cultural Foundations of Education.* New York: Merrill.

Pang, V. O. (2001). Asian Pacific American Students: A Diverse and Complex Population. In J. A. Banks & C. A. M. Banks (Eds.), *Handbook of Research on Multicultural Education* (pp. 412–424). San Francisco: Jossey-Bass.

Pang, V. O., & Cheng, L. R. C. (Eds.). (1998). *Struggling to Be Heard: The Unmet Needs of Asian Pacific American Children.* Albany: State University of New York Press.

Pang, V. O., Mizokawa, D. T., Morishima, J. K., & Olstad, R. G. (1985). Self-Concept of Japanese American Children. *Journal of Cross-Cultural Psychology, 16*(2), 99–108.

Persell, C. H. (1977). *Education and Inequality: A Theoretical and Empirical Synthesis.* New York: Free Press.

Ralph, J., Keller, D., & Crouse, J. (1994). How Effective Are American Schools? *Phi Delta Kappan, 76*(2), 144–150.

Shade, B. J. R. (Ed.). (1989). *Culture, Style, and the Educative Process.* Springfield, IL: Thomas.

Spindler, G., & Spindler, L. (1993). The Processes of Culture and Person: Cultural Therapy and Culturally Diverse Schools. In P. Phelan & A. L. Davidson (Eds.), *Renegotiating Cultural Diversity in American Schools* (pp. 27–51). New York: Teachers College Press.

U.S. Civil Rights Commission. (1971–1974). *Mexican-American Educational Study* (Reports I–VI). Washington, DC: U.S. Government Printing Office.

U.S. Department of Education. (n.d.). NAEP: The Nation's Report Card. Retrieved May 22, 2003, from http://nces.ed.gov/nationsreportcard/sitemap.asp.

U.S. Department of Education. (1994). *NAEP 1992 Trends in Academic Progress.* Washington, DC: U.S. Government Printing Office.

U.S. Department of Education. (1995). *Characteristics of American Indian and Alaska Native Education.* Washington, DC: U.S. Government Printing Office.

U.S. Department of Education. (1999a). *Digest of Education Statistics, 1998.* Washington, DC: U.S. Government Printing Office.

U.S. Department of Education. (1999b). *The Condition of Education, 1999.* Washington, DC: U.S. Government Printing Office.

U.S. Department of Education. (1999c). NAEP 1998 Civics Report Card for the Nation. Retrieved May 22, 2003, from http://nces.ed.gov/pubsearch/pubsinfo.asp?pubid=2000457.

U.S. Department of Education. (2002a). *The Nation's Report Card: Fourth Grade Reading Highlights 2002.* Jessup, MD: ED Pubs.

U.S. Department of Education. (2002b). *The Nation's Report Card, 2000: Science Highlights.* Jessup, MD: ED Pubs.

U.S. Department of Education. (2002c). *The Condition of Education, 2002.* Washington, DC: U.S. Government Printing Office.

Verdugo, R. R. (1986). Educational Stratification and Hispanics. In M. A. Olivas (Ed.), *Latino College Students* (pp. 325–347). New York: Teachers College Press.

Winkler, J. D., Stravelson, R. J., Stasz, C., Robyn, A., & Fiebel, W. (1984). *How Effective Teachers Use Microcomputers in Instruction.* Santa Monica, CA: RAND.

Yu, E. S. H., Doi, M., & Chang, C. (1986, November). *Asian American Education in Illinois: A Review of the Data.* Springfield: Illinois State Board of Education.

CHAPTER 10

Approaches to Multicultural Curriculum Reform

James A. Banks

THE MAINSTREAM-CENTRIC CURRICULUM

The United States is made up of many different racial, ethnic, religious, language, and cultural groups. In the year 2000, people of color—such as African Americans, Latinos, and Asian Americans—made up 28 percent of the U.S. population. These groups are projected to make up 48 percent of the U.S. population by 2050 (Martin & Midgley, 1999). Despite the deepening ethnic texture within the United States, the U.S. school, college, and university mainstream curriculum is organized around concepts, paradigms, and events that reflect the experiences of mainstream Americans (Banks, 1996, 2004b). The dominant, mainstream curriculum has been challenged and fractured within the last thirty-five years, beginning with the civil rights movement of the 1960s and 1970s. Consequently, the mainstream curriculum and textbooks today are much more multicultural than they were when the civil rights movement began. Progress has been made, and it should be acknowledged. However, the reforms have been neither as extensive nor as institutionalized as is needed, and the process of curriculum transformation needs to continue. Curriculum transformation is a process that never ends because of the changes that are continuing within the United States and throughout the world (Banks, 2004a).

A curriculum that focuses on the experiences of mainstream Americans and largely ignores the experiences, cultures, and histories of other ethnic, racial, cultural, language, and religious groups has negative consequences for both mainstream students and students of color. A mainstream-centric curriculum is one major way in which racism and ethnocentrism are reinforced and perpetuated in the schools, in colleges and universities, and in society at large.

A mainstream-centric curriculum has negative consequences for mainstream students because it reinforces their false sense of superiority, gives them a misleading conception of their relationship with other racial and ethnic groups, and denies them the opportunity to benefit from the knowledge, perspectives, and frames of reference that can be gained from studying and experiencing other cultures and groups. A mainstream-centric curriculum also denies mainstream U.S. students the opportunity to view their culture from the perspectives of other cultures and groups. When people view their culture from the point of view of another culture, they are able to understand their own culture more fully, to see how it is unique and distinct from other cultures, and to understand better how it relates to and interacts with other cultures.

A mainstream-centric curriculum negatively influences students of color, such as African Americans, Latinos, and Asian Americans. It marginalizes their experiences and cultures and does not reflect their dreams, hopes, and perspectives. It does not provide them social equality within the school, an essential characteristic of democratic institutions (Gutmann, 2004). Students learn best and are more highly motivated when the school curriculum reflects their cultures, experiences, and perspectives. Many students of color are alienated in the school in part because they experience cultural conflict and discontinuities that result from the cultural differences between their school and community (Delpit & Dowdy, 2002). The school can help students of color mediate between their home and school cultures by implementing a curriculum that reflects the culture of their ethnic groups and communities. The school can and should make effective use of the community cultures of students of color when teaching them such subjects as writing, language arts, science, and mathematics (Delpit & Dowdy).

In the mainstream-centric curriculum, events, themes, concepts, and issues are viewed primarily from the perspective of mainstream Americans and Europeans. Events and cultural developments such as the European explorations in the Americas and the development of American music are viewed from Anglo and European perspectives and are evaluated using mainstream-centric criteria and points of view (Bigelow & Peterson, 1998).

When the European explorations of the Americas are viewed from a Eurocentric perspective, the Americas are perceived as having been "discovered" by the European explorers such as Columbus and Cortés (Loewen, 1995; Zinn, 1999). The view that native peoples in the Americas were discovered by the Europeans subtly suggests that Indian cultures did not exist until they were "discovered" by the Europeans and that the lands occupied by the American Indians were rightfully owned by the Europeans after they settled on and claimed them.

When the formation and nature of U.S. cultural developments, such as music and dance, are viewed from mainstream-centric perspectives, these art forms become important and significant only when they are recognized or legitimized by mainstream critics and artists. The music of African American musicians such as Chuck Berry and Little Richard was not viewed as significant by the mainstream society until White singers such as the Beatles and Rod Stewart publicly acknowledged the significant ways in which their own music had been deeply influenced by these African American musicians. It often takes White artists to legitimize ethnic cultural forms and innovations created by Asian Americans, African Americans, Latinos, and Native Americans.

Public Sites and Popular History

Anglocentric history is not only taught in the nation's schools, colleges, and universities but is also perpetuated in popular knowledge in the nation's parks, museums, and other public sites. Loewen (1999) describes the ways in which public history in the nation's historic sites often distort history in order to present a positive image of Anglo Americans. The title of his book is *Lies across America: What Our Historic Sites Get Wrong*.

I have seen several examples of markers in public sites that perpetuate Anglocentric views of American history. The first appears on a marker in a federal park on the site where a U.S. Army post once stood in Fort Townsend in the state of Washington. With the choice of words such as *settlers* (instead of *invaders*), *restive*, and *rebelled*, the author justifies the taking of the Indians' lands and depicts their resistance as unreasonable.

Fort Townsend

A U.S. Army Post was established on this site in 1856. In [the] mid–nineteenth century the growth of Port Townsend caused the Indians to become *restive. Settlers* started a home guard, campaigned wherever called, and defeated the Indians in the Battle of Seattle. Indians *rebelled* as the government began enforcing the Indian Treaty of 1854, by which the Indians had ceded most of their territory. Port Townsend, a prosperous port of entry on Puget Sound, then asked protection of the U.S. army. (emphasis added)

The second example is in Marianna, Arkansas, my hometown, which is the city center for Lee County. The site commemorates the life and achievements of Confederate soldiers from Lee County and the life of Robert E. Lee, a general of the Confederate Army and a southern hero. The marker reads in part, "In loving memory of Lee County's Confederate soldiers. No braver bled for a brighter land. No brighter land had a cause so grand." The final example is from a marker in the Confederate Park in Memphis, Tennessee, which commemorates the life of Jefferson Davis, president of the Confederate States of America. The marker reads, in part: "Before the war Between the States, he served with distinction as a United States Congressman and twice as a United States Senator. He also served as Secretary of War of the U.S. He was a true American patriot." Describing Davis as a "true American patriot" is arguable.

EFFORTS TO ESTABLISH A MULTICULTURAL CURRICULUM

Since the civil rights movement of the 1960s, educators have been trying, in various ways, to better integrate the school curriculum with multicultural content and to move away from a mainstream-centric and Eurocentric curriculum (Banks, 2002). These have proven to be difficult goals for schools to attain for many complex reasons. The strong assimilationist ideology embraced by most U.S. educators is one major reason (Banks, 2001). The assimilationist ideology makes it difficult for educators to think differently about how U.S. society and culture developed and to acquire a commitment to make the curriculum multicultural. Individuals who have a strong assimilationist ideology believe that most important events and developments in U.S. society are related to the nation's British heritage and that the contributions of other ethnic and cultural groups are not very significant by comparison. When educators acquire a multicultural ideology and conception of U.S. culture, they are then able to view the experiences and contributions of a wide range of cultural, ethnic, language, and religious groups as significant to the development of the United States.

Ideological resistance is a major factor that has slowed and is still slowing the development of a multicultural curriculum, but other factors have also affected its growth and development. Political resistance to a multicultural curriculum is closely related to ideological resistance. Many people who resist a multicultural curriculum believe that knowledge is power and that a multicultural perspective on U.S. society challenges the existing power structure. They believe that the dominant mainstream-centric curriculum supports, reinforces, and justifies the existing social, economic, and political structure. Multicultural perspectives and points of view, in the opinion of many observers, legitimize and promote social change and social reconstruction.

During the 1980s and 1990s a heated debate occurred about how much the curriculum should be Western and European-centric or reflect the cultural, ethnic, and racial diversity in the United States. At least three major positions in this debate can be identified. The Western traditionalists argue that the West, as defined and conceptualized in the past, should be the focus in school and college curricula because of the major influence of Western civilization and culture in the United States and throughout the world (Ravitch, 1990; Schlesinger, 1991). Afrocentric scholars contend that the contributions of Africa and of African peoples should receive major emphasis in the curriculum (Asante, 1998; Asante & Ravitch, 1991). The multiculturalists argue that although the West should receive a major emphasis in the curriculum, the West should be reconceptualized so that it reflects the contributions that people of color have made to the West (Zinn & Kirschner, 1995). In addition to teaching about Western ideals, the gap between the ideals of the West and its realities of racism, sexism, and discrimination should be taught (Dilg, 2003). Multiculturalists also believe that in addition to learning about the West, students should study other world cultures, such as those in Africa, Asia, the Middle East, and the Americas as they were before the Europeans arrived (Gates, 1999).

Other factors that have slowed the institutionalization of a multicultural curriculum include the focus on high-stakes testing and accountability that has emerged within the last decade, the low level of knowledge about ethnic cultures that most educators have, and the heavy reliance on textbooks for teaching. Many studies have revealed that the textbook is still the main source for teaching, especially in such subjects as the social studies, reading, and language arts (Goodlad, 1984).

Teachers need in-depth knowledge about ethnic cultures and experiences to integrate ethnic content, experiences, and points of view into the curriculum. Many teachers tell their students that Columbus discovered America and that America is a "new world" because they know little about the diverse Native American cultures that existed in the Americas more than 40,000 years before the Europeans began to settle in the Americas in significant numbers in the sixteenth century. As Gary Howard (1999) states in the title of his cogent and informative book, *We Can't Teach What We Don't Know.*

LEVELS OF INTEGRATION OF MULTICULTURAL CONTENT

The Contributions Approach

I have identified four approaches to the integration of multicultural content into the curriculum (see Figure 10.1). The contributions approach to integration (Level 1) is frequently used when a school or district first attempts to integrate multicultural content into the mainstream curriculum.

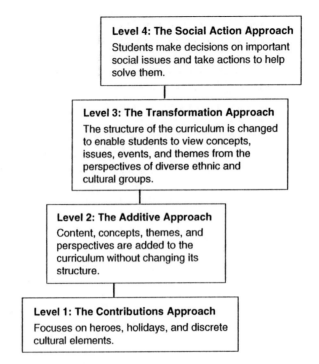

Figure 10.1   Banks's Four Levels of Integration of Multicultural Content

The contributions approach is characterized by the insertion of ethnic heroes/heroines and discrete cultural artifacts into the curriculum, selected using criteria similar to those used to select mainstream heroes/heroines and cultural artifacts. Thus, individuals such as Crispus Attucks, Benjamin Bannaker, Pocahontas, Martin Luther King, Jr., and Cesar Chavez are added to the curriculum. They are discussed when mainstream American heroes/heroines such as Patrick Henry, George Washington, Thomas Jefferson, Betsy Ross, and Eleanor Roosevelt are studied in the mainstream curriculum. Discrete cultural elements such as the foods, dances, music, and artifacts of ethnic groups are studied, but little attention is given to their meanings and importance within ethnic communities.

An important characteristic of the contributions approach is that the mainstream curriculum remains unchanged in its basic structure, goals, and salient characteristics. Prerequisites for the implementation of this approach are minimal. They include basic knowledge about U.S. society and knowledge about ethnic heroes/heroines and their roles and contributions to U.S. society and culture.

Individuals who challenged the dominant society's ideologies, values, and conceptions and advocated radical social, political, and economic reform are seldom included in the contributions approach. Thus, Booker T. Washington is more likely to be chosen for study than is W. E. B. Du Bois, and Pocahontas is more likely to be chosen than is Geronimo. The criteria used to select ethnic heroes/heroines for study and to judge them for success are derived from the mainstream society, not from the ethnic community. Consequently, use of the contributions approach usually results in the study of ethnic heroes/heroines who represent only one important perspective within ethnic communities. The more radical and less conformist individuals who are heroes/heroines only to the ethnic community are often invisible in textbooks, teaching materials, and activities used in the contributions approach.

The heroes/heroines and holidays approach is a variant of the contributions approach. In this approach, ethnic content is limited primarily to special days, weeks, and months related to ethnic events and celebrations. Cinco de Mayo, Martin Luther King, Jr.'s, birthday, and African American History Week are examples of ethnic days and weeks celebrated in the schools. During these celebrations, teachers involve students in lessons, experiences, and pageants related to the ethnic group being commemorated. When this approach is used, the class studies little or nothing about the ethnic or cultural group before or after the special event or occasion.

The contributions approach (Level 1 in Figure 10.1) provides teachers with a way to integrate ethnic content into the curriculum quickly, thus giving some recognition to ethnic contributions to U.S. society and culture. Many teachers who are committed to integrating their curricula with ethnic content have little knowledge about ethnic groups and curriculum revision. Consequently, they use the contributions approach when teaching about ethnic groups. These teachers should be encouraged, supported, and given the opportunity to acquire the knowledge and skills needed to reform their curricula by using one of the more effective approaches described later in this chapter.

There are often strong political demands from ethnic communities for the school to put their heroes/heroines, contributions, and cultures into the school curriculum. These political forces may take the form of demands for heroes and contributions because mainstream heroes, such as Washington, Jefferson, and Lincoln, are highly visible in the school curriculum. Ethnic communities of color want to see their own heroes/heroines and contributions alongside those of the mainstream society. Such contributions may help give them a sense of structural inclusion, validation, and social equality. Curriculum inclusion also facilitates the quests of marginalized ethnic and cultural groups for a sense of empowerment, efficacy, and social equality. The school should help ethnic group students acquire a sense of empowerment and efficacy. These factors are positively correlated with academic achievement (Coleman et al., 1966).

The contributions approach is also the easiest approach for teachers to use to integrate the curriculum with multicultural content. However, this approach has several serious limitations. When the integration of the curriculum is accomplished primarily through the infusion of ethnic heroes/heroines and contributions, students do not attain a global view of the role of ethnic and cultural groups in U.S. society. Rather, they see ethnic issues and events primarily as an addition to the curriculum and consequently as an appendage to the main story of the development of the nation and to the core curriculum in the language arts, the social studies, the arts, and other subject areas.

Teaching ethnic issues with the use of heroes/heroines and contributions also tends to gloss over important concepts and issues related to the victimization and oppression of ethnic groups and their struggles against racism and for power. Issues such as racism, poverty, and oppression tend to be avoided in the contributions approach to curriculum integration. The focus tends to be on success and the validation of the Horatio Alger myth that all Americans who are willing to work hard can go from rags to riches and "pull themselves up by their bootstraps."

The success stories of ethnic heroes such as Booker T. Washington, George Washington Carver, and Jackie Robinson are usually told with a focus on their success, with little attention to racism and other barriers they encountered and how they succeeded despite the hurdles they faced. Little attention is also devoted to the *process* by which they become heroes/heroines. Students should learn about the process by which people become heroes/heroines as well as about their status and role as heroes/heroines. Only when students learn the process by which individuals become heroes/heroines will they understand fully how individuals, particularly individuals of color, achieve and maintain hero/heroine status and what the process of becoming a hero/heroine means for their own lives.

The contributions approach often results in the trivialization of ethnic cultures, the study of their strange and exotic characteristics, and the reinforcement of stereotypes and misconceptions. When the focus is on the contributions and unique aspects of ethnic cultures, students are not helped to view them as complete and dynamic wholes. The contributions approach also tends to focus on the *lifestyles* of ethnic groups rather than on the *institutional structures*, such as racism and discrimination, that significantly affect their life chances and keep them powerless and marginalized.

The contributions approach to content integration may provide students with a memorable one-time experience with an ethnic hero/heroine, but it often fails to help them understand the role and influence of the hero/heroine in the total context of U.S. history and society. When ethnic heroes/heroines are studied apart from the social and political context in which they lived and worked, students attain only a partial understanding of their roles and significance in society. When Martin Luther King, Jr., and Rosa Parks are studied outside the social and political context of institutionalized racism in the U.S. South in the 1940s and 1950s, and without attention to the more subtle forms of institutionalized racism in the North during this period, their full significance as social reformers and activists is neither revealed nor understood by students.

The Additive Approach

Another important approach to the integration of ethnic content into the curriculum is the addition of content, concepts, themes, and perspectives to the curriculum without changing its basic structure, purposes, and characteristics. The additive approach (Level 2 in Figure 10.1) is often accomplished by the addition of a book, a unit, or a course to the curriculum without changing it substantially. Examples of this approach include adding a book such as *The Color Purple* to a unit on the twentieth century in an English class, the use of the film *Miss Jane Pittman* during a unit on the 1960s, and the addition of a videotape on the internment of the Japanese Americans, such as *Rabbit in the Moon*, during a study of World War II in a class on U.S. history.

The additive approach allows the teacher to put ethnic content into the curriculum without restructuring it, a process that would take substantial time, effort, and training as well as a rethinking of the curriculum and its purposes, nature, and goals. The additive approach can be the first phase in a transformative curriculum reform effort designed to restructure the total curriculum and to integrate it with ethnic content, perspectives, and frames of reference.

However, this approach shares several disadvantages with the contributions approach. Its most important shortcoming is that it usually results in the viewing of ethnic content from the perspectives of mainstream historians, writers, artists, and scientists because it does not involve a restructuring of the curriculum. The events, concepts, issues, and problems selected for study are selected using mainstream-centric and Eurocentric criteria and perspectives. When teaching a unit entitled "The Westward Movement" in a fifth-grade U.S. history class, the teacher may integrate the unit by adding content about the Oglala Sioux Indians. However, the unit remains mainstream-centric and focused because of its perspective and point of view.

A unit called "The Westward Movement" is mainstream and Eurocentric because it focuses on the movement of European Americans from the eastern to the western part of the United States. The Oglala Sioux were already in the West and consequently were not moving westward. The unit might be called "The Invasion from the East" from the point of view of the Oglala Sioux. Black Elk, an Oglala Sioux holy man, lamented the conquering of his people, which culminated in their defeat at Wounded Knee Creek on December 29, 1890. Approximately 200 Sioux men, women, and children were killed by U.S. troops. Black Elk said, "The [Sioux] nation's hoop is broken and scattered. There is no center any longer, and the sacred tree is dead" (Neihardt, 1972, p. 230).

Black Elk did not consider his homeland "the West," but rather the center of the world. He viewed the cardinal directions metaphysically. The Great Spirit sent him the cup of living water and the sacred bow from the West. The daybreak star and the sacred pipe originated from the East. The Sioux nation's sacred hoop and the tree that was to bloom came from the South (Black Elk's Prayer, 1964). When teaching about the movement of the Europeans across North America, teachers should help students understand that different cultural, racial, and ethnic groups often have varying and conflicting conceptions and points of view about the same historical events, concepts, issues, and developments. The victors and the vanquished, especially, often have conflicting conceptions of the same historical event (Limerick, 1987). However, it is usually the point of view of the victors that becomes institutionalized within the schools and the mainstream society. This happens because history and textbooks are usually written by the people who won the wars and gained control of the society, not by the losers—the victimized and the powerless. The perspectives of both groups are needed to help us fully understand our history, culture, and society.

The people who are conquered and the people who conquered them have histories and cultures that are intricately interwoven and interconnected. They have to learn each others' histories and cultures to understand their own fully. White Americans cannot fully understand their own history in the western United States and in America without understanding the history of the American Indians and the ways their histories and the histories of the Indians are interconnected.

James Baldwin (1985) insightfully pointed out that when White Americans distort African American history, they do not learn the truth about their own history because the history of Blacks and Whites in the United States is tightly bound together. This is also true for African American history and Indian history. The history of African Americans and Indians in the United States is closely interconnected, as Katz (1986) documents in *Black Indians: A Hidden Heritage.*

The histories of African Americans and Whites in the United States are tightly connected, both culturally and biologically, as Ball (1998) points out when he describes the

African Americans ancestors in his White family and as Gordon-Reed (1997) reveals when she describes the relationship between Thomas Jefferson and Sally Hemings, his slave mistress. The additive approach fails to help students view society from diverse cultural and ethnic perspectives and to understand the ways in which the histories and cultures of the nation's diverse ethnic, racial, cultural, and religious groups are interconnected.

Multicultural history enables students and teachers to understand America's complexity and the ways in which various groups within the United States are interconnected (Takaki, 1993). Sam Hamod (cited in Reed, 1997) describes the way in which diverse ethnic perspectives enrich our understandings and lead to more accurate versions of U.S. society: "Our dual vision of 'ethnic' and American allows us to see aspects of the U.S. that mainstream writers often miss; thus, our perspectives often allow us a diversity of visions that, ironically, may lead us to larger truth—it's just that we were raised with different eyes" (p. xxii).

Content, materials, and issues that are added to a curriculum as appendages instead of being integral parts of a unit of instruction can become problematic. Problems might result when a book such as *The Color Purple* or a film like *Miss Jane Pittman* is added to a unit when the students lack the concepts, content background, and emotional maturity to deal with the issues and problems in these materials. The effective use of such emotion-laden and complex materials usually requires that the teacher help students acquire, in a sequential and developmental fashion, the content background and attitudinal maturity to deal with them effectively. The use of both of these materials in different classes and schools has resulted in major problems for the teachers using them. A community controversy arose in each case. The problems developed because the material was used with students who had neither the content background nor the attitudinal sophistication to respond to them appropriately. Adding ethnic content to the curriculum in a sporadic and segmented way can result in pedagogical problems, trouble for the teacher, student confusion, and community controversy.

The Transformation Approach

The transformation approach differs fundamentally from the contributions and additive approaches. In those two approaches, ethnic content is added to the mainstream core curriculum without changing its basic assumptions, nature, and structure. The fundamental goals, structure, and perspectives of the curriculum are changed in the transformation approach.

The transformation approach (Level 3 in Figure 10.1) changes the basic assumptions of the curriculum and enables students to view concepts, issues, themes, and problems from several ethnic perspectives and points of view. The mainstream-centric perspective is one of only several perspectives from which issues, problems, concepts, and issues are viewed. Richard White (1991), a historian of the American West, indicates how viewing the American West from a transformative perspective can provide new insights into U.S. history. He writes, "The first Europeans to penetrate the West arrived neither as conquerors nor as explorers. Like so many others history has treated as discoverers, they were merely lost" (p. 5).

It is neither possible nor desirable to view every issue, concept, event, or problem from the point of view of every U.S. ethnic and cultural group. Rather, the goal should be to enable students to view concepts and issues from more than one perspective and from the point of view of the cultural, ethnic, and racial groups that were the most active participants in, or were most cogently influenced by, the event, issue, or concept being studied.

The key curriculum issues involved in multicultural curriculum reform is not the addition of a long list of ethnic groups, heroes, and contributions but the infusion of various perspectives, frames of references, and content from different groups that will extend students' understandings of the nature, development, and complexity of U.S. society. When students are studying the revolution in the British colonies, the perspectives of the Anglo revolutionaries, the Anglo loyalists, African Americans, Indians, and the British are essential for them to attain a thorough understanding of this significant event in U.S. history (see Figure 10.2). Students must study the various and sometimes divergent meanings of the revolution to these diverse groups to understand it fully (Gay & Banks, 1975).

In the language arts, when students are studying the nature of U.S. English and proper language use, they should be helped to understand the rich linguistic and language diversity in the United States and the ways in which a wide range of regional, cultural, and ethnic groups have influenced the development of U.S. English. Students should also examine how normative language use varies with the social context, the region, and the situation. The use

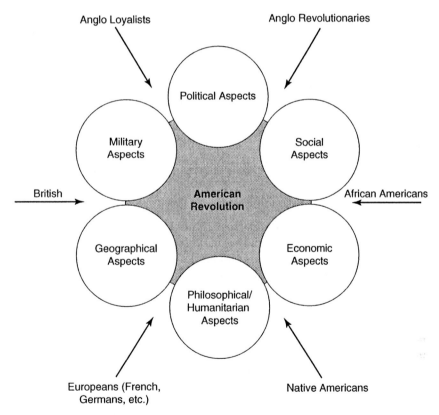

Figure 10.2   A Multicultural Interdisciplinary Model for Teaching the American Revolution

Source: James A. Banks and Geneva Gay, "Teaching the American Revolution: A Multiethnic Approach," *Social Education*, Vol. 39, No. 7 (November–December 1975): 462. Used with permission of the National Council for the Social Studies.

of Black English is appropriate in some social and cultural contexts and inappropriate in others (Delpit & Dowdy, 2002). This is also true of standard U.S. English. The United States is rich in languages and dialects. The nation had more than 35 million Latino citizens in 2000; Spanish is the first language for most of them. Most of the nation's approximately 34.6 million African Americans speak both standard English as well as some form of Black English or Ebonics. The rich language diversity in the United States includes more than twenty-five European languages; Asian, African, and Middle Eastern languages; and American Indian languages. Since the 1970s, languages from Indochina, spoken by groups such as the Hmong, Vietnamese, Laotians, and Cambodians, have further enriched language diversity in the United States (Ovando & McLaren, 2000).

When subjects such as music, dance, and literature are studied, the teacher should acquaint students with the ways these art forms among U.S. ethnic groups have greatly influenced and enriched the nation's artistic and literary traditions. The ways in which African American musicians such as Bessie Smith, W. C. Handy, and Leontyne Price have influenced the nature and development of U.S. music should be examined when the development of U.S. music is studied. African Americans and Puerto Ricans have significantly influenced the development of American dance. Writers of color, such as Langston Hughes, Toni Morrison, N. Scott Momaday, Carlos Bulosan, Maxine Hong Kingston, Rudolfo A. Anaya, and Piri Thomas, have not only significantly influenced the development of American literature but have also provided unique and revealing perspectives on U.S. society and culture (Gillan & Gillan, 1994; Rico & Mano, 1995).

When studying U.S. history, language, music, arts, science, and mathematics, the emphasis should not be on the ways in which various ethnic and cultural groups have contributed to mainstream U.S. society and culture. *The emphasis should be on how the common U.S. culture and society emerged from a complex synthesis and interaction of the diverse cultural elements that originated within the various cultural, racial, ethnic, and religious groups that make up U.S. society.* I call this process *multiple acculturation* and argue that even though Anglo Americans are the dominant group in the United States—culturally, politically, and economically—it is misleading and inaccurate to describe U.S. culture and society as an Anglo-Saxon Protestant culture (Banks, 2001). Other U.S. ethnic and cultural groups have deeply influenced, shaped, and participated in the development and formation of U.S. society and culture. African Americans, for example, profoundly influenced the development of the southern culture, even though they had very little political and economic power. One irony of conquest is that those who are conquered often deeply influence the cultures of the conquerors.

A multiple acculturation conception of U.S. society and culture leads to a perspective that views ethnic events, literature, music, and art as integral parts of the common, shared U.S. culture. Anglo American Protestant culture is viewed as only a part of this larger cultural whole. Thus, to teach American literature without including significant writers of color, such as Maxine Hong Kingston, Carlos Bulosan, and Toni Morrison, gives a partial and incomplete view of U.S. literature, culture, and society.

The Social Action Approach

The social action approach (Level 4 in Figure 10.1) includes all the elements of the transformation approach but adds components that require students to make decisions and take actions related to the concept, issue, or problem studied in the unit (Banks & Banks, with Clegg, 1999). Major goals of instruction in this approach are to educate students for social criticism and social change and to teach them decision-making skills. To empower students and help them acquire *political efficacy*, the school must help them become reflective social critics and skilled participants in social change. The traditional goal of schooling has been to socialize students so they would accept unquestioningly the existing ideologies, institutions, and practices within society and the nation-state (Banks, 2004a; Hahn, 1998).

Political education in the United States has traditionally fostered political passivity rather than political action. A major goal of the social action approach is to help students acquire the knowledge, values, and skills they need to participate in social change so that marginalized and excluded racial, ethnic, and cultural groups can become full participants in U.S. society and the nation will move closer to attaining its democratic ideals (Banks, 2004a). To participate effectively in democratic social change, students must be taught social criticism and helped to understand the inconsistency between our ideals and social realities, the work that must be done to close this gap, and how students can, as individuals and groups, influence the social and political systems in U.S. society. In this approach, teachers are agents of social change who promote democratic values and the empowerment of students. Teaching units organized using the social action approach have the components described below.

1. *A decision problem or question.* An example of a question is: What actions should we take to reduce prejudice and discrimination in our school?

2. *An inquiry that provides data related to the decision problem.* The inquiry might consist of these kinds of questions:
   a. What is prejudice?
   b. What is discrimination?
   c. What causes prejudice?
   d. What causes people to discriminate?
   e. What are examples of prejudice and discrimination in our school, community, nation, and the world?
   f. How do prejudice and discrimination affect the groups below? How does each group view prejudice? Discrimination? To what extent is each group a victim or a perpetuator of prejudice and discrimination?
   g. How has each group dealt with prejudice and discrimination?
      (Groups: White mainstream Americans, African Americans, Asian Americans, Hispanic Americans, Native Americans)

The inquiry into the nature of prejudice and discrimination would be interdisciplinary and would include readings and data sources in the various social sciences, biography, fiction, poetry, and drama. Scientific and statistical data would be used when students investigated how discrimination affects the income, occupations, frequency of diseases, and health care within these various groups.

3. *Value inquiry and moral analysis.* Students are given opportunities to examine, clarify, and reflect on their values, attitudes, beliefs, and feelings related to racial prejudice and discrimination. The teacher can provide the students with case studies from various sources, such as newspapers and magazines. The case studies can be used to involve the students in discussions and role-playing situations that enable them to express and to examine their attitudes, beliefs, and feelings about prejudice and discrimination.

Poetry, biography, and powerful fiction are excellent sources for case studies that can be used for both discussion and role playing. Countee Cullen's powerful poem "Incident" describes the painful memories of a child who was called "nigger" on a trip to Baltimore. Langston Hughes's poem "I, Too" poignantly tells how the "darker brother" is sent into the kitchen when company comes. The teacher and the students can describe verbally or write about incidents related to prejudice and discrimination they have observed or in which they have participated. The following case, based on a real-life situation, was written by the author for use with his students. After reading the case, the students discuss the questions at the end of it.

Trying to Buy a Home in Lakewood Island[1]

About a year ago, Joan and Henry Green, a young African American couple, moved from the West Coast to a large city in the Midwest. They moved because Henry finished his Ph.D. in chemistry and took a job at a big university in Midwestern City. Since they have been in Midwestern City, the Greens have rented an apartment in the central area of the city. However, they have decided that they want to buy a house. Their apartment has become too small for the many books and other things they have accumulated during the year. In addition to wanting more space, they also want a house so that they can receive breaks on their income tax, which they do not receive living in an apartment. The Greens also think that a house will be a good financial investment.

The Greens have decided to move into a suburban community. They want a new house and most of the houses within the city limits are rather old. They also feel that they can obtain a larger house for their money in the suburbs than in the city. They have looked at several suburban communities and decided that they like Lakewood Island better than any of the others. Lakewood Island is a predominantly White community, which is comprised primarily of lower-middle-class and middle-class residents. There are a few wealthy families in Lakewood Island, but they are exceptions rather than the rule.

---

[1] Reprinted with permission from James A. Banks (2003). *Teaching Strategies for Ethnic Studies* (7th ed.). Boston: Allyn & Bacon, pp. 217, 219.

Joan and Henry Green have become frustrated because of the problems they have experienced trying to buy a home in Lakewood Island. Before they go out to look at a house, they carefully study the newspaper ads. When they arrived at the first house in which they were interested, the owner told them that his house had just been sold. A week later they decided to work with a realtor. When they tried to close the deal on the next house they wanted, the realtor told them that the owner had raised the price $10,000 because he had the house appraised since he put it on the market and had discovered that his selling price was much too low. When the Greens tried to buy a third house in Lakewood Island, the owner told them that he had decided not to sell because he had not received the job in another city that he was almost sure he would receive when he had put his house up for sale. He explained that the realtor had not removed the ad about his house from the newspaper even though he had told him that he had decided not to sell a week earlier. The realtor the owner had been working with had left the real estate company a few days ago. Henry is bitter and feels that he and his wife are victims of racism and discrimination. Joan believes that Henry is too sensitive and that they have been the victims of a series of events that could have happened to anyone, regardless of their race.

Questions: What should the Greens do? Why?

4. *Decision making and social action* (synthesis of knowledge and values). Students acquire knowledge about their decision problem from the activities in item 2 above. This interdisciplinary knowledge provides them with the information they need to make reflective decisions about prejudice and discrimination in their communities and schools. The activities in item 3 enable them to identify, clarify, and analyze their values, feelings, and beliefs about prejudice and discrimination. The decision-making process enables the students to synthesize their knowledge and values to determine what actions, if any, they should take to reduce prejudice and discrimination in their school. They can develop a chart in which they list possible actions to take and their possible consequences. They can then decide on a course of action to take and implement it.

Mixing and Blending Approaches

The four approaches for the integration of multicultural content into the curriculum (see Table 10.1) are often mixed and blended in actual teaching situations. One approach, such as the contributions approach, can be used as a vehicle to move to other, more intellectually challenging approaches, such as the transformation and social action approaches. It is unrealistic to expect a teacher to move directly from a highly mainstream-centric curriculum to one that focuses on decision making and social action. Rather, the move from the first to higher levels of multicultural content integration is likely to be gradual and cumulative.

Table 10.1   Banks's Approaches for the Integration of Multicultural Content

Approach	Description	Examples	Strengths	Problems
Contributions	Heroes, cultural components, holidays, and other discrete elements related to ethnic groups are added to the curriculum on special days, occasions, and celebrations.	Famous Mexican Americans are studied only during the week of Cinco de Mayo (May 5). African Americans are studied during African American History Month in February but rarely during the rest of the year. Ethnic foods are studied in the first grade with little attention devoted to the cultures in which the foods are embedded.	Provides a quick and relatively easy way to put ethnic content into the curriculum. Gives ethnic heroes visibility in the curriculum alongside mainstream heroes. Is a popular approach among teachers and educators.	Results in a superficial understanding of ethnic cultures. Focuses on the lifestyles and artifacts of ethnic groups and reinforces stereotypes and misconceptions. Mainstream criteria are used to select heroes and cultural elements for inclusion in the curriculum.
Additive	This approach consists of the addition of content, concepts, themes, and perspectives to the curriculum without changing its structure.	Adding the book *The Color Purple* to a literature unit without reconceptualizing the unit or giving the students the background knowledge to understand the book. Adding a unit on the Japanese American internment to a U.S. history course without treating the Japanese in any other unit. Leaving the core curriculum intact but adding an ethnic studies course, as an elective, that focuses on a specific ethnic group.	Makes it possible to add ethnic content to the curriculum without changing its structure, which requires substantial curriculum changes and staff development. Can be implemented within the existing curriculum structure.	Reinforces the idea that ethnic history and culture are not integral parts of U.S. mainstream culture. Students view ethnic groups from Anglocentric and Eurocentric perspectives. Fails to help students understand how the dominant culture and ethnic cultures are interconnected and interrelated.
Transformation	The basic goals, structure, and nature of the curriculum are changed to enable students to view concepts, events, issues, problems, and themes from the perspectives of	A unit on the American Revolution describes the meaning of the revolution to Anglo revolutionaries, Anglo loyalists, African Americans, Indians, and the British. A unit on 20th-century U.S. literature includes works by William Faulkner, Joyce	Enables students to understand the complex ways in which diverse racial and cultural groups participated in the formation of U.S. society and culture. Helps reduce racial and ethnic encapsulation.	The implementation of this approach requires substantial curriculum revision, inservice training, and the identification and development of materials written from the perspectives of various racial and cultural groups.

Table 10.1 Continued

Approach	Description	Examples	Strengths	Problems
	diverse cultural, ethnic, and racial groups.	Carol Oates, Langston Hughes, N. Scott Momaday, Saul Bellow, Maxine Hong Kingston, Rudolfo A. Anaya, and Piri Thomas.	Enables diverse ethnic, racial, and religious groups to see their cultures, ethos, and perspectives in the school curriculum. Gives students a balanced view of the nature and development of U.S. culture and society. Helps to empower victimized racial, ethnic, and cultural groups.	Staff development for the institutionalization of this approach must be continual and ongoing.
Social Action	In this approach, students identify important social problems and issues, gather pertinent data, clarify their values on the issues, make decisions, and take reflective actions to help resolve the issue or problem.	A class studies prejudice and discrimination in their school and decides to take actions to improve race relations in the school. A class studies the treatment of ethnic groups in a local newspaper and writes a letter to the newspaper publisher suggesting ways that the treatment of ethnic groups in the newspaper should be improved.	Enables students to improve their thinking, value analysis, decision-making, and social action skills. Enables students to improve their data-gathering skills. Helps students develop a sense of political efficacy. Helps students improve their skills to work in groups.	Requires a considerable amount of curriculum planning and materials identification. May be longer in duration than more traditional teaching units. May focus on problems and issues considered controversial by some members of the school staff and citizens of the community. Students may be able to take few meaningful actions that contribute to the resolution of the social issue or problem.

A teacher who has a mainstream-centric curriculum might use the school's Martin Luther King, Jr., birthday celebration as an opportunity to integrate the curriculum with ethnic content about King as well as to think seriously about how content about African Americans and other ethnic groups can be integrated into the curriculum in an ongoing fashion. The teacher could explore with the students these kinds of questions during the celebration:

1. What were the conditions of other ethnic groups during the time that King was a civil rights leader?

2. How did other ethnic groups participate in and respond to the civil rights movement?

3. How did these groups respond to Martin Luther King, Jr.?

4. What can we do today to improve the civil rights of groups of color?

5. What can we do to develop more positive racial and ethnic attitudes?

The students will be unable to answer all the questions they have raised about ethnic groups during the celebration of Martin Luther King, Jr.'s, birthday. Rather, the questions will enable the students to integrate content about ethnic groups throughout the year as they study such topics as the family, the school, the neighborhood, and the city. As the students study these topics, they can use the questions they have formulated to investigate ethnic families, the ethnic groups in their school and in schools in other parts of the city, ethnic neighborhoods, and various ethnic institutions in the city such as churches, temples, synagogues, mosques, schools, restaurants, and community centers.

As a culminating activity for the year, the teacher can take the students on a tour of an ethnic community in the city. However, such a tour should be both preceded and followed by activities that enable the students to develop perceptive and compassionate lenses for seeing ethnic and cultural differences and for responding to them with sensitivity. A field trip to an ethnic community or neighborhood might reinforce stereotypes and misconceptions if students lack the knowledge and insights needed to view ethnic cultures in an understanding and caring way. Theory and research indicate that contact with an ethnic group does not necessarily lead to more positive racial and ethnic attitudes (Allport, 1979; Schofield, 2004). Rather, the conditions under which the contact occurs and the quality of the interaction in the contact situation are the important variables.

GUIDELINES FOR TEACHING MULTICULTURAL CONTENT

The following fourteen guidelines are designed to help you better integrate content about racial, ethnic, cultural, and language groups into the school curriculum and to teach effectively in multicultural environments.

1. You, the teacher, are an extremely important variable in the teaching of multicultural content. If you have the necessary knowledge, attitudes, and skills, when you encounter racist content in materials or observe racism in the statements and behavior of students, you can use these situations to teach important lessons about the experiences of ethnic, racial, and cultural groups in the United States. An informative source on racism is Gary Howard (1999), *We Can't Teach What We Don't Know: White Teachers, Multiracial Schools.* Another helpful source on this topic is Chapter 11 in this book.

2. Knowledge about ethnic groups is needed to teach ethnic content effectively. Read at least one major book that surveys the histories and cultures of U.S. ethnic groups. One book that includes historical overviews of U.S. ethnic groups is James A. Banks (2003), *Teaching Strategies for Ethnic Studies.*

3. Be sensitive to your own racial attitudes, behaviors, and the statements you make about ethnic groups in the classroom. A statement such as "Sit like an Indian" stereotypes Native Americans.

4. Make sure that your classroom conveys positive and complex images of various ethnic groups. You can do this by displaying bulletin boards, posters, and calendars that show the racial, ethnic and religious diversity within U.S. society.

5. Be sensitive to the racial and ethnic attitudes of your students and do not accept the belief, which has been refuted by research, that "kids do not see colors." Since the pioneering research by Lasker (1929), researchers have known that very young children are aware of racial differences and that they tend to accept the evaluations of various racial groups that are normative within the wider society (Van Ausdale & Feagin, 2001). Do not try to ignore the racial and ethnic differences that you see; try to respond to these differences positively and sensitively. Chapter 11 of this book provides thoughtful guidelines for avoiding the "colorblind" stance. Also see Walter Stephan (1999), *Reducing Prejudice and Stereotyping in Schools.*

6. Be judicious in your choice and use of teaching materials. Some materials contain both subtle and blatant stereotypes of groups. Point out to the students when an ethnic, racial, cultural, or language group is stereotyped, omitted from, or described in materials from Anglocentric and Eurocentric points of view.

7. Use trade books, films, videotapes, and recordings to supplement the textbook treatment of ethnic, cultural, and language groups and to present the perspectives of these groups to your students. Many of these sources contain rich and powerful images of the experience of being a person of color in the United States. Numerous books and videotapes are annotated in James A. Banks (2003), *Teaching Strategies for Ethnic Studies.*

8. Get in touch with your own cultural and ethnic heritage. Sharing your ethnic and cultural story with your students will create a climate for sharing in the classroom, will help motivate students to dig into their own ethnic and cultural roots, and will result in powerful learning for your students.

9. Be sensitive to the possibly controversial nature of some ethnic studies materials. If you are clear about the teaching objectives you have in mind, you can often use a less controversial book or reading to attain the same objectives. *The Color Purple*, by Alice Walker (1982), for example, can be a controversial book. A teacher, however, who wants his or her students to gain insights about African Americans in the South can use *Roll of Thunder, Hear My Cry*, by Mildred D. Taylor (1976), instead of *The Color Purple.*

10. Be sensitive to the developmental levels of your students when you select concepts, content, and activities related to racial, ethnic, cultural, and language groups. Concepts and learning activities for students in kindergarten and the primary grades should be specific and concrete. Students in these grades should study such concepts as *similarities, differences, prejudice,* and *discrimination* rather than higher-level concepts such as *racism* and *oppression.* Fiction and biographies

are excellent vehicles for introducing these concepts to students in kindergarten and the primary grades. As students progress through the grades, they can be introduced to more complex concepts, examples, and activities.

(If you teach in a racially or ethnically integrated classroom or school, you should keep the following guidelines in mind.)

11. View your students of color as winners. Many students of color have high academic and career goals. They need teachers who believe they can be successful and are willing to help them succeed. Both research and theory indicate that students are more likely to achieve highly when their teachers have high academic expectations for them.

12. Keep in mind that most parents of color are very interested in education and want their children to be successful academically even though the parents may be alienated from the school. Do not equate education with schooling. Many parents who want their children to succeed have mixed feelings about the schools. Try to gain the support of these parents and enlist them as partners in the education of their children.

13. Use cooperative learning techniques and group work to promote racial and ethnic integration in the school and classroom. Research indicates that when learning groups are racially integrated, students develop more friends from other racial groups and race relations in the school improve. A helpful guide is Elizabeth G. Cohen's *Designing Groupwork: Strategies for the Heterogeneous Classroom*.

14. Make sure that school plays, pageants, cheerleading squads, publications, and other formal and informal groups are racially integrated. Also make sure that various ethnic and racial groups have equal status in school performances and presentations. In a multiracial school, if all of the leading roles in a school play are filled by White actors, an important message is sent to students and parents of color whether such a message was intended or not.

SUMMARY

This chapter describes the nature of the mainstream-centric curriculum and the negative consequences it has for both mainstream students and students of color. This curriculum reinforces the false sense of superiority of mainstream students and fails to reflect, validate, and celebrate the cultures of students of color. Many factors have slowed the institutionalization of a multicultural curriculum in the schools, including ideological resistance, lack of teacher knowledge of ethnic groups, the heavy reliance of teachers on textbooks, and the focus on high-stakes testing and accountability. However, the institutionalization of ethnic content into the school, college, and university curriculum has made significant progress within the last thirty years. This process needs to continue because curriculum transformation is a development that never ends.

Four approaches to the integration of ethnic content into the curriculum are identified in this chapter. In the *contributions approach*, heroes/heroines, cultural components, holidays, and other discrete elements related to ethnic groups are added to the curriculum without changing its structure. The *additive approach* consists of the addition of content, concepts, themes, and perspectives to the curriculum, with its structure remaining unchanged. In the *transformation approach*, the structure, goals, and nature of the curriculum are changed to enable students to view concepts, issues, and problems from diverse ethnic perspectives.

The *social action approach* includes all elements of the transformation approach, as well as elements that enable students to identify important social issues, gather data related to them, clarify their values, make reflective decisions, and take actions to implement their decisions. This approach seeks to make students social critics and reflective agents of change. The final part of this chapter presents guidelines to help you teach multicultural content and to function more effectively in multicultural classrooms and schools.

Questions and Activities

1. What is a mainstream-centric curriculum? What are its major assumptions and goals?
2. Examine several textbooks and find examples of the mainstream-centric approach. Share these examples with colleagues in your class or workshop.
3. How does a mainstream-centric curriculum influence mainstream students and students of color?
4. According to Banks, what factors have slowed the development of a multicultural curriculum in the schools? What is the best way to overcome these factors?
5. What are the major characteristics of the following approaches to curriculum reform: the contributions approach, the additive approach, the transformation approach, the social action approach?
6. Why do you think the contributions approach to curriculum reform is so popular and widespread within schools, especially in the primary and elementary grades?
7. In what fundamental ways do the transformation and social action approaches differ from the other two approaches identified above?
8. What are the problems and promises of each of the four approaches?
9. What does the author mean by "multiple acculturation"? Do you think this concept is valid? Why or why not?
10. What problems might a teacher encounter when trying to implement the transformation and social action approaches? How might these problems be overcome?
11. Assume that you are teaching a social studies lesson about the westward movement in U.S. history and a student makes a racist, stereotypic, or misleading statement about Native Americans, such as, "The Indians were hostile to the White settlers." How would you handle this situation? Give reasons to explain why you would handle it in a particular way.
12. Since September 11, 2001, and the United States/British–Iraq War in 2003, there has been an increased emphasis on patriotism in U.S. society. Some groups have called for

more emphasis on the teaching of patriotism in the schools. What is patriotism? Describe ways in which multicultural content can be used to teach reflective patriotism. A useful reference for this exercise is *A Patriot's Handbook: Songs, Poems, Stories and Speeches Celebrating the Land We Love*, edited by Caroline Kennedy (2003). It contains selections by authors from diverse racial, ethnic, and cultural groups. Gwendolyn Brooks, Thomas Jefferson, Langston Hughes, Gloria Anzaldúa, E. B. White, and Paul Lawrence Dunbar are among the writers included in this comprehensive and useful collection.

References

Allport, G. W. (1979). *The Nature of Prejudice* (25th anniversary ed.). Reading, MA: Addison-Wesley.

Asante, M. K., & Ravitch, D. (1991). Multiculturalism: An Exchange. *The American Scholar, 60*(2), 267–276.

Asante, M. K. (1998). *The Afrocentric Idea* (rev. ed.). Philadelphia: Temple University Press.

Baldwin, J. (1985). *The Price of the Ticket: Collected Nonfiction 1948–1985.* New York: St. Martin's.

Ball, E. (1998). *Slaves in the Family.* New York: Farrar, Straus & Giroux.

Banks, J. A. (Ed.). (1996). *Multicultural Education, Transformative Knowledge, and Action: Historical and Contemporary Perspectives.* New York: Teachers College Press.

Banks, J. A. (2001). *Cultural Diversity and Education: Foundations, Curriculum, and Teaching* (4th ed.). Boston: Allyn & Bacon.

Banks, J. A. (2002). *An Introduction to Multicultural Education* (3rd ed.). Boston: Allyn & Bacon.

Banks, J. A. (2003). *Teaching Strategies for Ethnic Studies* (7th ed.). Boston: Allyn & Bacon.

Banks, J. A. (Ed.). (2004a). *Diversity and Citizenship Education: Global Perspectives.* San Francisco: Jossey-Bass.

Banks, J. A. (2004b). Race, Knowledge Construction, and Education in the United States: Lessons from History. In J. A. Banks & C. A. M. Banks (Eds.), *Handbook of Research on Multicultural Education* (2nd ed., pp. 228–239). San Francisco: Jossey-Bass.

Banks, J. A., & Banks, C. A. M., with Clegg, A. A., Jr. (1999). *Teaching Strategies for the Social Studies* (5th ed.). New York: Longman.

Bigelow, B., & Peterson, B. (1998). *Rethinking Columbus: The Next 500 Years.* Milwaukee, WI: Rethinking Schools.

Black Elk's Prayer from a Mountaintop in the Black Hills, 1931. (1964). In J. D. Forbes (Ed.), *The Indian in America's Past* (p. 69). Englewood Cliffs, NJ: Prentice-Hall.

Cohen, E. G. (1994). *Designing Groupwork: Strategies for the Heterogeneous Classroom* (2nd ed.). New York: Teachers College Press.

Coleman, J. S., Campbell, E. Q., Hobson, C. J., McPartland, J., Mood, A. M., Weinfeld, F. D., & York, R. L. (1966). *Equality of Educational Opportunity.* Washington, DC: U.S. Government Printing Office.

Delpit, L., & Dowdy, J. K. (Eds.). (2002). *The Skin That We Speak: Thoughts on Language and Culture in the Classroom.* New York: New Press.

Dilg, M. (2003). *Thriving in the Multicultural Classroom: Principles and Practices for Effective Teaching.* New York: Teachers College Press.

Gates, H. L., Jr. (1999). *Wonders of the African World.* New York: Knopf.

Gay, G., & Banks, J. A. (1975). Teaching the American Revolution: A Multiethnic Approach. *Social Education, 39,* 461–465.

Gillan, M. M., & Gillan, J. (Eds.). (1994). *An Anthology of Contemporary Multicultural Poetry.* New York: Penguin.

Goodlad, J. I. (1984). *A Place Called School.* New York: McGraw-Hill.

Gordon-Reed, A. (1997). *Thomas Jefferson and Sally Hemings: An American Controversy.* Charlottesville: University Press of Virgina.

Gutmann, A. (2004). Unity and Diversity in Democratic Multicultural Education: Creative and Destructive Tensions. In J. A. Banks (Ed.), *Diversity and Citizenship Education: Global Perspectives* (pp. 71–96). San Francisco: Jossey-Bass.

Hahn, C. L. (1998). *Becoming Political: Comparative Perspectives on Citizenship Education.* Albany: State University of New York Press.

Howard, G. (1999). *We Can't Teach What We Don't Know: White Teachers, Multiracial Schools.* New York: Teachers College Press.

Katz, W. L. (1986). *Black Indians: A Hidden Heritage.* New York: Atheneum.

Kennedy, C. (Ed.). (2003). *A Patriot's Handbook: Songs, Poems, Stories, and Speeches Celebrating the Land We Love.* New York: Hyperion.

Lasker, B. (1929). *Race Attitudes in Children.* New York: Holt.

Limerick, P. N. (1987). *The Legacy of Conquest: The Unbroken Past of the American West.* New York: Norton.

Loewen, J. W. (1995). *Lies My Teacher Taught Me: Everything Your American History Textbook Got Wrong.* New York: New Press.

Loewen, J. W. (1999). *Lies across America: What Our Historic Sites Get Wrong.* New York: New Press.

Martin, P., & Midgley, E. (1999). Immigration to the United States. *Population Bulletin, 54*(2), 1–44. Washington, DC: Population Reference Bureau.

Neihardt, J. G. (1972). *Black Elk Speaks.* New York: Pocket Books.

Ovando, C. J., & McLaren, P. (Eds.). (2000). *The Politics of Multiculturalism and Bilingual Education.* Boston: McGraw-Hill.

Ravitch, D. (1990, Spring). Diversity and Democracy: Multicultural Education in America. *American Educator,* pp. 16–48.

Reed, I. (Ed.). (1997). *MultiAmerica: Essays on Cultural Wars and Cultural Peace.* New York: Viking.

Rico, B. R., & Mano, S. (Eds.). (1995). *American Mosaic: Multicultural Readings in Context* (2nd ed.). Boston: Houghton Mifflin.

Schlesinger, A. M., Jr. (1991). *The Disuniting of America: Reflections on a Multicultural Society.* Knoxville, TN: Whittle Direct Books.

Schofield, J. W. (2004). Improving Intergroup Relations among Students. In J. A. Banks & C. A. M. Banks (Eds.), *Handbook of Research on Multicultural Education* (2nd ed., pp. 799–812). San Francisco: Jossey-Bass.

Stephan, W. (1999). *Reducing Prejudice and Stereotyping in Schools.* New York: Teachers College Press.

Takaki, R. (1993). *A Different Mirror: A History of Multicultural America.* New York: Little, Brown.

Taylor, M. (1976). *Roll of Thunder, Hear My Cry.* New York: Dial.

Walker, A. (1982). *The Color Purple.* New York: Harcourt Brace.

White, R. (1991). *"It's Your Misfortune and None of My Own:" A New History of the American West.* Norman: University of Oklahoma Press.

Van Ausdale, D., & Feagin, J. R. (2001). *The First R: How Children Learn Race and Racism.* Lanham, MD: Rowman & Littlefield.

Zinn, H. (1999). *A People's History of the United States* (20th anniversary ed.). New York: HarperCollins.

Zinn, H., & Kirschner, G. (1995). *A People's History of the United States: The Wall Charts.* New York: New Press.

CHAPTER 11

The Colorblind Perspective in School: Causes and Consequences

Janet Ward Schofield

INTRODUCTION

Race matters, or at least it has historically in the United States, although it is a scientifically imprecise construct the meaning of which is heavily influenced by social context (Jones, 1997). Racial group membership is the basis on which individuals were treated as the property of others and denied the basic rights of citizenship even after the formal abolition of slavery. The civil rights laws passed in the middle of the twentieth century were designed to do away with such group-based discrimination—to dismantle dual school systems, to ensure political rights, and to prevent discrimination in employment and housing, among other things. However, the passage of these laws created a situation that Jones (1998) has called the "New American Dilemma"—a conflict between "the values embodied in the democratic principles of freedom and equality without regard to race, and . . . the belief that current as well as cumulative racial biases persist making it necessary to take race into account in order to realize the principles of freedom and equality" (p. 645). The first of these perspectives was given voice by Supreme Court Justice John Marshall Harlan in his famous call for a color-blind society in his dissenting opinion in *Plessy v. Ferguson*. A colorblind society is one in which racial or ethnic group membership is irrelevant to the way individuals are treated (Rist, 1974). People in favor of colorblind approaches to policy argue that taking cognizance of group membership in decision making is illegitimate since it is likely to lead either to discrimination against minority groups or to reverse discrimination in their favor. Neither of these actions is viewed as desirable. The people aligned with this side of the debate argue that, since the laws that systematically disadvantaged African Americans were overturned decades ago, a fair system is now in place and this system can only be truly fair to the extent that it completely ignores group membership—treating individuals solely as individuals and striving to ignore race or ethnicity completely.

Yet others, such as Bonilla-Silva (2003) and Levin (2003), argue that such an approach is the antithesis of fairness—that it is akin to a race between a well-nourished and well-trained athlete whom most of the spectators are rooting for and an individual who has just been released from an unjust prison term during which food was sparse and opportunities for exercise and training were denied. People taking this perspective agree with Justice Harry Blackmun, who wrote in the *Regents of the University of California v. Bakke* (1978) case that "in order to get beyond racism, we must first take account of race. In order to treat persons equally, we must treat them differently" (pp. 2806–2808). They contend that the reality of continuing racism (Jones, 1997; Sidanius & Pratto, 1999; Trent et al., 2003) as well as the continuing impact of prior discrimination, such as the striking difference in net worth among African Americans and Whites with similar incomes due at least in part to larger inheritances received by Whites (Jaynes & Williams, 1989), make policies designed specifically to promote the inclusion of African Americans in the economic and political life of the country both just and wise. Thus, they tend to support affirmative action and other related policies designed to do this by explicitly taking account of the relative participation rates of various groups—an approach at direct odds with the colorblind perspective.

This tension between views that see taking cognizance of racial or ethnic group membership positively and those that see it negatively is strongly reflected in controversy over how our educational system should function (Wolsko, Park, Judd, & Wittenbrink, 2000). Specifically, one approach to education in our increasingly diverse society calls for redoubling efforts to teach all students core information and values in an attempt to strengthen a unified American identity (Bennett, 1987; Hirsch, 1996; Schlesinger, 1992). This approach, which typically decries bilingual and multicultural approaches to education, is quite consistent with the colorblind perspective in that it seeks to ignore or deemphasize subgroup identities and differences in an effort to create a unified citizenry. In contrast, another approach, typically endorsed by proponents of multicultural education, argues that responding to diversity by including material about many groups and using approaches to teaching that recognize cultural differences is needed to serve students well and to build harmony and respect between those from different backgrounds (Banks, 2001; Nieto, 2004; Takaki, 1993; Yinger, 1994).

Interestingly, this tension between ignoring or focusing on group membership is reflected in theoretical stances with sharply differing implications even in social psychological research on improving intergroup relations, as Wolsko et al. (2000) point out. Specifically, one major line of theorizing and research suggests that it is the categorization of individuals into groups that lays the basis for stereotyping and discrimination (Brewer & Miller, 1984, 1988; Tajfel, 1978). From this perspective, the logicial solution to the problem is to minimize the salience of the group or to redefine the in-group in a more inclusive way so that old "out-groups" join together in assuming a new, more expansive shared identity (Gaertner, Dovidio, Anastasio, Bachman, & Rust, 1993). Another perspective, clearly much less common, suggests that intergroup relations can be improved by careful and explicit focus on group differences (Lee & Duenas, 1995; Randolph, Landis, & Tzeng, 1977; Triandis, 1976).

The issues raised by the New American Dilemma are complex and unlikely to be easily resolved. Full consideration of them would of necessity involve work from fields as disparate as philosophy, history, psychology, law, ethics, economics, and politics. Thus, this chapter does not try to solve this dilemma. Rather, it has a more modest but nonetheless important goal: to provide a glimpse of how the colorblind perspective works in reality in one of the most important institutions in our society—its schools.

I did not set out initially to explore this question. Rather, as a scholar deeply interested in the potential of interracial school settings for improving intergroup relations, I embarked on a longitudinal ethnographic study designed to illuminate the nature of peer relations in a desegregated school and the impact that school policies, structures, and culture have on those relations (Schofield, 1989). It just so happened that having chosen a particular school for study, as described below, I found myself in an environment that strongly endorsed the colorblind perspective. Furthermore, over time, it became apparent that the institution's endorsement of this perspective had important consequences that educators at the school did not anticipate and often did not recognize. Thus, the causes and consequences of this perspective became the focus of the part of my research reported here.

I argue that two basic factors make understanding the implications of the colorblind perspective important. First, evidence suggests that this perspective is widespread in schools both within the United States and elsewhere, either as part of official policy or as an informal but nonetheless powerful social norm that applies in many situations (Eaton, 2001; Gillborn, 1992; Jervis, 1996; Pollock, 2000; Rist, 1978; Sagar & Schofield, 1984; Sleeter, 1993). Second, the colorblind approach is also frequently espoused as a goal to be sought in many other realms, including employment practices and judicial proceedings. This research led me to conclude that although in many ways the colorblind perspective is appealing because it is consistent with a long-standing American emphasis on the importance of the individual, it easily leads to a misrepresentation of reality in ways that allow and sometimes even encourage discrimination against minority group members, as later parts of this chapter demonstrate.

THE RESEARCH SITE: WEXLER MIDDLE SCHOOL

In choosing a site for the research, I adopted a strategy that Cook and Campbell (1976) call "generalizing to target instances." The aim was not to study what happens in a typical desegregated school, if such an entity can even be said to exist. Rather, it was to explore peer relations under conditions that theory suggests should be relatively conducive to positive relations between African Americans and Whites.

In his classic book *The Nature of Prejudice*, Allport (1954) proposed that intergroup contact may reinforce previously held stereotypes and increase intergroup hostility unless the contact situation is structured in a way that (1) provides equal status for minority and majority group members, (2) encourages cooperation toward shared, strongly desired goals, and (3) provides the support of law, authority, and customs for positive relations. These ideas, as elaborated and refined by subsequent theoretical and empirical work (Amir, 1969, 1976; Cook, 1969, 1985; Hewstone & Brown, 1986; Pettigrew, 1986, 1998; Pettigrew & Tropp, 2000; Schofield, 2001; Schofield & Eurich-Fulcer, 2001; Stephan & Stephan, 1996), constitute a useful foundation for understanding the likely outcomes of interracial contact. For example, although equal status may be neither an absolutely necessary prerequisite nor a sufficient condition for change, it does appear to be very helpful (Amir, 1969, 1976; Brewer & Brown, 1998; Brown, 1995; Cohen, 1975, 1997; Cohen, Lockheed, & Lohman, 1976; Cook, 1978, 1985; Norvell & Worchel, 1981; Pettigrew, 1998; Riordan, 1978; Schofield & Eurich-Fulcer, 2001; Stephan & Stephan, 1996,

2001). In addition, a substantial body of research suggests that cooperation toward mutually desired goals is indeed generally conducive to improved intergroup relations (Aronson & Patnoe, 1997; Bossert, 1988/89; Cook, 1978, 1985; Johnson & Johnson, 1982; Johnson, Johnson, & Maruyama, 1984; Johnson, Maruyama, Johnson, Nelson, & Skon, 1981; Schofield, 2001; Sharan, 1980; Sherif, 1979; Slavin, 1995; Slavin & Cooper, 1999; Stephan & Stephan, 1996, 2001).

Wexler Middle School was constructed in a large northeastern city to serve as a model of high-quality integrated education. When it first opened, Wexler had a student body almost precisely 50 percent African American and 50 percent White, mirroring closely the proportion of Black and White students in the city's public schools. This school, which serves 1,200 children in sixth through eighth grades, was chosen for study because the decisions made in planning for it suggested that it would come reasonably close to meeting the conditions specified by Allport and the more recent theorists who have built on his work. The school's strong efforts to provide a positive environment for interracial education can be illustrated by examination of its staffing policy. The administration, faculty, and staff of the school are biracial, with about 25 percent of the faculty being African American. The top four administrative positions are filled by two African Americans and two Whites, clearly symbolizing the school's commitment to providing equal status for members of both groups.

The extent to which Wexler met the conditions specified by Allport and his intellectual heirs as conducive to the development of improved intergroup relations has been discussed at length elsewhere (Schofield, 1989). Here, I merely report the conclusion drawn in that discussion—that Wexler came considerably closer to these criteria than did most desegregated public schools. Yet it fell seriously short of meeting them completely in a number of ways, many of which were the direct result of societal conditions over which Wexler had little or no control. For example, in spite of Wexler's commitment to a staffing pattern that would provide equal formal status for African Americans and Whites, the proportion of Black teachers on its staff was considerably lower than the proportion of Black students in the school because the school system did not want to put too high a proportion of its Black teachers in one school.

In addition, a large majority of Wexler's White students came from middle- or upper-middle-class homes. Although some of the African American children were middle-class, the majority came from either poor or working-class families. These social-class differences had implications for the status of African American and White students within the school. For example, in the eighth grade, which divided students into a "regular" and a "gifted" track, a much higher proportion of the White than African American students achieved scores on standardized tests that led to their placement in the gifted track. Even in the sixth and seventh grades, which had academically heterogenous classes, this difference influenced students' status (Schofield, 1980), although not in a way emphasized and formalized by a tracking policy. In sum, Wexler made stronger than usual efforts to foster positive relations between African Americans and Whites but fell markedly short of being a theoretically ideal milieu for the accomplishment of this goal.

DATA GATHERING

The analysis that follows is based on an intensive four-year study of peer relations at Wexler. The basic data-gathering strategy was intensive and extensive observation in Wexler's classrooms, hallways, playgrounds, and cafeteria. Observers used the full field-note method for recording the events they witnessed (Olson, 1976). A large number of events were observed because they were representative of the events that filled most of the school day at Wexler. However, an important subgroup of events was oversampled in relation to their frequency of occurrence because of their direct relevance to the study's focus. This strategy, which Strauss (1987) call theoretical sampling, led to oversampling certain activities, such as affective education classes, designed to help students get to know each other, and meetings of Wexler's interracial student advisory group set up to handle the special problems students might face in a desegregated school. Over the course of the study, more than 500 hours were devoted to observation of students and staff at Wexler.

A wide variety of other data-gathering techniques ranging from sociometric questionnaires to experimental work to quantitative observational approaches were also used (Sagar & Schofield, 1980; Sagar, Schofield, & Snyder, 1983; Schofield, 1979; Schofield & Francis, 1982; Schofield & Sagar, 1977; Schofield & Whitley, 1983; Whitley & Schofield, 1984). Interviews were employed extensively. For example, randomly selected students participated in open-ended interviews twice a year. Teachers and administrators were also interviewed repeatedly. In addition, graffiti in the bathrooms and on the school walls were routinely recorded, school bulletins were collected, and careful note was taken of such things as wall decorations and public address system announcements.

Space does not allow full discussion of the many varied techniques used in collecting and analyzing the data on which this chapter is based. However, two general principles that guided the research must be mentioned. First, both data gathering and analysis were as rigorous and systematic as possible. For example, sampling techniques were employed where appropriate; trained coders, who were unaware of the race and sex of particular respondents, coded the open-ended interviews using reliable systems developed for this research; and field notes were carefully indexed so that all notes relevant to a given topic could be examined.

Second, because it is often impossible to achieve extremely high levels of precision and control in field research, strong efforts were made to triangulate the data (Webb, Campbell, Schwartz, & Sechrest, 1966). Great care was taken to gather many different types of information bearing on the same issue, to minimize the potential problems with each data source, and to be sensitive in analyzing and interpreting data that might reflect biases in the data set that could not be completely eliminated. The basic approach used in the analysis of the qualitative data is outlined in works such as Bogdan and Taylor (1975), Campbell (1975), Miles and Huberman (1984), and Strauss and Corbin (1990). Fuller details on data gathering and analysis are presented elsewhere, as is information on the strategies used to minimize observer reactivity and bias (Schofield, 1989; Schofield & Sagar, 1979).

THE COLORBLIND PERSPECTIVE AND ITS COROLLARIES

Wexler's faculty clearly tended to subscribe to the colorblind view of interracial schooling. Interviews with both African American and White teachers suggested that the majority of both groups tended to see Wexler as an institution that could help impart middle-class values and modes of behavior to lower-class students so that they could break out of the cycle of poverty and become middle-class persons themselves. Even though most of these lower-class students were African American, race was seen as quite incidental to the anticipated class assimilation process.

An African-American administrator, with perhaps more candor than many similarly oriented White administrators and teachers, made her class assimilation goals explicit and, at the same time, made it clear just which students needed to be so assimilated:

> I really don't address myself to group differences when I am dealing with youngsters. . . . I try to treat youngsters, I don't care who they are, as youngsters and not as Black, White, green or yellow. . . . Many of the Black youngsters who have difficulty are the ones who . . . have come from communities where they had to put up certain defenses and these defenses are the antithesis of the normal situation . . . like they find in school. It is therefore [difficult] getting them to become aware that they have to follow these rules because [they] are here . . . not over there in their community. . . . I think that many of the youngsters [from the] larger community have a more normal set of values that people generally want to see, and therefore do not have [as] much difficulty in coping with their school situation. . . . [The Black children] do have difficulty in adjusting because they are just not used to it. Until we can adjustively counsel them into the right types of behavior . . . I think we're going to continue to have these types of problems.

The only thing atypical in the preceding remarks is the frank acknowledgment that the children perceived as lacking "the normal set of values that people generally want to see" are typically African American. More usually, this was implicit in remarks emphasizing the negative effects of growing up in a poor family or a low-income neighborhood.

As a reaction to the invidious distinctions that have traditionally been made in the United States on the basis of race, the colorblind perspective is understandable and, from a social policy standpoint, it seems laudable. However, this orientation was accompanied at Wexler by a number of other logically related beliefs, which taken together with it had some important though largely unrecognized negative consequences. These beliefs and their basis in the ongoing social reality at Wexler are discussed individually. Then the consequences of this belief system are discussed in some detail.

Race as an Invisible Characteristic

It is not a very great leap from the colorblind perspective, which says that race is a social category of no relevance to one's behaviors and decisions, to a belief that individuals should not or perhaps even do not notice each other's racial group membership. At Wexler, acknowledging that one was aware of another's race was viewed by many people as a possible sign of prejudice, as illustrated by the following excerpt from project field notes:

> When I was arranging the student interviews, I mentioned to Mr. Little [White] that I thought there was only one White girl in one of his classes. I asked if I was right about this and he said, "Well, just a minute. Let me check." After looking through the class roster in his roll book he said, "You know, you're right. I

never noticed that. . . . I guess that's a good thing." Our data suggest that teachers not only denied that they noticed children's race when the researchers were present, but also did so among themselves. For example, when complying with a request to mark down the race of his students on a class roster for research purposes, a White teacher remarked, "Did you ever notice those teachers who say, 'I never notice what they are'?"

Although there was less unanimity on the issue of whether students noticed the race of others than of whether teachers did, a substantial proportion of Wexler's faculty asserted that the students rarely noticed race. This point of view is exemplified by the following excerpt from an interview with an African American science teacher:

MS. MONROE: You know, I hear the things the students usually fight about. As I said before, it's stupid things like someone taking a pencil. It's not because [the other person] is Black or White. . . . At this age level . . . I don't think it's Black or White.

INTERVIEWER: There's something I'm wondering about. It is hard to believe, given the way our society is, that you can just bring kids together and they won't be very much aware.

MS. MONROE: They just go about their daily things and don't . . . I don't think they think about it really. . . . I see them interacting with one another on an adult basis. . . . They are not really aware of color . . . or race or whatever.

INTERVIEWER: You really don't see that as a factor . . . in their relationships?

MS. MONROE: No.

Although the faculty at Wexler saw themselves, and to a lesser extent their students, as oblivious to the race of others, a wide variety of data suggest that this view was not accurate. Most removed from the specific situation at Wexler, but nonetheless pertinent, is a substantial body of data from research on stereotyping and person perception. This work suggests that individuals tend to use preexisting categories in perceiving and responding to others (Brewer & Brown, 1998; Brown, 1995; Fiske & Neuberg, 1990). More specifically, research suggests that individuals spontaneously use the physical appearance of other people as a basis for categorizing them by race. Further, this categorization has an impact on how individuals are perceived and on how others respond to them (Devine, 1989; Dovidio et al., 1997; Duncan, 1976; Fazio, Jackson, Dunton, & Williams, 1995; Katz, Wackenhut, & Hass, 1986; Katz, 1976; Malpass & Kravitz, 1969; Sagar & Schofield, 1980; Taylor, Fiske, Etcoff, & Ruderman, 1978).

The teachers and students at Wexler were to some extent self-selected members of an interracial institution and thus might conceivably be less prone to use race as a category for processing information about others than would the college student populations used in most studies on person perception cited above. However, given the importance of race as a social category in many aspects of life in the United States, it seems highly unlikely that the prevailing tendency at Wexler was for individuals not even to notice each other's race.

Interviews with students made it clear that many of them were very conscious of their race or of the race of other students, which is hardly surprising given the fact that interracial schooling was a new and somewhat threatening experience for many of them. The following excerpt from an interview in which the interviewer had not herself previously mentioned race suggests just how salient racial categories were to the children.

INTERVIEWER: Can you tell me who some of your friends are?

BEVERLY [AFRICAN AMERICAN]: Well, Stacey and Lydia and Amy, even though she's White.

Similarly, students' awareness of racial group membership is seen in an excerpt from field notes taken in a seventh-grade class with a higher-than-average proportion of African American students because the teachers had decided to put many lower-achieving children in a class by themselves.

Howard, a White male, leaned over to me (a White female observer) and said, "You know, it just wasn't fair the way they set up this class. There are sixteen Black kids and only nine White kids. I can't learn in here." I said, "Why is that?" Howard replied, "They copy and they pick on you. It just isn't fair."

Race as a Taboo Topic

Before discussing why the view that they and their students tended not even to notice race gained considerable popularity among Wexler's teachers in spite of everyday indications that this was often not the case, this section discusses two other phenomena closely related to the development of the colorblind perspective. The first was the development of a norm strong enough to be labeled a virtual taboo against the use of the words *white* and *black* in a context in which they referred to racial group membership. Thus, for example, in almost 200 hours of observations in classrooms, hallways, and teachers' meetings during Wexler's first year, fewer than twenty-five direct references to race were made by school staff or students (Schofield, 1989). Any use of the words *black* and *white* in a context in which they referred to an individual or group was classified as a reference to race, as were racial epithets and words and phrases used almost exclusively within one group to express solidarity (e.g., "Hey, Brother") or the like.

The extremely infrequent reference to race was all the more surprising when one considers that our observations included a wide variety of formal and informal situations, ranging from workshops funded by the Emergency School Assistance Act, federal legislation that provided funds to desegregating schools to help them handle special problems that might arise as a result of desegregation, to informal student interactions on the playgrounds and in the hallways.

Students' awareness of the taboo is shown clearly in the following field notes, which recount a conversation with a White social worker whose work at Wexler on the extracurricular program was funded by a local foundation concerned with race relations. Perhaps not surprisingly under these circumstances, she showed much less reluctance than did most staff to deal in a straightforward manner with the issue of race.

> Ms. Fowler said that a short while ago she had heard from
> Martin [Black] that another child had done something wrong. The
> offense was serious enough so that she wanted to track down this
> individual. She asked Martin to describe the child who had
> committed the offense. Martin said, "He has black hair and he's
> fairly tall." He didn't give the race of the other person even
> though he went on to give a fairly complete description otherwise.
> Finally, Ms. Fowler asked, "Is he Black or White?" Martin replied,
> "Is it all right for me to say?" Ms. Fowler said that it was all
> right. . . . Martin then said, "Well, the boy was White."

Students were well aware that making references to race displeased many of their teachers and might also offend peers.

INTERVIEWER: You know, the other day I was walking around the school and heard a
sixth-grade student describing a student from the seventh grade to a teacher who
needed to find this student in order to return something she had lost. The sixth
grader said the seventh grader was tall and thin. She described what the girl had
been wearing and said her hair was dark, but she didn't say whether the girl was
Black or White. . . . Why do you think she didn't mention that?

SYLVIA [AFRICAN AMERICAN]: The teacher might have got mad if she said whether
she was White or Black.

INTERVIEWER: Do some teachers get mad about things like that?

SYLVIA: Some do . . . they holler. . . .

INTERVIEWER: Now, when you talk to kids who are Black, do you ever mention that
someone is White or Black?

SYLVIA: No.

INTERVIEWER: What about when you're talking with kids who are White?

SYLVIA: Nope.

INTERVIEWER: You never mention race? Why not?

SYLVIA: They might think I'm prejudiced.

Social Life as a Web of Purely Interpersonal Relations

Consistent with the view that race is not, or at least should not be, a salient aspect of other individuals and with the practice of not speaking about race were tendencies to conceptualize social life as a web of interpersonal rather than intergroup relations and to assume that interpersonal relations are not much influenced by group membership. As one teacher put it:

> Peer-group identity here in middle school . . . has nothing to
> do with race. There's a strong tendency to group that exists
> independent of . . . racial boundaries. . . . We started in September
> with these students letting them know we weren't going to fool
> around with that. . . . You're a student and we don't care what
> color you are.

This tendency to minimize the potential importance of intergroup processes was illustrated clearly during an inservice training session, the stated purpose of which was to help teachers deal effectively with the racially heterogeneous student body. The facilitator, a White clinical psychologist employed by a local foundation, began by making some general statements about the importance of understanding cultural differences between students. Although the facilitator kept trying to nudge and finally to push the group to discuss ways in which the racially-mixed nature of the student body influenced peer relations, appropriate curricular materials, and the like, the group ended up discussing issues such as the problems caused by individual children who acted out aggressively in the classroom, the difficulty that overweight children have in gaining peer acceptance, and the fact that children with disabilities were sometimes taunted by their classmates.

Contrasting sharply with the teachers' tendency to insist that they and their students reacted to each other exclusively as individuals and to deemphasize the importance of intergroup as opposed to interpersonal processes was the students' willingness to discuss with interviewers the important role race played in Wexler's social life.

INTERVIEWER: I have noticed . . . that [in the cafeteria] very often White kids sit with White kids and Black kids sit with Black kids. Why do you think that this is?

MARY [WHITE]: 'Cause the White kids have White friends and the Black kids have Black friends. . . . I don't think integration is working. . . . Blacks still associate with Blacks and Whites still associate with Whites. . . .

INTERVIEWER: Can you think of any White kids that have quite a few Black friends or of any Black kids who have quite a few White friends?

MARY: Not really.

The tendency for students to group themselves by race in a variety of settings was very marked. For example, on a fairly typical day at the end of the school's second year of operation 119 White and 90 African American students attended the seventh-grade lunch period. Of these more than 200 children, only 6 sat next to someone of the other race (Schofield & Sagar, 1977).

Of course, it is possible that race itself was not a factor in producing such interaction patterns, but something correlated with race such as socioeconomic status, academic achievement, or the opportunity for previous contact with each other. Such factors did appear to reinforce the tendency to prefer intragroup interactions and were often cited by teachers as the actual cause of the visually apparent tendency of students to cluster with those of their own race. Yet the results of an experiment conducted at Wexler demonstrate that race itself was a real factor in peer relations. In this study, eighty male sixth graders were presented with carefully drawn pictures of a number of ambiguously aggressive types of peer interactions that were quite common at Wexler, such as poking another student with a pencil. For each type of interaction, some students were shown pictures in which both students were African American, others saw pictures in which both students were White, and others saw mixed-race dyads with the Black student shown as either the initiator of the behavior or as the student to whom it was directed.

The results suggested that the race of the person initiating the behavior influenced how mean and threatening the behavior was interpreted as being (Sagar & Schofield, 1980) (see Table 11.1). Such a finding is, of course, inconsistent with the notion that students take no

Table 11.1   Mean Ratings of Both White and Black Actors' Ambiguously Aggressive Behaviors by White and Black Subjects

Subject Group	Actor Race	Rating Scale: Mean/Threatening
White	White	8.28
	Black	8.99
Black	White	7.38
	Black	8.40

Note. Means are based on sums of paired 7-point scales indicating how well the given adjective described the behaviors, from 1 (not at all) to 7 (exactly). N = 40 in each group. Each subject rated two White and two Black actors (e.g., the perpetrator of the ambiguously aggressive act) and two White and Black targets. The 4 × 4 nature of the Latin square required treating the race permutations as four levels of a single factor. Significant F values on this factor provided justification for testing actor race, target race, and interaction effects with simple contrasts, using the error variance estimate generated by the ANOVA. The significant main effect of race permutations on the summed mean/threatening scales, $F(3,192) = 3.02$, $p < .05$, was found to reflect, as predicted, a tendency for subjects to rate the behaviors by Black actors more mean/threatening than identical behaviors by White actors, $t(144) = 2.90$, $p < .01$. Means are not broken down by target race because no statistically significant main effects or interactions were found for this variable.

Source: From Sagar, H. A., and Schofield, J. W. (1980). Racial and Behavioral Cues in Black and White Children's Perceptions of Ambiguously Aggressive Acts. *Journal of Personality and Social Psychology, 39*(4) 590–598. Copyright 1980 by the American Psychological Association. Adapted with permission.

notice of others' race. It is also incompatible with the idea that intergroup processes have no influence on students' reactions to their peers because the data suggest that the perception of an individual's behavior is influenced by the group membership of the person performing it.

THE FUNCTIONS AND CONSEQUENCES OF THE COLORBLIND PERSPECTIVE AND ITS COROLLARIES

Regardless of the fact that the colorblind perspective and its corollaries were not completely accurate views of the social processes occurring at Wexler, they appeared to influence the development of the social fabric at Wexler in ways that had a number of important consequences, some positive and some negative. The following discussion of the functions of this set of beliefs suggests why the colorblind perspective was attractive to teachers and how it affected both the education and social experiences of Wexler's students.

Reducing the Potential for Overt Conflict

One concern that typifies many desegregated schools, and that is often especially salient in newly desegregated situations, is a desire to avoid dissension and conflict that are or could appear to be race related (Sagar & Schofield, 1984). The adoption of colorblind policies is often seen as useful in achieving this goal, because if such policies are implemented fully, they can help protect the institution and people in positions of responsibility in it from charges of discrimination. This is not to say that such policies lead to equal outcomes for members of all groups. Indeed, when there are initial group differences on criteria relevant to success in a given institution, such policies are likely to lead to differential outcomes, a situation that some people would characterize as institutional racism (Jones, 1997). However, as noted earlier, the colorblind perspective is consistent with notions of fairness that have long held sway in the United States and thus that can be relatively easily defended. Policies that give obvious preference to either minority or majority group members are much more likely to spark controversy and conflict.

An example from Wexler illustrates how the operation of the colorblind perspective helps to minimize overt conflict in situations in which the outcomes for Blacks and Whites as a whole are extremely different. The suspension rate for African American students at Wexler was roughly four times that for White students. The strong correlation between race and socioeconomic background at Wexler made it predictable that the African American students' behavior would be less consistent than that of White students with the basically middle-class norms prevailing in the school. However, the colorblind perspective appeared instrumental in helping to keep Wexler's discipline policies from becoming a focus of contention. To my knowledge, the disparity in suspension rates was never treated as a serious issue that needed attention. When researchers asked faculty and administrators about it, some, perhaps not altogether candidly, denied having noticed it. Others argued that it was not a problem in the sense that individual students were generally treated fairly. In fact, teachers often emphasized strongly the effort they made to treat discipline problems with White and African American students in exactly the same way.

On the relatively rare occasions when charges of discrimination were raised by students unhappy with the way a teacher had dealt with them, teachers tended to discount the complaints by reiterating their commitment to the colorblind perspective:

> MS. WILSON [WHITE]: I try not to let myself listen to it [the charge of discrimination]. Maybe once in a while I ask myself, "Well, why would he make that statement?" But I know in my mind that I do not discriminate on the basis of race. . . . And I will not have someone create an issue like that when I know I have done my best not to create it.

Only an occasional teacher, more often than not African American, suggested that the colorblind perspective actually worked to help create the disparity in suspension rates; this issue is addressed later in this chapter. Be that as it may, the colorblind perspective clearly fostered an atmosphere that minimized the chances that the disparity itself was likely to become the focus of either overt discontent or constructive action.

Minimizing of Discomfort or Embarrassment

Many of the faculty and students at Wexler had little prior experience in desegregated schools. Also, most of them lived in neighborhoods that were either heavily White or heavily African American. Thus, for many, there was an initial sense of awkwardness and anxiety, like the intergroup anxiety Stephan and Stephan (1985) discuss. Under such circumstances, avoiding mention of race and contending that it rarely influenced relations between individuals seemed to minimize the potential for awkward or embarrassing social situations. This is related to the aforementioned conflict-avoidance function of these beliefs, but it can be distinguished conceptually because feelings of awkwardness and embarrassment can but do not always lead to conflict. In fact, the colorblind perspective and the related norms against mention of race seemed to help maintain the veneer of politeness that Clement, Eisenhart, and Harding (1979) have argued is part of the etiquette of race relations in some desegregated situations.

One way to illustrate the ways in which the colorblind perspective and the associated beliefs and norms helped smooth social relations between Blacks and Whites is to compare the situation at Wexler to another sort of interaction that is often rather strained, at least initially—interaction between individuals who have visible disabilities and those who do not. In a fascinating analysis of this latter situation, Davis (1961) argues that the emotion aroused in the person without disabilities by the sight of a person with disabilities creates tension and an uncertainty about what is appropriate behavior; this tension interferes with normal interaction patterns. There is a tendency for the disability to become the focus of attention and to foster ambiguity about appropriate behavior. Davis argues that the initial reaction to this situation is often a fictional denial of the disability and of its potential effect on the relationship, that is, a tendency to pretend to ignore the existence of the disability, which at least temporarily relieves the interactants of the necessity of dealing with its implications.

Analogously, one can think of the racial group membership of individuals in a biracial interaction, be they Black or White, as a sort of visually apparent disability. Like a disability, one's group membership may provoke an affective response in other people that predisposes them to avoidance or at least raises questions about appropriate behavior. Of course, just as some individuals will feel more awkward than will others when interacting with a person with a disability, so some individuals will more likely be more affected by interacting with someone of the other race. However, to the extent that either person is perceived as a potential threat to a smooth, relaxed, and pleasant interaction, one way of handling that threat is to pretend to be unaware of the attribute that creates it.

Although Davis (1961) argues that initial interactions between people with disabilities and other people are characterized by a fictional denial of the disability, he also suggests that with time this fiction is discarded because, being based on an obvious falsehood, it is inherently unstable and in the long run dysfunctional. Similarly, I argue that although the colorblind perspective and the accompanying taboo may have made the initial adjustment to Wexler easier, in the long run they tended to inhibit the development of positive relations between African American and White students. These students were vividly aware of differences and of tensions between them that were related to their group membership. Yet such issues could not be dealt with in a straightforward manner in the colorblind climate. Thus, anger sometimes festered and stereotypes built when fuller discussion of the situation might have made it easier for individuals to see each other's perspectives.

This is not to suggest that schools have the responsibility to function as giant T-groups or as therapeutic institutions. Rather, it is to say that the refusal of many of Wexler's faculty to recognize the fundamental role that race played in peer relationships meant that they played a less constructive role than they might have in guiding students through a new and sometimes threatening experience. Jervis (1996) observed a similar phenomenon with similar results in her study of a multiethnic middle school. Furthermore, the norms discouraging discussion of race not only undercut potentially constructive teacher–students interactions related to this topic; they discouraged student discussion of this topic with peers as well. This clearly minimized the potential for conflict. But it also minimized the potentially constructive impact of such discussions, suggested by research demonstrating that discussion of race between more and less prejudiced students can actually reduce prejudice in the former without increasing it in the latter (Aboud & Doyle, 1996; Aboud & Fenwick, 1999).

Increasing Teachers' Freedom of Action

The colorblind perspective and its corollaries undoubtedly gained some of their appeal because they tended to simplify life for Wexler's staff and to increase their freedom of action. An example can illustrate both points. After being asked by one member of the research team about the outcome of a closely contested student council election, a White teacher disclosed that she had purposely miscounted votes so that a "responsible child" (a White boy) was declared the winner rather than the "unstable child" (an African American girl) who had actually received a few more votes. The teacher seemed ambivalent about and somewhat embarrassed by her action, but the focus of her concern was her subversion of the democratic process. She reported that she had looked at the two children as individuals and decided that one was a more desirable student council representative than the other. As far as I could tell from an extended discussion with her, she did not consciously consider the race of the students involved. Further, she did not appear to consider the fact that her action had changed the racial composition of the student council.

The failure to consider such issues clearly simplified the decision-making process because there was one less item, and an affect-laden one at that, to be factored into it. Related to this, such a colorblind approach increased teachers' freedom of action because actions that sometimes appeared acceptable if one were to think about them in a colorblind way often appeared much less acceptable from a perspective that was not colorblind. Indeed, the colorblind perspective and its corollaries fostered an environment that research suggests is conducive to discriminatory behavior, at least on the part of certain types of individuals. First, work by Snyder, Kleck, Strenta, and Mentzer (1979) demonstrates that people are more likely to act in accordance with feelings they prefer not to reveal when they can appear to be acting on some other basis than when no other obvious explanation for their behavior is available. Specifically, they found that individuals avoided people with physical disabilities when such avoidance could easily be attributed to preference for a certain kind of movie.

However, when the situation did not provide this sort of rationale for avoidance behavior, the tendency to avoid people with physical disabilities disappeared. Thus, by analogy, one might expect that an environment that minimizes the importance of race and even forbids overt consideration or discussion of the topic would free individuals whose basic tendency is to discriminate (a normatively unacceptable orientation at Wexler) to do so. The vast majority of Wexler's faculty espoused basically egalitarian racial attitudes and would quite rightly be insulted by the idea that they would intentionally discriminate against their African American students. Yet the work of Gaertner and Dovidio (1981, 1986) demonstrates that one need not be an old-fashioned racist to discriminate against African Americans when the conditions are conducive to doing so.

Specifically, Gaertner and Dovidio (1981, 1986) argue that a great many liberal Whites are highly motivated to maintain an image of themselves as egalitarian individuals who neither discriminate against others on the basis of race nor are prejudiced. However, the desire to maintain such an image is coupled with some negative affect and with certain beliefs that predispose them to react negatively to African Americans. This predisposition is expressed primarily in circumstances that do not threaten an egalitarian self-concept. One important relevant circumstance is the availability of non-race-related rationales for the behavior in question (Dovidio & Gaertner, 1998; Gaertner & Dovidio, 1986). It is precisely this aspect of the situation that is influenced by the colorblind perspective and its corollaries. To the extent that they help remove awareness of race from conscious consideration, they make other explanations for one's behavior relatively more salient. Thus, they free the aversive racist to act in a discriminatory fashion. Further, to the extent that the taboo at Wexler inhibited individuals from challenging the behavior of other people as racist in outcome or intent, it removed a potential barrier to racist behavior because it minimized the probability that such behavior would pose a threat to a liberal self-concept.

Ignoring the Reality of Cultural Differences between Students

Although the colorblind perspective and its corollaries served some useful purposes, they also had several unrecognized negative effects, as indicated. One important negative consequence of this mind-set was a predisposition to ignore or deny the possibility of cultural differences between White and Black children that influenced how they functioned in school. For example, the differential suspension rate for African American and White children may have stemmed partially from differences between these students in what Triandis and his colleagues (Triandis, 1994; Triandis, Vassiliou, Vassiliou, Tanaka, & Shanmugam, 1972) call their "subjective culture." Specifically, data from the Sagar and Schofield (1980) experiment described earlier suggested that African American boys saw certain types of ambiguously aggressive acts as less mean and threatening and as more playful and friendly than did their White peers. These behaviors were ones that sometimes began conflicts between students that resulted in suspensions. Awareness of the differential meaning of such behaviors to White and African American students might at least have suggested ways of trying to reduce the disproportionate suspension of Black students.

Other research suggests that Black-White differences in culture relevant to education are not limited to this one area (Hill, 1971; Irvine, 1990; Jones, 1986, 1997; Lee & Slaughter-Defoe, 2001). For example, Kochman (1981) has argued convincingly that Black and White students use widely differing styles in classroom discussion and that misunderstanding the cultural context from which students come can lead peers and teachers to misinterpret involvement for belligerence. Heath's (1982) research suggests that the types of questions teachers typically pose in elementary school classrooms are quite similar to those asked in White middle-class homes but differ substantially from those typically addressed to young children in poor African American homes. Thus, there is reason to think that in assuming a completely colorblind perspective teachers may rule out awareness and use of information that would be helpful in deciding how best to structure materials in ways that work well for the range of students they teach as well as in interpreting many aspects of their students' behavior.

Failing to Respond to and Capitalize on Diversity

There were numerous less subtle ways in which the colorblind perspective and the accompanying deemphasis on the biracial nature of the school worked to the disadvantage of Wexler's students—and more often to the disadvantage of African American than of White students. One of the more obvious of these concerned the extent to which efforts were made to use instructional materials and pedagogical approaches that were likely to reflect the interests and life experiences of Wexler's African American students, an approach that has been called "using culturally responsive pedagogy" (Carter & Goodwin, 1994; Irvine, 1991; Nieto, 2004; Ramsey, 1987). Wexler operated as part of a school system that made some effort to use multicultural texts. In addition, some teachers, a disproportionate number of whom were African American, took special care to relate class work to the concerns and interests likely to be found in their Black students as well as their White ones.

The prevailing tendency, however, was to abjure responsibility for making sure instructional materials reflected the diversity of the student body. Interviews with teachers suggested that many saw no reason to try to locate or develop instructional materials that reflected African Americans' participation in and contributions to our society. For example, one math teacher who used a book in which all individuals in the illustrations were White contended that "math is math" and that an interview question about the use of biracial or multicultural materials was irrelevant to his subject matter. Perhaps more surprisingly, similar claims were made by other teachers, including some who taught reading, language arts, and social studies.

The colorblind perspective and its corollaries not only made it more likely that individual faculty members would ignore the challenge of trying to present all students with materials that related in motivating ways to their own experiences, but they actually led to a constriction of the education provided to students. For example, in a lesson on the social organization of ancient Rome, one social studies teacher discussed at length the various classes in Roman society, including the patricians and plebeians, but avoided all reference to slaves. Another teacher included George Washington Carver on a list of great Americans from whom students could pick individuals to learn about but specifically decided not to mention that Carver was African American for fear of raising racial issues. In the best of all worlds, there would be no need to make such mention because children would have no preconceptions that famous people are generally White. However, in a school in which one White child was surprised to learn from a member of our research team that Martin Luther King, Jr., was African American, not White, it would seem reasonable to argue that highlighting the accomplishments of African Americans and making sure that students do not assume famous figures are White are reasonable practices.

Such constriction based on a desire to avoid racial problems is not unique at Wexler. For example, Scherer and Slawski (1979) report that a desegregated high school they studied eliminated the lunch hour and study halls to minimize the sort of loosely supervised contact between students that seemed to be likely to lead to conflict. However, the nature of the constriction at Wexler was influenced by the colorblind perspective and its corollaries. At Wexler, the tendency was to ignore or avoid certain topics. Such a tendency, while undeniably a low-risk one, failed to take advantage of the diversity of experiences and perspectives of Wexler's students as a resource for the educational process. Furthermore, in some cases, it literally distorted the education all students received as teachers attempted to avoid potentially controversial facts or issues.

CONCLUSIONS

Since Supreme Court Justice Harlan first spoke of a colorblind society as a goal to be striven for more than 100 years ago, the colorblind approach has often been held up as a needed antidote to the virulent racism in our society that traditionally consigned certain individuals to subordinate positions on the basis of their color and their color alone. However, this chapter takes the position that the colorblind perspective is not without some dangers. It may ease initial tensions and minimize the frequency of overt conflict. Nonetheless, it can also foster such phenomena as the taboo against ever mentioning race or connected issues and the refusal to recognize and deal with the existence of intergroup tensions. Thus, it fosters an environment in which aversive racists, who are basically well intentioned, are prone to act in a discriminatory manner. In addition, it can foster lack of recognition of problems that might be dealt with constructively if they were acknowledged. Further, the colorblind perspective makes it unlikely that the opportunities inherent in a pluralistic institution will be fully realized and that the challenge facing such an institution of providing all its students with an engaging and effective education will be met.

Although the colorblind approach clearly has many disadvantages, this finding does not lead to the conclusion that it is best to constantly call students' attention to group membership. There are several reasons to be wary of an unrelenting emphasis on group membership, and especially on group differences. First, there is substantial evidence that liking of others is enhanced by the perception of similarity (Berscheid & Reis, 1998), so a constant emphasis on difference is likely to be unproductive. Second, an emerging body of research about a phenomenon called stereotype threat also suggests that it may be unwise to make race constantly salient. For example, researchers studying this phenomenon have found that merely raising the issue of race by having students indicate their group membership before completing a task can lead to markedly decreased performance by African American students on tasks relevant to existing negative stereotypes about their ability (Steele & Aronson, 1995). Further, a large body of social psychological research mentioned earlier in this chapter has demonstrated that categorization of individuals into in-groups and out-groups tends to promote stereotyping and biased behavior.

What, then, is likely to be the most effective stance for schools to take? A full answer to this question would be an entire chapter in itself. However, I would suggest that at least three things are highly desirable. First, the education system needs to make a concerted effort to be responsive to our society's diversity in planning curriculum, in making staffing choices, and in thinking about how best to serve students. This seems likely to help make schools institutions that students from different backgrounds can feel engaged with and connected to, in addition to providing them with the breadth of information and perspectives necessary to function effectively in our increasingly diverse society. Second, schools need to help students and teachers see that groups are composed of individuals with their own unique characteristics who may be both similar to and different from those in both their in-group and in out-groups, which should help undercut the tendency to stereotype and to see group membership as defining an individual's characteristics. Finally, schools should provide students with opportunities to build meaningful shared identities as members of the school, the community, and the nation that complement and supplement, rather than replace or undermine, their identities as members of specific social groups.

Acknowledgments

The author expresses her deep appreciation to the students and staff of Wexler School. The research on which this chapter is based was funded by the author's contract with the National Institute of Education (Contract 400–76–0011). Other expenses relating to the chapter's preparation were covered by the Learning Research and Development Center, which was partly funded by the NIE when this research was conducted. However, all opinions expressed herein are solely those of the author, and no endorsement of the ideas by the NIE is implied or intended.

Questions and Activities

1. According to the author, how does the social context influence the expression of racism and discrimination?

2. What is the *colorblind perspective?* Give some examples of it. On what major beliefs and assumptions is it based?

3. In what ways does the colorblind perspective contribute to racial discrimination and institutionalized racism in schools? Give specific examples.

4. How does the colorblind perspective often lead to what the author calls a "misrepresentation of reality"? Which realities are often misrepresented by the colorblind perspective?

5. Why did the teachers at Wexler deny that they were aware of the race of their students? What were some consequences of their denial? How was their denial inconsistent with many realities related to race in the school?

6. What did the interviews with Wexler students reveal about their conceptions of race? How did their conceptions of race differ from those of the teachers? Why?

7. Why do teachers often embrace the colorblind perspective? According to the author, what are its benefits and costs?

8. How does the colorblind perspective make it easier for liberal White teachers to discriminate? Give specific examples from this chapter and from your own observations and experiences in schools and in other settings and contexts.

9. How does the colorblind perspective negatively affect the development of a multicultural curriculum? What are the most promising ways to counteract the colorblind perspective? Give specific examples.

References

Aboud, F. E., & Doyle, A. B. (1996). Does Talk of Race Foster Prejudice or Tolerance in Children? *Canadian Journal of Behavioral Science, 28*(3), 161–170.

Aboud, F. E., & Fenwick, V. (1999). Exploring and Evaluating School-Based Interventions to Reduce Prejudice. *Journal of Social Issues, 55*(4), 767–785.

Allport, G. W. (1954). *The Nature of Prejudice.* Cambridge, MA: Addison-Wesley.

Amir, Y. (1969). Contact Hypothesis in Ethnic Relations. *Psychological Bulletin, 71*(5), 319–342.

Amir, Y. (1976). The Role of Intergroup Contact in Change of Prejudice and Ethnic Relations. In P. A. Katz (Ed.), *Towards the Elimination of Racism* (pp. 245–308). New York: Pergamon.

Aronson, E., & Patnoe, S. (1997). *The Jigsaw Classroom* (2nd ed). New York: Longman.

Banks, J. A. (2001). Multicultural Education: Characteristics and Goals. In J. A. Banks & C. A. McGee Banks (Eds.), *Multicultural Education: Issues & Perspectives* (4th ed., pp. 3–30). New York: Wiley.

Bennett, W. (1987). *James Madison High School: A Curriculum for American Students.* Washington, DC: U.S. Department of Education.

Berscheid, E., & Reis, H. T. (1998). Attraction and Close Relationships. In D. T. Gilbert, S. T. Fiske, & G. Lindzey (Eds.), *The Handbook of Social Psychology* (4th ed., pp. 193–281). New York: McGraw-Hill.

Bogdan, R. C., & Taylor, S. J. (1975). *Introduction to Qualitative Research Methods: A Phenomenological Approach to the Social Sciences.* New York: Wiley.

Bonilla-Silva, E. (2003). *Racism Without Racists: Color-blind Racism and the Persistence of Racial Inequality in the United States.* New York: Rowman and Littlefield.

Bossert, S. T. (1988/89). Cooperative Activities in the Classroom. In E. Z. Rothkopt (Ed.), *Review of Research in Education* (Vol. 15, pp. 225–250). Washington, DC: American Educational Research Association.

Brewer, M. B., & Brown, R. J. (1998). Intergroup Relations. In D. T. Gilbert, S. T. Fiske, & G. Lindzey (Eds.), *The Handbook of Social Psychology* (4th ed., pp. 554–594). New York: McGraw-Hill.

Brewer, M. B., & Miller, N. (1984). Beyond the Contact Hypothesis: Theoretical Perspectives on Desegregation. In N. Miller & M. B. Brewer (Eds.), *Groups in Contact: The Psychology of Desegregation* (pp. 281–302). Orlando, FL: Academic Press.

Brewer, M. B., & Miller, N. (1988). Contact and Cooperation: When Do They Work? In P. A. Katz & D. A. Taylor (Eds.), *Eliminating Racism: Profiles in Controversy* (pp. 315–328). New York: Plenum.

Brown, R. (1995). *Prejudice: Its Social Psychology.* Oxford, UK: Blackwell.

Campbell, D. T. (1975). Degrees of Freedom and the Case Study. *Comparative Political Studies, 8*(2), 178–193.

Carter, R. T., & Goodwin, A. L. (1994). Racial Identity and Education. In L. Darling-Hammond (Ed.), *Review of Research in Education* (pp. 291–336). Washington, DC: American Educational Research Association.

Clement, D. C., Eisenhart, M., & Harding, J. R. (1979). The Veneer of Harmony: Social-Race Relations in a Southern Desegregated School. In R. C. Rist (Ed.), *Desegregated Schools* (pp. 15–62). New York: Academic Press.

Cohen, E. G. (1975). The Effects of Desegregation on Race Relations. *Law and Contemporary Problems, 39*(2), 271–299.

Cohen, E. G. (1997). Understanding Status Problems: Sources and Consequences. In E. G. Cohen & R. A. Lotan (Eds.), *Working for Equity in Heterogeneous Classrooms: Sociological Theory in Practice* (pp. 61–76). New York: Teachers College Press.

Cohen, E., Lockheed, M., & Lohman, M. (1976). The Center for Interracial Cooperation: A Field Experiment. *Sociology of Education, 49,* 47–58.

Cook, S. W. (1969). Motives in the Conceptual Analysis of Attitude-Related Behavior. In W. J. Arnold & D. Levine (Eds.), *Nebraska Symposium on Motivation* (Vol. 17, pp. 179–235). Lincoln: University of Nebraska Press.

Cook, S. W. (1978). Interpersonal and Attitudinal Outcomes in Cooperating Interracial Groups. *Journal of Research and Development in Education, 12*(1), 97–113.

Cook, S. W. (1985). Experimenting on Social Issues: The Case of School Desegregation. *American Psychologist, 40,* 452–460.

Cook, T., & Campbell, D. (1976). The Design and Conduct of Quasi-Experiments and True Experiments in Field Settings. In M. Dunnette (Ed.), *Handbook of Organizational Psychology* (pp. 223–281). Chicago: Rand McNally.

Davis, F. (1961). Deviance Disavowal: The Management of Strained Interaction by the Visibly Handicapped. In H. S. Becker (Ed.), *The Other Side: Perspectives on Deviance* (pp. 119–137). New York: Free Press.

Devine, P. G. (1989). Stereotyping and Prejudice: Their Automatic and Controlled Components. *Journal of Personality and Social Psychology, 56,* 5–18.

Dovidio, J. F., & Gaertner, S. L. (1998). On the Nature of Contemporary Prejudice: The Causes, Consequences, and Challenges of Aversive Racism. In J. L. Eberhardt & S. T. Fiske (Eds.), *Confronting Racism: The Problem and the Response* (pp. 3–32). Thousand Oaks, CA: Sage.

Dovidio, J. F., Gaertner, S. L., Voulidzic, A., Matoka, A., Johnson, B., & Frazier, S. (1997). Extending the Benefits of Recategorization: Evaluations, Self-Disclosure, and Helping. *Journal of Experimental Social Psychology, 33,* 401–420.

Duncan, B. L. (1976). Differential Racial Perception and Attribution of Intergroup Violence. *Journal of Personality and Social Psychology, 35,* 590–598.

Eaton, S. E. (2001). *The Other Boston Busing Story.* New Haven, CT: Yale University Press.

Fazio, R. H., Jackson, J. R., Dunton, B. C., & Williams, C. J. (1995). Variability in Automatic Activation as Unobtrusive Measure of Racial Attitudes: A Bona Fide Pipeline? *Journal of Personality and Social Psychology, 69,* 1013–1027.

Fiske, S. T., & Neuberg, S. L. (1990). A Continuum of Impression Formation, from Category-Based to Individuating Processes: Influences of Information and Motivation on Attention and Interpretation. In M. P. Zanna (Ed.), *Advances in Experimental Social Psychology* (Vol. 23, pp. 1–74). New York: Academic Press.

Gaertner, S. L., & Dovidio, J. F. (1981). Racism among the Well-Intentioned. In E. Clausen & J. Bermingham (Eds.), *Pluralism, Racism, and Public Policy: The Search for Equality* (pp. 208–222). Boston: Hall.

Gaertner, S. L., & Dovidio, J. F. (1986). The Aversive Form of Racism. In J. F. Dovidio & S. L. Gaertner (Eds.), *Prejudice, Discrimination, and Racism* (pp. 61–89). Orlando, FL: Academic Press.

Gaertner, S. L., Dovidio, J. F., Anastasio, P. A., Bachman, B. A., & Rust, M. C. (1993). The Common Ingroup Identity Model: Recategorization and the Reduction of Intergroup Bias. In W. Stroebe & M. Hewstone (Eds.), *European Review of Social Psychology* (pp. 1–26). Chichester, UK: Wiley.

Gillborn, D. (1992). Citizenship, Race, and the Hidden Curriculum. *International Studies in Sociology of Education, 2*(1), 57–73.

Heath, S. B. (1982). Questioning at Home and at School: A Comparative Study. In G. Spindler (Ed.), *Doing the Ethnography of Schooling: Educational Anthropology in Action* (pp. 102–131). New York: Holt, Rinehart & Winston.

Hewstone, M., & Brown, R. (Eds.). (1986). *Contact and Conflict in Intergroup Encounters*. Oxford, UK: Blackwell.

Hill, J. (1971). *Personalized Education Programs Utilizing Cognitive Style Mapping*. Bloomfield Hills, MI: Oakland Community College Press.

Hirsch, E. D. (1996). *The Schools We Need, And Why We Don't Have Them*. New York: Doubleday.

Irvine, J. J. (1990). *Black Students and School Failure: Policies, Practices, and Prescriptions*. Westport, CT: Greenwood.

Irvine, J. J. (1991, January). *Culturally Responsive and Responsible Pedagogy: The Inclusion of Culture, Research, and Reflection in the Knowledge Base of Teacher Education*. Paper presented at the annual meeting of the American Association of Colleges for Teacher Education, Atlanta.

Jaynes, G. D., & Williams, R. M., Jr. (1989). *A Common Destiny: Blacks and the American Society*. Washington, DC: National Academy Press.

Jervis, K. (1996). How Come There Are No Brothers on That List? Hearing the Hard Questions All Children Ask. *Harvard Educational Review, 66*(3), 546–576.

Johnson, D. W., & Johnson, R. T. (1982). The Study of Cooperative, Competitive, and Individualistic Situations: State of the Area and Two Recent Contributions. *Contemporary Education: A Journal of Reviews, 1*(1), 7–13.

Johnson, D. W., Johnson, R. T., & Maruyama, G. (1984). Goal Interdependence and Interpersonal Attraction in Heterogeneous Classrooms: A Meta-Analysis. In N. Miller & M. B. Brewer (Eds.), *Groups in Contact: The Psychology of Desegregation* (pp. 187–212). Orlando, FL: Academic Press.

Johnson, D. W., Maruyama, G., Johnson, R. T., Nelson, D., & Skon, L., (1981). Effects of Cooperative, Competitive, and Individualistic Goal Structures on Achievement: A Meta-Analysis. *Psychological Bulletin, 89*, 47–62.

Jones, J. M. (1986). Racism: A Cultural Analysis of the Problem. In J. F. Dovidio & S. L. Gaertner (Eds.), *Prejudice, Discrimination, and Racism* (pp. 279–313). Orlando, FL: Academic Press.

Jones, J. M. (1997). *Prejudice and Racism* (2nd ed.). New York: McGraw-Hill.

Jones, J. M. (1998). Psychological Knowledge and the New American Dilemma of Race. *Journal of Social Issues, 54*(4), 645.

Katz, I., Wackenhut, J., & Hass, R. G. (1986). Racial Ambivalence, Value Duality, and Behavior. In J. F. Dovidio & S. L. Gaertner (Eds.), *Prejudice, Discrimination, and Racism* (pp. 35–59). Orlando, FL: Academic Press.

Katz, P. A. (1976). The Acquisition of Racial Attitudes. In P. Katz (Ed.), *Toward the Elimination of Racism* (pp. 125–156). New York: Pergamon.

Kochman, T. (1981). *Black and White Styles of Conflict*. Chicago: University of Chicago Press.

Lee, C. D., & Slaughter-Defoe, D. T. (2001). Historical and Sociocultural Influences on African American Education. In J. A. Banks & C. A. McGee Banks (Eds.), *Handbook of Research on Multicultural Education* (pp. 348–371). San Francisco: Jossey-Bass.

Lee, Y. T., & Duenas, G. (1995). Stereotype Accuracy in Multicultural Business. In Y. T. Lee, L. J. Jussim, & C. R. McCauley (Eds.), *Stereotype Accuracy: Toward Appreciating Group Differences* (pp. 157–188). Washington, DC: American Psychological Association.

Levin, S. (2003). Social Psychological Evidence on Race and Racism. In M. J. Chang, D. Witt, J. Jones, & K. Hakuta (Eds.), *Compelling Interest: Examining the Evidence on Racial Dynamics in Colleges and Universities* (pp. 97–125). Stanford, CA: Stanford University Press.

Malpass, R. S., & Kravitz, J. (1969). Recognition for Faces of Own and Other Races. *Journal of Personality and Social Psychology, 13*, 330–334.

Miles, M. B., & Huberman, A. M. (1984). *Qualitative Data Analysis: A Sourcebook of New Methods.* Newbury Park, CA: Sage.

Nieto, S. (2004). *Affirming Diversity: The Sociopolitical Context of Multicultural Education* (4th ed.). Boston: Allyn & Bacon.

Norvell, N., & Worchel, S. (1981). A Reexamination of the Relation between Equal Status Contact and Intergroup Attraction. *Journal of Personality and Social Psychology, 41,* 902–908.

Olson, S. (1976). *Ideas and Data: Process and Practice of Social Research.* Homewood, IL: Dorsey.

Pettigrew, T. (1986). The Intergroup Contact Hypothesis Reconsidered. In M. Hewstone & R. Brown (Eds.), *Contact and Conflict in Intergroup Encounters* (pp. 169–195). Oxford, UK: Blackwell.

Pettigrew, T. F. (1998). Intergroup Contact Theory. *Annual Review of Psychology, 49,* 65–85.

Pettigrew, T. F., & Tropp, L. R. (2000). Does Intergroup Contact Reduce Prejudice: Recent Meta-Analytic Findings. In S. Oskamp (Ed.), *The Claremont Symposium on Applied Social Psychology* (pp. 93–114). Mahwah, NJ: Erlbaum.

Pollock, M. (2000). *Racing, De-Racing, and Erasing: The Paradoxes of Racial Description in School.* Unpublished doctoral dissertation, Stanford University, Stanford, CA.

Ramsey, P. G. (1987). *Teaching and Learning in a Diverse World.* New York: Teachers College Press.

Randolph, G., Landis, D., & Tzeng, O. C. S. (1977). The Effects of Time and Practice on Cultural Assimilator Training. *International Journal of Intercultural Relations, 1,* 105–119.

Regents of the University of California *vs.* Baake, 76–811 U.S. (1978).

Riordan, C. (1978). Equal-Status Interracial Contact: A Review and Revision of the Concept. *International Journal of Intercultural Relations, 2*(2), 161–185.

Rist, R. C. (1974). Race, Policy, and Schooling. *Society, 12*(1), 59–63.

Rist, R. C. (1978). *The Invisible Children: School Integration in American Society.* Cambridge, MA: Harvard University Press.

Sagar, H. A., & Schofield, J. W. (1980). Racial and Behavioral Cues in Black and White Children's Perceptions of Ambiguously Aggressive Acts. *Journal of Personality and Social Psychology, 39*(4), 590–598.

Sagar, H. A., & Schofield, J. W. (1984). Integrating the Desegregated School: Problems and Possibilities. In M. Maehr & D. Bartz (Eds.), *Advances in Motivation and Achievement: A Research Annual* (pp. 203–241) Greenwich, CT: JAI Press.

Sagar, H. A., Schofield, J. W., & Snyder, H. N. (1983). Race and Gender Barriers: Preadolescent Peer Behavior in Academic Classrooms. *Child Development, 54,* 1032–1040.

Scherer, J., & Slawski, E. J. (1979). Color, Class, and Social Control in an Urban Desegregated School. In R. C. Rist (Ed.), *Desegregated Schools* (pp. 117–153). New York: Academic Press.

Schlesinger, A. M. (1992). *The Disuniting of America: Reflections on a Multicultural Society.* New York: Norton.

Schofield, J. W. (1979). The Impact of Positively Structured Contact on Intergroup Behavior: Does It Last under Adverse Conditions? *Social Psychology Quarterly, 42*(3), 280–284.

Schofield, J. W. (1980). Cooperation as Social Exchange: Resource Gaps and Reciprocity in Academic Work. In S. Sharon, P. Hare, C. Webb, & R. Hertz-Lazarowitz (Eds.), *Cooperation in Education* (pp. 160–181). Provo, UT: Brigham Young University Press.

Schofield, J. W. (1989). *Black and White in School: Trust Tension or Tolerance?* New York: Teachers College Press.

Schofield, J. W. (2001). Improving Intergroup Relations among Students. In J. A. Banks & C. A. M. Banks (Eds.), *Handbook of Research on Multicultural Education* (pp. 635–645). San Francisco: Jossey-Bass.

Schofield, J. W., & Eurich-Fulcer, R. (2001). When and How School Desegregation Improves Intergroup Relations. In R. Brown & S. Gaertner (Eds.), *Handbook of Social Psychology* (Vol. 4, pp. 474–494). New York: Blackwell.

Schofield, J. W., & Francis, W. D. (1982). An Observational Study of Peer Interaction in Racially-Mixed "Accelerated" Classrooms. *Journal of Educational Psychology, 74*(5), 722–732.

Schofield, J. W., & Sagar, H. A. (1977). Peer Interaction Patterns in an Integrated Middle School. *Sociometry, 40*(2), 130–138.

Schofield, J. W., & Sagar, H. A. (1979). The Social Context of Learning in an Interracial School. In R. Rist (Ed.), *Inside Desegregated Schools: Appraisals of an American Experiment* (pp. 155–199). San Francisco: Academic Press.

Schofield, J. W., & Whitley, B. E. (1983), Peer Nomination versus Rating Scale Measurement of Children's Peer Preferences. *Social Psychology Quarterly, 46*(3), 242–251.

Sharan, S. (1980). Cooperative Learning in Teams: Recent Methods and Effects on Achievement, Attitudes and Ethnic Relations. *Review of Educational Research, 50*(2), 241–272.

Sherif, M. (1979). Superordinate Goals in the Reduction of Intergroup Conflict: An Experimental Evaluation. In W. G. Austin & S. Worchel (Eds.), *The Social Psychology of Intergroup Relations* (pp. 257–261). Monterey, CA: Brooks/Cole.

Sidanius, J., & Pratto, F. (1999). *Social Dominance: An Intergroup Theory of Social Hierarchy and Oppression.* Port Chester, NY: Cambridge University Press.

Slavin, R. E. (1995). *Cooperative Learning: Theory, Research, and Practice* (2nd ed.). Boston: Allyn & Bacon.

Slavin, R. E., & Cooper, R. (1999). Improving Intergroup Relations: Lessons Learned from Cooperative Learning Programs. *Journal of Social Issues, 55*(4), 647–663.

Sleeter, C. E. (1993). How White Teachers Construct Race. In C. McCarthy & W. Crichlow (Eds.), *Race Identity and Representation in Education* (pp. 157–171). New York: Routledge.

Snyder, M. L., Kleck, R. E., Strenta, A., & Mentzer, S. J. (1979). Avoidance of the Handicapped: An Attributional Ambiguity Analysis. *Journal of Personality and Social Psychology, 12*, 2297–2306.

Steele, C. M., & Aronson, J. (1995). Stereotype Threat and the Intellectual Test Performance of African Americans. *Journal of Personality and Social Psychology, 69*(5), 797–811.

Stephan, W. G., & Stephan, C. W. (1985). Intergroup Anxiety. *Journal of Social Issues, 41*(3), 157–175.

Stephan, W. G., & Stephan, C. W. (1996). *Intergroup Relations.* Boulder, CO: Westview.

Stephan, W. G., & Stephan, C. W. (2001). *Improving Intergroup Relations.* Thousand Oaks, CA: Sage.

Strauss, A. (1987). *Qualitative Analysis for Social Scientists.* New York: Cambridge University Press.

Strauss, A., & Corbin, J. (1990). *Basics of Qualitative Research.* Newbury Park, CA: Sage.

Tajfel, H. (1978). *Differentiation between Social Groups: Studies in the Social Psychology of Intergroup Relations.* New York: Academic Press.

Takaki, R. (1933). *A Different Mirror: A History of Multicultural America.* Boston: Little, Brown.

Taylor, S., Fiske, S., Etcoff, N., & Ruderman, A. (1978). Categorical and Contextual Basis of Person Memory and Stereotyping. *Journal of Personality and Social Psychology, 36*(7), 778–793.

Trent, W., Owens-Nicholson, D., Eatman, T., Burke, M., Daugherty, J., & Norman, K. (2003). Justice, Equality of Educational Opportunity, and Affirmative Action in Higher Education. In M. J. Chang, D. Witt, J. Jones, & K. Hakuta (Eds.), *Compelling Interest: Examining the Evidence on Racial Dynamics in Colleges and Universities* (pp. 22–48). Stanford, CA: Stanford University Press.

Triandis, H. C. (Ed.). (1976). *Variations in Black and White Perceptions of the Social Environment.* Urbana: University of Illinois Press.

Triandis, H. C. (1994). *Culture and Social Behavior.* New York: McGraw-Hill.

Triandis, H. C., Vassiliou, V., Vassiliou, G., Tanaka, Y., & Shanmugam, A. (Eds.). (1972). *The Analysis of Subjective Culture.* New York: Wiley.

Webb, E. J., Campbell, D. T., Schwartz, R. D., & Sechrest, L. (1966). *Unobtrusive Measures: Nonreactive Research in the Social Sciences.* Chicago: Rand McNally.

Whitley, B. E., & Schofield, J. W. (1984). Peer Preference in Desegregated Classrooms: A Round Robin Analysis. *Journal of Personality and Social Psychology, 46*(4), 799–810.

Wolsko, C., Park, B., Judd, C., & Wittenbrink, B. (2000). Framing Interethnic Ideology: Effects of Multicultural and Color-Blind Perspectives on Judgments of Groups and Individuals. *Journal of Personality and Social Psychology, 78*(4), 635–654.

Yinger, J. M. (1994). *Ethnicity: Source of Strength? Source of Conflict?* Albany: State University of New York Press.

CHAPTER 12

Language Diversity and Education

Carlos J. Ovando

> Language is a shared and sharing part of culture that cares
> little about formal classifications and much about vitality and
> connection, for culture itself perishes in purity or isolation.
> (Fuentes, 1988, p. 27)

> In nature's talent show we are simply a species of primate with
> our own act, a knack for communicating information about who
> did what to whom by modulating the sounds we make when we
> exhale. (Pinker, 1994, p. 19)

Language diversity has a strong influence on the content and process of schooling practices for both language-minority and language-majority students in the United States. As a system of communication linking sound, written or visual symbols, and meaning, language is an indispensable bridge for sharing knowledge, skills, values, and attitudes within and across cultures. It has tremendous power as the paramount instrument of cognitive development, and it can open or close the door to academic achievement. How, then, is the educational inequality often experienced by language-minority students related to the extent of their ability to understand, speak, read, and write standard English?

To present an overview of how language diversity is related to educational outcomes, this chapter is organized into three sections. The first section considers what language is and how children and adults acquire their first and second languages. The second section surveys varieties of nonstandard English as well as non-English-language diversity in the United States. The third section discusses classroom adaptations to meet the needs of language-minority students.

THE SOCIOCULTURAL NATURE OF LANGUAGE AND LANGUAGE ACQUISITION

Language is a powerful and transformative part of culture. Like culture, language is learned, it is shared, and it evolves and changes over time. It is much more than a set of words and grammar rules. It is a forceful instrument for giving individuals, groups, institutions, and cultures their identity. Through language, we communicate our values, attitudes, skills, and aspirations as bearers of culture and as makers of future culture.

Language can be analyzed from many different points of view. At the physical level, it is a system of sounds and movements made by the human body and decoded by the listener's auditory system. From the cognitive point of view, it is a tool for the expression of thought. From the anthropological point of view, it is an intricate and pervasive component of culture. From the semiotic point of view, it can also be studied as a system of signs and symbols that have socially determined meanings (Shaumyan, 1987).

From the pedagogical point of view, what has been learned by someone who is said to have gained communicative competence in a particular language? To begin with, there are the more familiar components of language that have to be developed:

1. Phonetics and phonology—the sound system

2. Morphology—how units of meaning are formed into words

3. Syntax—the grammar of sentence formation

4. Lexicon—the vocabulary

Beyond these four components, however, there are other culture-related domains that must be mastered in order for communicative competence to be achieved. These five domains illustrate the subtleties and sociocultural aspects of the process of learning a language:

1. Discourse—how the language is organized in speech and writing beyond the sentence level; for example, how paragraphs or conversations are structured

2. Appropriateness—the way language use is adjusted according to the social situation; for example, "Hit the lights, will ya?" versus "Would you mind turning the lights off, please?"

3. Paralinguistics—distance between speakers, intonation, volume and pitch of speech, gestures, facial expressions, and other body language

4. Pragmatics—the interaction of discourse, appropriateness, and paralinguistics; for example, pragmatics involve implicit and explicit cultural norms for when it is and is not appropriate to talk, how speech is paced, the correct way to listen, when to be direct and when to be indirect, how to take turns in conversation, and how to adapt language according to roles, social status, attitudes, settings, and topics

5. Cognitive-academic language proficiency (Cummins, 1979, 1981, 1991a, 2000a)— mastery of the language skills needed to learn and develop abstract concepts in such areas as mathematics, science, and social studies (Ovando, Collier, & Combs, 2003)

Even such a cursory listing of the components and domains of language clearly suggests that language acquisition is a complicated, subtle, culture-specific, and lifelong process. Educators thus need to realize that the difference between English and Spanish, for example, or even between standard English and Black English, is much more than a difference in phonology, morphology, syntax, and lexicon (Ogbu, 1999; Perry & Delpit, 1998). It has often been said that learning basic communication in one's first language is a simple process—child's play, so to speak. When examined carefully, however, full development of one's first language—including literacy skills and knowledge about the structure and function of the language—is a complex process requiring years to reach communicative competence. When teachers understand this, they are more likely to develop respect for and sensitivity to students who arrive in the classroom speaking anything other than standard English. For non-English speakers, in particular, teachers should be realistic about the years of language development that will be needed for speakers to move from basic communication in English to full communicative competence.

Languages grow and develop as tools of communication within a given environment. In this sense, there is no such thing as "right" or "wrong" language, only language that is appropriate or inappropriate in a given context. Languages and language varieties develop and thrive because they meet the needs of communities. If a given community of speakers finds it necessary to maintain a language because it satisfies spiritual, social, intellectual, technical, scientific, economic, or political needs, then the chances that this particular linguistic community will survive are greatly enhanced. Thus, for example, Yupik (an Eskimo Aleut language) is alive in Akiachak, Alaska, despite the powerful influence of English, because Yupik fulfills the people's need for continuity with their heritage. Within the domain of English itself, the United States teems with a variety of linguistic microcultures representing a diversity of experiences—American Indian varieties of English, creoles, Black English, and a broad array of regional accents, vocabularies, and styles (Ovando, 1999).

Because through multicultural education we seek to promote equity and excellence across such variables as race, ethnicity, nationality, gender, social class, regional group, religion, exceptionality, literacy background, age, and language background, it is vital for educators to understand the function that language can play in either helping or inhibiting the educational fulfillment of individuals. As Hymes (1981) states:

> The law of the land demands that equal educational opportunity not be denied because of language. "Language" has been understood most readily in terms of "languages," such as Spanish, and structurally definable varieties of a language, such as Black English Vernacular. If one defines "language," as I do, in terms of ways of speaking, as involving both structure and ways of using structure, there are even deeper implications, implications not yet legally explored. One's language affects one's chances in life, not only through accent, but also through action. Access to opportunities in the form of access to schools, jobs, positions, memberships, clubs, and homes may depend on ways of using language that one has no chance to master, or chooses not to master. (pp. vii–viii)

Within and outside the school setting, it is important to consider how people come to acquire and value the particular types of first and second languages they prefer to use in formal and informal situations. Therefore, I now turn to research on first and second language acquisition and its application in classrooms. I focus here on the process by which non-English speakers acquire English language skills.

First- and Second-Language Acquisition

For the past thirty years, linguists and cognitive psychologists have made considerable progress in understanding first- and second-language acquisition. It would be impossible to provide a complete overview of this complex field of study here (for more extensive examinations of this field, see Cummins, 2000a; Minami & Ovando, 1995). This section focuses on aspects of language acquisition that relate closely to the effective education of language-minority students.

The research indicates that language learning is an instinctual (Pinker, 1994) and developmental process that involves predictable stages. We acquire our first language as children, in the context of natural, interesting, and meaningful interactions within our social and physical environment. In such an environment, children are exposed on a daily basis to peer and adult language models in a context that gives meaning to language. Because of this strongly contextualized environment, speakers tend to learn communication shortcuts such as incomplete responses and many nonverbal cues.

Although it is now more commonly called social or playground language, Cummins (1981) initially referred to this type of language as basic interpersonal communicative skills (BICS). Doing research with English-language learners in Canada, Cummins (1981, 2000a) suggested that an average non–English-speaking student could learn to communicate at this level in English after about two years of instruction in an acquisition-rich environment similar to that of a child learning a first language. This ability to get along in the world conversationally enables English-language learners to make everyday conversational contact with their English-speaking peers. Such contact, in turn, plays a pivotal role in the acculturation of these students, especially to the school culture. In addition, face-to-face communication serves as a platform for beginning to build a self-concept in social relationships. In other words, the acquisition of social language serves a powerful and important sociolinguistic function in the lives of those who are learning their second language.

Even though a student of limited English proficiency may seem to be making rapid progress in the acquisition of English, having a command of social language does not necessarily equip that student for the more cognitively demanding tasks of the curriculum. Cognitive tasks require a second developmental level, beyond conversational language, that consists of the language used in school and in many facets of adult life. Here, the context is less clear. This level of communication depends on a speaker's (or writer's) ability to manipulate the vocabulary and syntax and discourse style with precision (Ovando, 1983). Cummins has referred to this type of language competence as cognitive-academic language proficiency (CALP). Again, research by Cummins (1981) indicates that, as measured by standardized tests, children with little or no prior schooling experience attain the cognitive-academic language proficiency of a native English speaker in about five to seven years. For the past ten years, Cummins's research (initially reported in 1981) has been replicated and expanded in a series of studies by Collier and Thomas (for a synthesis of their work, see Collier, 1995; Thomas & Collier, 1999). Affirming Cummins's earlier research, they conclude (cited in Collier, 1995):

> In our studies we have found that in U.S. schools where all
> instruction is given through the second language (English), non-
> native speakers of English with no schooling in their first language

take 7–10 years or more to reach age and grade-level norms of their native English-speaking peers. Immigrant students who have had 2–3 years of first language in their home country before they come to the U.S. take at least 5–7 years to reach typical native-speaker performance. (p. 8)

Cummins (1986) has long examined the pattern of minority students' academic success and failure, and stressed ways in which educators can promote the empowerment of minority students and their parents and communities so that those children can become confident and capable in the academic environment. To provide a balanced view, we should acknowledge that some researchers (Edelsky et al., 1983; MacSwan, 2000; Martin-Jones & Romaine, 1986; Wiley, 1996) disagree with Cummins's views on academic and social language. Carole Edelsky (1991), for instance, strongly criticizes Cummins's position on the grounds that his analysis of the social and cognitive nature of children's language skills relies heavily on test scores. According to Edelsky, while advocating the empowerment of minority students, Cummins is in reality using culturally biased conventional test scores to measure their academic progress. Edelsky claims that what Cummins is measuring has nothing to do with the extent to which minority children have become truly confident and capable in the academic environment. She concludes that Cummins's ideal and practice are contradictory. In response to this criticism, Cummins (2000b) points out that the construct of academic language proficiency entails no reliance on test scores as support for either its construct validity or its relevance to education.

Consequently, equitable assessment is necessary to monitor bilingual children's progress not only in language development but also in the development of language skills such as literacy. It is certainly true that standardized tests do not always serve as an accurate or fair measure of language-minority students' diverse strengths (Edelsky, 1991; McCloskey & Enright, 1992). Yet, as Cummins emphasizes, the function of educators and policy makers should be to create contexts of empowerment for minority students. Moreover, as Collier (1992) argues, ignoring minority students' performance on standardized tests means denying those students "access to a meaningful education and equal opportunity to benefit in life from their education" (p. 194). Additionally, as a recent trend, the Bilingual Verbal Ability Tests (BVAT), which reflects ideas developed by Cummins (1980, 1991b)—particularly the notion of CALP—were developed by researchers, educators, and classroom teachers (Muñoz-Sandoval, Cummins, Alvarado, & Ruef, 1998). The tests are administered to (1) measure an individual child's English language proficiency, (2) measure a child's bilingual verbal ability (e.g., verbal cognitive ability in English and Japanese combined), and (3) predict a child's academic progress. The major objective of the BVAT is, therefore, to measure the unique combination of cognitive and academic language abilities possessed by bilingual individuals in English and another language (for further discussion on these issues, see Minami & Ovando, 2004).

Just because children speak little or no English does not mean that they come to school as blank slates. These children bring to the classroom a wealth of home experiences and of skills and competence in their home language. All of this provides a basis for future learning. Again, Cummins (1981) concludes that previously acquired knowledge and skills in the home language transfer to the new language. This transfer is known as the common underlying proficiency (CUP). Thus, for example, a Filipino student who already knows in Tagalog how to manipulate the language involved in the solution of word problems will be able to transfer those skills into the second language as he or she acquires new mathematical vocabulary in English. In other words, knowledge acquired through the student's first language is not only useful but also crucial in the continuous cognitive development of the student in the second language (Ramírez, 1991). In fact, ample research evidence suggests that cognitive and academic development in the first language can have a very positive effect on second-language schooling (for a synthesis of the research on the role of the first language on second-language schooling, see Collier, 1995). Of importance to language-minority educators is Cummins's (1981) conclusion on the instructional use of both the home language (L1) and English (L2):

> The results of research on bilingual programs show that minority children's L1 can be promoted in school at no cost to the development of proficiency in the majority language. . . . The data clearly show that well-implemented bilingual programs have had remarkable success in developing English academic skills and have proved superior to ESL-only programs in situations where direct comparisons have been carried out. (p. 28)

Tracking and expanding on the work of Cummins, Collier (1995) reports:

> In our examination of large datasets across many different research sites, we have found that the most significant student background variable is the amount of formal schooling students have received in their first language. Across all program treatments, we have found that non-native speakers being schooled in second language for part or all of the school day typically do reasonably well in the early years of schooling (kindergarten through second or third grade). But from fourth grade on through middle school and high school, when the academic and cognitive demands of the curriculum increase rapidly with each succeeding year, students with little or no academic and cognitive development in their first language do less and less well as they move into the upper grades.
>
> What about students schooled bilingually in the U.S.? It still takes a long time to demonstrate academic proficiency in second language comparable to a native speaker. But the difference in student performance in a bilingual program, in contrast to an all-English program, is that students typically score at or above grade level in their first language in all subjects areas, while they are building academic development of second language. When students are tested in their second language, they typically reach and surpass native speakers' performance across all subject areas after 4–7 years in a quality bilingual program. Because they have not fallen behind in cognitive and academic growth during the 4–7 years that it takes to build academic proficiency in second

language, bilingually schooled students typically sustain this level of academic achievement and outperform monolingually schooled students in the upper grades. (p. 9)

Thus, native-language support in a quality bilingual program can provide academic development through comprehensible instruction. This development can then be applied to students' academic and language growth in English.

LANGUAGE VARIETY IN THE UNITED STATES

As a language laboratory, the United States is truly remarkable. Of the scores of American Indian languages that existed prior to European contact, about 175 have survived the overwhelming assimilative powers of English in the United States, and about 35 such languages have survived in Canada (Krauss, 1995). Languages other than English used by the colonizers of North America—such as Spanish and French—not only have survived but also continue to serve as lively communicative and cultural instruments in various regions of the country. The successive waves of immigrants to the United States have added to the nation's linguistic richness (Ovando, 1999). Today, the country's language assets range from such languages as Navajo—still spoken in the same communities in which it was spoken hundreds of years ago— to Hmong, spoken by refugees from the highlands of Laos, Thailand, and Cambodia.

In addition to the mix of languages, language contact in the United States has produced many indigenous language varieties known as pidgins, creoles, and dialects. A *pidgin* is a type of language that evolves through contact between groups speaking different languages. It mixes components of the contact languages and has its own grammar system. A *creole* is the adoption of a pidgin as the accepted language of a community. As Anttila (1972) puts it, "This happened often on the plantations of the New World, where slaves from different language backgrounds were forced to use a pidgin among themselves, and between themselves and the masters. After escape, freedom, or revolution the pidgin was all they had, and it had to become the first language of the community" (p. 176). Three examples of creole varieties in the United States are Gullah, a creole of English and West African origin that is spoken on the Sea Islands, from the Carolinas to northern Florida; Louisiana French Creole, which coexists with two local varieties of French and another local variety of English; and Hawaiian Creole, which has been influenced by Hawaiian, Japanese, Chinese, Portuguese, English, and Ilocano. Complementing the rich indigenous creole traditions of the United States is Black English, which is spoken by a large segment of the African American population. To gain a better understanding of these indigenous language varieties, the next section examines more closely the nature of Gullah, Louisiana French Creole, Hawaiian Creole, and Black English.

Gullah

Gullah originated among African Americans who settled in South Carolina in the 1700s. Nichols (1981) has estimated that in the early 1980s there were about 300,000 African Americans who spoke Gullah in an area including South Carolina, Georgia, and parts of lower North Carolina and northern Florida. Gullah is different from standard English in a number of ways. For example, its West African ancestry is reflected in certain vowel sounds and some vocabulary items, such as *goober* for "peanut," *cooter* for "turtle," and *buckra* for "White man" (Nichols, 1981, p. 75). There are structural differences as well. Instead of using *he* and *she*, the neuter pronoun *ee* is used for both males and females. *Fuh* is used to indicate an infinitive clause, as in "I came *fuh* get my coat." Progressive action can be indicated by *duh* plus the verb: "Greg *duh* hide" instead of "Greg is hiding" (Nichols, 1981, pp. 73–75).

Most members of the Gullah-speaking community are not strictly creole speakers. Instead, individuals "show greater or lesser use of creole features along a continuum of language use ranging from creole to a dialect of English" (Nichols, 1981, p. 73). Not surprisingly, there is a strong association of Gullah use with age and amount of formal schooling. The very old and the very young tend to use Gullah more extensively. School-age children tend to switch back and forth between Gullah—referred to as "country talk"—and the prestige variety of standard English, especially for the benefit of teachers, who usually do not understand Gullah.

Gullah has been analyzed extensively by linguists, and much is known about its phonology, grammar, vocabulary, and sociolinguistic usage. The language has also been popularized through literature such as the stories of Ambrose González and the novels and Gullah sketches of Pulitzer Prize winner Julia Peterkin (Nichols, 1981). Yet children who speak Gullah have been stigmatized in the schools, and there has not been a vigorous effort to incorporate their language into the curriculum in order to create bridges to standard English. Although some teachers are addressing literacy development for these children through such means as the language-experience approach, by and large Gullah-speaking children may not be receiving equal educational opportunities in classrooms in which standard English is the accepted medium of instruction.

Louisiana French Creole

Like Gullah, Louisiana French Creole exhibits a linguistic structure that sets it apart from English. Its speakers may have difficulty understanding English, and vice versa. Louisiana French Creole, a contemporary of Gullah, seems to have evolved among West African slaves who were introduced to southern Louisiana by French colonists and needed a common language to communicate with each other. Louisiana French Creole has structural similarities to English-related creoles such as Gullah. For example, the pronoun *li* is used for both *he* and *she*. Also, as in Gullah, the verb *to be* is not used in equative clauses. In contrast to Gullah, however, most of the Louisiana French Creole vocabulary is derived from French rather than from English, with some use of African vocabulary items (Nichols, 1981).

Although Acadian and standard French are officially affirmed in the school curriculum in Louisiana, Louisiana French Creole traditionally has not had the same status. Like Gullah-speaking children, children who speak Louisiana French Creole therefore run the risk of not receiving equal educational opportunities. Furthermore, they and their parents may interpret the neglect of their primary language as a devaluation of their sociolinguistic background in the eyes of school personnel and society at large.

Hawaiian Creole

Hawaiian Creole is a relative newcomer to the family of indigenous creoles in U.S. society. Its use dates back to the late nineteenth century. In contrast to Louisiana French Creole, there is considerably more careful scholarly documentation about its origin, structure, and function (Nichols, 1981). Hawaiian Creole evolved as a pidgin during the late nineteenth century, when plantations were being developed and the Hawaiian Islands came under the influence of English speakers from the U.S. mainland. Similar to Gullah, Hawaiian Creole is English-related, and its lexicon is predominantly English, with the aforementioned influence from Hawaiian, Japanese, Chinese, Portuguese, and Ilocano. This rich linguistic mixture in the Hawaiian Islands has led language scholars to view Hawaiian English "in terms of three coexistent systems—a pidgin, Creole, and dialect of English—none of which occurs in unadulterated forms but only in combinations of different proportions" (Nichols, 1981, p. 48).

Whether Hawaiian English is a dialect of English or a creole language is a complex issue. As is true to some extent of Gullah, its degree of similarity to English ranges along a continuum, depending on the community and the context. For example, linguists note a highly decreolized language variety in the more urbanized population centers such as Oahu and more creolized traditional patterns in the more remote islands of Kauai and Hawaii (Nichols, 1981).

In any event, Hawaiian Creole is a lively language that plays a key social and academic role in the lives of many Hawaiian children. Like Gullah and Louisiana French Creole, Hawaiian Creole, or Pidgin English, as it is known by island residents, is a highly stigmatized language variety that until the 1970s was singled out by educational policy makers as a cause of the many academic problems experienced by Hawaiian students. According to Nichols (1981), the policy at that time was to decreolize the students' language. Because this posture was not successful in achieving the elimination of Hawaiian Creole, however, education policies since then have tended toward acceptance of the language in the lives of the students. Yet there has remained a sense that it is a "deficient language" and thus in need of correction (Nichols, 1981, p. 86). The attempt in Hawaii to eradicate Hawaiian Creole confirms once more that when a cultural component as important as a language is threatened, its users tend to protect and defend it. This is what happened in the islands, where speakers of Hawaiian Creole began to view its use as an important symbol of solidarity in their community.

Black English

> Speaking a standard dialect certainly has advantages in certain settings, but it can also present a dilemma for a person in terms of local community norms. Not everyone needs to speak a standard dialect for all social occasions. Furthermore, there are consequences that go along with the use of both a standard and local dialect. (Wolfram, 1987, p. 10)

Although Black English is a dialect of English rather than a creole, it shows parallels with creole languages in its historical development. Black English reflects influences from British and American English as well as English-based pidgin from sixteenth-century West Africa. In situations involving language contact, it is important to understand the nature of social relationships both within and outside the involved communities. The inhumanity of master–slave relationships was certainly not conducive to an egalitarian communicative process. But it was in this socially strained context that Black English and standard English coexisted and influenced each other. From the late 1700s until the early 1900s, approximately 90 percent of the African American population lived in the southern states (Whatley, 1981). With such a high concentration of speakers, Black English was able to mature into a highly sophisticated and rule-governed "subsystem within the larger grammar of English" (Whatley, 1981, p. 64).

Unlike Gullah, Louisiana French Creole, and Hawaiian Creole, Black English spread throughout the United States. In the twentieth century, many African Americans began to migrate to the large urban centers of the North. Through this connection between Black communities in the rural South and the industrial North, Black English continued to evolve. As Whatley observes, "Funerals, homecoming celebrations at churches, and family reunions took northerners 'down home' at least annually" (Whatley, 1981, p. 94). Strong regional and familial ties between South and North generated much cross-fertilization of old and new communication patterns.

On the other hand, de facto segregation in the large urban centers of the North tended to insulate African American and White communities from each other. That meant that, given the social distance created between the speakers of Black English and standard English, the two languages had minimal influence on one another. Thus, Black English continued to develop its own structures, functional patterns, and styles.

Despite its presence throughout the United States, many people have a highly distorted perception of Black English. As Whatley points out, most people's understanding of Black English is based on its portrayal by Hollywood and the electronic media. The world of entertainment has given us a highly stylized, stereotyped version of Black speech—jiving, copping, playing the dozens, boasting, preaching, and fussing, for example. This, however, is just the tip of the linguistic iceberg. There are many aspects of Black English other than those represented in the media (Whatley, 1981).

As is true of any language, there is great speech variation among speakers of Black English. Also, speech behavior is highly contextualized. That is, individuals tend to assess the communicative situation and respond accordingly. Most speakers of English use a variety of styles of language in their daily lives, these variations being determined by degrees of formality and social status. Within the African American experience, praising, fussing, teasing, lying, preaching, jiving, boasting, and joking are carefully determined by the age, gender, and status of speakers. For example, the eldest members of the African American community tend to have greater latitude and prestige in language use, and children are the lowest-ranking members of the speech community (Whatley, 1981). This does not mean, of course, that African American children are not allowed to interact with adults in creative and expressive ways. What it does mean is that there is a speech protocol that is sensitive to such variables as age, social status, gender, and formal and informal settings (Smitherman, 1999).

Because of African Americans' historical status as an oppressed minority, Whites have tended to perceive Black English as "a mass of random errors committed by Blacks trying to speak English" (Labov, Cohen, Robins, & Lewis, 1968, p. 366). The language varieties used by African Americans, however, are valid linguistic systems (Perry & Delpit, 1998; Smitherman, 1999). They have an internal linguistic infrastructure and a set of grammar rules just as any other language does. For example, the use of the verb *to be* follows different rules in Black English than in standard English. Speakers of standard English tend to contract forms of *to be*, as in the sentence "She's tall" instead of "She is tall." Black English deletes *is* entirely, so that the sentence becomes "She tall." Black English also has a use for *be* that standard English does not. The sentences "He always be walkin' on a desert on TV" and "He jus' be walkin' dere sometime" use what linguists call the "invariant *be*." This use of the verb refers to action that takes place habitually over a period of time, and for this there is no exact standard English equivalent (Whatley, 1981).

Multiple negation is perhaps one of the most stigmatized aspects of Black English for speakers who enter the formal school system. Yet there is no logical basis for such stigmatization. Acceptance or nonacceptance of the double negative as a socially correct form is essentially a historical accident. According to language scholars, multiple negation was an integral part of the English language up to the time of Shakespeare. Also, it is useful to know that although Latin is credited with having influenced the "correctness" of single negation in English, other Romance languages, such as Spanish, French, and Italian, use the double negative as part of their standard speech patterns (Whatley, 1981).

A fair curricular process is one that builds on the sociocultural and linguistic backgrounds that students bring with them. Yet the use of Black English has had negative consequences for Black students. Many African American youth have not prospered in U.S. schools, and in the process of searching for the reasons, some educators have singled out their communication patterns as an important contributor to their academic failure. In the past, a common perception among educators, although not necessarily articulated, was that speakers of Black English are language-deficient. From this point of view, the use of Black English is seen as detrimental to a student's cognitive development. Thinking skills, however, can be demonstrated in any language; they are not the exclusive domain of standard English. Consider as an example the following conversation between two young speakers of Black English (Whatley, 1981, p. 99):

A: Do you know 'bout factors and all that stuff?

B: Yeah, I know all that.

A: Well, how come you only made a 50 on that test?

B: That test was tough—she ain't no good teacher anyway.

A: But you have been in the other math class, the one dat ain't done factors like we have.

B: Yeah, but I can do spelling—and you can't.

Whatley (1981) interprets the above playful interaction as follows:

> It is clear in this boasting episode that child A had collected highly specific information to support his boast, and he set child B up to a challenge by asking a seemingly innocent question. The strategies and information to support these were planned in advance. Child A wins this sequence, because child B must shift topic and begin another boast. (p. 30)

Although these children are not using standard English, they are certainly not language-deficient. If anything, the pair reflect a high level of creativity and spontaneity with language behavior, which is highly desirable for cognitive development. The children's language is different from standard English, but the language they use is not deficient. Their linguistic behavior and vocabulary inventory serve their communication needs extremely well.

Building on Students' Home Languages

Gullah, Louisiana French Creole, Hawaiian Creole, and Black English have much in common. They are rule-governed and legitimate linguistic expressions, just as standard English is. They are a link to our past, and they have a right to exist and to be accepted. Yet they are not given much recognition in the larger society. Rather, they are viewed by many people as aberrant and inferior language varieties. Consequently, a great unfounded fear exists on the part of educators that affirmation of such languages among students will perpetuate school failure. Because teaching practices are not always linguistically enlightened, language can become a primary source of inequality for students who come to school with a speech variety that marks them for stigmatization.

Cognitive psychologists, educators, and anthropologists, on the other hand, tell us that we build our cognitive repertoire on prior knowledge, experiences, attitudes, and skills (Ogbu, 1999; Perry & Delpit, 1998; Pinker, 1994; Wertsch, 1985). It is a layering process. Rather than destroy what was there before, the goal for educators should be to build on and add to what is already present in the lives of students. Creative bridges using the early socialization patterns of the home language and culture can be useful in motivating students to learn. These students will come to see their teachers as professionals who understand the value of their nonstandard languages. Such teachers, while respecting the structure and function of the home language, will help to build another layer of linguistic skill that will enable these students to negotiate the prestige variety of English in the larger society and thus to have more options in their lives.

Language use in society is also about issues of power and identity. Therefore, the creation of culturally and linguistically compatible classroom practices can lead to much political controversy (Ovando & McLaren, 2000). Responding to the alarming school failure, absenteeism, and suspension rates of African American students attending Prescott Elementary School, the African American Task Force in Oakland, California, recommended to the school board that Black English be used in schools. Task force members argued that Black English would serve as a springboard to affirm African American students' linguistic and cultural experiences, to develop competency in standard English, and to enhance academic achievement. Affirming the task force's recommendation, the school board unanimously endorsed the Ebonics Resolution on December 21, 1996.

Criticized by the media and key African American leaders as a concession that would lower academic standards, the war of words that followed the passage of the resolution was intense. This prompted the editors of *Rethinking Schools* to write, "The irrational and racist discourse that followed the school board's approval of the Ebonics Resolution has made it almost impossible to have a careful conversation about the important educational, political, and linguistic issues embedded in the resolution" (cited in Perry & Delpit, 1998, p. xii).

The Demographics of Students from Non–English-Language Backgrounds

As a result of shifting demographics, the number of English-language learners in U.S. schools is increasing. Since the passage of the 1968 Title VII Bilingual Education Act and the landmark

U.S. Supreme Court Decision *Lau v. Nichols* (Waugh & Koon, 1974), which provided a legal basis for equitable treatment of students from a non-English-speaking background in U.S. schools, educational policy for non-English-language communities has put linguistic minorities in the national spotlight. Many foreign-born children come to U.S. schools speaking only the language of their home country. Their families may be voluntary immigrants or involuntarily uprooted refugees, such as the Hmong. They may reside in the United States legally or as undocumented immigrants. There are also U.S.-born language-minority students. This group includes speakers of American Indian languages. It also includes groups who have maintained over generations the use of colonial and early immigration languages such as Spanish, French, German, and Swedish. And today it includes the offspring and subsequent generations of immigrants of virtually every nationality. Upon entering school, these students may fall anywhere along a broad continuum of language status. A child may be entirely monolingual in the non-English language, bilingual in the home language and English, or dominant in English with only a few fragmentary skills in his or her ancestral language.

The diversity of languages in the United States is truly amazing. In Anchorage, Alaska, students speaking more than a hundred different languages, from virtually every region of the world, have been identified in the local school district's bilingual education program. As of 1992, the Los Angeles School District, whose identified language-minority students spoke at least eighty different languages, offered bilingual instruction in Spanish, Cantonese, Vietnamese, Korean, Filipino, and Armenian. With its large language-minority population, California has become the Ellis Island of the 1990s. California has an ethnic minority population between 40 and 50 percent. Over 50 percent of its school population consists of ethnic minorities.

Other data show that during the ten years between 1980 and 1990, U.S. society became increasingly multiracial, multicultural, and multilingual. The demographic trend shows that in these ten years the total population of the United States grew by 9.8 percent. However, groups in which the most language-minority students are found were growing at a much faster rate. The American Indian population (including Eskimo and Aleut) grew by 37.9 percent, Asian and Pacific Islanders by 107.8 percent, Hispanic Americans by 53 percent, and "others" by 45.1 percent (National Association for Bilingual Education, n.d.). Increased immigration from Latin America and Asia and the high fertility rates within these populations are among the major factors contributing to this demographic shift.

The upswing in immigration has resulted in large numbers of school entrants whose first language is not English (Minami & Ovando, 2004). Summarizing census data concerning demographic changes from 1980 to 1990, the *New York Times* of April 28, 1993 (Barringer, 1993) reported that the number of U.S. residents for whom English is a foreign/second language had increased nearly 40 percent to 32 million. The U.S. Department of Education (1992) estimated that in 1990–1991, approximately 2.3 million children lived in language-minority households, made substantial use of minority languages, and were of limited proficiency in English. According to the Stanford Working Group (1993), the number of such children is much greater, perhaps as many as 3.3 million children between the ages of 5 and 17. Language-minority children are now the fastest-growing group in schools in the United States (McKeon, 1992). Spanish-speaking households are the fastest-growing sector among language-minority groups. The U.S. Census (cited in Martin & Midgley, 1999) projects that by 2025 Hispanics will be 18 percent of the U.S. population.

While these figures are useful in giving at least an imperfect glimpse at the approximate number of children from language-minority homes, they do not begin to scratch the surface when it comes to figuring out who is eligible for bilingual services and how long they are to be served. Thus, as Ulibarri (1986) suggests:

> Differences in estimates of the limited-English-proficient population derive from efforts to count the number of children according to different definitions and interpretations of eligibility for services. At issue are the criteria for determining which language minority children are in need of English and native language related services. Thus, the problem is not simply one of differences in number of eligible children, but one in which the actual definition of who is eligible also varies. (p. 57)

Although there is great variation depending on a student's background and schooling opportunities, a disproportionate number of English-language learners do not achieve well academically. In fact, they are all too often overrepresented at the bottom of the test score ladder. Despite the research-based knowledge we have gained over the past thirty years about how individuals learn their first and second languages and about how acculturative and assimilative forces work with immigrants and indigenous groups, there is still a wide gap between theory and practice. Consider, for example, the strong resistance that bilingual instruction has encountered in educational circles despite the evidence indicating that English-language learners who develop a strong sociocultural, linguistic, and cognitive base in their primary language tend to transfer those attitudes and skills to the other language and culture. Moreover, the chronically poor track record that schools have had in educating American Indians suggests that the schooling of most language minorities has generally been surrounded by political and ideological controversy at the expense of sustained and well-founded curricular development.

ADDRESSING LANGUAGE NEEDS IN THE MULTICULTURAL CLASSROOM

The debate about the schooling of language-minority students has to do essentially with the kind of citizens we want and need in our society. Should the school curriculum affirm cultural and linguistic pluralism through an additive process? Or should the schools pursue an ideologically conservative agenda of assimilating language minorities into mainstream U.S. society by subtracting their ancestral cultures and languages?

These questions raise some pointed and difficult issues regarding the nature and extent of cultural and linguistic pluralism in the United States. Rather than thinking in either–or terms of pluralism or assimilation, however, perhaps it would be useful to view U.S. society as a dynamic and complex cultural and linguistic organism—one that is constantly evolving and changing in accordance with the nature of circumstances. With this framework, we can envision a constructive pluralism in which cultural and linguistic maintenance, diversification, and assimilation are taking place simultaneously under varying circumstances. Within such an environment of constructive pluralism, it cannot be acceptable to blame the student's genetic, environmental, cultural, or linguistic background for his or her lack of academic success in the English-dominated classroom. Programs and practices can be implemented to redress some of the past inequities experienced by all language-minority students—English-background students who come to our schools speaking stigmatized nonstandard versions of English as well as students whose primary language is not English. Given the political climate at the beginning of the twenty-first century, however, trying to implement such programs can be like trying to paddle a canoe against a powerful tide while being buffeted from the sides by strong, cold winds. Not to do so, on the other hand, suggests abdicating responsibility for the basic tenets of a sound multicultural education.

A good place to start in designing quality programs for language-minority students is by examining effective teaching and learning classroom climates for students in general, taking into account the important school reform movements currently evolving. Summarizing and endorsing the case for constructivist classrooms in the educational reform efforts of the 1990s, Fosnot (1993) states:

> Constructivism is not a theory about teaching. It's a theory
> about knowledge and learning. Drawing on a synthesis of current
> work in cognitive psychology, philosophy, and anthropology, the
> theory defines knowledge as temporary, developmental, socially and
> culturally mediated, and thus, non-objective. Learning from this
> perspective is understood as a self-regulated process of resolving
> inner cognitive conflicts that often become apparent through
> concrete experience, collaborative discourse, and reflection. (p. vii)

Fosnot identifies five key principles of such constructive pedagogy: (1) posing problems of emerging relevance to learners, (2) structuring learning around "big ideas" or primary concepts, (3) seeking and valuing students' points of view, (4) adapting curriculum to address students' suppositions, and (5) assessing student learning in the context of teaching (Fosnot, 1993).

These principles provide an important reminder of certain basic pedagogical practices that may have validity for all students, regardless of language background; such practices should not be overlooked in the attempt to create a "special" program for language-minority students. Nevertheless, a variety of language issues in classroom instruction are unique to addressing the needs of language-minority students.

One issue pertaining to the education of speakers of nonstandard varieties of English, such as Black English, Appalachian English, and Hawaiian Creole, is whether their home languages should be used formally in the classroom. Also, should students be trained to be *bidialectical*, that is, to be able to switch from their home variety of English to standard English according to the situation? Some educators interpret bidialectalism as a waste of educational effort, suggesting that students need to discard their home language and replace it with standard English, preferably by the time they leave kindergarten. Yet most linguists remind us that suppressing such dialects is confusing and detrimental to the academic and social well-being of students.

As evidenced by the repeated attempts over the last fifty years to eradicate nonstandard varieties of English from the schools, such efforts have not been positively correlated with achievement gains among language-minority students (Ovando et. al., 2003). The use of nonstandard English itself cannot be singled out as the cause for school failure. As Torrey puts it, "Teachers should not judge children's language abilities by their schoolyard grammar" (Torrey, 1983, p. 627). Instead, among the sources of poor academic performance are the school's reaction and approach to nonstandard English. A more positive pedagogical position, states Torrey (1983), is one that

> affirms the importance of home dialect and its appropriate use within the community in which it is spoken while at the same time students are taught the standard variety. Affirming home language means that students may produce utterances in the classroom in native dialect without being told that they are wrong or that what they say is vulgar or bad. Instead, the teacher analyzes with the students the differences between their dialect and the standard variety: grammatical patterns, pronunciation, vocabulary items, varying social contexts, and so on. (p. 627)

The challenge for English-language learners, of course, is not that they speak a stigmatized variety of English but rather that their first language is one other than English. A variety of important instructional approaches have been developed to meet the unique needs of these students. Such curricular approaches support the idea that creating bridges between the world of the language-minority student and the world of the school will produce positive cognitive, linguistic, and cultural outcomes. In 1980, for example, the California Office of Bilingual Education launched the Case Studies Project, based on leading theories of cognitive development, second-language acquisition, and cross-cultural communication. An integrated curriculum incorporating home-language instruction, communication-based sheltered English, and mainstream English has produced excellent results in reading, language arts, and mathematics for language-minority students. Five principles serve as the pedagogical platform for the Case Studies Project (Crawford, 1999, p. 161):

1. Language development in the home language as well as in English has positive effects on academic achievement.

2. Language proficiency includes proficiency in academic tasks as well as in basic conversation.

3. [English-language learners] should be able to perform a certain type of academic task in [their] home language before being expected to perform the task in English.

4. Acquisition of English language skills must be provided in contexts in which the student understands what is being said.

5. The social status implicitly ascribed to students and their languages affects student performance. Therefore, majority and minority students should be in classes together in which cooperative learning strategies are used. English speakers should be provided with opportunities to learn the minority languages, and teachers and administrators should model using the minority languages for some noninstructional as well as instructional purposes.

A two-way bilingual program is specifically designed to give both languages equal status. The English-speaking children learn the minority language at the same time that the language-minority students are learning English. Collier (1995) found the following five elements to be important for effective two-way bilingual instruction. It is interesting and important to note the important role of sociocultural issues and community involvement among these elements for a successful bilingual program.

> (1) integrated schooling, with English speakers and language
> minority students learning academically through each other's
> languages; (2) perceptions among staff, students, and parents that it
> is a "gifted and talented" program, leading to high expectations for
> student performance; (3) equal status of the two languages
> achieved, to a large extent, creating self-confidence among
> language minority students; (4) healthy parent involvement among
> both language minority and language majority parents, for closer
> home-school cooperation; and (5) continuous support for staff
> development, emphasizing whole language approaches, natural
> language acquisition through all content areas, cooperative
> learning, interactive and discovery learning, and cognitive
> complexity for all proficiency levels. (pp. 15–16)

Bilingual programs by definition include an English as a Second Language (ESL) component, since a main goal is to develop the language-minority student's proficiency in English. Many communities, however, do not or are unable to provide bilingual instruction for all language-minority students. This occurs for a variety of reasons, involving such factors as politics, the availability of bilingual teachers, and demographics. In such situations, English-language learners are provided with ESL instruction alone, without any significant instruction in their home language. Among the skills important to the ESL teacher are (1) a sound knowledge of theory and methods of language acquisition; (2) an understanding of the relationships among culture and language, identity, and adjustment to the new school environment; and (3) the ability to design instruction in such a way that students are helped to become as proficient as possible in content areas such as math, science, and social studies at the same time that they are learning English.

Regarding the knowledge of language acquisition, the ESL teacher strives to enable the English-language learner to develop phonology, morphology, syntax, and vocabulary primarily through real communicative activities rather than through such approaches as lecture and drills (Heath, 1986). Crawford (1987) describes such language-rich instruction as follows:

> (a) Content is based on the students' communicative needs;
> (b) instruction makes extensive use of contextual clues; (c) the teacher
> uses only English, but modifies speech to students' level and confirms
> student comprehension; (d) students are permitted to respond in their
> native language when necessary; (e) the focus is on language function
> or content, rather than grammatical form; (f) grammatical accuracy is
> promoted, not by correcting errors overtly, but by providing more
> comprehensible instruction; and (g) students are encouraged to
> respond spontaneously and creatively. (p. 43)

With respect to cultural knowledge, effective ESL teachers do not necessarily need to speak the first languages of their students, but they do need to have as broad an understanding as possible of the history, folklore, traditions, values, attitudes, and current sociocultural situation of the cultural groups with which they work. This knowledge gives the teacher a better understanding of the behavior of ESL students as they adjust to life in the United States, and, equally important, it shows the students and their parents that the teacher values the family's cultural background and recognizes that students come to school not as blank slates but rather as unique individuals with a rich background.

We must also consider the role of the ESL teacher in enabling English-language learners to develop cognitive-academic language proficiency. Two such curricular and instructional approaches are communication-based sheltered English classes and the cognitive-academic language learning approach (CALLA). Sheltered English is an immersion type of methodology that "shelters" English-language learners from "input beyond their comprehension, first in subjects that are less language-intensive, such as mathematics, and later in those that are more so, such as social studies" (Crawford, 1987, p. 177). In sheltered English classes, teachers, who may be familiar with the students' first languages and cultures, adjust subject-matter content and methodology for students who represent a variety of linguistic backgrounds and who are at about the same level of competence in the target language (Richard-Amato, 1988). As reflected in the case studies design, sheltered English classes require that

> teachers change their speech register by slowing down; limiting
> their vocabulary and sentence length; repeating, emphasizing, and
> explaining key concepts, and using examples, props, visual clues,
> and body language to convey and reinforce meaning carried by the
> language of instruction. (cited in Crawford, 1999, p. 132)

Like sheltered English, CALLA is a content-based ESL instructional model originally developed by Chamot and O'Malley (1986) in response to the lack of academic success of English-language learners. The model supports the notion that by adding academic content to the ESL curriculum and following a specific set of instructional strategies, English-language learners can be prepared for grade-level content classrooms (Chamot & O'Malley, 1994). Buttressed by cognitive theory, research, and ongoing classroom use, CALLA is aimed at English-language learners who are at the advanced beginning and intermediate levels of English-language proficiency. As developed by Chamot and O'Malley (1994), CALLA is compatible with such instructional approaches as language across the curriculum, language experience, whole language, process writing, cooperative learning, and cognitive instruction.

Reflecting the bilingual and ESL principles discussed throughout this section, the California Commission on Teacher Credentialing (1993) has adopted a design for the preparation of teachers who serve English-language learners. The design includes two credential variations—a cross-cultural, language, and academic development (CLAD) emphasis for non-bilingual contexts, and the bilingual cross-cultural, language, and academic development (BCLAD) emphasis for bilingual contexts. The CLAD/BCLAD credentials include the following six domains of knowledge and skills in which teachers must show competence: (1) language structure and first- and second-language development; (2) methodology of bilingual, English-language development and content instruction; (3) culture and cultural diversity; (4) methodology for primary-language instruction; (5) the culture of emphasis; and (6) the language of emphasis. (Culture and language of emphasis refer to the particular group with whom the teacher is preparing to work, such as Vietnamese, Korean, or Chinese.)

Whether we are talking about speakers of nonstandard varieties of English or non-English speakers, and whether we are talking about bilingual programs, ESL programs, or mainstream classrooms, two common threads run through this entire section on how to address language needs in the multicultural classroom. First, the languages that children bring to the classroom must be respected and used as valuable cognitive tools and as bridges to the development of the language skills that will enable them to succeed academically. Second, all language-minority students need opportunities to develop the complex language skills they will use in literacy-related school activities and throughout their lives as lifelong learners and thinking, active citizens. In other words, it is not enough for students to be able to converse with their peers only on the playground or in the halls, or to be able to recite a few rules about standard English. They need to be able to use the context-reduced language associated with extracting meaning from the printed word, for synthesizing and evaluating materials, and for writing. The importance of the development of such high-level skills is illustrated in Collier's (1987) research on non–English-speaking students who entered school in the United States at seventh grade and who were not provided with native-language content instruction. Even though they may have had a solid academic background in their home language, in the U.S. school system they tended to fall behind in standardized test norms, except in mathematics, by the time they reached the eleventh grade. Collier (1987) points out that

> as they master enough BICS and develop a wide enough range of vocabulary in English to move into deeper development of CALP in second language, they have in the meantime lost 2–3 years of CALP development at their age-grade level. This puts them significantly behind in mastery of the complex material required for high school students. (p. 12)

The Sociolinguistic Context of Classroom Language Development

An important principle to keep in mind when working with language-minority students—either English-speaking or non–English-speaking—is that their cognitive development must be launched from within the existing sociolinguistic context. There is no such thing as an exportable model that works everywhere without adaptation. As Heath (1986) points out, language arts curricula are based on an assumption of a path of language development that is the same for all children, regardless of their ethnic origin. Yet the research that establishes such lines of development is based predominantly on middle-class English-speaking families. Only in the last two decades have ethnographers working in language-minority communities begun to identify culturally different patterns of language socialization experienced by children. One implication of this variation in language development is that the academic success of language-minority students may hinge to some degree on how these children are able to manipulate language in a variety of contexts and for different purposes, rather than on the specific language they use.

In describing the nature of language earlier in this chapter, we listed the culturally influenced domains of language beyond phonology, morphology, syntax, and vocabulary—such factors as body language, degrees of formality, organizational styles, styles of speech, and appropriate speaking and listening etiquette. Related to these domains is Heath's research on genres. Regarding the specific linguistic elements that are essential for academic success in school regardless of language background, Heath (1986) has summarized the research on genre, which she defines as the

> kind of organizing unit into which smaller units of language, such as
> conversations, sentences, lists, or directives may fit. Each cultural
> group has fundamental genres that occur in recurrent situations; and
> each genre is so patterned as a whole that listeners can anticipate by
> the prosody or opening formulae what is coming—a joke, a story, or
> a recounting of shared experiences. . . . Moreover, each sociocultural
> group recognizes and uses only a few of the total range of genres
> that humans are capable of producing. (p. 166)

Heath (1986) then argues that in order to function well in formal U.S. school settings, students must be able to use a variety of genres typical of U.S. pedagogy, such as label quests, meaning quests, recounts, accounts, event casts, and stories. Label quests are activities in which adults ask children to say their name or to identify an item—"What's that?" or "What kind of _____ is that?" Meaning quests are activities in which an unstated or partly stated meaning is inferred from an oral or written language source. For example, a teacher might ask, "What did the author mean when she wrote, 'Andy kicked the book out of his way'?" In recounts, the child retells an experience that is already known to the teller and the listener. The speaker may be prompted with guiding questions by the adult. Accounts are activities in which the child provides new information to the listener. Accounts are often judged by their logical sequence and their truthfulness. Such accounts are the predecessors of research and creative writing assignments in the upper grades. Event casts are running narratives of events occurring or about to occur. For example, making a gelatin dessert may be accompanied by the mother's sequenced narrative (Heath, 1986).

Heath (1986) indicates that such genres exist in mainstream U.S. school-based activities in a predictable and consistent manner but that genres may or may not be consistently present in the same way in the language-minority child's home context. Heath suggests that it is the school's responsibility to help students acquire these genres by working closely with the ethnolinguistic community. Teachers can thereby cross-culturally broaden the base of linguistic experiences to maximize their students' opportunities for acquiring such genres. Language-minority students should have access first to these genres in their dominant language. Also, parents who have a limited grasp of English should be encouraged to use their primary language rather than English with their children. Given their limited command of the English language, they will not be able to use English across the variety of suggested genres and thus will limit the quality and range of linguistic interaction with their children. Instead, such parents ideally should concentrate on engaging their children in conversations in their home language that are interesting and also representative of the variety of genres—written and oral—that schools require. Heath suggests that teachers in a creative partnership with ethnolinguistic communities should make a sustained and creative effort to expose students to these school-valued genres, at the same time capitalizing on community genres available.

As noted earlier, there is no single model for addressing the cognitive, linguistic, and cultural needs of all language-minority students. But the principles and designs, and their practical implications discussed here, can help educators who are genuinely interested in putting into practice in their classrooms what we have learned over the past thirty years or so about how children acquire their first and second languages, about how they develop cognitively in their primary and secondary languages, and about how they adjust socioculturally to the dominant culture.

Language diversity, as a powerful and ubiquitous ingredient of the U.S. multicultural mosaic, enriches the lives of the people who use these languages. It also enriches the lives of monolingual English speakers as they live, study, and work with people of non–English-language background. As educators, we have the power to ensure that the valuable and varied sociolinguistic experiences of language minorities do not continue to be translated into negative cognitive, cultural, and linguistic outcomes. As suggested in this chapter, we now have some of the conceptual, programmatic, and curricular tools with which to begin the job.

Unfortunately, bilingual education has become entangled in the politics of the English Only movement. With the passage of Proposition 227 on June 2, 1998, Californians voted to eliminate bilingual education. This draconian initiative puts a very negative spin on biculturalism, bilingualism, and biliteracy in U.S. society. It also denigrates the positive value that first-language instruction can have on academic achievement for language-minority students. Finally, it rejects the accumulated knowledge base generated for the past twenty-five years by linguists, cognitive psychologists, and bilingual educators; this knowledge supports the idea that quality-controlled bilingual programs do yield positive outcomes (Crawford, 2000; Ovando & Collier, 1998; Ovando & Pérez, 2000).

SUMMARY

This chapter stresses the power that language issues have to affect schooling outcomes for language-minority students. The first section discusses how language is interwoven with cultural styles and values. Thus, language comprises more than grammar rules, vocabulary, and a sound system. To have communicative competence in a language requires not only these things but also many others, such as the appropriate facial and body gestures, the use of varying levels of formality in the appropriate contexts, correct styles of conversation, and the ability to express abstract concepts.

By studying language learning among children, psycholinguists and cognitive psychologists have determined that it is a developmental process involving predictable stages. Researchers such as Cummins, Collier, and Thomas have identified two levels of language proficiency that are particularly important in designing educational programs for language-minority students: social language skills, which take approximately two years to develop, and cognitive academic language proficiency, which may take five to seven years or longer to acquire. Equally important is the common underlying proficiency (CUP) proposed by Cummins—the notion that skills learned in the first language will transfer to the second language. This concept is one of the major underpinnings for the value of bilingual instruction.

The second section of the chapter surveys the extent of language variety in the United States. An examination of nonstandard English and creole languages emphasizes that language changes fulfill sociohistorical needs. Likewise, the language varieties resulting from these changes have their own grammatical and phonological rules and appropriate cultural styles, and they are valid means of expression rather than "deficient" language systems. This section also documents that the proportion of students from non–English-speaking backgrounds continues to increase in the United States and that these students are present in significant numbers throughout the United States.

The final section of the chapter describes some principles for the instruction of language-minority students. In the case of speakers of nonstandard English, the home language cannot be blamed for school failure. On the contrary, one cause for language-related school failure is the educator's negative attitude toward the home language. Through an additive process, the value of the home language can be affirmed, while models are also provided for use of the standard language in appropriate contexts.

For students who come from non–English-speaking backgrounds, an active, hands-on teaching style rather than a lecture style is needed, with frequent checking for understanding. Concepts, a knowledge base, and thinking skills ideally should be developed in the home language through bilingual instruction, which, of course, includes an ESL component. Regarding ESL instruction, social communicative skills—which may be acquired fairly rapidly—are not sufficient for academic success. Schools must continue to provide support for language-minority students to help them achieve cognitive-academic language proficiency in English.

Finally, there is a need for the continued development and maintenance of social and cultural bridges between the language-minority student's home life and school life. An awareness of how language is used in the home community will enable educators to be sensitive to school genres that are different. Efforts to equalize the social and linguistic status of majority and minority students within the school setting will produce positive results for all students in the classroom and, ultimately, in society.

Questions and Activities

1. What are some of the major characteristics of a language? What role does language play in the maintenance of a culture?

2. How can teachers draw on the home experiences of non-English speakers and speakers of nonstandard varieties of English to help these students develop competence in standard English?

3. What are some common misconceptions about Black English and how can they be overcome? How can a knowledge of the nature of Black English be helpful to teachers of African American students?

4. What special problems do language-minority students experience in schools? What programs and practices can schools implement to help these students experience educational success?

5. Prepare a debate on the pros and cons of bilingual education.

6. Interview officials in a nearby school district to get a profile of local language diversity. Find out how many different languages are spoken by the students in the district and what programs are being implemented to address the needs of these students.

7. Identity some principles for working effectively with language-minority students. What support and training might teachers need to implement these principles in the classroom? Interview an ESL teacher, a bilingual teacher, or a teacher who has many nonstandard English speakers in his or her classroom. Discuss what concepts, principles, and methods this teacher uses for students' language and academic development.

References

Anttila, R. (1972). *An Introduction to Historical and Comparative Linguistics.* New York: Macmillan.

Barringer, F. (1993, April 28). Immigration in 80s Made English a Foreign Language for Millions. *New York Times,* pp. Al, A10.

California Commission on Teacher Credentialing. (1993). *CLAD/BCLAD: California's New Design for the Preparation and Credentialing of Teachers of Limited-English-Proficient Students.* Sacramento: Author.

Chamot, A. U., & O'Malley, J. M. (1986). *A Cognitive Academic Language Learning Approach: An ESL Content-Based Curriculum.* Washington, DC: National Clearinghouse for Bilingual Education.

Chamot, A. U., & O'Malley, J. M. (1994). *The CALLA Handbook: Implementing the Cognitive Academic Language Learning Approach.* Reading, MA: Addison-Wesley.

Collier, V. P. (1987, April). *Age and Rate of Acquisition of Cognitive-Academic Second Language Proficiency.* Paper presented at the American Educational Research Association meeting, Washington, DC.

Collier, V. P. (1992). A Synthesis of Studies Examining Long-Term Language-Minority Student Data on Academic Achievement. *Bilingual Research Journal, 16*(1 & 2), 187–212.

Collier, V. P. (March 1995). *Second Language Acquisition for School: Academic, Cognitive, Sociocultural and Linguistic Processes.* Paper presented at the Georgetown University Round Table (GURT), Washington, DC.

Crawford, J. (1987, April 1). Bilingual Education: Language, Learning, and Politics. *Education Week: A Special Report,* p. 43.

Crawford, J. (1999). *Bilingual Education: History, Politics, Theory and Practice* (4th ed.). Los Angeles: Bilingual Education Services.

Crawford, J. (2000). Language Politics in the United States: The Paradox of Bilingual Education. In C. J. Ovando & P. McLaren (Eds.), *The Politics of Multiculturalism and Bilingual Education* (pp. 106–125). Boston: McGraw-Hill.

Cummins, J. (1979). Cognitive/Academic Language Proficiency, Linguistic Interdependence, the Optimal Age Question, and Some Other Matters. *Working Papers on Bilingualism, 9,* 1–43.

Cummins, J. (1980). The Cross-Lingual Dimensions of Language Proficiency: Implications for Bilingual Education and Optimal Age Issue. *TESOL Quarterly, 14*(2), 175–187.

Cummins, J. (1981). The Role of Primary Language Development in Promoting Educational Success for Language Minority Students. In California State Department of Education, *Schooling and Language Minority Students: A Theoretical Framework.* Los Angeles: National Evaluation, Dissemination, and Assessment Center, California State University.

Cummins, J. (1986). Empowering Minority Students: A Framework for Intervention. *Harvard Educational Review, 56*(1), 18–36.

Cummins, J. (1991a). Language Development and Academic Learning. In L. M. Malavé & G. Duquette (Eds.), *Language, Culture and Cognition* (pp. 161–175). Clevedon, England: Multilingual Matters.

Cummins, J. (1991b). Interdependence of First- and Second-Language Proficiency in Bilingual Children. In E. Bialystok (Ed.), *Language Processing in Bilingual Children* (pp. 70–89). New York: Cambridge University Press.

Cummins, J. (2000a). Beyond Adversarial Discourse: Searching for Common Ground in the Education of Bilingual Students. In C. J. Ovando & P. McLaren (Eds.), *The Politics of Multiculturalism and Bilingual Education: Students and Teachers Caught in the Cross Fire* (pp. 126–147). Boston: McGraw-Hill.

Cummins, J. (2000b). *Language, Power and Pedagogy: Bilingual Children in the Crossfire.* Clevedon, England: Multilingual Matters.

Edelsky, C. (1991). *With Literacy and Justice for All.* Bristol, PA: Falmer.

Edelsky, C., Hudelson, S., Flores, B., Barkin, F., Altweger, J., & Jilbert, K. (1983). Semilingualism and Language Deficit. *Applied Linguistics, 4,* 1–22.

Fosnot, C. T. (1993). Preface. In J. G. Brooks & M. G. Brooks (Eds.), *In Search of Understanding: The Case for Constructivist Classrooms* (pp. vii–viii). Alexandria, VA: Association for Supervision and Curriculum Development.

Fuentes, C. (1988). *Myself with Others: Selected Essays.* New York: Farrar, Straus & Giroux.

Heath, S. B. (1986). Sociocultural Contexts of Language Development. In California State Department of Education, *Beyond Language: Social and Cultural Factors in Schooling Language Minority Students* (pp. 143–186). Los Angeles: National Evaluation, Dissemination, and Assessment Center, California State University.

Hymes, D. H. (1981). Foreword. In C. A. Ferguson & S. B. Heath (Eds.), *Language in the USA* (pp. v–ix). New York: Cambridge University Press.

Krauss, M. (1995, February 3). *Endangered Languages: Current Issues and Future Prospects.* Keynote address presented at Dartmouth College, Hanover, NH.

Labov, W., Cohen, P., Robins, C., & Lewis, J. (1968). *A Study of the Non-Standard English of Negro and Puerto Rican Speakers in New York City* (Report on Cooperative Research Project 3288). New York: Columbia University.

MacSwan, J. (2000). The Threshold Hypothesis, Semilingualism, and Other Contributions to a Deficit View of Linguistic Minorities. *Hispanic Journal of Behavior Sciences, 20*(1), 3–45.

Martin, P., & Midgley, E. (1999). Immigration to the United States. *Population Bulletin, 54*(2), 1–44. Washington, DC: Population Reference Bureau.

Martin-Jones, M., & Romaine, S. (1986). Semilingualism: A Half-Baked Theory of Communicative Competence. *Applied Linguistics, 7,* 26–38.

McCloskey, M. L., & Enright, D. S. (1992). America 2000: A TESOL Response. In *TESOL Resource Packet* (pp. 1–9). Alexandria, VA: Teachers of English to Speakers of other Languages (TESOL).

McKeon, D. (1992). Introduction. In *TESOL Resource Packet* (p. i). Alexandria, VA: Teachers of English to Speakers of other Languages (TESOL).

Minami, M., & Ovando, C. J. (1995). Language Issues in Multicultural Contexts. In J. A. Banks & C. A. M. Banks (Eds.), *Handbook of Research on Multicultural Education* (pp. 427–444). New York: Macmillan.

Minami, M., & Ovando, C. J. (2004). Language Issues in Multicultural Contexts. In J. A. Banks & C. A. M. Banks (Eds.), *Handbook of Research on Multicultural Education* (2nd ed., pp. 567–588). San Francisco: Jossey-Bass.

Muñoz-Sandoval, A. F., Cummins, J., Alvarado, C. G., & Ruef, M. L. (1998). *Bilingual Verbal Ability Tests: Comprehensive Manual.* Itasca, IL: Riverside.

National Association for Bilingual Education. (n.d.). *Fact Sheet: Need for Additional Funding for the Federal Bilingual Education Act.* Washington, DC: Author.

Nichols, P. (1981). Creoles of the USA. In C. A. Ferguson & S. B. Heath (Eds.), *Language in the USA* (pp. 69–91). New York: Cambridge University Press.

Ogbu, J. U. (1999). Beyond Language: Ebonics, Proper English, and Identity in a Black-American Speech Community. *American Educational Research Journal, 36*(2), 147–184.

Ovando, C. J. (1983). Bilingual/Bicultural Education: Its Legacy and Its Future. *Phi Delta Kappan, 64*(8), 564–568.

Ovando, C. J. (1999 April). *Bilingual Education in the United States: Historical Development and Current Issues.* Paper presented at the annual meeting of the American Education Research Association, Montreal, Canada.

Ovando, C. J., & Collier, V. P. (1998) *Bilingual and ESL Classrooms: Teaching in Multicultural Contexts* (2nd ed.). New York: McGraw-Hill.

Ovando, C. J., Collier, V. P., & Combs, M. C. (2003). *Bilingual and ESL Classrooms: Teaching in Multicultural Contexts* (3rd ed.). Boston: McGraw-Hill.

Ovando, C. J., & McLaren, P. (Eds.). (2000). *The Politics of Multiculturalism and Bilingual Education: Students and Teachers Caught in the Cross Fire.* Boston: McGraw-Hill.

Ovando, C. J., & Pérez, R. (2000). The Politics of Bilingual Immersion Programs. In C. J. Ovando & P. McLaren (Eds.), *The Politics of Multiculturalism and Bilingual Education: Students and Teachers Caught in the Cross Fire* (pp. 148–165). Boston: McGraw-Hill.

Perry, T., & Delpit, L. (1998). *The Real Ebonics Debate.* Boston: Beacon.

Pinker, S. (1994). *The Language Instinct: How the Mind Creates Language.* New York: Morrow.

Richard-Amato, P. A. (1998). *Making It Happen: Interaction in the Second Language Classroom.* New York: Longman.

Shaumyan, S. (1987). *A Semiotic Theory of Language.* Bloomington: Indiana University Press.

Smitherman, G. (1999). *Talkin That Talk: Language, Culture, and Education in African America.* New York: Routledge.

Stanford Working Group. (1993). *Federal Education for Limited-English-Proficient Students: A Blueprint for the Second Generation.* Palo Alto, CA: Stanford University.

Thomas, W. P., & Collier, V. P. (1999, April). *Evaluation That Informs School Reform of Programs for Language Minority Students.* Paper presented at the annual meeting of the American Educational Research Association Meeting, Montreal, Canada.

Torrey, J. W. (1983). Black Children's Knowledge of Standard English. *American Educational Research Journal, 20*(4), 627–643.

Ulibarri, D. M. (1986). Issues in Estimates of the Number of Limited English Proficient Students. In *A Report of the Compendium of Papers on the Topic of Bilingual Education of the Committee on Education and Labor House of Representatives, 99th Congress, 2nd Session.* Washington, DC: U.S. Government Printing Office.

U.S. Department of Education. (1992). *The Condition of Bilingual Education: A Report to the Congress and the President.* Washington, DC: U.S. Government Printing Office.

Waugh, D., & Koon, B. (1974). *Breakthrough for Bilingual Education.* Washington, DC: U.S. Commission on Civil Rights.

Wertsch, J. V. (1985). *Vygotsky and the Social Formation of Mind.* Cambridge, MA: Harvard University Press.

Whatley, W. (1981). Language among Black Americans. In C. A. Ferguson & S. B. Heath (Eds.), *Language in the USA* (pp. 92–107). New York: Cambridge University Press.

Wiley, T. (1996). *Literacy and Language Diversity in the United States.* Washington, DC: Center for Applied Linguistics; and McHenry, IL: Delta Systems.

Wolfram, W. (1987). *American Tongues: An Instructional Guide.* New York: Center for New American Media.

Teachers need to find creative and democratic ways to satisfy the needs of students with special talents and characteristics.

Exceptionality

Expanded rights for students with disabilities was one major consequence of the civil rights movement of the 1960s and 1970s. The Supreme Court's Brown decision, issued in 1954, established the principle that to segregate students solely because of their race is inherently unequal and unconstitutional. This decision, as well as other legal and social reforms of the 1960s, encouraged advocates for the rights of students with disabilities to push for expanded rights for them. If it was unconstitutional to segregate students because of their race, it was reasoned, segregating students because of their disabilities could also be challenged.

The advocates for the rights of students with disabilities experienced a major victory in 1975, when Congress enacted Public Law 94-142, the Education for All Handicapped Children Act. This act is unprecedented and revolutionary in its implications. It requires free public education for all children with disabilities, nondiscriminatory evaluation, and an individualized education program (IEP) for each student with a disability. The act also stipulates that each student with a disability should be educated in the least restricted environment. This last requirement has been one of the most controversial provisions of Public Law 94-142. Most students who are classified as having disabilities—about 85 percent—have mild disabilities.

Exceptionality intersects with factors such as gender and race or ethnicity in interesting and complex ways. Males and students of color are more frequently classified as special education students than are females and White mainstream students. Nearly twice as many males as females are classified as special education students. Consequently, males of color are the most likely group to be classified as mentally retarded or learning disabled. The higher proportion of males and students of color in special education programs is related to the fact that mental retardation is a socially constructed category (see Chapter 1).

Students with disabilities as well as gifted students are considered exceptional. Exceptional students are those who have learning or behavioral characteristics that differ substantially from most other students and that require special attention in instruction. Concern for U.S. students who are gifted and talented increased after the Soviet Union successfully launched Sputnik in 1957. A Gifted and Talented Children's Education Act was passed by Congress in 1978. However, the nation's concern for the gifted is ambivalent and controversial. In 1982, special funding for gifted education was consolidated with 29 other educational programs. The controversy over gifted education stems in part from the belief by many people that it is elitist. Others argue that gifted education is a way for powerful mainstream parents to acquire an excellent education for their children in the public schools. The fact that few students of color are classified as gifted is another source of controversy. Despite the controversies that surround programs for gifted and talented youths, schools need to find creative and democratic ways to satisfy the needs of these students.

The three chapters in this part describe the major issues, challenges, and promises involved in creating equal educational opportunities for students who are exceptional—those with disabilities as well as those who are intellectually gifted and talented.

CHAPTER 13

Educational Equality for Students with Disabilities

William L. Heward, Rodney A. Cavanaugh, and
Sara C. Ernsbarger

Children differ from one another. Look in any classroom in any school and you will immediately notice differences in children's height, weight, style of dress, hair and skin color, and
other physical characteristics. Look a bit closer and you will see some obvious differences in
children's language and their academic and social skills. Closely observe the interactions
among students, curriculum, and instruction, and you will begin to see how individual children respond differently to the curriculum content and to the instructional methods.

Children also differ from one another in ways that are usually not apparent to a casual
observer. Differences in the educational opportunities children receive and the benefits they
derive from their time in school are two examples. The educational implications of gender,
race, social class, religion, ethnicity, and language diversity not only influence how children
may respond to curriculum and instruction but also affect the structure and design of educational systems in general.

While diversity in social class, race, culture, and language differences increasingly
characterizes U.S. classrooms, every classroom can also be characterized by students' *skill
diversity.* Some children learn quickly and easily apply what they learn to new situations.
Other children need repeated practice to perform a simple task and then may have difficulty
successfully completing the same task the next day. Some children begin a lesson with a large
store of relevant experience and background knowledge; others come to the same lesson with
little or no relevant prerequisite skills or knowledge. Some children are popular and have
many friends. Others are ostracized because they have not learned how to be friendly.

The skill differences among most children are relatively small, allowing these children to
benefit from the general education program offered by their schools. When the physical,
social, and academic skills of children differ to such an extent that typical school curricula or
teaching methods are neither appropriate nor effective, however, equitable access to and benefits from educational programs are at stake.

Since 1975, federal legislation has mandated educational equality for learners with disabilities through individualized programs of special education. Like the others in this book,

this chapter is not about surface or educationally irrelevant differences among children. Nor does it propose that teachers are casual observers. Teachers must have the knowledge and skills to recognize and to be instructionally responsive to the diversity their students represent. This chapter extends the concept of diversity to include children with disabilities, and it lays the foundation for teachers to examine educational equity for learners with diverse skills.

This chapter briefly outlines the history of exclusion and educational inequality experienced by many students with disabilities in our nation's schools. It also examines the progress made during the past three decades, paying particular attention to the Individuals with Disabilities Education Act (IDEA), federal legislation that requires that all children, regardless of the type or severity of their disabilities, be provided with a free and appropriate public education. We look at the key features of this landmark law, the outcomes of its implementation, and the major barriers that impede true educational equity for students with disabilities. But first, let us take a closer look at the concept of disability and examine when skill diversity necessitates special education.

WHO ARE STUDENTS WITH DISABILITIES?

A variety of related terms are used to refer to children with special learning needs. When the term *exceptional* is used to describe students, it includes both children who have difficulty learning and children whose performance is advanced. The performance of exceptional children differs from the norm (either above or below) to such an extent that individualized programs of special education are necessary to meet their diverse needs. *Exceptional* is an inclusive term that describes not only students with severe disabilities but also those who are gifted and talented. This chapter focuses on children with disabilities—those students for whom learning presents a significant challenge.

The term *disability* refers to the loss or reduced function of a certain body part or organ; *impairment* is often used synonymously with *disability*. A child with a disability cannot perform certain tasks (e.g., walking, speaking, seeing) in the same way in which nondisabled children do. A disability does not constitute a handicap, however, unless the disability leads to educational, personal, social, vocational, or other difficulties for the individual. For example, a child with one arm who can function in and out of school without special support or accommodations is not considered handicapped. *Handicap* refers to the challenges a person with a disability experiences when interacting with the environment. Some disabilities pose a handicap in some environments but not in others. The child with a prosthetic arm may be handicapped (i.e., disadvantaged) when competing with nondisabled classmates on the playground but experience no handicap in the classroom. Individuals with disabilities also experience handicaps that have nothing to do with their disabilities but instead are the result of negative attitudes and inappropriate behavior of others who needlessly restrict their access and ability to participate fully in school, work, or community activities.

Children who are not currently identified as handicapped but are considered to have a higher-than-normal chance of developing a disability are referred to as *at risk*. This term is used with infants and preschoolers who, because of difficulties experienced at birth or conditions in the home environment, may be expected to have developmental problems as they grow older. Some educators also use the term to refer to students who are having learning problems in the regular classroom and are therefore "at risk" of being identified as disabled and in need of special education services. Physicians also use the terms *at risk* or *high risk* to identify pregnancies in which there is a higher-than-usual probability of the baby being born with a physical or developmental disability.

A physical, behavioral, or cognitive disability is considered a handicap when it adversely affects the educational performance of a student. Students with disabilities are entitled to special education because their physical or behavioral attributes conform to one or more of the following categories of disability:

- Mental retardation or developmental disabilities (Beirne-Smith, Patton, & Ittenbach, 2002)
- Learning disabilities (Mercer, 2001)
- Behavior disorders or emotional disturbances (Kauffman, 2001)
- Communication (speech and language) disorders (Shames & Anderson, 2002)
- Hearing loss (Moores, 2001)
- Blindness and low vision (Barraga & Erin, 1992)
- Physical and health impairments (Bigge, Best, & Heller, 2001)
- Traumatic brain injury (Hill, 1999)
- Severe and multiple disabilities (Snell & Brown, 2000)
- Autism (Scheuermann & Webber, 2002)

It is beyond the purpose and scope of this chapter to describe the defining characteristics and educational implications of each type of disability. Interested readers should refer to the sources identified in the References section to obtain information about each area.

Regardless of the terms used to refer to students who exhibit diversity in academic, vocational, and social skills, it is incorrect to believe that there are two distinct kinds of students—those who are exceptional and those who are typical. All children differ from one another to some extent. Exceptional students are those whose skill diversity is significant enough to require a specially designed program of instruction in order to achieve educational equality.

Students with disabilities are more like other students than they are different from them. All students are alike in that all students can benefit from an appropriate education, an education that enables students to do things they were previously unable to do and to do them with greater independence and enjoyment.

Disability as a Social Construct?

The proposition that some (perhaps all) disabilities are social constructs merits attention in any discussion of educational equity for exceptional children (Danforth, 1995; Elkind, 1998; Smith, 1999). The issue is perhaps particularly relevant to a text about multicultural education (Huebner, 1994). The establishment of membership criteria in any group is, by definition, socially constructed because the criteria have been created by human beings (Banks, 2000). How educational communities respond to the cultural-, ethnic-, gender-, and class-specific attributes children bring to the classroom is more important than how they perceive the establishment of membership criteria for a particular group. Education's response to the diversity children represent will influence their achievement as well as the professional and societal judgments about that achievement.

Children who are poor or whose ethnicity is not White European American are generally underrepresented in programs for children who are gifted and talented and overrepresented in programs for children who experience learning difficulties (Artiles, Aguirre-Munoz, & Abedi, 1998; Daugherty, 2001; Ford, 1998; MacMillan & Reschly, 1998; Oswald & Coutinho, 2001; Patton, 1998). There is evidence that some children's so-called disabilities are primarily the result of culture, class, or gender influences that are at odds with the culture, class, or gender that has established a given category of disability and the assessment procedures used to make those determinations (Gollnick & Chinn, 2002; Langdon, Novak, & Quintanar, 2000). As is discussed later in this chapter, a significant focus of special education litigation and legislation has been directly on these inequities.

Deconstructing the traditional sociopolitical view of exceptionality, changing social group membership, or passing legislation will not, however, eliminate the real challenges students with disabilities experience in acquiring fundamental academic, self-help, personal-social, and vocational skills. While the criteria for determining the presence or absence of a disability may be hypothetical social constructions, the handicaps created by educational disabilities are not (Fuchs & Fuchs, 1995a; Sugai, 1998).

School-age learners with disabilities, those who have pronounced difficulty acquiring and generalizing new knowledge and skills, are real children, with real needs, in real classrooms. Be wary of the conception that disabilities are merely socially constructed phenomena, that all children who are identified as disabled would achieve success and behave well if others simply viewed them more positively. This romantic ideology is seldom, if ever, promoted by individuals with disabilities themselves or by their parents and families.

Our discussion of students with disabilities and of the role special education plays in addressing their needs assumes that a child's physical, behavioral, or cognitive skill diversity is influenced by, but also transcends, other variables such as ethnicity and social class. We also assume that the educational challenges students with disabilities experience represent real and significant barriers to their ability to experience independence and personal satisfaction across a wide range of life experiences and circumstances. Many factors will contribute to educational equality for children with disabilities. Among the most important of these factors is carefully planned and systematically delivered instruction with meaningful curricula and future-oriented learning objectives (Heward & Dardig, 2001).

How Many Students with Disabilities Are There?

It is impossible to know for certain how many students with disabilities there are in U.S. schools for many reasons, including the following:

- The use of different criteria by state and local school systems for identifying exceptional students
- The relative degree to which different school systems provide services that prevent at-risk students from becoming special education students

- The imprecise nature of assessment and the large part that subjective judgment plays in interpreting assessment data
- The fact that a student might be identified as disabled at one time and as not disabled (or included in another disability category) at another time

The most complete and systematic information about the number of students with disabilities in the United States is found in the U.S. Department of Education's annual report to Congress on the education of children with disabilities. The most recent information available is for the 2000–2001 school year (U.S. Department of Education, 2003):

- Nearly 6.5 million children with disabilities, from birth to age twenty-one, received special education services during the 2000–2001 school year.
- The number of children and youth who receive special education has increased every year since a national count was begun in 1976.
- New early-intervention programs have been major contributors to the increases since 1986. During 2000–2001, 620, 195 preschoolers (aged three to five) and 247, 433 infants and toddlers (birth through age two) were among those receiving special education.
- Children with disabilities in special education represent approximately 11.5 percent of the entire school-age population.
- The number of children who receive special education increases from age three through age nine. The number served decreases gradually with each successive year after age nine until age seventeen. After age seventeen, the number of students receiving special education decreases sharply.
- Of all school-age children receiving special education, 86 percent are reported under four disability categories: learning disabilities (49 percent), speech and language impairment (18.3 percent), mental retardation (10.6 percent), and emotional disturbance (8.1 percent).
- The percentage of school-age students with learning disabilities receiving special education has grown dramatically since 1976 (from 23.8 percent to 49 percent), while the percentage of students with mental retardation has decreased by more than half (from 24.9 percent to 10.3 percent).
- About twice as many males as females receive special education.
- The vast majority—approximately 85 percent—of school-age children receiving special education have "mild disabilities."

Classification of Students with Disabilities

The classification and labeling of exceptional students have been widely debated for many years. Some educators believe the classification and labeling of exceptional students serve only to stigmatize and exclude them from the mainstream of educational opportunities (Danforth & Rhodes, 1997; Reschly, 1996; Stainback & Stainback, 1991). Others argue that a workable system of classification is necessary to obtain the special educational services and programs that are prerequisite to educational equality for exceptional students (Kauffman, 1999; MacMillan, Gresham, Bocian, & Lambros, 1998). Like most complex questions, there are valid perspectives on both sides of the labeling issues, with political, ethical, and emotional concerns competing with educational, scientific, and fiscal considerations (Luckasson & Reeve, 2001). The most common arguments for and against the labeling of students with exceptional learning needs are the following (Heward, 2003a):

Possible Advantages of Labeling

- Labeling recognizes meaningful differences in learning or behavior and is a first and necessary step in responding responsibly to those differences.
- Labeling helps professionals communicate with one another and to classify and assess research findings.
- Funding and resources for research and other programs are often based on specific categories of exceptionality.
- Labels allow disability-specific advocacy groups (e.g., parents of children with autism) to promote specific programs and to spur legislative action.
- Labeling helps make the special needs of exceptional children more visible to policy makers and the public.

Possible Disadvantages of Labeling

- Because labels usually focus on disability, impairment, and performance deficits, some people may think only in terms of what the individual cannot do instead of what he or she can do or might be able to learn to do.
- Labels may stigmatize the child and lead peers to reject or ridicule the labeled child.
- Labels may negatively impact the child's self-esteem.
- Labels may cause other people to react to and hold low expectations of a child based on the label, resulting in a self-fulfilling prophecy.
- Labels that describe a child's performance deficit often mistakenly acquire the role of explanatory constructs (e.g., "Sherry acts that way because she is emotionally disturbed.").
- Labels suggest that learning problems are primarily the result of something wrong within the child, thereby reducing the systematic examination of and accountability for instructional variables as the cause of performance diversity. This is an especially damaging outcome when the label provides educators with a built-in excuse for ineffective instruction (e.g., "Jalen hasn't learned to read because he's learning disabled.").
- Special education labels have a certain permanence; once labeled, a child has difficulty ever achieving the status of simply being just another kid.
- Labels may provide a basis for keeping students out of the regular classroom.
- The classification of exceptional children is costly and requires the expenditure of much professional and student time that could be better spent in planning, delivering, and receiving instruction.

There are strong arguments both for and against the classification and labeling of exceptional students. Research conducted to assess the effects of labeling has been of little help, with most of the studies contributing inconclusive, often contradictory, evidence. Two important issues are how the use of categorical labels affects a child's access to special education services and the quality of instruction that he or she receives as a result of classification.

Eligibility for Special Education

Under current law, to receive an individualized program of special educational services to meet his or her needs, a student must first be identified as having a disability, that is, must be labeled and then, with few exceptions, further classified into one of the categories, such as learning disabilities or visual impairment. So, in practice, membership in a given disability category, and therefore exposure to the potential disadvantages that label carries with it, is prerequisite to receiving the special education services necessary to achieve educational equality.

Kauffman (1999) points out the reality of labels as a necessary first step in serving students with important differences in behavior and learning: "Although universal interventions that apply equally to all, regardless of their behavioral characteristics or risks of developing disorders, can be implemented without labels and risk of stigma, no other interventions are possible without labels. Either all students are treated the same or some are treated differently. Any student who is treated differently is inevitably labeled" (p. 452).

Impact on Instruction

The classification of students according to the various categories of exceptionality is done largely under the presumption that students in each category share certain physical, behavioral, and learning characteristics that hold important implications for planning and delivering educational services. It is a mistake, however, to believe that once a child has been identified by a certain disability category his or her educational needs and the manner in which those needs should be met have also been identified. Regardless of what labels may or may not do for children with disabilities, labels do not teach. Although written three decades ago, the advice of Becker, Engelmann, and Thomas (1971) is still pertinent today: "For the most part the labels are not important. They rarely tell the teacher who can be taught in what way. One could put five or six labels on the same child and still not know what to teach him or how" (pp. 435–436).

HISTORY OF EDUCATIONAL EQUALITY FOR STUDENTS WITH DISABILITIES

If a society can be judged by the way it treats people who are different, our educational system does not have a distinguished history. Students who are different, whether because of race, culture, language, gender, or disability, have often been denied equal access to educational opportunities. For many years, educational opportunity of any kind did not exist for many students with disabilities. Students with severe disabilities were completely excluded from public schools. Before 1970, many states had laws permitting local school districts to deny access to children whose physical or intellectual disability caused them, in the opinion of school officials, to be unable to benefit from instruction (Murdick, Gartin, & Crabtree, 2002).

Most students with disabilities were enrolled in school, but perhaps half of the nation's children with disabilities were denied an appropriate education through what H. R. Turnbull and A. P. Turnbull (2001) call "functional exclusion." The students were allowed to come to school but were not participating in an educational program designed to meet their special needs. Students with mild learning and behavior problems remained in the regular classroom but were given no special help. If they failed to make satisfactory progress in the curriculum, they were called "slow learners"; if they acted out in class, they were called "disciplinary problems" and were suspended from school.

For students who did receive a program of differentiated curriculum or instruction, special education usually meant a separate education in segregated classrooms and special schools isolated from the mainstream of education. These children were labeled *mentally retarded, crippled,* or *emotionally disturbed.* Special education often meant a classroom specially reserved for students who could not measure up in the regular classroom. The following passage exemplified what was too often a common occurrence:

> I accepted my first teaching position in a special education
> class in a basement room next door to the furnace. Of the fifteen
> "educable mentally retarded" children assigned to work with me,
> most were simply nonreaders from poor families. One child had
> been banished to my room because she posed a behavior problem
> to her fourth-grade teacher. My class and I were assigned a recess
> spot on the opposite side of the play yard, far away from the
> "normal" children. I was the only teacher who did not have a
> lunch break. I was required to eat with my "retarded" children
> while the other teachers were permitted to leave their students.
> (Aiello, 1976, p. 14)

As society's concepts of equality, freedom, and justice have expanded, education's response to students with disabilities has changed slowly but considerably over the past several decades. Educational opportunity has gradually shifted from a pattern of exclusion and isolation to one of integration and participation. But change has not come easily, nor has it occurred by chance. Judiciary and legislative authority has been necessary to begin to correct educational inequities for children with disabilities. Recent efforts to ensure educational equality for students with disabilities can be viewed as an outgrowth of the civil rights movement. All of the issues and events that helped shape society's attitudes during the 1950s and 1960s affected the development of special education for exceptional students, particularly the 1954 landmark case of *Brown v. Board of Education of Topeka.* This case challenged the practice, common at the time, of segregating schools according to the race of the children. The U.S. Supreme Court ruled that education must be available to all children on equal terms and that it is unconstitutional to operate segregated schools under the premise that they are separate but equal.

The *Brown* decision that public school education should be provided to African American and White children on equal terms initiated a period of intense questioning by parents of children with disabilities who wondered why the same principles of equal access to education did not also apply to their children. Numerous cases challenging the exclusion and isolation of children with disabilities by the schools were brought to court by parents and advocacy groups. At issue in these cases were numerous questions, including (1) the fairness of intelligence testing and the legitimacy of placing children in special education classes solely on the basis of those tests; (2) intelligence testing and other assessment instruments that were not administered in a child's native language or were otherwise culturally biased; and (3) arguments by schools that they could not afford to educate exceptional students. One of the most influential court cases in the development of educational equality for exceptional students was *Pennsylvania Association for Retarded Children v. Commonwealth of Pennsylvania* (1972). The association (PARC) brought the class-action suit to challenge a state law that enabled public schools to deny education to children they considered "unable to profit from public school attendance."

The attorneys and parents who represented PARC argued that it was neither rational nor necessary to assume that the children were uneducable. Because the state could neither prove that the children were uneducable nor demonstrate a rational basis for excluding them from public school programs, the court decided that the children were entitled to a free public education. Other court cases followed with similar rulings—children with disabilities, like all other people in the United States, are entitled to the same rights and protection under the law as guaranteed in the Fourteenth Amendment, which declares that people may not be deprived of their equality or liberty on the basis of any classification such as race, nationality, or religion. (For a summary of these court cases, see Heward, 2003a.)

The term *progressive integration* (Reynolds, 1989) has been used to describe the history of special education and the gradual but unrelenting progress of ensuring equal educational opportunity for all children. Of the many court cases involving education for children with disabilities, no single case resulted in sweeping educational reform. With each instance of litigation, however, the assembly of what was to become the Individuals with Disabilities Education Act became more complete. Together, all of these developments contributed to the passage of a federal law concerning educational equality for students with disabilities.

THE INDIVIDUALS WITH DISABILITIES ACT: A LEGISLATIVE MANDATE FOR EDUCATIONAL EQUALITY FOR STUDENTS WITH DISABILITIES

Public Law 94–142 (1975), originally titled the Education for All Handicapped Children Act, but since amended as the Individuals with Disabilities Education Act (IDEA), was reluctantly signed by President Gerald Ford, who expressed concern that the federal government was promising more than it could deliver. Shortly after its passage, PL 94–142 was called "blockbuster legislation" (Goodman, 1976) and hailed as the law that "will probably become known as having the greatest impact on education in history" (Stowell & Terry, 1977, p. 475).

These predictions have proven accurate; IDEA is a landmark piece of legislation that has changed the face of education in the United States. This law has affected every school in the United States and has changed the roles of regular and special educators, school administrators, parents, and many other people involved in the educational process. Its passage marked the culmination of the efforts of a great many educators, parents, and legislators to bring together in one comprehensive bill this country's laws regarding the education of children with disabilities. The law reflects society's concern for treating people with disabilities as full citizens, with the same rights and privileges that all other citizens enjoy.

The purpose of IDEA is to

> assure that all children with disabilities have available to them . . .
> a free appropriate public education which emphasizes special
> education and related services designed to meet their unique needs,
> to assure that the rights of children with disabilities and their
> parents or guardians are protected, to assist states and localities to
> provide for the education of all children with disabilities, and to
> assess and assure the effectiveness of efforts to education children
> with disabilities. (IDEA, 20 U.S.C. § 1400[c])

Major Components of the Individuals with Disabilities Education Act

IDEA is directed primarily at the states, which are responsible for providing education to their residents. The majority of the many rules and regulations defining how IDEA operates are related to six major principles that have remained unchanged since 1975 (Turnbull & Cilley, 1999; H. R. Turnbull & A. P. Turnbull, 2001). [*Note:* As this text went to press, Congress was debating the reauthorization of IDEA. It is possible that some of the IDEA requirements described here were modified in the amended version of the law.]

Zero Reject

Schools must educate *all* children with disabilities. This principle applies regardless of the nature or severity of the disability; no child with disabilities may be excluded from a public education. This requirement of the law is based on the proposition that all children with disabilities can learn and benefit from an appropriate education and that schools, therefore, do not have the right to deny any child access to equal educational opportunity. The mandate to provide special education to all students with disabilities is absolute between the ages of six and seventeen. If a state provides educational services to children without disabilities between the ages three to five and eighteen to twenty-one, it must also educate all children with disabilities in those age groups. Each state education agency is responsible for locating, identifying, and evaluating all children, from birth to age 21, residing in the state who have disabilities or are suspected of having disabilities. This requirement is called the *child find system*.

Nondiscriminatory Identification and Evaluation

IDEA requires that students with disabilities be evaluated fairly. Assessment must be nondiscriminatory. This requirement is particularly important because of the disproportionate number of children from non-White and non–English-speaking cultural groups who are identified as having disabilities, often solely on the basis of a score from standardized intelligence tests. The intelligence tests that have been used most often in the identification of students with learning problems were developed based on the performance of White, middle-class children. Because of their Anglocentric nature, the tests are often considered to be unfairly biased against children from diverse cultural groups who have had less of an opportunity to learn the knowledge sampled by the test items (Venn, 2000). IDEA states clearly that the results of one test cannot be used as the sole criterion for placement into a special education program. Ortiz and colleagues (Ortiz, 1997; Ortiz & Wilkinson, 1991) have developed a prereferral process for preventing inappropriate placements of culturally diverse students in special education.

In addition to nondiscriminatory assessment, testing must be multifactored to include as many tests and observational techniques as necessary to fairly and appropriately identify an individual child's strengths and weaknesses. A child who has been referred for a multifactored assessment for a learning disability, for example, must be evaluated by several individuals across several different social and academic areas. The school psychologist may administer several different tests in order to obtain reliable data about the child's ability and achievement levels. The school counselor may observe the child in various academic as well as nonacademic settings such as the playground and lunchroom. Observational data from the child's teachers and samples of the child's work should be compiled. A speech and language therapist, occupational therapist, rehabilitation counselor, or social worker may also be included in the assessment process. Parental input and the child's own perceptions of his or her needs complete a thorough and well-rounded multifactored assessment. The result of these efforts should be an accurate picture of the child's current levels of performance, with clear indications as to what type of educational program will be most appropriate.

Free, Appropriate Public Education

All children with disabilities, regardless of the type or severity of their disability, shall receive a free, appropriate public education. This education must be provided at public expense—that is, without cost to the child's parents. An *individualized education program* (IEP) must be developed and implemented for each child with a disability. The law is specific in identifying the kind of information an IEP must include and who is to be involved in its development. Each IEP must be created by an *IEP team* consisting of (at least) the child's parents (or guardians), at least one regular education teacher of the child, at least one special education teacher, a representative of the local school district, and, whenever appropriate, the child. Many IEP teams also include professionals from various disciplines such as school psychology, physical therapy, and medicine. (For suggestions on how IEP teams can work effectively and involve parents and students with disabilities in the IEP process, see Al-Hassan & Gardner, 2002; Martin, Hughes, Huber Marshall, Jerman, & Maxson, 1999; Menlove, Hudson, & Suter, 2001; Peters, 2003; A. P. Turnbull & H. R. Turnbull, 2001.)

The IEP is the foundation of the special education and related services a child with a disability receives. A carefully and collaboratively prepared IEP specifies the skills the child needs to learn in relation to his or her present levels of performance, the procedures that will be used to occasion that learning, and the means of determining the extent to which learning has taken place (Bateman & Linden, 1998). Although IEP formats vary widely across school districts, and schools may go beyond the requirements of the law and include additional information, all IEPs must include the following seven components:

1. A statement of the child's present levels of educational performance, including
   - How the child's disability affects the child's involvement and progress in the general curriculum; or
   - For preschool children, as appropriate, how the disability affects the child's participation in appropriate activities;

2. A statement of measurable annual goals, including benchmarks or short-term objectives, related to
   - Meeting the child's needs that result from the child's disability to enable the child to be involved in and progress in the general curriculum; and
   - Meeting each of the child's other educational needs that result from the child's disability;

3. A statement of the special education and related services and supplementary aids and services to be provided to the child, or on behalf of the child, and a statement of the program modifications or support for school personnel that will be provided for the child
   - To advance appropriately toward attaining the annual goals;
   - To be involved in and progress in the general curriculum and to participate in extracurricular and other nonacademic activities; and
   - To be educated and participate with other children with disabilities and nondisabled children in [such] activities;

4. An explanation of the extent, if any, to which the child will not participate with nondisabled children in the regular class and in the activities described in paragraph 3;

5. A statement of
   - Any individual modifications in the administration of state or district-wide assessments of student achievement that are needed in order for the child to participate in such assessment; and
   - If the IEP team determines that the child will not participate in a particular state or district-wide assessment of student achievement (or part of an assessment), a statement of
     - Why that assessment is not appropriate for the child; and
     - How the child will be assessed;

6. The projected date for the beginning of the services and modifications described in paragraph 3 and the anticipated frequency, location, and duration of those services and modifications; and

7. A statement of:
   - How the child's progress toward the annual goals described in paragraph 2 will be measured; and

- How the child's parents will be regularly informed (through such means as periodic report cards), at least as often as parents are informed of their nondisabled children's progress, of
- Their child's progress toward the annual goals; and
- The extent to which that progress is sufficient to enable the child to achieve the goals by the end of the year.
- IEPs for students age fourteen and older must also include information on how the child's transition from school to adult life will be supported. (20 U.S.C. Section 1414 [d] [1] [A])

Essentially, the IEP is a system for spelling out where the child is, where he or she should be going, how he or she will get there, how long it will take, and how to tell when he or she has arrived. Although the IEP is a written document signed by both school personnel and the child's parents, it is not a legally binding contract. That is, parents cannot take their child's teachers or the school to court if all goals and objectives stated in the IEP are not met. However, schools must be able to document that the services described in the IEP have been provided in a systematic effort to meet those goals (Yell, 1998). IEPs must be reviewed by the IEP team at least annually.

Of all the requirements of IDEA, the IEP is "probably the single most unpopular aspect of the law, not only because it requires a great deal of work, but because the essence of the plan itself seems to have been lost in the mountains of paperwork" (Gallagher, 1984, p. 228). Properly including all of the mandated components in an IEP is no guarantee that the document will guide the student's learning and teacher's teaching in the classroom, as intended by IDEA. Although most educators agree with the idealized concept of the IEP, inspection and evaluation of IEPs often reveal inconsistency between what is written on the document and what students experience in the classroom (e.g., Grigal, Test, Beattie, & Wood, 1997; Smith, 1990; Smith & Brownell, 1995).

Several tools have been developed that IEP teams can use to create IEPs that go beyond compliance with the law and actually serve as a meaningful guide for the "specially designed instruction" a student with disabilities needs (e.g., Bateman & Linden, 1998; Gibb & Dyches, 2000; Lignugaris/Kraft, Marchand-Martella, & Martella, 2001). For example, *Choosing Outcomes and Accommodations for Children (COACH)* is a field-tested program that guides child-study teams through the assessment and planning stages of IEP development in a way that results in goals and objectives directly related to functional skills in integrated settings (Giangreco, Cloninger, & Iverson, 1998).

Least Restrictive Environment

IDEA mandates that students with disabilities be educated in the *least restrictive environment* (LRE). Specifically, the law states that

> to the maximum extent appropriate, children with disabilities,
> including children in public or private institutions or other care
> facilities, [will be] educated with children who are not disabled,
> and that special classes, separate schooling or other removal of

children with disabilities from the regular educational environment
[may occur] only when the nature or severity of the disability is
such that education in regular classes with the use of
supplementary aids and services cannot be achieved satisfactorily.
(20 U.S.C. Section 1412[a][5])

The LRE requirement has been one of the most controversial and least understood aspects of IDEA. During the first few years after its passage, some professionals and parents erroneously interpreted the law to mean that all children with disabilities, regardless of type or severity of their disabilities, had to be placed in regular classrooms. Instead, the LRE principle requires that each child with a disability be educated in a setting that most closely resembles a regular class placement in which his or her individual needs can be met. Although some people argue that any decision to place a child with a disability in a special class or school is inappropriate, most educators and parents realize that a regular classroom placement can be overly restrictive if the child's academic and social needs are not met. Two students who have the same disability should not necessarily be placed in the same setting. LRE is a relative concept; the least restrictive environment for one student with a disability would not necessarily be appropriate for another.

Children with disabilities need a wide range of special education and related services. Today, most schools provide a *continuum of services*—that is, a range of placement and service options to meet the individual needs of students with disabilities. The continuum can be symbolically depicted as a pyramid, with placements ranging from least restrictive (regular classroom placement) at the bottom to most restrictive (special schools, residential programs, and hospital or homebound programs) at the top (see Figure 13.1). The regular classroom is at the bottom of the pyramid and is widest to show that the greatest number of exceptional students should be placed there. Moving up from the bottom of the pyramid, each successive placement option represents an environment in which increasingly more restrictive, specialized, and intensive instructional and related services can be offered. Typically, as the severity of a child's disability increases, so too does the need for more specialized services. As noted, however, the majority of students who receive special education services experience mild disabilities; hence, the pyramid grows smaller at the top to show that more restrictive settings are required for fewer students.

Placement of a student with disabilities should not be viewed as all-or-nothing at any one level on the continuum. The IEP team should consider the extent to which the student can effectively be integrated in each of three dimensions of school life—the general academic curriculum, extracurricular activities (e.g., clubs), and other school activities (e.g., recess, mealtimes). The LRE "provision allows for a 'mix and match' where total integration is appropriate under one dimension and partial integration is appropriate under another dimension" (Turnbull & Cilley, 1999, p. 41).

In addition, placement must not be regarded as permanent. The continuum concept is intended to be flexible, with students moving from one placement to another as dictated by their individual educational needs. The IEP team should periodically review the specific goals and objectives for each child—they are required to do so at least annually—and make new placement decisions if warranted. Note that in the first three placement options, students with disabilities spend the entire school day in regular classes with their nondisabled peers.

Figure 13.1   Continuum of Educational Services for Students with Disabilities

Source: From W. L. Heward. (2003a). *Exceptional Children: An Introductory Survey of Special Education* (7th ed., p. 70).
Upper Saddle River, NJ: Merrill/Prentice-Hall. Used by permission.

Nearly three out of four students with disabilities receive at least part of their education in regular classrooms with their nondisabled peers (see Figure 13.2). Many of these students, however, spend a portion of each school day in a resource room, where they receive individualized instruction from a specially trained teacher. Approximately one of every five students with disabilities is educated in a separate classroom in a regular public school. Special schools and residential facilities provide the education for less than 4 percent of children with disabilities, usually students with the most severe disabilities.

Neither IDEA nor the regulations that accompany it specify exactly how a school district is to determine LRE. After reviewing the rulings on litigation in four LRE suits that

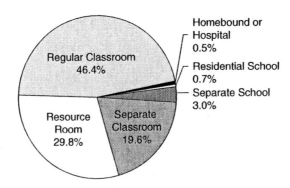

Figure 13.2   Percentage of All Students with Disabilities Ages 3 through 21 in Six Educational Placements

Note: Separate school includes both public and private separate school facilities. Residential school includes both public and private residential facilities.

Source: From U.S. Department of Education. (2003). *Twenty-fifth Annual Report to Congress on the Implementation of the Individuals with Disabilities Act* (Table AS2). Washington, DC: U.S. Government Printing Office.

have reached the U.S. courts of appeals, Yell (1995) concluded that the courts have held that IDEA does not require the placement of students with disabilities in the regular classroom but fully supports the continuum of services.

Although the continuum-of-services model represents well-established practice in special education, it is not without controversy. A number of specific criticisms have been leveled at this approach to providing services to exceptional students. Some critics have argued that the continuum overly legitimizes the use of restrictive placements, implies that integration of persons with disabilities can take place only in least restrictive settings, and may infringe on the rights of people with disabilities to participate in their communities (e.g., Stainback & Stainback, 1996; Taylor, 1988).

The relative value of providing services to students with disabilities outside of the regular classroom, and especially in separate classrooms and schools, is a hotly contested issue (e.g., Fuchs & Fuchs, 1994, 2003; Giangreco, 2003; Kauffman & Hallahan, 1994; O'Neil, 1995; Sasso, 2001; Shanker, 1995; Taylor, 1995). Virtually all special educators, however, support the responsible inclusion of students with disabilities in which systematic modifications in curriculum and instruction provide the student with frequent and meaningful IEP goals (Kochar, West, & Taymans, 2000; Schwartz, 2000; Smith & Hilton, 1997). Responsible inclusion models have been developed for children ranging in age from preschool (Sandall, Schwartz, & Joseph, 2000) through high school (Bauer & Brown, 2001) and for students whose disabilities range from mild (Hock, Schumaker, & Deshler, 1999) to severe (Fisher & Ryndak, 2001). Numerous strategies have been developed to help teachers, administrators, parents, and students work together to build inclusive classrooms and schools (Giangreco, Cloninger, Dennis, & Edelman, 2000; Salend, 2001; Snell & Janney, 2000; Thomas, Correa, & Morsink, 2001; Wood, 2002).

Due Process Safeguards

IDEA acknowledges that students with disabilities are people with important legal rights. The law makes it clear that school districts do not have absolute authority over exceptional students. Schools may not make decisions about the educational programs of children with disabilities in a unilateral or arbitrary manner.

Due process is a legal concept that is implemented through a series of procedural steps designed to ensure fairness of treatment among school systems, parents, and students. Specific due process safeguards were incorporated into IDEA because of past educational abuses of children with disabilities. In the past, special education placements were often permanent, void of periodic reviews, and made solely on the basis of teacher recommendations. Further, students with severe and profound disabilities were automatically excluded from public school programs and placed in residential programs, where the quality of instructional programs often was very poor. The fact that children from minority cultural groups were disproportionately placed into special education programs was another factor in mandating the due process procedures.

Key elements of due process as it relates to special education are the parents' right to the following:

- Be notified in writing before the school takes any action that may alter the child's program (testing, reevaluation, change in placement)
- Give or withhold permission to have their child tested for eligibility for special education services, reevaluated, or placed in a different classroom or program
- See all school records about their child
- Have a hearing before an impartial party (not an employee of the school district) to resolve disagreements with the school system
- Receive a written decision following any hearing
- Appeal the results of a due process hearing to the state department of education (school districts may also appeal)

A. P. Turnbull and H. R. Turnbull (2001), who are special educators and parents of a young man with disabilities, describe due process as the legal technique that seeks to achieve fair treatment, accountability, and a new and more equal "balance of power" between professionals, who have traditionally wielded power, and families, who have felt they could not affect their children's education.

Parent and Student Participation and Shared Decision Making

IDEA recognizes the benefits of active parent and student participation. Parents not only have a right to be involved in their child's education, but parents can also help professionals select appropriate instructional goals and provide information that will help teachers be more effective in working with their children. As noted, parents (and, whenever appropriate, students) are to take an active role as full members of the IEP team; their input and wishes must be considered in determining IEP goals and objectives, placement decisions, and related services needs (e.g., sign language interpreting, special transportation). Of course, parents cannot be forced to do so and may waive their right to participate.

Section 504 of the Rehabilitation Act of 1973

Another important law that extends civil rights to people with disabilities is Section 504 of the Rehabilitation Act of 1973. This regulation states, in part, that "no otherwise qualified handicapped individual shall, solely by reason of his handicap, be excluded from the participation in, be denied the benefits of, or be subjected to discrimination in any program or activity receiving federal financial assistance." This law, worded almost identically to the Civil Rights Act of 1964 (which prohibited discrimination based on race, color, or national origin), promises to expand opportunities to children and adults with disabilities in education, employment, and various other settings. It calls for provision of "auxiliary aides for students with impaired sensory, manual, or speaking skills"—for example, readers for students who are blind, interpreters for students who are deaf, and people to assist students with physical disabilities in moving from place to place. This requirement does not mean that schools, colleges, and employers must have *all* such aides available at *all* times; it simply mandates that no person with disabilities may be excluded from a program because of the lack of an appropriate aide.

Architectural accessibility for students, teachers, and other people with physical and sensory impairments is an important feature of Section 504; however, the law does not call for a completely barrier-free environment. Emphasis is on accessibility to programs, not on physical modification of all existing structures. If a chemistry class is required for a premedical program of study, for example, a college might make this program accessible to a student with physical disabilities by reassigning the class to an accessible location or by providing assistance to the student in traveling to an otherwise inaccessible location. All sections of all courses need not be made accessible, but a college should not segregate students with disabilities by assigning them all to a particular section, regardless of disability. Like the IDEA, Section 504 calls for nondiscriminatory placement in the "most integrated setting appropriate" and has served as the basis for many court cases over alleged discrimination against individuals with disabilities, particularly in their right to employment.

The Americans with Disabilities Act

The Americans with Disabilities Act (PL 101–336) was signed into law on July 26, 1990. Patterned after Section 504 of the Rehabilitation Act of 1973, the Americans with Disabilities Act (ADA) extends civil rights protection to persons with disabilities in private-sector employment, in all public services, and in public accommodations, transportation, and telecommunications. A person with a disability is defined in the ADA as a person (1) with a mental or physical impairment that substantially limits that person in a major life activity (e.g., walking, talking, working, self-care); (2) with a record of such an impairment (e.g., a person who no longer has heart disease but is discriminated against because of that history); or (3) who is regarded as having such an impairment (e.g., a person with significant facial disfiguration due to a burn who is not limited in any major life activity but is discriminated against). The major provisions of the ADA are as follows:

- Employers with fifteen or more employees may not refuse to hire or promote a person because of a disability if that person is qualified to perform the job. Also, the employer must make reasonable accommodations that will allow a person with a disability to perform essential functions of the job. Such modifications in job requirements or situation must be made if they will not impose undue hardship on the employer.

- All new vehicles purchased by public transit authorities must be accessible to people with disabilities. All rail stations must be made accessible, and at least one car per train in existing rail systems must be made accessible.

- It is illegal for public accommodations to exclude or refuse persons with disabilities. Public accommodations are everyday businesses and services, such as hotels, restaurants, grocery stores, parks, and so on. All new buildings must be made accessible, and existing facilities must remove barriers if the removal can be accomplished without much difficulty or expense.

- Companies offering telephone service to the general public must offer relay services to individuals who use telecommunications devices for the deaf (such as TDDs) twenty-four hours a day, seven days a week.

EDUCATIONAL EQUALITY FOR STUDENTS WITH DISABILITIES: PROGRESS MADE BUT CHALLENGES REMAIN

What impact has IDEA had? The most obvious effect is that many more students with disabilities are receiving special education and related services than before the law's passage. But this is what the law requires and is only one aspect of its impact.

Educational equality for students with disabilities is also evidenced in the ways that today's schools function as complex human services agencies. Since the passage of IDEA, there has been a dramatic increase in the number of both special education teachers and support staff. Providing the related services necessary to meet the diverse needs of students with disabilities requires that the number of nonclassroom professionals be nearly equal to that of special education teachers. School psychologists, social workers, speech and language therapists, occupational therapists, physical therapists, audiologists, recreational therapists, adaptive physical educators, vocational specialists, and mental health professionals all lend support and expertise to the education of learners with special needs.

Perhaps the law has had its most dramatic effect on students with severe disabilities, many of whom had been completely denied the opportunity to benefit from an appropriate education. No longer can schools exclude students with disabilities on the premise that they are uneducable. IDEA is based on the presumption that all students can benefit from an appropriate education, and it states clearly that the local school has the responsibility to modify curriculum content and teaching methods according to the needs of each student. In essence, the law requires schools to adapt themselves to the needs of students rather than allowing schools to deny educational equality to students who do not fit the school. Most people would agree that IDEA has contributed positively to the education of students with disabilities, but significant barriers remain to full educational equality for exceptional students in the United States. We briefly examine five of these issues. If a truly appropriate educational opportunity is to be a reality for students with disabilities, U.S. schools must work hard to (1) bridge the research-to-practice gap with regard to effective instruction,

(2) improve cooperation and collaboration between special and regular educators, (3) provide more and better early intervention programs for young children with disabilities, (4) increase the success of young adults with disabilities as they make the transition from school to adult life, and (5) ensure relevant, individualized education to students with disabilities from culturally and linguistically diverse backgrounds.

Effective Instruction

Educational equality for students with disabilities is required by IDEA. The letter of the law can be met by following the mandates for multifactored evaluations, IEPs, due process, and placements in the least restrictive environment. None of these mandated processes, however, teach. True educational equality for children with disabilities can be achieved only through effective instruction (Heward & Dardig, 2001).

Special education is not a slowed-down, watered-down version of general education. It is a systematic, purposeful approach to teaching students with disabilities the academic and social skills they will need to live independent, satisfying, and productive lives, and to do it more effectively and efficiently than could be accomplished by general education alone.

Effective teaching is much more than simply assigning something to learn. One role of all teachers, but especially special educators, is to ensure that the instruction they deliver is measurably effective in meeting the needs of their students. When this occurs, the education that students with disabilities receive will be truly special (Heward, 2003b).

Special education can be nothing more, or less, than the quality of instruction provided by teachers. Teachers, of course, are ultimately responsible for providing effective instruction to exceptional students. With this responsibility come several obligations. Working collaboratively with their regular education colleagues and parents (Heron & Harris, 2001), special educators must (1) target instructional objectives that will improve the quality of students' lives in school, home, community, and workplace; (2) use research-validated methods of instruction (Gersten, 1998; Lovitt, 2000); (3) continually evaluate the effectiveness of instruction with direct measures of student performance (Greenwood & Maheady, 1997); and (4) change an instructional program when it does not promote achievement and success (Bushell & Baer, 1994).

Teachers must demand effectiveness from their instructional approaches. For many years conventional wisdom has fostered the belief that it takes unending patience to teach children with disabilities. We believe this view is a disservice to students with special needs and to the educators—both special and general education teachers—whose job it is to teach them. Teachers should not wait patiently for exceptional students to learn, attributing lack of progress to some inherent attribute or faulty process within the child, such as mental retardation, learning disability, attention-deficit disorder, or emotional disturbance. Instead, the teacher should use direct and frequent measures of the student's performance as the primary guide for modifying instruction in order to improve its effectiveness. This, we believe, is the real work of the educator (Heward, 2003a).

Although IDEA does not state that the job of a teacher is to change behavior, that is what good teachers do. When a teacher helps a child who previously could not add, spell, compose, tie his or her shoes, apply for a job, or make a friend, behavior has been changed. Effective instruction does not change children's behavior by chance. Effective instruction is deliberate in its intent (Heward & Silvestri, in press). Chance has no place in assuring children's equal opportunity to lead productive, independent, and satisfying lives.

In order to remove chance from the equation for children with disabilities, special education must bridge the research-to-practice gap regarding instructional practice in the classroom (Carnine, 1997; Gersten, 2001). Contrary to the contentions of some people, special education research has produced a significant and reliable knowledge base about effective teaching practices (Spear-Swerling & Sternberg, 2001; Vaughn, Gersten, & Chard, 2000). No knowledgeable person will argue that research has discovered everything that is important to know about teaching exceptional students. There are many questions to be answered, the pursuit of which will no doubt lead to other questions yet to be asked.

While there is a significant gap between what is relatively well understood and what is poorly understood or not understood at all, the more distressing gap may be between what research has discovered about teaching and learning and what is practiced in many classrooms. For example, scientific research has helped us discover a great deal about the features of early reading instruction that can reduce the number of children who later develop reading problems (Grossen, 1997) and the components of secondary special education programs that can increase students' success in making the transition from school to work (Wehman, 1998), but the beginning reading instruction and transition plans implemented for many students with disabilities do not reflect that knowledge.

Regular and Special Education Partnership

Traditionally, regular and special education have been viewed as separate disciplines, each serving a different student population. Today, general and special education teachers are becoming partners in meeting the needs of all learners. The concept of "your kids" and "my kids" is gradually being replaced by that of "our kids."

Mainstreaming has traditionally been thought of as the process of integrating students with disabilities into regular schools and classes. Today, the term *inclusive education* is changing not only the language of special education reform but also its intent. Inclusive education can be successful only with full cooperation of and collaboration among those people responsible for the educational programs of students with disabilities (Bauer & Brown, 2001; Giangreco et al., 2000; Snell & Janney, 2000). Although IDEA does not specifically mention mainstreaming or inclusion, it creates a presumption in favor of the regular classroom by requiring that educational services be provided in the least restrictive environment, which in turn necessitates cooperation between general and special educators.

The effects of IDEA on general education are neither entirely clear nor without controversy. This dissonance is further complicated by the tone and content of many discussions about how special education can or should reform while ensuring that the best interests of students with disabilities are appropriately served (Fuchs & Fuchs, 1994, 1995a, 1995b; Taylor, 1995). What is clear, however, is that the entire educational community has the responsibility to do the best job it can in meeting the needs of children with diverse skills. In the final analysis, issues of labeling, classification, placement, and teaching assignments are secondary to the quality of instruction that takes place in the classroom (Heward & Dardig, 2001).

Improved collaboration between special education and general education is important not only for the more than six million students with disabilities in U.S. schools. In addition to the 11.5 percent of school-age children with disabilities who receive special education, it is estimated that another 10 to 20 percent of the student population have mild to moderate learning or behavior problems that interfere with their ability to progress and succeed in the general education program. Both special and regular educators must develop strategies for working together and sharing their skills and resources to prevent these millions of students, who are at risk, from becoming failures of our educational system.

Early Intervention

The years from birth to school age are critical to a child's learning and development. The typical child enters school with a large repertoire of intellectual, language, social, and physical skills on which to build. For many children with disabilities, unfortunately, the preschool years represent a long period of missed opportunities. Without systematic instruction, most young children with disabilities do not acquire many of the basic skills their nondisabled peers seemingly learn without effort. Parents concerned about their child's inability to reach important developmental milestones have often been told by professionals, "Don't worry. He'll probably grow out of it before too long." Many children with disabilities, as a result, fall further and further behind their nondisabled peers, and minor delays in development often become major delays by the time the child reaches school age.

Twenty-five years ago, there were very few early-intervention programs for children with disabilities from birth to school age; today, early childhood special education is the fastest-growing area in the field of education. As with special education of school-age exceptional students, federal legislation has played a major role in the development of early-intervention programs (Shonkoff & Meisels, 2000). By passing Public Law 99–457, the Education of the Handicapped Act Amendments of 1986, Congress reaffirmed the basic principles of the original PL 94–142 and added two major sections concerning early-intervention services.

Only about 70 percent of the preschoolers aged three to five with disabilities were being served under the incentive provisions of IDEA (which did not require states to provide a free public education to children with disabilities under the age of six). PL 99–457 requires each state to show evidence of serving all three- to five-year-old children with disabilities in order to receive any preschool funds. The second major change brought about by PL 99–457 is that incentive grants are available to states for developing systems of early identification and intervention for infants and toddlers with disabilities from birth to age two. The services must be planned by a multidisciplinary team that includes the child's parents and must be implemented according to an *individualized family services plan (IFSP)* that is similar in concept to the IEP for school-age students with disabilities.

Nearly every special educator today now realizes the critical importance of early intervention for both children who are at risk and those who have disabilities, and most also agree that the earlier intervention is begun, the better (Guralnick, 1997; Sandall, McLean, & Smith, 2000). Fortunately, many educators are working to develop the programs and services so desperately needed by the increasing numbers of babies and preschoolers who are at risk for developing disabilities due to poverty or prenatal exposure to drugs and alcohol (Carta, 2003; Howard, Williams, & McLaughlin, 1994). Early intervention is necessary to give these children a fighting chance to experience educational equality when they enter school.

Transition from School to Adult Life

If the degree of educational equality afforded to students who are exceptional is to be judged, as we think it should, by the extent to which students with disabilities can function independently in everyday environments, then we still have a long way to go. Follow-up studies of young adults who have graduated or left public school secondary special education programs have produced disquieting results. Data from the National Longitudinal Transition Study (NLTS) (Blackorby & Wagner, 1996), an ongoing study of more than 8,000 youths with disabilities after they left secondary special education programs, show an unemployment rate of 36.5 percent after being out of school for three to five years. And much of the work for those who do find jobs is part-time and at or below minimum wage. The probability of a person with moderate or severe disabilities finding real work in the community is much lower. The NLTS found extremely low employment rates three to five years after high school for young adults with orthopedic impairments (22 percent), visual impairments (29 percent), and multiple disabilities (17 percent).

Employment problems are not the only difficulties faced by adults with disabilities. Many youths with disabilities find every aspect of adult life a challenge (Knoll & Wheeler, 2001; Tymchuk, Lakin, & Luckasson, 2001). For example, in a statewide follow-up study of graduates of secondary special education programs in Iowa, Sitlington, Frank, and Carson (1993) found only 5.8 percent of 737 students with learning disabilities, 5 of 142 students with mental retardation (3.5 percent), and 1 of 59 students with behavior disorders could be judged as having made a "successful adult adjustment" one year after they had completed high school (p. 230).

Education cannot be held responsible for all the difficulties faced by adults with disabilities, but the results of these and other studies make it evident that many young people leave public school special education programs without the skills necessary to function in the community. Many educators today see the development of special education programs that will effectively prepare exceptional students for adjustment and successful integration into the adult community as the ultimate measure of educational equality for students with disabilities (Patton, Cronin, & Jairrels, 1997; Sitlington, Clark, & Kolstoe, 2000).

Special Education in a Diverse Society

Both special and general educators face major challenges in providing relevant, individualized education to students with disabilities from culturally diverse backgrounds (Correa & Heward, 2003). Many students with disabilities experience discrimination or inadequate educational programs because their race, ethnicity, social class, or gender is different from that of the majority. Students from culturally and linguistically diverse backgrounds are often under- or overrepresented in educational programs for exceptional children (Artiles, Aguirre-Munoz, & Abedi, 1998; Artiles & Zamora-Durán, 1997; Baca & Cervantes, 1998; Correa, Blanes-Reyes, & Rapport, 1995; Daugherty, 2001; Kauffman, Hallahan, & Ford, 1998; Oswald & Coutinho, 2001). For example, Native Americans are in classes for students with learning disabilities in disproportionately high numbers, whereas their representation in classes for students who are gifted is consistently low (Montgomery, 2001).

The 1997–1998 school year was the first time the federal government required states to report the race and ethnicity of students receiving special education (U.S. Department of

Education, 2000). Those data show some disparities between the distribution by race/ethnicity in the general population and participation in special education, particularly for African American students. Although they constitute about 15 percent of the general school population, African American students make up 34.3 percent of students classified with mild mental retardation and 26.4 percent of students with severe emotional disturbance. While a student's ethnicity or language should never be the basis for inclusion in or exclusion from special education programs, increased numbers of students from culturally and linguistically diverse backgrounds will require that educators attend to three important issues.

First, the adequacy of assessment and placement procedures must be assured. Multifactored assessments must be conducted in ways that will be appropriately sensitive to the students' culture and language to ensure that a special education placement is a function of the student's documented needs rather than of biased referral and assessment practices (Utley & Obiakor, 2001).

Second, providing appropriate support services that are responsive to the cultural and linguistic needs of the student may enhance the child's educational program. For example, bilingual aides, inservice training for teachers, and multicultural education for peers may be necessary to ensure that the child's education is meaningful and maximally beneficial.

Third, teachers and other school staff may need to learn about the values and standards of behavior present in the child's home. Since most teachers are White (Nieto, 2000; Pavri, 2001), learning not only to understand but also to respect and appreciate the child's culture as it is reflected in his or her home will be important to understanding the child's behavior in the classroom and in communicating with parents (Harry, Rueda, & Kalyanpur, 1999; Robins, Lindsey, Lindsey, & Terrell, 2002). Good intentions or token attempts at cultural sensitivity, of course, will do little to provide an appropriate IEP for students with disabilities from culturally diverse backgrounds. The instructional materials educators use and the methods they employ while teaching must be responsive to the differing cultural backgrounds of their students. For example, Gersten and Baker (2000) found that effective instruction for students who are not proficient in English is "more than just 'good teaching.' It is teaching that is tempered, tuned, and otherwise adjusted, to the correct 'path' at which English-language learners will best 'hear' the content (i.e., find it most meaningful)" (p. 461).

Does this mean that a teacher with students from four different cultural backgrounds needs four different methods of teaching? The answer is both "no" and "yes." For the first answer, it is our view that systematic instruction benefits children from all cultural backgrounds. When students with disabilities must also adjust to a new or different culture or language, it is especially important for the teacher to plan individualized activities, convey expectations clearly, observe and record behavior precisely, and give the child specific, immediate feedback during instruction. When coupled with a respectful attitude, these procedures will increase the motivation and achievement of most students.

Good teachers must also be responsive to changes (or lack of change) in individual students' performance. It thus can also be argued that the effective teacher needs as many different ways of teaching as there are students in the classroom. Cultural diversity adds another dimension to the many individual characteristics students present each day. While the basic methods of systematic instruction apply to all learners, teachers who will be most effective in helping children with disabilities from culturally diverse backgrounds achieve will be those who are sensitive to and respectful of their students' heritage and values.

As with all children with disabilities, the teacher of culturally diverse students must be flexible in teaching style, establish a positive climate for learning, and use a variety of approaches to meet individual student needs. Through careful assessment and observation of behavior, and the use of appropriate materials and community resources, the teacher can do a great deal to help culturally and linguistically diverse children with disabilities and their families experience success in school.

SUMMARY

The task of providing educational equality for students with markedly diverse skills is enormous. By embracing the challenge, U.S. schools have made a promise to exceptional students, to their parents, and to society. Progress has been made, but significant challenges must still be overcome if the promise is to be kept. The views of our society are changing and continue to be changed by people who believe that our past practice of excluding people with disabilities was primitive and unfair. As an institution, education reflects society's changing attitudes.

Common expressions of humanity and fair play dictate that all children are entitled to educational equality; but the history of exclusion and inequality for students with disabilities tells us that humanity and fair play have not driven a great deal of educational policy for children with disabilities in the absence of legislation or litigation. While much progress has been made in achieving educational equality for students with disabilities, much work remains to be done.

Educational equality for children with disabilities must ultimately be assessed by the effects of the schooling those children receive. If educational equality means simply having access to curriculum and instruction in schools and classrooms attended by students without disabilities, it has largely been attained. But equal access alone does not guarantee equal outcomes. Special education must ultimately be judged by the degree to which it is effective in helping individuals with disabilities to acquire, maintain, and generalize skills that will appreciably improve their lives. New skills are needed that will promote real participation and independence in the changing school, workplace, and community environments of the twenty-first century.

Providing educational equality for students with disabilities does not mean either ignoring a child's disability or pretending that it does not exist. Children with disabilities do have differences from children who do not have disabilities. But, as stated at the beginning of this chapter, students who are exceptional are more like than unlike other students. Every exceptional student must be treated first as an individual, not as a member of a labeled group or category.

There is a limit to how much educational equality can be legislated. In many cases it is possible to meet the letter but not necessarily the spirit of the law. Treating every student with a disability as a student first and as an individual with a disability second may be the most important factor in providing true educational equality. This approach does not diminish the student's exceptionality, but instead it might give us a more objective and positive perspective that allows us to see a disability as a set of special needs. Viewing exceptional students as individuals tells us a great deal about how to help them achieve the educational equality they deserve.

Questions and Activities

1. Why are both children who are learning disabled and those who are gifted considered exceptional?

2. In what ways are students with disabilities similar to and different from other students?

3. What are the advantages and disadvantages of labeling and classifying students with disabilities? Be sure to consider the views of educators, parents, and students.

4. How did the civil rights movement influence the movement for educational equality for students with disabilities?

5. Interview a local special education school administrator to determine (a) how many students in the district receive special education services; (b) how many of these students are English-language learners, bilingual, males, females, and/or are students of color; (c) how many students are in each of the ten categories of disability; and (d) how many students with disabilities receive some or all of their education in the regular classroom, the portion of the school day in which they are included in the regular classroom, and the curriculum areas or other school activities in which they participate in inclusive settings.

6. What is an IEP and how can it benefit students with disabling conditions? Visit a special education classroom and talk with the teacher about how an IEP might influence regular classroom teachers when students are mainstreamed.

7. How does the concept of least restrictive environment influence alternative placements for students with disabilities?

8. Do you think all students with disabilities should be educated in regular classrooms? Why or why not?

9. Why are collaboration and teaming between special educators and general classroom teachers so critical to the quality of education experienced by children with disabilities?

10. In your view, what is the most critical challenge currently facing the education of exceptional students? What suggestions would you make for meeting that challenge?

References

Aiello, B. (1976, April 25). Up from the Basement: A Teacher's Story. *New York Times*, p. 14.

Al-Hassan, S., & Gardner, R., III. (2002). Involving Immigrant Parents of Students with Disabilities in the Educational Process. *Teaching Exceptional Children, 35*(2), 12–16.

Artiles, A. J., Aguirre-Munoz, Z., & Abedi, J. (1998). Predicting Placement in Learning Disabilities Programs: Do Predictors Vary by Ethnic Group? *Exceptional Children, 64*, 543–559.

Artiles, A. J., & Zamora-Durán, G. (1997). *Reducing Disproportionate Representation of Culturally Diverse Students in Special and Gifted Education.* Reston, VA: Council for Exceptional Children.

Baca, L. M., & Cervantes, H. T. (1998). *The Bilingual Special Education Interface* (3rd ed.). Upper Saddle River, NJ: Merrill/Prentice-Hall.

Banks, J. A. (2000). *Cultural Diversity and Education: Foundations, Curriculum, and Teaching* (4th ed.). Boston: Allyn & Bacon.

Barraga, N. C., & Erin, J. N. (1992). *Visual Handicaps and Learning* (3rd ed.). Austin, TX: PRO-ED.

Bateman, B. D., & Linden, M. L. (1998). *Better IEPs: How to Develop Legally Correct and Educationally Useful Programs* (3rd ed.). Longmont, CO: Sopris West.

Bauer, A. M., & Brown, G. M. (2001). *Adolescents and Inclusion: Transforming Secondary Schools.* Baltimore: Brookes.

Becker, W. C., Engelmann, S., & Thomas, D. R. (1971). *Teaching: A Course in Applied Psychology.* Chicago: Science Research Associates.

Beirne-Smith, M., Patton, J. R., & Ittenbach, R. (2002). *Mental Retardation: Foundations of Educational Programming* (6th ed.). Upper Saddle River, NJ: Merrill/Prentice-Hall.

Bigge, J. L., Best, S. J., & Heller, K. W. (2001). *Teaching Individuals with Physical, Health, or Multiple Disabilities* (4th ed.). Upper Saddle River, NJ: Merrill/Prentice-Hall.

Blackorby, J., & Wagner, M. (1996). Longitudinal Postschool Outcomes of Youth with Disabilities: Findings from the National Longitudinal Transition Study. *Exceptional Children, 62,* 399–413.

Brown v. *Board of Education of Topeka.* (1954). 347 U.S. 483.

Bushell, D., Jr., & Baer, D. M. (1994). Measurably Superior Instruction Means Close, Continual Contact with the Relevant Outcome Data. Revolutionary! In R. Gardner III, D. M. Sainato, J. O. Cooper, T. E. Heron, W. L. Heward, J. Eshleman, & T. A. Grossi (Eds.), *Behavior Analysis in Education: Focus on Measurably Superior Instruction* (pp. 3–10). Pacific Grove, CA: Brooks/Cole.

Carnine, D. (1997). Bridging the Research to Practice Gap. *Exceptional Children, 63,* 513–521.

Carta, J. J. (2003). Perspectives on Educating Young Children Prenatally Exposed to Illegal Drugs. In W. L. Heward, *Exceptional Children: An Introduction to Special Education* (7th ed., pp. 168–169). Upper Saddle River, NJ: Merrill/Prentice-Hall.

Chinn, P. C., & Hughes, S. (1987). Representation of Minority Students in Special Education Classes. *Remedial and Special Education, 8,* 41–46.

Correa, V. I., & Heward, W. L. (2000). Special Education in a Culturally Diverse Society. In W. L. Heward, *Exceptional Children: An Introduction to Special Education* (6th ed., pp. 82–114). Upper Saddle River, NJ: Merrill/Prentice-Hall.

Danforth, S. (1995). Toward a Critical Theory Approach to Lives Considered Emotionally Disturbed. *Behavioral Disorders, 20*(2), 136–143.

Danforth, S., & Rhodes, W. C. (1997). On What Basis Hope? Modern Progress and Postmodern Possibilities. *Remedial and Special Education, 18,* 357–366.

Daugherty, D. (2001). IDEA '97 and Disproportionate Placement. Retrieved June, 20, 2003, from http://www.naspcenter.org/teachers/IDEA_disp.html.

Elkind, D. (1998). Behavior Disorders: A Postmodern Perspective. *Behavioral Disorders, 23,* 153–159.

Fisher, D., & Ryndak, D. L. (Eds.). (2001). *The Foundations of Inclusive Education: A Compendium of Articles on Effective Strategies to Achieve Inclusive Education.* Baltimore: Association for Persons with Severe Handicaps.

Ford, D. Y. (1998). The Underrepresentation of Minority Students in Gifted Education: Problems and Promises in Recruitment and Retention. *Journal of Special Education, 32,* 4–14.

Fuchs, D., & Fuchs, L. S. (1994). Inclusive Schools Movement and the Radicalization of Special Education Reform. *Exceptional Children, 60,* 294–309.

Fuchs, D., & Fuchs, L. S. (1995a). What's "Special" about Special Education? *Phi Delta Kappan, 76*(7), 531–540.

Fuchs, D., & Fuchs, L. S. (1995b). Sometimes Separate Is Better. *Educational Leadership, 52*(4), 22–25.

Fuchs, D., & Fuchs, L. S. (2003). Inclusion versus Full Inclusion. In W. L. Heward, *Exceptional Children: An Introduction to Special Education* (7th ed., pp. 80–81). Upper Saddle River, NJ: Merrill/Prentice-Hall.

Gallagher, J. J. (1984). The Evolution of Special Education Concepts. In B. Blatt & R. J. Morris (Eds.), *Perspectives in Special Education: Personal Orientations* (pp. 210–232). Glenview, IL: Scott, Foresman.

Gersten, R. (1998). Recent Advances in Instructional Research for Students with Learning Disabilities: An Overview. *Learning Disabilities Research and Practice, 13,* 162–170.

Gersten, R. (2001). Sorting Out the Roles of Research in the Improvement of Practice. *Learning Disabilities Research and Practice, 16,* 45–50.

Gersten, R., & Baker, S. (2000). What We Know about Effective Instructional Practices for English-Language Learners. *Exceptional Children, 66,* 454–470.

Giangreco, M. F. (2003). Moving toward Inclusion. In W. L. Heward, *Exceptional Children: An Introduction to Special Education* (7th ed., pp. 78–79). Upper Saddle River, NJ: Merrill/Prentice-Hall.

Giangreco, M. F., Cloninger, C., Dennis, R., & Edelman, S. (2000). Problem-Solving Methods to Facilitate Inclusive Education. In J. S. Thousand, R. A. Villa, & A. I. Nevin (Eds.), *Restructuring for Caring and Effective Education: Piecing the Puzzle Together* (2nd ed., pp. 293–327). Baltimore: Brookes.

Giangreco, M. F., Cloninger, C. J., & Iverson, V. S. (1998). *Choosing Options and Accommodations for Children: A Guide to Educational Planning for Students with Disabilities* (2nd ed.). Baltimore: Brookes.

Gibb, G. S., & Dyches, T. T. (2000). *Guide to Writing Quality Individualized Education Programs.* Boston: Allyn & Bacon.

Gollnick, D. M., & Chinn, P. G. (2002). *Multicultural Education in a Pluralistic Society* (6th ed.). Upper Saddle River, NJ: Merrill/Prentice-Hall.

Goodman, L. V. (1976). A Bill of Rights for the Handicapped. *American Education, 12*(6), 6–8.

Greenwood, C. R., & Maheady, L. (1997). Measurable Change in Student Performance: Forgotten Standard in Teacher Preparation? *Teacher Education and Special Education, 20,* 265–275.

Grigal, M., Test, D. W., Beattie, J., & Wood, W. (1997). An Evaluation of Transition Components of Individualized Education Programs. *Exceptional Children, 63,* 357–372.

Grossen, B. (1997). *Thirty Years of Research: What We Now Know about How Children Learn to Read: A Synthesis of Research on Reading from the National Institute of Child Health and Human Development.* Santa Cruz, CA: Center for the Future of Teaching and Learning.

Guralnick, M. J. (1997). *The Effectiveness of Early Intervention*. Baltimore: Brookes.

Harry, B., Rueda, R., & Kalyanpur, M. (1999). Cultural Reciprocity in Sociocultural Perspective: Adapting the Normalization Principle for Family Collaboration. *Exceptional Children, 66,* 123–136.

Heron, T. E., & Harris, K. C. (2001). *The Educational Consultant: Helping Professionals, Parents, and Mainstreamed Students* (4th ed.). Austin, TX: PRO-ED.

Heward, W. L. (2003a). *Exceptional Children: An Introduction to Special Education* (7th ed.). Upper Saddle River, NJ: Merrill/Prentice-Hall.

Heward, W. L. (2003b). Ten Faulty Notions about Teaching and Learning That Hinder the Effectiveness of Special Education. *Journal of Special Education, 36*(4), 186–205.

Heward, W. L., & Dardig, J. C. (2001, Spring). What Matters Most in Special Education. *Education Connection*, pp. 41–44.

Heward, W. L., & Silvestri, S. M. (in press). The Neutralization of Special Education. In J. W. Jacobson, J. A. Mulick, & R. M. Foxx, (Eds.). *Fads: Dubious and Improbable Treatments for Developmental Disabilities*. Hillsdale, NJ: Erlbaum.

Hill, J. L. (1999). *Meeting the Needs of Students with Special Physical and Health Care Needs*. Upper Saddle River, NJ: Merrill/Prentice-Hall.

Hock, M. F., Schumaker, J. B., & Deshler, D. D. (1999). Closing the Gap to Success in Secondary Schools: A Model for Cognitive Apprenticeship. In D. D. Deshler, J. B. Schumaker, K. R. Harris, & S. Graham (Eds.), *Teaching Every Adolescent Every Day: Learning in Diverse Middle and High School Classrooms* (pp. 1–51). Cambridge, MA: Brookline Books.

Howard, V. F., Williams, B. F., & McLaughlin, T. F. (1994). Children Prenatally Exposed to Alcohol and Cocaine: Behavioral Solutions. In R. Gardner III, D. M. Sainato, J. O. Cooper, T. E. Heron, W. L. Heward, J. Eshleman, & T. A. Grossi (Eds.), *Behavior Analysis in Education: Focus on Measurably Superior Instruction* (pp. 131–146). Pacific Grove, CA: Brooks/Cole.

Huebner, T. A. (1994). Understanding Multiculturalism. *Journal of Teacher Education, 45*(5), 375–377.

Kauffman, J. M. (1999). How We Prevent the Prevention of Emotional and Behavioral Disorders. *Exceptional Children, 65,* 448–468.

Kauffman, J. M. (2001). *Characteristics of Emotional and Behavioral Disorders of Children and Youth* (7th ed.). Upper Saddle River, NJ: Merrill/Prentice-Hall.

Kauffman, J. M., & Hallahan, D. K. (1994). *The Illusion of Full Inclusion: A Comprehensive Critique of a Current Special Education Bandwagon*. Austin, TX: PRO-ED.

Kauffman, J. M., Hallahan, D. P., & Ford, D. Y. (Guest Eds.). (1998). Special section: Disproportionate Representation of Minority Students in Special Education. *Journal of Special Education, 32,* 3–54.

Knoll, J. A., & Wheeler, C. B. (2001). My Home: Developing Skills and Supports for Adult Living. In R. W. Flexer, T. J. Simmons, P. Luft, & R. M. Baer (Eds.), *Transition Planning for Secondary Students with Disabilities* (pp. 499–539). Upper Saddle River, NJ: Merrill/Prentice-Hall.

Kochar, C. A., West, L. L., & Taymans, J. M. (2000). *Successful Inclusion: Practical Strategies for a Shared Responsibility*. Upper Saddle River, NJ: Merrill/Prentice-Hall.

Langdon, H. W., Novak, J. M., & Quintanar, R. S. (2000). Setting the Teaching–Learning Wheel in Motion in Assessing Language Minority Students. *Multicultural Perspectives, 2*(2), 3–9.

Lignugaris/Kraft, B., Marchand-Martella, N., & Martella, R. C. (2001). Writing Better Goals and Short-Term Objectives or Benchmarks. *Teaching Exceptional Children, 34*(1), 52–58.

Lovitt, T. C. (2000). *Preventing School Failure: Tactics for Teaching Adolescents* (2nd ed.). Austin, TX: PRO-ED.

Luckasson, R., & Reeve, A. (2001). Naming, Defining, and Classifying in Mental Retardation. *Mental Retardation, 39*, 47–52.

MacMillan, D. L., Gresham, F. M., Bocian, K. M., & Lambros, K. M. (1998). Current Plight of Borderline Students: Where Do They Belong? *Education and Training in Mental Retardation and Developmental Disabilities, 33*, 83–94.

MacMillan, D. L., & Reschly, D. J. (1998). Overrepresentation of Minority Students: The Case for Greater Specificity or Reconsideration of the Variables Examined. *Journal of Special Education, 32*, 15–24.

Martin, J. E., Hughes, W., Huber Marshall, L., Jerman, P., & Maxson, L. L. (1999). *Choosing Personal Goals*. Longmont, CO: Sopris West.

Menlove, R. R., Hudson, P. J., & Suter, D. (2001). A Field of IEP Dreams: Increasing General Education Teacher Participation in the IEP Development Process. *Teaching Exceptional Children, 33*(5), 28–33.

Mercer, C. D. (2001). *Students with Learning Disabilities* (6th ed.). Upper Saddle River, NJ: Merrill/Prentice-Hall.

Moores, D. F. (2001). *Educating the Deaf: Psychology, Principles, and Practices* (5th ed.). Boston: Houghton Mifflin.

Nieto, S. (2000). *Affirming Diversity: The Sociopolitical Context of Multicultural Education* (3rd ed.). New York: Longman.

O'Neil, J. (1995). Can Inclusion Work? A Conversation with Jim Kauffman and Mara Sapon-Sevin. *Educational Leadership, 52*(4), 7–11.

Ortiz, A. (1997). Learning Disabilities Occurring Concomitantly with Linguistic Differences. *Journal of Learning Disabilities, 30*, 321–333.

Ortiz, A. A., & Wilkinson, C. Y. (1991). Assessment and Intervention Model for the Bilingual Exceptional Student (AIM for the BEST). *Teacher Education and Special Education, 14*, 35–42.

Oswald, D. P., & Coutinho, M. J. (2001). Trends in Disproportionate Representation: Implications for Multicultural Education. In C. Utley & F. Obiakor (Eds.), *Special Education, Multicultural Education, and School Reform: Components of Quality Education for Learners with Mild Disabilities* (pp. 53–73). Springfield, IL: Thomas.

Patton, J. M. (1998). The Disproportionate Representation of African Americans in Special Education: Looking behind the Curtain for Understanding and Solutions. *The Journal of Special Education, 32*, 25–31.

Patton, J. R., Cronin, M. E., & Jairrels, V. (1997). Curricular Implications of Transition: Life-Skills Instruction as an Integral Part of Transition Education. *Remedial and Special Education, 18*, 294–306.

Pavri, S. (2001). Developmental Delay or Cultural Differences? Developing Effective Child Find Practices for Young Children from Culturally and Linguistically Diverse Families. *Young Exceptional Children, 4*, 2–9.

Pennsylvania Association for Retarded Children v. *Commonwealth of Pennsylvania.* (1972). 343 F., Supp. 279.

Peters, M. T. (2003). Someone's Missing: The Student as an Overlooked Participant in the IEP Process. In W. L. Heward, *Exceptional Children: An Introduction to Special Education* (6th ed., pp. 64–65). Upper Saddle River, NJ: Merrill/Prentice-Hall.

Public Law 94–142: The Education of All Handicapped Children Act. (1975). Section 612(5)B.

Reschly, D. J. (1996). Identification and Assessment of Students with Disabilities. *Future of Children, 6*(1), 40–53.

Reynolds, M. C. (1989). An Historical Perspective: The Delivery of Special Education to Mildly Disabled and At-Risk Students. *Remedial and Special Education, 10,* 6–11.

Robins, K. N., Lindsey, R. B., Lindsey, D. B., & Terrell, R. D. (2002). *Culturally Proficient Instruction: A Guide for People Who Teach.* Thousand Oaks, CA: Corwin.

Salend, S. J. (2001). *Creating Inclusive Classrooms: Effective and Reflective Practices* (4th ed.). Upper Saddle River, NJ: Merrill/Prentice-Hall.

Sandall, S., McLean, M. E., & Smith, B. J. (Eds.). (2000). *DEC Recommended Practices in Early Intervention/Early Childhood Special Education.* Reston, VA: Council for Exceptional Children, Division for Early Childhood.

Sandall, S., Schwartz, I., & Joseph, G. (2000). A Building Blocks Model for Effective Instruction in Inclusive Early Childhood Settings. *Young Exceptional Children, 4*(3), 3–9.

Sasso, G. (2001). The Retreat from Inquiry and Knowledge in Special Education. *The Journal of Special Education, 34,* 178–193.

Scheuermann, B., & Webber, J. (2002). *Autism: Teaching Does Make a Difference.* Belmont, CA: Wadsworth.

Schwartz, I. (2000). Standing on the Shoulders of Giants: Looking Ahead to Facilitating Membership and Relationships for Children with Disabilities. *Topics in Early Childhood Special Education, 20,* 123–128.

Shames, G. H., & Anderson, N. B. (2002). *Human Communication Disorders: An Introduction* (6th ed.). Boston: Allyn & Bacon.

Shanker, A. (1995). Full Inclusion Is Neither Free Nor Appropriate. *Educational Leadership, 52*(4), 18–21.

Shonkoff, J. P., & Meisels, S. J. (Eds.). (2000). *Handbook of Early Childhood Intervention* (2nd ed.). New York: Cambridge University Press.

Sitlington, P. L., Clark, G. M., & Kolstoe, O. P. (2000). *Comprehensive Transition Education and Services for Adolescents with Disabilities* (3rd ed.). Needham Heights, MA: Allyn & Bacon.

Sitlington, P. L., Frank, A. R., & Carson, R. (1993). Adult Adjustment among High School Graduates with Mild Disabilities. *Exceptional Children, 59,* 221–233.

Smith, J. D., & Hilton, A. (1997). The Preparation and Training of the Educational Community for the Inclusion of Students with Developmental Disabilities: The MRDD Position. *Education and Training of Mental Retardation and Developmental Disabilities, 32,* 3–10.

Smith, P. (1999). Drawing New Maps: A Radical Cartography of Developmental Disabilities. *Review of Educational Research, 69,* 117–144.

Smith, S. W. (1990). Individualized Education Programs (IEPs) in Special Education: From Intent to Acquiescence. *Exceptional Children, 57,* 6–14.

Smith, S. W., & Brownell, M. T. (1995). Individualized Education Programs: From Intent to Acquiescence. *Focus on Exceptional Children, 28*(1), 1–12.

Snell, M. E., & Brown, F. (Eds.). (2000). *Instruction of Students with Severe Disabilities* (5th ed.). Upper Saddle River, NJ: Merrill/Prentice-Hall.

Snell, M. E., & Janney, R. E. (2000). *Practices for Inclusive Schools: Collaborative Teaming.* Baltimore: Brookes.

Spear-Swerling, L., & Sternberg, R. J. (2001). What Science Offers Teachers of Reading. *Learning Disabilities Research and Practice, 16,* 51–57.

Stainback, S., & Stainback, W. (Eds.). (1991). *Teaching in the Inclusive Classroom: Curriculum Design, Adaptation, and Delivery.* Baltimore: Brookes.

Stainback, S., & Stainback, W. (Eds.). (1996). *Inclusion: A Guide for Educators* (2nd ed.). Baltimore: Brookes.

Stowell, L. J., & Terry, C. (1977). Mainstreaming: Present Shock. *Illinois Libraries, 59,* 475–477.

Sugai, G. (1998). Postmodernism and Emotional and Behavioral Disorders: Distraction or Advancement. *Behavioral Disorders, 23,* 171–177.

Taylor, S. J. (1988). Caught in the Continuum: A Critical Analysis of the Principle of Least Restrictive Environment. *The Journal of the Association for Persons with Severe Handicaps, 13,* 41–53.

Taylor, S. J. (1995). On Rhetoric: A Response to Fuchs and Fuchs. *Exceptional Children, 61,* 301–302.

Thomas, C., Correa, V., & Morsink, C. (2001). *Interactive Teaming: Enhancing Programs for Students with Special Needs* (3rd ed.). Upper Saddle River, NJ: Merrill/Prentice-Hall.

Turnbull, A. P., & Turnbull, H. R. (2001). *Families, Professionals, and Exceptionality: A Special Partnership* (4th ed.). New York: Macmillan.

Turnbull, H. R., & Turnbull, A. P. (2001). *Free Appropriate Public Education: The Law and Children with Disabilities* (6th ed.). Denver, CO: Love.

Turnbull, R., & Cilley, M. (1999). *Explanations and Implications of the 1997 Amendments to IDEA.* Upper Saddle River, NJ: Merrill/Prentice-Hall.

Tymchuk, A. J., Lakin, K. C., & Luckasson, R. (2001). *The Forgotten Generation: The Status and Challenges of Adults with Mild Cognitive Limitations.* Baltimore: Brookes.

U.S. Department of Education. (2000). *Twenty-second Annual Report to Congress on the Implementation of the Individuals with Disabilities Education Act.* Washington, DC: U.S. Government Printing Office.

U.S. Department of Education. (2003). *Twenty-fifth Annual Report to Congress on the Implementation of the Individuals with Disabilities Education Act.* Washington, DC: U.S. Government Printing Office.

Utley, C. A., & Obiakor, F. E. (2001). Learning Problems or Learning Disabilities of Multicultural Learners: Contemporary Perspectives. In C. Utley & F. Obiakor (Eds.), *Special Education, Multicultural Education, and School Reform: Components of Quality Education for Learners with Mild Disabilities* (pp. 90–117). Springfield, IL: Thomas.

Vaughn, S., Gersten, R. L., & Chard, D. J. (2000). The Underlying Message in LD Intervention Research: Findings from Research Syntheses. *Exceptional Children, 67,* 99–114.

Venn, J. J. (2000). *Assessing Students with Special Needs* (2nd ed.). Upper Saddle River, NJ: Merrill/Prentice-Hall.

Wehman, P. (1998). *Developing Transition Plans.* Austin, TX: PRO-ED.

Wood, J. W. (2002). *Adapting Instruction to Accommodate Students in Inclusive Settings* (4th ed.). Upper Saddle River, NJ: Merrill/Prentice-Hall.

Yell, M. L. (1995). Least Restrictive Environment, Inclusion, and Students with Disabilities: A Legal Analysis. *Journal of Special Education, 28,* 389–404.

Yell, M. L. (1998). *The Law and Special Education.* Upper Saddle River, NJ: Merrill/Prentice-Hall.

CHAPTER 14

School Inclusion and Multicultural Issues in Special Education

Luanna H. Meyer, Jill Bevan-Brown,
Beth Harry, and Mara Sapon-Shevin

Before the passage of Public Law 94–142 by Congress in 1975, children with disabilities could be excluded from the public school system altogether if they were not performing academically at the level of their age-peers. If they did attend public school, there was no obligation that schools adapt curricula and instruction to meet their educational needs so that they might ultimately graduate with qualifications for meaningful adult roles.

The advent of the legislation now known as the Individuals with Disabilities Education Act (IDEA) changed the situation dramatically: IDEA requires that all children, regardless of the severity or extent of their disability, be provided with a free and appropriate education. Various due process protections are included in the law to ensure that schools not only cannot deny access but also must adapt curricula to meet diverse student needs, with no exceptions.

Throughout its history, special education has signified access to equality of educational opportunity as well as a commitment to meeting individualized student needs. Special education has also intersected with movements within general education—such as multicultural education—focused on pedagogical reform to address the diverse student population in today's schools. The relationship between special and general education is a complex one that can provide a measure of the extent to which our public education system is succeeding in its responsibility for equality of educational opportunity.

This chapter highlights this relationship and challenges the reader to acknowledge and promote future directions in both multicultural education and special education that do not compromise this fundamental responsibility. We believe that the fields of multicultural education and special education have been conceptualized all too separately. Increased awareness of the inequities inherent in the structure of special education services is demanding a call for attention to the intersection of these two fields. Three leading journals, *Teacher Education and Special Education* (Tyler & Smith, 2000), *The Journal of the Association for Persons with Severe Handicaps* (Park & Lian, 2001), and *Remedial and Special Education* (Torres-Velasquez, 2000) have recently published special issues on this topic, focusing on the "ethics, power, and privilege" and the theoretical and empirical aspects of sociocultural perspectives in special education. As Patton and Townsend (1999) have said, the time is ripe for a critical analysis of special education and a shift from a "search for deficits within the student and/or the family to a critique of educational processes and structures that result in unethical consequences for African American learners" (p. 284).

THE SPECIAL EDUCATION MANDATE TO EDUCATE ALL CHILDREN

Special education has come to occupy "the high ground of many contemporary educational debates," located at "the forefront of pedagogical innovation and judicial reform" (Richardson, 1994, p. 713). Following the passage of national legislation, special education rose to the challenge of developing diverse instructional strategies that resulted in significant educational achievement even in children once labeled "uneducable" (Horner, Meyer, & Fredericks, 1986). Furthermore, this evolution of effective specialized services in public education emerged at a time when general education continued, for the most part, to maintain the myth of homogeneity—a "one size fits all" approach. Special educators became the reformers, willing to address the complexities of educating children as they are, not as they are supposed to be. This is the generous and idealistic interpretation of the history of special education.

Special Education as Segregation from the Mainstream

There is another view, which Richardson (1994) describes as the consequence of the impact of compulsory education in linking three worlds of children—the typical, the delinquent, and the special. With the advent of compulsory education, students who had previously been excluded or absent voluntarily began to come to school. Richardson points to data from the state of California—a leader in the early special education movement before the passage of national legislation—that illustrates well the scenario that followed compulsory attendance requirements in general education. In 1947, a "separation of races" clause that had existed unchallenged since 1883 was under attack as the basis for segregating Mexican Americans in school. The California court ruled that because Mexican Americans were not one of the "great races of man" they could not be segregated. Richardson argues that this judicial decision became the impetus for the establishment of segregated, special education classes in California for students diagnosed as educably mentally retarded (EMR). At the same time, there was a dramatic increase in school use of long-term suspensions for behavior problems as the student population increased and became more diverse as a result of compulsory attendance requirements (*Divergent Youth*, 1963; Richardson, 1994). The original function of special education to provide programs for students with intellectual disabilities was also expanded to include a new behavioral category—educationally handicapped (EH)—rapidly populated by the same children previously excluded from school.

Special education in these early days was synonymous with special classes, which appeared to be the contemporary placement for many children who had previously been excluded from school. Thus, Richardson (1994) argues, special education emerged not primarily to meet individual needs but, instead, to provide a mechanism to continue to send some children to school elsewhere, apart from the mainstream. Dunn (1968) argued this same point in his influential article, "Special Education for the Mildly Retarded: Is Much of It Justifiable?" He highlighted the disproportionate overrepresentation of children of color in segregated special classes and noted the increase of these segregated programs in the 1950s and 1960s, just as the *Brown* v. *Board of Education* decision was otherwise challenging racial segregation. Dunn also presented evidence that the special education classes were not so very special: Children in those segregated programs did less well academically than did similar children who had remained in general education without special education services. Special education was being used, Dunn charged, to achieve socially acceptable racial segregation. His scathing critique, widely discussed for many years, was accompanied by continued evidence that children of color were disproportionately represented in special education programs.

Mercer (1973) studied the phenomenon labeled the "six-hour retarded child" used to describe the irony of children who had been diagnosed as EMR in school while doing just fine outside the school day and in their communities. She argued that both school structure and the nature of diagnostic measures (such as IQ) used to identify mental retardation were culturally biased in favor of Anglo children and against children of color. Hence, Anglo children would be conservatively diagnosed as EMR by these biased measures, resulting in more accurate identification of those children in need of special education. In contrast, the majority of children of color labeled EMR through existing measures were not retarded at all but were mislabeled. To remediate this situation, Mercer (1979) developed and validated the System of Multicultural Assessment (SOMPA), which became the model for culture-free cognitive assessment. Her pioneering work was also instrumental in the design of certain procedural safeguards incorporated into IDEA, with key provisions requiring nondiscriminatory assessment and the use of both intellectual and adaptive behavior evaluations to establish eligibility for special education services. Of course, a continuing dilemma for the diagnostic category of mild mental retardation was also an issue for categories such as learning disabilities and emotional disturbance: These are the "soft" disability categories for which diagnosis is primarily determined by professional judgment influenced heavily by existing classroom ecologies (Adelman & Taylor, 1993).

Special Education as Racial Discrimination

As attacks on the concept and practice of "educably mentally retarded" became more pronounced, a shift in the pattern of diagnosis occurred. The population of students labeled EMR (more recently referred to as "mildly mentally retarded") declined dramatically during the 1970s and 1980s, while the percentage of children labeled as learning disabled (LD) or educationally handicapped (EH) grew just as dramatically. Nationally, the EH category became that of "serious emotional disturbance" (SED), with patterns of identification and referral that were just as troubling (Webb-Johnson, 1999). G. Smith (1983) noted that African Americans continued to be overrepresented in EMR classes in some parts of the United States; where there were decreases in the EMR category, a corresponding increase in disproportionate labeling as LD occurred. Increasingly, the overrepresentation of children of color in EMR classes was paralleled by similar patterns in LD and EH/SED programs (Argulewicz, 1983; Finn, 1982; MacMillan, Jones, & Meyers, 1976; Oswald, Coutinho, Best, & Singh, 1999; Tucker, 1980). Meier, Stewart, and England (1989) reported the results of a large-scale study conducted in nearly 200 school districts examining the effects of socioeconomic status and race on educational opportunities. They found widespread evidence of "second-generation discrimination," including various sorting practices resulting in overrepresentation of African American students in special education classrooms as well as in punishment and suspension statistics. In contrast, "a White student was 3.2 times more likely to be assigned to a gifted class than is a black student" (Meier et al., 1989, p. 5). In their study of New York City referral patterns, Gottlieb, Alter, Gottlieb, and Wishner (1994) found that only 15 percent of LD students in a 1992 sample actually fit the criteria for this clinical disability, while the majority were poor children with low achievement and low scores on cognitive measures. What was happening, they argued, was that special education was being asked to accept "regular education fallout" (p. 458). They added, "The current state of urban education, so woefully underfunded relative to its needs, provides students little access to intensive resources outside of special education" (p. 459).

Oswald and his colleagues (1999) analyzed the extant data reported by nearly 4,500 U.S. school districts in the fall of 1992 for a survey of compliance with civil rights requirements. They found that African American students were two times as likely to be identified as EMR and just as likely to be identified as SED compared to their non–African American peers. These authors maintain that the issue is further complicated by national problems of general under-identification of students in both disability categories. A major purpose for their analysis, however, was to control for the effects of poverty and other demographic variables that are also known to be associated with mild developmental delay and emotional and behavioral problems—perhaps legitimately so, signifying actual special education needs. Ethnic minority status is known to be associated with greater poverty in the United States. Knowing that overrepresentation of ethnic minorities in special education statistics might actually be a function of the impact of poverty would lead to one set of intervention implications. What Oswald and his colleagues found, however, was that even after the effects of demographic variables were accounted for, placement in special education was still significantly influenced by ethnicity.

While it is very likely that discriminatory practices are responsible for much of the overrepresentation of minorities in special education, the potential effects of poverty cannot be ignored (Donovan & Cross, 2002; Fujiura & Yamaki, 2000). The National Academy of Sciences has implicated both school environments and community environments in this matter (Donovan & Cross, 2002). Data on detrimental environmental influences on the health and development of minority children who live in poverty are sobering, and we interpret these as further examples of structural discrimination in U.S. society.

Finding that ethnic minorities are disproportionately represented in special education even after controlling for the effects of demographic variables such as poverty requires that we revisit and reform discriminatory educational practices. Given that the vast majority of teachers and administrators in the U.S. educational system are White, evidence of widespread referral of ethnic minority children away from the mainstream (whether into special education or exclusion through suspension) represents a significant challenge to equality of educational opportunity.

Eliminating Racial Bias in Educational Practice

Oswald and his colleagues (1999) conclude that "further work is warranted to determine the impact of other factors not included in these models, such as educators who mistake cultural difference for cognitive or behavioral disabilities during the prereferral, referral, assessment, or eligibility process" (p. 203). Patton (1998) believes that the fundamental school structures of general and special education represent the dominant Anglo European culture such that our knowledge base and educational practices inevitably devalue the contributions of African Americans at all levels. He challenges the research community to adopt qualitatively different knowledge-producing approaches that are "culturally and interculturally competent" (p. 27). In Aotearoa, New Zealand, similar concerns have been raised regarding the place of Maori in school and society, in a nation formally committed to Maori–Anglo biculturalism but reflecting predominantly Anglo cultural infrastructures. The call for culture-specific research approaches for indigenous people to counter traditional research methodologies, seen as disempowering non-European groups, focuses on "decolonizing methodologies" and the validation of Maori knowledge (Smith, 1999). The education of Maori children in New Zealand includes emphasis on the availability of immersion Kura Kaupapa Maori schools from early years through university level, in educational units and institutions where only Te Reo Maori is spoken. Tertiary degrees are taught entirely in the indigenous language and are based on indigenous Maori knowledge rather than on a translation of Western knowledge into Te Reo; since 2000, doctoral degree level Maori education has been available.

Artiles (1998) locates competence within one's culture and emphasizes that we must deepen our understanding about how teachers deal with student diversity in the classroom. The message of contemporary work on multicultural education is not primarily fixed on remediation of racial discrimination and adoption of unbiased educational practices in schools and classrooms, although this is a part of what needs to be done whenever such discrimination and bias exists. Current multicultural education theory and practice highlight pedagogy in cultural context and prescribe a future classroom and school in which culturally diverse learners will find educational practices that value and develop their individual behavioral styles and culture-specific knowledge base (Banks & Banks, 2001).

Hence, work by Cronin (1998), Townsend (1998), and Webb-Johnson (1999) examining and intervening with the clash in cultural repertoire between teacher and child represents an important step in resolving the place of African American and other ethnically diverse students in today's classrooms. But even more fundamental reform at the preservice teacher education level will be required if the result is to be an educational system that no longer discriminates by institutionalizing "dominant" Western cultural structures, values, and practices. Research by Artiles and Trent and their colleagues examines the process of learning to teach in culturally diverse schools (Artiles & McClafferty, 1998; Artiles & Trent, 1994, 1997; Trent, Artiles, & Englert, 1998). Their approach is data-based, whereby strategies are ultimately informed by evidence regarding outcomes rather than by professional opinion about what teachers need to know and do.

Bevan-Brown's (1998a, 1999) Cultural Audit Process was designed for use by teachers in Aotearoa, New Zealand, to ensure that their educational practices are culturally appropriate for Maori students. Bevan-Brown bases her definition of *cultural appropriateness* on existing tradition and entitlements (e.g., the Treaty of Waitangi between Maori and English, signed in the nineteenth century), comprising the criteria of partnership, participation, active protection, empowerment and *tino rangatiratanga*, equality and accessibility, and integration. The various components of programs and services offered at schools are to be measured against these criteria, and educators are challenged to describe specific actions (and action planning for vacant cells) to address each intersection on the framework. By aggregating individual teacher responses and structuring collaborative planning across teachers, teacher aides, and the principal within the school, a Maori cultural input action plan may be developed for the entire school, including specification of objectives, planned strategies to achieve objectives, and designation of who is responsible and by what target date. Ongoing research, with both the teacher and the school as units of analysis, provides a basis for evaluating the effectiveness of such proactive planning.

Based on these principles, Bevan-Brown (2001) has developed the more generic Checklist for ethnically appropriate evaluation and research in special education (see Table 14.1), intended for use by educators from the dominant professional culture for the design and conduct of assessments, evaluation, and/or research involving learners from different cultures. Given the likelihood of differences in cultural and linguistic identities between the majority of children and their families on the one hand and the majority of educators, administrators, and researchers on the other (Tyler & Smith, 2000), formal prompts such as this could better promote systemic educational thinking and actions that are culturally appropriate (Trent, Artiles, Fitchett-Bazemore, McDaniel, & Coleman-Sorrell, 2002).

Table 14.1 A Checklist for Ethnically Appropriate Evaluation and Research in Special Education

---

The Right Person

- Is the interviewer from the same ethnic group as the person being questioned/receiving the special education service?

- If not, does the interviewer have the cross-cultural competence needed to interview people from a different culture and to accurately interpret the information given?

- Are the interviewer and the interviewee suitably matched (e.g., same gender, similar age, and socioeconomic status)?

- Where interviewers from the ethnic community are employed—has the method of recruitment been culturally appropriate? Have the interviewers received adequate training? Is involvement an empowering experience for the interviewers?

Asking the Right Questions

- Has the ethnic group's concept of special needs been incorporated into the evaluation/research?

- Have different cultural concepts, beliefs, values, attitudes, norms, customs, experiences, skills, knowledge, and practices been taken into account?

- Are culturally appropriate and relevant standards and measures used to evaluate special education services?

- Are differing language patterns, cognitive structures, and dialects taken into account?

- Is the evaluation/research important, relevant, empowering, and beneficial to the ethnic community concerned?

- Have both the service providers and the ethnic community been involved in formulating evaluation/research questions?

Of the Right People

- Has evaluation/research involved wide, in-depth consultation (e.g., have all relevant groups been included)?

- Has the ethnic community involved been consulted in the selection of appropriate interviewees?

(continued)

Table 14.1   Continued

In the Right Way

- Have culturally appropriate practices and protocols been incorporated into the evaluation/research process?
- Have approval and support of the evaluation/research been gained from the community concerrned or their representatives?
- Have culturally appropriate means been used and sufficient time allowed for rapport building prior to commencing interviews?
- Are culturally appropriate evaluation/research designs and methods used?
- Have interviewees been given the option of inviting family members or colleagues to support them in the interview situation?
- Are interviews conducted in the first language of the people being interviewed?
- Where an interpreter is used, is this person appropriate, and have confidentiality and privacy concerns been addressed?
- Has jargon been avoided?
- When evaluation/research is complete, have appropriate means been used to share findings with interviewees and the ethnic community concerned?

At the Right Place and the Right Time

- Is the interview being conducted at a place that is both convenient and comfortable for the interviewee?
- Does the interview venue afford privacy?
- Is the interview being conducted at a time that is convenient to the interviewee?

Source: Bevan-Brown, J. (2001). Evaluating Special Education Services for Learners from Ethnically Diverse Groups: Getting It Right. *The Journal of the Association for Persons with Severe Handicaps, 26,* 138–147. Reprinted with permission of the author.

PARENT PARTICIPATION AND MULTICULTURAL SPECIAL EDUCATION

The importance of parental involvement is not unique to special education. However, parental involvement is particularly crucial for children with disabilities for two reasons. First, students with disabilities are more vulnerable because their performance and behavior may be misinterpreted through the use of inappropriate and incorrect assessments. Students with cognitive and language impairments may not be able to report negligent or abusive practices to their parents. Parental input is essential to ensure professional understanding of the student as well as to protect the student. Second, the historical fact that students with significant disabilities were traditionally excluded from schools necessitated greater specification of student rights and, consequently, of parental rights to ensure adequate provision of educational services to which a child is entitled.

For children of color, parental involvement becomes even more critical given the overrepresentation of these children in special education services and the likely negative impacts of poverty on minority families with children who have disabilities (Park, Turnbull, & Turnbull, 2002). Parental involvement can function as a protection against the misinterpretation of cultural behavioral differences by dominant-culture professionals. At the same time, low-income and ethnic minority parents are the least likely to participate in aspects of their children's schooling (Harry, 1992).

This section of the chapter analyzes how parental participation plays out for these families—or fails to work for them—in special education. Understanding why these parents are apparently disempowered by the special education system helps us develop alternative strategies enabling families to advocate effectively for their children's needs. The focus of the discussion is on families from diverse cultures who are expected to fit within a special education (and general education) structure designed to match dominant cultural values.

The Structure of Parent Participation in the Context of Special Education

IDEA specifies a series of due process requirements for a parent–professional partnership that should be reflected in special education throughout the steps of referral, evaluation, placement, and instruction of a student with a disability (Turnbull & Turnbull, 1997). Policy makers, practitioners, researchers, and theorists in special education attempted to implement an equitable parent–professional foundation for the prescription of services to meet children's individual needs with the best of intentions. Unfortunately, the designers of the special education model established a culturally biased structure that is firmly rooted in Western European cultural values. Many difficulties in implementing that model occur because the model is not always well suited to a multicultural population. Furthermore, the team of specialists involved at every stage of the special education process is most likely to be White and from a middle-class background, and thus culturally discontinuous with most of the people receiving special education services. The special education cultural tensions include the following:

1. The focus in special education on deficit behavior and on one person as the target of intervention is not a cultural universal.

For example, Pacific Nation and Native American peoples may find many principles and practices of IDEA culturally foreign, including the structure of the individualized education program (IEP) and the focus on the individual and his or her behaviors and skills in a formal, professional planning structure. In an interview with the parent of a child in Kohanga Reo, an immersion Maori preschool, a parent explains:

> After identifying the problem, the first step is always to talk about it, you know, and with Maori people they would rather communicate with their elders first, their whanau [family] . . . they would rather do that than have to be sitting in an office with these specialists who . . . it's frightening, it's daunting for parents to come into that situation. . . . The other thing too [is that] it's not appropriate to talk about yourself, not even your own problems as Maori people. The kumera doesn't go around talking about how sweet it is . . . that's why we do things in the whanau. (cited in Bevan-Brown, 1998b, p. 6)

2. The formal prescriptions for due process are grounded in Anglo legal traditions, so that written consent and legalistic entitlements actually disempower culturally diverse families.

IDEA specifies that parents must consent to the initial evaluation; if they disagree with the results of that evaluation, they may seek an independent evaluation that must be paid for by the district if the results do not concur. Parents must also formally participate in the annual IEP process and must sign their concurrence to the intervention plan developed for their child at the formal IEP meeting. At one level, these seem like reasonable due process guarantees that parental rights will be respected from referral to placement as well as throughout special education placement.

However, these very formalistic notions of legal accountability differ considerably from the interaction styles of most families. Research on such parent conferences reveals that it is not uncommon for professionals to hold low expectations of parent involvement at these meetings (Turnbull & Turnbull, 1997). Observations of meetings reveal that parents are not generally expected to participate actively and that the agenda is usually structured to relegate the parent to the position of passive recipient of professional opinions and signatory to their recommendations (Bennett, 1988; Harry, 1992; Mehan, Hartwick, & Meihls, 1986). Harry, Allen, and McLaughlin (1995) report the comments of an African American mother: "They lay it out [the IEP]. If you have a question, you can ask them. Then you sign it" (cited p. 372).

Maori parents would expect to bring the *whanau* (family) to such a meeting, and the *whanau* might comprise a group even larger than the professional team. Everyone in the *whanau* would be involved in setting goals, because intervention to meet the child's needs would also be seen as intervention with the entire *whanau*. In an interview with a parent at a Kura Kaupapa Maori, an immersion elementary school, one parent said:

> This was one of the main reasons why we came together . . .
> so that any issues arising came back and we could deal with them
> together. . . . We don't just look at the individual. It is the whanau
> katoa . . . we have specifics with culture, we have specifics with
> language. . . . [We need to] get services that look at us holistically,
> that look at whanau; . . . they look at these kids in isolation. (cited
> in Bevan-Brown, 1998c, pp. 3, 9, 10)

3. Further cultural discontinuities arise from the fact that the influence of culture is embedded in all aspects of special education service delivery. Specifically, we address here process factors such as communication style, goal setting, and psychological assessment.

The special education structure of written communication and formal face-to-face conferences assigns a passive role to parents unless they possess the professional language, cultural, and legalistic skills integral to the process. The distinct middle-class quality of these events is a source of discomfort for many low-income and working-class parents.

In her well-known guide for parents, Coyne Cutler (1993), herself a parent, exhorts parents to develop various skills to advocate for their children in the following ways: making effective telephone calls and writing formal letters to school principals and other profes-sionals, reviewing school records, and keeping records themselves. The framework of pro-ductive assertiveness and confrontation in which these activities are suggested illustrates how difficult such advocacy would be for a parent whom professionals perceive as having low social status and less education, and whose literacy skills or experience with schools and bureaucracies are not adequate to these tasks.

Add to this the virtual certainty that the majority of the educational team (if not the entire team) will themselves be White and middle class, while most parents of children with disabilities are neither White nor middle class. Neither within nor outside these two sets of events is there any avenue for the voice of parents who do not use the language of the sys-tem. Logistical barriers to participation such as lack of transportation and child-care needs may be much more surmountable in comparison to the numerous barriers related to the structure and process of the special education system itself. Bennett (1988), for example, used ethnographic data with Caribbean Hispanic families to illustrate how school personnel deter-mined what could be discussed at the IEP conference and, in so doing, effectively excluded a parent's concern with classroom climate as a factor in her child's education. Studies by Figler (1981), Harry (1992), and Harry, Allen, and McLaughlin (1995) of the perspectives of Puerto Rican and African American families offer vivid pictures of the progressive alienation of parents, who gradually withdrew from interaction with professional educators in the face of legal and formal diagnostic frameworks described here that were incompatible with the more personal and less technological cultural frameworks more familiar to the parents. These studies also identified a pattern of deferential parental behavior that masked the parents' real reactions to the process.

Dominant-culture professionals also often assume that the values driving their interven-tions and goal setting are universally applicable. Kalyanpur and Harry (1999) have argued that the principle of normalization, while a powerful tool for individualized planning for indi-viduals with disabilities, is in itself culturally specific and is a frequent source of discontinu-ity for families from societies where equity and individualism are not highly valued. Geenen, Powers, and Lopez-Vasquez (2001), in a study of service providers' and culturally and lin-guistically diverse families' views of transition planning, found contrasting interpretations of "parent involvement." The service providers viewed European American families as much more involved in planning than the Hispanic and African American families. However, the latter two groups perceived themselves as highly involved in "launching" their youngsters into adulthood, but their family and community-based focus differed dramatically from the more formal and program-based goals envisioned by service providers.

With regard to psychological assessment, cognitive processes assumed to be universal that actually represent culture-specific behavior have become institutionalized in the diag-nostic process. As a Maori mother explained:

> One of the big barriers . . . is those people who train up to
> be specialists [who] don't know anything about Te Reo [Maori
> language] and how the speaking of the language and the living of
> the language in Kohanga [immersion preschool] . . . this specialist
> would do these games and always ask the same question what isn't
> there. And I kept saying to her he doesn't understand what you're

saying, he's come through Kohanga. We don't speak about what's not there, we speak about what is there, . . . it's the culture of the language, the structure of the language and how you implement it, the way you say things. Maori people do not ask what isn't there, what they ask is "What is in front of you, what you see, what you do know?" they don't ask you what don't you know. This is what I kept telling this specialist and she was really young and she just kept brushing me off; . . . it was culturally inappropriate for her to be asking questions like that.

Improving Practices in Supporting Parent Participation

Effective practices ensuring representation of family members of color will require strategies that begin with trust between parents and professionals. Such strategies are not likely to be illustrated solely through the more narrow framing of participation required by law, such as attendance at formal meetings and signatures at selected meetings arranged by professionals. Furthermore, where formal meetings are held, perhaps the structure and composition of the group meeting should shift toward including the child's family members—whoever the family feels is relevant to the educational process rather than restricting attendance to selected "advocates."

We have also suggested elsewhere that ongoing communications between home and school could become a valued role performed by teacher aides who themselves come from the school community and thus are more likely to share cultural membership with the family (Meyer, Park, Grenot-Scheyer, Schwartz, & Harry, 1998). Similarly, Evans, Okifuji, and Thomas (1995) describe the role of school partners who were paraprofessional staff hired by their urban school district to serve as mediators and go-betweens, to advocate for both parents and teachers, and to interpret each group's needs. This does not preclude the effectiveness of sensitive "border crossers," however, as illustrated by Harry's (1992) description of how a culturally sensitive American family liaison worker succeeded in increasing the participation of Puerto Rican parents. Because of her efforts to personalize and clarify the special education process for parents, families' perceptions of this service provider changed from "una Americana" ("an American woman") to "someone you can trust." However it is achieved, only ongoing communication between the family and the school will enable a true partnership to emerge.

The educational community must, however, address the cultural discontinuity between the teacher (most often White and middle class as well as English speaking) and the family (increasingly ethnically diverse and speaking a first language other than English). Harry (1992) and Harry, Grenot-Scheyer, and colleagues (1995) have reported on some strategies that professionals can and do use even where such cultural discontinuities exist in order to carry out exemplary parent–teacher conferences. Successful conferences are the result of sensitive responding of individual professionals or teams to the concerns expressed by parents during those meetings. Of course, truly exemplary conferences must be based on a systemic structure that incorporates parental participation, rather than relying on the goodwill and personality characteristics of individual professionals and the initiative of parents (Correa, 1987; Goldstein & Turnbull, 1982; Malmberg, 1984; Thompson, 1982). More research is needed to identify the specifics of successful conference communication strategies as part of educators' professional preparation (Harry & Kalyanpur, 1994). Several researchers have emphasized the need for increased use of qualitative methods that can use the voices of families from disenfranchised communities to instruct mainstream professionals (Sanchez, 1999; Skinner, Rodriguez, & Bailey, 1999). We also maintain that educators who choose to work in culturally diverse schools will have to make a commitment to multiculturalism themselves and develop a rich personal cultural repertoire that goes beyond the monocultural experiences with which they entered the educational profession—they will need to demonstrate what Lindsey, Robins, and Terrell (1999) labeled "culturally proficient leadership."

QUALITY INCLUSIVE SCHOOLING: BUILDING SCHOOL COMMUNITIES

IDEA has been a bold social experiment, signaling our acceptance of the responsibility to educate all children. Yet, while we adhere to the principles of compulsory education for all children, our ambivalence regarding its practice evidences itself in varied strategies for labeling and separating children who seem to fall outside the margins of a hypothetical mainstream that still fails to accommodate diversity. The persistent overrepresentation of children of color in special education is possible because disability itself can be a social judgment, most likely made about culturally diverse children and their families by the dominant school cultures.

As long as predominant models of special education involve segregation from the mainstream, special education can become a vehicle for legitimizing continued segregation of children whose behavior and learning differs from dominant cultural norms. The intentions of special education may be noble, but its practice can further delay the evolution of a public school system with the capacity to serve all children as they are. Students are diverse in many ways; no single response to that diversity is appropriate. Some differences can be celebrated, others redefined, others remediated. Each response to diversity has implications for how educational programs are organized and services delivered. Inclusive schools are purposely heterogeneous and attempt to meet individual educational needs within a shared, common social context, without the requirement or expectation that a child must go elsewhere for services (Meyer, 1997; Roach, 1994; Sapon-Shevin, 2001).

The movement for quality inclusive schooling in special education and general education began with a focus on enabling students with disabilities to attend their neighborhood schools and classrooms with their peers (Will, 1986). However, the inclusive schooling movement is now centered within the broader agenda of de-tracking and merging previously fragmented and categorical services for children (Cohen, 1994/1995; Meyer, 1997; Roach, 1994; Sapon-Shevin, 1994). From this broader perspective, inclusion entails a system that responds sensitively and constructively to racial, ethnic, religious, and all other student differences within a cohesive school community—accepting that children are different rather than expecting them to be the same (Ayres, 1993; Sapon-Shevin, 1999). Requiring schools to accommodate all children in the general education classroom is seen as the basis for creating multicultural schools to replace monocultural schools that exclude and separate children into groups of those who belong and those who do not. How we treat students with disabilities can, in practice, be how we treat children who are culturally different from the mainstream; and the messages schools give about who belongs in the mainstream classroom reveals our larger, lifelong agenda about who really belongs in our communities.

Ramsey's (1998) goals for teaching from a multicultural perspective represent the kinds of interpersonal and intrapersonal attitudes and behaviors also regarded as critical to quality inclusive schooling. These goals include teaching children to appreciate and value the contributions of others, to see themselves as members of a larger society, to respect different perspectives, and to accept responsibility for their social environment and society. Teaching children to be knowledgeable about difference, supportive of others, and active in changing structures that are oppressive to various groups can begin within inclusive classrooms. Effective strategies now exist for the inclusion of even those students with the most severe disabilities, and Fisher and Meyer (2002) have documented that quality inclusive programs are associated with significantly greater gains on measures of development and social competence in comparison to gains made by students educated in self-contained settings. We now have a rich database demonstrating the benefits to individual children (those with and without disabilities), professional school personnel, and the community as a function of the development of quality inclusive schooling (Meyer & Park, 1999).

Delivering Special Education within the Context of General Education

In inclusive schools, special services to meet the needs of individual children are delivered within the general education classroom and context. For example, Shakira may need speech therapy. Rather than sending her down the hall for a fifteen-minute pullout individual speech therapy session, the speech therapist plans with the general education classroom teacher how to meet Shakira's speech needs within the regular classroom. The speech therapist would most likely come into the classroom and work with Shakira and a small group of children—who can also be positive models for her and for the speech therapist, who might otherwise lose touch with how children Shakira's age actually do speak and converse. The speech therapist may also coach the teacher on how to work with Shakira during her usual reading group activities. Because Shakira is African American, the speech therapist must be sensitive to issues of her dialect of English as she plans what speech patterns do and do not require remediation. Shakira must be viewed as a person with multiple identities, and these identities must be dealt with in an integrated fashion within the classroom and social context (Vygotsky, 1978)

All individuals are multifaceted. Banks (see Chapter 1) emphasizes that all persons bring with them to any interaction a racial identity, an ethnic background, their age, their religion, their social class, as well as other group identities. Mee Wong is a ten-year-old girl. She is also Korean, lives in the city, has two working-class parents, and is a practicing Buddist. Having a learning disability may be part of her identity, but it does not define who she is. All of her characteristics help define who she is and must be respected in the classroom. Having a learning disability should not preclude her from participation in the schooling experiences of her peer group (including attending the general education classroom) any more than being Buddhist should exclude her from interactions with her peers in the neighborhood. Grant and Sleeter (Chapter 3) explain that race, social class, and gender are used to construct major groups of people in society. Because all students are members of all three status groups, each group and the interactions among these groups affect students' perceptions and actions.

When issues of disability are added to these categories, the number of interactions and spheres of influence increase exponentially. Adapting a Christmas craft activity for Joshua, who has cerebral palsy and uses a communication board, may not be an appropriate or adequate response to his individual identity when we know that Joshua is Jewish and does not celebrate Christmas. If we define Joshua according to only one dimension of his identity, we cannot meet his needs and treat him with respect. Shamika is African American, lives with her mother, and has difficulty reading. When she is given books at her level, we must be thoughtful about not limiting reading materials to books that portray only European American, two-parent families. We should create classroom environments in which children are comfortable revealing all aspects of their backgrounds and experiences that matter to them.

Classrooms must support the diversity of students by responding to each of their identities and by not stereotyping students according to unidimensional and narrow notions of who they are. Social context is critical for virtually all learning, and a child's experiences are the foundation of mastery of everything new (Tharp & Gallimore, 1989; Vygotsky, 1978). Putting our educational theories about social contexts for learning into action requires that we model the realities of children's personal and social lives throughout their academic lives in the general education classroom.

Sapon-Shevin (1992, 1999) has detailed the ways in which teachers can structure their classrooms so that students learn about racial, cultural, family, gender, religious, and skill differences as part of the curriculum. This information need not be limited to learning facts about other groups but can be extended so that students are actively working to understand and combat prejudices and stereotypes they encounter in school and society. Work by Derman-Sparks and the ABC Task Force (1989) and by Cronin (1998) provide examples of how even very young children can be empowered through antibias curricula to challenge injustices and inequities in society. Inclusive classroom communities must also model social and academic interactions between and among children and adults that build capacities for lifelong competence in multicultural communities outside school. Cooperative learning strategies enable students to achieve academic mastery within the context of positive, collaborative social interactions that reflect student diversity. These alternatives to tracking and ability grouping can be adapted to enable the inclusion of the full range of differences in the classroom, and they can also send powerful messages about individual responsibility to work together in order to achieve goals (Meyer & Fisher, 1999; Sapon-Shevin, Ayres, & Duncan, 2002).

Meyer, Minondo, et al (1998) describe the range of possible social relationships in children's lives, evident in their research, that can be fostered by educational practices and the organization of schooling. Their work highlights the importance of attention to the implementation of inclusive schooling, which is much more than the physical presence of students with disabilities in the classroom or even the provision of special education services within the general education environment. They found that when teachers communicated through actions and words that did not fully include children with disabilities, children mirrored those social patterns in their peer interactions. Thus, when the teacher always refers to "helping" the student with disabilities rather than working together, and fails to identify meaningful opportunities for academic participation for the student with disabilities, children without disabilities are most likely to see their peers with disabilities as students to be ignored, helped, or treated "specially," much as one would interact with a very young child or even a plaything (Evans, Salisbury, Palombaro, Berryman, & Hollowood, 1992). When classroom practices

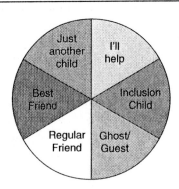

Question to ask to assess informally the nature of children's social relationships:

Ghost / Guest: Does the child frequently get "passed over" as if he or she were not there (ghost)? Do staff talk about another placement as soon as there is a problem (guest)?

Inclusion Child: Does the teacher say "I have 27 students plus 2 included students"?

I'll Help: Do classmates use the words "work with" or "help" whenever they refer to time spent with the child?

Just Another Child: Is the child expected to participate in the class activity along with everyone else?

Regular Friend: Has the child ever been invited to a party by a classmate?

Best Friend: Does the child have one or more friends who call him or her on the telephone at home and/or visit after school or on weekends?

Figure 14.1   Six Frames of Friendship Characterizing a Student's Social Relationships at School

Source: L. H. Meyer, H. Park, M. Grenot-Scheyer, I. S. Schwartz, & B. Harry (Eds.) (1998). *Making Friends: The Influences of Culture and Development* (p. 216). Baltimore: Paul H. Brookes. Reprinted with permission of the publisher.

support full participation in the range of academic and social activities occurring in school, students with even the most severe disabilities experience social lives that include being part of the group in some contexts as well as enjoying regular and best friendships (Meyer, Minondo, et al., 1998; Schnorr, 1997). Figure 14.1 provides some examples of how teachers can assess their practices to support different social outcomes for children in inclusive classrooms.

Inclusive Classrooms, Inclusive Pedagogy

An inclusive classroom requires not only that a full range of students be represented and respected within the classroom context but also that the teaching strategies respond to and include those differences. Narrow, inflexible teaching practices that assume all students learn best in the same way and bring the same experiences, background, learning style, and interests to the task are neither inclusive nor sensitive to student needs. Inclusive pedagogy can be described in terms of both the content of what is taught and the process.

Banks (Chapter 10) discusses the ways in which the "mainstream-centric curriculum" can be modified to incorporate multiple perspectives; he describes four levels of integration of multicultural content (see Chapter 10 for a more extensive discussion of these levels). In keeping with Banks's levels of integration, issues of ability/disability can be seen to have been incorporated into the practices of teaching and learning at each level as well, with substantial differences in the extent to which the status quo is accepted or challenged.

The *contributions* level focuses on heroes, holidays, and discrete cultural elements. This approach is reflected in having the class read a book about Helen Keller and then teaching a unit on blindness. Students may come to appreciate that persons who are blind can make important contributions, but this level does not challenge the more fundamental notions of segregation and exclusion of *most* people who are blind and who are not seen as making exemplary contributions.

At the *additive* level, teachers "put ethnic content into the curriculum without restructuring it" (Banks, 2001, p. 232). A special education parallel to the additive approach is to mainstream students with special education needs while leaving the curriculum of the classroom intact. Special activities may be implemented for the students with disabilities, but these activities are not integrated into the main life and curriculum of the classroom. Operationally, this level alone would result in an island in the mainstream, consisting of a special education student or small group working with a special educator (or teacher aide) on a separate activity while classmates are engaged in the larger-group, *real* academic activity. Early exemplars of integration differed from today's inclusive efforts in their fundamental practices of creating small tutorials within the general education classroom rather than modifying ongoing instructional activities to enable the student with disabilities to participate fully.

The *transformational* approach "changes the basic assumptions of the curriculum and enables students to view concepts, issues, events, and themes" from the perspectives of diverse ethnic and cultural groups (Banks, 2001, p. 233). This approach from an inclusive perspective involves not only having students with special needs become part of the classroom but also rethinking and reinventing the curriculum so that it is inclusive and multilevel. All students—across a diverse range of abilities and needs—would be engaged in educational experiences appropriate to their level but as part of a common topic, focus, and lesson (Putnam, 1998).

The *social action* approach "includes all the elements of the transformation approach but adds components that require students to make decisions and take actions related to the concept, issue, or problem studied in the unit" (Banks, 2001, p. 236). This requires both reshaping and reinventing the nature of general education classrooms and making them multilevel and inclusive as well as thinking about how schools and teaching can be part of a broader social goal of changing arbitrary and limiting notions of ability, expectations, and the need for segregation (Bigelow, Harvey, Karp, & Miller, 2001). This level has implications for school-based and systemwide decisions about outcomes evaluation, diplomas, testing of students, and curriculum design. Portfolio assessment of student outcomes—as opposed to using a uniform psychometric test—is one example of flexible educational practices that can better accommodate the richness of the repertoires of all students and their achievements (Kleinart, Kearns, & Kennedy, 1997). Other examples of fundamental change at this level are the National Council of the Teachers of Mathematics (1993) standards that reconceptualize broader outcomes, such as critical thinking and problem solving. These goals relate meaningfully to the use of mathematics in life and can be readily adapted to represent the wide range of mathematics skill levels of students found in any given classroom. Thus, students with and without disabilities might be working on their problem-solving skills in mathematics, but each student would have an individually appropriate learner objective, and the instructional unit would be adapted to accommodate differences rather than assuming everyone is learning at the same level.

Inclusive Pedagogy

Inclusive pedagogy can be described as a set of teaching practices and structures that acknowledge student differences and are responsive to that diversity. Banks's (Chapter 10) transformation and social action levels represent inclusive pedagogy. Cooperative learning and other strategies to support multilevel instruction are examples of pedagogy that can be structured inclusively (Kagan, 1998; Putnam, 1998; Sapon-Shevin et al., 2002). In cooperative learning structures, students work together to achieve common goals. Social skills (listening, compromising, asking questions, encouraging) are taught both formally and informally, and the task is structured so that students must work together in order to achieve a successful outcome. A cooperatively structured math lesson, for example, may involve students generating and then solving their own multistep math problems. A student with a disability who cannot write could contribute to the task as the checker for the group, doing the problem on a calculator and confirming the group's answer. Tasks can be structured so that students generate problems related to their own lives and experiences. Because students are working together, student differences can contribute to successful task completion rather than being viewed as obstacles to some standard curriculum.

Multilevel instruction involves structuring lessons so that different modalities, different content areas, and different levels of performance can be accommodated within current educational practices (Putnam, 1998). A thematic unit on families could be constructed involving math activities (graphing family demographics), language (writing biographies of family members, taking oral histories), and exploration of music and arts activities related to different cultures. All students could be involved in reading, writing, and mathematics activities appropriate to their level and interests, so that even a student with the most profound disabilities could be meeting his or her educational objective in such a unit.

For example, a student with multiple disabilities might be working on operating a switch to activate a computer, small appliances, or a tape recorder. Depending on the student's communication goals, two needs could be met within the context of this hypothetical thematic unit on the family. First, the student could be telling a biography of a family member by listing some descriptive facts about a brother or sister—this might be part of a communication goal for that student involving describing important personal characteristics and using an augmentative communication system to write the list. Second, the student could be working on operating a switch to activate a tape recording of that list read out by a classmate. When it is the student's turn to read the biography to the class, he or she must operate the switch to start the recording and then again to stop it at the end. There are numerous examples of successfully including students with special needs through adaptations to good instruction and educational best practices for all students (Fisher, Bernazzani, & Meyer, 1998; Hedeen, Ayres, & Tate, 2001; Meyer, Williams, Harootunian, & Steinberg, 1995; Ryndak, Morrison, & Sommerstein, 1999; Salisbury, Palombaro, & Hollowood, 1993; Sapon-Shevin et al., 2002; Smith, 1997).

Inclusive School Supports and Teacher Education

Before the advent of quality inclusive schooling, the delivery of special education services occurred in separate schools, classrooms, and/or resource rooms. Both general and special educators were professionally prepared to teach their respective students in separate environments. Teacher education, curricula, classroom organization, instructional practices, and structures of educational teaming to support students have evolved for two parallel systems— one general and one special—over a period of decades. Winn and Blanton (1997) describe the major implications for changes in teacher education and school collaboration that will be needed if inclusive schools are to become a reality. Early movements toward the integration of students with disabilities into general education were characterized by attempts to transplant specialized special education approaches into the mainstream (Meyer & Park, 1999). In contrast, the contemporary inclusive schooling movement recognizes that fundamental school reform will be required for both special and general education—indeed, merger toward one unified system of education—if quality inclusive schooling is to become a reality (Gartner & Lipsky, 1987; Meyer, 1997; Pugach & Johnson, 1995).

Goessling (1998) describes the changes that were required in thinking and practice by both general and special educators in fourteen different elementary schools following the decision to provide special education services within K–8 classrooms. She contrasts the traditions (e.g., homogeneity vs. heterogeneity), language (e.g., scope and sequence vs. goals and objectives), rituals (e.g., report cards vs. IEPs), and symbols (e.g., worksheets vs. graphs of student performance) of general versus special education programs as background to the restructuring efforts undertaken by the fourteen schools in her sample. For example, the traditional pullout system of service delivery in special education had been supplanted by a more collaborative consultation model, with all special education services provided within the context of general education activities and lessons. Her research report chronicles the "process of assimilation" for the special education teachers in particular as they moved from special education into general education. Their presence within the general education classroom had an impact on them as well as on the culture of general education itself:

> This research indicated that these fourteen teachers of students
> with severe disabilities were assimilated into the culture of general
> education and that their presence in general education could bring
> about changes within the culture of general education itself. . . .
> The presence of students with severe disabilities appeared to
> influence the push forward of school restructuring efforts and
> helped create schools that were less bureaucratic and more
> personalized and caring. . . . Perhaps there will be another study in

a few years that does not discuss the cultural assimilation of special
education teachers into general education, but rather the creation
of a third school culture that incorporates the best of both.
(Goessling, 1998, p. 249)

The model of the methods and resource (M&R) teachers develop as an alternative to
the traditional special education teacher exemplifies specialized school support personnel who
are staffed to assist the learning of all students, working in collaboration with the classroom
teacher. Porter and Stone (1998) describe the role and responsibilities of the M&R teacher
and the school-based student services team structure that evolved in New Brunswick, Canada,
once the school district had made the commitment to quality inclusive schooling. School district officials recognized that significant restructuring of teachers' roles and responsibilities
was needed to operationalize inclusion. This model does not involve placing students with
disabilities into the mainstream without support services, nor does the model deny that some
students do have disabilities that require significant services. The model does change the
nature of those support services and creates a new "special education" support teacher role
charged to work collaboratively with the classroom teacher to meet the diverse needs of all
students—not only those with a disability label.

A major argument advanced in support of quality inclusive schooling is capacity building: schools and teachers within those schools would be committed to and capable of delivering effective instruction to all children, not only to those judged to be typical or tracked
according to various criteria (Gartner & Lipsky, 1987; Roach, 1994; Sapon-Shevin, 1994).
Yet the evidence is that today's teachers are not confident of their abilities to manage and
accommodate the diverse range of student characteristics in their classrooms. Gottlieb et al.
(1994) reported that 63 percent of the teachers who referred children out of the classroom
to special education said they did not know what resources would enable them to teach those
children within their classrooms. Only 16 percent believed they could be trained with the
skills to enable them to teach children whom they had referred. Only 10 percent of the referring general education teachers could even describe a curricular adaptation they might make
to accommodate the child. It is no wonder, then, that Gottlieb and his colleagues (1994)
conclude that without "massive staff development efforts," the mainstreaming movement was
unlikely to improve children's academic status (p. 462).

Similarly, in their 1994 study in New York City—again showing disproportionate referrals to special education for students whose needs were not much different from the needs
of other students—referring classroom teachers had made only one attempt to address the
learner's needs before seeking placement elsewhere. That one attempt did not involve making curricular adaptations, modifying instruction, or even seeking additional professional
technical assistance from within their school or district; the teachers called the students'
home and asked the parent to fix the problem! Given stressed economic circumstances and
both cultural and language differences from that of the school professional staff, it is difficult to envision what parents would be expected to do to address the academic learning and
behavioral difficulties their children were experiencing in school.

Who, then, will staff the quality inclusive schools and classrooms of the future? What
are the implications of teaching staff in schools who were themselves prepared in teacher
education programs tracked for either special or general education? We believe that just as

cultural diversity demands preparation in multicultural education for all teachers, individual learning differences (including disabilities) and multiple intelligences (Gardner, 1993) demand the preparation of a new generation of teachers with a repertoire of values and strategies that match the demands of inclusive classrooms. The National Association of State Boards of Education (1992) recognized the implications of inclusion for teacher preparation programs and called for the development of new directions in teacher education consistent with the merger of general and special education. Historically, many preservice teacher education programs have included dual-certification options in both general and special education, but a truly merged program incorporating multicultural education as well as both special and general education preparation is still a rarity (Winn & Blanton, 1997).

An early example of a merged and unified inclusive teacher education program was implemented at Syracuse University in 1990 (Meyer, Mager, Yarger-Kane, Sarno, & Hext-Contreras, 1997). Its graduates are in strong demand, and graduate follow-up indicates that they enter the teaching profession with the commitment and professional repertoire for successful inclusion (Meyer et al., 1997). Ornelles and Goetz (2001) describe the University of Hawaii's post-baccalaureate program to recruit and train teachers with cultural competence who are better prepared to work with ethnically diverse students who have special needs (for other examples, see also Blanton, Griffin, Winn, & Pugach, 1997). The recent Wingspread Conference coordinated by the Teacher Education Division of the Council for Exceptional Children (CEC) focused on the development of guiding principles and specific action steps if we are to prepare teachers to work with diverse learners (Dieker, Voltz, & Epanchin, 2002; see also CEC, 2001). Achieving quality inclusive schooling will require significant reform of teacher education at all levels, both preservice and inservice.

DIVERSITY AND CARING COMMUNITIES: OUTCOMES FOR THE SOCIAL GOOD

We believe that the existence and perpetuation of pullout solutions to student differences inevitably generates (and reflects) some perhaps unintended but nonetheless real negative side effects:

1. As long as the belief persists that general education classrooms are homogenous, the cycle of referral for differences will continue and will, ultimately, exceed the resources of marginalized systems.

Our current dual system of general and special education encourages the school to conceptualize homogeneous typical groupings as the only functional structures for teaching and learning. Language which implies that the optimal response to differences is to make them invisible is particularly problematic because it does not help teachers or students learn to be responsive and proactive when faced with differences and oppression (Sapon-Shevin, 2001). Systems that allow and even encourage narrowing of commitment and capacity to serve diverse needs, that expect children to fit curriculum rather than adapting schooling to meet children's needs, and that institutionalize the identification of difference through segregation and tracking will increasingly reduce tolerance for differences and restrict the range of those who are viewed as being typical and who are seen as belonging. This is particularly dysfunctional now, when new immigrant groups, increased poverty, and proportionately greater numbers of culturally and linguistically diverse students and families are facts of life in the United States. The inevitable result will be an increasing cycle of referrals that will ultimately exceed the resources of the various special systems that are both marginalized and devalued by the mainstream society.

2. In the long run, efforts to reduce class size and restrict general education enrollment to smaller groups of students ready to learn will fail. Instead, as children leave the mainstream, resources will follow, and the cycle will repeat.

Gottlieb and his colleagues (1994) note that the current system of special education reduces any need for the general education system to develop meaningful instructional and student support programs and services for children in the general education classrooms. Teachers seemed to believe that the only mechanism available to them to reduce class size and the instructional challenges confronting them in the short run was to fully access referrals to special education—which, in large urban areas, continued to mean placement in a separate educational environment. But as children do leave general education, resources must be provided to them at their new destination—and those resources must come from somewhere. Increasingly, resources have declined in general education as our many entitlement programs have increased. While the relationship may not be a simple one, we believe that declining resources will be spread ever more thinly—and, ultimately, that those resources will come from the same budget and require subsequent increases in class size in general education.

A major argument advanced by proponents of quality inclusive schooling is that our educational system cannot afford separate and fragmented systems. Children with disabilities must return to the general education classroom and attend school with their peers. But the resources supporting those children must return as well—and those resources must be restructured and capacities enhanced to better serve all children, both those with and without disabilities.

3. When children with and without disabilities grow up in isolation from one another, everyone loses. Children will "do as I do, and not as I say." If we model segregation and rejection in a social system as central to our democratic institutions as the public schools, we will have a great deal to answer for when those exclusionary models play out in the domains of daily living.

When children with disabilities are segregated from their nondisabled peers, they lose the mainstream social context as a major teaching and learning environment. They become increasingly dependent on teacher-directed, highly structured learning and on adults in particular as the source of all new knowledge and support. On the other hand, they give up peer groups and participation in their neighborhood and community. Increasingly, as natural supports are thwarted from developing, persons with disabilities become more and more dependent on costly professional and paid services to fill the void.

More than fifty years ago, Adorno, Frenkel-Brunswik, Levinson, and Sanford (1950) advanced their theory that one's attitudes toward persons who are viewed as different is part of a consistent pattern that affects all aspects of the individual's behavior and beliefs. Their studies of racial prejudice and political conservatism were premised on the theory that cultural acceptance would be associated with democratic principles and that the promotion of cultural acceptance would thus have broad benefits for the social good. The movement for diversity in education makes a similar point while acknowledging the futility of ignoring the pluralism that now dominates the population of U.S. schoolchildren. Learning to accept individual differences and to celebrate diversity as an enriching experience are broad principles consistent with democratic values and the creation of caring schools that support children's growth and development.

In addition to multicultural education, various other general education reform movements emphasize the need for caring school communities. Berman (1990) builds a case for such school communities if we are to address the basic societal needs of our democracy for the "nurturing in young people of a sense of social responsibility and social efficacy" (p. 1); he notes with irony that "we teach reading, writing, and math by doing them, but we teach democracy by lecture" (p. 2). In her writings, Noddings (1992) has long emphasized that the creation of educational environments that support learning involves the creation of caring communities, where teachers supplement the emphasis on academic excellence with relational ethics and moral education. She emphasizes that teachers must model caring throughout their teaching and interactions with students, a concern that can be traced to John Dewey's writings.

Wells and Grain (1994) note that a thirty-year research literature on school desegregation has most often focused on the immediate effects of racial integration on individual students—their achievement, their self-esteem, and their intergroup relations. These researchers argue that another perspective focused on the life chances of African American students requires a longer-term outlook. According to a sociological perspective referred to as *perpetuation theory*, "the goal of desegregation is also to break the cycle of segregation and increase access to high status institutions and the powerful social networks within them" (p. 531). What is the purpose of our educational system and public education in the United States? Is it exclusively intended to meet the needs of each individual child? We think not. At least in part, our educational system was conceptualized as a pathway to a democratic community and the betterment of all its citizenry. Our challenge is, of course, to examine the rhetoric and practices within education with the goal of reaching a better balance between meeting unique needs and building community.

Questions and Activities

1. Why, according to the authors, are students of color and low-income students overrepresented in special education classes and programs?

2. Why is it especially important for parents of color and low-income parents to be involved in special education programs for their children? What are some effective ways in which these parents can become involved in special education programs?

3. Why do parents, especially low-income parents and parents of color, often find it difficult to participate meaningfully in special education programs even though laws exist to ensure their participation?

4. In what ways do the research and assessment work by Jane R. Mercer reveal that special education is a social construction? Give specific examples from this chapter to support your response.

5. According to the authors, what are some of the major characteristics of quality *inclusive* schools? On what major assumptions and beliefs are they based? How do inclusive schools exemplify and foster the idea of "the school as a community" described by the authors?

6. What do the authors mean by "inclusive pedagogy"? Give specific examples of this concept.

7. The authors believe that special education students should be educated in the same schools and classrooms as general education students. What problems and opportunities does this practice pose for classroom teachers? What changes might need to occur within teacher education to prepare teachers for inclusive classrooms? What guidelines, tips, and insights do the authors provide that may help teachers deal with the challenges and problems posed by inclusive education?

8. The authors maintain that a commitment to the principles and practices of inclusive education not only will benefit special education students but also will lead to classrooms and schools that reflect diversity and can thus better serve all students with and without disabilities. How might fully inclusive schools prepare our children for fully inclusive communities?

References

Adelman, H. S., & Taylor, L. (1993). *Learning Problems and Learning Disabilities: Moving Forward.* Pacific Grove, CA: Brooks/Cole.

Adorno, T. W., Frenkel-Brunswik, E., Levinson, D. J., & Sanford, R. N. (1950). *The Authoritarian Personality* (Vols. 1 & 2). New York: Wiley.

Argulewicz, E. N. (1983). Effects of Ethnic Membership, Socioeconomic Status, and Home Language on LD, EMR, and EH Placements. *Learning Disabilities Quarterly, 6,* 195–200.

Artiles, A. J. (1998). The Dilemma of Difference: Enriching the Disproportionality Discourse with Theory and Context. *The Journal of Special Education, 32,* 32–36.

Artiles, A. J., & McClafferty, K. (1998). Learning to Teach Culturally Diverse Learners: Charting Change in Preservice Teachers' Thinking about Effective Teaching. *The Elementary School Journal, 98,* 189–220.

Artiles, A. J., & Trent, S. C. (1994). Overrepresentation of Minority Students in Special Education: A Continuing Debate. *The Journal of Special Education, 27,* 410–437.

Artiles, A. J., & Trent, S. C. (1997). Forging a Research Program on Multicultural Preservice Teacher Education in Special Education: A Proposed Analytic Scheme. In J. W. Lloyd, E. J. Kameenui, & D. Chard (Eds.), *Issues in Educating Students with Disabilities* (pp. 275–304). Mahwah, NJ: Erlbaum.

Ayres, B. J. (1993). *Equity, Excellence, and Diversity in the "Regular" Classroom.* Unpublished doctoral dissertation, Syracuse University, Syracuse, NY.

Banks, J. A. (2001). Approaches to Multicultural Curriculum Reform. In J. A. Banks & C. A. McGee Banks (Eds.), *Multicultural Education: Issues and Perspectives* (4th ed., pp. 225–246). New York: Wiley.

Banks, J. A., & Banks, C. A. McGee. (Eds.). (2001). *Multicultural Education: Issues and Perspectives* (4th ed.). New York: Wiley.

Bennett, A. T. (1988). Gateways to Powerlessness: Incorporating Hispanic Deaf Children and Families into Formal Schooling. *Disability, Handicap, and Society, 3*(2), 119–151.

Berman, S. (1990). The Real Ropes Course: The Development of Social Consciousness. *ESR Journal: Educating for Social Responsibility, 1,* 1–18.

Bevan-Brown, J. (1998a). *A Cultural Audit for Teachers: Looking Out for Maori Learners with Special Needs. SET: Special Education 2000.* Wellington, New Zealand: New Zealand Council for Educational Research.

Bevan-Brown, J. (1998b). [Kohanga reo interview transcript, No. 3]. Unpublished raw data.

Bevan-Brown, J. (1998c). [Kura kaupapa Maori interview transcript, No. 1]. Unpublished raw data.

Bevan-Brown, J. (1999). *Catering for Maori Learners with Special Needs.* Paper presented at the 23rd Annual International Conference of the Association for Persons with Handicaps, Seattle.

Bevan-Brown, J. (2001). Evaluating Special Education Services for Learners from Ethnically Diverse Groups: Getting It Right. *Journal of the Association for Persons with Severe Handicaps, 26,* 138–147.

Bigelow, B., Harvey, B., Karp, S., & Miller, L. (Eds.). (2001). *Rethinking our Classrooms: Teaching for Equity and Justice* (Vol. 2). Milwaukee, WI: Rethinking Schools.

Blanton, L. P., Griffin, C. C., Winn, J. A., & Pugach, M. C. (Eds.). (1997). *Teacher Education in Transition: Collaborative Programs to Prepare General and Special Educators.* Denver, CO: Love Publishing.

Cohen, F. (1994/1995). Prom Pictures: A Principal Looks at Detracking. *Educational Leadership, 52*(4), 85–86.

Correa, V. I. (1987). Involving Culturally Diverse Families in the Educational Process. In S. H. Fradd & M. J. Weismantel (Eds.), *Meeting the Needs of Culturally and Linguistically Different Students: A Handbook for Educators* (pp. 130–144). Boston: College Hill.

Council for Exceptional Children (CEC). (2001). *What Every Special Educator Must Know: The Standards for the Preparation and Licensure of Special Educators.* Reston, VA: Author.

Coyne Cutler, B. (1993). *You, Your Child, and "Special" Education: A Guide to Making the System Work.* Baltimore: Brookes.

Cronin, S. (1998). Culturally Relevant Antibias Learning Communities: Teaching Umoja. In L. H. Meyer, H. S. Park, M. Grenot-Scheyer, I. S. Schwartz, & B. Harry (Eds.), *Making Friends: The Influences of Culture and Development* (pp. 341–351). Baltimore: Brookes.

Derman-Sparks, L., & ABC Task Force. (1989). *Anti-Bias Curriculum: Tools for Empowering Young Children.* Washington, DC: National Association for the Education of Young Children.

Dieker, L., Voltz, D., & Epanchin, B. (2002). Report of the Wingspread Conference: Preparing Teachers to Work with Diverse Learners. *Teacher Education and Special Education, 25,* 1–10.

Divergent Youth (Report of the Senate Fact Finding Committee on Education: Subcommittee on Special Education). (1963). Washington, DC: U.S. Government Printing Office.

Donovan, S., & Cross, C. (2002). *Minority Students in Special and Gifted Education.* National Academy of Sciences. Washington, DC: National Academy Press.

Dunn, L. (1968). Special Education for the Mildly Retarded: Is Much of It Justifiable? *Exceptional Children, 35,* 5–22.

Evans, I. M., Okifuji, A., & Thomas, A. D. (1995). Home–School Partnerships: Involving Families in the Educational Process. In I. M. Evans, T. Cicchelli, M. Cohen, & N. P. Shapiro (Eds.), *Staying in School: Partnerships for Educational Change* (pp. 23–40). Baltimore: Brookes.

Evans, I M., Salisbury, C. L., Palombaro, M. M., Berryman, J., & Hollowood, T. M. (1992). Peer Interactions and Social Acceptance of Elementary-Age Children with Severe Disabilities in an Inclusive School. *Journal of the Association for Persons with Severe Handicaps, 17,* 205–212.

Figler, C. S. (1981). *Puerto Rican Families with and without Handicapped Children.* Paper presented at the Council for Exceptional Children Conference on the Exceptional Bilingual Child, New Orleans. (ERIC Document Reproduction Service No. ED 204 876)

Finn, J. D. (1982). Patterns in Special Education Placement as Revealed by the OCR Surveys. In K. A. Heller, W. H. Holtzman, & S. Mesrick (Eds), *Placing Children in Special Education: A Strategy for Equity* (pp. 322–381). Washington, DC: National Academy Press.

Fisher, M., Bernazzani, J., & Meyer, L. H. (1998). Participatory Action Research: Supporting Social Relationships in the Cooperative Classroom. In J. Putnam (Ed.), *Cooperative Learning and Strategies for Inclusion: Celebrating Diversity in the Classroom* (2nd ed., pp. 137–165). Baltimore: Brookes.

Fisher, M., & Meyer, L. H. (2002). Development and Social Competence after Two Years for Students Enrolled in Inclusive and Self-Contained Educational Programs. *Research and Practice for Persons with Severe Disabilities, 27,* 165–174.

Fujiura, G. T., & Yamaki, K. (2000). Trends in Demography of Childhood Poverty and Disability. *Exceptional Children, 66,* 187–199.

Gardner, H. (1993). *Multiple Intelligences: The Theory in Practice.* New York: Basic Books.

Gartner, A., & Lipsky, D. K. (1987). Beyond Special Education: Toward a Quality System for All Students. *Harvard Educational Review, 57,* 367–395.

Geenen, S., Powers, L. E., & Lopez-Vasquez, A. (2001). Multicultural Aspects of Parent Involvement in Transition Planning. *Exceptional Children, 67,* 265–282.

Goessling, D. P. (1998). Inclusion and the Challenge of Assimilation for Teachers of Students with Severe Disabilities. *Journal of the Association for Persons with Severe Handicaps, 23,* 238–251.

Goldstein, S., & Turnbull, A. P. (1982). The Use of Two Strategies to Increase Parent Participation in IEP Conferences. *Exceptional Children, 48,* 360–361.

Gottlieb, J., Alter, M., Gottlieb, B. W., & Wishner, J. (1994). Special Education in Urban America: It's Not Justifiable for Many. *Journal of Special Education, 27,* 453–465.

Harry, B. (1992). *Cultural Diversity, Families, and the Special Education System: Communication for Empowerment.* New York: Teachers College Press.

Harry, B., Allen, N., & McLaughlin, M. (1995). Communication vs. Compliance: African American Parents' Involvement in Special Education. *Exceptional Children, 61,* 364–377.

Harry, B., Grenot-Scheyer, M., Smith-Lewis, M., Park, H.-S., Xin, F., & Schwartz, I. (1995). Developing Culturally Inclusive Services for Individuals with Severe Disabilities. *Journal of the Association for Persons with Severe Handicaps, 20,* 99–109.

Harry, B., & Kalyanpur, M. (1994). The Cultural Underpinnings of Special Education: Implications for Professional Interactions with Culturally Diverse Families. *Disability, Handicap, and Society, 9*(2), 145–166.

Hedeen, D. L., Ayres, B. J., & Tate, A. (2001). Getting Better, Happy Day, Problems Again! The Ups and Downs of Supporting a Student with Autism in Her Home School. In M. Grenot-Scheyer, M. Fisher, & D. Staub (Eds.), *At the End of the Day: Stories of Ordinary Lives of Children and Youth in Inclusive Schools and Communities* (pp. 47–72). Baltimore: Brookes.

Horner, R. H., Meyer, L. H., & Fredericks, H. D. B. (Eds.). (1986). *Education of Learners with Severe Handicaps: Exemplary Service Strategies.* Baltimore: Brookes.

Kagan, S. (1998). New Cooperative Learning, Multiple Intelligences, and Inclusion. In J. W. Putnam (Ed.), *Cooperative Learning and Strategies for Inclusion* (2nd ed.). Baltimore: Brookes.

Kalyanpur, M., & Harry, B. (1999). *Culture in Special Education: Building Reciprocal Parent–Professional Relationships.* Baltimore: Brookes.

Kleinert, H. L., Kearns, J. F., & Kennedy, S. (1997). Accountability for All Students: Kentucky's Alternate Portfolio Assessment for Students with Moderate and Severe Cognitive Disabilities. *Journal of the Association for Persons with Severe Handicaps, 22,* 88–101.

Lindsey, R. B., Robins, K. N., & Terrell, R. D. (1999). *Cultural Proficiency: A Manual for School Leaders.* Thousand Oaks, CA: Corwin.

MacMillan, D. L., Jones, R. L., & Meyers, C. E. (1976). Mainstreaming the Mildly Retarded: Some Questions, Cautions and Guidelines. *Mental Retardation, 14,* 3–10.

Malmberg, P. A. (1984). *Development of Field Tested Special Education Placement Committee Parent Education Materials.* Unpublished doctoral dissertation, Virginia Polytechnic Institute and State University, Blacksburg.

Meier, K. J., Stewart, J., & England, R. E. (1989). *Race, Class, and Education: The Politics of Second-Generation Discrimination.* Madison: University of Wisconsin Press.

Mercer, J. R. (1973). Labeling the Mentally Retarded: Clinical and Social System Perspectives on Mental Retardation. Berkeley: University of California Press.

Mercer, J. R. (1979). *System of Multicultural Pluralistic Assessment: Technical Manual.* Cleveland, OH: The Psychological Corporation.

Meyer, L. H. (1997). Tinkering around the Edges? *Journal of the Association for Persons with Severe Handicaps, 22,* 80–82.

Meyer, L. H., & Fisher, M. (1999). Participatory Research on Strategies to Support Inclusion. In *SET 1999: Special Education.* Wellington, New Zealand: New Zealand Council for Educational Research.

Meyer, L. H., Mager, G. M., Yarger-Kane, G., Sarno, M., & Hext-Contreras, G. (1997). Syracuse University's Inclusive Elementary and Special Education Program. In L. P. Blanton, C. C. Griffin, J. A. Winn, & M. C. Pugach (Eds.), *Teacher Education in Transition: Collaborative Progams to Prepare General and Special Educators* (pp. 18–38). Denver, CO: Love.

Meyer, L. H., Minondo, S., Fisher, M., Larson, M. J., Dunmore, S., Black, J. W., & D'Aquanni, M. (1998). Frames of Friendship: Social Relationships among Adolescents with Diverse Abilities. In L. H. Meyer, H.-S. Park, M. Grenot-Scheyer, I. S. Schwartz, & B. Harry (Eds.), *Making Friends: The Influences of Culture and Development* (pp. 189–221). Baltimore: Brookes.

Meyer, L. H., & Park, H.-S. (1999). Contemporary Most Promising Practices for People with Disabilities. In J. S. Scotti & L. H. Meyer (Eds.), *Behavioral Intervention: Principles, Models, and Practices* (pp. 25–45). Baltimore: Brookes.

Meyer, L. H., Park, H. S., Grenot-Scheyer, M., Schwartz, I. & Harry, B. (1998). Participatory Research: New Approaches to the Research to Practice Dilemma. *Journal of the Association for Persons with Severe Handicaps, 23,* 165–177.

Meyer, L. H., Williams, D. R., Harootunian, B., & Steinberg, A. (1995). An Inclusion Model to Reduce At-Risk Status among Middle School Students: The Syracuse Experience. In I. M. Evans, T. Chicchelli, M. Cohen, & N. Shapiro (Eds.), *Staying in School: Partnerships for Educational Change* (pp. 83–110). Baltimore: Brookes.

National Association of State Boards of Education. (1992). *Winners All: A Call for Inclusive Schools.* Alexandria, VA: Author.

National Council of Teachers of Mathematics. (1993). *Curriculum and Evaluation Standards for School Mathematics*. Reston, VA: Author.

Noddlings, N. (1992). *The Challenge to Care in Schools: An Alternative Approach to Education*. New York: Teachers College Press.

Ornelles, C., & Goetz, L. (2001). Considerations for Changing Populations: Supporting Nontraditional Students in Acquiring Special Educators Licensure. *Journal of the Association for Persons with Severe Handicaps, 26*, 171–179.

Oswald, D. P., Coutinho, M. J., Best, A. M., & Singh, N. N. (1999). Ethnic Representation in Special Education: The Influence of School-Related Economic and Demographic Variables. *The Journal of Special Education, 32*, 194–206.

Park, H. S., & Lian, M-G. J. (Eds.). (2001). Culturally and Linguistically Diverse Learners: Issues and Practices [Special issue]. *The Journal of the Association for Persons with Severe Handicaps, 26*(3).

Park, J., Turnbull, A. P., & Turnbull, H. R. (2002). Impacts of Poverty on Quality of Life in Families of Children with Disabilities. *Exceptional Children, 68*, 151–170.

Patton, J. M. (1998). The Disproportionate Representation of African Americans in Special Education: Looking behind the Curtain for Understanding and Solutions. *The Journal of Special Education, 32*, 25–31.

Patton, J. M., & Townsend, B. (1999). Ethics, Power, and Privilege: Neglected Considerations in the Education of African American Learners with Special Needs. *Teacher Education and Special Education, 22*, 276–286.

Porter, G. L., & Stone, J. A. (1998). The Inclusive School Model: A Framework and Key Strategies for Success. In J. W. Putnam (Ed.), *Cooperative Learning and Strategies for Inclusion: Celebrating Diversity in the Classroom* (2nd ed., pp. 229–248). Baltimore: Brookes.

Pugach, M. C., & Johnson, L. J. (1995). *Collaborative Practitioners, Collaborative Schools*. Denver, CO: Love.

Putnam, J. (Ed.). (1998). *Cooperative Learning and Strategies for Inclusion: Celebrating Diversity in the Classroom* (2nd ed.). Baltimore: Brookes.

Ramsey, P. G. (1998). *Teaching and Learning in a Diverse World: Multicultural Education for Young Children* (2nd ed.). New York: Teachers College Press.

Richardson, J. G. (1994). Common, Delinquent, and Special: On the Formalization of Common Schooling in the American States. *American Educational Research Journal, 31*, 695–723.

Roach, V. (1994). The Superintendent's Role in Creating Inclusive Schools. *The School Administrator, 52*(4), 64–70.

Ryndak, D. L., Morrison, A. P., & Sommerstein, L. (1999). Literacy before and after Inclusion in General Education Settings: A Case Study. *Journal of the Association for Persons with Severe Handicaps, 24*, 5–22.

Salisbury, C. L., Palombaro, M. M., & Hollowood, T. M. (1993). On the Nature and Change of an Inclusive Elementary School. *Journal of the Association for Persons with Severe Handicaps, 18*, 75–84.

Sanchez, S. (1999). Learning from the Stories of Culturally and Linguistically Diverse Families and Communities. *Remedial and Special Education, 20*, 351–359.

Sapon-Shevin, M. (1992). Celebrating Diversity, Creating Community: Curriculum That Honors and Builds on Differences. In S. Stainback & W. Stainback (Eds.), *Curriculum Considerations in Inclusive Classrooms: Facilitating Learning for All Students* (pp. 19–36). Baltimore: Brookes.

Sapon-Shevin, M. (1994). *Playing Favorites: Gifted Education and the Disruption of Community.* Albany: State University of New York Press.

Sapon-Shevin, M. (1999). *Because We Can Change the World: A Practical Guide to Building Cooperative, Inclusive Classroom Communities.* Boston: Allyn & Bacon.

Sapon-Shevin, M. (2001). Making Inclusive Visible: Honoring the Process and the Struggle. *Democracy and Education, 14,* 24–27.

Sapon-Shevin, M., Ayres, B., & Duncan, J. (2002). Cooperative Learning and Inclusion. In J. Thousand, R. Villa, & A. Nevin (Eds.), *Creativity and Collaborative Learning: The Practical Guide to Empowering Students, Teachers and Families* (2nd ed., pp. 209–221). Baltimore: Brookes.

Schnorr, R. F. (1997). From Enrollment to Membership: "Belonging" in Middle and High School Classes. *Journal of the Association for Persons with Severe Handicaps, 22,* 1–15.

Skinner, D., Rodriguez, P., & Bailey, D. B., Jr. (1999). Qualitative Analysis of Latino Parents' Religious Interpretations of their Childrens' Disabilities. *Journal of Early Intervention, 22,* 271–285.

Smith, G. R. (1983). Desegregation and assignment of children to classes for the mentally retarded and learning disabled. *Integrated Education, 21,* 208–211.

Smith, L. T. (1999). *Decolonizing Methodologies: Research and Indigenous Peoples.* London: Zed.

Smith, R. M. (1997). Varied Meanings and Practice: Teachers' Perspectives Regarding High School Inclusion. *Journal of the Association for Persons with Severe Handicaps, 22,* 235–244.

Tharp, R. G., & Gallimore, R. (1989). *Rousing Minds to Life: Teaching, Learning and Schooling in Social Context.* New York: Cambridge University Press.

Thompson, T. M. (1982). An Investigation and Comparison of Public School Personnel's Perception and Interpretation of P.L. 94–142. *Dissertation Abstracts International, 43,* 2840A.

Torres-Velasquez, D. (Ed.). (2000). Sociocultural Perspectives in Special Education [Special issue]. *Remedial and Special Education, 21*(2).

Townsend, B. L. (1998). Social Friendships and Networks among African American Children and Youth. In L. H. Meyer, H. S. Park, M. Grenot-Scheyer, I. S. Schwartz, & B. Harry (Eds.), *Making Friends: The Influences of Culture and Development* (pp. 225–241). Baltimore: Brookes.

Trent, S. C., Artiles, A. J., & Englert, C. S. (1998). From Deficit Thinking to Social Constructivism: A Review of Theory, Research, and Practice in Special Education. *Review of Research in Education, 23* (pp. 277–307). Washington, DC: American Educational Research Association.

Trent, S. C., Artiles, A. J., Fitchett-Bazemore, K., McDaniel, L., & Coleman-Sorrell, A. (2002). Addressing Theory, Ethics, Power, and Privilege in Inclusion Research and Practice. *Teacher Education and Special Education, 25,* 11–22.

Tucker, J. A. (1980). Ethnic Proportions in Classes for the Learning Disabled: Issues in Nonbiased Assessment. *Journal of Special Education, 14,* 93–105.

Turnbull, A. P., & Turnbull, H. R. (1997). *Families, Professionals, and Exceptionality: A Special Partnership* (3rd ed.). Upper Saddle River, NJ: Prentice-Hall.

Tyler, N., & Smith, D. D. (2000). Preparation of Culturally and Linguistically Diverse Special Educators [Special issue]. *Teacher Education and Special Education, 23*(4).

U. S. Department of Education, Office of Civil Rights. (1994). *1992 Elementary and Secondary Civil Rights Compliance Report.* Washington, DC: U.S. Government Printing Office.

Vygotsky, L. S. (1978). *Mind in Society: The Development of Higher Psychological Processes* (M. Cole, V. John-Steiner, S. Scribner, & E. Souberman, Eds. and Trans.). Cambridge, MA: Harvard University Press.

Webb-Johnson, G. C. (1999). Cultural Contexts: Confronting the Overrepresentation of African American Learners in Special Education. In J. S. Scotti & L. H. Meyer (Eds.), *Behavioral Intervention: Principles, Models, and Practices* (pp. 449–464). Baltimore: Brookes.

Wells, A. S., & Crain, R. L. (1994). Perpetuation Theory and the Long-Term Effects of School Desegregation. *Review of Educational Research, 64,* 531–555.

Will, M. (1986). Educating Children with Learning Problems: A Shared Responsibility. *Exceptional Children, 52,* 411–415.

Winn, J., & Blanton, J. (1997). The Call for Collaboration in Teacher Education. In L. P. Blanton, C. C. Griffin, J. A. Winn, & M. C. Pugach (Eds.), *Teacher Education in Transition: Collaborative "Programs" to Prepare General and Special Educators* (pp. 1–17). Denver, CO: Love.

CHAPTER 15

Recruiting and Retaining Gifted Students from Diverse Ethnic, Cultural, and Language Groups

Donna Y. Ford

One of the most persistent and pervasive educational problems is the underrepresentation of African American, Hispanic American, and Native American students in gifted education programs and services. More than seven decades of reports indicate that these students have always been inadequately represented and underserved in gifted education (Artiles, Trent, & Palmer, 2004; Donovan & Cross, 2002; Ford, 1998). Statistics show that these three groups are underrepresented by 50 to 70 percent (U.S. Department of Education [USDE], 1993). The data in Table 15.1 support the notion that "a mind is a terrible thing to waste," a statement popularized by the United Negro College Fund. These data also support the reality that a mind is a

Table 15.1   Demographics of Gifted Education Programs

	School Population %	Gifted Education %
White, non-Hispanic	62.1	75.53
African American	17.2	8.40
Hispanic	15.6	8.63
Asian American	4.0	6.57
Native American/Alaskan Native	1.2	0.87

Sources: Elementary and Secondary School Civil Rights Survey (1998): www.demo.beyond2020.com/ocrpublic/eng. National Center for Education Statistics. (2001). *Common Core of Data (CCD), State Nonfiscal Survey of Public Elementary/Secondary Education, 1999–2000* (Appendix E, Table 5). Washington, DC: U.S. Department of Education. Available online at: http://nces.ed.gov/ccd/pdf/stNfis99genr.pdf.

terrible thing to erase. In other words, many African American, Hispanic American, and Native American students are gifted but unidentified. Consequently, they are neither challenged nor given the opportunity to develop their gifts and talents, which atrophy.

ASSUMPTIONS OF THE CHAPTER

This chapter explores barriers to and recommendations for recruiting and retaining racial and ethnic minority students into gifted education programs. In particular, I present data on the underrepresentation of African Americans students in gifted education. Asian Americans are also racial and ethnic minority students. However, I have yet to find a report indicating that Asian Americans students are underrepresented in gifted education. Consequently, they are not discussed in this chapter. Asian Americans, unlike African American, Hispanic American, and Native American students, frequently experience positive stereotypes. Many are high achieving. By omitting Asian American students from this chapter, I am not ignoring the social injustices they have experienced and continue to experience in society and in the schools (Pang et al., 2004).

This chapter is grounded in several assumptions and propositions. First, I propose that the majority of past and current efforts to redress the underrepresentation problem have been inadequate and misdirected, resulting in what may be the most segregated programs in our public schools. Second, gifted education is a need—not a privilege. By not being identified as gifted and placed in gifted programs, gifted students from racial, ethnic, and language minorities are being denied an education that meets their needs. Consequently, educators need to examine their views about the purposes of education in general and gifted education in particular.

A third assumption and proposition is that no group has a monopoly on "giftedness." Giftedness exists in every cultural group and across all economic strata (USDE, 1993). Consequently, there should be little or no underrepresentation of racial and ethnic minority students in gifted education. A fourth assumption and proposition is that giftedness is a social construct; subjectivity guides definitions, assessments, and perceptions of giftedness (Sternberg, 1985). This subjectivity contributes to segregated gifted education programs in numerous and insidious ways. Sapon-Shevon (1996) states that "the ways in which gifted education is defined, constituted, and enacted lead directly to increased segregation, limited educational opportunities for the majority of students, and damage to children's social and political developments" (p. 196).

The fifth guiding assumption is that all decisions made on behalf of students should be made with their best interests in mind. Education should be additive for students, not subtractive. We should be about the business of building on what students have when they enter and leave our schools. Finally, I believe that efforts to recruit and retain racial and ethnic minority students in gifted education must be comprehensive and systematic. Educators, families, and children themselves need to work together to ensure that gifted education is desegregated.

This chapter is divided into three major sections. The first section focuses on recruitment issues and barriers, the second on recruitment recommendations, and the third on retention recommendations. The guiding question of the chapter is: How can we recruit and retain more racial and ethnic minority students in gifted education?

RECRUITMENT ISSUES AND BARRIERS

Most of the scholarship that explains underrepresentation focuses on recruitment. Specifically, it is assumed that racial and ethnic minority students are underrepresented because of problems associated with screening and identification instruments, specifically tests. Little attention has been given to retention, which is discussed later in this chapter.

The first step in addressing (or redressing) the underrepresentation of racial and ethnic minority students in gifted education is to focus on recruitment. Recruitment relates to screening, identification, and placement (or getting students into gifted education). Perceptions about racial and ethnic minority students combined with a lack of cultural understanding significantly undermine the ability of educators to recruit diverse students into gifted education and to retain them. Elsewhere, I have argued that a "cultural deficit" perspective pervades decisions made about and on behalf of African American, Hispanic American, and Native American students (Ford, Harris, Tyson, & Frazier Trotman, 2002). This phenomenon is described below.

Deficit Thinking

> The more we retreat from the culture and the people, the less
> we learn about them. The less we know about them, the more
> uncomfortable we feel among them. The more uncomfortable we
> feel among them, the more inclined we are to withdraw. The more
> we withdraw from the people, the more faults we find with them.
> The less we know about their culture, the more we seem to dislike it.
> And the worst of it is that, in the end, we begin to believe the very
> lies we've invented to console ourselves (Storti, 1989, pp. 32–34).

A major premise of this chapter is that a deficit orientation held by educators hinders access to gifted programs for diverse students, as reflected in the above quote. This thinking hinders the ability and willingness of educators to recognize the strengths of students from diverse ethnic, racial, and language groups. Deficit thinking exists when educators interpret differences as deficits, dysfunctions, and disadvantages. Consequently, many diverse students quickly acquire the "at-risk" label and there is a focus on their shortcomings rather than their strengths. With deficit thinking, differences are interpreted negatively as if they are abnormal, substandard, or otherwise inferior. For example, when a student speaks nonstandard English and is making good grades in school, he may not be referred to screening and identification if the teacher neither understands nor appreciates nonstandard English. Likewise, if a student has excellent math skills but weak writing skills, she may not be perceived as gifted or intelligent. All children have strengths and weaknesses. Educators need to move beyond a deficit orientation in order to recognize the strengths of students from racial, ethnic, and language minorities.

Ideas about racial groups influence the development of definitions, policies, and practices designed to understand and deal with differences. For instance, Gould (1981/1995) and Menchaca (1997) noted that deficit thinking contributed to past (and, no doubt, current) beliefs about race/ethnicity and intelligence. Gould takes readers back two centuries to demonstrate how *a priori* assumptions and fears associated with different ethnic groups, particularly African Americans, led to conscious fraud—dishonest and prejudicial research methods, deliberate miscalculations, convenient omissions, and data misinterpretation among scientists studying intelligence. These early assumptions and practices gave way to the prevailing belief that human races could be ranked in a linear scale of mental worth, as evidenced by the research of Cyril Burt, Paul Broca, and Samuel Morten on craniometry (Gould, 1981/1995).

Later, as school districts faced increasing ethnic/racial diversity (often attributable to immigration), educators resorted to increased reliance on biased standardized tests (Armour-Thomas, 1992; Gould, 1981/1995; Helms, 1992; Menchaca, 1997). These tests almost guaranteed low test scores for immigrants and racial and ethnic minority groups who were unfamiliar with U.S. customs, traditions, values, norms, and language. These tests measured familiarity with mainstream American culture and English proficiency, not intelligence. According to Gould (1981/1995), intelligence tests provide limited information about racial and ethnic minority populations. The results from these tests often limited the educational opportunities of diverse students, who tended not to score high on them. Menchaca (1997) stated:

> Racial differences in intelligence, it was contended, are most
> validly explained by racial differences in innate, genetically
> determined abilities. What emerged from these findings regarding
> schooling were curricular modifications ensuring that the
> "intellectually inferior" and the social order would best be served
> by providing these students concrete, low-level, segregated
> instruction commensurate with their alleged diminished intellectual
> abilities. (p. 38)

The publication of *The Bell Curve* (Herrnstein & Murray, 1994) revived deficit thinking. Seeking to influence public and social policy, Herrnstein and Murray, like researchers of earlier centuries, interpreted—or misinterpreted and misrepresented—their data to confirm institutionalized prejudices. As Gould (1981/1995) noted, the hereditarian theory of IQ is a homegrown American product that persists in current practices of testing, sorting, and discarding. Issues associated with screening support this assertion.

Screening Issues and Barriers

To be considered for placement in gifted education, students often undergo screening in which they are administered assessments with predetermined criteria (e.g., cutoff scores). If students meet the initial screening requirements, they may be given additional assessments, which are used to make final placement decisions. In most schools, entering the screening pool is based on teacher referrals (Colangelo & Davis, 2003). This practice hinders the effective screening of racial and ethnic minority students because they are seldom referred by teachers for screening (Ford, 1996). Specifically, a Hispanic American student may meet the school district's criteria for giftedness but be overlooked because she has not been referred for screening. The teacher may not refer this student because of her biases and stereotypes about Hispanic Americans (deficit thinking), because the student's English skills are not strong, or because of many of the teacher's perceptual and attitudinal barriers. Intuitively, it makes sense that teacher referrals should be used as part of the screening or decision-making process. As the above example illustrates, however, this practice may negatively affect racial and ethnic minority students.

Similarly, teachers and other adults (e.g., counselors, parents, community members) may be required to complete checklists on the referred students. If the checklists ignore cultural diversity—how giftedness manifests itself differently in various cultures—then gifted diverse students may receive low ratings that do not accurately capture their strengths, abilities, and potential. A framework proposed by Frasier et al. (1995) describes how the core attributes of giftedness vary by culture. They contended that educators should define and assess giftedness with each group's cultural differences in mind. As an illustration, one core characteristic of giftedness is a keen sense of humor. A common verbal game—or match—among low-income African Americans is "playing the dozens" or "signifying" (Lee, 1993). African American students are exemplifying two characteristics of giftedness when playing the dozens—humor and verbal skills. Teachers may be offended by the students' humor, blinding them from seeing this core characteristic of giftedness.

Another core characteristic of giftedness is strong verbal skills. However, if the student does not speak standard English (but, e.g., Ebonics) or has limited English proficiency, the teacher may not recognize the student's strong verbal skills. A third example relates to independence, which is another essential characteristic of giftedness. Racial and ethnic minority students who have communal values, such as interdependence and cooperation, may be social and prefer to work in groups rather than individually (Ramírez & Castañeda, 1974). Consequently, the teacher may not consider such students to be independent workers.

In addition to checklists being "culture-blind," they frequently focus on demonstrated ability and performance. As a result, they overlook students who are gifted but lack opportunities to demonstrate their ability and achievement. These "potentially gifted" students and/or gifted underachievers are those who live in poverty and/or are culturally different from mainstream students. A study by Smith, Constantino, and Krashen (1997) sheds light on this issue. These researchers compared the number of books in the homes and classrooms of three California communities. There was an average of 199 books in the homes of Beverly Hills children, 4 in the homes of Watts children, and 2.7 in the homes of Compton children. In terms of classrooms, there was an average of 392 books in Beverly Hills classrooms, 54 in Watts classrooms, and 47 in Compton classrooms. Essentially, because of exposure to books and educational opportunities, children from Beverly Hills homes and schools are more likely to demonstrate their giftedness (e.g., have a large vocabulary, be able to read at an early age) than are children from the other homes and schools. Many children in Compton and Watts are gifted but lack essential academic experiences and exposure to develop their abilities and potential.

In 1993, the U.S. Department of Education recognized that our schools are filled with potentially gifted students. To help educators improve the recruitment of diverse students into gifted education, the department issued the following definition of giftedness, one that relies heavily on the notion of talent development:

> Children and youth with outstanding talent perform or show
> the potential for performing at remarkably high levels of
> accomplishment when compared with others of their age,

experience, or environment. These children and youth exhibit high performance capacity in intellectual, creative, and/or artistic areas, possess an unusual leadership capacity, or excel in specific academic fields. They require services or activities not ordinarily provided by the schools. Outstanding talents are present in children and youth from all cultural groups, across all economic strata, and in all areas of human endeavor. (USDE, 1993, p. 3)

The percentage of school districts adopting this definition or some version of it is unknown. The ramifications of not adopting the federal definition, or some version of it, are clear—continued underrepresentation of students from racial, ethnic and language minorities in gifted education.

Identification/Assessment Issues and Barriers

Monolithic definitions of *giftedness* pose serious barriers to recruiting diverse students into gifted education. Monolithic definitions ignore human differences in general and cultural diversity in particular. They ignore the fact that what is valued as giftedness in one culture may not be valued in another. For example, most European Americans highly value cognitive and academic ability over spatial, musical, interpersonal, and other abilities (Gardner, 1993) and tend to value academic knowledge and skills over tacit or practical knowledge and skills (Sternberg, 1985). Conversely, navigational skills or hunting skills may be prized in another culture. These differences raise the question: "If a student is not gifted in the ways that are valued by my culture, is she gifted?" Based on current practice, most culturally different students are not likely to be perceived as gifted.

Perceptions and definitions also influence the instruments or tests selected to assess giftedness. Dozens of intelligence and achievement tests exist. What determines which instrument a school district selects? If we value verbal skills, we will select an instrument that assesses verbal skills. If we value logic and/or problem-solving skills, we will select an instrument that assesses these skills. If we value creativity, the instrument we select will assess creativity. We are not likely to choose an instrument that measures a construct or skill that we do not value.

Accordingly, many schools use intelligence and achievement tests—more than other types of tests—to assess giftedness. Test scores play a dominant role in identification and placement decisions. For example, a study by Van Tassel-Baska, Patton, and Prillaman (1989) revealed that 88.5 percent of states rely primarily on standardized, norm-referenced tests to identify gifted students, including those from economically and culturally diverse groups. More than 90 percent of school districts use scores from these types of tests for labeling and placement (Colangelo & Davis, 2003; Davis & Rimm, 1997). These tests measure verbal skills, abstract thinking, math skills, and other skills considered indicative of giftedness (or intelligence or achievement) by educators. Likewise, they ignore skills and abilities that may be also valued by other groups (e.g., creativity, communication skills, interpersonal skills, problem-solving skills, navigational skills, musical skills). Consequently, racial and ethnic minority students are more likely than others to display characteristics that place them at a disadvantage in testing situations (Helms, 1992). Monolithic definitions result in the adoption of unidimensional, ethnocentric tests that contribute significantly to racially homogeneous gifted education programs. These tests are more effective at identifying giftedness among middle-class White students than among racial and ethnic minority students, particularly if these students are from low socioeconomic status (SES) backgrounds.

An additional concern related to tests is the extensive use of cutoff scores, referred to earlier. The most frequently used cutoff score for placement in gifted education is an IQ score of 130 or above, two standard deviations above the average IQ of 100 (Colangelo & Davis, 2003). Decades of data indicate that groups such as African Americans, Puerto Rican Americans, and Native Americans have mean IQ scores lower than White students, even at the highest economic levels. For the most part, the average IQ of African Americans is 83 to 87, compared to 97 to 100 for White students (see Helms, 1992; Kaufman, 1994). I have consulted with several psychologists who believe that because the "average" IQ score of African Americans is about 85, giftedness would mean an IQ of 115 or higher among this population. The same holds for children who live in poverty, regardless of racial background. Their average IQ is about 85.

Sadly, those holding racist ideologies will attribute these differences to genetics and argue that giftedness is inherited. This position implies that the environment is less important than heredity in the development of talents and abilities. Such a view is counterproductive in education, which is supposed to build upon and improve the skills and abilities of students.

Conversely, those who recognize the influence of the environment and culture on performance attribute these different scores primarily to social, environmental and cultural factors. For instance, it has been demonstrated in numerous studies on "environmental racism" that poverty, exposure to lead, malnutrition, and poor educational experiences negatively affect test performance (Baugh, 1991; Bryant & Mohai, 1992; Bullard, 1993; Dwight, 1994; Grossman, 1991). Thus, cutoff scores cannot be selected arbitrarily and in a culture-blind fashion. If used at all, cutoff scores should be used with caution and should take into consideration the different mean scores of different racial, ethnic, cultural, and language groups.

A final issue related to testing is interpreting results. When other information is considered, it is possible to select and use a test that effectively assesses the strengths of racial and ethnic minority students. However, perceptions can prevent a teacher, counselor, or psychologist from interpreting the results in a culturally fair way. What if a teacher, counselor, or psychologist interpreting the test results holds negative stereotypes about African Americans? What if the counselor holds stereotypes about groups who have limited English proficiency? What if a student from these two groups receives a high IQ or achievement test score? How would this affect the psychologist's and counselor's interpretation of the results? Test interpretation is heavily subjective and interpretations are influenced by the quantity and quality of training to work with diverse cultural, ethnic, and language groups. Results from a "good" test can be poorly interpreted if the interpreter has little understanding of how culture influences test performance.

In a collaborative effort, the American Educational Research Association (AERA), the American Psychological Association (APA), and the National Council on Measurement in Education (NCME) (1999) addressed the myriad problems of interpreting test scores. They noted the harmful effects of misinterpreting test results, especially with racial and ethnic minority groups: "The ultimate responsibility for appropriate test use and interpretation lies predominantly with the test user. In assuming this responsibility, the user must become knowledgeable about a test's appropriate uses and the populations for which it is appropriate" (p. 112). They advise, as do others (e.g., National Council for Gifted Children, 1997), that test-users collect extensive data on students to complement tests and use a comprehensive approach in the assessment process (Armour-Thomas, 1992; Helms, 1992). Test-users are encouraged to consider the validity of a given instrument or procedure as well as the cultural characteristics of the student when interpreting results (Office of Ethnic Minority Affairs, 1993).

In sum, the data collected on all students should be multidimensional—a variety of information collected from multiple sources. For example, data are needed from school personnel, family members, and community members. Data on intelligence, achievement, creativity, motivation, and learning styles are essential when making decisions about students. In this era of high-stakes testing, educators should err on the side of having "too much" information rather than too little.

The data collected should also be multimodal and collected in a variety of ways. Information should be collected verbally (interviews, conversations) and nonverbally (e.g. observations, writing, performances), and both subjective and objective information should be gathered. Further, if the student speaks a first language other than English, educators should use an interpreter. Essentially, assessment should be made with the students' best interests in mind and the principle of "do no harm" should prevail. As noted by Sandoval, Frisby, Geisinger, Scheuneman, and Grenier (1998): "In any testing situation, but particularly high stakes assessments, examinees must have an opportunity to demonstrate the competencies, knowledge, or attributes being measured" (p. 183). Few equitable opportunities exist when assessments are ethnocentric and unidimensional, and when interpretations of test results ignore or trivialize the impact of culture.

After screening, the next step is placement considerations. As with screening, placement considerations are complex and riddled with potential problems.

Placement Issues and Barriers

Too often, giftedness is equated with achievement or productivity. To most educators and laypersons alike, the notion of a "gifted underachiever" may seem paradoxical. However, any educator who has taught students identified as gifted knows that gifted students can and do underachieve—some are unmotivated, some are procrastinators, some have learning disabilities, and some are uninterested in school. In my work with gifted African American students, I have observed about 80 percent of them underachieving (Ford, 1996). Other researchers, such as Rimm (1995) and Silverman (1993), believe that at least 20 percent of gifted students underachieve, especially gifted females (Reis & Callahan, 1989).

One problem associated with placement, therefore, is the belief that gifted students should receive gifted education services *if* they are high achievers and motivated. That is, achievement needs to be manifested (e.g., high grade point average [GPA] or high achievement test scores). Gifted underachievers are not likely to be referred or placed in gifted education. If placement occurs, it is often provisional. For example, several school districts will remove gifted students from a program if their GPA falls below a designated level, they fail a course, or have poor attendance that is unexcused. This situation of students meeting gifted education criteria (e.g., high test scores) but underachieving often arises when testing has been unidimensional—educators have focused solely on determining the students' IQ scores. Conversely, if intelligence *and* achievement data were collected during screening, educators would know whether the student is: (1) gifted and achieving or (2) gifted and underachieving. And they would make placement decisions based on these data. For example, they could place gifted underachievers in gifted education classes and provide them with a tutor. The objective would be to help gifted underachievers become achievers and experience success in gifted education classrooms.

Many students from racial, ethnic, and language minorities are likely to be gifted underachievers or potentially gifted students (Ford, 1996). Some educators do not wish to place these students in gifted education programs because they believe that the level and pace of the schoolwork may frustrate them. In theory, the issue of underachievers being overwhelmed in gifted education programs may be a valid concern, depending on why the students are underachieving. In practice, it has harmed gifted students who are members of racial, ethnic, and language minority groups.

Instead of supporting diverse students and helping them to overcome their weaknesses, educators have often chosen the option of least resistance under the guise of altruism. ("I don't want him to be frustrated." "She'll be unhappy." "He'll just fall further behind.") As we seek to prevent students from being frustrated, we should ask: "What are we doing to help to alleviate their frustration?" Tutoring, counseling, and other support systems are essential. When placement is combined with support, gifted underachieving students are more likely to be successful in gifted education programs.

As described below, recruiting students from diverse groups into gifted education programs is one thing; retaining them is another. What policies, practices, procedures, philosophies, and supports should be in place for diverse students to remain in gifted education?

RECRUITMENT RECOMMENDATIONS

Recruiting students from diverse groups into gifted education is the first half of resolving their underrepresentation in gifted education. As described below, recruitment should include a talent-development philosophy, changes in standardized tests and assessment practices, culturally sensitive tests, multicultural assessment preparation, and the development of policies and procedures.

Talent Development Philosophy

Educators who support a talent-development philosophy and culturally sensitive definitions of giftedness are more likely than others to have supports in place to assist students from diverse groups. For example, school districts would begin screening and placing students in gifted education at the preschool and primary levels. Currently, most gifted education programs begin in grades 2–4, which may be too late for potentially gifted students and those beginning to show signs of underachievement, commonly referred to as the second-grade syndrome. Abilities and talents should be recognized and nurtured early (USDE, 1993), especially among students already at risk of being unrecognized as gifted.

Changes in Standardized Tests and Assessment Practices

Tests standardized on middle-class White populations are here to stay, despite the reality that they are another form of discrimination favoring the privileged (Sowell, 1993). However, educators concerned about improving the test performance of diverse students on these instruments have a number of options to consider. First and foremost, they should never select, use, and interpret tests that lack validity for students from racial, ethnic, and language minorities. Second, they need to mesh the process of assessment with the cultural characteristics of the group being studied while recognizing that assessment is made culturally sensitive through a continuing and open-ended series of substantive and methodological insertions and adaptations (Suzuki, Meller, & Ponterotto, 1996). In essence, equitable and culturally sensitive assessment necessitates a combination of changed attitudes, accumulation of more knowledge, thoughtful practice, and development of keen insight into the dynamics of human behavior (Heubert & Hauser, 1999; Kornhaber, 2004; Sandoval et al. 1998). Tests should never be given so much power that other data are ignored—tests simply assist educators in making *conditional probability statements* on the basis of the particular test (Sandoval et al., 1998).

Culturally Sensitive Tests

Tests vary in the amount of language used in the directions and in the items. Educators need to recognize the limitations of information gathered from tests normed or standardized on middle-class White students. Much data indicate that the results from such tests may underestimate what students from racial, ethnic, and language minorities can do or misjudge behaviors to be abnormal and in need of intervention when, in reality, they are normal within a different cultural context (Dana, 1993; Mercer, 1973). To address these issues, educators will need to include more culturally sensitive tests, such as nonverbal tests, in screening and identification procedures (Naglieri & Ford, 2003; Sandoval et al., 1998). To date, the most promising instruments for assessing the strengths of African American students are such nonverbal tests of intelligence as the Naglieri Non-Verbal Abilities Test and Raven's Matrix Analogies Tests, which are considered less culturally loaded than traditional tests (Kaufman, 1994; Saccuzzo, Johnson, & Guertin, 1994).

Contrary to popular misconceptions, nonverbal tests do not mean that students are nonverbal. Rather nonverbal tests measure abilities nonverbally and rely less on language proficiency. Thus, the intelligence of students with limited English proficiency, bilingual students, and students who speak nonstandard English can be assessed with less reliance on language skills. Jensen (1980) distinguished between culturally loaded and culturally reduced tests. Culturally reduced tests are often performance based and include abstract figural and nonverbal content; culturally loaded tests have printed instructions, require reading, have verbal content, and require written responses. Essentially, nonverbal tests decrease the confounding effects of language skills on test performance and consequently increase the chances of students from diverse groups being identified as gifted.

Other testing accommodations in the best interest of diverse students include using tests that have been translated into different languages, using interpreters and translators when students are not proficient in English, and having educators who are bilingual and bicultural administer the tests.

Multicultural Assessment Preparation

Finally, on the issue of testing, multicultural assessment preparation is essential for any educator who administers, interprets, and uses results based on tests with diverse students

(AERA, APA, & NCME, 1999). As stated earlier, the test results are only as good as the test-taking situation, including the qualifications and competencies of the educator administering the test. Comas-Diaz (1996) has developed a list of cultural assessment variables with which educators should be familiar when making comprehensive assessments and interpreting results. These cultural assessment variables include information about the individual's heritage, religion, history of immigration, child-rearing practices, views about assimilation, language skills, gender roles, and views about authority figures and family structure.

Policies and Procedures

Students should be placed in gifted education based on multiple data, which are then used to create profiles of students' strengths and weaknesses. Consequently, recruitment becomes diagnostic and prescriptive. Strengths are used to place students in gifted education, and weaknesses are remediated rather than used as an excuse to avoid placement.

If teacher referral is the first step in the screening and placement process, and diverse students are underreferred and underidentified, then teachers are serving as gatekeepers and schools should reevaluate this practice. To qualify as a valid referral source, teachers require preparation in at least three areas: (1) gifted education, (2) urban and multicultural education, and (3) multicultural assessment (Ford & Frazier Trotman, 2001). Preparation in these areas prepares educators to be knowledgeable about gifted students from diverse groups, as well as the limitations of testing them.

RETENTION RECOMMENDATIONS

Half of our efforts to desegregate gifted education should focus on recruitment and half on retention. This section centers almost extensively on how multicultural education can be used to retain diverse students in gifted education. Just as important, teachers require substantive preparation in multicultural education to ensure that classrooms are culturally responsive and responsible (Ford & Frazier Trotman, 2001).

Multicultural Instruction

Boykin (1994), Saracho and Gerstl (1992), and Shade, Kelly, and Oberg (1997) are just a few of the scholars who have presented convincing research supporting the notion that culture influences learning styles and thinking styles. Due to space limitations, only Boykin's (1994) work will be discussed in this chapter. Before doing so, I want to add a word of caution. As noted by Irvine and York (2001), we must never adhere so strongly to generalizations or frameworks that they become stereotypes. Irvine and York point out that "negative teacher expectations can be fueled if teachers incorporate generalized and decontextualized observations about children of color without knowledge of the limitations of learning-styles labels" (p. 492). Although each of us belongs to several groups, we are nonetheless individuals first and foremost.

In his Afrocentric model, Boykin (1994) identifies nine cultural styles commonly found among African Americans: spirituality, harmony, oral tradition, affective orientation, communalism, verve, movement, social time perspective, and expressive individualism.

Movement refers to African Americans being tactile and kinesthetic learners who show a preference for being involved in learning experiences. They are active learners who are engaged when they are physically and psychologically involved. Otherwise, they may be easily distracted and go off-task. Harmony refers to an ability to read the environment well and to read nonverbal behaviors proficiently. Thus, students who feel unwelcome in their classes may become unmotivated and uninterested in learning. Communalism refers to a cooperative, interdependent style of living and learning in which competition—especially with friends—is devalued. Students with this learning preference may be unmotivated in highly individualistic and competitive classrooms, preferring instead to learn in groups.

Harmony and communalism may explain why an increasing number of African American students—especially middle school and high school students—are choosing not to be in gifted programs. They recognize that such programs are primarily composed of White students and express concerns about alienation and isolation (Ford, 1996). Further, communalism may result in some African American students shunning participation in gifted programs and equating high achievement with "acting White" (Fordham, 1988; Fordham & Ogbu, 1986). Educators who take the time to get to know racial and ethnic minority students and their families can avoid what I refer to as "drive-by teaching"—driving into racial and ethnic minority communities, teaching students who are strangers, and driving out of the community immediately after school. Drive-by teaching is counterproductive to students and the educational process in general. It does not give educators time to get to know and understand their students and fails to give students opportunities to get to know their teachers in meaningful ways.

Teachers should learn to modify their teaching styles to accommodate different learning styles. For example, to accommodate students' preference for communalism, teachers can use cooperative learning strategies and place students in groups (Cohen & Lotan, 2004). To accommodate the oral tradition as well as verve and movement, teachers can give students opportunities to write and perform skits, to make oral presentations, and to participate in debates. More examples of ways in which teachers can use culturally responsive teaching activities are described by Ford (1998), Shade et al. (1997), and Lee (1993).

Multicultural Gifted Curriculum

In the area of retention, curricular considerations are also critical. How to teach and what to teach gifted students have been discussed extensively by other scholars (e.g., Maker & Nielson, 1996; Tomlinson, 1995; VanTassel-Baska, 1994). These strategies, such as curriculum compacting, independent study, acceleration, and grade skipping will not be discussed here because of space limitations. While these strategies are certainly appropriate for gifted students from diverse groups, an equally important but overlooked retention recommendation is the need to create culturally responsive and responsible learning environments (Gay, 2000) and to ensure that the curriculum for gifted students is multicultural.

Ford and Harris (1999) have created a framework that uses Bloom's (1985) taxonomy and Banks's (2002; Chapter 10, this volume) multicultural education model to assist educators in developing learning experiences that are multicultural and challenging. The result is a twenty-four-cell matrix. The model is presented in Table 15.2. Four of the twenty-four levels in the model are described below (for a more complete discussion of the mode', see Ford & Harris, 1998).

Table 15.2   Ford-Harris Multicultural Gifted Education Framework—Description of Levels

	Knowledge	Comprehension	Application	Analysis	Synthesis	Evaluation
Contributions	Students are taught and know facts about cultural artifacts, events, groups, and other cultural elements.	Students show an understanding of information about cultural artifacts, groups, etc.	Students are asked to and can apply information learned about cultural artifacts, events, etc.	Students are taught to and can analyze (e.g., compare and contrast) information about cultural artifacts, groups, etc.	Students are required to and can create a new product from the information on cultural artifacts, groups, etc.	Students are taught to and can evaluate facts and information based on cultural artifacts, groups, etc.
Additive	Students are taught and know concepts and themes about cultural groups.	Students are taught and can understand cultural concepts and themes.	Students are required to and can apply information learned about cultural concepts and themes.	Students are taught to and can analyze important cultural concepts and themes.	Students are asked to and can synthesize important information on cultural concepts and themes.	Students are taught to and can critique cultural concepts and themes.
Transformation	Students are given information on important cultural elements, groups, etc., and can understand this information from different perspectives.	Students are taught to understand and can demonstrate an understanding of important cultural concepts and themes from different perspectives.	Students are asked to and can apply their understanding of important concepts and themes from different perspectives.	Students are taught to and can examine important cultural concepts and themes from more than one perspective.	Students are required to and can create a product based on their new perspective or the perspective of another group.	Students are taught to and can evaluate or judge important cultural concepts and themes from different viewpoints (e.g., minority group).
Social action	Based on information about cultural artifacts, etc., students make recommendations for social action.	Based on their understanding of important concepts and themes, students make recommendations for social action.	Students are asked to and can apply their understanding of important social and cultural issues; they make recommendations for and take action on these issues.	Students are required to and can analyze social and cultural issues from different perspectives; they take action on these issues.	Students create a plan of action to address a social and cultural issue(s); they seek important social change.	Students critique important social and cultural issues, and seek to make national and/or international change.

Note: Actions taken on the social action level can range from immediate and small scale (e.g., classroom and school level) to moderate (e.g., community or regional level) to large scale (state, national, and international levels). Likewise, students can make recommendations for action or actually take social action.

Source: Ford & Harris, 1999. Adapted from Banks, Chapter 10, this volume; Bloom, 1956.

At the knowledge–contributions level, students are provided information and facts about cultural heroes, holidays, events, and artifacts. For example, students might be taught about Martin Luther King, Jr., and then asked to recall three facts about him on a test. They might be introduced to Cinco de Mayo and be required to recite the year when it became a holiday.

At the comprehension–transformation level, students are required to explain what they have been taught—but from the perspective of another group or individual. For instance, students might be asked to explain the events that led to slavery in the United States and then to discuss how enslaved persons might have felt about being held captive. They might discuss the Trail of Tears from the perspective of a Native American child living when this event occurred.

At the analysis–social action level, students are asked to analyze an event from more than one point of view. Students might be asked to compare and contrast events during slavery with events associated with infractions of child labor laws today. Following these comparisons, students could be asked to develop a social action plan for eliminating illegal child labor.

At the evaluation–social action level, students might be asked to conduct a survey about prejudice in their local stores. This information could be given to store owners, along with a plan of action for change, such as developing a diversity-training program.

Multicultural education can engage students and give them opportunities to identify with, connect with, and relate to the curriculum. It consists of deliberate, ongoing, planned, and systematic opportunities to avoid drive-by teaching—to make learning meaningful and relevant to students, and to give racial and ethnic minority students mirrors in order to see themselves reflected in the curriculum. Multicultural gifted education challenges students culturally, affectively, academically, and cognitively.

Multicultural Counseling

Fordham and Ogbu (1986), Fordham (1998), and Ford (1998) have conducted research examining the concerns that high-achieving, gifted African American students have about being academically successful. A common finding is that many of these students are accused of "acting White" by other African American students because of their academic success. Such accusations can be frustrating, overwhelming, and unmotivating for students. Should an anti-achievement ethic be present in schools, educators should provide students—the accused and the accusers—with social-emotional and psychological supports. The students accused of acting White will need assistance with coping skills, conflict resolution skills, and anger management. The accusers will need assistance examining the negative implications—the self-defeating thoughts and behaviors—of an anti-achievement ethic. Peer-group counseling is one potentially powerful method for addressing these issues.

Skills-Based Supports

Retention efforts must also address and rectify skill deficits. As stated earlier, many diverse students are gifted but need support to maintain an acceptable level of achievement. Supportive systems include test-taking skills, study skills, time-management skills, and organizational skills.

Ongoing Professional Development in Multicultural Education and Counseling

In order to implement the above recommendations, educators should participate in ongoing and formal preparation in multicultural education and counseling. Whether in the form of courses or workshops, such preparation should focus on educators becoming culturally competent in the following areas:

1. Understanding cultural diversity and its impact on (a) teaching, (b) learning, and (c) assessment

2. Understanding the impact of biases and stereotypes on (a) teaching, (b) learning, and (c) assessment (e.g., referrals, testing, expectations)

3. Working effectively and proactively with (a) students from racial, ethnic, and language minorities, (b) their families, and (c) their community

4. Creating multicultural (a) curricula and (b) instruction

5. Creating culturally responsive (a) learning and (b) assessment environments

SUMMARY AND CONCLUSIONS

Gifted students are gifted twenty-four hours of the day. Racial and ethnic minority students are racial and ethnic minorities twenty-four hours of the day.

In 1954 the U.S. Supreme Court ruled deliberate (*de jure*) school segregation unconstitutional. Yet, *de facto* segregation persists in schools and in gifted education programs. Educators should focus extensively, consistently, and systematically on the many factors that contribute to and exacerbate the underrepresentation of students from racial, ethnic, and language minorities in gifted education. I have argued that a deficit orientation among educators, based primarily on a lack of understanding of culture, permeates all areas of recruitment and retention in gifted education programs. Deficit thinking has no place in education. Instead, educators should acknowledge the realities of the diversity in the world, in the United States, and in schools, and seek the resources and preparation needed to become culturally responsive and responsible professionals. Culturally competent educators are advocates for students from diverse racial, ethnic, cultural, and language groups. The multicultural philosophy and preparation of teachers will guide their referrals, instrument selection, test interpretation, and placement decisions that are essential for recruiting and retaining diverse students into gifted education programs.

Questions and Activities

1. Why, according to the author, are ethnic minority and low-income students underrepresented in school programs for gifted and talented youths?

2. What does the author mean by "deficit orientation" among educators regarding the education of gifted and talented minority students? In her view, how does deficit

thinking contribute to the underrepresentation of minority students in programs for gifted and talented students?

3. Why are many ethnic minority and low-income students likely to be gifted underachievers or potentially gifted students? Describe some specific actions that teachers can take to identify these students and to provide them the support they need to achieve at higher levels.

4. The author describes some ways in which culture influences learning and thinking. How might theories about culture and learning, such as those by Boykin and Shade and her colleagues, help teachers to better meet the needs of gifted talented and minority students? Do these theories have drawbacks and limitations? If so, what are they?

5. Visit a school in your community and interview teachers to determine: (1) the criteria used to identify students for gifted and talented programs; (2) the percentage of students from ethnic and language minority students who are in gifted and talented programs in the school; and (3) the steps that are taken by the school to recruit and retain students from low-income and minority groups into programs for gifted and talented students.

References

American Educational Research Association (AERA), American Psychological Association (APA), & National Council on Measurement in Education (NCME). (1999). *Standards for Educational and Psychological Testing.* Washington, DC: Author.

Armour-Thomas, E. (1992). Intellectual Assessment of Children from Culturally Diverse Backgrounds. *School Psychology Review, 21,* 552–565.

Artiles, A. J., Trent, S. C., & Palmer, J. D. (2004). Culturally Diverse Students in Special Education: Legacies and Prospects. In J. A. Banks & C. A. M. Banks (Eds.), *Handbook of Research on Multicultural Education* (2nd ed., pp. 716–735). San Francisco: Jossey-Bass.

Banks, J. A. (2002). *An Introduction to Multicultural Education* (3rd ed.). Boston: Allyn & Bacon.

Baugh, J. H. (1991). African Americans and the Environment: A Review Essay. *Policy Studies Journal, 19*(2), 182–191.

Bloom, B. (Ed.). (1956). *Taxonomy of Educational Objectives: The Classification of Educational Goals.* New York: McKay.

Boykin, A. W. (1994). Afrocultural Expression and Its Implications for Schooling. In E. R. Hollins, J. E. King, & W. C. Hayman (Eds.), *Teaching Diverse Populations: Formulating a Knowledge Base* (pp. 225–273). Albany: State University of New York Press.

Byrant, B., & Mohai, P. (Eds.). (1992). *Race and the Incidence of Environmental Hazards: A Time for Discourse.* Boulder, CO: Westview.

Bullard, R. D. (Ed.). (1993). *Confronting Environmental Racism: Voices from the Grassroots.* Boston: South End Press.

Cohen, E. G., & Lotan, R. A. (2004). Equity in Heterogeneous Classrooms. In J. A. Banks & C. A. M. Banks (Eds.), *Handbook of Research on Multicultural Education* (2nd ed., pp. 736–750). San Francisco: Jossey-Bass.

Colangelo, N., & Davis, G. A. (2003). *Handbook of Gifted Education* (3rd ed.). Boston: Allyn & Bacon.

Dana, R. H. (1993). *Multicultural Assessment Perspectives for Professional Psychology*. Boston: Allyn & Bacon.

Davis, G. A., & Rimm, S. B. (1997). *Education of the Gifted and Talented*. Boston: Allyn & Bacon.

Donovan, M. S., & Cross, C. T. (Eds.). (2002). *Minority Students in Special and Gifted Education*. Washington, DC: National Academy Press.

Dwight, H. (1994). Overcoming Racism in Environmental Decision Making. *Environment, 36*, 10–27.

Ford, D. Y. (1996). *Reversing Underachievement among Gifted Black Students: Promising Practices and Programs*. New York: Teachers College Press.

Ford, D. Y. (1998). The Under-Representation of Minority Students in Gifted Education: Problems and Promises in Recruitment and Retention. *The Journal of Special Education, 32*(1), 4–14.

Ford, D. Y., & Frazier Trotman, M. (2001). Teachers of Gifted Students: Suggested Multicultural Characteristics and Competencies. *Roeper Review, 23*(4), 235–239.

Ford, D. Y., & Harris, J. J., III. (1999). *Multicultural Gifted Education*. New York: Teachers College Press.

Ford, D. Y., Harris, J. J., III, Tyson, C. A., & Frazier Trotman, M. (2002). Beyond Deficit Thinking: Providing Access for Gifted African American Students. *Roeper Review, 24*(2), 52–58.

Fordham, S. (1988). Racelessness as a Strategy in Black Students' School Success: Pragmatic Strategy or Pyrrhic Victory? *Harvard Educational Review, 58*, 54–84.

Fordham, S., & Ogbu, J. (1986). Black Students' School Success: Coping with the "Burden of 'Acting White,'" *The Urban Review, 18*, 176–203.

Frasier, M. M., Martin, D., Garcia, J., Finley, V. S., Frank, E., Krisel, S., & King, L. L. (1995). *A New Window for Looking at Gifted Children*. Storrs: University of Connecticut, National Research Center on the Gifted and Talented.

Gardner, H. (1993). *Frames of Mind: The Theory of Multiple Intelligences*. New York: Basic Books.

Gay, G. (2000). *Culturally Responsive Teaching: Theory, Research, and Practice*. New York: Teachers College Press.

Gould, S. J. (1995). *The Mismeasure of Man* (rev. ed.). New York: Norton. (Original work published 1981).

Grossman, K. (1991). Environmental Racism. *Crisis, 98*(4), 14–17, 31–32.

Helms, J. E. (1992). Why is There No Study of Cultural Equivalence in Standardized Cognitive Ability Testing? *American Psychologist, 47*, 1083–1101.

Herrnstein, R. J., & Murray, C. (1994). *The Bell Curve: Intelligence and Class Structure in American Life*. New York: Free Press.

Heubert, J. P., & Hauser, R. M. (Eds.). (1999). *High Stakes: Testing for Tracking, Promotion, and Graduation*. Washington, DC: National Academy Press.

Irvine, J. J., & York, D. E. (2001). Learning Styles and Culturally Diverse Students: A Literature Review. In J. A. Banks & C. A. McGee Banks (Eds.), *Handbook of Research on Multicultural Education* (pp. 484–497). San Francisco: Jossey-Bass.

Jensen, A. R. (1980). *Bias in Mental Testing*. New York: Free Press.

Kaufman, A. S. (1994). *Intelligent Testing with the WISC-III*. New York: Wiley.

Kornhaber, M. (2004). Assessment, Standards and Equity. In J. A. Banks & C. A. M. Banks (Eds.), *Handbook of Research on Multicultural Education* (2nd ed., pp. 91–109). San Francisco: Jossey-Bass.

Lee, C. (1993). *Signifying as a Scaffold for Literary Interpretation: The Pedagogical Implications of an African American Discourse Genre.* Urbana, IL: National Council of Teachers of English.

Maker, J., & Nielson, A. B. (1996). *Curriculum Development and Teaching Strategies for Gifted Learners* (2nd ed.). Austin, TX: PRO-ED.

Menchaca, M. (1997). Early Racist Discourses: The Roots of Deficit Thinking. In R. Valencia (Ed.), *The Evolution of Deficit Thinking* (pp. 13–40). New York: Falmer.

Mercer, J. R. (1973). *Labeling the Mentally Retarded.* Berkeley: University of California Press.

Naglieri, J. A., & Ford, D. Y. (2003). Addressing Under-Representation of Gifted Minority Children Using the Naglieri Nonverbal Ability Test (NNAT). *Gifted Child Quarterly, 47,* 155–160.

National Council for Gifted Children. (1997). Position Paper on Testing. Washington, DC: Author.

Office of Ethnic Minority Affairs. (1993). Guidelines for Providers of Psychological Services to Ethnic, Linguistic, and Culturally Diverse Populations. *American Psychologist, 48,* 45–48.

Pang, V. O., Kiang, P. N., & Pak, Y. K. (2004). Asian Pacific American Students: Challenging a Biased Educational System. In J. A. Banks & C. A. M. Banks (Eds.), *Handbook of Research on Multicultural Education* (2nd ed., pp. 542–563). San Francisco: Jossey-Bass.

Ramírez, M., III, & Castañeda, A. (1974). *Cultural Democracy, Bicognitive Development, and Education.* New York: Academic Press.

Reis, S. M., & Callahan, C. M. (1989). Gifted Females—They've Come a Long Way—or Have They? *Journal for the Education of the Gifted, 12,* 99–117.

Rimm, S. B. (1995). *Why Bright Kids Get Poor Grades—and What You Can Do about It.* New York: Crown.

Saccuzzo, D. P., Johnson, N. E., & Guertin, T. L. (1994). *Identifying Underrepresented Disadvantaged Gifted and Talented Children: A Multifaceted Approach* (Vols. 1–2). San Diego: San Diego State University.

Sandoval, J., Frisby, C. L., Geisinger, K. F., Scheuneman, J. D,, & Grenier, J. R. (1998). *Test Interpretation and Diversity: Achieving Equity in Assessment.* Washington, DC: American Psychological Association.

Sapon-Shevon, M. (1996). Beyond Gifted Education: Building a Shared Agenda for School Reform. *Journal for the Education of the Gifted, 19,* 194–214.

Saracho, O. N., & Gerstl, C. K. (1992). Learning Differences among At-Risk Minority Students. In H. C. Waxman, J. Walker de Felix, J. E. Anderson, & H. P. Baptiste (Eds.), *Students at Risk in At-Risk Schools: Improving Environments for Learning* (pp. 105–136). Newbury Park, CA: Corwin.

Shade, B. J., Kelly, C., & Oberg, M. (1997). *Creating Culturally Responsive Classrooms.* Washington, DC: American Psychological Association.

Silverman, L. K. (1993). *Counseling the Gifted and Talented.* Denver, CO: Love.

Smith, C., Constantino, R., & Krashen, S. (1997). Differences in Print Environment for Children in Beverly Hills, Compton, and Watts. *Emergency Librarian, 24*(4), 8–9.

Sowell, T. (1993). *Inside American Education: The Decline, the Deception, the Dogma.* New York: Free Press.

Sternberg, R. J. (1985). *Beyond IQ: A Triarchic Theory of Human Intelligence.* New York: Cambridge University Press.

Storti, C. (1989). *The Art of Crossing Cultures* (2nd ed.). Yarmouth, ME: Intercultural Press.

Suzuki, L. A., Meller, P. J., & Ponterotto, J. G. (Eds.). (1996). *Handbook of Multicultural Assessment: Clinical, Psychological, and Educational Adaptations.* San Francisco: Jossey-Bass.

Tomlinson, C. A. (1995). *How to Differentiate Instruction in Mixed-Ability Classrooms.* Alexandria, VA: Association for Supervision and Curriculum Development.

U.S. Department of Education (USDE). (1993). *National Excellence: A Case for Developing America's Talent.* Washington, DC: Author.

VanTassel-Baska, J. (1994). *Comprehensive Curriculum for Gifted Learners.* Boston: Allyn & Bacon.

VanTassel-Baska, J., Patton, J., & Prillaman, D. (1989). Disadvantaged Gifted Learners At-Risk for Educational Attention. *Focus on Exceptional Children, 22,* 1–16.

Schools should be reformed so that all students will have an equal opportunity to succeed.

P
A
R
T
VI

School Reform

Reforming schools so that all students have an equal opportunity to succeed requires a new vision of education and social actors who are willing to advocate for and participate in change. The two chapters in Part VI discuss effective ways to conceptualize and implement school reform within a multicultural framework. In Chapter 16, Sonia Nieto presents and analyzes five conditions that will promote student achievement within a multicultural perspective. According to Nieto, schools should (1) be antiracist and antibiased; (2) reflect an understanding and acceptance of all students as having talents and strengths that can enhance their education; (3) be considered within the parameters of critical pedagogy; (4) involve those people most intimately connected with teaching and learning; and (5) be based on high expectations and rigorous standards for all learners.

Cherry A. McGee Banks, in Chapter 17, discusses ways to involve parents in schools. She argues that parent involvement is an important factor in school reform and student achievement and that parents can be a cogent force in school reform. Parents, perhaps more than any other group, can mobilize the community to support school reform. Parents have first-hand knowledge about the school's effectiveness and can be vocal advocates for change. As consumers of educational services, parents can raise questions that are difficult for professional educators and administrators to raise, such as: "What is the proportion of males in special education classes?" and "What is the ethnic breakdown of students enrolled in higher-level math and science classes?"

Banks argues that parents are more willing to work for school reform when they are involved in schools. They are more likely to become involved in schools when parent involvement opportunities reflect their varied interests, skills, and motivations. Banks suggests ways to expand traditional ideas about parent involvement and to increase the number and kinds of parents involved in schools.

CHAPTER 16

School Reform and Student Learning: A Multicultural Perspective

Sonia Nieto

Learning is at the heart of schooling. If this is the case, then it makes sense that student learning be a major focus of school reform efforts. This means that educational policies and practices need to be viewed in terms of how they affect the learning and academic achievement of students. But some school policies, especially as espoused in the reform movement that began with the publication of *A Nation at Risk* (National Commission on Excellence in Education, 1983) and that are now institutionalized through the No Child Left Behind federal legislation, as well as similar legislation in many states, pay scant attention to whether and to what extent students actually learn. These reform efforts often end up punishing schools, teachers, districts, and ultimately students who have not measured up to norms of success predetermined by politicians, policy makers, and others who know little about schools. Longer school days and years, strict retention policies, placement of schools "on probation," more high-stakes testing (that is, tests used as the sole or primary criterion for such crucial decisions as class placement and college admission), and less attention to pedagogy and curricula have been the result. Students who are most at risk of receiving an inadequate education are often the ones most jeopardized by such reform efforts.

This chapter begins with the assumption that student learning can be positively influenced by changes in school policies and practices that affirm students' identities and that are part of systemic school reform measures. Given the social nature of schooling, it is impossible to ascribe a fixed causal relationship between student learning and schooling. Many complex forces influence student learning, including personal, psychological, social, cultural, community, and institutional factors (Erickson, 1993; Nieto, 2004). That is, we cannot simply say that eliminating tracking will help all students succeed or that native-language instruction will guarantee success for all language-minority students. Neither can we state unequivocally that culturally responsive pedagogy is always the answer. Although these changes may in fact substantially improve educational outcomes for many more students than are now achieving academic success, taken in isolation, they may fail to reflect the complex nature of student learning.

A comprehensive view of student learning that takes into account the myriad influences on achievement can help explain why some students succeed academically while others do not. For example, a number of years ago, my colleague Manuel Frau-Ramos and I did a study of Puerto Rican students who had dropped out of school in a particular city. We found that 68 percent of those who had never been in bilingual programs dropped out of school, while only 39 percent of those who had been in bilingual classrooms for at least part of their school experience dropped out (Frau-Ramos & Nieto, 1993). The difference in dropout rates was dramatic, but a 39 percent dropout rate is still unacceptably high. It suggests that other conditions also were involved. We found that these included the students' perceptions of fitting in and their previous educational preparation; teachers' limited knowledge of their students' backgrounds and their negative attitudes about diversity; and school policies and practices that led some students to feel like outsiders. In this case, although bilingual education was significant in mediating the school retention of some students, it was insufficient to ensure that all students would succeed academically.

Culturally responsive education, an approach based on using students' identities and backgrounds as meaningful sources of their education, can go a long way toward improving the education of students whose cultures have been maligned, denied, or omitted in school curricula (Au & Kawakami, 1994; Gay, 2000; Irvine, 1997; Ladson-Billings, 1994). This approach offers crucial insights for understanding the lack of achievement of students from culturally subordinated groups. However, by itself, culturally responsive pedagogy cannot guarantee that all students will learn. For example, if viewed simply as "cultural sensitivity" or as including a few activities in the curriculum, culturally responsive education offers little hope for substantive change. Moreover, there are cases in which culturally marginalized students have been successfully educated *in spite* of what might be considered culturally incompatible settings. As a case in point, Catholic schools might seem at first glance to be culturally inappropriate for some children because bilingual programs are seldom offered, classes are usually overcrowded, and formal environments stress individual excellence rather than cooperation. Yet many students of African American and Latino backgrounds who attend Catholic schools have been academically successful (Bryk, Lee, & Holland, 1993; Irvine & Foster, 1996).

In the case of Catholic schools, we need to look beyond just cultural responsiveness to explain student academic success. Because of generally limited resources, Catholic schools tend to offer *all* students a less differentiated curriculum, less tracking, and more academic classes, in addition to having clear, uncomplicated missions and strong social contracts (Bryk, Lee, & Holland, 1993; Irvine & Foster, 1996). What at first glance might appear to be incongruous in terms of cultural compatibility can nevertheless reflect high expectations for all students. This example illustrates the complex relationship of academic success to a multiplicity of conditions, and it again indicates that there is no one simple solution to academic failure.

In this chapter, I explore the meaning of school reform with a multicultural perspective and consider implications for student learning. I begin by defining school reform with a multicultural perspective, including how a school's policies and practices implicitly illustrate beliefs about who deserves the benefits of a high-quality education. That is, certain school policies and practices may exacerbate the inequalities that exist in society. I then describe a set of five interrelated conditions for successful school reform within a multicultural perspective. These conditions are intimately interconnected, but for the purpose of expediency, I explain the five conditions separately, with implications for increasing student achievement.

SCHOOL REFORM WITH A MULTICULTURAL PERSPECTIVE

Many people assume that multicultural education consists of little more than isolated lessons in sensitivity training or prejudice reduction, or separate units about cultural artifacts or ethnic holidays. Sometimes, it is used to mean education geared for inner-city schools or, more specifically, for African American students. If conceptualized in this limited way, multicultural education will have little influence on student learning.

When conceptualized as broad-based school reform, however, multicultural education can have a major influence on how and to what extent students learn. When it focuses on conditions that can contribute to student underachievement, multicultural education allows educators to explore alternatives to systemic problems that may lead to academic failure and it fosters the design and implementation of productive learning environments, diverse instructional strategies, and a deeper awareness of how cultural and language differences can influence learning.

To approach school reform with a multicultural perspective, we need to begin with an understanding of multicultural education within its *sociopolitical context* (Nieto, 2004). A sociopolitical context underscores that education is part and parcel of larger societal and political forces, such as inequality based on stratification due to race, social class, gender, and other differences. Given this perspective, decisions concerning such practices as ability tracking, high-stakes testing, native-language instruction, retention, curriculum reform, and pedagogy are all influenced by broader social policies.

As Freire (1985) states, every educational decision, whether made at the classroom, city, state, or national level, is imbedded within a particular ideological framework. Such decisions can be as simple as whether a classroom should be arranged in rows with all students facing the teacher, or in tables with groups of students to encourage cooperative work, or in a variety of ways depending on the task at hand. Alternatively, these decisions can be as far-reaching as eliminating tracking in an entire school system, or teaching language-minority students by using both their native language and English, or by using English only. Within each educational decision are assumptions about the nature of learning, about what particular students are capable of achieving, about whose language is valued, and about who should be at the center of the educational process. Even seemingly innocent decisions carry an enormous amount of ideological and philosophical baggage, which is in turn communicated to students either directly or indirectly.

As stated more extensively elsewhere, I define multicultural education within a sociopolitical context as (Nieto, 2004)

> a process of comprehensive school reform and basic education for all
> students. It challenges and rejects racism and other forms of
> discrimination in schools and society and accepts and affirms the
> pluralism (ethnic, racial, linguistic, religious, economic, and gender,
> among others) that students, their communities, and teachers reflect.

> Multicultural education permeates the schools' curriculum and
> instructional strategies, as well as the interactions among teachers,
> students, and families, and the very way that schools conceptualize
> the nature of teaching and learning. Because it uses critical pedagogy
> as its underlying philosophy and focuses on knowledge, reflection,
> and action (*praxis*) as the basis for social change, multicultural
> education promotes democratic principles of social justice. (p. 346)

This definition of multicultural education assumes a comprehensive school reform effort rather than superficial additions to the curriculum or one-shot treatments about diversity, such as workshops for teachers or assembly programs for students. As such, I use this definition as a lens to view conditions for systemic school reform that can improve the learning of all students.

CONDITIONS FOR SYSTEMIC SCHOOL REFORM WITH A MULTICULTURAL PERSPECTIVE

Failure to learn does not develop out of thin air; it is scrupulously created through policies, practices, attitudes, and beliefs. In a very concrete sense, the results of educational inequality explain by example what a society believes its young people are capable of achieving and what they deserve. For instance, offering only low-level courses in schools serving culturally diverse and poor youngsters is a clear message that the students are not expected to achieve to high levels; in like manner, considering students to be "at risk" simply because of their ethnicity, native language, family characteristics, or social class is another clear sign that some students have been defined by conventional wisdom as uneducable based simply on their identity.

As a result, we cannot think about education reform without taking into account both micro- and macro-level issues that may affect student learning. Microlevel issues include the cultures, languages, and experiences of students and their families and how these are considered in determining school policies and practices (Cummins, 1996; Nieto, 1999). Macrolevel issues include the racial stratification that helps maintain inequality, and the resources and access to learning that schools provide or deny (Kozol, 1991; Orfield, 2001; Spring, 2002). In addition, how students and their families view their status in schools and society must be considered. Ogbu (1994), for instance, has argued that school performance gaps persist because of racial stratification and the unequal treatment of dominated groups, as well as the responses of dominated groups to these experiences.

Conditions such as inequitable school financing (National Center for Education Statistics, 2000), unrepresentative school governance (Meier & Stewart, 1991), and large class size (Mosteller, 1995) may play a powerful role in promoting student underachievement. For example, inequities in school financing have remained quite stable since Jonathan Kozol's (1991) landmark study of more than a decade ago (National Center for Educational Statistics, 2000). Yet reform strategies such as longer school days, more rigorous graduation standards, and increased standardized testing often do not take such issues into account. The evidence is growing, for example, that school size makes a difference in student learning and that it may also influence students' feelings of belonging, and thus their engagement with learning. One study, for example, concluded that elementary schools of fewer than 400 students tend to display stronger teacher collective responsibility for student learning and greater student achievement in math (Lee & Loeb, 2000). In fact, equalizing just two conditions of schooling—funding and class size—would probably result in an immediate and dramatic improvement in learning for students who have not received the benefits of these two conditions.

School reform strategies that do not acknowledge such macrolevel disparities are bound to be inadequate because they assume that schools provide all students with a level playing field. The conditions described below, while acknowledging these disparities, nevertheless provide hope for school systems where such changes as equitable funding or small class size may not occur in the near future. Rather than wait for these changes to happen, schools and teachers can begin to improve the conditions for successful student learning. Five such conditions are described below (these conditions are described in greater detail in Nieto, 1999). These conditions, along with changes in funding and resource allocation, would help create schools where all students have a better chance to learn.

School Reform Should Be Antiracist and Antibiased

An antiracist and antibias perspective is at the core of multicultural education. This is crucial because too often people believe that multicultural education automatically takes care of racism; but this is far from the reality. In fact, multicultural education without an explicit antiracist focus may perpetuate the worst kinds of stereotypes if it focuses only on superficial aspects of culture and the addition of ethnic tidbits to the curriculum.

In contrast, being antiracist means paying attention to all areas in which some students may be favored over others, including the curriculum and pedagogy, sorting policies, and teachers' interactions and relationships with students and their communities. Schools committed to multicultural education with an antiracist perspective need to examine closely both school policies and the attitudes and behaviors of their staff to determine how these might be complicit in causing academic failure. The kind of expectations that teachers and schools have for students (Nieto, 2002/2003; Zeichner, 1996), whether native-language use is permitted or punished (Gebhard, Austin, Nieto, & Willet, 2002), how sorting takes place (Oakes, Wells, Jones, & Datnow, 1997), and how classroom organization, pedagogy, and curriculum may influence student learning (Bennett deMarrais & LeCompte, 1999) each need to be considered.

To become antiracist, schools also need to examine how the curriculum may perpetuate negative, distorted, or incomplete images of some groups while exalting others as the makers of all history. Unfortunately, many textbooks and children's books are still replete with racist and sexist images and with demeaning portrayals of people from low-income communities. Although the situation is improving, and the stereotypes that exist are not as blatant as they once were, there are still many inaccuracies and negative portrayals (Harris, 1997; Loewen, 1995, 2000; Willis, 1998).

In a related vein, most of the women and men presented as heroes or heroines in the standard curriculum—whether from dominant or nondominant cultures—are "safe"; that is, they do not pose a challenge to the status quo. Other people who have fought for social justice are omitted, presented as bizarre or insane, or made safe by downplaying their contributions. A now-classic article by Kozol (1975) graphically documents how schools bleed the life and soul out of even the most impassioned and courageous heroes, such as Helen Keller and Martin Luther King, Jr., in the process making them boring and less-than-believable caricatures. A powerful article by Kohl (1993) demonstrates how Rosa Parks, the mother of the civil rights movement, has been made palatable to the mainstream by portraying her not as a staunch civil rights crusader who consciously battled racist segregation but rather as a tired woman who simply did not want to give up her seat on the bus (Kohl, 1993). Taking another example, few children learn about the slave revolt led by Nat Turner (Aptheker, 1943/1987), although most learn that "Abraham Lincoln freed the slaves all by himself." These are examples of at best misleading, and at worst racist, representations.

Through this kind of curriculum, students from dominant groups learn that they are the norm, and consequently they often assume that anyone different from them is culturally or intellectually disadvantaged. On the other hand, students from subordinated cultures may internalize the message that their cultures, families, languages, and experiences have low status, and they learn to feel inferior. The result may be what has been called "stereotype threat," or the impact on Blacks, other people of color, and women of their devaluation in schools and society (Steele, 1999). All students suffer as a result of these messages, but students from dominated groups are the most negatively affected.

The issue of institutional power is also at play here. The conventional notion of racism is that it is an *individual* bias toward members of other groups. This perception conveniently skirts the issue of how institutions themselves, which are much more powerful than individuals, develop harmful policies and practices that victimize American Indians, African Americans, Latinos, poor European Americans, females, and other people from powerless groups. The major difference between *individual racism* and *institutional racism* is the wielding of power, because it is primarily through the power of the people who control institutions such as schools that oppressive policies and practices are reinforced and legitimated (Tatum, 1997; Weinberg, 1990). That is, when racism is understood as a systemic problem, not just as an individual dislike for a particular group of people, we can better understand its negative and destructive effects.

I do not wish to minimize the powerful effect of individual prejudice and discrimination, which can be personally very painful, nor to suggest that individual discrimination occurs only in one direction, for example, from Whites to African Americans. No group monopolizes prejudice and discrimination; they occur in all directions, and even within groups. But interethnic hostility, personal prejudices, and individual biases, while certainly hurtful, do not have the long-range and life-limiting effects on entire groups of people that *institutional* racism and bias have. Testing practices, for example, may be institutionally discriminatory because they label students from culturally and socially dominated groups as inferior as a result of their performance on these tests (McNeil, 2000). Rather than critically examining the tests themselves, the underlying purpose of such tests, or their damaging effects, the students themselves are often blamed (Orfield & Kornhaber, 2001). In addition, the fact that textbook companies and companies that develop tests earn huge profits from test construction and dissemination is often unmentioned, yet it, too, is a reality (Kohn, 2000).

An antiracist perspective is also apparent in schools when students are permitted, and even encouraged, to speak about their experiences with racism and other biases. Many White teachers feel great discomfort when racism is discussed in the classroom. They are uncomfortable for several reasons: their lack of experience in confronting such a potentially explosive issue, the conspiracy of silence about racism (as if not speaking about it will make it disappear), the guilt they may feel being a member of the group that has benefited from racism, the generally accepted assumption that we live in a colorblind society, or a combination of these reasons (Fine, 1991; Kailin, 1999; McIntyre, 1997; Sleeter, 1994; Tatum, 1997). Yet when students are given time and support for expressing their views, the result can be compelling because their experiences are legitimated and used in the service of their learning. For example, both Levin (2001) and Landsman (2001) have written eloquently about the impact of addressing issues of racism and discrimination in the classroom. In a related vein, Donaldson (1996) described how urban high school students used the racism they and their peers experienced in school as the content of a peer-education assembly program. The result was a critical examination of the impact that race can have on their education. Rather than shying away from such topics, these researchers found that directly confronting issues of bias can help students become more critical and reflective learners.

In my own research on the views of students concerning their education, they mentioned racism and other examples of discrimination on the part of fellow students and teachers (Nieto, 1994). Manuel, a Cape Verdean student who moved to the United States at age eleven, described how it felt to be the butt of jokes from his peers: "When American students see you, it's kinda hard [to] get along with them when you have a different culture, a different way of dressing and stuff like that. So kids really look at you and laugh, you know, at the beginning" (cited p. 414). Avi, a Jewish American young man, discussed a number of incidents of anti-Semitism, including one in which a student walked by him and whispered, "Are you ready for the Second Holocaust?" Other students talked about discrimination on the part of teachers. Marisol, a Puerto Rican student, and Vinh, who was Vietnamese, specifically mentioned language discrimination as a major problem. In Marisol's case, it happened when a teacher did not allow her to use Spanish in the classroom. For Vinh, it concerned teachers' attitudes about his language. He explained: "Some teachers don't understand about the language. So sometimes, my language, they say it sounds funny" (cited p. 414).

As these examples make clear, an antiracist perspective is essential in schools if all students are to be given equitable environments for learning. An antiracist perspective is a vital lens through which to analyze a school's policies and practices, including the curriculum, pedagogy, testing and tracking, discipline, faculty hiring, student retention, and attitudes about and interactions with parents.

School Reform Should Reflect an Understanding and Acceptance of All Students as Having Talents and Strengths That Can Enhance Their Education

Many educators believe that students from culturally subordinated groups have few experiential or cultural strengths that can benefit their education. A classic example comes from Ryan (1972), who coined the expression "blaming the victim" for the tendency to place responsibility on students and their families for their failure to achieve in school. These students, generally low-income children of all groups and children of color specifically, are often considered deficient or "culturally deprived," a patronizing term popularized in the

1960s (Reissman, 1962). But Ryan turned the perspective of "cultural deprivation" on its head when he wrote:

> We are dealing, it would seem, not so much with culturally
> deprived children as with culturally depriving schools. And the task
> to be accomplished is not to revise, amend, and repair deficient
> children, but to alter and transform the atmosphere and operations
> of the schools to which we commit these children. (p. 61)

Students may be thought of as culturally deprived simply because they speak a language other than English as their native language or because they have just one parent or live in poverty. Sometimes they are labeled in this way just because of their race or ethnicity. Rather than begin with this kind of deficit view, however, it makes sense to begin with a more positive and, in the end, more realistic and hopeful view of students and their families. Thus, school reform measures based on the assumption that children of all families bring cultural and community strengths to their education would go a long way toward providing more powerful learning environments for a greater number of youngsters. Moll and González's (1997) research on incorporating "funds of knowledge" into the curriculum—that is, using the experiences and skills of all families to encourage student learning—is a more promising and productive way of approaching families than is the viewpoint that they have only deficits that must be repaired.

If we begin with the premise that children and their families have substantial talents that can inform student learning, a number of implications for improving schools follow (Kiang, 1995). Instead of placing the blame for failure to learn solely on students, teachers need to become aware of how their own biases can act as barriers to student learning. Teachers also need to consider how their students best learn and how their own pedagogical practices need to change as a result. This implies that teachers need to learn culturally responsive ways of teaching all of their students (Irvine, 2003; Ladson-Billings, 2001).

Teachers also need to consider how the native language of students influences their academic achievement. For this to happen, they need to "unlearn" some of the conventional myths surrounding native-language use (Snow, 1997). For instance, it is common practice in schools to try to convince parents whose native language is other than English that they should speak only English with their children. This recommendation makes little sense for at least three reasons. First, these parents often speak little English themselves, and their children are thus provided with less than adequate models of English. Second, this practice often results in cutting off, rather than stimulating, communication between parents and children. Likewise, if young people are encouraged to learn English at the expense of their native language, rather than in conjunction with it, they may lose meaningful connections that help maintain close and loving relations with family members (Beykont, 2000; Wong Fillmore, 1991).

A more reasonable recommendation, and one that would honor the contributions parents can make to their children's education, is to encourage rather than discourage them to speak their native language with their children, to speak it often, and to use it consistently. In schools, this means that students would not be punished for speaking their native languages; rather, they would be encouraged to do so, and to do so in the service of their learning (Fránquiz & Reyes, 1998). A rich communicative legacy, both in school and at home, could be the result.

Another example of failing to use student and community strengths can be found in the curriculum. Young children are frequently presented with images of community helpers who may be unrelated to their daily lives. A perspective that affirms the talents and experiences of students and their families can expand the people and roles included in the curriculum. Not only would children study those community helpers traditionally included, such as police officers, mail carriers, and teachers, but they could also learn about local merchants, community activists, and street vendors. These people are also community helpers, although they have not generally been sanctioned as such by the official curriculum.

A further consideration concerning the talents and strengths of students and their families is what Cummins (1996) has called the "relations of power" in schools. In proposing a shift from "coercive" to "collaborative" relations of power, Cummins argues that traditional teacher-centered transmission models can limit the potential for learning, especially among students from communities whose cultures and languages are devalued by the dominant canon. For instance, an in-depth study of schools by Poplin and Weeres (1992) found that students frequently reported being bored and seeing little relevance in the school curriculum to their lives and futures. The researchers concluded that as the curriculum, texts, and assignments became more standardized, students became even more disengaged in their learning (Poplin & Weeres, 1992). That is, the more school experiences were unrelated to their own community experiences, the less relevant schooling became for students.

Their findings suggest that using students and their families as collaborators in developing the curriculum would help promote student learning. By encouraging collaborative relations of power, schools can begin to recognize other sources of legitimate knowledge that have been overlooked. This practice can, in turn, positively affect the degree to which students learn.

School Reform Should Be Considered within the Parameters of Critical Pedagogy

According to Banks (2003), the main goal of a multicultural curriculum is to help students develop decision-making and social action skills. Consequently, when students learn to view situations and events from a variety of viewpoints, critical thinking, reflection, and action are promoted. The connection between critical pedagogy and a multicultural perspective is a promising avenue for expanding and informing both of these philosophical frameworks (Lee, Menkart, & Okazawa-Rey, 1998; May, 1999; Sleeter & McLaren, 1995; Walsh, 1996). Critical pedagogy is an approach through which students and teachers are encouraged to view what they learn in a critical light, or, in the words of Freire (1970), by learning to read both "the word and the world." According to Freire, the opposite of a critical or empowering approach is "banking education," where students learn to regurgitate and passively accept the knowledge they are given. A critical education, on the other hand, expects students to seek their own answers, to be curious, and to question.

Many students do not have access to a wide range of viewpoints, but such access is essential if they are to develop the critical judgment and decision-making skills they will need to become productive members of a democratic society. Because a critical perspective values diverse viewpoints and encourages critical thinking, reflection, and action, students are empowered as learners because they are expected to become problem solvers. Critical pedagogy is based on using students' present reality as a foundation for their further learning, rather than on doing away with or belittling what they know and who they are. As a result, critical pedagogy acknowledges diversity of all kinds instead of suppressing or supplanting it.

Shor's (1992) analysis concerning critical pedagogy is instructive. He begins with the assumption that because no curriculum can be truly neutral, it is the responsibility of schools to present students with the broad range of information they will need to learn to read and write critically and in the service of social change. Thus, critical pedagogy is not simply the transfer of knowledge from teacher to students, even though it may be knowledge that has heretofore not been made available to them. A critical perspective does not simply operate on the principle of substituting one truth for another; instead, students are encouraged to reflect on multiple and contradictory perspectives in order to understand reality more fully. For instance, learning about the internment of Americans of Japanese descent and Japanese residents in the United States during World War II is not in itself critical pedagogy; it only becomes so when students analyze different viewpoints and use them to understand the inconsistencies they uncover (Daniels, 1971). They can then begin to understand the role played by racist hysteria, economic exploitation, and propaganda as catalysts for the internment, and they can judge this incident through the stated ideals of our nation.

Without a critical perspective, reality is often presented to students as if it were static, finished, and flat; underlying conflicts, problems, and inherent contradictions are omitted. As we have seen, textbooks in all subject areas generally exclude information about unpopular perspectives or the perspectives of disempowered groups in society. Few of the books to which students have access present the viewpoints of people who have built our country, from enslaved Africans to immigrant labor to other working-class people, even though they have been the backbone of society (Zinn, 2003).

Likewise, the immigrant experience, shared by many groups in the United States, is generally treated, if at all, as a romantic and successful odyssey instead of as a more complicated process that has been also a wrenching experience of loss. Moreover, the European immigrant experience is generally presented in our history books as the sole model for all immigrants, although the historical context, the racial politics and hostility, and the economic structures awaiting more recent immigrants are very different and more complicated than was true for the vast majority of Europeans who arrived during the late nineteenth and early twentieth centuries (Carnoy, 1994; Takaki, 1993).

Using critical pedagogy as a basis for school reform renders very different policies for schools than do traditional models of school reform. Even more important than just increasing curricular options, critical pedagogy helps to expand teachers' and schools' perspectives about students' knowledge and intellectual capabilities. In terms of students, using critical pedagogy helps them become agents of their own learning so they can use what they learn in productive and critical ways. The knowledge they learn can be used to explore the reasons for certain conditions in their lives and to design strategies for changing them.

A number of recorded accounts of critical pedagogy in classrooms are compelling examples of the positive and empowering influence that teachers' guidance can have on student learning. Mercado (1993), working collaboratively with Marceline Torres, a middle school teacher and her students, designed a project in which the young people became researchers about conditions in their Bronx neighborhood. Students learned a variety of sophisticated academic skills at the same time that they learned to think more deeply about the reasons for the situations such as drug abuse, homelessness, teenage pregnancy, and intergenerational conflicts. In many cases, students used their research skills in social action projects to improve their community.

In a now-classic essay, Peterson (1991) wrote about how he used critical pedagogy to teach literacy, debunk myths, and provide a rich environment for learning in his fifth-grade classroom. He describes how class meetings became "problem-posing" exercises (Freire, 1970) as students listed the concerns or problems they wanted to discuss and then decided which one to tackle on a particular day. He described the five-step plan they used by listing a series of questions students needed to answer:

1. What is the problem?
2. Are you sure about it?
3. What can we do about it?
4. Try it.
5. How did it work? (p. 166)

Peterson (1991) does not propose this process as a panacea. Instead, he states, "While many of the problems poor and minority children and communities face cannot be easily or immediately 'solved,' a 'problem-posing' pedagogy can encourage a questioning of why things are the way they are and the identification of actions, no matter how small, to begin to address them" (p. 166).

More recently, Patty Bode, a gifted art teacher who incorporates a multicultural perspective in her teaching, reflected on her experience with a first-grade child who was concerned about unfair representation in some of the books she was reading. In "A Letter from Kaeli" (Nieto, 1999), Patty discussed how she had received in her mailbox at school the following letter, using invented spelling, from a first-grade student:

> Dear !!!!!! mis Boudie
> Ples! halp. my moom was spcing to me abut wite piple leving
> bran and blak piple out of books.
>
> Love Kaeli
>
> [Dear Ms. Bode,
> Please help! My mom was speaking to me about White people
> leaving Brown and Black people out of books.
>
> Love, Kaeli] (cited p. 125)

In the letter she sent to Kaeli as a response, Patty wrote, in part, "I am glad you asked for help. This is a problem that we need to help each other with. We need to ask our friends and teachers and families for help so we can work together. . . . I think we should work on this problem in art class" (cited p. 126). As a result, when Kaeli's class came to the art room, she read her letter aloud. She also showed her classmates the book that was the basis for her letter to Patty. It was a book about the human body that had been published fairly recently by a prominent publishing house. Out of the many illustrations in the book, Kaeli found only a small number of pictures of Brown and Black people. When the students discussed why this might be a problem, Patty recounted:

> In their first-grade voices and six-year-old vocabulary, they
> discussed "fair" and "unfair," "discrimination," "stereotypes," and
> more. Through their dialogue, they decided—without my
> prompting—that it was OK for some books to exclusively depict

> Black people or Brown people or White people or others if it was
> a story about a specific family or event. But books that claimed to
> be about the "HUMAN BODY" or about "PEOPLE OF THE
> WORLD" needed to be much more balanced to pass the
> scrupulous eye of this first grade class. (cited p. 127)

After engaging in a number of art activities—color theory, self-portraits, face shapes—the students discussed terminology and why some terms for people of different ethnic, racial, and social groups might be more appropriate than others. As a result of this discussion, the students concluded that "using words like *Black* or *African American, White* or *European American, Latino* or *Hispanic,* and *Asian* or *Chinese-American* were important decisions that required lots of thinking" (cited p. 127). Patty also gave the students examples of various books for analysis. At this point, the students decided that the publishers should receive some letters of information from them and some of their artwork to display good examples of fair pictures. Erika, one of the first-grade students, wrote the following letter, again in inverted spelling:

> Dear publisher,
>   Make your books faire! And if you don't me and my famyuliy
> will never by or read your unfaire books. we want fairenes.
>   From, Erika
> [Make your books fair! And if you don't, me and my family will
> never buy or read your unfair books. We want fairness.] (cited
> p. 128)

In a moving description of the impact of this kind of pedagogy and curriculum on students, Patty went on to describe what happened when she prepared a bulletin board around the theme of diversity in textbook representation:

> I filled the walls of the artroom with photographs of children's
> faces. I spent a great deal of time choosing images of children to
> reflect the enormous variety of ethnicity and race that our society
> holds. One European American boy looked at the photo display
> and said, "Ms. Bode, you left out the White people." (cited p. 127)

Patty asked him to count the number of people he thought were of different backgrounds (an activity through which he realized that this was not always easy to do), and, to his surprise, he discovered that the bulletin board actually included many Whites. When Patty asked him why he had thought that European Americans were missing from the display, he answered "Maybe it's 'cuz I'm used to seeing more of them" (cited p. 128).

Patty's reflection ended with the following words:

> This unit proved to be a good reminder to me that it is the
> responsibility of the entire community to work for social justice.
> One individual or one group should not be burdened to fight for
> their rights in solitude nor exempt from the responsibility of
> democracy. It requires careful observation, attentive listening, and
> critical thought to facilitate sociopolitical consciousness effectively
> within a first grade classroom. (cited pp. 128–129)

Experiences such as Patty Bode's reinforce the idea that critical multicultural education should not be reserved for the college classroom or just for classes in history or English. Even an art class for six-year-olds is fertile ground for planting the seeds of critical thinking and social justice. Other accounts of critical pedagogy in action, written mostly by classroom teachers, are contained in publications by Rethinking Schools (Bigelow, Christensen, Karp, Miner, & Peterson, 1994; Bigelow, Harvey, Karp, & Miller, 2001) and Teaching for Change (Lee et al., 1998). In these inspiring accounts, which discuss specific curricular and pedagogical innovations, critical pedagogy is the force behind student learning.

The People Most Intimately Connected with Teaching and Learning (Teachers, Families, and Students) Need to Be Meaningfully Involved in School Reform

Fine (1994), describing the massive school reforms in Philadelphia that began in 1988, wrote, "Democratic change is frustrating, loud, but possible" (p. 10). In fact, research on involvement by families, students, and teachers has consistently indicated that democratic participation by people closest to learners can dramatically improve student learning. This is especially true in urban schools and in schools that serve poor, African American, Latino, and immigrant students (Epstein, 2001; Olsen, Jaramillo, McCall-Perez, White, & Minicucci, 1999). Yet these are the people who are most often excluded from discussions and implementation of school reform measures.

Cummins (1996) reviewed programs that included student empowerment as a goal and concluded that students who are encouraged to develop a positive cultural identity through interactions with their teachers experience a sense of control over their own lives and develop the confidence and motivation to succeed academically. School reform measures that stress the meaningful involvement of teachers, families, and students look quite different from traditional approaches. They begin with the assumption that these groups have substantial and insightful perspectives about student learning. Rather than thinking of ways to bypass their ideas, school reformers actively seek the involvement of students, families, and teachers in developing, for instance, disciplinary policies, curriculum development, and decisions concerning tracking and the use of tests. Similarly, allowing time in the curriculum for students to engage in critical discussions about issues such as whose language is valued in schools can help to affirm the legitimacy of the discourse of all students.

At the same time, these kinds of discussions also acknowledge the need to learn and become comfortable with the discourse of the larger society (Delpit, 1995). In addition, involving families in curriculum development enriches the curriculum, affirms what families have to offer, and helps students overcome the shame they may feel about their cultures, languages, and values, an all-too-common attitude for students from culturally subordinated groups (Nieto, 2004; Olsen, 1997).

School Reform Needs to Be Based on High Expectations and Rigorous Standards for All Learners

Many students cope on a daily basis with complex and difficult problems, including poverty, violence, racism, abuse, families in distress, and lack of health care and proper housing. In addition to such situations, many students come to school with experiences and conditions that some teachers and schools consider as placing them at risk for learning, including speaking a language other than English or simply belonging to a particular racial or ethnic group. But beginning with this perspective leaves teachers and schools with little hope. Rather than viewing language and cultural differences as impediments to learning, they can be viewed as resources that students bring to their education. In this way, instead of using these differences as a rationalization for low expectations of what students are capable of learning, they can be used to promote student learning. In addition, in our society we have always expected schools to provide an equal and equitable education for all students, not just for those who have no problems in their lives or who fit the image of successful students due to race, class, or language ability. The promise of an equal education for all students of all backgrounds in the United States has yet to be realized, as is evident from a number of classic critiques of the myth of our schools as "the great equalizer" (Bowles & Gintis, 1976; Katz, 1975; Spring, 1989). Nevertheless, the ideal of equitable educational opportunity is worth defending and vigorously putting into practice.

It is undeniably true that many students face unimaginably difficult problems, and the school cannot be expected to solve them all. Neither can we dismiss the heroic efforts of many teachers and schools who, with limited financial and other material resources, teach students who live in dire circumstances under what can best be described as challenging conditions. Nevertheless, the difficult conditions in which some students live need not be viewed as insurmountable barriers to their academic achievement. It is too often the case that society's low expectations of students, based on these situations, pose even greater obstacles to their learning. For example, if students do not speak English, teachers may assume that they cannot learn; or if they do not have consistent experiences with or access to libraries, museums, or other cultural institutions considered essential for preparing students for schools, teachers may assume that these children are not even, to use the language of current reform efforts, "ready to learn."

If we are serious about giving all students more options in life, particularly students from communities denied the necessary resources with which to access these options, then we need to begin with the assumption that these students are academically capable, both individually and as a group. Too many students have been dismissed as uneducable simply because they were not born with the material resources or family conditions considered essential for learning. The conventional attitude that students who do not arrive at school with such benefits are incapable of learning is further promoted by assertions of race-based genetic inferiority, an assumption that is unfortunately still too prevalent (Herrnstein & Murray, 1994).

Numerous examples of dramatic success in the face of adversity are powerful reminders that great potential exists in all students. Consider, for example, the case of Garfield High School in East Los Angeles, California. Here, the mostly Mexican American students taught by Jaime Escalante, the protagonist of the popular film *Stand and Deliver,* were tremendously successful in learning advanced mathematics. In fact, when they took the Advanced Placement (AP) calculus test, they did so well that the test-makers assumed they had cheated. As a result, they had to take it a second time, and this time their performance was even better.

The success of the Algebra Project in Cambridge, Massachusetts, is another example. In this project, young people who had previously been denied access to algebra because they were thought to be incapable of benefiting from it became high achievers in math. When they went on to high school, 39 percent of the first graduating class of the project were placed in honors geometry or honors algebra classes; in fact, none of the graduates was placed in a lower-level math course. The Algebra Project has now spread to other school systems throughout the United States (Moses & Cobb, 2002).

Central Park East Elementary School in East Harlem, New York, a school with a student body made up overwhelmingly of Latino and African American students, provides another example of academic success among youngsters who might not have been thought capable of succeeding (Meier, 1995). The school, which accepts students from the neighborhood and not from elite or favored groups, has documented astonishing success: an in-depth study of the first seven graduating classes of the school revealed that 90 percent earned high school diplomas and two-thirds went on to college, nearly double the rate for the city as a whole.

Although students' identities are often perceived to be handicaps to learning by an assimilationist society that encourages cultural and linguistic homogeneity, numerous success stories of students who use their cultural values and traditions as strengths have been reported in the educational research literature (Deyhle & Swisher, 1997; Igoa, 1995; McCarty, 2002; Nieto, 2004; Soto, 1997; Zentella, 1997). This result leads us to the inevitable conclusion that before fixing what they may consider to be problems in students, schools and society need to change their own perceptions of students and view them as capable learners.

CONCLUSION

There is no simple formula for increasing student learning. A step-by-step blueprint for school reform is both unrealistic and inappropriate because each school differs from all others in its basic structure, goals, and human dimensions. Moreover, inequitable conditions such as school funding and the distribution of resources for learning also help explain why some students are successful and others are not. However, certain conditions can dramatically improve the learning of many students who are currently marginalized from the center of learning because of school policies and practices based on deficit models. If we begin with the assumptions that students cannot achieve at high levels, that their backgrounds are riddled with deficiencies, and that multicultural education is a frill that cannot help them to learn, we will end up with school reform strategies that have little hope for success.

This chapter presented and analyzed five conditions to promote student achievement within a multicultural perspective:

1. School reform should be antiracist and antibiased.
2. School reform should reflect an understanding and acceptance of all students as having talents and strengths that can enhance their education.
3. School reform should be considered within the parameters of critical pedagogy.
4. The people most intimately connected with teaching and learning (teachers, parents, and students themselves) need to be meaningfully involved in school reform.
5. School reform needs to be based on high expectations and rigorous standards for all learners.

This chapter is based on two related assumptions: (1) that students, families, and teachers bring strengths and talents to teaching and learning, and (2) that a comprehensive and critical approach to multicultural education can provide an important framework for rethinking school reform. Given these assumptions, we have a much more promising scenario for effective learning and for the possibility that schools can become places of hope and affirmation for students of all backgrounds and situations.

Questions and Activities

1. What does the author mean by "culturally responsive education"? Why does she think it is important? According to the author, is culturally responsive education sufficient to guarantee academic success for students of color and low-income students? Why or why not?

2. What does it mean to say that multicultural education takes place within a sociopolitical context? What social, political, and economic factors must be considered when multicultural education is being implemented? How can a consideration of sociopolitical factors help multicultural school reform to be more effective?

3. What five conditions does the author believe are needed to improve students' academic achievement? How are these factors interrelated?

4. How does the author distinguish *individual* and *institutional racism?* Why does she think this distinction is important? Give examples of each type of racism from your personal experiences and observations.

5. What is an antiracist perspective? Why does the author believe that an antiracist perspective is essential for the implementation of multicultural education? Give specific examples of antiracist teaching and educational practices with which you are familiar.

6. The author briefly describes Moll's concept of incorporating community knowledge into the curriculum. How does this concept help teachers to implement "culturally sensitive" teaching?

7. What is critical pedagogy? How, according to the author, can it be used to enrich and strengthen multicultural education?

8. What positive contributions can parents and students make to creating an effective multicultural school? Give specific examples.

References

Aptheker, H. (1987). *American Negro Slave Revolts.* New York: International Publishers. (Original work published 1943)

Au, K. A., & Kawakami, A. J. (1994). Cultural Congruence in Instruction. In E. R. Hollins, J. E. King, & W. C. Hayman (Eds.), *Teaching Diverse Populations: Formulating a Knowledge Base* (pp. 5–24). New York: State University of New York Press.

Banks, J. A. (2003). *Teaching Strategies for Ethnic Studies* (7th ed.). Boston: Allyn & Bacon.

Bennett deMarrais, K., & LeCompte, M. G. (1999). *The Way Schools Work: A Sociological Analysis of Education* (3rd ed.). New York: Longman.

Beykont, Z. (Ed.). (2000). *Lifting Every Voice: Pedagogy and Politics of Bilingual Education.* Cambridge, MA: Harvard Educational Publishing Group.

Bigelow, B., Christensen, L., Karp, S., Miner, B., & Peterson, B. (Eds.). (1994). *Rethinking Our Classrooms: Teaching for Equity and Justice* (Vol. 1) Milwaukee, WI: Rethinking Schools.

Bigelow, B., Harvey, B., Karp, S., & Miller, L. (Eds.). (2001). *Rethinking Our Classrooms: Teaching for Equity and Justice* (Vol. 2) Milwaukee, WI: Rethinking Schools.

Bowles, S., & Gintis, H. (1976). *Schooling in Capitalist America: Educational Reform and the Contradictions of Economic Life.* New York: Basic Books.

Bryk, A. S., Lee, V. E., & Holland, P. B. (1993). *Catholic Schools and the Common Good.* Cambridge, MA: Harvard Educational Review.

Carnoy, M. (1994). *Faded Dreams: The Politics and Economics of Race in America.* New York: Cambridge University Press.

Cummins, J. (1996). *Negotiating Identities: Education for Empowerment in a Diverse Society.* Ontario, CA: California Association for Bilingual Education.

Daniels, R. (1971). *Concentration Camps, U.S.A.: Japanese Americans and World War II.* New York: Holt.

Delpit, L. (1995). *Other People's Children: Cultural Conflict in the Classroom.* New York: New Press.

Deyhle, D., & Swisher, K. (1997). Research in American Indian and Alaska Native Education: From Assimilation to Self-Determination. In M. W. Apple (Ed.), *Review of Research in Education* (Vol. 22, pp. 113–194). Washington, DC: American Educational Research Association.

Donaldson, K. (1996). *Through Students' Eyes.* New York: Bergin & Garvey.

Epstein, J. L. (2001). *School, Family, and Community Partnerships: Preparing Educators and Improving Schools.* Boulder, CO: Westview.

Erickson, F. (1993). Transformation and School Success: The Politics and Culture of Educational Achievement: In E. Jacob & C. Jordan (Eds.), *Minority Education: Anthropological Perspectives* (pp. 27–51). Norwood, NJ: Ablex.

Fine, M. (1991). *Framing Dropouts: Notes on the Politics of an Urban Public High School.* Albany: State University of New York Press.

Fine, M. (Ed.). (1994). *Chartering Urban School Reform: Reflections on Public High Schools in the Midst of Change.* New York: Teachers College Press.

Fránquiz, M. E., & Reyes, M. de la Luz (1998). Creating Inclusive Learning Communities through English Language Arts: From *Chanclas* to *Canicas. Language Arts,* 75(3), 211–220.

Frau-Ramos, M., & Nieto, S. (1993). "I Was an Outsider": An Exploratory Study of Dropping Out among Puerto Rican Youths in Holyoke, Massachusetts. In R. Rivera & S. Nieto (Eds.), *The Education of Latino Students in Massachusetts: Issues, Research, and Policy Implications* (pp. 147–169). Boston: Gastón Institute.

Freire, P. (1970). *Pedagogy of the Oppressed.* New York: Seabury.

Freire, P. (1985). *The Politics of Education: Culture, Power, and Liberation.* South Hadley, MA: Bergin & Garvey.

Gay, G. (2000). *Culturally Responsive Teaching: Theory, Research, and Practice.* New York: Teachers College Press.

Gebhard, M., Austin, T., Nieto, S., & Willett, J. (2002). "You Can't Step on Someone Else's Words": Preparing All Teachers to Teach Language Minority Students. In Z. Beykont (Ed.), *The Power of Culture: Teaching across Language Difference* (pp. 219–243). Cambridge, MA: Harvard Educational Publishing Group.

Harris, V. J. (Ed.). (1997). *Using Multiethnic Literature in the K–8 Classroom*. Norwood, MA: Christopher-Gordon.

Herrnstein, R. J., & Murray, C. (1994). *The Bell Curve: Intelligence and Class Structure in American Life*. New York: Free Press.

Igoa, C. (1995). *The Inner World of the Immigrant Child*. Mahwah NJ: Erlbaum.

Irvine, J. J. (Ed.). (1997). *Critical Knowledge for Diverse Teachers and Learners*. Washington, DC: American Association of Colleges for Teacher Education.

Irvine, J. J. (2003). *Educating Teachers for Diversity: Seeing with a Cultural Eye*. New York: Teachers College Press.

Irvine, J. J., & Foster, M. (Eds.). (1996). *Growing up African American in Catholic Schools*. New York: Teachers College Press.

Kailin, J. (1999). How White Teachers Perceive the Problem of Racism in Their Schools: A Case Study of "Liberal" Lakeview. *Teachers College Record, 100*(4), 724–750.

Katz, M. B. (1975). *Class, Bureaucracy, and the Schools: The Illusion of Educational Change in America*. New York: Praeger.

Kiang, P. N. (1995). Bicultural Strengths and Struggles of Southeast Asian Americans in School. In A. Darder (Ed.), *Culture and Difference: Critical Perspectives on the Bicultural Experience in the United States* (pp. 201–225). Westport, CT: Bergin & Garvey.

Kohl, H. (1993). The Myth of "Rosa Parks the Tired." *Multicultural Education, 1*(2), 6–10.

Kohn, A. (2000). *The Case against Standardized Testing: Raising the Scores, Ruining the Schools*. Portsmouth, NH: Heinemann.

Kozol, J. (1975, December). Great Men and Women (Tailored for School Use). *Learning Magazine*, pp. 16–20.

Kozol, J. (1991). *Savage Inequalities: Children in America's Schools*. New York: Crown.

Ladson-Billings, G. (1994). *The Dreamkeepers: Successful Teachers of African American Children*. San Francisco: Jossey-Bass.

Ladson-Billings, G. (2001). *Crossing over to Canaan: The Journey of New Teachers in Diverse Classrooms*. San Francisco: Jossey-Bass.

Landsman, J. (2001). *A White Teacher Talks about Race*. Lanham, MD: Scarecrow.

Lee, E., Menkart, D., & Okazawa-Rey, M. (1998). *Beyond Heroes and Holidays: A Practical Guide to K–12 Anti-Racist, Multicultural Education and Staff Development*. Washington, DC: Teaching for Change.

Lee, V. E., & Loeb, S. (2000). School Size in Chicago Elementary Schools: Effects on Teachers' Attitudes and Students' Achievement. *American Educational Research Journal, 37*, 3–31.

Levin, M. (2001) *"Teach Me!" Kids Will Learn When Oppression Is the Lesson*. Lanham, MD: Rowman & Littlefield.

Loewen, J. W. (1995). *Lies My Teacher Taught Me: Everything Your American History Textbook Got Wrong*. New York: Free Press.

Loewen, J. W. (2000). *Lies across America: What Our Historic Sites Got Wrong*. New York: New Press.

May, S. (Ed.). (1999). *Rethinking Multicultural and Antiracist Education: Towards Critical Multiculturalism*. London: Falmer.

McCarty, T. L. (2002). *A Place to Be Navajo: Rough Rock and the Struggle for Self-Determination in Indigenous Schooling*. Mahwah, NJ: Erlbaum.

McIntyre, A. (1997). *Making Meaning of Whiteness: Exploring Racial Identity with White Teachers*. Albany: State University of New York Press.

McNeil, L. (2000). *Contradictions of School Reform: Educational Costs of Standardized Testing*. New York: Routledge.

Meier, D. (1995). *The Power of Their Ideas: Lessons for America from a Small School in Harlem*. Boston: Beacon.

Meier, K. J., & Stewart, J., Jr. (1991). *The Politics of Hispanic Education: Un Paso Pálante y Dos Pátras*. Albany: State University of New York Press.

Mercado, C. I. (1993). Caring as Empowerment: School Collaboration and Community Agency. *Urban Review, 25*(1), 79–104.

Moll, L., & González, N. (1997). Teachers as Social Scientists: Learning about Culture from Household Research. In P. M. Hall (Ed.), *Race, Ethnicity, and Multiculturalism* (Vol. 1, pp. 89–114). New York: Garland.

Moses, R. P., & Cobb, C. E. (2002). *Radical Equations: Math Literacy and Civil Rights*. Boston: Beacon.

Mosteller, F. (1995). The Tennessee Study of Class Size in the Early School Grades. *The Future of Children, 5*(2), 113–127.

National Center for Education Statistics. (2000). *Trends in Disparities in School District Level Expenditures per Pupil*. Washington, DC: U.S. Department of Education, Office of Educational Research and Improvement.

National Commission on Excellence in Education. (1983). *A Nation at Risk: The Imperative for Educational Reform*. Washington, DC: Author.

Nieto, S. (1994). Lessons from Students on Creating a Chance to Dream. *Harvard Educational Review, 64*(4), 392–426.

Nieto, S. (1999). *The Light in Their Eyes: Creating Multicultural Learning Communities*. New York: Teachers College Press.

Nieto, S. (2002/2003). Profoundly Multicultural Questions. *Educational Leadership, 60*(4), 6–10.

Nieto, S. (2004). *Affirming Diversity: The Sociopolitical Context of Multicultural Education* (4th ed.). Boston: Allyn & Bacon.

Oakes, J., Wells, A. S., Jones, M., & Datnow, A. (1997). Detracking: The Social Construction of Ability, Cultural Politics, and Resistance to Reform. *Teachers College Record, 98*(3), 482–510.

Ogbu, J. U. (1994). Racial Stratification and Education in the United States: Why Inequality Persists. *Teachers College Record, 96*(2), 264–298.

Olsen, L. (1997). *Made in America: Immigrant Students in Our Public Schools*. New York: New Press.

Olsen, L., Jaramillo, A., McCall-Perez, Z., White, J., & Minicucci, C. (1999). *Igniting Change for Immigrant Students: Portraits of Three High Schools*. Oakland, CA: California Tomorrow.

Orfield, G. (2001). *Schools More Separate: Consequences of a Decade of Resegregation*. Cambridge, MA: Harvard Civil Rights Project.

Orfield, G., & Kornhaber, M. L. (Eds.). (2001). *Raising Standards or Raising Barriers? Inequality and High-Stakes Testing in Public Education*. New York: Century Foundation Press.

Peterson, R. E. (1991). Teaching How to Read the World and Change It: Critical Pedagogy in the Intermediate Grades. In C. E. Walsh (Ed.), *Literacy as Praxis: Culture, Language, and Pedagogy* (pp. 156–182). Norwood, NJ: Ablex.

Poplin, M., & Weeres, J. (1992). *Voices from the Inside: A Report on Schooling from Inside the Classroom.* Claremont, CA: Claremont Graduate School, Institute for Education in Transformation.

Reissman, F. (1962). *The Culturally Deprived Child.* New York: Harper & Row.

Ryan, W. (1972). *Blaming the Victim.* New York: Vintage.

Shor, I. (1992). *Empowering Education: Critical Teaching for Social Change.* Chicago: University of Chicago Press.

Sleeter, C. E. (1994). White Racism. *Multicultural Education, 1*(4), 5–8, 39.

Sleeter, C. E., & McLaren, P. L. (1995). *Multicultural Education, Critical Pedagogy, and the Politics of Difference.* Albany: State University of New York Press.

Snow, C. (1997). The Myths around Bilingual Education. *NABE News, 21*(2), 29.

Soto, L. D. (1997). *Language, Culture, and Power: Bilingual Families and the Struggle for Quality Education.* Albany: State University of New York Press.

Spring, J. (1989). *The Sorting Machine Revisited: National Educational Policy Since 1945.* White Plains, NY: Longman.

Spring, J. (2002). *American Education* (10th ed.). Boston: McGraw-Hill.

Steele, C. M. (1999). Thin Ice: "Stereotype Threat" and Black College Students. *The Atlantic Monthly, 284*(2), 44–54.

Takaki, R. (1993). *A Different Mirror: A History of Multicultural America.* Boston: Little, Brown.

Tatum, B. D. (1997). *"Why Are All the Black Kids Sitting Together in the Cafeteria?" and Other Conversations about Race.* New York: HarperCollins.

Walsh, C. E. (Ed.). (1996). *Education Reform and Social Change: Multicultural Voices, Struggles, and Visions.* Mahwah, NJ: Erlbaum.

Weinberg, M. (1990). *Racism in the United States: A Comprehensive Classified Bibliography.* Westport, CT: Greenwood.

Willis, A. (Ed.). (1998). *Teaching and Using Multicultural Literature in Grades 9–12: Moving beyond the Canon.* Norwood, MA: Christopher-Gordon.

Wong Fillmore, L. (1991). When Learning a Second Language Means Losing the First. *Early Childhood Research Quarterly, 6,* 323–346.

Zeichner, K. (1996). Educating Teachers to Close the Achievement Gap: Issues of Pedagogy, Knowledge, and Teacher Preparation. In B. Williams (Ed.), *Closing the Achievement Gap: A Vision for Changing Beliefs and Practices* (pp. 76–96). Alexandria, VA: Association for Supervision and Curriculum Development.

Zentella, A. C. (1997). *Growing Up Bilingual: Puerto Rican Children in New York.* Malden, MA: Blackwell.

Zinn, H. (2003). *A People's History of the United States: 1492–Present* (rev. ed.). New York: HarperCollins.

CHAPTER 17

Communities, Families, and Educators Working for School Improvement

Cherry A. McGee Banks

Mr. Watson looked over at Ms. Taylor with an exasperated expression on his face and just shook his head. Ms. Taylor wasn't sure what to say, and so she didn't say anything. Mr. Watson was the principal at Vine Middle School and Ms. Taylor chaired the school's Academic Council. They had just completed a meeting with several members of the Eastside Improvement Club, a high-status and influential group in the community. After seeing a newspaper article on the school's low test scores, the club members had decided to put their energy into improving academic achievement at the school. Vine had the lowest test scores in the district.

Mr. Watson had organized the Academic Council shortly after he arrived at Vine. The council included teacher representatives from all the academic departments at the school. Under Ms. Taylor's leadership, the council had begun to discuss curriculum issues, review disciplinary procedures, survey students and parents about after-school programs, and generate ideas about ways to encourage parents and community groups to participate in school events. Even though the council had been in existence for less than a year, it was a visible sign that Vine was being revitalized. Teachers were excited about their jobs and were talking to each other about how to work more effectively with Vine students. Mr. Watson believed that this was an important change and a necessary foundation for improving students' academic performance.

When the Eastside Improvement Club offered their services to the school, the staff was delighted. Mr. Watson and the teachers believed that the prestige that members of the club had in the community would open doors for the school and help Vine secure resources for field trips, materials, and other extras that students could not afford and that the school could not provide. While the club did provide a number of "extras" for the school, its support was not exactly free. As one teacher commented, "Everytime I look up, someone from the Eastside Improvement Club is in the building. You never know when one of them will show up at your door." Mr. Watson was amazed at the amount of time he spent with club members talking to them about the school and what he and the teachers were trying to do. However, their talks seemed more like debates than conversations. After several months, club members still didn't seem to understand how schools work, grasp the length of time it takes for school improvements to take hold, or really seem to appreciate the multiple factors that influence student achievement. More than once, Mr. Watson had overheard teachers talking about the Eastside Improvement Club and noting that "they only seem to be concerned about test scores." He had also heard teachers say, "They act like they know more about education than we do." Unlike other community and parent groups that had volunteered at the school in the past, the members of the Eastside Improvement Club wanted to insert themselves into all aspects of decision making at the school. They wanted to observe teachers teaching and help select new texts—and they didn't mind telling teachers what they liked and didn't like.

The club members were very disappointed that, after a year, Vine was still near the bottom of the district when test scores were reported in the local newspaper. They told Mr. Watson and Ms. Taylor that they wanted less talk on the Academic Council and more action. They threatened to withdraw their support from the school if student test scores didn't improve by the end of the school year.

After a long pause while she thought about what had just happened, Ms. Taylor finally found the words she was looking for. She turned to Mr. Watson and said, "Even though I don't want to admit it, the club members have a point. It is time for action. The only problem is that we don't define *action* in the same way. The teachers think we're already taking action. The club members don't seem to care about our small steps; they want us to make some dramatic changes." "You're right, but the bottom line is that we don't know how to work with high-powered community groups," said Mr. Watson. "If this relationship is going to work, we're going to have to come together as a team. Right now we seem more like adversaries."

This hypothetical incident raises questions about how and when community groups and parents should be involved in schools. For example, how involved should parents and members of the community be in determining curriculum, instruction, and staffing? What does it mean for parents and community groups to be partners with teachers and administrators? What roles should parents and teachers play in that partnership? How important is it for parents, members of community groups, and teachers with different points of view and from different backgrounds to work together? Since community groups don't always represent parent concerns and issues, how important is it for schools to make sure that parents aren't left out of decision making?

These are the kinds of questions Mr. Watson, Ms. Taylor, and the teachers at Vine Middle School will need to answer to work effectively with the Eastside Improvement Club and other community groups, parents, and family members. They will also need people skills, confidence in their ability to work with community groups and parents, and a clear understanding of how and why students benefit when parents and teachers are partners. Teachers who are unsure of the importance of working with parents and members of the community and are uncomfortable reaching out to critical parents and groups will likely have difficulty collaborating with them. They may also have a skewed view of the opinions, concerns, and interests of parents and other members of the community.

When confronted with concerns like those raised by the Eastside Improvement Club, Mr. Watson, Ms. Taylor, and the teachers at Vine may conclude that most parents and members of the community are concerned only about test scores. As a result, they may narrowly focus their energy on test performance. This would be unfortunate because there is a growing body of evidence that raises doubts about the value of high-stakes testing. A comprehensive study of high-stakes tests conducted by researchers at Arizona State University found that even though students performed better on state exams, they did not perform as well on other measures of academic achievement. When school curricula are narrowly focused on state exams, students have difficulty understanding and applying the information they learn to other problems and issues (Winter, 2002). It is important for educators to be able to communicate these and other facts about testing to parents and community groups.

To be effective communicators, teachers have to be good listeners. Ms. Taylor and Mr. Watson need to be able to hear and respectfully respond to the Eastside Improvement Club's concerns about test scores. Club members may not have an accurate understanding about the complexities of academic achievement or how to implement school change, but as influential members of the community they should not be ignored. As school leaders, Ms. Taylor and Mr. Watson should serve as resources for groups like the Eastside Improvement Club. They can share information with them, invite them to read the texts and materials used at the school, arrange for them to talk with parents who understand the school's goals, and invite them to take an active role in improving Vine Middle School. In that way, club members aren't simply on the sidelines critiquing teachers and the school. They become a part of the school and can take ownership of both the challenges and opportunities that exist there. These steps can help minimize the difficulties that arise when communication breaks down and when there is a lack of trust and respect.

In addition to differences of opinion, teachers must be aware of possible cultural boundaries that could limit their communication with parents and members of community groups. Frequently, the kind of cultural boundaries that are discussed when talking about parent involvement in schools focus on differences in religion, language, and ethnic characteristics. Those differences can make communication between parents and teachers difficult and strained. The example involving the Eastside Improvement Club suggests that cultural boundaries can also exist when parents or members of community groups have more education, higher incomes, and more cultural capital than the educators with whom they work. In both cases cultural boundaries have to be crossed, and it is not surprising that communication sometimes breaks down and that trust and respect are called into question. In school communities with large numbers of low-income parents, educators may need to focus on ways to welcome and support parent and community involvement. In such communities, educators may feel superior to parents and members of the community and see themselves as benign helpers. Educators in communities with large numbers of upper-middle-class parents may find that they are working with parents and community groups that are similar to the Eastside Improvement Club. In these cases, parents and members of community groups may feel superior to educators and see themselves as benign helpers who politely, but firmly, demand that the school listen and respond to their concerns.

The diversity of parent and community groups, with their different concerns and issues, illustrates one of the important complexities of parent and community involvement in schools (De Carvalho, 2001). That complexity, which may be reflected in different interaction styles, expectations, and concerns, complicates but does not negate the need for parent and community involvement in schools (DeSteno, 2000). Educators lose an important voice for school improvement when parents and community groups are not involved in schools. They can give teachers a unique and important view of the students as well as help the school garner resources and opportunities that are available in the community.

In a comprehensive review of research on parent involvement, Henderson and Berla (1994) found compelling evidence that parent involvement improves student achievement. Parent involvement is also associated with improvements in students' attendance and social behavior. However, to capitalize on the benefits of parent and community involvement, strategies must be broadly conceptualized. Parents should be given an opportunity to contribute to school improvement by working in different settings and at different levels of the educational process (Mannan & Blackwell, 1992). For example, some parents may want to focus their energies on working with their own children at home. Other parents may want to work on decision-making committees. Still others may be able to provide in-class assistance to teachers.

Parents, other family members, and community groups can also work with teachers to reform schools. Many tasks involved in restructuring schools, such as setting goals and allocating resources, are best achieved through a collaborative problem-solving structure that includes parents, educators, and family and community members (Mannan & Blackwell, 1992).

Family and community members can form what Goodlad (1984) calls "the necessary coalition of contributing groups" (p. 293). Educational reform needs their support, influence, and activism. Schools are highly dependent on and vulnerable to citizens who can support or impede change. Family members and community leaders can validate the need for educational reform and can provide an appropriate forum for exploring the importance of education. They can also extend the discussion on school improvement issues beyond formal educational networks and can help generate support for schools in the community at large. Family members and community leaders can help provide the rationale, motivation, and social action necessary for educational reform.

WHY IS PARENT AND FAMILY INVOLVEMENT IN SCHOOLS IMPORTANT?

Parent involvement is important because it acknowledges the importance of parents in the lives of their children, recognizes the diversity of values and perspectives within the community, provides a vehicle for building a collaborative problem-solving structure, and increases the opportunity for all students to learn in school. Parents, however, are not the only adults who support and contribute to the care of children. The role of grandparents and other family members as primary caregivers is becoming more significant. In 2000, 4.5 million children under eighteen lived in grandparent-headed households. This was a 29.7 percent increase from 1990 in the number of grandchildren in grandparent-headed households. Grandparents caring for grandchildren occurs in all ethnic and income groups. About one-third of the children living in their grandparents' homes do not have parents living with them (U.S. Bureau of the Census, 2000).

Students, parents, and teachers all benefit when parents and family members are involved in schools (Comer, Ben-Avie, Haynes, & Joyner, 1999). When parents help their children at home, the children perform better in school (Booth & Dunn, 1996). Although we do not know exactly why students show improvements when their parents are involved in their education, we know that parent involvement increases the number of people who are supporting the child's learning. Parent involvement also increases the amount of time the child is involved in learning activities.

Parent involvement allows parents and teachers to reinforce skills and provides an environment that has consistent learning expectations and standards. Parents also become more knowledgeable about their child's school, its policies, and the school staff when they are involved in schools. Perhaps most important, parent involvement provides an opportunity for parents and children to spend time together. During that time, parents can communicate a high value for education, the importance of effort in achievement, and a high positive regard for their children.

Parents and family members are often children's first and most important teachers. Students come to school with knowledge, values, and beliefs they have learned from their parents and in their communities. Parents directly or indirectly help shape their children's value system, orientation toward learning, and view of the world (Stratton, 1995). Most parents want their children to succeed in school. Schools can capitalize on the high value most parents put on education by working to create a school environment that respects the students' home and community (Hidalgo, Sau-Fong, & Epstein, 2004). When schools are in conflict with their students' home and community, they can alienate students from their families and communities.

To create harmonious relations among the school, home, and community, teachers need to understand their students' community and home life. Teachers need to know the educational expectations parents have for their children, the languages spoken at home, the family's values and norms, and how children are taught in their homes and communities. Parents also need information about the school. They need to know what the school expects their children to learn, how they will be taught, and the required books and materials their children will use in school. Most important, parents need to know how teachers assess students and how they can support their children's achievement.

Teachers and principals who know parents treat them with greater respect and show more positive attitudes toward their children (Berger, 2003). Teachers generally see involved parents as concerned individuals who support the school. Parents who are not involved in schools are frequently seen as parents who do not value education.

Historical Overview

While parent involvement in education is not new, its importance and purpose have varied over time. In the early part of the nation's history, families were often solely responsible for educating children. Children learned values and skills by working with their families in their communities.

When formal systems of education were established, parents continued to influence their children's education. During the colonial period, schools were viewed as an extension of the home. Parental and community values and expectations were reinforced in the school. Teachers generally came from the community and often personally knew their students' parents and shared their values.

At the beginning of the twentieth century, when large numbers of immigrants came to the United States, schools became a major vehicle for assimilating immigrant children into U.S. society (Banks, 2003). In general, parents were not welcomed in schools. Students were taught that their parents' ways of speaking, behaving, and thinking were inferior to those of mainstream Americans. In his study of the sociology of teaching, Waller (1932/1965) concluded that parents and teachers lived in a state of mutual distrust and even hostility. There were, however, some notable exceptions.

One such exception was Benjamin Franklin High School (BFHS) in East Harlem, New York. Leonard Covello, principal at BFHS, instituted a program of intergroup education at Franklin in the 1930s. Parents were welcome at Franklin, and teachers encouraged students to appreciate their parents' language, values, and customs. Community groups were also actively involved at BFHS. Covello saw parent and community involvement as a way to promote democractic values, reduce prejudice, and increase cross-cultural understanding and appreciation.

Over time, as society changed and education became more removed from the direct influence of parents, responsibility for transmitting knowledge from generation to generation was transferred from the home and community to the school. Education was seen as a job for trained professionals. Schools became autonomous institutions staffed by people who were often strangers in their students' home communities. Teachers did not necessarily live in their students' neighborhoods, know the students' parents, or share their values. Schools were given more and more duties that traditionally had been the responsibility of the home and community. Schools operated under the assumption of *in loco parentis*, and educators were asked to assume the role of both teacher and substitute parent.

In a pluralist society, what the school teaches as well as who and how the school teaches can create tensions between parents and schools. Issues ranging from what the school teaches about the role of women in our society to mainstreaming students with disabilities point to the need for teachers, parents, and community leaders to work together (Schneider & Coleman, 1996). However, parents, community leaders, and teachers do not always agree on meaningful ways to cooperate and partner in the educational process (Cibulka & Kritek, 1996).

The Changing Face of the Family

Parent/family diversity mirrors student diversity. Involving parents in schools means that teachers have to be prepared to work with a range of parents, including single parents, parents with special needs, low-income parents, parents with disabilities, and parents who do not speak English as their first language. Working with parents from diverse backgrounds requires a sensitivity to and an understanding of their circumstances and worldviews (Chavkin & Gonzalez, 1995; Kagan, 1995; Pena, 2000; Schneider & Coleman, 1996).

It is especially important that teachers be sensitive to and understand the changing nature of the ethnic and racial makeup of their students and their students' parents. The ethnic landscape of U.S. schools includes an increasing number of Arab, Jewish, Eastern European, and African students (Pollard & O'Hare, 1999). African Americans constituted 8 percent of the nation's total foreign-born population in 1999. In 2000, about 80 percent of the African American foreign-born population came from Latin America, and about 63 percent of that number came from the Caribbean (U.S. Bureau of the Census, 2000). For many of these individuals, their ethnic identity has primacy over their racial identity. Such individuals, for example, would identify themselves as Cuban Americans or Puerto Ricans, not as Blacks or Whites. Their phenotype, however, might conflict with physical characteristics that traditionally have been used to identify races in the United States. For example, a Cuban American with brown skin may consider himself White.

The lines between racial groups are becoming blurred. A growing number of students and parents are members of more than one racial group. Even though marriage between people from different races is still an exception rather than the rule, more and more people are marrying interracially. As a result, the number of students with parents or grandparents of different races is increasing. In 2000, about 2.4 percent of the U.S. population, or about 6.8 million people, identified with two or more races (U.S. Census Bureau, 2000). While this is a relatively small percentage of the U.S. population, the percentage of people who are multiracial is more salient when geographic regions and subgroups within the population are examined. For example, children are more likely to be multiracial than adults and racial groups that have small populations tend to include higher percentages of multiracial people. Additionally, urban areas tend to have higher rates of interracial marriage than rural areas. In 2000, about 1.9 percent of U.S. adults identified themselves as multiracial compared to 4.0 percent of children.

Among all the racial groups, American Indians were the most likely to marry someone outside their racial group (Pollard & O'Hare, 1999). Data from the 2000 census indicate that approximately 40 percent of American Indians are multiracial. Asians also tend to marry at a high rate outside their racial group; consequently, a growing number of Asians are multiracial. The 2000 census indicates that about 14 percent of Asians report that they are multiracial compared to 5 percent of Blacks and 3 percent of Whites (Lee, 2001). About

52 percent of the total number of the multiracial Asians are Asian and White. Historically this population has been referred to as Amerasians and associated with the interracial marriages of service personnel stationed in Asian countries after WWII and the Vietnam War. Today the term "Hapa," a Hawaiian term meaning half White and half Hawaiian, is frequently used to refer to Asians of mixed-race ancestry (Krebs, 2000).

The increase in interracial marriage has resulted in an increase of interracial children. Between 1977 and 1997, the number of babies born to interracial couples increased from less than 2 percent of the total births to about 5 percent. In 1997, interracial births were the third-largest racial or ethnic category of U.S. births. In California, the number of interracial births surpassed Asian, Black, and American Indian births. Of all the ethnic and racial groups, interracial births were highest for American Indians. Approximately 50 percent of American Indians born in 1997 were biracial. About 20 percent of births to Asian women and 5 percent of births to African American women were biracial (Pollard & O'Hare, 1999). Also adding to the increasing number of interracial families are the growing number of children adopted from other countries. Foreign-born children, usually Asian, are being adopted by American families, usually White families, in growing numbers. In 2000, immigration visas were issued to 5,053 orphans from China, 4,269 orphans from Russia, and 1,794 orphans from South Korea. The vast majority of the adoptees are girls (Lee, 2001).

Diversity in parent and community groups can be a tremendous asset to the school. However, it can also be a source of potential conflicts and tensions. Some parents are particularly difficult to involve in their children's education. They resist becoming involved for several reasons (Harry, 1992; Walker, 1996). In a national survey, parents indicated that a lack of time was the primary reason they were not involved in their children's schools (Clark, 1995). The pressures to earn a living and take care of a home and children can result in a great deal of stress. At the end of the day, some parents just want to rest. Other parents do not believe they have the necessary educational background to be involved in their children's school. They feel intimidated by educators and believe that education should be left to teachers. Still others feel alienated from their children's schools because of negative experiences they had in school or because they believe the school does not support their values (Berger, 2003; Clark, 1995; Rasinski, 1990).

Three groups of parents are frequently underrepresented in school activities: parents with special needs, single parents, and low-income parents. These are not the only groups that are underrepresented in school activities; however, their experiences and needs illustrate particular problem areas. The specific groups of parents discussed should not be viewed as an indication that only parents from these groups are difficult to involve in schools or that all parents from these groups resist participation in schools. Parents from all groups share many of the concerns discussed below. Moreover, there are examples of parents from each of the groups discussed below who are actively involved in schools.

Parents with Special Needs

Parents with special needs include a wide range of individuals. They are found in all ethnic, racial, and income groups. Chronically unemployed parents, parents with long-term illnesses, abusive parents, and parents with substance-abuse problems are examples of parents with special needs. Abusive parents require special attention from the school. Most schools have policies on how to treat suspected cases of child neglect and abuse. The policies should be written and available to all school personnel. All states require schools to report suspected cases of child abuse.

Although parents with special needs frequently have serious problems that the school cannot address, teachers should not ignore the importance of establishing a relationship with them. Knowing the difficulties students are coping with at home can help teachers create environments that are supportive during the time students are in school (Swadener & Niles, 1991). Schools can help compensate for the difficult circumstances students experience at home. The school, for some students, is the only place during the day where they are nurtured.

Working with special-needs families requires district or building support in identifying places for family referrals and support for students and teachers. Although some special-needs parents may resist the school's help, they need to know that their problems can negatively affect their children's success in school. Working with these parents can show students who are in difficult home environments that they are not alone. Most parents want to feel that they are valued and adequate human beings and that they can help their children succeed. When they are willing to be involved in school, they do not want to be humiliated (Berger, 2003).

Some parents with special needs will be able to be actively involved in schools, but many will be unable to sustain ongoing involvement. An important goal for working with parents with special needs is to keep lines of communication open. Most important, try to get to know the parents. Do not accept a stereotypical view of them without ever talking to them. Encourage parents to become involved whenever and however they feel they are able to participate. Be prepared to recommend appropriate community agencies to the family. Try to develop a clear understanding of your student's home environment so that you can provide appropriate intervention at school.

Members of the community who are involved in school may be willing to serve as intermediaries between the school and uninvolved parents and in some cases as surrogate parents. In an ethnography of an inner-city neighborhood, Shariff (1988) found that adults shared goods and services and helped each other. Educators can build on the sense of extended family that may exist in some neighborhoods to form or connect with community support groups for students whose parents cannot be involved in school.

Working with students whose parents have special needs is complicated and challenging. However, regardless of the circumstances students confront at home, teachers have a responsibility to help them perform at their highest level at school. Schools with large numbers of parents with special needs require experienced and highly qualified teachers. Traditionally, however, these schools have many teachers who are relatively new to the field and are not certified in the areas in which they teach (Darling-Hammond, 2004).

Single Parents

One of the most significant social changes in the United States in the last thirty years is the increase in the percentage of children living with one parent. In 1997, 32 percent of U.S. households with children under eighteen were headed by a single parent. The number of single-parent families is particularly significant in the African American community. In 1997, 64 percent of African American families with children under eighteen were headed by one parent (U.S. Census Bureau, 1998). Twenty-six percent of White and 36 percent of Hispanic families with children under eighteen were headed by one parent (U.S. Census Bureau, 1998).

Most children who live with one parent are from divorced homes or are the children of unwed mothers. In 1997, approximately 50 percent of all marriages in the United States ended in divorce (U.S. Bureau of the Census, 1998). The number of years from the dissolution of the first marriage until remarriage for women varies tremendously by race. Within one year after a divorce, 21.9 percent of White women are remarried, compared to 10.9 percent of Black women. Five years after divorcing, 53 percent of White women are remarried, compared to 25 percent of Black women (U.S. Census Bureau, 1998).

This trend is reflected in the increase in the nation's unmarried households and the fifty-year decline in the number of married couples. In 2000, only 51.7 percent of U.S. households contained a married couple. This was down from 55 percent in 1990, 60.8 percent in 1980, 70.5 percent in 1970, and 78 percent in 1950 (U.S. Census, 2000). If this trend continues, in the near future the majority of U.S. households will be headed by unmarried adults.

Single-parent families have many of the same hopes, joys, and concerns about their children's education as two-parent families. However, because these parents have a lower rate of attendance at school functions, they are frequently viewed as not supporting their children's education. When teachers respond sensitively to their needs and limitations, they can be enthusiastic partners with teachers. Four suggestions for working with single parents are listed below. Many of these suggestions apply to other groups of parents as well.

1. Provide flexible times for conferences, such as early mornings, evenings, and weekends.
2. Provide baby-sitting service when activities are held at the school.
3. Work out procedures for acknowledging and communicating with noncustodial parents. For instance, under what circumstances are noncustodial parents informed about their children's grades, school behavior, or attendance? Problems can occur when information is inappropriately given to or withheld from a noncustodial parent.
4. Use the parent's correct surname. Students will sometimes have different names from their parents.

Low-Income Parents

The poverty rate in the United States was 11.7 percent in 2001, with 6.8 million families and 32.9 million people living in poverty. The number of people living below the poverty line increased by 1.3 million from 2000 to 2001. The poverty rate for children was 16.3 percent in 2001. The poverty level is an official governmental estimate of the income necessary to maintain a minimally acceptable standard of living. Poverty rates vary by family type. Households headed by single women have the highest poverty rate at 28.6 percent. The poverty rate for married couples is 5.7 percent (Proctor & Dalaker, 2002). A family of four in 2000 with a total income less than $18,104 was considered to be living below the poverty line (Proctor & Dalaker, 2002).

Even though the number of individuals of color in the highest income brackets has more than doubled since 1980, race continues to be a salient factor in poverty. The poverty rate in 2001 was 7.8 percent for non-Hispanic Whites, 22.7 percent for African Americans, and 10.2 percent for Asians and Pacific Islanders. Most minorities earn less than Whites. However, Asians earn more than all ethnic groups. In 2001, their median income was $5 ,635 per year, compared to $46,305 per year for non-Hispanic Whites, $33,565 for Hispanics, $32,116 for American Indians and Alaska Natives, and $29,470 for Blacks (U.S. Census Bureau, 2002).

Low-income parents are often among the strongest supporters of education, seeing it as a means to a better life for their children. However, they may define "support for education" and may see their role in supporting their children's education differently than the school staff. Additionally, they are often limited in their ability to buy materials and to make financial commitments that can enable their children to participate in activities such as field trips or extracurricular programs. Many of the suggestions listed for single parents also apply to low-income parents. Schools can provide workbooks and other study materials for use at home as well as transportation for school activities and conferences. The school can also support low-income parents by establishing community service programs. For example, students can help clean up neighborhoods and distribute information on available social services. The schools can provide desk space for voter registration and other services.

Perhaps the most important way for schools to work with low-income parents is to recognize that they can contribute a great deal to their children's education. Even though their contributions may not be in the manner traditionally associated with parent involvement, they can be very beneficial to teachers and students. The positive values and attitudes parents communicate to their children and their strong desire for their children to get a good education in order to have a better chance in life than they had are important forms of support for the school.

TEACHER CONCERNS WITH PARENT AND FAMILY INVOLVEMENT

Even though teachers often say they want to involve parents, many are suspicious of parents and are not sure what parents expect from them. Some teachers think parents may disrupt their routine, may not have the necessary skills to work with students, may be inconvenient to have in the classroom, and may be interested only in helping their own child, not the total class. Even teachers who would like to involve parents may not be sure that they have the time, skill, or knowledge to involve parents in the school. Many teachers believe that they already have too much to do and that working with parents would make their already-overburdened jobs impossible.

Many of these concerns derive from a limited view of the possibilities for parent involvement. Frequently, when parents and teachers think of parent involvement, they think it means doing something for the school generally at the school or having the school teach parents how to become better parents. In today's ever-changing society, a traditional view of parent involvement inhibits rather than encourages parents and teachers to work together. Traditional ideas about parent involvement have a built-in gender and social-class bias and are a barrier to many men and low-income parents. Moreover, they tend to focus on parents, not on community groups. With a national focus on education, more and more community groups are interested in working with schools. More consideration will need to be given to how to work effectively with community groups. It is not uncommon for schools to have corporate or community sponsors. While these are generally supportive and cooperative relationships, they can be time consuming and present new challenges for schools. Educators will need to think carefully about how to involve these groups in schools, their expectations for the relationship, and how the goals they established will be evaluated.

When parent involvement is viewed as a means of getting support for the school, parents are encouraged to bake cookies, raise money, or work at the school as unpaid classroom, playground, library, or office helpers. This form of parent recruitment is generally directed to mothers who do not work outside the home. However, the number of mothers available for this form of involvement is decreasing. In 1997, 71.1 percent of married women with children under six years old worked full-time outside the home (U.S. Census Bureau, 1998).

The parent-as-helper idea is geared toward parents who have the skills, time, and resources to become school helpers. Not all parents want to or feel they can or should do things for the school. Whether parents are willing to come to school is largely dependent on the parent's attitude toward school. This attitude results in part from the parent's own school experiences.

Cultural perspectives play an important role in the traditional approach to parent involvement. Bullivant (1993) points out the importance of understanding a social group's cultural program. To be effective, strategies for parent and community involvement should reflect what Bullivant calls the core of the social group's cultural program, which consists of the knowledge and conceptions embodied in the group's behaviors and artifacts and the values subscribed to by the group.

When teachers do not understand a group's cultural program, they may conceptualize parent involvement as a means to help deficient parents become better parents (Linn, 1990). This view of parent involvement is often directed toward culturally different and low-income parents (Jennings, 1990). Teachers are presented as more skilled in parenting than are parents. Instead of helping parents and teachers work cooperatively, this attitude can create barriers by suggesting that parents are the cause of their children's failure in school. Parents and teachers may even become rivals for the child's affection (Lightfoot, 1978).

Involvement efforts based on "the parent in need of parenting skills" assume that there is one appropriate way to parent and that parents want to learn it. Both "the parent as helper" and "the parent in need of parenting skills" are conceptualizations derived from questionable assumptions about the character of contemporary parents and reflect a limited cultural perspective.

STEPS TO INCREASE PARENT AND FAMILY INVOLVEMENT

Teachers are a key ingredient in parent and family involvement. They play multiple roles, including facilitator, communicator, and resource developer. Their success in implementing an effective parent/community involvement program is linked to their skill in communicating and working with parents and community groups. Teacher attitudes are also very important. Parents are supportive of the teachers they believe like their children and want their children to succeed. Teachers who have a negative attitude toward students will likely have a similar attitude toward the students' parents. Teachers tend to relate to their students as representatives of their parents' perceived status in society. Teachers use such characteristics as class, race, gender, and ethnicity to determine students' prescribed social category.

There are five steps you can take to increase parent/community involvement in your classroom: establishing two-way communication, enlisting support from staff and students, enlisting support from the community, developing resource materials for home use, and broadening the activities included in parent involvement.

Establish Two-Way Communication between the School and the Home

Establishing two-way communication between the school and the home is an important step in involving parents (Decker & Majerczyk, 2000). Most parents are willing to become involved in their children's education if you let them know what you are trying to accomplish and how parents can help. Teachers should be prepared to engage in outreach to parents and not to wait for them to become involved. Actively solicit information from parents on their thoughts about classroom goals and activities. When you talk with parents and community members, be an active listener. Listen for their feelings as well as for specific information. Listed below are seven ways you can establish and maintain two-way communication with parents and community members.

1. If possible, have an open-door policy in your classroom. Let parents know they are welcome to assist in your classroom. When parents visit, make sure they have something to do.

2. Send written information home about school assignments and goals so that parents are aware of what is going on in the classroom. Encourage parents to send notes to you if they have questions or concerns.

3. Talk to parents by phone. Let parents know when they can reach you by phone. Call parents periodically and let them know when things are going well. Have something specific to talk about. Leave some time for the parent to ask questions or make comments.

4. Report problems to parents, such as failing grades, before it is too late for them to take remedial action. Let parents know what improvements you expect from their children and how they can help.

5. Get to know your students' community. Take time to shop in their neighborhoods. Visit community centers and attend religious services. Let parents know when you will be in the community and that you are interested in talking to them.

6. If you teach in an elementary school, try to have at least two in-person conferences a year with parents. When possible, include the student in at least part of the conference. Be prepared to explain your curriculum to parents and have books and materials that students use available for them to examine. Let the parents know in specific terms how their children are doing in class. Find out how parents feel about their children's levels of achievement, and let them know what you think about their children's achievement levels. Give the parents some suggestions on what their children can do to improve and how they can help.

7. Solicit information from parents about their views on education. Identify their educational goals for their children, ways they would like to support their children's education, and their concerns about the school. There are a number

of ways to get information from parents, including sending a questionnaire home and asking parents to complete it and return it to you, conducting a telephone survey, and asking your students to interview their parents. Don't forget high-tech solutions for staying in touch with parents. These include school web pages, homework hotlines, e-mail conferences, videotaped events, and televised meetings.

Enlist the Support of Other Staff Members and Students

Teachers need support from staff, students, the principal, and district-level administrators to support and enhance their parent-involvement activities. Teachers generally have some flexibility in their classrooms but are not always able to influence some of the other important factors that influence their ability to have a strong parent-involvement program. For example, when teachers are consulted about the type and amount of supplies purchased for their classroom, they should be able to decide whether they want to have enough supplies to be able to send paper, pencils, and other materials home for parents to use with their children. If the school cannot provide extra supplies for teachers to send home with students, community groups may be able to provide them. Also, if teachers are allowed to modify their schedules, they can find free time to telephone parents, write notes, and hold morning or evening conferences with parents. Additionally, school climate influences parent involvement, but school climate is not determined by one individual; it is influenced by a broad range of individuals, including students, teachers, the principal, and the school secretary.

Your students can help solicit support for parent and community involvement from staff and other students. Take your class on a tour of the school. Ask the students to think about how their parents would feel if they came to the school. Two obvious questions for students are: Is there a place for visitors to sit? Are there signs welcoming visitors and inviting them to the school office? Ask your students to list things they could do to make the school a friendlier place for parents.

Invite your principal to come to your classroom and discuss the list with your students. Divide the class into small groups and have them discuss how they would like their parents to become involved in their education. Ask them to talk to their parents and get their views. Have each group write a report on how parents can be involved in their children's education. Each group could make presentations to students in the other classrooms in the building on how they would like to increase parent involvement in their school. They could also publish a newsletter on parent involvement in schools. The newsletter could be sent to the students, parents, and other schools in the district.

If funds or other forms of support are needed from the district office for parent-involvement activities, have the students draw up a petition requesting funding and solicit signatures from teachers, students, and parents. When all the signatures are gathered, they can be delivered to an appropriate district administrator. The petition could also be used to inform community groups about school issues and solicit their support.

Building principals and district administrators can give teachers the support they need to do the following:

1. Help create and maintain a climate for positive parent/community involvement. This can include supporting flexible hours for teachers who need to be out of the classroom to develop materials or to work with parents. Teachers can be given

time out of the classroom without negatively affecting students. Time can be gleaned from the secondary teacher's schedule by combining homerooms one day a week, by team-teaching a class, or by combining different sections of a class for activities such as chapter tests. At the elementary school level, team teachings, having released time during periods when students are normally out of the classroom for specialized subjects such as music and art, or having the principal substitute in the classroom are ways to provide flexible hours for teachers.

2. Set up a parent room. The parent room could be used for a number of functions, including serving as a community drop-in center where parents could meet other parents for a cup of coffee or as a place for parents to work on school activities without infringing on the teachers' lounge. It could also be used as a waiting room for parents who need to see a student or a member of the school staff.

3. Host parent nights during which parents can learn more about the school, the curriculum, and the staff.

4. Send a personal note to students and to their parents when students make the honor roll or do something else noteworthy.

5. Develop and distribute a handbook that contains the names and phone numbers of students, PTA or other parent-group contacts, and staff.

6. Ask the school secretary to make sure visitors are welcomed when they come to the school and are given directions as needed.

7. Encourage students to greet visitors and help them find their way around the building.

Enlist Support from the Community

To enlist support from the community, you need to know something about it. The following are some questions you should be able to answer.

1. Are there any drama, musical, dance, or art groups in the community?

2. Is there a senior-citizen group, a public library, or a cooperative extension service in the community?

3. Are employment services such as the state employment security department available in the community?

4. Are civil rights organizations such as the Urban League, Anti-Defamation League, or National Association for the Advancement of Colored People (NAACP) active in the community?

5. What is the procedure for referring people to the Salvation Army, Goodwill, or the state department of public assistance for emergency assistance for housing, food, and clothing?

6. Does the community have a mental health center, family counseling center, or crisis clinic?

7. Are programs and activities for youth—such as Boys and Girls Clubs, Campfire Girls, Boy Scouts, Girl Scouts, YMCA, and YWCA—available for your students?

As you learn about the community, you can begin to develop a list of community resources and contacts that can provide support to families, work with your students, and provide locations for students to perform community service projects. Collecting information about your students' community and developing community contacts should be viewed as a long-term project. You can collect information as your schedule permits and organize it in a notebook. This process can be shortened if several teachers work together. Each teacher could concentrate on a different part of the community and share information and contacts.

Community groups can provide support in several ways. They can develop big sister and big brother programs for students, provide quiet places for students to study after school and on weekends, donate educational supplies, help raise funds for field trips, set up mentor programs, and tutor students.

Community-based institutions and groups can also provide opportunities for students to participate in community-based learning programs. Community-based learning programs provide an opportunity for students to move beyond the textbook and experience real life. They give students an opportunity to see how knowledge is integrated when it is applied to the real world. It puts them in touch with a variety of people and lets them see how people cope with their environment. Community-based learning also enhances career development. It can help students learn about themselves, gain confidence, and better understand their strengths and weaknesses. Students can learn to plan, make decisions, negotiate, and evaluate their plans. Here are some examples of community work students can do:

- Paint an apartment for an ill neighbor
- Clean alleys and backyards for the elderly
- Write letters for people who are ill
- Read to people who are unable to read
- Prepare an empty lot as a play area for young children
- Plant a vegetable garden for the needy
- Collect and recycle newspapers

Develop Learning Resources for Parents to Use at Home

Many of the learning materials teachers use with students at school can be used by parents at home to help students improve their skills. The materials should be in a format suitable for students to take home and should provide clear directions for at-home completion. Parents could let the teacher know how they liked the material by writing a note, giving their child a verbal message for the teacher, or by calling the school. Clark (1995) has written a series of math home-involvement activities for kindergarten through eighth grade. The activities are included in a booklet and are designed to help students increase their math skills. Parents are able to use the creative activities to reinforce the skills their children learn at school. These kinds of materials are convenient for both parents and teachers to use.

It is important for teachers to have resources available for parents to use. This lets parents know that they can help increase their children's learning and that you want their help. Simply telling parents they should work with their children is not sufficient. Parents generally need specific suggestions. Once parents get an idea of what you want them to do, some will develop their own materials. Other parents will be able to purchase materials. You can suggest specific books, games, and other materials for parents to purchase and where these learning materials are available.

Some parents will not have the financial resources, time, or educational background to develop or purchase learning materials. With your principal's help or help from community groups, you can set up a learning center for parents. The learning center could contain paper, pencils, books, games, a portable typewriter, a portable computer, and other appropriate resources. The learning center could also have audiocassettes on such topics as instructional techniques, classroom rules, educational goals for the year, and readings from books. Parents and students could check materials out of the learning center for use at home.

Broaden the Conception of Parent and Community Involvement

Many barriers to parent/community involvement can be eliminated by broadly conceptualizing parent/community involvement. Parents can play many roles, depending on their interests, skills, and resources. It is important to have a variety of roles for parents so that more parents will have an opportunity to be involved. It is also important to make sure that some roles can be performed at home as well as at school. Below are four ways parents and community members can be involved in schools. Some of the roles can be implemented by the classroom teacher. Others need support and resources from building principals or central office administrators.

Parents Working with Their Own Children

Working with their own children is one of the most important roles parents can play in the educational process. Parents can help their children develop a positive self-concept and a positive attitude toward school as well as a better understanding of how their effort affects achievement. Most parents want their children to do well in school and are willing to do whatever they can to help them succeed. Teachers can increase the support they receive from their students' homes by giving parents a better understanding of what is going on in the classroom, by letting parents know what is expected in the classroom, and by suggesting ways in which they can support their childrens' learning.

Teachers can work with parents to support the educational process in these three ways:

1. Involve parents in monitoring homework by asking them to sign homework papers.

2. Ask parents to sign a certificate congratulating students for good attendance.

3. Give students extra points if their parents do things such as sign their report card, attend conferences, or read to them.

Some parents want a more active partnership with the school. These parents want to help teach their children. Below are three ways you can help parents work with their children to increase their learning:

1. Encourage parents to share hobbies and games, discuss news and television programs, and talk about school problems and events with their children.

2. Send information home on the importance of reading to children and include a reading list. A one-page sheet could be sent home stating, "One of the best ways to help children become better readers is to read to them. Reading aloud is most

helpful when you discuss the stories, learn to identify letters and words, and talk about the meaning of the words. Encourage leisure reading. Reading achievement is related to the amount of reading kids do. It increases vocabulary and reading fluency." Then list several books available from the school library for students to check out and take home.

3. Supply parents with materials they can use to work with their children on skill development. Students can help make math games, crossword puzzles, and other materials that parents can use with them at home.

Professional Support Person for Instruction

Many parents and community members have skills that can be shared with the school. They are willing to work with students as well as teachers. These people are often ignored in parent- and community-involvement programs. A parent or community member who is a college professor could be asked to talk to teachers about a topic that interests him or her or to participate in an inservice workshop. A bilingual parent or community member could be asked to help tutor foreign-language students or to share books or magazines written in his or her language with the class. Parents who enjoy reading or art could be asked to help staff a humanities enrichment course before or after school or to recommend materials for the course. Parents and community members who perform these kinds of duties could also serve as role models for your students and would demonstrate the importance of education in the community. Review the list below and think of how you could involve parents and community members in your classroom. Parents and community members can do the following:

- Serve as instructional assistants
- Use carpentry skills to build things for the school
- Tutor during school hours or after school
- Develop or identify student materials or community resources
- Share their expertise with students or staff
- Expand enrichment programs offered before, after, or during school, such as a program on great books or art appreciation
- Sew costumes for school plays
- Type and edit a newsletter

General Volunteers

Some parents are willing to volunteer their time, but they do not want to do a job that requires specific skills. When thinking of activities for general volunteers, be sure to include activities that can be performed at the school as well as ones that can be performed at home. Some possible activities include:

- Working on the playground as a support person
- Working in the classroom as a support person
- Working at home preparing cutouts and other materials that will be used in class
- Telephoning other parents to schedule conferences

Decision Makers

Some parents are interested in participating in decision making in the school. They want to help set school policy, select curriculum materials, review budgets, or interview prospective staff members. Roles for these parents and community members include school board member, committee member, and site council member. Serving on a site council is an excellent way for parents to participate in decision making. Site councils are designed to increase parent involvement in schools, empower classroom teachers, and allow decisions to be made at the school level.

The Comer (1995; Comer et al., 1999) model is an effective way to involve parents, classroom teachers, and other educators in decision making. Comer (1997) believes schools can be more effective when they are restructured in ways that encourage and support cooperation among parents and educators. Comer did much of his pioneering work on parent involvement and restructuring schools in Prince George's County, Maryland. There he implemented two committees—the School Planning and Management Team (SPMT) and the Student Staff Services Team (SSST).

The SPMT included the school principal, classroom teachers, parents, and support staff. Consensus was used to reach decisions. The committee also had a no-fault policy, which encouraged parents not to blame the school and educators not to blame parents. The SPMT provided a structure for parents and educators to create a common vision for their school; reduce fragmentation; and develop activities, curriculum, and inservice programs. It also developed a comprehensive school plan, designed a schoolwide calendar of events, and monitored and evaluated student progress. The SPMT met at least once a month. Subcommittees of the SPMT met more frequently.

The second committee that Comer implemented was the SSST, which included the school principal, guidance counselor, classroom teachers, and support staff, including psychologists, health aides, and other appropriate personnel. Teachers and parents were encouraged to join this group if they had concerns they believed should be addressed. The SSST brought school personnel together to discuss individual student concerns. It also brought coherence and order to the services that students receive.

Summary

Parent and community involvement is a dynamic process that encourages, supports, and provides opportunities for teachers, parents, and community members to work together to improve student learning. Parent and community involvement is also an important component of school reform and multicultural education. Parents and community groups help provide the rationale, motivation, and social action necessary for educational reform.

Everyone can benefit from parent/community involvement. Students tend to perform better in school and have more people supporting their learning. Parents know more about what is going on at school, have more opportunities to communicate with their children's teachers, and are able to help their children increase their learning. Teachers gain a partner in education. Teachers learn more about their students through their parent and community contacts and are able to use that information to help increase their students' performance.

Even though research has consistently demonstrated that students have an advantage in school when their parents support and encourage educational activities, not all parents know how they can support their children's education or feel they have the time, energy, or other resources to be involved in schools. Some parents have a particularly difficult time supporting their children's education. Three such groups are parents who have low incomes, single parents, and parents with special needs. Parents from these groups are often dismissed as unsupportive of education. However, they want their children to do well in school and are willing to work with the school when the school reaches out to them and responds to their needs.

To establish an effective parent/community involvement program, you should establish two-way communication with parents and community groups, enlist support from the community, and have resources available for parents to use in working with their children. Expanding how parent/community involvement is conceptualized can increase the number of parents and community members able to participate. Parents can play many roles. Ways to involve parents and community members include parents working with their own children, parents and community members sharing their professional skills with the school, parents and community groups volunteering in the school, and parents and community members working with educators to make decisions about school reform.

Questions and Activities

1. Compare the role of parents in schools during the colonial period to that which exists today. Identify and discuss changes that have occurred and changes you would like to see occur in parent involvement.

2. Consider this statement: Regardless of the circumstances students experiences at home, teachers have a responsibility to help them perform at their highest level at school. Do you agree? Why or why not?

3. Interview a parent of a bilingual, ethnic minority, religious minority, or low-income student to learn more about the parent's views on schools and the educational goals for his or her children. This information cannot be generalized to all members of these groups, but it can be an important departure point for learning more about diverse groups within our society.

4. Consider this statement: All parents want their children to succeed in school. Do you agree? Why or why not?

5. Interview a classroom teacher and an administrator to determine his or her perceptions of parent/community involvement.

6. Write a brief paper on your personal views of the benefits and drawbacks of parent/community involvement.

7. Form a group with two other members of your class or workshop. One person in the group will be a teacher, the other a parent, and the third an observer. The teacher and the parent will role-play a teacher–parent conference. Afterwards, discuss how it felt to be a parent and a teacher. What can be done to make the parent and teacher feel more comfortable? Was the information shared at the conference helpful? The observer can share his or her view of the parent and teacher interaction.

References

Banks, J. A. (2003). *Teaching Strategies for Ethnic Studies* (7th ed.). Boston: Allyn & Bacon.

Berger, E. H. (2003). *Parents as Partners in Education: Families and Schools Working Together* (7th ed.). New York: Macmillan.

Booth, A., & Dunn, J. F. (Eds.). (1996). *Family–School Links: How Do They Affect Educational Outcomes?* Mahwah, NJ: Erlbaum.

Bullivant, B. M. (1993). Culture: Its Nature and Meaning for Educators. In J. A. Banks & C. A. M. Banks, *Multicultural Education: Issues and Perspectives* (2nd ed., pp. 29–47). Boston: Allyn & Bacon.

Chavkin, N. F., & Gonzalez, D. L. (1995). *Forging Partnerships between Mexican American Parents and the Schools.* Charleston, WV: Clearinghouse on Rural Education and Small Schools, Appalachia Educational Laboratory.

Cibulka, J. A., & Kritek, W. J. (Eds.). (1996). *Coordination among Schools, Families, and Communities: Prospects for Educational Reform.* Albany: State University of New York Press.

Clark, C. S. (1995). Parents and Schools. *CQ-Researcher, 5*(3), 51–69.

Comer, J. P. (1995). *School Power: Implication of an Intervention Project.* New York: Free Press.

Comer, J. P. (1997). *Waiting for a Miracle: Why Schools Can't Solve Our Problems—And How We Can.* New York: Dutton.

Comer, J. P., Ben-Avie, M., Haynes, N. M., & Joyner, E. T. (1999). *Child by Child: The Comer Process for Change in Education.* New York: Teachers College Press.

Darling-Hammond, L. (2004). What Happens to a Dream Deferred? The Continuing Quest for Equal Educational Opportunity. In J. A. Banks and Cherry A. McGee Banks, *Handbook of Research on Multicultural Education* (2nd. ed., pp. 525–547). San Francisco: Jossey-Bass.

De Carvalho, M. E. P. (2001). *Rethinking Family–School relations.* Mahwah, NJ: Erlbaum.

Decker, J., & Majerczyk, D. (2000). *Increasing Parent Involvement through Effective Home/School Communication.* Chicago: Saint Xavier University. (ERIC Document Reproduction Service No. ED 439790)

DeSteno, N. (2000). Parent Involvement in the Classroom: The Fine Line. *Young Children, 55*(3), 13–17.

Goodlad, J. I. (1984). *A Place Called School: Prospects for the Future.* New York: McGraw-Hill.

Harry, B. (1992). Restructuring the Participation of African-American Parents in Special Education. *Exceptional Children, 59*(2), 123–131.

Henderson, A. T., & Berla, N. (Eds.). (1994). *A New Generation of Evidence: The Family Is Critical to Student Achievement.* Washington, DC: National Committee for Citizens in Education.

Hidalgo, N. M., Sau-Fong, S., & Epstein, J. L. (2004). Research on Families, Schools, and Communities: A Multicultural Perspective. In J. A. Banks & C. A. M. Banks (Eds.), *Handbook of Research on Multicultural Education* (2nd ed., pp. 631–655). San Francisco: Jossey-Bass.

Jennings, L. (1990, August 1). Parents as Partners. *Education Week,* pp. 23, 35.

Kagan, S. L. (1995). *Meeting Family and Community Needs: The Three C's of Early Childhood Education.* Paper presented at the Australia and New Zealand Conference on the First Years of School, Tasmania, Australia.

Krebs, N. B. (2000). For Students with Multicultural Heritage. *Multicultural Education, 8*(2), 25–27.

Lee, S. M. (2001). *Using the New Racial Categories in the 2000 Census: A Kids Count/PRB Report on Census 2000.* Baltimore, MD: The Annie E. Casey Foundation.

Lightfoot, S. L. (1978). *Worlds Apart: Relationships between Families and Schools.* New York: Basic Books.

Linn, E. (1990). Parent Involvement Programs: A Review of Selected Models. *Equity Coalition, 1*(2), 10–15.

Mannan, G., & Blackwell, J. (1992). Parent Involvement: Barriers and Opportunities. *Urban Review, 24*(1), 219–226.

Pena, D. C. (2000). Parent Involvement: Influencing Factors and Implications. *Journal of Educational Research, 94*(1), 42–54.

Pollard, K. M., & O'Hare, W. P. (1999). America's Racial and Ethnic Minorities. *Population Reference Bulletin, 54*(3), 1–48. Washington, DC: Population Reference Bureau.

Proctor, B. D., and Dalaker, J. (2002). Poverty in the United States: 2001. Washington, DC: U.S. Government Printing Office.

Rasinski, T. (1990). Reading and the Empowerment of Parents. *Reading Teacher, 42,* 226–231.

Schneider, B., & Coleman, J. S. (Eds.). (1996). *Parents, Their Children, and Schools.* Boulder, CO: Westview.

Shariff, J. W. (1998). Free Enterprise and the Ghetto Family. In J. S. Wurzel (Ed.), *Toward Multiculturalism: A Reader in Multicultural Education,* (pp. 30–54). Yarmouth, ME: Intercultural Press.

Stratton, J. (1995). *How Students Have Changed: A Call to Action for Our Children's Future.* Arlington, VA: American Association of School Administration.

Swadener, B. B., & Niles, K. (1991). Children and Families "At Promise": Making Home–School–Community Connections. *Democracy and Education, 6,* 13–18.

U.S. Census Bureau. (1998). *Statistical Abstract of the United States* (118th ed.). Washington, DC U.S. Government Printing Office.

U.S. Census Bureau. (2000). *Statistical Abstract of the United States, 2000* (120th ed.). Washington, DC: U.S. Government Printing Office.

Walker, V. S. (1996). *Their Highest Potential: An African American School Community in the Segregated South.* Chapel Hill: University of North Carolina Press.

Waller, W. (1965). *The Sociology of Teaching.* New York: Wiley. (Original work published 1932.)

Winter, G. (2002, December 28). Rigorous School Tests Grow, but Big Study Doubts Value. *New York Times,* p. A1.

APPENDIX

Multicultural Resources

Issues and Concepts

Banks, J. A. (Ed.). (1996). *Multicultural Education, Transformative Knowledge, and Action: Historical and Contemporary Perspectives.* New York: Teachers College Press.

Banks, J. A. (1997). *Educating Citizens in a Multicultural Society.* New York: Teachers College Press.

Banks, J. A. (2001). *Cultural Diversity and Education: Foundations, Curriculum, and Teaching* (4th ed.). Boston: Allyn & Bacon.

Banks, J. A. (Ed.). (2004). *Diversity and Citizenship Education: Global Perspectives.* San Francisco: Jossey-Bass.

Banks, J. A., & Banks, C. A. M. (Eds.). (2004). *Handbook of Research on Multicultural Education* (2nd ed.). San Francisco: Jossey-Bass.

Dilg, M. (1999). *Race and Culture in the Classroom: Teaching and Learning through Multicultural Education.* New York: Teachers College Press.

Gay, G. (2000). *Culturally Responsive Teaching: Theory, Research, and Practice.* New York: Teachers College Press.

Howard, G. (1999). *We Can't Teach What We Don't Know: White Teachers, Multiracial Schools.* New York: Teachers College Press.

Irvine, J. J. (2003). *Educating Teachers for Diversity: Seeing with a Cultural Eye.* New York: Teachers College Press.

May, S. (Ed.). (1999). *Critical Multiculturalism: Rethinking Multicultural and Antiracist Education.* Philadelphia: Falmer.

Nieto, S. (1999). *The Light in Their Eyes: Creating Multicultural Learning Communities.* New York: Teachers College Press.

Noguera, P. A. (2003). *City Schools and the American Dream: Reclaiming the Promise of Public Education.* New York: Teachers College Press.

Sleeter, C. E., & Grant, C. A. (2002). *Making Choices for Multicultural Education: Five Approaches to Race, Class, and Gender* (4th ed.). New York: Wiley.

Vavrus, M. (2002). *Transforming the Multicultural Education of Teachers: Theory, Research, and Practice.* New York: Teachers College Press.

Social Class

Anyon, J. (1997). *Ghetto Schooling: A Political Economy of Urban Educational Reform.* New York: Teachers College Press.

Blank, R. M. (1997). *It Takes a Nation: A New Agenda for Fighting Poverty.* New York: Russell Sage Foundation.

Collins, C., Leondar-Wright, B., & Sklar, H. (1999). *Shifting Fortunes: The Perils of the Growing American Wealth Gap.* Boston: United for a Fair Economy.

Conley, D. (1999). *Being Black, Living in the Red: Race, Wealth, and Social Policy in America.* Berkeley: University of California Press.

Gans, H. (1995). *The War against the Poor: The Underclass and Antipoverty Policy.* New York: Basic Books.

Hernandez, D. J. (Ed.). (1999). *Children of Immigrants: Health, Adjustment, and Public Assistance.* Washington, DC: National Academy Press.

Lucas, S. R. (1999). *Tracking Inequality: Stratification and Mobility in American High Schools.* New York: Teachers College Press.

Quint, S. (1994). *Schooling Homeless Children: A Working Model for America's Public Schools.* New York: Teachers College Press.

Romer, D. (Ed.). (2003). *Reducing Adolescent Risk: Toward an Integrated Approach.* Thousand Oaks, CA: Sage.

Wilson, W. J. (1999). *The Bridge over the Racial Divide: Rising Inequality and Coalition Politics.* Berkeley: University of California Press.

Religion

Bowker, J. (1997). *World Religions: The Great Faiths Explored and Explained.* New York: DK Publishing.

Carpenter, J. A. (1999). *Revive Us Again: The Reawakening of American Fundamentalism.* New York: Oxford University Press.

Corbett, J. M. (2000). *Religion in America* (4th ed.). Upper Saddle River, NJ: Prentice-Hall.

Doniger, W. (1999). *Merriam-Webster's Encyclopedia of World Religions.* Springfield, MA: Merriam-Webster.

Eck, D. L. (2001). *A New Religious America: How a "Christian Country" Has Become the World's Most Religiously Diverse Nation.* New York: Harper.

Esposito, J. L. (1998). *Islam: The Straight Path* (3rd ed.). New York: Oxford University Press.

Housden, R. (1999). *Sacred America: The Emerging Spirit of the People.* New York: Simon & Schuster.

Lippy, C. H. (2000). *Pluralism Comes of Age: American Religious Culture in the Twentieth Century.* Armonk, NY: Sharpe.

Lippy, C. H., & Williams, P. W. (Eds.). (1988). *Encyclopedia of the American Religious Experience* (Vols. 1–3). New York: Scribner's.

Nord, W., & Haynes, C. (1998). *Taking Religion Seriously across the Curriculum.* Alexandria, VA: Association for Supervision and Curriculum Development.

Sears, J. T., with Carper, J. C. (Eds.). (1998). *Curriculum, Religion, and Public Education.* New York: Teachers College Press.

Swatos, W. H., Jr., & Wellman, J. K., Jr. (Eds.). (1999). *The Power of Religious Publics: Staking a Claim in American Society.* Westport, CT: Praeger.

Yoo, D. K. (Ed.). (1999). *New Spiritual Homes: Religion and Asian Americans.* Honolulu: University Press of Hawaii.

Gender

American Association of University Women Foundation. (1998). *Gender Gaps: Where Schools Still Fail Our Children.* Washington, DC: Author.

Andersen, M. L., & Collins, P. H. (Eds.). (1998). *Race, Class, and Gender: An Anthology* (3rd ed.). Belmont, CA: Wadsworth.

Anderson, K. (1996). *Changing Women: A History of Racial Ethnic Women in Modern America.* New York: Oxford University Press.

Anzaldúa, G. E., & Keating, A. (Eds.). (2002). *This Bridge We Call Home: Visions of Transformation.* New York: Routledge.

Benedek, E. (1995). *Beyond the Four Corners of the World: A Navajo Woman's Journey.* New York: Knopf.

Boyd, H., & Allen, R. L. (Eds.). (1995). *Brotherman: The Odyssey of Black Men in America—An Anthology.* New York: Ballantine.

Collins, P. H. (2000). *Black Feminist Thought: Knowledge, Consciousness, and the Politics of Empowerment* (2nd ed.). New York: Routledge.

Guy-Sheftall, B. (Ed.). (1995). *Words of Fire: An Anthology of African-American Feminist Thought.* New York: New Press.

Harding, S. (1998). *Is Science Multicultural? Postcolonialisms, Feminisms, and Epistemologies.* Bloomington: Indiana University Press.

Harfo, J., & Bird, G. (Eds.). (1997). *Reinventing the Enemy's Language: Contemporary Native Women's Writing in North America.* New York: Norton.

Katz, J. (Ed.). (1995). *Messengers of the Wind: Native American Women Tell Their Life Stories.* New York: Ballantine.

Kimmel, M. (2000). *The Gendered Society.* New York: Oxford University Press.

Maccoby, E. E. (1998). *The Two Sexes: Growing Up Apart, Coming Together.* Cambridge, MA: Harvard University Press.

Maher, F. A., & Tetreault, M. K. (1994). *The Feminist Classroom.* New York: Basic Books.

Mankiller, W., Mink, G., Navarro, M., Smith, B., & Steinem, G. (Eds.). (1998). *The Reader's Companion to U.S. Women's History.* Boston: Houghton Mifflin.

Morales, A. L. (1998). *Remedios: Stories of Earth and Iron from the History of Puertoriqueñas.* Boston: Beacon.

Moya, P. (2002). *Learning from Experience: Minority Identities, Multicultural Struggles.* Berkeley: University of California Press.

Orenstein, P. (1994). *School Girls: Young Women, Self-Esteem, and the Confidence Gap.* New York: Doubleday.

Pollack, W. (1998). *Real Boys: Rescuing Our Sons from the Myths of Boyhood.* New York: Holt.

Sadker, M., & Sadker, D. (1994). *Failing at Fairness: How America's Schools Cheat Girls.* New York: Scribner's.

Sarasohn, E. S. (Ed.). (1998). *Issei Women: Echoes from Another Frontier.* Palo Alto, CA: Pacific Books.

Zinn, M. B., & Dill, B. T. (Eds.). (1994). *Women of Color in U.S. Society.* Philadelphia: Temple University Press.

Race, Ethnicity, and Language

Banks, J. A. (2003). *Teaching Strategies for Ethnic Studies* (7th ed.). Boston: Allyn & Bacon.

Banks, J. A., & Banks, C. A. M. (Eds.). (2004). *Handbook of Research on Multicultural Education* (2nd ed.). San Francisco: Jossey-Bass.

Beykont, Z. F. (Ed.). (2000). *Lifting Every Voice: Pedagogy and Politics of Bilingualism.* Cambridge, MA: Harvard Education Publishing Group.

Crawford, J. (1999). *Bilingual Education: History, Politics, Theory, and Practice* (4th ed.). Los Angeles: Bilingual Educational Services.

Delpit, L., & Dowdy, J. K. (Eds.). (2002). *The Skin That We Speak: Thoughts on Language and Culture in the Classroom.* New York: New Press.

Garcia, E. (2001). *Hispanic Education in the United States.* Lanham, MD: Rowman & Littlefield.

Gay, G. (Ed.). (2003). *Becoming Multicultural Educators: Personal Journey toward Professional Agency.* San Francisco: Jossey-Bass.

Ladson-Billings, G. (2001). *Crossing over to Canaan: The Journey of New Teachers in Diverse Classrooms.* San Francisco: Jossey-Bass.

Moreno, J. F. (Ed.). (1999). *The Elusive Quest for Equality: 150 Years of Chicano/Chicana Education*. Cambridge, MA: Harvard Educational Review.

Ovando, C. J., & Collier, V. P. (1998). *Bilingual and ESL Classrooms: Teaching in a Multicultural Context* (2nd ed.). Boston: McGraw-Hill.

Romero, M., Hondagneu-Sotelo, P., & Ortiz, V. (Eds.). (1997). *Challenging Fronteras: Structuring Latina and Latino Lives in the U.S.* New York: Routledge.

Smith, V. (Ed.). (1998). *Not Just Race, Not Just Gender: Black Feminist Readings*. New York: Routledge.

Smitherman, G. (1999). *Talkin That Talk: Language, Culture, and Education in African America*. New York: Routledge.

Stephan, S. (1999). *Reducing Prejudice and Stereotyping in Schools*. New York: Teachers College Press.

Suárez-Orozco, C., & Suárez-Orozco, M. (2001). *Children of Immigration*. Cambridge, MA: Harvard University Press.

Valdés, G. (2001). *Learning and Not Learning English: Latino Students in American Schools*. New York: Teachers College Press.

Exceptionality

Artiles, A. J., & Trent, S. C. (2000). Representation of Culturally/Linguistically Diverse Students. In C. R. Reynolds & E. Fletcher-Jantzen (Eds.), *Encyclopedia of Special Education* (2nd ed., Vol. 1, pp. 513–517). New York: Wiley.

Artiles, A. J., Trent, S. C., & Palmer, J. D. (2004). Culturally Diverse Students in Special Education: Legacies and Prospects. In J. A. Banks & C. A. M. Banks (Eds.). *Handbook of Research on Multicultural Education* (2nd ed., pp. 716–735). San Francisco: Jossey-Bass.

Baca, L. M., & Cervantes, H. T. (1997). *The Bilingual Special Education Interface*. Englewood Cliffs, NJ: Prentice-Hall.

Bauer, A. M., & Brown, G. M. (2001). *Adolescents and Inclusion: Transforming Secondary Schools*. Baltimore: Brookes.

Bireley, M. (1995). *Crossover Children: A Sourcebook for Helping Children Who Are Gifted and Learning Disabled* (2nd ed.). Reston, VA: Council for Exceptional Children.

Carrasquillo, A. L., & Rodriguez, V. (1995). *Language Minority Students in the Mainstream Classroom*. Bristol, PA: Taylor & Francis.

Cummins, J. (1984). *Bilingualism and Special Education: Issues in Assessment and Pedagogy*. Bristol, PA: Taylor & Francis.

Ford, D. Y., & Harris, J. J., III. (1999). *Multicultural Gifted Education*. New York: Teachers College Press.

Gallagher, J. J. (1994). *Teaching the Gifted Child* (4th ed.). Boston: Allyn & Bacon.

George, D. (1995). *Gifted Education: Identification and Provision*. Bristol, PA: Taylor & Francis.

Golomb, C. (Ed.). (1995). *The Development of Artistically Gifted Children: Selected Case Studies*. Hillsdale, NJ: Erlbaum.

Grossman, H. (1994). *Special Education in a Diverse Society*. Boston: Allyn & Bacon.

Harry, B. (1992). *Cultural Diversity, Families, and the Special Education System*. New York: Teachers College Press.

Heward, W. L. (2003). *Exceptional Children: An Introduction to Special Education* (7th ed.). Upper Saddle River, NJ: Prentice-Hall/Merrill.

Lombardi, T. P. (Ed.). (1999). *Inclusion: Policy and Practice*. Bloomington, IN: Phi Delta Kappa.

Mercer, C. D., & Mercer, A. R. (1998). *Teaching Students with Learning Problems* (5th ed.). Upper Saddle River, NJ: Prentice-Hall/Merrill.

Meyer, L. H., Park, H., Grenot-Scheyer, M., Schwartz, I., & Harry, B. (Eds.). (1998). *Making Friends: The Influences of Culture and Development*. Baltimore: Brookes.

Putnam, J. W. (Ed.). (1993). *Cooperative Learning and Strategies for Inclusion: Celebrating Diversity in the Classroom*. Baltimore: Brookes.

Sapon-Shevin, M. (1999). *Because We Can Change the World: A Practical Guide to Building Cooperative, Inclusive Classroom Communities.* Boston: Allyn & Bacon.

Shapiro, A. (Ed.). (1999). *Everybody Belongs: Changing Negative Attitudes toward Classmates with Disabilities.* New York: Garland.

School Reform

Banks, J. A., Cookson, P., Gay, G., Hawley, W. D., Irvine, J. J., Nieto, S., Schofield, J. W., & Stephan, W. G. (2001). *Diversity within Unity: Essential Principles for Teaching and Learning in a Multicultural Society.* Seattle: Center for Multicultural Education, University of Washington.

Cohen, E. G., & Lotan, R. A. (Eds.). (1997). *Working for Equity in Heterogeneous Classrooms: Sociological Theory in Practice.* New York: Teachers College Press.

College Board. (1999). *Reaching the Top: A Report of the National Task Force on Minority High Achievement.* New York: Author.

Comer, J. P. (1997). *Waiting for a Miracle: Why Schools Can't Solve Our Problems—And How We Can.* New York: Dutton.

Comer, J. P., Ben-Avie, M., Haynes, N. M., & Joyner, E. T. (1999). *Child by Child: The Comer Process for Change in Education.* New York: Teachers College Press.

Darling-Hammond, L. (1997). *The Right to Learn: A Blueprint for Creating Schools That Work.* San Francisco: Jossey-Bass.

Gardner, H. (1999). *The Disciplined Mind: What All Students Should Understand.* New York: Simon & Schuster.

Hidalgo, N. M., Siu, S.-F. & Epstein, J. L. (1995). Research on Families, Schools, and Communities: A Multicultural Perspective. In J. A. Banks & C. A. M. Banks (Eds.), *Handbook of Research on Multicultural Education* (2nd ed., pp. 631–655). San Francisco: Jossey-Bass.

Levine, D. U., & Lezotte, L. W. (2001). Effective Schools Research. In J. A. Banks & C. A. M. Banks (Eds.), *Handbook of Research on Multicultural Education* (pp. 525–547). San Francisco: Jossey-Bass.

McNeil, L. M. (2000). *Contradictions of School Reform: Educational Costs of Standardized Testing.* New York: Routledge.

Mehan, H., Villanueva, I., Hubbard, L., & Linta, A. (1996). *Constructing School Success.* New York: Cambridge University Press.

Meier, D. (1995). *The Power of Their Ideas: Lessons for America from a Small School in Harlem.* Boston: Beacon.

Oakes, J., Quartz, K. H., Ryan, S., & Lipton, M. (2000). *Becoming Good American Schools: The Struggle for Civic Virtue in Educational Reform.* San Francisco: Jossey-Bass.

Olsen, L. (1997). *Made in America: Immigrant Students in Our Public Schools.* New York: New Press.

Perkins, D. (1995). *Outsmarting IQ: The Emerging Science of Learnable Intelligence.* New York: Free Press.

Rethinking Our Classrooms: Teaching for Equity and Justice. (1994). Milwaukee, WI: Rethinking Schools.

Glossary

African Americans U.S. residents and citizens who have an African biological and cultural heritage and identity. This term is used synonymously and interchangeably with *Blacks* and *Black Americans*. These terms are used to describe both a racial and a cultural group. According to the U.S. Census, there were 34,658,190 African Americans in the United States in 2000. This figure excludes African Americans of Hispanic origin.

The number of African Americans increased by 33 percent between 1980 and 2000 to about 12.3 percent of the U.S. population. The U.S. Census Bureau (2000) projects that African Americans will make up 14.7 percent of the nation's population by 2050; they were slightly outnumbered by Hispanic Americans in 2000. Today, African Americans make up 12.3 percent of the U.S. population, while Hispanics make up 12.5 percent. An excellent one-volume encyclopedia on African Americans is *Africana: The Encyclopedia of the African and African American Experience* (Appiah & Gates, 1999).

Afrocentric curriculum A curriculum approach in which concepts, issues, problems, and phenomena are viewed from the perspectives of Africans and African Americans. This curriculum is based on the assumption that students learn best when they view situations and events from their own cultural perspectives (Asante, 1998).

American Indian See *Native Americans*.

Anglo Americans Americans whose biological and cultural heritage originated in England, or Americans with other biological and cultural heritages who have assimilated into the dominant or mainstream culture in the United States. This term is often used to describe the mainstream U.S. culture or to describe most White Americans.

Antiracist education A term used frequently in the United Kingdom and Canada to describe a process used by teachers and other educators to eliminate institutionalized racism from the schools and society and to help individuals to develop nonracist attitudes. When antiracist educational reform is implemented, curriculum materials, grouping practices, hiring policies, teacher attitudes and expectations, and school policy and practices are examined and steps are taken to eliminate racism from these school variables. A related educational reform movement in the United States that focuses more on individuals than on institutions is known as *prejudice* reduction (see Stephan, 1999).

Asian Americans and Pacific Islanders Americans who have a biological and cultural heritage that originated on the continent of Asia or in the Pacific region. The largest groups of Asian Americans in the United States in 2000 were (in descending order) Chinese, Filipinos, Asian Indians, Vietnamese, Koreans, and Japanese.

Other groups include Laotians, Thai, Hmong, Taiwanese, Cambodians, Pakistanis, and Indonesians. Asians are the fastest-growing ethnic group in the United States. They increased 194 percent between 1980 and 2000. There were about 10.2 million Asian Americans in the United States in 2000. The U.S. Census projects that Asians will make up 9.3 percent of the nation's population by 2050 (Pollard & O'Hare, 1999; Population Reference Bureau, 2003; U.S. Census Bureau, 2000, 2002).

Cultural assimilation A phenomenon that takes place when one ethnic or cultural group acquires the behavior, values, perspectives, ethos, and characteristics of another ethnic group and sheds its own cultural characteristics. (For a further discussion of assimilation of ethnic groups in the United States since the 1960s, see Alba & Nee, 2003).

Culture The ideations, symbols, behaviors, values, and beliefs that are shared by a human group. *Culture* can also be defined as a group's program for survival and adaptation to its environment. Pluralistic nation-states such as the United States, Canada, and Australia are made up of an overarching culture, called a *macroculture*, that all individuals and groups within the nation share. These nation-states also have many smaller cultures, called *microcultures*, that differ in many ways from the macroculture or that contain cultural components manifested differently than in the macroculture. (See Chapters 1 and 2 for further discussions of *culture*.)

Disability The physical or mental characteristics of an individual that prevent or limit him or her from performing specific tasks.

Discrimination The differential treatment of individuals or groups based on categories such as race, ethnicity, gender, sexual orientation, social class, or exceptionality.

Ethnic group A microcultural group or collectivity that shares a common history and culture, values, behaviors, and other characteristics that cause members of the group to have a shared identity. A sense of peoplehood is one of the most important characteristics of an ethnic group. An ethnic group also shares economic and political interests. Cultural characteristics, rather than biological traits, are the essential attributes of an ethnic group. An ethnic group is not the same as a *racial group*. Some ethnic groups, such as Puerto Ricans in the United States, are made up of individuals who belong to several different racial groups. White Anglo-Saxon Protestants, Italian Americans, and Irish Americans are examples of ethnic groups. Individual members of an ethnic group vary considerably in the extent to which they identify with the group. Some individuals have a very strong identification with their particular ethnic group, whereas other members of the group have a very weak identification with it.

Ethnic minority group An ethnic group with several distinguishing characteristics. An ethnic minority group has distinguishing cultural characteristics, racial characteristics, or both, which enable members of other groups to identify its members easily. Some ethnic minority groups, such as Jewish Americans, have unique cultural characteristics. African Americans have unique cultural and physical characteristics. The unique attributes of ethnic minority groups make them convenient targets of racism and discrimination. Ethnic minority groups are usually a numerical minority within their societies. However, the Blacks in South Africa, who are a numerical majority in their nation-state, were often considered a sociological minority group by social scientists because they had little political power until the constitution of the Republic of South Africa was established in 1996 (Moodley & Adam, 2004).

Ethnic studies The scientific and humanistic analysis of behavior influenced by variables related to ethnicity and ethnic group membership. This term is often used to refer to special school, university, and college courses and programs that focus on specific racial and ethnic groups. However, any aspects of a course or program that includes a study of variables related to ethnicity can accurately be referred to as ethnic studies. In other words, ethnic studies can be integrated within the boundaries of mainstream courses and curricula.

Eurocentric curriculum A curriculum in which concepts, events, and situations are viewed primarily from the perspectives of European nations and cultures and in which Western civilization is emphasized. This approach is based on the assumption that Europeans have made the most important contributions to the development of the United States and the world. Curriculum theorists who endorse this approach are referred to as *Eurocentrists* or *Western traditionalists*.

European Americans See *Anglo Americans*.

Exceptional Term used to describe students who have learning or behavioral characteristics that differ substantially from those of most other students and that require special attention in instruction. Students who are intellectually gifted or talented as well as those who have disabilities are considered exceptional.

Gender A category consisting of behaviors that result from the social, cultural, and psychological factors associated with masculinity and femininity within a society. Appropriate male and female roles result from the socialization of the individual within a group.

Gender identity An individual's view of the gender to which he or she belongs and his or her shared sense of group attachment to other males or females.

Global education A curricum reform movement concerned with issues and problems related to the survival of human beings in the world community. International studies is a part of global education, but the focus of global education is the interdependence of human beings and their common fate, regardless of the national boundaries within which they live. Many teachers confuse global education and international studies with ethnic studies, which deal with ethnic groups within a particular national boundary, such as the United States.

Handicapism The unequal treatment of people who are disabled and related attitudes and beliefs that reinforce and justify discrimination against people with disabilities. The term *handicapped* is considered negative by some people. They prefer the term *disabled*. *People with disabilities* is considered a more sensitive phrase than *disabled people* because the word *people* is used first and given emphasis.

Hispanic Americans Americans who share a culture, heritage, and language that originated in Spain. Most of the Hispanics living in the United States have cultural origins in Latin America. Many Hispanics in the United States prefer to use the word *Latino* rather than *Hispanic*, as do the editors of this book. However, *Hispanic* is the term used by the U.S. Census. Most Hispanics in the United States speak Spanish and are

mestizos. A *mestizo* is a person of mixed biological heritage. Most Hispanics in the United States have an Indian as well as a Spanish heritage. Many of them also have an African biological and cultural heritage.

The largest groups of Hispanics in the United States are Mexican Americans (Chicanos), Puerto Ricans, and Cubans. According to the U.S. Census, 35,306,000 Hispanics lived in the United States in 2000, which was about 12.5 percent of the U.S. population. In 2000, there were 20.6 million Mexican Americans, 3.4 million Puerto Ricans in the mainland United States, 1.2 million Cubans, and 10 million Hispanics from other nations (U.S. Census Bureau, 2000, 2002).

Hispanics are one of the nation's fastest-growing ethnic groups of color. They increased 142 percent between 1980 and 2000, from 14.6 to 35.3 million. The nation's total population increased 24 percent between 1980 and 2000 (Pollard & O'Hare, 1999; U.S. Census Bureau, 2002). The U.S. Census Bureau (2000) projects that Hispanics will make up 24.3 percent of the nation's population in 2050.

It is misleading to view Hispanics as one ethnic group. Some Hispanics believe that the word *Hispanics* can help to unify the various Latino groups and thus increase their political power. The primary identity of most Hispanics in the United States, however, is with their particular group, such as Mexican American, Puerto Rican American, or Cuban American.

Mainstream American A U.S. citizen who shares most of the characteristics of the dominant ethnic and cultural group in the nation. Such an individual is usually White Anglo-Saxon Protestant and belongs to the middle class or a higher social-class status.

Mainstream-centric curriculum A curriculum that presents events, concepts, issues, and problems primarily or exclusively from the points of view and perspectives of the mainstream society and the dominant ethnic and cultural group in the United States—White Anglo-Saxon Protestants. The mainstream-centric curriculum is also usually presented from the perspectives of Anglo males.

Mainstreaming The process that involves placing students with disabilities into the regular classroom for instruction. They might be integrated into the regular classroom for part or all of the school day. This practice was initiated in response to Public Law 94–142 (passed by Congress in 1975), which requires that students with disabilities be educated in the least restricted environment.

Multicultural education A reform movement designed to change the total educational environment so that students from diverse racial and ethnic groups, both gender groups, exceptional students, and students from each social-class group will experience equal educational opportunities in schools, colleges, and universities. A major assumption of multicultural education is that some students, because of their particular racial, ethnic, gender, and cultural characteristics, have a better chance of succeeding in educational institutions as they are currently structured than do students who belong to other groups or who have different cultural and gender characteristics. See Chapter 1 in the *Handbook for Research on Multicultural Education* (Banks & Banks, 2004) for a further discussion of multicultural education.

Multiculturalism A philosophical position and movement that assumes that the gender, ethnic, racial, and cultural diversity of a pluralistic society should be reflected in all of the institutionalized structures of educational institutions, including the staff, the norms and values, the curriculum, and the student body.

Native Americans U.S. citizens who trace their biological and cultural heritage to the original inhabitants in the land that now makes up the United States. The term *Native American* is sometimes used synonymously with *American Indian.* There were about 2.5 million Native Americans (including American Indians, Eskimos, and Aleuts) in the United States in 2000. In 2000, only four tribes—the Cherokee, Navajo, Chippewa, and Sioux—had a population of more than 100,000 persons. Most tribes had a population of less than 10,000. The two largest tribes were the Cherokee (281,000) and the Navajo (269,000) (Banks, 2003; U.S. Census, 2002).

People of color Groups in the United States and other nations who have experienced discrimination historically because of their unique biological characteristics that enabled potential discriminators to identify them easily. African Americans, Asian Americans, and Hispanics in the United States are among the groups referred to as *people of color.* Most members of these groups still experience forms of discrimination today.

Positionality An idea that emerged out of feminist scholarship stating that variables such as an individual's gender, class, and race are markers of her or his relational position within a social and economic context and influence the knowledge that she or he produces. Consequently, valid knowledge requires an acknowledgment of the knower's position within a specific context. (See Chapter 7.)

Prejudice A set of rigid and unfavorable attitudes toward a particular individual or group that is formed without consideration of facts. Prejudice is a set of attitudes that often leads to discrimination, the differential treatment of particular individuals and groups.

Race A term that refers to the attempt by physical anthropologists to divide human groups according to their physical traits and characteristics. This has proven to be very difficult because human groups in modern societies are highly mixed physically. Consequently, different and often conflicting race typologies exist. An excellent book on race is *Whiteness of a Different Color: European Immigrants and the Alchemy of Race* (Jacobson, 1999).

Racism A belief that human groups can be validly grouped according to their biological traits and that these identifiable groups inherit certain mental, personality, and cultural characteristics that determine their behavior. Racism, however, is not merely a set of beliefs but is practiced when a group has the power to enforce laws, institutions, and norms, based on its beliefs, that oppress and dehumanize another group. An informative reference on racism is *Racism: A Short History* (Fredrickson, 2002).

Religion A set of beliefs and values, especially about explanations that concern the cause and nature of the universe, to which an individual or group has a strong loyalty and attachment. A *religion* usually has a moral code, rituals, and institutions that reinforce and propagate its beliefs.

Sex The biological factors that distinguish males and females, such as chromosomal, hormonal, anatomical, and physiological characteristics.

Sexism Social, political, and economic structures that advantage one sex group over the other. Stereotypes and misconceptions about the biological characteristics of each sex group reinforce and support sex discrimination.

In most societies, women have been the major victims of sexism. However, males are also victimized by sexist beliefs and practices.

Social class A collectivity of people who have a similar socioeconomic status based on such criteria as income, occupation, education, values, behaviors, and life chances. *Lower class, working class, middle class,* and *upper class* are common designations of social class in the United States.

References

Alba, R. D., & Nee, V. (2003). *Remaking the American Mainstream: Assimilation and Contemporary Immigration.* Cambridge, MA: Harvard University Press.

Appiah, K. A., & Gates, H. L., Jr. (Eds.). (1999). *Africana: The Encyclopedia of the African and African American Experience.* New York: Perseus.

Asante, M. K. (1998). *The Afrocentric Idea* (rev. ed.). Philadelphia: Temple University Press.

Banks, J. A. (2003). *Teaching Strategies for Ethnic Studies* (7th ed.). Boston: Allyn & Bacon.

Banks, J. A., & Banks, C. A. M. (Eds.). (2004). *Handbook of Research on Multicultural Education* (2nd ed.). San Francisco: Jossey-Bass.

Fredrickson, G. M. (2002). *Racism: A Short History.* Princeton, NJ: Princeton University Press.

Jacobson, M. F. (1999). *Whiteness of a Different Color: European Immigrants and the Alchemy of Race.* Cambridge, MA: Harvard University Press.

Moodley, K. A., & Adam, H. (2004). Citizenship Education and Political Literacy in South Africa. In J. A. Banks (Ed.), *Diversity and Citizenship Education: Global Perspectives* (pp. 159–183). San Francisco: Jossey-Bass.

Pollard, K. M., & O'Hare, W. P. (1999). America's Racial and Ethnic Minorities. *Population Bulletin, 54*(3), 1–48. Washington, DC: Population Reference Bureau.

Population Reference Bureau. (2003). *A First Look at Asian Americans in the Census.* Retrieved June 12, 2003, from http://www.prb.org/pdf/asianamericans.pdf.

Stephan, W. (1999). *Reducing Prejudice and Stereotyping in Schools.* New York: Teachers College Press.

U.S. Census Bureau. (2000). *Resident Population by Race and Hispanic Origin—Status Projections: 2005 to 2050.* Retrieved June 12, 2003, from http://www.census.gov/population/www/projections/natsum-T3.html.

U.S. Census Bureau. (2002). *USA Statistics in Brief—Population and Vital Statistics.* Retrieved June 12, 2003, from http://www.census.gov/statab/www/poppart.html.

Contributors

Cherry A. McGee Banks is professor of education at the University of Washington, Bothell. She is associate editor of the *Handbook of Research on Multicultural Education*, co-editor of *Multicultural Education: Issues and Perspectives*, and co-author of *Teaching Strategies for the Social Studies*. In 1997, she received the Distinguished Teaching Award from the University of Washington, Bothell, and was named a Worthington Distinguished Professor in 2000.

James A. Banks is Russell F. Stark University Professor and director of the Center for Multicultural Education at the University of Washington, Seattle. His books include *Educating Citizens in a Multicultural Society; Teaching Strategies for the Social Studies; Cultural Diversity and Education: Foundations, Curriculum and Teaching; Diversity and Citizenship Education;* and the *Handbook of Research on Multicultural Education*. Professor Banks is a past president of the American Educational Research Association (AERA) and the National Council for the Social Studies (NCSS). He is also a member of the National Academy of Education and holds honorary Doctorates of Humane Letters from four universities.

Jill Bevan-Brown is a senior lecturer in inclusive education at Massey University College of Education, New Zealand. Being of Maori heritage (the indigenous people of New Zealand), she has a particular interest in the special education needs of Maori children and has concentrated her writing and research efforts in this area. Her most recent publication is a workbook for schools entitled *The Cultural Self-Review: Providing Culturally Effective, Inclusive Education for Maori Learners*. Dr. Bevan-Brown has been a member of National Advisory Committees on Autism and Gifted Education and has had responsibility for the Maori component of two government-commissioned, national research projects evaluating special education and gifted education policies and provisions in New Zealand.

Johnnella E. Butler is associate dean and associate vice provost of the graduate school, professor of American Ethnic Studies, and adjunct professor of English and Women Studies at the University of Washington, Seattle. Professor Butler is a specialist in African American literature, American ethnic literature and criticism, and multicultural studies. She is particularly interested in the relationships among American ethnic literatures, their theory and pedagogy. She is editor and lead contributor of *Color Line to Borderlands: Ethnic Studies and the Matrix of Higher Education*. She is also co-editor of the *Encyclopedia of American Studies*.

Rodney A. Cavanaugh is an associate professor of special education at the State University of New York, Plattsburgh. A former teacher of students with learning and behavior disorders in Michigan and Ohio, he currently teaches graduate and undergraduate courses in special education and research methods and supervises practice teaching. He is a past president of the New York

State Council for Exceptional Children Subdivision of Mental Retardation/Developmental Disabilities. His current interests focus on effective teaching strategies and teacher-as-researcher components in teacher education. Dr. Cavanaugh was named the 1995 New York State Professor of the Year by the Carnegie Foundation for the Advancement of Teaching.

Diana L. Eck is a professor of comparative religion and Indian studies in the Faculty of Arts and Sciences at Harvard University and is also a member of the Faculty of Divinity. Professor Eck's work on India has produced several books, including *Benares, City of Light* and *Darsan: Seeing the Divine Image in India*. Her work also deals with issues of religious diversity, Christian theology, and interfaith dialogue in the context of American pluralism. Since 1991 she has been the director of Harvard University's Pluralism Project, which explores the new religious diversity of the United States. Her most recent book is *A New Religious America: How a "Christian Country" Has Become the World's Most Religiously Diverse Nation*.

Frederick Erickson is the George F. Kneller Professor of Anthropology of Education at the University of California, Los Angeles, where he teaches in the Graduate School of Education and Information Studies. His publications include *The Counselor as Gatekeeper: Social Interaction in Interviews; Sights and Sounds of Life in Schools*; a chapter on qualitative research methods in the *Handbook of Research on Teaching* (3rd ed.); and articles on ethnicity and on ethnographic description in *Sociolinguistics: An International Handbook of the Science of Language and Society*. He is a past president of the Council on Anthropology and Education of the American Anthropological Association. He received the council's George and Louise Spindler Award for outstanding scholarly contributions to educational anthropology in 1991. He is a past editor of the *Anthropology and Education Quarterly*. In 1998–99 he was a Spencer Fellow at the Center for Advanced Study in the Behavioral Sciences.

Sara C. Ernsbarger received her Ph.D. in special education from the Ohio State University in 2002. She is currently an instructional specialist in the Positive Behavior Change Program at the University of South Florida, where she teaches behavior-management classes for parents. Prior to working with parents, she was a special education teacher for adolescents with learning disabilities. Dr. Ernsbarger's research interests include effective and efficient instructional strategies and methods to help struggling readers acquire and generalize reading skills.

Donna Y. Ford is professor of education at the Ohio State University. She has written two books on multicultural education and gifted education and more than seventy-five articles on topics in these fields. Professor Ford consults with school districts nationally on recruiting and retaining culturally diverse students in gifted education, creating culturally responsive learning environments, and improving achievement among culturally diverse students. She has received several awards for her research and serves on numerous education boards and committees.

Geneva Gay is professor of education and associate of the Center for Multicultural Education at the University of Washington, Seattle. She is nationally and internationally known for her scholarship in multicultural education, particularly as it relates to curriculum design, staff development, classroom instruction, and culture and learning. Her writings include more than 135 book chapters, books, and journal articles. Among these are *At the Essence of Learning: Multicultural Education; Culturally Responsive Teaching: Research, Theory, and Practice*; and, as editor, *Becoming Multicultural Educators: Personal Journey toward Professional Agency*. International consultations on multicultural education have taken her to Canada, Brazil, Taiwan, Finland, Japan, England, and Scotland.

Carl A. Grant is a Hoefs-Bascom Professor at the University of Wisconsin, Madison. He has written or edited seventeen books on multicultural teacher education. These books include *Making Schooling Multicultural: Campus and Classroom* (with Mary L. Gomez); *Educating for Diversity; Making Choices for Multicultural Education* (with Christine E. Sleeter); *Research and Multicultural Education*; and *After the School Bell Rings* (with Christine E. Sleeter). Professor Grant has written more than 100 articles and book chapters. His writings and the programs that he has directed have received awards. He is a former teacher and administrator. He was a Fulbright Scholar in England and was chosen by the

Association of Teacher Education as a leader in teacher education. He is a past president of the National Association for Multicultural Education (NAME).

Beth Harry entered the field of special education as a parent of a child with cerebral palsy. She is professor of special education at the University of Miami, Florida, and her particular interests are families and cultural issues. Her research and teaching focus on the impact of culture and social status on the needs and perspectives of families of children with disabilities and on the disproportionate placement of ethnic minorities in special education. She is the author or co-author of three books on interactions with parents from culturally diverse backgrounds and of several articles published in leading educational journals.

William L. Heward is professor and coordinator of the Ph.D. program in special education at the Ohio State University. His more than 100 professional publications include *Applied Behavior Analysis* (2nd ed.) and *Exceptional Children: An Introduction to Special Education* (7th ed.), which has been used at more than 400 colleges and universities in the United States and translated into Spanish and Japanese. Professor Heward's current research interests focus on increasing the effectiveness of group instruction, improving the academic success of students with disabilities in general education classrooms, and promoting the generalization and maintenance of newly learned skills.

Charles H. Lippy is the LeRoy A. Martin Distinguished Professor of Religious Studies at the University of Tennessee, Chattanooga. Among his books are *Being Religious; American Style: A History of Popular Religiosity in the United States; Pluralism Comes of Age: American Religious Culture in the Twentieth Century;* and the forthcoming *Do Real Men Pray? Images of the Christian Man and Male Spirituality in White Protestant America.* He is also co-editor of the *Encyclopedia of the American Religious Experience* and the forthcoming second edition of the *Encyclopedia of Religion in the South.*

Luanna H. Meyer is assistant vice chancellor–academic, Massey University, Aotearoa, New Zealand, where she is responsible for academic affairs across all campuses of the university. Prior to her current position, she was pro-vice chancellor of the Massey University College of Education. She is internationally known for her work in special and inclusive education and has published more than 200 books, journal articles, and book chapters, carried out reviews of policy and practice in her areas of expertise, and been an invited speaker in several countries and thirty states in the United States.

Sonia Nieto is professor of education, University of Massachusetts, Amherst. Her research centers on multicultural education, the education of Latinos, teacher education, and Puerto Rican children's literature. Her books include *Affirming Diversity: The Sociopolitical Context of Multicultural Education; The Light in Their Eyes: Creating Multicultural Learning Communities;* and *What Keeps Teachers Going?* as well as the edited volume *Puerto Rican Students in U.S. Schools.* Dr. Nieto has received numerous awards for her scholarship, activism, and advocacy; in 1999, she was awarded an Honorary Doctorate in Humane Letters from Lesley College, Cambridge, Massachusetts.

Carlos J. Ovando is professor and associate dean for teacher education at Arizona State University. He has taught at Indiana University, Oregon State University, the University of Alaska, Anchorage, and the University of Southern California. Professor Ovando specializes in bilingual and multicultural education and has contributed numerous publications in these fields. He is senior author of *Bilingual and ESL Classrooms: Teaching in Multicultural Contexts* and senior editor of *The Politics of Multiculturalism and Bilingual Education.* With Colleen Larson he co-authored *The Color of Bureaucracy: The Politics of Equity in Multicultural School Communities.*

Caroline Hodges Persell is professor of sociology at New York University. A past president of the Eastern Sociological Society, she has received grants from the Carnegie Academy for the Scholarship of Teaching and Learning, the National Science Foundation, the Danforth Foundation, the Fund for the Improvement of Post-Secondary Education, and the U.S. Office of Education. Her books include *How Sampling Works* (with Richard Maisel); *Understanding Society: An Introduction to Sociology; Preparing for Power: America's Elite Boarding Schools* (with Peter W. Cookson, Jr.); and *Education and Inequality.* She was named Professor of the Year in sociology and selected for a Golden Dozen Teaching Award at New York University.

David Sadker is a professor at the American University in Washington, D.C. His research and writing document gender bias from the classroom to the boardroom. His work has been reported in *Harvard Educational Review; Educational Leadership; Phi Delta Kappan; USA Today; Business Week; The Washington Post; The Times* of London; *The New York Times; Time;* and *Newsweek*. Professor Sadker received the American Educational Research Association (AERA) Research Review Award in 1991, its professional service award in 1995, and the Eleanor Roosevelt Award from the American Association of University Women in 1995. Dr. Sadker coauthored *Failing at Fairness: How Our Schools Cheat Girls* and *Teachers, Schools and Society*.

Myra Sadker was a professor of education at the American University in Washington, D.C., and director of the Master of Arts in Teaching program. She also served as dean of the School of Education and director of the teacher preparation programs. Professor Sadker, who was a language arts teacher, contributed to numerous journals and books and offered workshops on sex equity in more than forty states. She and Professor David Sadker co-authored a number of books, including *Sex Equity Handbook for Schools* and *Failing at Fairness: How Our Schools Cheat Girls*.

Mara Sapon-Shevin is professor of inclusive education in the Teaching and Leadership Department of the School of Education at Syracuse University. She teaches in the university's Inclusive Elementary and Special Education Teacher Education Program, which prepares teachers for inclusive, heterogeneous classrooms. She is active in working with schools to promote the full inclusion of all students and the creation of cooperative school communities. Professor Sapon-Shevin is past co-president of the International Association for the Study of Cooperation in Education and the convenor of the Invisible College on Social Justice Teaching at AERA. Her most recent book is *Because We Can Change the World: A Practical Guide for Building Co-operative, Inclusive Classroom Communities* (Allyn & Bacon).

Janet Ward Schofield is professor of psychology and a senior scientist at the Learning Research and Development Center at the University of Pittsburgh. Her book *Black and White in School: Trust, Tension or Tolerance?* was awarded the Society for the Psychological Study of Social Issues Gordon Allport Intergroup Relations Prize. She is a contributing author of the *Handbook of Research on Multicultural Education*, a former member of the governing body of the American Psychological Association, and a member of the board on International Comparative Studies in Education at the National Research Council. She is the author of *Computers and Classroom Culture* and *Bringing the Internet to School: Lessons from an Urban District*.

Christine E. Sleeter is a professor of teacher education and multicultural education at California State University, Monterey Bay. She consults nationally and internationally in multicultural education and multicultural teacher education. She has published numerous books and articles in multicultural education. Her most recent books include *Culture, Difference and Power; Multicultural Education as Social Activism; Turning on Learning* (with Carl Grant); and *Multicultural Education, Critical Pedagogy and the Politics of Difference* (with Peter McLaren). She edits the series The Social Context of Education for the State University of New York Press. She served as program chair of the American Educational Research Association (AERA) annual meeting in 1998.

Mary Kay Thompson Tetreault is provost and vice president for academic affairs at Portland State University. Her research interests center around feminist pedagogy, social constructions of Whiteness, and the epistemology of knowing and learning. She is the author (with Frances Maher) of *The Feminist Classroom* (2nd ed., Rowman & Littlefield) and "They Got the Paradigm and Painted It White: Higher Education Classrooms and Legal Discourse" in the *Duke Journal of Gender Law and Policy*. She has also co-authored (with Maher) "Learning in the Dark: How Assumptions of Whiteness Shape Classroom Knowledge," published in the *Harvard Educational Review*.

Index

Printed in the United States
62170LVS00004B/137

9 780471 713630